Jewish Possibilities
The Best of MOMENT MAGAZINE

Jewish Possibilities

The Best of MOMENT MAGAZINE

Leonard Fein, editor

Jason Aronson Inc.
Northvale, New Jersey
London

Copyright © 1987 by Leonard Fein

10 9 8 7 6 5 4 3 2 1

All rights reserved. Printed in the United States of America.
No part of this book may be used or reproduced in any manner
whatsoever without written permission from *Jason Aronson Inc.*
except in the case of brief quotations in reviews for inclusion
in a magazine, newspaper, or broadcast.

Library of Congress Cataloging-in-Publication data pending.
ISBN 0-87668-969-1

The editor gratefully acknowledges permission to
use the following material:

"Jacob Schiff and My Uncle Ben Daynovsky,"
copyright © 1975 by Calvin Trillin.

"All God's Children," copyright © 1980 by
Julius Lester.

Manufactured in the United States of America.

For my father and teacher,
the bell-mender
Isaac Fein —
heretic, believer, skeptic,
but never cynic.

Contents

In All Its Parts: An Introduction xi

Part I
The American Jewish Experience: Explorations in Identity 1

Coming of Age in Morgantown (JANUARY 1976)
    Nancy Datan 3
Unbecoming and Rebecoming A Jew (JANUARY-FEBRUARY 1984)
    Kenneth Wolman 8
Noël Coward (DECEMBER 1976)
    Carol Kur 12
We Gather Together (NOVEMBER 1977)
    Carol Kur 14
Portraits at a Condominium (JANUARY-FEBRUARY 1983)
    Fern Kupfer 16
Searching for the Self: An Exchange of Letters (SEPTEMBER 1979)
    Janet Lehrman Brown and Leonard Fein 20
A Me Grows in Dayton (OCTOBER 1980)
    Carol Ewig 23
All God's Children (APRIL 1980)
    Julius Lester 27
Pesach in Katman — Who? (APRIL 1984)
    Shula Beyer 32
The Artificial Jewboy (OCTOBER 1985)
    Gene Lyons 35
On Becoming Jewish (SEPTEMBER 1980)
    Andrew Potok and Anita Landa 49

Part II
The American Jewish Experience: Threads and Themes 55

Anti-Semitism, Malignant Obsession (JUNE 1985)
    Harold Schulweis 57
Are Good Jewish Men a Vanishing Breed? (JANUARY-FEBRUARY 1980)
    William Novak 60
It Matters How the Dead Are Buried (APRIL 1980)
    Robert Kanigel 67
My Father's Ritual (APRIL 1978)
    Danny Siegel 72
A Walnut Tree, A Glass of Wine, and Thou (JUNE 1979)
    Phyllis Rose Eisenberg 74
"Your Mother," The Social Worker Says, "Is Having Some Trouble Adjusting."
  (DECEMBER 1978)
    Annette Henkin Landau 79
Jacob Schiff and My Uncle Ben Daynovsky (MAY-JUNE 1975)
    Calvin Trillin 83
An Extra Pair of T'fillin (APRIL 1980)
    Joel Grossman 86
Wanted Dead or Alive (JANUARY-FEBRUARY 1979)
    Jacob Neusner 89

Part III
Israel 93

Dual Citizenship (OCTOBER 1985)
    Nancy Datan 95

We the Homeborn (JULY-AUGUST 1985)
    Haim Guri 99
Back From the Front (JANUARY-FEBRUARY 1985)
    Judy Labensohn 103
Unofficial Rumors of the War (OCTOBER 1982)
    Matthew Nesvisky 106
The Kahane Controversy (JANUARY-FEBRUARY 1985)
    Walter Reich 116
Hebron, The Roots of Jewish Terror (APRIL 1985)
    Yossi Klein Halevi 126
The Ends and Means of Zionism (JULY-AUGUST 1985)
    Yossi Klein Halevi 144
Here We Beat Our Rugs out the Window (APRIL 1985)
    Wendy Leibowitz 147

Part IV
The Pursuit of Religious Meaning 149

Gym Shoes and Irises (JULY-AUGUST 1975)
    Danny Siegel 151
An I for An I (DECEMBER 1980)
    Harold Schulweis 157
Loving Kindness in New Jersey (DECEMBER 1981)
    Devra Weingart 161
Brother, Can You Spare a Dime? (NOVEMBER 1981)
    Arthur Kurzweil 164
Coming of Age at 66 (MAY 1981)
    Linda Kerber 169
A Symposium on Orthodoxy (SEPTEMBER 1978) 172
    Leonard Fein: Prologue
    Moshe Adler: Faith and Fear
    David Singer: Thumbs and Eggs
    Jacob Neusner: Arrogance and Authenticity
    Roundtable Discussion: Doing and Believing
The Shattered Tablets (OCTOBER 1985)
    Gerson Cohen 189
Jews By Choice: A Discussion (MARCH 1979) 194
"I've Had Nothing Yet So I Can't Take More" (SEPTEMBER 1983)
    Rachel Adler 201
How Do You Doo? (JULY 1983)
    Marc Gellman 206
The First Rosh Hashanah (SEPTEMBER 1977)
    Marc Gellman 208
13 Things Kids Don't Know About Tz'dakah (MAY 1980)
    Danny Siegel 211
The Riddle of the Ordinary (JULY-AUGUST 1975)
    Cynthia Ozick 216
A Moment Report: Who is a Jew? (SEPTEMBER 1981) 221

Part V
Interviews 233

Marie Syrkin and Trude Weiss-Rosmarin (SEPTEMBER 1983) 235
Isaac Bashevis Singer (SEPTEMBER 1976) 243
Abba Eban (JUNE 1980) 248
Marion Pritchard (DECEMBER 1983) 256
Barney Frank (MAY 1983) 262
Jacob Rader Marcus (MARCH-APRIL 1981) 267
Yitzchak Ben Aharon (OCTOBER 1979) 278
Jane Fonda (NOVEMBER 1984) 286
Thomas Friedman (JUNE 1985) 294

Father Theodore Hesburgh (JULY 1983) 300
Hyman Bookbinder (MAY 1981) 305
Helen Suzman (JANUARY-FEBRUARY 1981) 309
Immanuel Jakobovits (MAY 1980) 315
Arie Eliav (APRIL 1978) 322
Nahum Goldmann (SEPTEMBER 1977) 328

Part VI
The Editor's Pen: Leonard Fein 337

In the Wake of Peace (NOVEMBER 1978) 339
Vital Signs (JUNE 1979) 344
Israel, Summer 1979 (JULY-AUGUST 1979) 348
The Andrew Young Affair... To be Continued (OCTOBER 1979) 360
Autumnal Reflections (DECEMBER 1980) 365
Israel at 33 (MAY 1985) 370
Thinking About Lebanon (JULY-AUGUST 1982) 373
What, Then, Shall We Do (APRIL 1983) 378
The 91st Moment (DECEMBER 1984) 390

Part VII
Just a Moment... 393

How to Read A Yiddish Poem (DECEMBER 1981)
    Seth Wolitz 395

In All Its Parts: An Introduction

It seemed reasonable, back in late 1974 and early 1975 when *Moment* was gestating, to issue a manifesto announcing its imminent birth and offering a rationale for the effort. So, at least, many of my friends advised and urged. My own preference, however, was to let the magazine speak for itself. It's altogether too easy to prepare a passionate, high-minded statement of intent—but the challenge, no less in magazines than in, say, revolutions, is less in the describing than in the doing.

I still believe that. Besides, words, once published, belong at least as much to those who read them as to those who wrote (or published) them, and the needs and purposes of the reader may be quite different from those of the author. Why should the author get a second chance, be entitled to say, "No, *this* is what I meant, what I intended"? So I shall spare the reader of these introductory words a lofty proclamation of intent, presume that he/she is willing to stipulate that our intentions were in fact (and remain) honorable, and/or lofty, and allow those who read the pages that follow to do that which they will in any case do—to wit, come to their own conclusions regarding what we've achieved in ten years of publishing this magazine.

A word of caution: Every issue of a magazine is an anthology, a selection from among all the manuscripts, solicited and unsolicited, that are available to the editors. So this volume is, in a way, an anthology of anthologies. But it is an anthology that is constructed according to a very different principle from that which we invoke every month as we put *Moment* together. The monthly effort is to produce a balanced selection, one that reflects the enormous diversity of Jewish interests and concerns. An essay, a poem, a story, a report; the community, the individual; Israel, America, Soviet Jewry—all these, and more, confront us as choices to be made, and the beginning of wisdom is the understanding that a magazine is meant to roam the waterfront, in style and in substance. Ours, *Moment,* is a theme park—its rides, exhibits, tours, and restaurants are all tied together by the Jewish connection. In a good month, the whole is greater than the sum of its parts, for there are internal relationships between one article and another that provide a cumulative illumination to the reader.

But a volume that is announced as "The Best of . . ."—obviously, according to one person's taste—is put together in a different way, according to a different principle, and offers a different kind of illumination.

The reader will decide whether "the best" is good and what it all adds up to. In making the selection, this reader has been especially struck by how much of what we've published simply wouldn't exist, wouldn't have been written, if *Moment* had never happened. That's an important thing to know about magazines, and about writers—they feed each other. It's not only that editors commission particular articles, but also that the very existence of a magazine is an invitation, an incentive, to writers. In the case at hand, a majority of the articles here assembled were written specifically for *Moment*'s pages—and that brings me to the real subject of this brief essay.

Before *Moment* is about politics, it is about culture—specifically, about testing whether a serious Jewish culture is possible here in America. I do not delude myself that magazines a culture make, but I am convinced that a vigorous and ambitious community requires media of communication wherein its achievements and aspirations can be presented and debated.

One of my assets as an editor is that I travel about a good deal, and in the course of my travels, I get to meet a fair number of our readers. Although they are surely diverse in interests, they nonetheless seem to me to constitute a community within the community. They are linked not merely by their decision to subscribe to this magazine, but also by their appetite for a Jewish connection that's rooted in something more than nostalgia, something beyond guilt, beyond fear. They are, I think, alive to Jewish possibility. And it's the exploration of that possibility that is our underlying agenda.

The years from 1975 to 1985 were stormy, dense with political activity. In that decade, Israel and Egypt negotiated a peace treaty; Prime Minister Begin was succeeded by Yitzhak Shamir, who was followed by Shimon Peres and the Government of National Unity; Israel's economy came close to collapse, and is still seeking cure; Israel's invasion of Lebanon happened, and Sabra and Shatilla and the Kahan Commission; a different Kahane was elected to the Knesset; terrorism took on a new dimension. When we published our first issue, Gerald Ford was president of the United States, and that alone seems like forever ago. And halfway into that decade, Jimmy Carter was succeeded by Ronald Reagan, and the Reagan revolution began. Hunger and heroin, the worldwide rebirth of religious fundamentalism, the dramatic emergence in America of alternatives to the traditional nuclear family, the impending extinction of the family farm: to read the daily newspaper is to be assaulted by endless slings and arrows of what seems increasingly a genuinely outrageous fortune. And within our own community, these have been years of growing divisiveness, hardly even insulated any longer by the conventions of civility.

Where, in all this, is there room for culture? Or does culture become a kind of safe harbor in which to seek respite from the tempest?

If I speak of a serious Jewish culture, and of our interest in it, I do not intend high culture. I mean the word *culture* more as anthropologists mean it than as literary critics mean it. I mean the culture of our community: its ways, its manners, its values and commitments; its stance and its substance. And it is precisely in highly charged, profoundly political times that the content of a serious culture is best revealed.

Mordecai M. Kaplan described the Jews as an "evolving religious civilization." Either he was looking over his shoulder at what was even then, when he first used the term, on the verge of collapse, or he was peering into the distant future and providing us a goal rather than a description. The "is" of America's Jews (as distinguished from the "ought") hardly deserves to be called either a religion or a civilization. We are, for the most part, a community linked together by a smattering of nostalgic rememberings (and misrememberings), an assortment of fears that have more to do with yesterday's traumas than with tomorrow's prospects, a handful of rituals, and frenetic activity on Israel's behalf.

It does not seem to me likely that a voluntary community that depends on such links as these can long command the loyalty of its constituents. It is neither anti-Semitism nor assimilation that presents us the most sinister threat today; it is sheer boredom. For if, after all the *sturm und drang*, after 4,000 years of extraordinary time, we have become merely a SPAC (sentimental political action committee), our own offspring will not take our claims to grandeur seriously.

Or, to put it somewhat differently: As the first generation in 2,000 years of Jewish time to have more than a modicum of control over our own destiny, we face an awesome challenge. Henceforward, we will no longer be judged on the eloquence of our rhetoric; henceforward, the best evidence on the question of whether the Jews are who they say they are, of whether there is truth in Jewish self-advertising, is what we do, not what we say.

And if what we do is yawn, if what we are committed to is little more than making it, if our religion becomes a residual category rather than an impassioned challenge, if we succumb to all the diverse anesthetics of our time and are no longer able to hear the call, then the dismal truth will cry out: Jewishly, we are not making it; we are faking it.

Our tradition knows no radical distinction between politics and culture. Ours is a profoundly political religion, not a pietistic faith. We are enjoined to reject the world-as-it-is, to love it for what it might yet be, and to help transform it from the one into the other. To be interested in a serious Jewish culture means, necessarily, to be interested in politics—in whether the hungry are fed and the naked clothed, in whether justice is pursued and mercy loved. Judaism does not tell us which tax reform plan to favor; it does tell us that no tax plan that slights the downtrodden is acceptable.

Moment comes to fight against Jewish boredom. It comes not merely to satisfy curiosity (who are the Jews?) or to stimulate interest (what are the Jews?) but to arouse passion (where, oh where are the Jews?). It comes to propose an old-new link that will bind us to one another, the link of shared understanding that this world, our world, is not working as it was meant to and that we are implicated in its repair.

Whole chunks of what's appeared in the magazine have been excluded here. There's no TSB (*The Spice Box*) here. TSB works as a modest entertainment in each issue; but the one time we tried to go beyond that (several years back, for a Purim issue, we interspersed TSB throughout the magazine) we bombed. Nor do we present any of the many excerpts from forthcoming books that we (as do most magazines) publish in almost every issue. The books are no longer "forthcoming"; they've come, and, for the most part, gone. Principally for that reason, there's less, much less, on the Holocaust than we've actually published (another piece of evidence that our selection does not mirror the contents of our monthly efforts). We've avoided most (although not all) of the articles that were highly specific to the time of their writing. And we've not included any of my introductory *Alef* column, which is intended as ephemeral and appears to have lived up to its intentions.

Those were the only restrictions on the selection process. Actually, the word *process* implies a rather more systematic approach than we in fact employed. We simply browsed all our back issues, noting those articles that seemed, for one reason or another, memorable. The original list ran to about 200, and it was from that list that the "winners" were selected. In the course of making that selection, no attention was paid to the question of "balance." And that is why it was so interesting, when the work was done, to look back at what we'd selected and to learn how much of what we deemed memorable had to do with issues of identity. With all our talk about and commitment to politics, it came as something of a surprise to find we'd devoted as much attention as we evidently had to the more intimate, more personal questions of Jewish coping. A pleasant surprise, to be sure: a Judaism that does not speak to the intimate concerns of the individual, that does not make a private difference, cannot hope to make a public difference.

And yes, I do have some favorites. I shan't list them all, but if I am asked what I am proudest of, I know the answer. I am proud that we did not join the "Peace for Galilee" bandwagon, that we were skeptical of the wisdom of Israel's invasion from its inception. Given the mood of the community at the time, it wasn't a popular course to take; given what most or all of us have learned since, it was plainly the right course. Right, and realistic. I am repeatedly annoyed by those who assume that there's a distinction to be drawn between realism and morality, as if morality were some kind of fatuous self-indulgence. Over and over again, I am struck by how often the moral course is also, and definitively, the sensible course, the pragmatic course. And Lebanon is as good a recent example as we have, here reflected by some of my own pieces as well as by Matt Nesvisky's "Unofficial Rumors of the War."

That's one; the other, as different

as different can be, is called "How to Translate a Yiddish Poem." It doesn't fit logically into any of the larger categories of this volume, so we've placed it at the end. And I suspect a word to explain what it's doing here at all may be in order.

To the best of my knowledge, we're the only Jewish magazine that routinely prints the actual Hebrew (or Yiddish) text of such translated poetry as we publish. I have no idea how many of our readers can, or choose to, examine the original. The number is surely less than ten percent, and may be considerably less. But there's a statement implicit in our stubborn presentation of the original, a statement about sources, about knowing that when you're dealing with a translation, that is what you're dealing with, a statement even about the shape of the letters.

On the one hand, war; on the other, poetry in translation; Jewish life in all its parts.

And one final part: Naming things was the first responsibility given to man. *Moment* derives its name from one of the two leading Yiddish dailies of pre-war Warsaw, *Der Moment*. Our tradition suggests that one's progeny be named after one's deceased progenitors. That is one way we insure the future of our past.

Now, of course, knowing that our name (happily) does not describe our life expectancy, we are a bit more relaxed than we were at the beginning. Still, the appearance of this volume imposes a new kind of pressure on us: now, when we make each month's issue, we have to keep in mind that we are creating the past of our future, selecting the candidates for inclusion in *The Best of Moment's First Twenty-Five*. Barring unforeseen interruption, that volume should appear some time in the year 2001, 144 issues and more than 2,000 articles (from the time I make these complex calculations) down the road. So hang in; the new millennium is on its way.

P.S. A coincidence in timing makes this volume rather more a summing-up than I had foreseen. Its appearance coincides almost exactly with the publication of the last issue of the magazine under my editorship. New hands and new ideas now enter, and the next anthology, however many years from now, will be of articles chosen by a second generation of editors. So "the best of *Moment* Magazine" turns out to be the best of my years at *Moment*. (Well, not exactly; this book takes *Moment* through Volume 10, Number 10; I have taken *Moment* through Volume 12, Number 5. But let's not quibble.) It becomes, for that reason, my valediction. I couldn't have asked for a nicer graduation present, one I both get and give with delight and, yes, a bit of pride, too.

Leonard Fein

Jewish Possibilities
The Best of MOMENT MAGAZINE

Part I

The American Jewish Experience: Explorations in Identity

OUR PEOPLE

COMING OF AGE IN MORGANTOWN

Nancy Datan

"For a bat mitzvah?" as I pull an embroidered denim pantsuit off the rack.

"I don't think I can begin to tell you how tired I'm getting of that phrase," I tell my daughter, who has inspected every item of clothing in her size in every store in the town. Her size — or so it seems to me — I shall soon discover otherwise — is *not quite*. Although she has fortunately outgrown my shoes, she is not quite my height, and I wear the smallest size manufactured for adult women. But she is not quite a child's size either, not even the size of a large child, as we have learned by trying to zip up dresses from the preteen rack, getting no further than the middle of her rib cage before giving up:

We might have done better on selection if we had begun our planning before Christmas parties had emptied the stores throughout the town, although we are now able to take advantage of sale prices — a considerable advantage, it seems to me, since this dress (which is taking shape in my mind as a platonic ideal, forever sought and never attained) is manifestly destined for a single wearing. However, neither feature of

Nancy Datan, who died as this book was going to press, was, most recently, Professor of Human Development and Chairman of the Department of Women's Studies at the University of Wisconsin in Green Bay.

> She stands, splendid, at the threshold of womanhood, perfect in all respects except that the ruffles do not hide her hiking boots.

our present situation is the outcome of planning. On the contrary, I had made no plans at all and my daughter's plans had been quite different: "What should I wear for my bat mitzvah?"

"Whatever you like."

"Would my black and white body suit and my black jeans be all right?"

"For a bat mitzvah?" — it is I who bear responsibility for the phrase.

"Why not?"

"Well, it would be a little unusual," although in my mind I have begun to reflect that among the unusual features of this bat mitzvah, my daughter's choice of clothing is far from a major issue. As it is said, "Thou shalt love the Lord thy God with all thy heart, with all thy soul, and with all thy might. And these words which I command thee this day shall be upon thy heart. Thou shalt teach them diligently unto thy children . . . ." I learned the words myself, for I was a diligent child; but I learned no Hebrew, never celebrated my own bat mitzvah, and met the writings of Freud at the crest of my own adolescent skepticism, bringing *Civilization and Its Discontents* home in triumph to my mother as proof of the absence of God. Some years would pass before I learned that Scriptural fragment in Hebrew, found that those were the words tucked into *m'zzuzot*, posted one upon the doorpost of my own house, realized that Freud's concern was not with God but with men, and discovered that his skepticism and mine bore a surprising resemblance to a tradition of angry questioners of God found, of all places, among the Chassidim. I learned it from non-Jews.

2

I married a classmate out of those angry adolescent days, with whom I shared the unique joys of a liberal arts education at a small college. Though his father, a Protestant minister, performed our marriage ceremony, we wrote it ourselves. Eager to prove we were citizens of the world, but also anxious to avoid offending either side of the family, we produced a ceremony which, if it had had a cast of characters, would have included everyone from the Baal Shem Tov to the Holy Ghost.

The ecumenical spirit was short-lived, however. Although our personal nondenominational agnosticism remained untouched, we soon renounced citizenship of the world, became instead residents of Israel.

The credit and the blame for the renunciation is mine. Though the years which bring a daughter to bat mitzvah lie between that moment and this, I can recall the shock that came to me as a new life moved in my body and I found that I was not at all pregnant with a citizen of the world. I was pregnant with a Jew. My baptized, agnostic husband, who traced his forebears to the Mayflower, could not have been more surprised than I was myself when I told him, "We're going to raise this child as a Jew." The force of this declaration derived in part from my memories of childhood festivals, and certainly owed some of its strength to the fundamentalist tracts an aunt of his sent us from time to time. Since retreat to Orthodoxy was not in my repertoire, I intended to try to eliminate the question of a Jewish identity, to move to Israel.

In the course of time this daughter was joined by another and by a son; some years later, on a sojourn to the United States, my former college classmate and I became part of the statistics reflecting the high divorce rate which follows intermarriage. Upon my return to Israel with the children, I shed my married name, an Anglo-Saxon name, and took Datan, the name of a heretic

4/Moment

Jewish Possibilities: The Best of Moment

who rebelled against the establishment of the priesthood of Moses and Aaron at the time of the exodus from Egypt.

3

With this transformation, however, a decade of pioneering came to an end: Israel is a Garden of Eden for small children, but a harsh land for the adult, and it requires two working parents to rear a family. I needed an American income, a developmental psychology program, a small town where women and children were safe; and I found West Virginia University. And so I came to Morgantown with three children and a dog, four suitcases and a briefcase, to begin again.

The children's experiences as members of a minority group were limited. On our previous sojourn, in Chicago, they had attended a Jewish day school, and had wakened on the morning of the Yom Kippur holiday to disbelief:

"It can't be Yom Kippur!"
"Why not?"
"All the cars are moving."
"Those aren't Jews."
"They're not Jews?"
"No."

"I didn't know there were that many people who weren't Jews." Thus my firstborn daughter, who was descended from the Mayflower on one side and Moses on the other, and who, upon arrival in Morgantown three years later, soon learned more.

"They told me there's a kid in school who beats up other kids and calls them dirty Jews."

"That could be. It does happen sometimes."

"Well, but what would you do if it happened to *us*?"

"I would call the rabbi, I would call the principal, and I would call the police, but I wouldn't take you out of school, if that's what you're asking, because for 2,000 years there have been people who from time to time have beaten up children and called them dirty Jews. I think it may be just as important to know what *that* feels like as it is to know that the Jews have a land of their own," I heard my own voice declare, with some surprise. In the end, however, it turned out that the child in question was an indiscriminate bully, finding words appropriate to each victim. By chance, he never touched my children; and the discovery of new meanings to minority group identity was to be deferred until the season for my firstborn daughter to become a Bat Mitzvah drew near.

Consistent with the ongoing I-and-Thou of self-definition by silhouette against the Christian majority which had been true of my life to this point, I was first brought to consider a celebration of my daughter's bat mitzvah by a Lutheran, a provost at the university who, like myself, had come to his intellectual maturity at the University of Chicago. As we explored our academic kinship, it emerged that we had been neighbors as well, in a densely Jewish area where I spent my childhood.

"Of course," he told me, "I went to everybody's bar mitzvah. I still do, when I get the chance."

"I hope you'll come to my daughter's bat mitzvah too," although up to that very minute I had not given it any thought: My daughter's march toward maturity was proceeding more quickly than I realized. Prompted by my own words, I asked my daughter with some hesitation — for she had once declared with heat that she was not *Jewish*, an identification which seemed to her to rest upon acts of affirmation, but a *Jew*, born into a people — whether she wanted to celebrate her bat mitzvah.

"I guess so," and she warmed gradually to enthusiasm as she drew up a small list of guests and participants.

The Torah reading, for which American children endure years of Hebrew lessons, was a portion which she had first read in second grade in Israel. One of my friends remarked, "To be perfectly fair, she ought to be required to recite in Latin and go through all the agonies our kids have to suffer." And I agreed, for that aspect of the ceremony was, finally, to involve a total of one hour's investment in two casual rehearsal readings, as I sat in the bathtub and Merav on the bathroom floor.

"This is a rather peculiar way to prepare for a bat mitzvah."

"We can wait until you get out of the bathtub and I'll read in the bedroom."

"Never mind, just go ahead."

The ceremonies that mark the coming of age must nevertheless involve a fixed quantity of nervous tension, and we were soon to discover where ours lay: in the areas others take for granted, food and clothing.

Food was the first hurdle. While certain components of Jewish motherhood were clearly strong within me, others seemed to be absent; although I had packed for Israel without a second thought, I had never discovered the joys of feeding one's family. Indeed, after one day of a succession of meetings which blurred into the evening, at nightfall I was tucking the children into bed, and as I kissed my six-year-old son good night he asked, "Aren't we having any dinner tonight?" and it was not long before the instinct for survival led my daughters to cook for the family. No, baking for a large gathering held no attractions for me; as for Merav, she merely wanted the ritual:

"Can't I just read, and then be finished? I don't want a party."

"I don't see why not."

The Jews are a tribe, however, and tribal decisions are not made alone. When I mentioned my plans to a colleague, I was told: "Datan, that's out of the question, *nobody* has a bat mitzvah without food."

"All we want is the ceremony."

"The ceremony *includes* the food."

"Where is it written that a bat mitzvah includes food?"

"*Everybody* has food. Do you want your daughter to feel left out?"

"She's the one who just wants to read from the Torah in her jeans and make a quick getaway. Can't you elope at a bat mitzvah?"

"Datan, it doesn't have to be elaborate, but there has to be food. Let's think it through. You'll have baked goods, and then you would probably want to avoid the chopped liver, that gets complicated, but you'd have to have cold cuts and some sort of salad...."

"What salad? What cold cuts? What chopped liver? What baked goods?"

"You'll do what Shari did, just ask people to bake, and a few people will bring in honey cake and date bread and that's it."

"How can I possibly ask people to bake?" for I remembered the catered affairs of Chicago and Jerusalem.

"Datan, that's what people do here," he told me, and it seemed I had still a good deal to learn about the coming of age in a tiny Jewish community in a small city in West Virginia. I began with the rabbi's wife, who believed me when I insisted that I hadn't the slightest idea where to begin planning, and went straight to basics:

"The women will bring their baked goods in. The synagogue has serving dishes. You'll bring a couple of bottles of wine; paper napkins, and paper cups, and I'll be there to help you set it up, and so will everyone else" — and indeed they were, though that was yet to come, for the next hurdle was still to be crossed.

4

"What's wrong with my black and white body suit and my black jeans?"

The easy answers, the prohibition in Leviticus against a woman's putting on the clothing of a man (which might activate the heretic in my daughter's soul) or the injunction that *no one* does that (which had never held much force for me until my feet took their first steps on the path of small town Jewish tradition) did not seem promising. I tried negotiations: "Haven't you anything else?"

"My Arab shirt" — fading and slightly ragged — "and my Levis?"

I dropped the matter. But on a gray Saturday, the sort of bleak weekend day sometimes spent in shopping centers, the question seemed to surface of its own accord: "Would you like to go shopping for a dress for your bat mitzvah?"

"I don't know," and pursuing my policy of nonintervention I went no further; but sometime later in the day Merav asked suddenly: "Aren't

we going shopping for my bat mitzvah dress?"

"I didn't know you wanted to go."

"I didn't say I *didn't* want to go," and off we went to a large discount house. We were greeted by racks and racks of dresses, and it was in the dressing rooms of this store, whose supplies seemed boundless, that I found my daughter to be not quite a child, as she looked at herself in a long dress which reached to the shins and did not quite zip up the back; perhaps not quite a woman, but a new lust had begun to grow in her eyes. Her jeans 'round her ankles, hiking boots on her feet, and a dress not quite the right size not quite covering the rest of her, she gazed into the mirror and said, "I think I like this dress."

"It doesn't fit."

"Couldn't I wear tights with it?"

"It won't zip shut."

"I'll hold in my stomach."

"Do you think you can hold your breath for two hours?"

"I guess it's too small," and we are back scanning racks. We move to the women's section, and I discover that my daughter is, like me, a petite size 5.

"But I want a long dress," for the lust has not gone out of her eyes, and in this store there are none at all to fit her, and we return to the downtown shopping area. And there, in one of the town's most expensive stores, my daughter is zipped into a long red dress with a bodice of white lace and price tag of $30 and she stands before the mirror, in love. I consider for a moment making the purchase, for the sake of the light in her eyes; but no, I would spend the money in a minute for books, but the lesson to be learned from the purchase of that dress on my salary is not one I wish to teach.

"It would solve the problem of my dress and your present to me all at once."

"It would cost you $15 an hour to wear that dress," but I cannot tell my daughter how greatly I should like to give it to her; she will learn that for herself when her own daughter comes to maturity and she must choose among gifts.

Presently a compromise is achieved: I discover a reasonably priced long-sleeved ruffled dress which reaches my daughter's ankles, and in which she stands, splendid, at the threshold of womanhood, perfect in all respects except that the ruffles do not hide her hiking boots.

"We'll have to get you some shoes," and my mother once wished for me a daughter like myself in all ways, including a readiness to try on and reject every pair of shoes in a store, and her wish found fulfillment. We move from store to store and finally the Jewish community rescues us once more and a friend produces a pair of silver shoes.

"These make me look *grown up*."

"You *are* grown up."

"I'm not *this* grown up."

"As a matter of fact, you are."

"Why don't you just take the shoes home and try them on with the dress and see how you feel about them?" comes my friend's suggestion. She has dealt not only with years of customers but with three sons now grown to adulthood — "and if you don't feel comfortable with them, just bring them back. I know how you feel when it's hard to decide, and you certainly want to feel comfortable at your own bat mitzvah!"

As the event draws near, however, being comfortable looks like it's out of the question. Abruptly, on the Wednesday before the Saturday on which she is to celebrate her coming of age, Merav asks: "Could we just call it off?"

"Certainly not!" for I had been astonished at the community response. The president of the Sisterhood had come to the door a few days earlier with a honey cake, apologizing for the fact that she would be out of town on the date of the bat mitzvah, and explaining that she had therefore baked in advance, so that I could freeze the cake and have it ready when needed; another timed her vacation to end with enough time to bake. But when I spoke of my surprise to a friend, she told me simply: "We are a small and fragile community. Each child who comes of age is precious to us," and yes, this was what the ceremony would teach my daughter and me.

5

My uncle flew in on Friday afternoon to join us for the ceremony. I later learned that my son had declared that morning to his teacher, "Don't expect me to work today, because my UNCLE is coming HERE and I'm too EXCITED to do ANYTHING!" If I had dared, I might have made the same declaration myself.

Merav's bedroom, the most civilized of the options, was turned over to my uncle for the night, and Merav joined me in my double bed. "I'll sleep with my daughter on the night before her bat mitzvah too," she told me, and phantoms of priestesses danced briefly through my head as she turned over into slumber.

We wakened into Saturday morning and I dressed my daughter as though she were made of porcelain: Her brother and sister and my uncle were marshaled 'round her; time to go to synagogue; and suddenly the ceremony has begun.

A *Kohen* is called to bless the Torah, and it is my colleague; we have quarreled over the value of Ph.D. prelims and he is transformed in *tallit* and *kippah* and the ancient invocation with which my daughter's reading begins. Next a *Levi* recites a blessing, and it is a boy just recently come to bar mitzvah age himself. And the reading continues, with the five Israelites — Jews who are neither *Kohen* nor *Levi* — rising to recite their blessings in turn: first, our neighbor; next, my uncle, for whom an extra place had had to be made after he asked, "Don't I have an *aliyah*?" and when he rises for the blessing with his own *tallit* I remember with surprise that I was myself born only one generation away from Orthodoxy. And my daughter's voice, "And a new Pharaoh arose in Egypt who knew not Joseph . . . ." The Dean of Social Work, co-editor with me of proceedings from a conference we had organized, and echoes of arguments vanish in the magic of the recited blessing; a colleague whose training is in physiological psychology, and he adds his voice to the others' voices, and my daughter reads on, "And Moses went unto Pharaoh . . ." and finally my colleagues' sons, so that as the reading is concluded Merav stands among her own friends, come of age, and the blessing for parents is said, "Blessed art Thou who has given us life, sustained us, and brought us to see this day." The rabbi, who loves the celebration of Bar Mitzvah, speaks briefly: "I never thought I would see the day when a Datan would stand to declare the praises of Moses," and he goes on to explain Datan's rebellion and the tradition of dissent in Judaism. Neither did I, until the world taught me otherwise — though I am about to learn that this is only part of today's teaching.

Downstairs at the reception I discover that the women of the Sisterhood have prepared everything — "Isn't it luck that we turned out to have matching tablecloths?" I am asked by two of my friends, who set up the tables, splendid with flowers; but there is more than luck behind it. "Have you seen the napkins?" — no, I have not; I look and find not the flowered napkins I had brought in, but ceremonial napkins made to be imprinted with the name of the bar mitzvah child, and on the first flap a slot tidily cut with pinking shears, so that the second flap shows through, and typed on it, MERAV DATAN — "They were left over from Larry's bar mitzvah and I thought it might be nice," says a friend, dismissing my surprise and gratitude.

To this celebration I have brought three bottles of sacramental wine, five cans of Hawaiian Punch, paper cups and napkins, a cake, and a daughter, who, though eligible for the Daughters of the American Revolution, was reared in Israel and read Exodus in the original Hebrew before she read Dick and Jane in English. Jerusalem broods over the centuries and commands the heart: Morgantown is only a small citadel of decency in an undistinguished region. But the principal contribution to this celebration was made by this community, in which each coming of age is precious; and so it must have been for all our generations, as parents and children brought one another to their coming of age. ✦

UNBECOMING AND REBECOMING A JEW

KENNETH WOLMAN

Kenneth Wolman is a consulting technical writer and semi-professional photographer who lives in Wayne, NJ, with his wife and two sons. For Moment, *he has authored the present article, as well as "Son of My Father, Father of My Son" and "I Am Enraged."*

I.

It is an evening late in 1979, and our year-old son Jacob is in bed for the night. My wife and I sit and talk about him, and, like all parents of adored children, we speculate, plan and dream all at once. Inevitably, the subject turns to the education Jacob will receive in the nominal faith of his parents. On this subject, Ann is unequivocal.

"He's going to grow up knowing what he is," she says.

All marriages develop shorthand forms of communication. In this marriage of ten years' duration between two Jews, I understand that Ann's pronouncement means the following: We'll never bring a Christmas tree into the house masquerading as that bastard entity, the "Chanukah bush." We'll send him to Hebrew school to learn something about his people's religion, history and language. He'll become bar mitzvah when he's 13. He'll get at least as far as we did.

Yes. But.

It is an evening late in 1979, and our year-old son Jacob is in bed for the night. Daddy is having that most unfunny of clichés, the Spiritual Crisis. At the age of 35, he has only lately owned his belief in God, a belief accepted and asserted in fearful defiance of his years of secular education and presumed rationalism. Now his wife has had the exquisite timing to remind him that he is also a *Jew* and the father of a Jew. Despite the fact that he has spent the last six months reading around in the works of Georges Bernanos, Dietrich Bonhoeffer and the apostate (so he will later name her, a bit unfairly) Simone Weil...despite more than six years spent reading and writing about English Renaissance literature, none of which does much to glorify Yiddishkeit...despite all this, his is not the God of Milton, Herbert or Donne, but rather, of *Avraham, Yitzchak* and *Ya'akov.*

Turning inward, there are endless questions all pointing toward beginnings. How did this start? And—*what am I going to do about it?*

II.

It began—and all but ended—with a withdrawn nine-year-old boy (of whom I am the biological and spiritual continuation) being shepherded by his mother to enroll in a Young Israel Talmud Torah in the Bronx, there to purchase yarmulke, notebook and Shilo *siddur,* and to begin learning the *aleph-beis* and the first (and last) declaration of our faith: *Sh'ma Yisroel, Adonoi Eloheiu, Adonoi Echod*—Hear O Israel, the Lord our God, the Lord is One.

Hebrew school was really nobody's idea. My father, who endured unknown traumas as a child on the Lower East Side in the early 1900s, was against the entire enterprise as a waste of his money and my time. My mother, daughter of socialists, was largely indifferent. And my wish to attend was based not on any consuming desire to learn Torah, but because my friends from PS 102 all were going and I didn't want to be left out.

As it turned out, Hebrew school quickly became excruciating. Always given to hyperbole, I viewed it as the martyrdom of Rabbi Akiba prolonged over three-and-a-half years. *Eileh ezkerah...,* "These martyred ones I shall remember..."—indeed. It was the daily torture of sounding out words in a language I was never taught to understand. It was the weekly ordeal of being tested for fluency rather than comprehension (and failing on both counts, anyway). Worst of all, it was enduring an annual season of terror—particularly fierce in a neurotic child—that I had not been a sufficiently Good Boy to merit sealing in the Book of Life on Yom Kippur.

And it was the gradual—only semiconscious—disillusioning realization that despite my not being a Good Boy, somehow I was managing to beat The System all the same. *Other* kids (some of them unquestionably Good Boys) were getting run over on Tremont Avenue. *Other* kids were getting polio and waddling around in ten pounds of steel and leather. *Other* kids were dying of leukemia.

Although I could not verbalize what I felt—and probably would not have dared do so if I could—a question about what I was being taught was developing somewhere deep inside me. It was the kind of question that, by the very nature of being asked, was also its own answer: *Who's kidding whom?*

And yet I persisted from year to year, driven by peer pressure, inertia and a burgeoning sense of greed. For I knew that at the end of my thrice-weekly servitude in the House of Bondage, I would experience a secular Pesach of personal liberation: my bar mitzvah on *Shabbas Yisro*, January 19, 1957.

In the autumn of 1956, the rabbi, a gentle and dedicated man, began to teach me the text and the *trop* for my Haftarah. He also began to instruct me in the obligations of a Jewish male beginning his religious adulthood, especially the *mitzvah* of putting on *t'fillin*, phylacteries, six mornings a week while praying the *Shacharis* service. Shortly before the date fixed for my bar mitzvah, I brought my new *t'fillin* to the rabbi, who taught me the order for laying them while reciting the prescribed blessings.

But something was very wrong, and perhaps the rabbi sensed it.

"Do you have any questions for me, Kalman?" he asked, using my Hebrew name, which was the given name of my father's father.

I know it's a commandment, Rabbi. But I don't know how to pray. Nobody ever taught us about that. And you know I don't understand the words. No one ever taught us about that, either. I don't know if I even believe any of this stuff anymore. What will I pray for? For God to make me the toughest kid in school instead of the class punching bag? For Him to take away my stutter? For Him to make my father rise from the grave he went into when I was 10? How will delaying my breakfast to perform a complicated, inconvenient act six days a week for the rest of my life make me a better Jew or better anything at all?

Oh, what's the difference? It'll all be over in two weeks, anyway. Shut up and let the rabbi talk. Take the money and run.

"No questions, Rabbi."

III.

I shut up. And I ran.

On my bar mitzvah morning, I chanted my Haftarah flawlessly in a still-unbroken tenor that rose and fell in dramatic mockery of a faith about which I cared too little to question, let alone observe. I pocketed the checks surreptitiously palmed to me by my relatives (for this was an Orthodox shul where money was not to be handled on Shabbos!) and, satisfied that I had been properly indemnified for my time served in Hebrew school, I breathed an earnest, empty *Shehecheyanu* and hit the ground running.

Enough has been written about the phenomenon of the "Jewish Drop-Out" to provide careers for a generation of tenure-hungry academic sociologists, so I will add only this much to the data bank: for me and for most of the friends I made in high school, college and beyond, the common experience of Hebrew school Judaism made any subsequent form of religious Judaism all but irrelevant. Religious Judaism was the exclusive province of *zaydes* on Essex Street or in Boro Park. It was *payess, shtreimels* and long black coats. It was a collection of archaic rules about no lights, TV or travel on Saturday (in New York City, *vu den!*). It was something for The Professionals, the men you turned to when you decided to get married and your family got on your case to Do It Right—with a rabbi—instead of in front of a swami, guru or Criminal Court judge.

In other words, religious Judaism was not even the tremendous monolith of the Roman Catholic Church against which my lapsed Catholic friends railed even as they admitted the awe in which they held their early spiritual and intellectual training.

Instead, it was just silly.

And so I, like most others I knew, turned my back. *My* Judaism was the kosher-style pastrami sandwiches I devoured with ice cream sodas. And my rabbi was the guy with the strongest of all links to the *real* Judaism: an extensive vocabulary of Yiddish words and phrases depicting excretory functions, sexual activity and the hoped-for fate of one's enemies.

IV.

Above my desk in an office where I worked for three-and-a-half years hung a quotation from Carl Jung's *Essays on a Science of Mythology:* "'What can I do?' 'Become what you have always been.'"

Throughout my 20s and into my middle 30s, my Judaism silently pursued me, relegated though it was to the suburbs of my conscious life by a willful separation from a nature I nevertheless recognized as increasingly spiritual. Judaism, I continued to insist, was cultural, not religious. Living for the first time in my life in an area that was not predominantly Jewish (the Triple Cities region of upstate New York), I grew increasingly attuned to evidence of presumed—and often all-too-obvious—anti-Semitism. When the Black Septembrists massacred the Israeli Olympic team in Munich in 1972, I shared in both the hurt of my people and the world's outrage. In 1973, I was appalled by the treachery and carnage of the Yom Kippur attack by Egypt. And in July 1976, I was thrilled by the daring of the raid on Entebbe and the humiliation of the *behemma*, the beast, Idi Amin. I was, after all, a Jew, and all Jews were my brothers.

So long, that is, as those Jews did not wear their faith between their eyes or upon their sleeves.

For the fact of the matter is that religious Judaism *embarrassed* me. It filled me with distaste, an almost physical discomfort and a formless anxiety and fear. Rosh Hashanah and Yom Kippur remained the worst of all. For years, particularly during the early and middle 1960s, I went out of my way to flout what I remembered of the days' solemnity by hanging out with my friends, smoking grass in the park and eating anything that fell into my hands. But I was never quite able to forget that I was flouting something of enormous sanctity to a people I recognized, however fuzzily and sentimentally, as my own. As I got older, I felt obligated to attend *Yizkor* services to stumble throught the transliteration of the *Kaddish* for my father, but I never stopped feeling hypocritical, fearful, misplaced and exposed.

Periodically, while going through my dresser drawers, I came across something that somehow managed to travel with me through my years of moving from one place to another: the blue velvet bag containing my *t'fillin*. It was all but impossible for me to open the bag, if only to look at what was inside. I am not at all certain what I felt at those times. Perhaps the tug of childhood guilt. Perhaps the discomfort of someone who has stumbled upon a memory he would just as soon forget because it evokes a world momentarily glimpsed, but now unattainable and lost. Perhaps fear.

Perhaps nothing.

In graduate school, earning a PhD in English, I decided to specialize in Renaissance Literature. I developed and to this day harbor a fondness for the 17th century religious poets: Southwell, Donne, but most of all, George Herbert. If confronted, I would claim to be an agnostic (it sounded politer than the too-definitive "atheist"); and yet, the poetry of Herbert, an Anglican priest with extraordinary poetic gifts, moved me deeply with its explicit belief in a palpable, personal God.

I had contemporaries in graduate school who could explicate Herbert with ease and grace, but who adopted the evangelical faith of the German rabbi's grandson, Karl Marx. I had gone through a more-or-less radical period myself in the late 1960s, and, the older I became, the less attractive the classic Marxist solution to the problems of world-repairing appeared. I found far more courage in the struggles of an anti-Fascist Central American Catholic priest than in the death of Che Guevara. Indeed, religious approaches to existential problems loomed increasingly large in my thinking, and, almost without being aware of it, I gravitated toward an ideal of living *in* the world without necessarily being *of* it. Largely as the result of my studies, but also because religion began to exert an irresistable force on my consciousness, I developed a reasonably sound theological knowledge and fascination.

But by the time I was 35 years old, I realized that I had been cheating. It dawned on me that all my examples of ethical conduct in a religious framework were Christian. I knew more about Anglicanism and Roman Catholicism than I ever knew about Yiddishkeit. I could tell you the date Luther posted his 95 Theses on the church door, but I could not have identified Rabbi Yochanan ben Zakkai. Indeed, I could not even identify the first night of Pesach when asked by a Gentile colleague. I was ripe for that conversation with my wife on that evening late in 1979.

V.

It is standard wisdom that people become "religious" when they acquire the responsibility of children. More often than not, joining a church or synagogue is confused with acquiring a religious sense. My wife's comment to me that Jacob would grow up knowing what he is did not "bring me back to God"; instead, it merely helped focus what had begun long, long before.

From without, I now looked at myself as something I had already come to find contemptible in others: a type of Simone Weil, the classic deracinated intellectual who rejected her own faith but could not accept conversion to another. The question became for me not only what kind of Jew my son would become, but what kind of Jew I was. The answer disturbed me.

My decision to "come back" was deliberate and conscious. If I did not say aloud, "At the age of 13 I unmade myself as a Jew, and now, at the age of 37, I am going to re-become one," that indeed was my precise sentiment. The problem was in reconciling my initial skepticism with an increasingly powerful need for identification with a people and faith.

My attempt at reconciliation was conducted with the intellectual rigor I had learned through years of education. I began to hunt, quite methodically, for a form of Judaism that would not intimidate me or revive in me the religious traumas of Orthodoxy that really were part of the whole cloth of a childhood that was little more than an extended trauma. In the next few months I read books about modern American Judaism, Jewish history and the major Jewish denominations, and discovered a movement I had never heard of, Reconstructionism.

When I read the Reconstructionist program, I recognized myself. Here was a group who shared my needs and interests. It did not compel me to accept a fixed concept of God. It did not command me to live a particular lifestyle, one that felt inappropriate and impractical to me at that point.

After I had been reading for several months, I spent an evening talking with a Reconstructionist rabbi about what was happening inside of me. Shortly thereafter, I attended Shabbas services at his congregation, and a few months later, joined it with my family. I found in this "reentry" congregation many people whose stories paralleled mine, people who had fought their way back into Yiddishkeit by a curious combination of force of will and negation of will. I began to relearn—or, more truthfully, really learn—the Hebrew I had forgotten from my childhood.

And suddenly I discovered that even this much was not enough.

Martin Buber's question of *ba'al t'shuvah* ("returnee" to Judaism) Franz Rosenzweig comes to mind: "Do you put on *t'fillin*?" Rosenzweig's answer: "Not yet."

In the early spring of 1981, as we anticipated the April birth of our second son, Rosenzweig's answer became mine, as well. A few months before, in January, my mother-in-law had returned from a tour of Egypt and Israel bearing a suitcase crammed with all sorts of gifts. For me there was a large *tallis,* appropriate, she said, for the father of two sons. Shortly thereafter, she posed the question that brought me up short: "Do you put on *t'fillin*?"

Sherley did not ask the question because she is particularly religious. Her father, a hard-working, yeshiva-educated Jew from the Russian Pale, had made a comfortable living—enough to raise and educate three daughters—in Sag Harbor, Long Island, during the Depression. He was a shrewd but impeccably ethical merchant. He also—perhaps not incidentally—put on *t'fillin* every weekday of his life. Perhaps Sherley saw something in me that I myself was not yet aware of. In any case, I didn't know what to answer, and the words that came from my mouth came in innocence of the question Buber asked Rosenzweig:

"Not yet."

In a sense, Sherley's question set the mechanism in motion. I found myself reading once again, this time about prayer: not simply the philosophy behind it, but also its mechanics (for Jewish prayer, as anyone who prays regularly will verify, is as much craft as inspiration.)

The communal prayers of my congregation had often moved me, but they were not always sufficient if my own concentration and intention—what I later learned to call *kavannah*—were not fixed to the congregational "clock." I now found myself needing to move beyond the communal aspects of prayer and confront through private prayer my feelings about myself as an individual Jew and, even more critically, about the existence of something I could no longer avoid viewing as a real presence, and which I could now call God. The *t'fillin*, unused and still residing in my bureau drawer, came to represent a commitment to myself not only as an individual and as a member of *k'lal Yisrael,* but also as the father of two Jewish boys who would learn from my example long before they would learn from the well-meant preachments of a Hebrew school teacher or anyone else who would ever come into their lives.

In a very real sense, then, those *t'fillin* acquired the significance of a personal mitzvah fulfilled *and* of my acceptance of what I was and might become as a Jew.

Thus, one Thursday afternoon I brought my *t'fillin* to a Hebrew book dealer and had him adjust the straps to fit the head of the 37-year-old man who had once been a 12-year-old boy. The bookseller offered neither comments nor explanations. He asked me only one question: "Do you put them on Ashkenazic-style or Sephardic-style?" Fortunately, from the reading I had done I knew the differences.

The following Sunday morning, after a fitful night spent dreaming about what I was about to do, I skipped breakfast, retired to the bedroom and donned my *tallis* and *t'fillin* by the numbers. I then painfully battled my way through the major prayers and declarations of the morning service. It seemed to take forever, an exercise to conquer my own ignorance and intense discomfort.

I rewrapped the *t'fillin* and replaced them in their bag, folded my *tallis* and returned to the living room. Ann looked at me. I never asked her what she saw in my face at that moment, but I recall myself all but hyperventilating.

"This is what it was all for, wasn't it?" she asked. "It's probably been coming for a long time." And she was right.

But not entirely.

VI.

I am not an observant Jew. Instead, I am a Jew who has extracted from the whole cloth of Jewish law and tradition a single observance, one of the most sacred of Jewish rituals, and molded it around my life. I have discovered prayer as a central part of my existence, a need that I neither can nor will attempt to explain, justify or analyze.

Yes. But.

I do not know what kind of Jew I am or shall become. I no longer belong to the Reconstructionist congregation that brought me back into Judaism; I am active, instead, in a Conservative congregation nearer my home. This does not mean, however, that I have become insensitive to the need for change and creativity in Judaism. It suggests to me, instead, that my drive for change is complemented by my preservationist urge, my strong attraction to traditional forms of worship and behavior.

I have travelled an immense distance from what and where I was three years ago. In some ways, I have rejoined the nine-year-old I used to be, recognizing that the seeds sown then—however unwillingly or unawares—have begun to flower as I approach middle age. I have taken it upon myself to raise not two but three boys to Jewish awareness and observance: not only Jacob and Benjamin, my sons, but also the boy named Kenneth Wolman. This third boy is being brought slowly along toward a level of Jewishness he cannot predict but which he no longer avoids, denies or fears. This boy and I reject nothing, for all things may yet be possible. ✯

NOËL COWARD

CAROL KUR

Carol Kur, Moment's longtime managing editor, lives in Brookline, Massachusetts, where she now does freelance writing and editing.

Every year, we would take a ride to look at the lights. It was a family ritual. One evening, sometime between December 23 and January 1 (but never on *the* day), we would bundle into our coats and galoshes and climb into the old Dodge. The tire chains would thung-thung-thung-thung through the snow as we crept along the holiday-hushed neighborhood streets. Clandestine. Inevitably, someone would begin to hum the melody of a carol, and because singing together was commonplace for us, the others couldn't resist joining in. And before long, the thung-thung-thung of the tire chains was drowned out by pure, if restrained, four part harmony (but never *the* words). *"O come, let us adore hi-immmm, hum, hum, hu-hum."*

Always given to the dramatic, I pretended to be the Poor Little Match Girl. Was it really the way the stories described it? The neighbors worked hard to out-do themselves (and each other) every year. The lights were gloriously beautiful, and my fantasies projected detailed imaginings of the joy and festivity and warmth and glow that was happening inside all those sparkling, clean, well-lighted houses. And when we arrived home to our own dark house, we drank hot chocolate in subdued silence, despite the reminders from our parents that *we*, after all, had eight days, and *they* only had one. (*The* one.)

Unquestionably, this is not *our* season to be jolly, Chanukah notwithstanding. This is the season when Jewish marginality, never very far from the surface, emerges fully blown, disturbing the delicate ecumenical truce that governs our neighborly interactions from January through November. And we, who are noted for our ability to persevere in the face of adversity, do not cope well at all.

Witness: The Chanukah Bush becomes a seasonal tradition in any number of otherwise Jewish households. Or, it becomes custom for large families to congregate, have a holiday meal, and exchange "Chanukah" gifts on December 25—after all, everyone has the day off, and it is so convenient to hold the celebration on that day. Or, "Chanukah Joe" sneaks in the back door at the homes of good little *Jewish* boys and girls, while his merry old cousin Nick is busy pursuing the more conventional chimney route.

Nor does it do at all well to sermonize about the folly of such misguided behavior. That such actions are an infringement upon traditions that do not belong to us, that in our efforts to include ourselves we demean our own heritage and mock the heritage we so crudely emulate—that's clear. Yet it remains for all of us but the most isolated and insulated (read: ghettoized) it is impossible to be blind to the splendor of the season, and it is human to reach out for the camaraderie that it engenders.

So—otherwise sensible, if casual, Jews find all manner of rationalization acceptable in their charade of inclusion. "Oh, we don't celebrate it as a *religious* holiday. That's archaic. It's really become a secular holiday." Try that one out on an observant Christian friend, bent on doing *his* thing—putting the Christ back into Christmas. Or, "We only let the children hang stockings on Christmas Eve. There's nothing sacred about *that*. We don't have a tree or anything."

I remember returning home one Christmas Eve several years ago to find the fireplace mantle festooned with bright red knee socks to which our children had affixed white cotton balls. After we recovered from fits of uproarious laughter (probably more hysterical than gleeful), we pondered what to do. Ignore them? Tell the kids we never saw them? Humor them? Fill the stockings and have a heart-to-heart chat in the morning? Don't fill the stockings and wake them for the chat that very minute? Finally, we searched the house for any and every Jewish object we could lay our hands on. We stuffed silver kiddush cups, Chanukah candles, Hebrew notebooks, dreidels, Simchat Torah flags, hats and coins from our last trip to Israel, old copies of the Synagogue bulletin, and finally, on the very top of each stocking, we placed a shiny prisoner of conscience *magen david* necklace. I don't know if we did the right thing. I only know that it was our first and last "stocking caper." And, of course, we had the talk in the morning.

That our own Festival of Lights competes for seasonal honors is indeed a mixed blessing. On its own, Chanukah is a lovely holiday. Appreciation for its meaning can be shared by the very young, who delight in the story of the miracle of the little flask of oil, or by the more advanced, who can marvel at the miracle of deliverance from oppression and can grasp the significance of rededication. And so we have much to celebrate. But, that we count on those eight little candles to outshine the splendor of trees, tinsel, sparkling electricity of sight and sound, so dazzlingly packaged by Madison Avenue's best, is simply too much to ask. Even the Maccabees did not face such overwhelming odds.

Perhaps, as future generations of young Jews reach maturity, they will be armed with a stronger sense of security about themselves than we, their forebears. Perhaps pride in ethnicity will continue to grow stronger, and religious understanding expand. Until they do, the seasonal identity crisis will continue to be a problem to be acknowledged, to be managed. We may feel a bit of lust in our hearts—the harmonies *are* spectacular—but in the end, Christmas is *their* Christmas: at its best, our neighbors' Christmas, mangers and all, and season's greetings to them every one. Our compliments to the singers, the dancers, the players—and then home, to make our own warmth, a different warmth, not with the glow of candles alone, but with rich remembering, fervent dream, and lavish, unimitative present. ✡

"Over the river and through the woods

WE GATHER TOGETHER

CAROL KUR

At home, the Simchat Torah flag was the last remnant of the holiday season; the taste of apples and honey had long since faded.

And so we came to the brief time of congruence in our calendar of annual celebration, of sweet and relieving merger of our secular (public school) lives, and our Jewish ones, a respite from the tugs and tensions of a separate agenda, tem-

Pure nostalgia. Visions of Mrs. Stout, the elementary school music teacher, emerge from the recesses of childhood memory: a cheerful round face that perfectly matched her name, and a tightly coiled black chignon that bobbed just a bit as she led the chorus through the double *fortes*.

The song evokes the memory because it was the one she always used to in-

porarily at one with our non-Jewish classmates. For September marked not only the beginning of a new school year, but of our Jewish year, and, through most of October, we led double lives. Although we were enmeshed with new books and teachers and classmates, we missed chunks of school time as Rosh Hashanah and Yom Kippur, Sukkot and Simchat

Torah tumbled one upon the next. We were confronted by questions from our peers (and, not infrequently, from our teachers) such as: how come you stay out two days and Rochelle only stays out one?

Just ahead, the discomfort of December, the time of greatest separation, loomed large, with Bing Crosby, Mother Nature, and the genius of American mer-

chandising combining to remind us just how small a minority we are. November, and Thanksgiving, provide a resting place both comfortable and important.

As a family, we delighted in our Jewishness. We knew who we were; assimilation was never even a temptation. But for a seven or eight or nine-year-old, growing up as one of two or three Jews in a public

troduce Thanksgiving. Meanwhile, we neatly folded away the Nina, the Pinta, and the Santa Maria that had anchored "October" on the bulletin board, not so neatly soaped and scraped away the black cats and witches' hats, orange jack o'lanterns and fingernail slices of midnight moon painted on the classroom windows, and began cutting out pilgrim's hats with big silver buckles.

Carol Kur, Moment's *longtime managing editor, lives in Brookline, Massachusetts, where she now does freelance writing and editing.*

14/MOMENT

Jewish Possibilities: The Best of Moment

to Grandmother's house we go."

school class of more than 30, it was pleasant to be able to share a celebration of mutual significance, from the inside and at ease.

In his essay, "The Twelve Weeks of Christmas" (January 1963), Milton Himmelfarb says, "Thanksgiving seems made to order for Jews. As a friend and colleague has noted, it is celebrated by eating, and Jews eat rather than drink. . . . And what comes out of the mouth on Thanksgiving is equally Jewish—both the message and the tone. Thanksgiving is the great point of intersection between Judaism and the sacral tradition of America."

Indeed, Thanksgiving is so Jewish that we could have invented it. Examine it custom by custom, and you will see that we Jews could have packaged it, as is, no omissions or emendations, and presented it as our gift to America's heritage. (Not that we should take credit for it. Columbus may have been a Jew, but Miles Standish wasn't. Well, most likely wasn't.) In any case, its Jewish essence cannot be ignored. Consider:

★ It is a four-and-a-half day weekend. In preparation for the big day, schools release kids at noon on Wednesday, *erev* Thanksgiving. By sundown, it's *yomtov*.

★ It is a gastronomic field day, food centered, fattening, and strictly kosher, from the big bird through the cranberry relish and the pumpkin pie.

★ It is a family day. We may not have to go over the river and through the woods, and we opt for wings or wheels rather than a sleigh. Still, grandmother's house is a more than likely

destination. But if Bubbe is leaving for Florida right after the holiday, we'll have everybody at our house this year.

★ It is a day for—quite literally—giving thanks. We recite *Shehecheyanu* at our Thanksgiving table, and our non-Jewish neighbors are every bit as comfortable with that as we are with "We Gather Together" and "Bless This House." And

in the same frenzy of preparation, of shopping and baking and cooking, as everyone else. We can even go and cheer for the local high school football team, which in every other week of the season plays on Friday night or Saturday morning.

In short, there is not a single feature, a single element, a single custom in the celebration of Thanksgiving

the opportunity to offer thanks for the abundance of America, and for its freedoms, is especially meaningful for us.

There's more. Thanksgiving was not scheduled for Sunday, which would have made it, probably, much more church-oriented than family and home centered, and it never comes on Shabbat, therefore never excludes us. We can engage

that strikes a discordant note. And so we feel richly blessed, and thankful, indeed, for our own great bounty, and for our marvelous good fortune that the Pilgrims spotted that wild turkey for their very first Thanksgiving feast, and not, heaven forfend, a wild boar. Accordingly, from our house to yours, and without a trace of irony, *chag sameach*. ✡

We Gather Together

Moment/15

PORTRAITS AT A CONDOMINIUM
From Bialystok to Brooklyn to Boca Raton

FERN KUPFER

Fern Kupfer's novel Surviving the Seasons *will be published by Delacorte in 1987. She is currently living in Ames, Iowa, and is thinking about another novel.*

The Bronx, 1949
I am standing on a chair pulled up to the kitchen counter, watching my grandmother, her fingers clenched around a sharp cleaver, her knuckles protruding white and shiny, as she chops onions in a wooden bowl. I stare mesmerized as the doughy flabs of her busy arm sway rhythmically to the clop-clop of the blade against the wood, like horses' hooves on cobblestone.

The smells of pot roast, of soup greens simmering on the stove, fill the small apartment, clinging to brocade, to the overstuffed furniture in the other room. The apartment is European dark, heavy with pillows; oriental scatter rugs in dusky rose and faded teal; huge, brass-based floor lamps; and a sofa whose legs claw the living room floor.

My grandmother, who is always hot even in winter, wears a sleeveless cotton dress under her apron and fans herself as she looks out of the fifth-floor window at the grimy New York snow. She muses to my grandfather, who is drinking a glass of tea at the table.

"You know what I think, Lou? When one of us dies, I think I'll go to Florida."

West Palm Beach, 1982
My mother's arm, holding her tennis racket overhead, is sure and still for the serve. I make a mental "click-click" to preserve this shot, her shot, in my mind. My mother at 63, brown and freckled under that blue sky, running across the court, an overhand swing that sails the ball evenly toward the far right corner: It's in.

"Good shot, Grandma," yells my daughter from behind the fence.

"Oh, your kids are here already?" says my mother's tennis partner, wiping the sweat from her brow.

Only yesterday we were digging our way out of a snow-drifted driveway in Iowa. The teacher asks her fourth-grade class, "And what do you do for the holidays?"

"We go to my grandparents, to their condominium in Florida," says my daughter. Condominium is a word she has correctly pronounced since nursery school, when she knew that milk came from cows and babies grew in mothers' tummies and grandparents lived in condominiums.

The condominiums in West Palm Beach have elegant names—Poinciana Place, The Fountains, Lakewood Estates. My parents' complex has an attempted quaintness: Like a New England fishing village, the streets surrounding the man-made lake are called Dorchester Court, Martha's Vineyard, Worcester Way. The condominium itself is named Covered Bridge, and a wooden bridge, new but authentically rickety, spans a narrow bit of lake.

It's Christmas vacation, and "the children are coming" is a cry spread across the Southern peninsula. The children are coming, pasty-faced from frigid New York and the blustery Midwest, ready for their week in the sun. Going to see Grandma no longer means a Sunday drive out to Brooklyn or the Bronx. Supermarkets near the condominiums prepare for the invasion, stocking up on Pampers and sand pails and first-cut briskets of beef.

The Florida sun is so bright that the landscape seems washed, splashed by light. The sky, the water, the black-paved roads all reflect the light, seem laminated by it. The women wear white pants and blouses in colorful hot pinks, yellows. They wear purple sandals and golden chains. They laugh a lot when they play bridge together and look forward to dinner parties and visits from the kids. They have enough money to be "comfortable" and are in good health, knock wood. As my mother says, "It's some life!"

My mother's tennis partner says that she can't play tomorrow.

"My boy is coming," she says proudly. I know her boy—a man approaching 40 with a thickening waist and thinning hair. She is going to make ready her home, to stock the shelves, to cook the favorite foods of his childhood. "My boy is coming." My boy, my light, my pearl. The son, Marty, is an anesthesiologist who, according to his mother, is doing "very well," pulling in the big bucks as he puts people to sleep.

Sons who become doctors are plentiful here; and now, especially among the new condominium dwellers, daughters will be, too. The status acclaimed by "my daughter who married

16/Moment

a doctor" will no longer be the ultimate *nachas;* today the daughters can *be* the doctors. Lawyers, too, are common as high blood pressure. And accountants. And college professors. Sometimes there is exaggeration among members of this group that has apparently spawned only professionals. Once, poolside, I heard a woman introduce her son as *the* therapist for the West Coast.

My mother's tennis partner walks off down the trail to her own village, Nantucket Circle. "So long, kids," she says to my husband and me. "Enjoy. Enjoy."

We, the "kids," are the third generation of immigrant Jews who left the poverty and persecution of Eastern Europe for a chance in the New World. My grandfather would tell me, "Two dollars to my name and didn't speak von vord of English," his voice trembling as it rose, as if to emphasize the peril. In America, he painted houses for a living, high, high on scaffolds taller than any building in his native village, and shared a tenement room with three other young men who had come off the boat with empty pockets and big dreams. I loved to hear his stories about life on the Lower East Side, about sleeping out on fire escapes on sweltering nights, of choosing a two-cent pickle from the barrel for an afternoon treat. It is a life that exists now only in memory and in those novels, the shtetl-to-success stories that are popular with my parents' friends. They read them as they lie on lounge chairs by the pool. Floridians now. Oh, what a strange tribal migration: From Bialystok to the Bronx to Boca Raton. The spirit of my grandparents hovers amid the palm trees. What would they think about this life? My grandfather, who had seen the Czar in a passing parade, in West Palm Beach? I have a flash of him standing by the pool in his long, blue overcoat, shrugging his narrow shoulders, paint chips still under his fingernails. He would say, "I don't know from swimming pools. Chlorine, feh!"

My grandmother, who never did make it to Florida, would be more appreciative. She had loved the beach. As a young woman, in this country not more than a year, she was "issued a citation" at Coney Island for taking off the black cotton stockings that, at the beginning of the century, were deemed appropriate beachwear. She was afraid of the big, blond policeman who wrote out the ticket (looking all the while at the stockings which lay across the blanket, the shape of her leg still outlined in them, evidence of her lewdness), afraid she would go to jail, or worse—perhaps even be deported. Removing the hose was not a political act. She just longed to feel the soft sand between her toes, the warmth on her bare skin. She would like it here, so near the beach.

Now, in my mother's bedroom, a room with white walls and white carpet and plenty of mirrors, we are haggling over a bathing suit, a gift she offers but which I'm not sure I want. My mother initially bought it for herself. The suit is an electric green with a high-cut leg. "French-cut," says my mother. Where did she learn such terms?

"Well, I liked it when I tried it on in the store but then when I got it home, I thought that it really wasn't for me," she says. (I get many such gifts this way.)

The suit is very provocative and uncomfortable. I'm not sure it's for me either. My mother tells me it looks great. "Go show your father," she says, pointing me out toward the living room. I am back to being ten years old, showing Daddy the new party dress, wanting to please. My own ten-year old daughter looks up from her Judy Blume book with raised eyebrows. But my father briefly seconds the opinion. "Looks great," he says and goes back to the newspaper.

I walk with my mother and my daughter to the pool in this new suit, my own good judgment clouded by my family's not impartial praise, self-conscious at the pads of buttock spilling out beneath the scanty brief. My husband is already at the pool and he whistles softly as I walk by his chair.

"*You* bought a suit like that?" he asks.

"No, Grandma bought it," says our daughter blandly, not in the least astonished at a tennis-playing grandmother who buys French-cut bathing suits.

The other sons and daughters of the

My daughter wants to know if they had condominiums in Europe.

> "How are you?" has become a condominium in-joke. "Better," they say in mock seriousness.

condominium owners lie spread-eagled, greased, across plastic chairs. Today in the shallow middle of the pool is a red-haired woman in her mid-60s bobbing towards deeper water with a little boy, also red-headed, in her arms. Her black bathing suit is low-cut, around her neck is a gold chain with the letters N-A-N-A dangling between two ample breasts. The child squeals with delight as the water hits his legs, then his waist, then his chest.

"More, Grandma! More," he yells, making giddy-up-horsie motions with his body. The red-haired woman continues to bob toward deeper water and covers his cheeks with noisy kisses until the water reaches his neck. Then she places him with a wet plop by the side of the pool and calls out.

"Carol. Put a shirt on him. This Florida sun is murder."

A woman in her late 20s with auburn hair and nails the color of late summer plums gets up from her chair, comes over with a tiny football jersey, number 66.

"Here you go, sweetheart," she says to the boy.

"Herb! Herb!" yells N-A-N-A from the pool to a man reading the New York *Times* in the shade of a palm frond.

"Herb, I want you to meet my family. This is my daughter Carol, from Westchester, and *this*," she waves her arm with a flourish to number 66, now shivering by the pool's edge, "*this* is Spencer!" Spencer smiles shyly up at the man.

"Can you say hi to Herb?" prods his grandmother.

The man asks silent Spencer, "Where'd you get that red hair from? You get your red hair from your Grandma, huh?"

"No," says red-headed N-A-N-A, still in the pool. "No, I was a blondie all my life. I took a look at him when he was born and went out and did *mine* red, too." Then laughing, "*I* got mine from *him*!"

The smells of roasting meats waft across the swimming pool. If I close my eyes, I can skip across three decades in my mind, back to that kitchen in the Bronx. By my reverie is interrupted by a harsh voice:

"Where's your tag? I don't see your I.D. tag."

There is a man, bald and round, standing in my sun. He is in a plaid bathing suit and shirtless, but he has the officious air of someone in uniform. As a matter of fact, he is wearing a button pinned onto the elastic waist band of his swim suit: Pool Committee, it says. The white identification tag, which reveals that I am indeed a bona fide guest of condominium residents and not a gate-crashing rowdy out for a free swim, is folded in my towel. Wordlessly, I hold it up.

"That's no good there. You have to wear your tag. It's gotta be visible at all times. Put it on."

I am not used to being spoken to so rudely, having lived the last ten years in the Midwest, where one would never be ordered about by a stranger or waiters or a clerk at the motor vehicle bureau.

I balk, slightly. "Well, you see I have it. Why do I have to wear it?"

" 'Cause that's the rule. Look, this is *our* place and you're a guest here. . . ." He is getting a nasty tone now, whereas before he was merely bossy. Cowed, I put the tag on my wrist and shut my eyes, feeling the sun again on my face as he moves off. I hear him yelling across the pool at someone who is about to jump in: "Did you shower? The rule says you hafta shower before you swim." The teenager sloughs off sourly toward the outdoor stall. Later I see another man with a Pool Committee button on his straw sun hat reprimanding some children who are too enthusiastic in their water play.

"No splashing," he bellows.

My daughter is afraid of these Pool Committee men and wants me to come in with her to swim.

"It's okay," I assure her. "Just wear your tag, and shower before you get into the pool, and don't dive or splash, and wear your cap. . . . "

"How come there are so many rules?" she asks.

I don't know, myself. There are people here who run the show, obsessed by rules and standards, frantic in their determination lest . . . lest what? Are they afraid of the neighborhood going bad? There does seem to be an over-zealous law-and-order streak to condominium life. A friend who was staying with her folks at their condo in Fort Lauderdale said that her teenagers ("who are really good kids") were continuously hassled whenever they used the facilities. "They must really hate kids," her daughter said. "Why don't they just put up one big sign: 'NO'?"

My daughter, who has heard this story, agrees—they must hate kids. No, of course not, I tell her. It's just that, well, the people here want a quiet place to live and they're retired so they have a lot of time on their hands. They do seem to make themselves busy with these committees, with drafting these endless rules and regulations. It goes deeper, perhaps, to the concepts of power and control for people who no longer effect changes in the real world, to minds set in the foundations of talmudic legality, to pride of ownership. This land is mine, God gave this land to me.

"And some older people are just grouchy," I tell my daughter. (But they were probably grouchy as younger people, too.)

In the *Condo News* this week, congratulations are announced to Rose and Abe Feinblatt, who have a new grandson Joshua Elliott. . . . Welcome back to Snowbirds Sylvia and Harold Hemmings. . . . Have you tried the poo-poo platter at the new Dragon Sky Restaurant at Oceanridge Plaza? Dee-licious! . . . Our best wishes for a speedy recovery to Al Ruben following his successful triple bypass surgery last week. We're waiting to see you back on the greens soon, Al.

My parents and their condo cohorts think of themselves as active members in life's community, a lively group. It is for them, released from the pressures and responsibilities of working and raising a family, a good time of life. My parents are healthy. They eat green vegetables and fiber and get plenty of exercise. My mother smiles, surprised at being able to pay senior citizen rates in the movie theater. "Am I old?" she says. "I don't feel old. I can't really believe my life went so damn fast."

At night, sitting with a cool drink on the patio, you can hear an ambulance wail down by the road. Always there is talk of someone's heart attack, someone's colostomy, of a woman who "just lost her husband." (Hearing that euphemism for the first time some years ago, my daughter thought that the man had wandered off at a shopping mall.)

My parents and their friends laugh sometimes at the infirmities, at themselves. Their reply to that casual cliché, "How are you?" has become a condominium in-joke. "Better," they say in mock seriousness.

One morning I walk with my father to buy some groceries, past a group of men riding bicycles down the tree-lined boulevard. They all know Dad. "Hi," they shout, "Hi ya," one after the other, waving merrily.

"What are they so happy about?" I say to my father.

He smirks sarcastically. "They're happy to be alive."

The supermarket is filled with shoppers, mostly the well-kept elderly from the condominiums. There are more men here than in an ordinary suburban market during daytime hours, some alone with their lists, adjusting reading glasses as they hold two packages of cereal aloft to compare prices. No one seems rushed. Some married couples shop together, although my parents never do. My mother complains that my father takes things out of the cart. "Then he puts in cookies when I'm not looking. I put in, he takes out. He puts in, I take out. I'd rather go by myself."

My mother says that she can always spot the second marriages in the supermarket, those peaceful and cooperative couples who take joy together in their discovery of specials on cans of tuna and 3/$1.00 yogurt. Some of the shoppers are in tennis shorts, the women in crisp culottes or sun dresses, looking tan and peppy. I mention to Dad that all the people here seem in such good shape. "Well, it's a younger crowd," he explains. "A younger *old* crowd."

Just then in the produce department we see a frail old woman, 90 if she's a day, taking tiny, bird-like steps as she moves about the oranges. Four peaches in a plastic bag. A small package of grapes. A boney arm moves slowly out over the lettuce. Coming up behind her is an even more ancient little man using his shopping cart as a walker. He calls, "So Sarah, vere ya running?"

Our last day of vacation, we go to the beach, and my mother, my daughter and I take a long walk by the ocean, picking up shells, stopping to look at the waves as they crest, lulled by the gentle roar. I stand flanked between the generations and explain to my child that when *I* was her age and went to the beach with *my* grandmother, we, too, would walk along and dig for crabs and find shells with silver-pink linings.

"And we'd look out over the ocean, only we were at a beach in New York, not Florida, and my grandma would tell me to look across and I'd see Europe—although I never could—that Europe was where she was born."

My daughter wants to know if they had condominiums in Europe. I say that they probably do now, although they didn't when her great-grandma was born, which was almost one hundred years ago.

"And she'd be too poor anyway to own one, right?" my daughter asks, having heard the immigrant stories third hand from me, so watered down by now that you could no longer taste the brine from those wooden pickle barrels.

So maybe it's goodbye to all that. Really, what's so great about fire escapes? Rusty cages. Dangerous eyesores, when you get right down to it. I do wonder if my daughter will tell her child tales of this condominium life. I wonder if there will be magic in the memories there for her as well. ✤

SEARCHING FOR THE SELF

AN EXCHANGE OF LETTERS

JANET LEHRMAN BROWN

Last year as part of my campaign to be nice to my parents, I went to Rosh Hashanah services at our local temple. It had been at least four years since I'd gone, and having mellowed somewhat with age—I'm thirty now—I was kind of hoping it would mark the beginning of a better relationship with Judaism. You see, I'm one of those younger Jews whom the Reform rabbis worry about. I grew up in a good Jewish home; I went to Hebrew school three afternoons a week; I even learned to speak Hebrew when I was sixteen and went to Israel, stars in my eyes, to be a *chalutz*. But since I've become an adult, I've been unable to see any reason, save nostalgia, for making a Jewish identity the center of my personal identity. Some of my friends are Jewish, but a lot aren't, and worse—in the eyes of my family and the Reform rabbis—I've fallen seriously in love with a wonderful man who isn't the least bit Jewish.

It's not that I'm not a religious person. No, in fact the problem may be that I am. Otherwise I might have gone to Temple this Rosh Hashanah, enjoyed looking at everyone's new clothing, let my mind wander during the sermon, and gone home smugly complimenting myself for being part of the Great Jewish People. But I didn't. What I did instead was listen carefully to what the Rabbi had to say, and as I did so I remembered why it was that I had stopped going to Temple in the first place.

The best way that I can explain it is to say that if this Rabbi had been speaking about Moses and the Children of Israel in the Desert he would have told his congregation about the case of a charismatic leader of an ethnic group that had been culturally and economically disadvantaged for a significant time span. He would then have explained that this leader, whose speech impediment had identified him as learning-impaired, had led his ethnic group on a forty-year encounter session in an ecologically unendangered area. After this would have come the punch line: we should all be proud because they, like us, were Jews.

You could almost hear the bodies of a thousand Jewish saints whirling as the Rabbi spoke—and maybe those of a few social scientists, since the sociological jargon dragged in to give the sermon relevance was often incorrectly used.

As the Rabbi droned on about the Great Jewish Tradition, I tried to imagine what message a stranger like my Goyish but open-minded boy friend would have extracted from this sermon, what answer he would have found here to the question, "What do Jews worship?" The answer would have been clear, I think. Jews—at least educated, middle-class, American Jews—worship an idea of Jewishness. The origin of that Jewishness? The worship by Jewish ancestors of a God, now retired, whom those ancestors had once believed it prudent to worship, praise, and extol.

I thought about this God a bit further, wondering why he's *been* retired. He was old, of course, but that wasn't reason enough. Then again, he was hard to get along with. The passages we read out loud from the Union Prayerbook make a point of stressing just how likely he was to visit us with a variety of misfortunes. Of course he was just as likely to rescue us from these misfortunes—that may even have been the point of the passages—but he sounded at best unstable, and unhealthily fond of praise. In short, a God no sensible, balanced, modern person was likely to be drawn to.

Fine. But is it enough to replace this God with the worship of Jewishness? For my father it is. I have only to think of my father's stories of his boyhood, when as a small, frightened, Jewish immigrant, he had to run home from school dodging the rocks thrown by Polish immigrant children who chased after him crying, "Christ-killer." There's no mystery about why my father has a strong Jewish identification: for him Jews are the people who are on his side. He finds no difficulty in being aggressively Jewish, even though anything vaguely supernatural—a belief in a God-force or an afterlife—he finds distastefully unscientific.

But for me clubhouse Judaism won't work. I grew up in America. The flack I've gotten hasn't come from anti-Semites. I've been discriminated against because I was a woman and wouldn't keep to my place, and I've been sent away from lunch counters unserved because I lived on a Hippy farm, but the closest I've come to anti-Semitism was the time I was fired from a job in a cocktail lounge because my hair was too frizzy—and that happened in the South. The people who have stood by my side in times of stress have not been distinguished from those who haven't by the fact of their being Jewish. Some were, some weren't. Just as some of the people who have done the things I've had to protest were Jewish, and some weren't. In spite of the rhetoric I've heard about "the Jewish community" I have yet to encounter it as a real entity. In no situation throughout my life have I been in a strange town and needed help and been able to turn instinctively to Jews simply because they were Jews—yet in many such situations I have turned to women, because they were women, or musicians because they were musicians, with no other introduction, and made an instant, helpful connection. If Judaism is going to command my devotion, it is going to have to offer me something more profound than a group identification. I already have several of those.

There are two explanations for

why the Jewish people have existed as long as they have. The first one, the depressing one, is that they survived because they were constantly persecuted. If this explanation is true, you can put the Jews among good-natured people who don't persecute them, and you will have solved the Jewish Question as thoroughly as any Nazi could wish. The fate of the Sephardic Jews who fled to China after the expulsion from Spain points a warning here. Welcomed by the Chinese merchant class for their intelligence and skill, they had all but disappeared through intermarriage and assimilation within a century or two. If all that Judaism can offer me and my generation is a reference group, we may well be on our way to a similar fate here in America.

There is, however, another explanation for the survival of Judaism. I think of my grandmother for whom God was a friend, albeit a demanding one, and who believed firmly that death was a gateway into a new existence. My grandmother lived a spiritual life in a Jewish fashion. She didn't harp on her Judaism, or brag that so-and-so, the famous such-and-such was Jewish. As a matter of fact her chauvinism was more likely to come out about Hungarians, since my grandmother was an immigrant from that unlucky land. What my grandmother did was radiate a sprightly joy which clearly was connected with her Jewish beliefs. The acts of charity she performed were not performed because the Jewish tradition prescribes good works, but because my grandmother had an understanding of the world, a spiritual understanding, which made good works natural. Yes, she brought her own plates when she visited us, but we knew, at least we children knew, that that was not the point. When my grandmother was told she had cancer, her spiritual understanding continued to give her strength. The last time I ever saw her she was lighting the shabbos candles from her bed; disease had shrivelled her to the size of a child, but her eyes still shone with faith. I'd give a lot to know what she knew. I've had a few flashes of what it was, but nothing I can sustain from day to day.

A Judaism that could teach me what it taught my grandmother would be a Judaism to which I could give my heart. But the Judaism I saw at my local temple cannot. As long as a good rabbi is one who does not alienate the town's business leaders, congregations will be made up, as they are now, of moderately well-off folks who need the reference group that Judaism provides, who enjoy weddings and bar-mitzvahs like any other party, and who are raising children for whom Judaism can have no real gut-relevance. They'll listen to the rabbi's psychological jargon, but when they have problems, you better believe they're going to go to a psychologist. Until Jewish congregations are led by people and filled with people who have dedicated themselves to a lifetime of learning and living the spiritual reality that animated my grandmother, I will have to leave undecided the question: Am I, by anything more significant than an accident of birth, a Jew?

LEONARD FEIN

Dear Janet Lehrman Brown:

Your letter is, of course, a question, even though it comes in the disguise of an attack. But since the real attack on Judaism and Jewish belonging is clad in indifference and speaks in the language of sullen silence, I know that you do not mean to destroy; you mean to understand.

So let's talk about the three main characters in your story: the rabbi, your grandmother—and, most important, JLB herself.

The rabbi: I hold no brief for the kind of rabbi you describe. I have met him in many synagogues and temples across the country. He wants to be with it, to be relevant. He may be a mite embarrassed at the title "Rabbi," preferring to be called "Doctor." The most that I can say for him is that it's no great joy to enter a calling that has teaching as its central aspect, and then to discover that your students cut almost all their classes. The rabbi you encountered may be a caricature, but even the best of his colleagues end up damnably frustrated. Come the high holidays, they look out at a sea of people—most of them as much in search as you—who sit there and say, "Show me." There is less an air of expectancy than a brooding skepticism. Strangers have come together, for a wide variety of reasons, for a wide variety of backgrounds, and the poor rabbi, who knows better than you that this is his own annual opportunity to work a piece of magic—and who also, if he's like most, has his own personal agenda with God that day—must charm, educate, inspire, convert. "Be charismatic," the audience (for it is not a congregation) says; "you've got two hours, or three, to defeat the massed forces of secularization, of modernism, of alienation and assimilation. Make it happen."

And that's the best of the assembly; the rest just want out as quickly as possible.

I don't know the rabbi you heard that day. From what you say about him, I suspect I'm fortunate not to know him. But I wonder, even about him, even after what you've said, what sort of an impression he might have made on you had you come to him and said, "Some of my friends and I would like to meet with you once a week, and really study. We did when we were kids, but that was a long time ago, and now we want a non-pediatric Judaism. No sociological jargon, no effort to make things 'relevant.' The texts, in their own terms. Will you help?"

The point, I guess, is that for a rabbi to work, you've got to know how to use him. With very, very few exceptions, the worst possible way to use a rabbi, any rabbi, is to have him do his high holiday number.

And then, of course, there's the problem of generalizing from one episode, from one case. We're dealing with a 4,000 year old tradition—one that includes and once nurtured your grandmother, and so cannot be casually dismissed as lightweight—and when you enter that tradition, it seems to me that you can't place the burden of proof on its representatives. Given its extravagant productivity, given its manifest power to sustain and enrich the lives of so very many different people in so very many different places and circumstances, the burden's on you—and on me, on all of us. A mediocre rabbi? Even a horrendous rabbi? So what? In what conceivable sense does that have any bearing at all on the meanings of Judaism and Jewishness?

Your father, as many of the congregants, came to the synagogue for reasons of which you do not entirely approve. Although he regards religious doctrine as "distastefully unscientific," he very much wants to assert his Jewishness. You are prepared, it appears, to understand and accept that, for him. You understand and accept that the experiences which shaped him—specifically, exposure to anti-Semitism as a child—are valid experiences. But they are not your experiences. You want something that is spiritually purer. You want something more evocative of your grandmother, that good woman who "lived a spiritual life in a Jewish fashion." You want your rabbi to teach what your grandmother knew. You would, as you say, "give a lot" to know what she knew.

Yet you rather casually dismiss a couple of obvious possibilities. You say that the "acts of charity she performed were not performed because the Jewish tradition prescribes good works, but because my grandmother had an understanding of the world, a spritual understanding, which made good works natural."

Perhaps. Such understandings of the world are by no means limited to Jews, nor are they ubiquitous among Jews. And yet, and yet: I suspect that your grandmother herself might have drawn a rather more direct connection between the prescriptions of the Jewish tradition and her own acts of charity. Understandings of the world are not, after all, genetically transmitted. They are formed by family and by culture, and your grandmother's culture was the historic culture of the Jews. Place her, on the high holidays, in your temple, and she would have felt as alienated as you. But she would have known that her alienation was from *that* temple, *that* rabbi, perhaps even *those* Jews—and not from Judaism. She knew the whole, and did not confuse it for the part.

But the bottom line, as they say, is you. I don't know, as you claim to, whether the survival of the Jews can adequately be explained by the kind of faith you saw in your grandmother's eyes. But that is what you seek, what you admire, what you wish you could claim as your own. Bravo! If one seeks to enter Judaism, best that it should be in order to lay claim to goodness, to acts of charity, to peace of mind and soul. And you, as you say, would "give a lot" for that.

I don't mean to sit as judge; I hope you can accept that. But I am bound to ask just what it is that you would give. For what is it that you go on to say? "Until Jewish congragations are led by people and filled with people who have dedicated themselves to a lifetime of learning and living the spiritual reality that animated my grandmother," you will have to leave undecided the question of the significance of your own Judaism. Janet: Where will those people who are needed to fill the congregations come from? Is this an Alphonse-Gaston routine, in which each of us stands on the steps of the temple and waits for someone else to enter its doors before we ourselves enter? If the congregation can somehow get itself filled with the "right" kind of people, with people who are "properly" motivated, *then* you will enter, and join?

But you are those people.

You do not want to be, because it is lonely, and because it is work, and because you are not quite sure where the payoff is. The fact is, of course, that you will not be your grandmother. (Most likely even she wasn't. Her conflicts she likely kept to herself.) And it is unfortunate, I agree, that the tradition has somewhere been ruptured, that one cannot simply enter the house of Judaism and find there an ongoing congregation, into which one fits most naturally. No, in our time we must create such congregations, and we must do so even though we lack many of the required resources.

There are, therefore, many people who walk away from the enterprise. It does not appear to them worth the effort. But you are ready for the effort; so you say. You would "give a lot." And the one fairly certain thing, the one thing that I can say to you with considerable confidence, is that only so will you get a lot, will you get what you seek. There are so very many others like you, in search. Look more carefully at the others next time; you will find that many of them are there with questions. The answers are there to be found; that much you know from your grandmother's life, as those who sit near you know it from their parents and grandparents, from their shaping experiences. You, and they, are the only people who can fill the congregations, who can make the dedication, who can reclaim the rightful inheritance.

No, you are not by anything more significant than the accident of birth a Jew. If there is to be meaning to the accident, your grandmother's meaning or your own, it is a meaning you will have to impose upon that accident, a meaning that you will have to work towards. There is no one to hand it to you; there are only hands to hold as you search for it, together with all of the rest of us who are searching. ✦

A ME GROWS IN DAYTON

CAROL EWIG

Carol Ewig teaches at Wright State University in Ohio.

For nearly four years now, I have been saying goodbye to Brooklyn. For twenty-one years, I had been fully defined by the Jewishness which was all around me. My friends were Jewish, my parents' friends Jewish, schoolmates and then office co-workers, shopkeepers and cab drivers, all Jewish. In fact, after a while it seemed to me that even the owner of the Chinese take-out place possessed a bit of a Semitic look, translated from the faces of his many faithful customers. Brooklyn's Jews defined me—so much so that I felt they had left me no room to define myself.

Yes, it is still the same place, Brooklyn, more or less. Perhaps it will never really change, at least in our perceptions of it. But people do change. And what once gave me a feeling of claustrophobia, as if I were stuck in the back of a crowded elevator, unable to do anything more than stare, with my eyes closed, at the familiar backs of too many complacently nodding heads, gives me now, many goodbyes later, a feeling of Whitmanesque joy: a sense of me and all of Brooklyn squashed onto the Staten Island ferry on a windy spring day, gliding smoothly through the same port that my ancestors—and those of my Brooklyn friends, co-workers, taxi cab drivers—once entered Brooklyn through, albeit somewhat less smoothly. For in these four years, it seems, I have come out here—to Lafayette and Bloomington, Indiana, and now to Dayton, Ohio—to become a Jew.

It might, at first, appear strange that someone living in such an intensely Jewish environment would only become *consciously* Jewish upon arriving in the Midwest, a place with few Jews and still fewer Jewish influences. Here, we have to seek out Chanukah candles at B'nai B'rith or a synagogue, for they won't be displayed on the neatly stacked shelves of most supermarkets. Our Passovers are shared with friends, both Jewish and non-Jewish, or families who will set an extra place, or two, for the wandering members of their tribe. And at Rosh Hashanah and Yom Kippur, we must announce that we will not be students, or teachers, or workers, for a while, to the surprised looks of the others.

But it is more than this; we must be more than Holiday Jews out here, if we are to be Jews at all. Here, if we're young—in our twenties and thirties, let's say—we have many non-Jewish friends, with a sprinkling of Jews mixed in, unless we don't want to be selective. If we're older, with our own children, we must become fully involved in our shuls, develop and then support our own Jewish network, for this is not the natural state of things. Even more, we must explain ourselves, who we are—telling our Gentile friends about the observance of *kashruth*, explaining the meaning of the Sabbath, or the difference between our Chanukah and their Christmas, which is not always as obvious as it would seem; and when we are confronted with a group which has just viewed a television *Holocaust*, we must reply—our voices faltering, our words coming slow—with a picture that is more real, or at least more honest.

This is how we consciously become Jews, then. For how can one describe *kosher*—not just what one is or is not allowed to eat, but the origins of the practice, and finally, our own feelings about it—if we have not begun to read, to study, to discover for ourselves? How can we talk about *Shabbat* without lighting at least two candles, saying the *brachot*, and sharing our homemade *cholent* with those non-Jewish friends who expect—who deserve—answers to their questions? And when we light our Chanukah candles, how can we explain to our friends that this is not just another rite evolving out of Christmas? None of these Midwesterners knows the story, whether miracle or parable, of Chanukah. So I have had to ask myself: What is that story? And in time, it matters less, after we have read all we could, that we can tell those others the story, as one *tells* a plot synopsis; what matters is the way we begin to create Chanukah as part of our lives—an illumination, a strength, a song in our own home. No less a miracle.

So we become, most of us for the first time, true *yiddische kinder*. We still may not *do* much more than we used to, when we lived in Brooklyn—we do not all become religious, true believers (whatever that means) in the Jewish God. But no longer are we merely fighting our past, or allowing ourselves to be completely unaware of it. We have developed in ourselves an awareness of Judaism which we can pass on to our children, and they to theirs; and thus we have, really, denied what so many Jews are calling assimilation, intermarriage, or simply a loss of faith—for we have created a future that reaches far beyond ourselves, and at the same time, holds us in its blessings.

It is not so strange, then, that I have found my Jewishness in the Midwest, among *goyim*. What is harder to understand, really, is why I could not find it in Brooklyn, within an environment which was created and nurtured for just that purpose. Perhaps it is because it was *too* easy there: too easy to caricature, to ridicule, the *things* of Jewishness I didn't like—*Goodbye Columbus* and all the Potemkins stand for, which seemed, in my naiveté, to be all that Judaism stood for. I am, after all, a child of the middle class, which could be comfortable—only it wasn't to me. Something seemed wrong with that world to me, growing up by its rules; only I could not see beyond it, and try as I might, had no tools to chip its surface—only a kind of spit, a contempt. Or so I thought.

So I got myself ready for my journey to the Middle West, to deny that Jewish world—until, that is, the day I actually stood, bags packed, novel ready for breezy reading on the plane, at my kitchen door. For my mother was not crying, as she stood rewrapping the containers of frozen stuffed cabbage she'd put together "to make your first few days a little easier." Or rather, she was red-eyed, but was trying hard not to cry, and because I'd seen her cry for so many lesser reasons—my more insignificant rebellious gestures—I began to understand what my leave-taking was really about. The mother who, after many arguments and tears, could not—or did not want to—understand why I was leaving Brooklyn, my home, while her friends' daughters and sons were not only staying but had never thought of leaving, looked me in the eyes and did not cry, because she did not, finally, want to hold me back. I have thought about this day many times, perhaps too many, and maybe it is just because she knew I would that she did not yield to that so-called "typical" Jewish mother's impulse: she did not, when it really mattered, make me feel guilty about leaving her. So there *was* a Jewish gift which my mother gave me that day: a gift of life, of such pure love that it did not need to announce its self-sacrifice.

But my first goodbye to Brooklyn did not end there. My father drove me to the airport—the grey in his temples, four years ago, just beginning to show—and talked to me, in his gentle way, of simple things: that he and my mother would always be here, that I would always have a home with them. He might not have said that he loved me—not with words, anyway. He didn't have to. For as I went to hug him—afraid, by now, that I would not have the strength to leave—I saw that it was he who was crying: my calm, rational father, who never cries. And so, as if completing a circle, I boarded my plane, and said my first farewell to Brooklyn—escaping, finally, to the tiny toilet in the back of the plane so that my now-fervent cries for my Brooklyn home would be drowned out by the engine. It was the release I needed. And when I was back in my seat, staring at the giant cotton clouds in a bright blue sky, I was reminded of those childhood dioramas my parents had helped me design; but I was no longer playing with shoeboxes and glue. I had to admit, then, that I was exactly where I needed to be. *What were we crying about, really?* I asked myself, beginning to laugh. *We are not saying goodbye forever*—I was just a short plane ride, a telephone call away. It didn't much help, though, not even then; for if these same ties have been ridiculed so often as being out of proportion, and binding, they had also offered me security in a world that, more often than not, is a lonely place.

That was how I found myself at Purdue University, with Gentile classmates and professors and a *shikse* roommate. When I first met the woman with whom I'd be sharing an apartment—beautifully blonde, a New England goddess—I allowed us at least five minutes for the usual rundown of our lives, and then sprang this at her: "I feel I should explain, before we go any further" (that is, because you still have time to get away) "that I'm . . . Jewish." I expected to hear a hiss of hate, or at least to see one glance at my hair for the horn marks, for what other way did I have of dealing with a non-Jew in a truly personal situation? But instead, very nonchalantly, she said, "Oh, that's great, I have a Jewish boyfriend," and proceeded to unpack her suitcase. What does this *really* mean? I wondered. *Can* she be this accepting? Can she *like* Jews? In the next few weeks, as we learned about each other and began to be friends, I felt relieved, as if I had escaped somehow from that sense of persecution and prejudice I had heard so much about in Brooklyn, but had never really been able to believe in. Brooklyn had always seemed to me a kind of *shtetl* (though I didn't know the meaning of that word then): a tiny Jewish village that was so well-barricaded, so protected, that no marching Cossacks or SS men would ever penetrate its walls. And it seemed, in those first few weeks, that this *shtetl* extended its protection even as far as a place where Brooklyn was just another name of a city, the birthplace of Coney Island and its famous hot dog; nothing more.

Until, that is, the composition one of my students wrote about the glories of Hitler and the horrors of the "money loving Jews." I remember, quite clearly, my anger as I read the paper again and again, which changed to disbelief and fear until I felt, instead, ashamed—of myself. For what was the difference, really, between my own rebellious feelings, bred out of experience, and those of my student, who was uninformed and misguided? He was taught prejudice, that was all; I had learned it all by myself.

It was not to be my only experience with anti-Semitism, and I was more surprised than I should have been. How could I, really, have imagined Brooklyn as a stone-walled fortress, when I had thought to crack its foundation myself? It was not, I was well aware, very hard to do: spit turns too easily to yellow star; tools become guns; and sturdy Brooklyn, my home, could crumble into dust and ash. I had forgotten—or I had never realized—that a *shtetl* has no walls.

From that time, an emerging, conscious Jewishness began to shape, rather than define, my life: a Jewishness that could never be taught to me back in Hebrew school in Brooklyn, or by parental lectures, or by my Jewish friends and imagined enemies, but that I had to teach myself. Of course, not everyone develops this same feeling out in the Midwest. But more often than not, the Jewish friends, acquaintances, and professors I have met out here have been more intensely Jewish—even religious—than the people I know back home.

In Brooklyn, I have friends who keep kosher homes, have two complete sets of dishes just for Passover, though they do not necessarily believe in this. They do this, simply, because their parents require that they do. I am not criticizing them for this; in fact, theirs is the way that traditions were passed on: a simple way. But it was always, to some extent, a passage of faith. It is out here too, but in a different way. In Bloomington, where Indiana University is situated, I knew a Jewish woman who kept a kosher home, although she lived in a house with six other women, none of them Jewish. There is no real contradiction here, though it might appear so if one believes in only a single definition of *kosher*. Of course, she shared a sink with these women and their *treife;* on a graduate student's budget, she could not afford her own set of dishes—much less two—so she shared these as well. But she wouldn't eat meat unless it was kosher—and kosher meat being very hard to obtain in Bloomington, and prohibitively expensive if one could, she became a vegetarian. Her roommates did more than merely respect her feelings; when they cooked together, they avoided combinations of milk and meat, or at least made sure there was always something she could eat—something good. Not particularly amazing—except that it was she, from a suburb of Chicago in which there were no other Jews, who had brought Judaism back to her family as well as to her own life.

But it is the first seder of Passover at their house last year that I remember most clearly. It was a warm and brilliant spring after another devastating Midwestern winter, but we had to walk quickly, our eyes partially closed, to get moving at all—our exams, papers, and the like taking precedence over all else. Tense, irritable, exhausted, we prepared for our Seder: searching for Haggadahs wherever we could find them, rushing off to the big supermarket for a few extra boxes of Matzos when my "CARE package" hadn't arrived on time. But when I entered the house in my favorite blouse and skirt—having decided, only moments before I was to leave, that an external change might help my internal mood—all of the guests, my friends, were also wearing their favorite clothes. Three Jews, four Gentiles, we sat around the table laden with the things that made this Passover, and our faces were glowing—could it have been the wine?—our voices sounded sweet as we chanted the blessings—even mine, normally off-key—our non-Jewish friends helped by transliterations our hostess had carefully prepared. We recited the story of Passover in English as I had done, with my family, for so many years before; and we did not need to explain anymore. Not even to ourselves.

It was Rosh Hashanah and my husband—then fiance—had come from Dayton, where he was working, to share it with me in Bloomington. We could have gone to the services held for students and faculty in the large auditorium, where I had been the year before; I was amazed then, new to the campus, at the numbers of Jews streaming towards this makeshift synagogue, as if there were no corners of this small Indiana town we had left untouched. But this year we had been invited to Bloomington's one *shul* by one of my professors, an intelligent, kind man who belongs to it, and whom, at the time, I did not know well. I suppose the magic of this Rosh Hashanah started there, when we realized that his other guests were family, close friends; instead of feeling awkward, we felt ourselves welcomed into this small, loving circle of a family not our own. Then, in the tiny synagogue, we listened to a service that was intimate and close, as if the congregation had been to a single dinner, widening the circle still further. Each member of the congregation was able to take some part in the reading that night, standing at his or her turn. And after services, there were rows of tables laden with homemade strudels, cookies, and other *noshes*, the crowd of people crying, as if with one voice, "*A gut Yom Tov*," so that there was an echo that lasted long after everyone had gone. The next day, a woman—obviously, wonderfully pregnant—read from the Torah in a clear, melodious voice, and what a lovely sound that was to hear. What was this *shul*? Conservative, mostly, but also a bit of Orthodox, of Reform. It served everyone's needs. And because of that, it felt right, there in Bloomington, Indiana; we felt, truly, a part of those days, and even more, we felt an almost Chassidic joy, as if we might at any moment begin to dance and sing. We felt like Jews. At the same time, we knew that it could never happen in Brooklyn, with its overflowing congregations; but we would be able to feel, from then on, as if it might.

And what of my present stopping point, Dayton, Ohio, the "typical American city"? We have Renaldo's here, and its owner is Italian, true, but also a Jew. This is the one place in town for our Danish, our chalahs; here you can find a woman imploring, "Make it a *nice* assortment, I want it should be a little special," like anywhere in Brooklyn. There are a few signs proclaiming "pareve" foods, but many customers don't know what this means; *we* know, though. And the Chicago Deli, where any weekend we can meet other Jews picking out a whitefish, some lox, and of course a few bagels. More expensive to those of us from New York, certainly, but worth it for that special craving; and to those who have lived here all their lives, it is simply the way things are. In Dayton, the Jewish Community Center took fifteen years to plan and build; it, too, serves as a meeting place, a common ground. The difference between a city like Cincinnati, only fifty miles away, where there are, of course, many Jews, and Dayton, is that in the former, we are very visible, helping to mold the character of the place; here, we have to know where we can go to allow ourselves visibility, where we will feel at home.

Home. I've said goodbye to my Brooklyn many times, and each time, it's been a little harder. Just over a year ago, during a holiday visit to New York, my grandmother died suddenly, in Florida, of a heart attack. Mechanically, I made new plane reservations. I sat with my family as the decisions were made about where the *shiva* would be held—my grandmother's children living in Brooklyn, on Long Island and Staten Island, and my grandfather, grieving, someplace in between. I went through the funeral, took my place at the side of a new grave in one of those city cemeteries where it always seems colder, windier than it should; those, like my grandmother, who were immigrants to this country and who spent most of their lives in crowded tenements now shoved too close to one another in death. I remembered visiting them in Miami one year, my grandfather walking too briskly, too fast, inhaling the air of "God's Country" as if it could rid him of the fumes of paint and plaster from all his years of work; my grandmother hiding under the shade of trees, shopping daily in air-conditioned supermarkets for the items no longer needed: two old people who had worked too hard, worried too much, and for whom it was too late to be at peace.

Back in my house to begin the *shiva,* I helped to cover the mirrors, boil the eggs, make the coffee, telling my mother to sit, to mourn, that I would take care of everything— the ability to go through the routines somehow proving that I was an adult. But too quickly, I was back on yet another plane, going down one more straightaway cutting through the Indiana cornfields; and my daily routine—my life— which had begun to be satisfying, was no longer. The Midwest had offered me a different perspective, true, and in so doing it had given my family and friends back to me, had allowed me to see Brooklyn whole. I was not mourning my grandmother's death as much as her life, any life: too short, too filled with routines that, done too often, define one's life, one's way of living, and which then become nearly impossible to shake off. I had come to the Midwest to get away from one routine, to define myself; I had not yet been here long enough to get into another, but soon I would be. Soon, too soon, the relationship between myself and my family would be defined by our infrequent times together, by our lives apart. I wanted to come home.

But it is not death which is finally bringing me home; it is, moreover an affirmation of life. I have not fully undergone a conversion in these four years in the Midwest, my stopping ground; there are still many facets of Brooklyn life which I can never like or fully accept. And still it is mine: my Jewish home. I criticize from within, linking my life with Brooklyn's; whatever the outcome, I have no other home.

In June, my husband-to-be and I stood under the chuppah we had made from a tallis, but our decision to link our lives together was not as simple as that woven cloth. With the help of our rabbi—our friend—we were simply continuing the search that our Midwestern lives had begun. We examined the rituals surrounding Jewish marriage, eliminating those elements which had no relation to our lives or which had not evolved out of simplicity and faith, adding to our ceremony those which would make it only ours, and retaining those traditions which would help to shape our new lives. Our stumbling block had been the actual, necessary words which would force my husband to "buy me"; resolving this as best we could, we "bought" each other, attempting to cancel out a prerequisite of generations. There were no revolving chuppahs, statues of bride and groom sculpted out of chopped liver, or hours of photographed wedding "rehearsals," pastel party dresses and strained smiles; but these things are not Jewish.

Surrounded by our family, our friends—both Jewish and not— holding up the chuppah poles on all sides, we repeated those words which had been said so many times before, and the words we had written for each other, which were as new as our own lives. We held each other's hands, smiled into each other's eyes and those of our family and friends, and began our life together, from the start, whole: as individuals, as Jews. The "Mazel Tovs" were shouted as always upon the breaking of the glass, reminding us, in our most joyful times, of the destruction of the Second Temple—and symbolizing the idea that our life together should be as long as the time it would take to put the glass back together. There are many traditions, after all, that are worth keeping. ✡

AFFIRMATIONS | ALL GOD'S CHILDREN | JULIUS LESTER

Let us speak of the racism each of us carries. For, though racism is political, it also resides in our persons. It could not be otherwise, because anti-Semitism and anti-Black racism are an integral part of Western culture. As a Gentile I grew up absorbing anti-Semitism without even knowing that it was anti-Semitism; so, too, Jews and/or whites have absorbed anti-Black racism.

Our task is not to flagellate ourselves with guilt. Our task is to learn how to cast away the unholy birthrights bequeathed us by this culture. To do this is difficult, because we must do it as solitary individuals in the privacy and terror of our souls, where angels sing and demons scream and God is deaf to our cries for help.

I begin with a story. It is a story about a young black child, around seven or eight. Each summer he went with his mother to his grandmother's house in the backwoods of Arkansas. The boy didn't enjoy these visits, for his grandmother's home was so rural, there were no other children around, and the adults were too busy doing whatever adults do to know he was there—except when he did something wrong. So, he lived his days listening to the sounds of the bees, wondering if the buzz of the bees seemed louder because of the deep summer silence, or was the silence made deeper by the sound of the bees? You think about things like that when you're seven.

A high point of each day was to walk to the road, sit beside the mailbox and await the mailman. The boy didn't expect mail, but went because he wanted to solve the mystery of the name on his grandmother's mailbox. He could read, but he could not pronounce the name painted rudely there in black: A-L-T-S-C-H-U-L. It was an odd name, made even odder by the fact that his grandmother's name was Smith. Why then was A-L-T-S-C-H-U-L painted on her mailbox? Of course, her brother lived with her, but his name was Uncle Rudolph. Who was A-L-T-S-C-H-U-L?

The boy dared not ask, because his family did not appreciate questions and answered them, generally, with a "No," even if the questions began with "Why?". So, the boy sat by the mailbox and stared and wondered.

One day he was in town with his parents and while walking along a street, he looked up to see a large clock suspended above a store front. Around the clock was the name on his grandmother's mailbox, followed by the word, "Jeweller's."

"That's the same name on grandmama's mailbox," he said, with that calculated innocence of which seven-year-olds are masters.

His mother gave a short, bitter laugh. Later that day, she told him a story.

It was of a man named Adolf Altschul, a German Jew who came to Arkansas sometime after the Civil War. He came with his brothers and, while the boy's mother did not know what the brothers did, Adolf Altschul became a peddler. And perhaps it was in the course of his rounds that he met a woman, a half-African, half Cherokee ex-slave, named Maggie Carson. As improbable as it was in that time and that place when hooded Klansmen rode at night bringing death as if it were a present, Adolf and Maggie came to love each other.

Even in the most propitious of circumstances, love requires courage, because what is more dangerous than to look at another and say, "I give myself to you." In that time and that place, it was acceptable for a white man to be in relationship to a black woman only if the relationship were for the white man's sexual pleasure. So, the courage of Adolf and Maggie was great, because they chose to accept the consequences of courageous love and do the unacceptable: They married.

Adolf's brothers disowned him. Adolf became a farmer, buying the land and building the house where the little boy's grandmother still lived. Adolf and Maggie had five children, including the boy's grandmother and the man the boy knew as Uncle Rudolph, whose surname it was on the mailbox.

The boy was, of course, me. Adolf Altschul was my great-grandfather. I share this deeply personal story not because I claim any Jewish ancestry. I do not and I could not. (Parenthetically, I must add that I know there will be some who will use this story as the explanation they've needed to "explain" my recent essay articulating my support of Israel which appeared in the *Village Voice,* and reprinted in the Sunday New York *Times.* Indeed, there seem to be those so baffled by the essay that I was told recently that I supported Israel because my wife is Jewish. This was said by someone who has never met my wife, who, incidentally, is not Jewish.)

My great-grandfather was a Jew, but what does that mean? I doubt that he was Jewish in any living sense, for no hint of Judaism or Jewish culture survive in my family. In all likelihood, Adolf Altschul did not live as a Jew. Perhaps he was buried as one, because when he died, his brothers, the ancestors of the jewelry story owners, took his body for burial.

Maggie never talked about her husband, or much else, it seems. My

---

Julius Lester holds a joint appointment in the Afro-American Studies Department and the Near Eastern and Judaic Studies Program at the University of Massachusetts in Amherst. He converted to Judaism in 1982.

mother knew her and asked her once what slavery had been like. Her response was, "I don't talk about that," which in itself says a lot about slavery. How fraught with terror her nights must have been if memory contained naught except pain, a pain so total that she could open her mouth only wide enough to say, "I don't talk about that."

I imagine that my great-grandfather lay beside her in the night and helped her stare down terror and if he could not dissolve that memory-filled-with-pain, he could whisper into night's-dread-silence, "It's over, Maggie. You're not there anymore."

What an extraordinary couple they must have been, because they trusted their souls. They trusted their love, not only for each other, but for something wider and higher and nameless. At least, that is what their story is about for me.

Learning that my great-grandfather was a Jew was a curious fact, but nothing more. Jews had no substance or reality in my child-consciousness. I had noticed that my classmates at school liked to call me by the first syllable of my name when they taunted me, standing before me and spitting out, "Ju! Ju!" I knew they were trying to hurt me, but not knowing how calling me "Ju!" was to accomplish that, I was unfazed.

I perceived dimly that it had something to do with Jews, but those were the people my father preached about. It is only recently, however, that I've realized that when Jews were presented as a model, they weren't called Jews. They were Hebrews, or the children of Israel — Moses parting the Red Sea; Daniel in the lion's den; Samson bringing down the temple walls; David killing Goliath. Those were Hebrews. Jews were the people who demanded that Pontius Pilate free Barabbas and crucify Jesus.

I never told my father, but I wasn't too sure that I wouldn't have cast my vote for Barabbas, too. At age seven, Jesus couldn't compare with The Lone Ranger, or even Tonto, and Barabbas did.

Occasionally I'd overhear one of my parents refer to someone as a "Shylock," or my father would come home with a purchase, saying with a chuckle, "I jewed him down to five dollars," and maybe once or twice I heard my mother say, "Oh, he's like an ol' Jew. You can't trust him."

None of this had a context for me, because I could see only two kinds of people in the world—black and white. Anyway, in the 1940s and 1950s, as I blundered my way toward some imitation of adulthood, it was hard enough to make sense of a world that was harsh, violent and hateful to me because I was black, a world I had to prepare myself to enter.

I went to college, a black college with many white teachers. If there were Jews among them, they never said so. I studied nothing by or about Jews. Exactly how a program of study can be called liberal education and omit Judaism, Jewish history and culture, is beyond me. I remember reading Marlowe's "The Jew of Malta," and Shakespeare's "Merchant of Venice," but the professor didn't talk about Jews. So, I continued absorbing anti-Semitism.

But one day, Rhoda Miller, a classmate and fellow English major, on whom I had a crush of extraordinary proportions, thrust a book at me and told me to read it. Thinking that it would give me something to say to her other than "Duh, duh, duh," I read it. The book was *Exodus*. I haven't read it since 1958, but its impact on me was so extraordinary that I wanted to go and fight for Israel, even die, if need be, for Israel. Rhoda and I had much to talk about, because she wanted to do the same. I realized, finally, that if she wouldn't go on a date with me, she certainly wouldn't go to Israel with me. So my fantasies of living on a kibbutz with her faded.

Israel did not fade. Israel spoke to the need I had as a young black man for a place where I could be free of being an object of hatred. I did not wish I were Jewish, but was glad that Jews had a land of their own, even if blacks didn't.

There was another day, a year or so later, a mouse-gray day that an English major finds romantic. I was walking across campus and Roma Jones called me. I was into the third year, at least, of my crush on Roma, and indeed, was in real danger of dying of terminal heartache and galloping acne. No matter. Roma had called my name. My name had touched her lips and as far as I was concerned, that was enough to consummate the relationship. She said she was going to visit a synagogue and did I want to come? I would have read poetry to a brussel sprout if Roma had asked me. Of course I wanted to go to the synagogue and I'd find out what it was when I got there.

Life is always intruding with such accidents, such strange occurrences, which are really invitations from God, and if you're male, God's agent is generally female, not giving you what you think you want, but offering what you could not know you needed, would not know that you needed for many years.

We went to the synagogue. I remember how strange I felt in a place of worship whose rites I could not imagine. The rabbi talked, but about what, I don't remember. But maybe there was something about the way we listened, or maybe he developed a crush on Roma. Whatever it was, he said, "I'm not supposed to do this, but . . . ." He took us up to the Ark, parted the curtains, and showed us the Torah. Even now, I can see myself standing there, gazing at the Torah, not knowing at what I was looking, but knowing that it was a moment that would remain with me.

The spring semester of my junior year, 1959, I transferred to San Diego State College for a semester, where I happened to meet, among my three roommates, a Palestinian named Khalid Tuck-Tuck. "Tuck," as we called him, was an adumbration of the Middle Eastern nightmare that was to come; I have never known a human being so filled with rage. He began each day, literally, cursing Jews. Once he came near tears describing what had been his family's home in Palestine and the beauty of the surrounding orange groves. Such a moment of tenderness was singular. The primary force of his life was hatred, and it was difficult to live with, day in, day out. Eventually, I began responding by reading passages aloud from *Exodus*, which did not help our relationship. And once I interrupted one of his tirades with a loud rendition of *Hava Nagila*. At least I began, because in an instant, his hands were around my throat, and our roommates had to pull him off me. After that Tuck and I were never in the apartment at the same time.

I forgot him until the '67 war, and every time I hear of a Palestinian raid or bombing, I wonder if he was involved. If he is still alive, I have no doubt that he is.

All of these were isolated events, significant, but occurring on the outskirts of my life. I graduated from college in 1960, and after a year of bridge-playing (what else can you do with a B.A. in English?), I moved to New York City, where I also graduated from crushes to love affairs, learning painfully that crushes have a loveliness and integrity of their own, which is devalued when the crush is asked to rise to the plateau of love.

Many people, especially those who are twenty years younger than I, look back on the 1960s with a yearning, a regret at having been born too late to participate in the excitement of marches in Alabama, organizing in Mississippi, demonstrating against the war in Vietnam at the Pentagon. Yes, it was an exciting time, a time of incredible hope, a time of intense belief that the ideals of freedom and justice could be made manifest.

But it was also a time too big to grasp, or to understand, or even to know what it was you were experiencing. Events that shook you to the soul happened too often and too frequently: The assassinations of a president, that president's brother, Martin Luther King Jr., Malcolm X, Che Guevara. Not to mention the martyrs of the civil rights movement—Jimmie Lee Jackson, Viola Liuzzo, Jonathan Daniels, Rev. James Reeb, James Chaney, Andrew Goodman, Michael Schwerner, William Moore. Not to mention those who were killed in the riots of the long, hot summers. The decade that began with the singing of "We Shall Overcome" came to its end with shouts of "Burn, Baby, Burn." That is too long and too arduous a journey to travel in a mere ten years. The decade that began with blacks and whites working together to create what we called "the beloved community" ended with blacks and whites alienated, hurt and angry with each other. Many of those whites were Jews.

The turning point was in 1966 when black nationalism became the dominant tone of "the movement" and Black Power its rallying cry. I was stunned when many Jews responded by accusing us of kicking them out of "the movement." I was hurt and angered when people we had thought were friends denounced us and called us racists. I had thought that if anyone would understand the need for black nationalism, it would be Jews. After all, black nationalism was a form of Zionism. Black Power was our attempt to create institutions that were controlled by black people alone. We didn't have a nation, but we had to have something.

Many Jews did not understand, did not try to understand, and in a rage, I struck back by publishing an article attacking Jews and Israel. It was worthy of Jesse Jackson, I am ashamed to say, but all the anti-Semitism I had imbibed came forth, though I did not recognize it as such. I knew only that I had been deeply hurt, and I wanted to hurt Jews in return and I knew exactly how to do it.

That was not to be the end, for in the fall of 1968, there was a bitter school strike in New York City over the issue of community control. The adversaries were Blacks and Jews.

I had a radio show then, and a black teacher read an anti-Semitic poem on it, written by one of his students. I asked him to read the poem because I wanted to illustrate the psychological impact of the strike on black children. I took great care to explain to my listeners that my purpose in having the poem read was not to insult Jews, but to begin a dialogue. For three weeks I took phone calls on the air about the poem, and talked with Jews about Jewish racism. Not one caller objected to my having aired the poem.

A month after the poem's airing, the New York *Times* carried a front page story about the broadcasting of an anti-Semitic poem, but without mentioning the context in which it was broadcast. Suddenly I found myself labeled an anti-Semite.

Elements in the Jewish community pressured the radio station to fire me, which it didn't. The Jewish Defense League passed out leaflets reading, "Cancel Out Julius Before He Cancels Out You." There were threats on my life and my children's lives. The FBI called to tell me that they had uncovered a plot to kidnap me, but couldn't act until I'd been carried across state lines.

But there were also Jews who defended me. Two sets of friends in particular—the parents of Micky Schwerner and Andrew Goodman—supported me personally and publicly.

I was left branded an anti-Semite, however. And, for the first time since spelling out that name on my grandmother's mailbox, I remembered my great-grandfather. Remembering him, I was flooded with a deep and abiding shame, because I had betrayed him. And the betrayal had little to do with the fact that he was a Jew, but with something else I could not yet name.

That is when my education began, as true education must begin—in the awful experience of shame. I, who had suffered because of how others regarded my race, had grievously hurt many who suffered because of their religion and cultural identity. It did not matter that my intention had been to create a dialogue between blacks and Jews. It did not matter that the New York *Times* had used me as a pawn to rally support against black community control of the schools. The fact remained that I had not dissociated myself from the sentiments expressed in the anti-Semitic poem. How, then, could I be viewed except as an anti-Semite?

So, I learned with agonizing pain that being a victim of racism did not give me automatic immunity from carrying and spreading the disease.

But what to do about it? That was not so easy. Especially since I was still angry at those Jews who had denounced black nationalism. I was still angry at those Jews who refused to recognize the legitimacy of community control. How could I reconcile the anger and the shame?

The 1970s came and another confrontation between blacks and Jews, this time over affirmative action. I was again angry, but this time my anger did not take the form of striking back. Instead, I shed myself of one of the worst remnants of anti-Semitism, the one which says that "Jews should know better, because they have suffered, too." In and of itself, suffering does not bring knowledge, I was beginning to learn. In and of itself, suffering brings only pain, and sometimes, the desire to cause others pain, as I had done. Angered and hurt as I was by those Jews who opposed affirmative action, I began to accept that it was wrong, very wrong, to expect Jews to be better than anyone else, to expect Jews to understand more and to be more. Jews were human. That was hard enough, without demanding that they live up to my expectations.

Eventually I realized that it was condescending to say even that. It was not Jews whom I was allowing to be human. It was myself. The reconciliation of shame and anger came when I allowed myself to be a human being.

To be a human being. There is only one way to be human and that is found in how we use our suffering. And by suffering I do not mean the sentimentality of those who see themselves as victims, of those who define themselves as oppressed. By suffering I mean the pain which comes when you look at yourself and see yourself as you truly are — a mere mortal, limited, frail, full of pretense, bloated with self-importance, very alone and very afraid. And that is only the beginning.

Beneath that is that layer about which Maggie, my great-grandmother, said, "I don't talk about that." Old woman! I picture you as lean and black as an apple tree in autumn and as silent as Death. I picture you sitting on the front porch and staring across the fields with eyes so filled with pain that you are blind. And I feel that you passed your suffering down to your daughter, Emma Smith, who was my grandmother, and she didn't "talk about that, either," and she passed the accumulated suffering down to my mother, Julia Smith Lester, who doesn't talk about that, either, and she passed it all to me—a legacy of suffering passed down for three generations like a precious heirloom at which I stare and hear the wind in the sails of slave ships, and see the water spraying outward from the thrust of the pointed bow. And I hear the lash of whips and see blood fall like manna and one day at some time in the mid-seventies, I was plunged into that suffering, which had accumulated through the generations like a miser's hoard of gold. How did I get there? Well, in the tradition of my foremothers, I don't talk about that. I do not want to mislead you into thinking that because you might understand the words you therefore know the experience. There are experiences which elude the finest words one can find. Suffering is one. Love is another.

Suffice it to say that I dwelled in nothingness and that if God heard my cries, He did not respond because I was not screaming loud enough. Eventually, I emerged and within me, I discovered something quite new: in the embracing of my suffering as a black person, I embraced the pain that everyone carries. And that was not the end, for the end is always a paradox: The embrace of suffering does not bring pain, but a surprising shout of affirmation flung joyfully in the teeth of negation.

Let me illustrate what I mean with three brief stories. The first is from Elie Wiesel's *A Jew Today*. The setting is a train carrying Jews to a death camp.

They were pressed together so that they could hardly move or breathe. Suddenly an old rabbi exclaimed, "Today is Simhath Torah. Have we forgotten what Jews are ordered to do on Simhath Torah?" Somebody had managed to smuggle a small *Sefer Torah* aboard the train. He handed it to the rabbi. And they began to sing, to sway, since they could not dance. And they went on singing and celebrating the Torah, all the while knowing that every motion of the train was bringing them closer to their end.

The next story is from the affidavit of Hermann Graebe, an eyewitness to a massacre of Jews in the Ukraine in 1942.

I watched a family of about 8 persons, a man and woman, both about 50, with their children of about 1, 8, and 10, and two grown-up daughters of about 20 to 24. An old woman with snow-white hair was holding the one-year-old child in her arms and singing to it and tickling it. The child was cooing with delight. The couple were looking on with tears in their eyes. The father was holding the hand of a boy about 10 years old and speaking to him softly; the boy was fighting his tears. The father pointed toward the sky, stroked his head and seemed to explain something to him. At that moment the S.S. man at the pit shouted something to his comrade. The latter counted off about 20 persons. Among them was the family which I have mentioned.

The final story is again from Weisel's *A Jew Today,* adapted by him from the testimony of Leib Langfuss, who was a member of the Sonder Kommando, those Jews forced to burn the bodies.

Two Jews turned to a member of our Kommando and asked if they should recite the *Viddui,* the last confession before dying. And my comrade said yes. So they took a bottle of brandy and drank from it while shouting *l'chaim,* to life, to one another with true joy. And they insisted that my comrade drink, too, but he felt too embarrassed, and ashamed. And he said no, but they refused to let him go. They pressed him to drink, to drink and to say *l'chaim*.

Perhaps some read only passivity in these stories. Perhaps some people are uncomfortable and angry and even a little ashamed that those Jews did not go to their deaths trying to take a Nazi with them.

Resistance has many faces, and the most difficult to see and to appreciate is that tiny, prosaic act, which affirms life even as Death's jaws close upon us. Yet, the most enduring response to racism, and my response to anti-Semitism, is precisely this: To affirm Life.

Sometimes, affirming life means anger, protest, defiance, self-defense. But that is not enough. It is never enough, because anger is seductive and one can easily become trapped by and imprisoned by anger. It is easy to become so wholly focused on those who cause our suffering that, without knowing it, we become marionettes, dangling from the hands of the oppressors, who pull our strings, and we respond with the appropriate gestures, imprecations and slogans. We become what we hate. There is nothing else possible when we become mired in our suffering, when suffering becomes our badge of identity.

We must go into the suffering. A racist lies in wait there, eager to mock you, scorn you, spit on you, and laugh at you. Do not be cowed by that demon. Demons cannot abide the sight of tears and the sound of weeping. So, cry, cry your guilt, cry your shame. Life resides there.

Once we confront the demons within, the demons without lose some of their power. We do not meet their hatred with an equal hatred, but we suffuse our anger with compassion, our despair with joy. And always, we affirm that life is, and it is good, despite everything, and especially despite those who would have it be otherwise for those of us who are Black and who are Jews.

And that brings me full circle to those two people who affirmed Life. The mailbox is no longer there and the house that Adolf Altschul built burned, turning all his letters to ashes. I guess he didn't want to talk either. It doesn't matter now, because Adolf and Maggie offered themselves to Life. I want to say more, but I think I hear an old women's gruff voice saying, "Boy, hush! We don't talk about that." And I see a man looking at me in real confusion and he says, with a German accent: "Blacks! Jews! CHICKEN NOODLE SOUP!"

I look at him, shrug, and say, "You know? You're right." ✦

PESACH IN KATMAN— WHO?

Twenty-nine "Jewish dinners" and a bottle of Manischewitz wine in the Himalayas

SHULA BEYER

Shula Beyer lives in Hattiesburg, Mississippi, with her husband, an eye surgeon, and her infant son, David. She teaches journalism at the University of Southern Mississippi and is working on her first novel.

You can get almost anything in Katmandu. Just name it. Even though the Himalayan kingdom, wedged between India and Tibet, has been open to westerners only since the 1950s, you can find everything from pizza to tinned paté.

But a bottle of Manischewitz wine, kosher for Passover?

We arrived in Katmandu on Friday, March 23, 1983, in time, we thought, to get an invitation to the seder at the Israeli consulate the following Monday evening. My husband, Wayne, and I were six months into our year-long trip around the world, and thus far it had been 189 days, 10 countries, 95 beds (mostly clean) and nine awful days.

Two of those awful days had been spent trying to get from Darjeeling, India, high in the Himalayas east of Nepal, in time for Passover. We made our way to Nepal by local buses, vintage 1940s, a jeep that broke down several times and even a bicycle rickshaw. We spent the night at the Nepalese border in a room with no electricity or running water. The bus trip to Katmandu from the border took over 19 hours.

During Chanukah, we had lit candles in an improvised menorah in a small Balinese village. Tu B'shvat passed unnoticed in Malaysia. We celebrated Purim in a remote hamlet in northern Thailand. But Passover—a time to connect with other Jews in a night of common ancestral memory—is an important holiday to us, and we had carefully planned ahead to celebrate it in Katmandu.

"Avi" at the Israeli consulate was apologetic, but firm. The first night seder was only for Jews who work for the United Nations and other international organizations, and who live in Katmandu year-round. He invited us to a party planned for the second night for the Israeli travellers in town.

I was disappointed, even bitter. The invitation is explicit in the Haggadah: "Whoever is hungry shall come and eat." A party was not what I had in mind. I wanted a seder.

Our mood improved at the post office, where we found waiting for us a box of matzah and a Haggadah sent by thoughtful friends from our havurah in Miami. At least we now had the makings for a seder of our own.

Next morning, Wayne cycled to the nearby Kopan Buddhist manastery, where Jonathan Wolfson, a Berkeley philosopher/carpenter we had met on the train from Malaysia to Thailand, was studying Tibetan Buddhism. We had made tentative plans to hold a seder together.

Jonathan was not the only Jew in the monastery. Wayne returned five hours later with the names of four others who jumped at the chance to exchange Buddhist solitude for Jewish fellowship.

That same morning I also got ambitious and advertised the seder on the bulletin board of the Katmandu Guest House, our $4-a-night hostel. I then reserved a small room at a nearby restaurant called Le Bistro, which didn't serve anything even remotely French. The room would hold 12 people comfortably but wouldn't be too massive if it turned out to be just the seven of us. I was optimistic: I told the owner to expect 12 people for dinner.

It was still before the monsoon season; rhododendrons covered the hillsides, and Katmandu was filled with travellers who had come to catch the end of the Himalayan trekking season. We soon received the first response to my sign, a note from a Larry Bornstein and a Phyl Levine who said they were interested in participating. They asked if Wayne Beyer was the same fellow who attended the Bronx High School of Science.

"Sure I know him," Wayne said. "We had geometry together." In a further twist of Jewish geography, it turned out that Larry and I attended the same yeshiva day school.

Now there were nine of us.

During lunch a young traveller entered the restaurant. Wayne decided he looked Jewish. I agreed. I worked up some courage, went to his table and asked, "Excuse me. Do you have any plans for the Passover seder?"

His immediate shock at such an unexpected question turned to delight. He had forgotten about the holiday but

Pesach in Katman — Who?

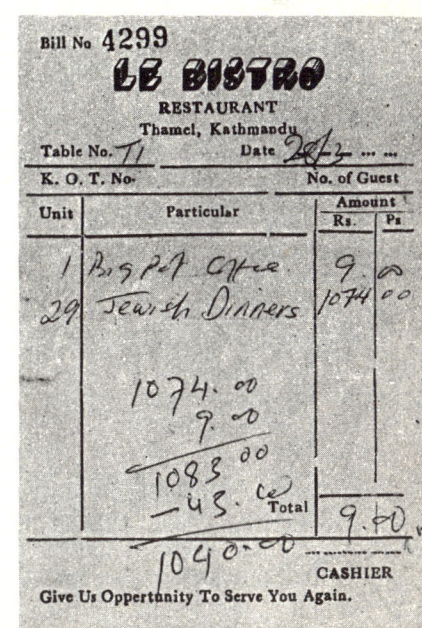

would be thrilled to join us. He was David Rydell, an 18-year-old travelling in Asia before beginning his freshman year at the University of Maryland. He volunteered to ask the four questions and to find a shank bone for the seder plate.

Sunday morning I sat in the garden of the guesthouse talking to a steady stream of Jews who had read the notice or had heard about the seder. There was Adam Stern, a DC environmentalist conducting a study on erosion in Nepal. Josh Plout, a Californian, turned out to be the nephew of a Miami dance teacher I know. Many Israelis dropped by, including a beautiful Yemenite woman named Ilana, who promised to bring a flute. Two former Israeli army buddies held an emotional reunion in the garden.

"Normally I don't like to go to a seder," one American confided. "I do it just to please my mother. But here, halfway around the world, it's important. I'm not sure why."

I returned to the restaurant and excitedly told the owner to prepare 23 roast chicken dinners. The cost per person would be $3. He offered to throw in bread and butter for no extra charge. I explained why that wasn't a good idea.

So far, there was something almost magical about the way things were falling into place. I had even found a special cup for Elijah—silver colored, long-stemmed with four stars of David, a common symbol in Nepal, carved along the rim. I saw it in a souvenir shop and explained to the owner that I needed it for one night and would like to rent it from him.

"Just take it and bring it back the next day," he said.

"I'll give you a deposit."

"No. No. Just take it."

Still, I had awakened that morning worried, wondering where we would find wine. We scoured the markets. The liquor stores in Katmandu carry rum, whiskey, brandy and beer, but no wine. Sunday afternoon we found a bottle of French wine at the exclusive Yak and Yeti Hotel, but it cost $18, much too expensive for us. Finally, on the other side of town, in a small hole-in-the-wall shop, we found two bottles of California cabernet sauvignon for $10 each. Manischewitz it was not, but it would have to do. Wayne immediately took out his pen and wrote, in Hebrew, on the label: "Kosher for Passover." He smiled sadly.

Monday morning, the Nepalese holiday of Holi was in full, boisterous swing. Since the Nepalese follow a lunar calendar, their holiday coincides with ours—although their way of celebrating is a bit different. Holi, a Hindu spring festival, is celebrated with a giant water fight. Water balloons are thrown at passersby from rooftops, windows and balconies. Crowds of teenagers roam the streets drenching each other. I put on a raincoat, pulled the canvas rickshaw over my head and asked the driver to take me to the Israeli consulate.

The consul's wife was expecting me. I had told her about my burgeoning seder and she had promised 10 haggadot and matzah. She also graciously offered real horseradish from her garden, and flowers. On my return trip, I managed to protect the matzah from the water fights by covering it with my raincoat. I, however, got drenched.

By four, the chicken soup was done, the chaharoset made and the tables set.

I rushed back to the guesthouse to shower and change. By the time I was finished it was almost five. We had told everyone to arrive at six.

A knock on the door. Two young, bearded travellers stood side by side. If my heart sank at the sight of them I hope I didn't show it. I had already increased the number of participants from 12 to 23. The owner had moved us to the main dining room, but even there I wasn't sure any more people could fit.

Still in my mind was the memory of the disappointment I had felt being turned away from the seder at the Israeli consulate. "Welcome," I said, and smiled.

If this story were an ancient tale, the author might have you believe that one of the visitors was really Elijah in disguise.

"Do you have wine for the seder?" asked one of the newcomers.

"We found some California wine," I said.

"Kosher for Passover?"

"Of course not."

He reached into his shoulder bag and pulled out a bottle of Manischewitz. It was kosher for Passover. It was red. It was wonderful.

He had just arrived in Katmandu for a trek in the Himalayas and had brought the wine, a box of matzah and a Haggadah, thinking he would hold a seder alone in his hotel room.

By the time we sat down an hour later, there were 29 of us, Americans, Israelis and Canadians, all strangers, all Jews tied together by a bond, re-enacting an ancient drama. Outside we could hear the laughter and revelry of Holi dying down as the sun set. It was time now to celebrate our own holiday on this night of Passover, a night of memory and liturgy, an acting out of the event "as if I were there."

David, the youngest, asked the four questions. We read and sang the entire Haggadah without leaving out a single word. It was so strange for all of us to be going through this familiar ritual in Katmandu, the Hidden Kingdom, the Roof of the World. Some of those assembled had come to Nepal hoping to find inner peace and spirituality in the monasteries and the silence of the Himalayas. The last thing they thought they would discover was a yearning for Jewish connections. We asked questions, we discussed, we debated; as it says, "the more one tells about the Exodus, the more praiseworthy."

Nepalese children, attracted by our singing, stood outside the restaurant, faces pressed into the window to see what we were doing. The king and queen of Nepal looked at us from their portrait on the restaurant wall.

We opened the door for Elijah. Surely he would come, even to Katmandu. ★

THE ARTIFICIAL JEWBOY

Gene Lyons

A young man maturing as I did in the Eastern provinces of our country during the Fifties — the period in American life which lasted from 1948 to 1967 — and aspiring to that form of endeavor that has been called "The Quality Lit Biz," particularly one whose entrance into the trade required the crossing of ethnic and class barriers, has had to learn to cope with the Jews. Such were the conditions of my growing up that intellectualism itself, that peculiar amalgam of restlessness and inertia most often rather smugly called "the life of the mind" during those years, first appeared to me as an almost exclusively "Jewish" phenomenon. At the times and places I was taught there was an unfailing, if often unspoken, association of those key words expressive of the highest values in life and art: "literature," "tragic," "ironic," "human," "moral," "symbol," "organic," and "Jew."

The intensive cultivation of morality, Jewishness, and literary intelligence as virtual synonyms has been noted elsewhere, perhaps most revealingly in Norman Podhoretz's *Making It*. Besides giving credence to the terms I am using by calling his version of the literary establishment a "Jewish Family," Podhoretz is irritatingly accurate in discussing

---

Gene Lyons is a freelance writer who lives in Arkansas, where he has become a fierce local patriot. Formerly a staff writer for Texas Monthly *and* Newsweek, *he has written for a number of magazines. Among them are the* New York Times, Esquire, Inside Sports, Southern Magazine, Triquarterly, *the* Nation *and* Harper's. *He contributes a monthly humor article to the Arkansas* Times. *His* Texas Monthly *article, "Why Teachers Can't Teach" won the National Magazine Award in 1980. A collection of his essays relating to language, bureaucracies, and propaganda will be published in 1987 by the University of Arkansas Press.*

> ... Jews were to be respected as possessing an erroneous but deeply held and coherent tradition.

the cultural synthesis of the generation that taught my own. An understandable reaction to the Holocaust, and Stalinism, and to what seemed to be the failure of ideology, resulted in the guilty enshrinement of the Jewish intellectual by gentiles and the simultaneous celebration of America as a land of freedom and plenty for almost all.

Scarcely are these words on the page than I feel compelled almost as a matter of reflex to disavow anti-Semitism, for my education has been such that one simply does not speak of these things. So overpowering is the moral authority of the Holocaust, so tangible are the achievements of many of the men and women I may seem to be slighting, and so pervasive the commercially valuable and ideologically useful *mythos* of Jewishness, that one hesitates before them. By way of avoiding semantic backflips and apologies that sound all the more insincere for their repetition let us imagine that a novel had appeared in 1957 in which a greedy Shylock of a landlord raised the rent on a humble Italian shopkeeper until that man was forced out of business in order to make room for a more profitable tenant. Let us further imagine that said Shylock had out of remorse gone to work for nothing, operating the Italian's pushcart when he fell ill, in the process falling in love with his Jew-hating *shicksa* daughter, and being gradually won over by their simple and heartfelt faith to the hope everlasting and a merciful Jesus, converting to Roman Catholicism on the last page. If such a book were published at all, there is little doubt that it would have been denounced as a clumsy slur, its degree of literary merit an index to its danger, and its appearance brooded upon as presaging some dark turn against the Jews by the American public. What is more the protesters would very likely have been correct.

Why then was I not as a young Catholic from the lower orders made at least uneasy by Bernard Malamud's *The Assistant*, the plot of which I have not parodied but simply turned inside out? Why did it move me as a work of literature expressive of Universal Truth rather than as the contrived exercise in ethnic self-indulgence that it is? Partly because the contrivance was not cheap. Malamud is a skillful literary artist and intended, I am sure, no slur. Occasional bows in the direction of St. Francis of Assisi are taken in the novel, although hardly vitiating its central force. Then, too, casual bias against Catholicism is so pervasive in American culture that it is hardly noticeable, particularly to those ex-Catholics like myself who partly share it. More important than any of that, though, was that like Malamud's Frank Alpine I was on my way to becoming an Artificial Jewboy and I was not alone. Let me explain:

I first became aware of Jewishness as an issue in the fall of 1952, when I was nine years old. My family lived on Magie Avenue in the Elmora section of Elizabeth, New Jersey, a gritty third-rate industrial city bordering on Newark and just opposite Staten Island. Because it was free I went to P.S. 12, two blocks east of my home, instead of St. Genevieve's school two blocks west. Only months before I had made my First Holy Communion, a sacrament received on a gloriously appropriate spring day entirely out of character with my memories of northern New Jersey. Walking home that morning in my white suit, black and white saddle oxfords and floppy bow tie, hair water parted and admiring God's daffodils, I had the only glimpse I have had, then or since, of a state of grace, and a fading glimmer of what it is people are after when they enter churches.

In early September of that year my father had brought home a 1953 DeSoto sedan, powder blue with a semi-automatic shift, to replace our 1946 Chevy. It was our first new car. We were the recent owners of a 19" Dumont console television set, also our first. I admired my father, a handsome freckle-shouldered Irishman whose uniformed pictures bear a striking resemblance to Mike Riordan of the Capitol Bullets, with uncritical abandon. The Old Man had played semi-pro baseball and football, as well as having recently been the center (at 6'2" and 215 pounds) of a Prudential Insurance Company basketball team which won the New Jersey State AAU championship but which the company had declined to send to the Nationals. One of our famous family legends concerns his thrashing of three men, including his older brother Jim, who tried to hold him down and make him drink whiskey. He once played the fourth quarter of a football game at fullback after dislocating his shoulder in the third and having his teammates pop it back into place. I thought that my mother, a redhead whose maiden name was Sheedy, was the loveliest woman in New Jersey.

My first Jewish acquaintance was Judy Peckerman, the daughter of a housepainter and seltzer salesman on my block who had provided his family with a television set. From 1948 until 1952 I spent at least two hours of every day in her home. From the time school let out until Howdy Doody was over at 5:30 and we all went home for dinner, every kid on the block — most of them Celtic Papists like me — could be found in front of the little round screen in the Peckerman living room ruining our eyes together. Judy also had a two-car garage cluttered with cases of empty chrome-fauceted seltzer bottles, the better to imitate Clarabelle the Clown with, and a large abandoned wardrobe chest inside of which she, Peggy MacNamara and I exhibited to each other our private particulars and pissed into empty Dutch Boy cans to demonstrate their use.

A regular feature on those afternoon children's shows from Channel 13 in Newark was a public service announcement on behalf of brotherhood, a cartoon in which a smug blonde trapeze artist swung back and forth refusing the grasp of successive minority partners until he fell, as the announcer cried, "Oh Joe, you schmo." Yiddish and all, we children received this as the gravest of truths, and on our block at least, I believe that we practiced it. If I knew that Judy was a Jew, or if she attached any significance to our Catholicism, I cannot recall it. Yet, while it may be my faulty memory, I do not remember her coming to my house.

Contrary to popular myth there was no hint of anti-Semitism in my Sunday school devotions at St. Genevieve's. My pre-communion training, what there was of it, stressed the belief that while only Catholics could enter the Kingdom of Heaven, Jews were to be respected as possessing an erroneous but deeply held and coherent tradition. Since I have noticed that theological anti-Semitism is often stronger among my co-religionists who attended parochial schools, it may be that the brotherhood stratagem was self-consciously assumed for public school students, but I doubt it. *The Assistant* notwithstanding, we were deemed in no immediate danger of becoming Jews. Such a conversion would have been mere pathology, like coming down with leukemia instead of polio. Closer at hand was a more insidious trap for our immortal souls: Protestantism.

Perhaps Simon Daedalus is right, and the Irish never persecuted the Jews because they never let them in. But there is also the fact of a common enemy on both sides of the Atlantic: the WASP. It is difficult not to feel foolish writing this down in 1975, and people outside the east coast may be forgiven treating it as a hopeless anachronism, but against all reason and most statistics, Irish Catholics there still see themselves essentially as landless peasants in a system run by and for their hereditary oppressors, an attitude they continue to share through the parish church with their fellow ex-peasants of Eastern and Southern European extraction — and which all of them share with increasingly equal dubiousness with the Jew. Still vivid in my mother's mind is her father's excuse for his besottedness: signs reading "Irish need not apply." Active among my father's resentments is the anti-Catholic bias of the Prudential Insurance Company, only very recently reported to be giving way.

So when the Jew is discussed in those circles it is with ambivalence. His alleged clannishness, like his other qualities, is a two-sided coin. Jews will stick together to defraud the simple Christian; but no Jew will allow another to go hungry. If he is an arrogant, self-seeking schemer, he is also a Real Go Getter. Grass Does Not Grow Under His Feet. For every disloyal intellectual and po-

The Artificial Jewboy

tential subversive there is a Smart Jew Lawyer, who knows the value of a good education, and is the only kind to have when you are in trouble. The same goes for doctors. So far as I know neither of my parents has ever gone to a gentile doctor for anything important. What is equally important I think is that perhaps because he cannot — anyone can spot one — the Jew does not as soon as he gets a few dollars ahead become a Republican and begin aping the gentry. And he is good to his family.

Behind all of this lies the suspicion that whatever else Jews are, they are serious people, little given to frivolity and waste. Although I have always found my grandfather's curses against the English dated and my father's forced, they are emotions that persist. I can recall quite vividly volunteering in a Sunday School discussion of religious tolerance that my best friend was a Presbyterian, and basking in self-congratulation because I forgave him in this world the sure knowledge that he would suffer an eternity of punishment in the next. To this day I continue to harbor an irrational mistrust and distaste for all varieties of Protestantism, and secretly regard the lot of them as self-seeking or deluded simpletons of the Pat Boone-Charles Colson variety, whose zeal for public righteousness masks the shallowest and most crocodilian morality.

In December of 1953 my family moved permanently to the largely gentile suburb of Chatham. Unlike so many others, though, we did not move west as a result of postwar prosperity so much as in search of it, purchasing a huge four-apartment investment of a home in what my mother, who hates it to this day, considers the remote provinces, twelve miles from the house she was born in, and my father more affectionately calls "the sticks," although it is scarcely more rural now than The Bronx.

My mother's objections to this migration might have been settled by a classier set of neighbors, although they would have terrified her, but the economics of the thing landed us smack in the middle of the only Jewish neighborhood in town, a sizeable tract known as the Chatham Colony Association. And such a neighborhood. These were not your upward mobile, country clubbing, assimilationist type of Jewish persons. They were first and second generation Russian and Yiddish speaking immigrants, former ghetto dwellers and long time ardent Zionists. We had purchased security at the expense of respectability. We had actually made a downward move to the suburbs, leaving a stable lower middle class environment to settle with a tribe of "friggin' Sheenies." Adlai Stevenson was all you got, you should live so long.

The Chatham Colony Association was founded in 1922 by a group of Polish, Russian, and German immigrants seeking to establish a cooperative community on Socialist principles in what was then the remote fastness of the Jersey woods. By the time we arrived, however, the membership was aging, many having died or moved away, their children long since departed and the old left to keep up fifty year old houses on wooded plots that they had cleared themselves by hand when the experiment was new.

As desperately as my parents wanted respectability there was something comforting about living among poor Jews, for in no case were they in a position to condescend. Besides which in their foreignness they were apt subjects for Aesopian fables of moral instruction. Although it was believed that all of our neighbors had vast sums hidden away and they were smuggling bags of loot to Israel, their outward need was evidence of yet another truth: the Jew in his greed was like the farrow that ate the sow, and the departed children of the elderly, having robbed their poor parents of life and goods, were leaving them to die in shame while they wintered in Miami. Two needs were thus taken care of. Jews without wealth were accounted for, and a powerful moral lesson was imparted: Don't ever leave home, my parents were telling us, do you want to be like a Jew? That the whole works conflicted with other fables of Jewish existence and was internally inconsistent anyway never bothered them, although being as literal minded as I was, it gave me no end of trouble.

As I write, moreover, I am in danger of falling into another kind of sentimentalizing fiction. By no means were all of our neighbors poor. Although most lived modestly, at least a few made trips to Israel, others to Europe and Russia, and some wintered in Florida, Arizona, or California, perhaps with their children. For all I know the others didn't have children, or lost them. And except for one proud woman whose son was a "big television producer" and who drove a Cadillac, none of us had any idea where those children were or what they did for the most part. When the Cadillac went by we sometimes shouted "Jew Canoe" as soon as it was out of range.

Our gentile neighbors were halfway specimens like ourselves: an alcoholic lawyer whose wife took in boarders and typing, and whose sons (as my mother never let me forget) ate Clark Bars and drank Pepsis for breakfast; a machinist whose wife conducted an open liaison with the town's garbage contractor (he arrived in his truck); Chatham's second-string dancing teacher, who conducted classes in her living room and whose husband was permitted inside the house only to stoke the furnace; a laborer and his wife whose two room shack smelled of gin and garbage (the wife was never once seen out of doors in ten years). That kind of thing. By coincidence there were several boys my age or my brother's, and we shared two things: fascination that sometimes edged over into revulsion for our strange neighbors, and a common social stigma derived from living near them; a stigma which grew all the stronger as the suburbs spread and the woods and fields filled up with executives and their kin. Having lost the sharp definitions of the city I only half comprehended, as we all did, what was going on. Without the sustaining categories of city life, I simply floated. From my father I learned to reject the smug and successful, from them I learned to reject my father, and from the Jews around us, I am now convinced, I learned how to maintain my dignity even as I half accepted and partly rejected the vicious anti-Semitic stereotypes of which my parents were intimately and my classmates more coolly convinced.

My father's Jew hatred, like his nigger phobia, grew sharply more pronounced as his own feelings of failure and my mother's barely submerged hysteria closed in on him. In 1956, by which time it was plain he was not going to make his fortune with the Prudential, he sunk his life's savings and all he could borrow, together with what remained of his belief in himself, nurtured by all those years of athletic triumph and personal charm, into a Dairy Queen franchise on a badly chosen country highway in Wayne, 20 miles from our home. As he had been with the Prudential (we had a painting of the Rock of Gibraltar in our living room) he became a Dairy Queen believer, a very Morris Bober of the soft ice cream trade. He could talk butterfat content for hours, extolling the merits of the Dairy Queen product over all competitors. How someone could actually put Carvel ice cream in their mouth was beyond his comprehension. I spent frustrated hours sweating over the spigot, the old man bellowing instructions over my shoulder in a fruitless attempt to perfect the trademarked curl that had to go on the top of every three ounce cone. I never saw myself what difference it made. I was not cut out for the retail business. By moving to the suburbs we skipped a generation in my family. I should have been a hustler and my own kids punks like me.

Whatever, we never made it to Easy Street. Instead of working from Easter to Halloween and going south for the winter, my father spent the next ten years putting in 16 to 18 hour days all during the warm months, commuting home from "The Pru," grabbing a sandwich and heading for the "D.Q." on the run, never making anything more than ten dollars a day he could skim off the top. It ended only when his cursed avaricious Kike of a landlord refused to renew the option on his lease so he could do it for ten more.

Whatever he thought of the "miserable Jewbastards" when the vapors were on him my father was unfailingly polite and helpful towards our elderly neighbors and became a community favorite. Sensing a soft touch, many of them came to count on him for tasks my brother and I were too young to do. Without public complaint, he hung shelves, unclogged pipes, moved furniture, played taxicab, and lifted things. The phone would ring at dinnertime, my sister would shout "It's one of the Jews" — all had heavy accents and depended upon them for identification, beginning conversations *in medias res:* "Lyons, in the attic is such a business with squirrels I couldn't sleep. You could fix it?" Whatever he was doing the Old Man would drop it and go. Katz had a stuck door; Sachs' car wouldn't start; Switzen wondered was he maybe going by the train station. "Meesthair Lynz," Fanny Sachs once told me, "is a good man."

The Artificial Jewboy

> Portnoy's story, up to the adult part of it anyway, was my own story...

At the same time the Dairy Queen was failing, the domestic sign of my father's inability to move us into the suburban mainstream was the Chatham Colony Association's only public enterprise, the most ramshackle swim club in northern New Jersey. Over a period of years the members had converted a swampy pond on a back corner of their property into something resembling a swimming pool by damming one end with a cement wall, digging an artesian well and dumping in granular chlorine at odd intervals from a rowboat. At a time when everyone else in town was joining country clubs and taking up golf, my brother, sister, and I wheedled eighty bucks out of the Old Man for a season membership at "The Colony," which had water the color of light coffee, bullfrogs, and a tarpaper shack for a dressing room, through the plywood walls of which Barry Irving and I drilled scores of peepholes. (A bolder voyeur than I, "Irv" once packed a lunch and spent an entire day sitting quietly in the open rafters over the Women's dressing room, which could be reached from the Men's side.) Even more significant in our gentile paradise, "The Colony" drew carloads of Jews without money from the hot streets of Newark, Elizabeth, Irvington, and Union. A few families from New York summered in flat roofed bungalows on the community property, serene in what they considered "the country." No tennis, golf, volleyball, or swim team. No cabanas, no sandwiches, no liquor. Even the showers didn't work. Just overweight, and some not so overweight, lower middle class housewives with their hair as often as not in curlers playing Mah-Jongg, canasta and bridge under the trees while their children pissed in the water. On weekends the husbands arrived to sit chewing cigars and reading the *Newark News*, dressed in sleeveless undershirts, bermuda shorts, and crepe-soled web sandals with calf-length black socks.

Fortunately for all of us, the pool was located at the end of a dead end street next to a power line right-of-way and most "Chathamites," as they were designated in the town's weekly paper, did not know it existed. Had it been more public I do not doubt that attempts would have been made to get the County Board of Health to shut it down. For me, lurching through adolescence in a suburb only slightly less caste-ridden than Calcutta, the pool was a multiple blessing. In order to avoid my father's stubborn self-defeating pride it was necessary that I continue to be only subliminally aware of class differences. The pool helped by providing me ready access to people to whom I did not have to feel inferior, both because of their faith and their social position. And not only was I introduced to that mysterious form of oriental sensuality known as the

---

Photo Credits

Norman Mailer/Wide World Photos
Saul Bellow/Jill Krementz
Philip Roth/Widener Library
Karl Marx/Widener Library
Sigmund Freud/Wide World Photos
Albert Einstein/Widener Library
Woody Allen/Wide World Photos
Mel Brooks/Wide World Photos
Lenny Bruce/Wide World Photos

Jewish girl, but by mutual consent I was able to keep my infatuations a secret. Whether copping a feel off Bambi Irving in the murky waters or dry-humping Ruth Kantrowitz against a tree in the woods I was safe from detection. And so were they.

I only wish I knew more than I do about the whole subject of Jewish girls and gentile boys, and hope that some scholar more learned in the ways of the world will appear to enlighten us. For now I offer these few comments: In my experience Jewish girls seemed to be on franker terms with their desires and less concerned with maintaining about their flesh an aura of mysticism than their *shicksa* counterparts. But then like a photographic negative of Alexander Portnoy's encounters, my limited erotic experiences during the period of adolescence were confined largely to *shicksas* who Didn't and Jewish girls who *Did*, or more frequently Almost Did, or Did Everything But. I wonder if Philip Roth is aware how badly all of us with murky class origins wanted the archetypal young snub-nosed cheerleader he calls Thereal McCoy? The kind of girl who knew the value of a good body and a fresh face and was not about to be pawed or spurted upon by anybody who couldn't afford her. To this day the sight of a girl like that in a tennis dress triggers in me contradictory impulses of near homicidal desire.

More matter of fact and less hysterical about it all, Jewish girls did not seem so anxious to make one pay for what one was getting. This was because there was a sometimes tacit and sometimes spoken assumption that we were not in it for the long haul. But then I only went out with the kind of Jewish girl who goes out with gentiles. When Ruth Kantrowitz and I were caught in a moderately compromising position on her grandmother's back porch we suffered politely the old woman's Yiddish accented lecture on tradition and the individual *goy* because it was less upsetting for her to fear that her son's daughter might marry a Christian than that she simply liked to do what she was doing. It was Ruth who introduced me to the idea, later to become familiar, that Jewish girls would be far more willing to play You Do It For Me and I'll Do It For You with one of us than with one of their co-religionists because of the lack of long-range prospects involved. More likely an explanation, I think, was that these were summertime games away from home where one's "reputation" could not be affected. In the 1950's that consideration would have been far more important than anybody's religion. For all of this petting and pawing, incidentally, I never in my life actually showed up at a Jewish girl's house for a date; we are speaking here of *ad hoc* arrangements. It strikes me that most of what I know on the subject is on a level with the kind of tribal superstition that created the complementary myth that Catholic girls screwed like mink because they could confess it all, but invariably became pregnant because they forbade the use of rubbers. Nice logic there. For all of the cross-religious carrying on that was conducted in parked cars all over northern New Jersey, during the period we stayed as ignorant about each other as so many stone age savages sharing a rain forest together.

So from the seventh grade until I left New Jersey permanently after college, I spent most of every day at the Colony pool, exchanging with the solstice gentile friends for Jews, and passing, as time went on, from member to lawn mower and drain skimmer, and from there eventually to head lifeguard, retaining at each step all of my former duties, so that when I attained my loftiest position with the organization I was performing (or rather malingering) at everything from teaching lifesaving to digging used Kotex pads out of the toilet. Had my duties required anything short of conversion to the faith of Abraham, I am sure I would have grudgingly performed them. Anything to stay out of the Dairy Queen. If my father was going to sink, he could man his own lifeboats.

Imagine my surprise then, when I began to learn that Jews were prejudiced against us and prejudiced in ways that could not have been better designed to contribute to my own secret conviction that I was a foundling unrelated by blood to anyone with whom I lived. That my mother's family was an almost parodic example and my father's just barely removed from what most Jews seemed willing to think that we were did not lessen my discomfort at gradually discovering that we Christians, and we Irish Catholics in particular it seemed, were held to be drunken undereducated philistines, Jew haters to the core, and prone to random outbursts of insensate violence. What civilized habits we attained, such as literacy, were held to be a thin veneer over a spirit only slightly advanced since the time when our ancestors painted themselves blue and worshipped totems. Explicit in Grandmother Kantrowitz's lecture, in fact, with me sitting right there trying to tuck my shirt in, was that there was no logical attitude for gentiles and Jews to take toward one another except mutual suspicion and dislike. I even suspected that there was a foreskin hidden in there somewhere, although like everybody else I knew I had been circumcised at birth. It reminded me of the time Mrs. Kaplan from down the street stood on the sidewalk in front of our house shaking her cane and shouting that my brother and I were "little Nazi pigs" for wrestling and hollering on our front lawn, leaving us bewildered and abashed and providing impetus for a twenty year grudge between my mother and her. In any case a *goy* with a book, I learned, was considered a contradiction in terms and was to be approached gingerly, like a trained bear in a tutu. Even if this theory was advanced most openly by people whose idea of literature was *Exodus* or *Only in America*, it hurt. Those were my ideas of literature too. Where was I supposed to learn any better? Neither of my parents has ever read a book.

My relationship with Eddie Zarin, fellow lifeguard, was a case in point, and premonition of more complicated relationships to come. For five consecutive summers we spent most of every day together. Although we attended the same college (Rutgers) and lived only ten miles apart, our friendship, if that was what it was, was confined to working hours only. Unathletic and given to plumpness, at least in my strenuous sense of what was athletic, Zarin had an abhorrence of physical labor that made me seem energetic by comparison, and devoted astonishing amounts of time to avoiding it with a barefaced chicanery that was almost ingratiating in its openness. He would scheme for days to be sure the lawn was mowed on his day off — usually dropping a hint to our aged employers that it was looking ragged as he went out the gate the night before. Where there was garbage to be collected or chlorine drums to be unloaded Eddie would usually be deep in conversation with one of the old ladies at the front entrance, with whom, as the only Jewish lifeguard, he was an assiduous favorite. He had a way of knowing (small cousins) which of the bathrooms had been befouled by a child and would volunteer to clean the others before anyone else knew what was up. When the rest of us complained, he would urge us to straighten things out with the handful of Christian mothers in the place, because obviously no Jew would do such a swinish thing. Zarin drove the rest of us to fits by beating everyone at an improvised handball game we had invented by mastering chops, spins, lobs, and undercuts while I lost three points to two setting him up for soul-satisfying smashes. He boasted but would never try to prove that he could beat me in the same way at basketball, which was more my game, although we both knew he couldn't, since I was by then my father's size and fairly proficient at a sport more suited to sheer physicality.

What is more, if my description of Zarin seems tainted with barely disguised anti-Semitism of the cheapest kind, it should be clear that Eddie not only cheerfully accepted these terms, he invented them himself. Implicit in all our dealings over a five year period was the often repeated assertion that *as a Jew* Zarin was shrewder, more cunning, and fundamentally saner than we coarse louts who were so stupidly vain as to hoist 100-pound chlorine barrels to our shoulders and carry them through the grounds for the sole purpose of showing off our muscles. If I were enough of a *putz* to strain my *goyische* back, it was fine with Eddie and would only serve to confirm his already low opinion of my intelligence. Zarin never let us forget that he was paid twenty dollars a week more than the rest of us for the same job, that he had been given it primarily as a kind of scholarship for a nice Jewish boy, and that the *goyim* were expected to do all the work. Furthermore, although he flirted with probation the whole four years we were at Rutgers together and had not yet graduated when I left, he treated his intellectual superiority as an unchallenged matter of fact.

For all of that I could never bring myself to dislike old Zarin, for while his chauvinism was sometimes annoying it was also simple, essentially amoral, and at bottom comic in a way that is very nearly sad. Would that it had always been so.

Shall I begin with Beethoven, with chess, or with physics? Or shall I simply observe that in arriving on the campus of Rutgers for my freshman year I was for the first time in my life confronted with persons far beyond my intellectual depth — almost my comprehension, as it seemed at the time — and who treated my obvious inferiority with patient, if kind, condescension. Here were young men of lower-middle-class origins who shared, or at least were conversant with, my own cultural enthusiasms — Jerry West, Willie Mays, Chuck Berry — but who were simultaneously able to distinguish by ear between Mozart and Stravinsky, to discuss the merits of various openings in chess, who seemed to know a lot of history, and not only had heard of relativity theory but professed to understand it. Do I need to say at this point that these young men were Jews?

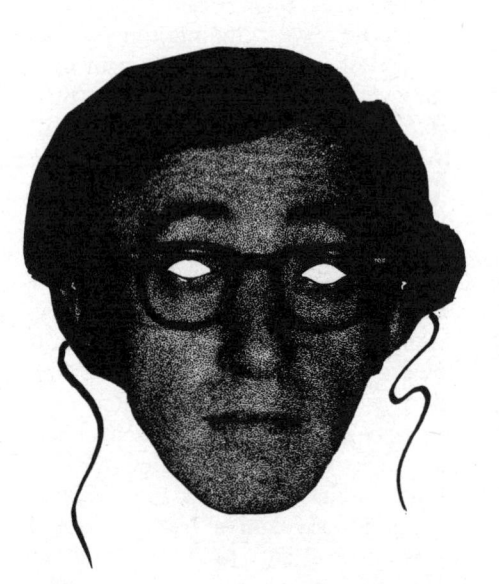

Whenever I read, in this autobiography or that article, of the formidable intellectual influence upon various individuals by the eminent Scholar and Professor X, I am puzzled and suspect either exaggeration or sycophancy. I arrived at college with a mind possessing all the density and rigor of silly putty, and was too inexperienced to do more than sit with my mouth agape taking notes in the presence of any of the real luminaries of the Rutgers faculty. Until I hid out in a gentile jock fraternity house at the end of my sophomore year, my real teachers were all students — and almost all Jews.

To hear them talk, most of my new pals in the dormitory had come at it from the other side. They settled for Rutgers after not quite making, or making and being unable to afford Harvard, Columbia, or Yale. While I was terrified of flunking out in my first semester and going home in disgrace, they were arguing the merits of Albert Schweitzer and Harvard Medical School and debating the relative stature of Chicago and Berkeley in physics or English — institutions of whose existence I had previously been virtually unaware. Having learned a bit more in academic life about bluffing, I suspect now that most of the earnest discussions we held deep into the night on Beauty, Art, Truth, Sex, and the Existence of God would have struck even college juniors as fairly jejune, but to me they were effusions of the pure ether of reason, virtually the first indication I had ever really had that ideas did matter. To assimilate and understand a culture and its values, always with the consciousness of being an outsider determined not to be swallowed alive by the majority; to transform oneself and one's expectations without being changed — that we shared.

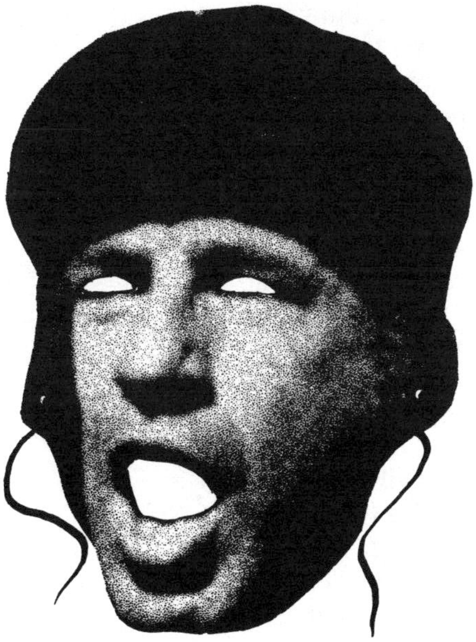

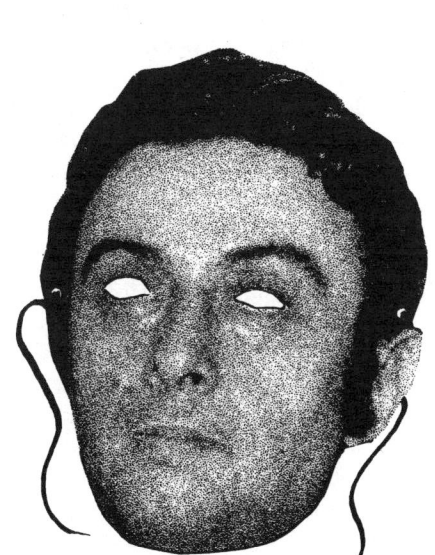

Ideas themselves, by God, that was the thing! One had neither to join nor fight, merely to become An Intellectual. In an altogether serious way — and for once I do not mean to be glib about this — those Jewboys saved my life.

In very short order, moreover, lessons begun at the pool were continued. Just as Sandy Koufax was unquestionably the best pitcher in baseball history, and just as Elizabeth Taylor could claim to be the loveliest woman on earth (now that she had done the sensible thing), so were Marx, Freud, and Einstein the three great geniuses of the modern age — and all of them, of course, were Jews like Irwin Cantor, who never took more than five moves to beat me at chess when he really wanted to, having taught me just enough about how to move the pieces to beat my dummy of a roommate, but not enough so that I could anticipate what he was doing to me. The only reason he played with me at all, I am sure, is that I puzzled him. Here I was tall, well set-up, and not bad looking. From one or two trips to the gym he knew that I was a natural athlete who had played at least creditably in high school competition. I probably did OK with the girls (little did he know); I was a *goy* in a Christian country. So what did I want with ideas? Ideas were for Jews. Better I should hang around with Dennis Murphy, Joe Helenowski, and Joe Gerassi, those misplaced louts, and go out for pizzas, than *kibbitz* at the chess games, or talk about *Crime and Punishment*.

Neither Cantor nor any of the other Jewish friends I had at the time had much reservation about admitting, or sometimes insisting, and much more seriously than Greenberg, that Jews as people were intellectually superior to the rest of us, and that the alleged superiority was, if not racial in origin, at least the product of a better genetic pool. My initial reaction to this idea was a kind of mild panic, because I knew I thought it was true, but had been trained by every respectable organ of public opinion since Joe the Schmo that such invidious distinctions between races and cultures were by their nature evil. How in the name of all that was holy could *they* say *that*? My second reaction was suppressed anger and some resentment — because I began to suspect that no one, least of all the persons who made up the terms of the debate, truly believed in either cultural or racial equality, and to realize that I could not argue back against the idea of Jewish superiority because to do so would be beyond the bounds of civilized discourse as I had internalized them.

Our discussions of the subject were often, in fact, protracted games of "Catch a Gentile by the Toe," in which the object (unconscious most of the time) is to needle the half-despised *goy* into revealing his own presumed hatred, then to recoil in horror while he turns against himself in shame. As useful a survival mechanism as this must be it was not easy to cope with. One was not even supposed to notice, in

The Artificial Jewboy

> Most appealing to me as a young man ... was the realization that one need not be Jewish to be a Jew.

those days, that there is sometimes such a thing as a "Jewish nose."

Perhaps nothing I have written or probably can write will convince some readers that I harbor no Nazi within, or explain what I mean by calling myself an "artificial Jewboy." I have neither knowledge of nor serious interest in Judaism — or in any religious doctrine for that matter. But neither did most of the Jews I am talking about. What attracted and repelled me then was the restless, skeptical, categorizing intellect I came to associate with Jews. Yes, and the pride, the intellectual arrogance, and the moral superiority. I had to get out of the hole I was in somehow, and at the time and in the place I was educated, literary Jewishness, a more complicated, subtle and serious version of the games I am describing, was the prestige ticket.

Looking back, it is not at all difficult to see how that cultural metamorphosis came about. In the aftermath of the most unimaginably "inhuman" cataclysm in European history it was perhaps inevitable and certainly healthy that the Jew assume a position of special moral and intellectual authority in American life. For one thing it freed artists, writers, and thinkers to be as openly "Jewish" in their preoccupations as they cared to be without needing to be fearful or apologetic. At least publicly, anti-Semitism was viewed by almost every serious person in the United States as an unthinkable perversion. The extraordinary and continuing burst of creative and intellectual activity by the American Jews and European immigrants reinforced this predisposition to see the Jew not as Superman but as Everyman. The Holocaust itself stood forth as the central historical event of our times: the suffering of European Jewry became the quintessential symbol for all that was mad in a maddened century. One could not look beyond or around it, and one could hardly call into question the credentials of anyone who wished to invoke its horrific shadow, even if one suspected at a level too deep for conscious articulation that the invocation was occasionally self-serving when used as a means of avoiding all criticism by persons no closer to the actual event than my father is to Belfast, and not so close as my grandfather (whose own parents fled it) was to deliberate starvation.

It was on the advice of friends in the dormitory that I first read *The Assistant*, a work which moved me at the time as very few books ever have, then or since. Most appealing to me as a young man almost wholly out of touch with himself and anything one could call a tradition, and I do not mean to be at all flippant about this, was the realization that one need not be Jewish to be a Jew.

Witness the following exchange between shopkeeper Morris Bober and repentant Italian thug Frank Alpine:

> "Nobody will tell me that I am not Jewish because I put in my mouth once in awhile, when my tongue is dry, a piece of ham. But they will tell me, and I will believe them, if I forget the Law. This means to other people. Our life is hard enough. Why should we hurt somebody else? For everybody should be the best, not only for you or me. We ain't animals. This is why we need the Law. This is what a Jew believes —"
> "I think other religions have those ideas too," Frank said. "But tell me why it is the Jews suffer so damn much, Morris? It seems they like to suffer, don't they?"
> "Do you like to suffer? They suffer because they are Jews."

Or, to reverse the near tautology that the novel creates by its end: "They are Jews because they suffer." My God, how I wanted to suffer when I first read that book in 1961 or 1962. Not in any immediate or palpable way, of course, for while I hoped for a life of moral anguish and difficulty I expected no pain. Thus novels like *The Assistant* and the cultural climate that exalted them cultivated a sense of tragedy, of ambiguity, and of contradiction that was the only "mature" attitude that one could take toward life — life in those days being a more vivid but unforgivably random source of images from which to produce "art." The intensive emphasis upon the literature of high contemplation, if not of literary criticism itself, into the characteristic "human" act — was inextricably tied up, it seems to me, as it seemed to me then with much different implications, with the idea of Jewishness. For those of us who were only imaginatively involved in an event which had transpired before we assumed consciousness, and in another land, after all, the disaster of the European Jews provided a kind of eschatological thrill. More than anything else it served to convince us that a life of passive virtue could have the tragic consequences we half-desired without having any more idea what we were talking about than so many children. Otherwise why not Hiroshima, Nagasaki, or even Dresden as similarly symbolic totems?

I envied my new friends the ready-made identity, to risk another cliché of the period, that they had, and for which I was obliged, heaven help me, to search. For a lost boy in a neurotic civilization that was losing confidence even as it tried to insist on itself as a classless capitalist country in which the parameters of political debate conformed almost exactly to those of human possibility — for such a young man and such a country, what figure could have been more appealing than one who had a historical identity whenever he wanted it, an identity moreover, that did not require belief or commitment (not in Cold War America anyway) and which might be claimed or denounced almost at will? In which ethnic and racial chauvinism of the mild sort I have described was not only permitted but looked upon favorably, at least in public.

I have learned remarkably little in the intervening years about the peculiar habits of mind and emotion that I have attempted to describe except that I have read a good many more books and have grown skeptical in my dotage. Nor is there any point in discussing my personal dealings with those more formidable people I was to encounter later on. Not only are some of them public or semi-public figures whom I do not wish to embarrass for attitudes that some readers may conclude to be projections of my own, but as I have said, in Zarin and Cantor the pattern was laid.

Throughout my remaining years at Rutgers and four more at the University of Virginia I never wavered in my private conviction that what I was getting was essentially a "Jewish" education. It was not just the big three, Sigmund, Karl, and Albert, but all the rest: Kazin, Trilling, Fiedler, Howe, Rahv, Hook, Arendt, Fromm, Bellow, Mailer, Roth, *et al*. Truly it never occurred to me to think, nor did it occur to anyone to encourage me to think, that there could be such an animal as a Roman Catholic or an ex-Roman Catholic intellectual. James Joyce, I suppose, would have qualified, but he had, after all, this thing about Jews himself. And who taught me Joyce? Why Robert Langbaum of course. In any case we are talking America here, and American delusions.

So I know exactly what Leslie Fiedler means when he calls Ralph Ellison a "black Jew" and have no doubt that he is correct. Consider that unmatched set of affirmations in the Epilogue to *Invisible Man*, another novel I encountered at roughly the same time as *The Assistant* and which likewise bore the imperishable stamp of "art":

> So it is now that I denounce and defend, or feel prepared to defend. I condemn and affirm, say no and say yes, yes and say no. I denounce because though implicated and partially responsible, I have been hurt to the point of abysmal pain, hurt to the point of invisibility. And I defend because in spite of all I love. In order to get some of it down I *have* to love . . . too much of your life will be lost, its meaning lost, unless you approach it as much through love as through hate. So I approach it through division. So I denounce and I defend and I hate and I love.

Denounce and defend what, one asks? Why literature itself, of course. Doubtless Ellison's rhetoric and its overwhelming acceptance at the time it was written was made easier by the lack of direct objects to all those high-sounding verbs. Who, after all, was there to be troubled by a dense and beautifully written novel of social injustice, moral blindness and self-deception which proved literary intellectuals to have made the only possible choice? Ah, but to be human: to be above or outside the battle without proclaiming oneself indifferent. May I be pardoned for saying that for all its brilliance the novel is a period piece? — a contrivance not so bold as *The Assistant* perhaps, but mechanical and strained nonetheless.

Nor is this entirely to discount Ellison's achievement, for in the moribund cultural climate of the Cold War we were all made artificial Jewboys, and the bookish among us were prone to seek our coherence, poor things, through literature. One finishes one's books as one finishes them, and a writer can be pardoned a certain degree of aesthetic enthusiasm for having done so. If *Invisible Man* now seems to lack the consolations of "organic form," "imaginative wholeness," or whatever one chooses to call it, the fault may lie in the concept rather than in the novel. For when one writes honestly about a neurotic and disintegrating culture one has relatively few choices about endings; either one destroys one's characters or one reverses the Aristotelian formula and concludes in the middle of things, in which case the mere survival of a voice is no mean thing. Better that than the contrived and sentimental apotheoses of an Updike or a Malamud.

And then the Vietnam years, the fragile intellectual and emotional compromises I have spoken of beginning to disintegrate visibly on the great centrifuge of American life. During the worst of it (1969-1972), I did a three year stretch as Assistant Professor of English at the University of Massachusetts in Amherst, a place my colleagues seemed to regard as a kind of academic heaven, but was very near to driving me mad. There the traditional righteousness of the New England gentry and the kind I have been describing combined to produce an atmosphere of guilt-ridden smugness the likes of which, I pray, I may never live with again. For many the Cambodian invasion of 1970 and the subsequent killings were the culmination, and very soon afterward the end of a five year battle to preserve that sense of self-importance and passive virtue we had based our lives upon. We had gone so far in opposition to that hated but for us still imaginary war as to call off classes and demonstrate. We read statistics to each other through loudspeakers, trying to convince ourselves that Vietnam was a real place and that our own country was conducting an aerial program as vile as that whose memory had formed us. More than anything else we wanted our rebellion taken seriously, because if it was not, than we were not and then . . .

So when those shootings were announced we were for the briefest of moments confirmed, our world in order. They were coming after us at last as we had always known they would, those rednecks in the executive suites, those Fascist gentile hordes. The whole idea, even by those who claimed to abjure the worship of books a good deal more unequivocally than I had done, was to insult, belittle, offend, and mock *them* into attacking *us*, so demonstrating our ethical superiority to the world — and to each other. I was back in that Rutgers dorm, except that by this time I had at least halfway switched sides.

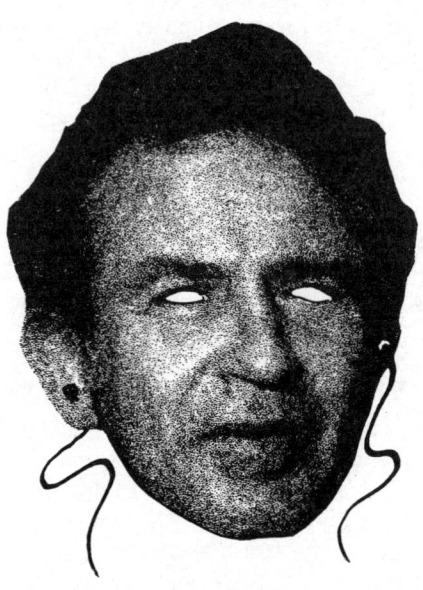

Only nobody was picking on us, not really. Unless we made deliberate pests of ourselves no one, least of all our government, seemed to care what we did. Lies, cunning and brutality more or less ended the war, while moral scrupulousness and literary intellectuals did less than nothing. And still they kept raising our salaries. Wasn't anyone going to punish us at all?

But I am representing myself as having been a good deal more comfortable with all that than I was at the time. For in spite of all the rage and anguish, office politics continued in the academic world as usual, with the Higher Politics temporarily substituted for the Higher Literature as the shibboleth by which one knew the chosen. Amherst confused me no end, because for a state university in which so many of the students were hirsute metamorphoses of my adolescent self, the faculty was comprised almost entirely of older versions of my high school classmates, my dormitory friends, and my old professors. And as much as I had altered myself to fit the mold, a buried grain of rebelliousness yet remained, a stubbornness that made me suspicious of the habit of equating what appeared to me to be unearned self-rightousness with virtue. Caught in the middle, I felt trapped and cheated, with exactly nowhere to go. I couldn't make myself — to use pop shorthand — into either Abbie Hoffman or Norman Podhoretz (ever scanning the horizon for a classy Herman Wouk). So I tried to prove myself to people I did not respect by acting as if I had nothing to prove and becoming sullen when persons who had no reason to do so failed to take me at my own valuation of myself.

Into all this came Alexander Portnoy, pulling his pud. At first I found the novel simply and sheerly hilarious — the male adolescent mind, my own male adolescent mind anyway, revealed and parodied in all its enraged tumescence. Doubtless it helped that Portnoy's background in terms of geography and class were very nearly identical to my own — give or take a few years. And the Jewishness alongside of all that made not one damned bit of difference; had I Roth's talent and social perceptiveness, I felt, I could have written every word of it with certain minor changes of emphasis. Portnoy's story, up to the adult part of it anyway, was my own story, his guilt, isolation, resentment and confusion over the question of where he had come from and where he was going so exactly parallel to mine that so small a difference as the exact nature of one's childhood beliefs made no real difference at all.

So they said about the *goyim* at the Portnoy dinner table things as primitively tribal as we said about the kikes — and apparently with a good deal more frequency and less ambivalence. So what? I knew that already. So what, if it did help to free me from the guilt I felt for other people's crimes and the consequent reverence for all things Jewish, as if a Jew could do no serious wrong? Was that a bad thing? Wasn't it about time we got over all that and started taking one another seriously?

More important here was a real (if imaginary) Jewboy who was coming apart as I was in danger of coming apart, who wanted some degree of continuity between his public and his private lives and with the ideas and values all of us claimed to reverence so dearly; who wanted, in brief, to mature and prosper in contemporary America without surrendering either to the thuggishness of the gentiles we imagined or to the even more insidiously fashionable life of angst as value and staggering self-contradiction that seemed to me to be the essence of Amherst — and, I was sure, of Cambridge, New Haven, Ann Arbor, Berkeley and most of the way stations in between.

I do not, after all this, intend to overstate the impact of one novel, or even of a whole body of significant work. Nor is it my intention to defend Roth against his critics, either the Professional Jews or Irving Howe. Still it was disappointing to find the latter, a sophisticated critic with an unsparing eye for other people's sentimentalities both defining the problem and missing his own point in his famous *Commentary* assault upon Roth's work:

> When we say . . . that a writer betrays a thin personal culture we mean, among other possibilities, that he comes at the end of a tradition which can no longer nourish his imagination, or that he has, through an act of fiat, chosen to tear himself away from that tradition . . . It is of course, a severe predicament for a writer to find himself in this situation; it forces him into self-consciousness, improvisation, and false starts.

Oh it does exactly that. Indeed it does. And not just in writing books either. But can he really imagine, this man of his own generation, that the Idea of Literature is going to get ours through too? Elsewhere Howe has spoken of feeling "the difficulties of keeping alive a high civilization without a sustaining belief," to which there is but one response. What high civilization? In contemporary America? We are all too far from Europe now to preserve that sense of continuity intact. Or let us rather say we are unable to shut out the rest of it. The madness, the lies, the unimaginable daily assaults upon reason and sensibility that every day's newspapers bring us. For most of the last thirty years American literary intellectuals, like the secularized Jews I have spoken of, have been attempting to preserve the empty *forms* of a cultural tradition that has been progressively emptied of *content*. It is no wonder that our visions of coherence tend to be, when they are not strained and artificial, as "vulgar," to use the word Howe applied to the book, as Alexander Portnoy's.

Beyond that there is very little more to report. Things never became that clear for me in Amherst, and my wife's and my own desire for coherence of the old-fashioned kind led us to wish, rather wistfully, that it could be had in the South, so we picked up and moved to Little Rock, where she had been raised as a part of a tiny Catholic minority. What Arkansas offered, I now see, was the 1950's all over again, this time 1,500 miles from home, where I could shed this truculence and discomfort of mine and get on with the business of affirmation. I could be the Camel Filter Man I aspired to be at Chatham High (tieless but disdainful of extremes), making my way *ambiguously* up the middle class ladder without seeming to want to — and where the possibilities of genuine social change were so remote that one could have one's moral superiority and live well too

The Artificial Jewboy

with a liberalism so tepid that it would qualify for the Ripon Society anywhere else. Arkansas is in a time-warp of ten to fifteen years proportion, and is now in the midst of a regional version of Camelot, with Senator Dale Bumpers and a new Governor named David Pryor sharing the title roles. But we fucked up, my wife and I. The farce is so transparent here, the swindles and brutalities so barefaced and callow, and the people who run things so generally incompetent or unwilling to cover up the mess they are making that I have been forced to be a different kind of Jewboy, whether artificial or real only a handful of people here know the difference — we are all Easterners to them.

So it is that I have finally begun to sort out the things that most bewildered me in that Rutgers dorm 14 years ago. Literature was a hell of a way to try to assimilate anyway and I ought to have known better. Zarin and Cantor themselves, I am sure, might have used the ideas for the protection and advantage they offered, but even if they believed them they wouldn't have expected the world to concur. Not for very long, that is. Like them I am all sharp edges and suspicion now, restless, cynical, convinced that it is my duty to be a permanent member of the semi-disloyal opposition, touchy for signs of betrayal among my friends, and with the suspicion that one has to be an abrasive *schmuck* if one is to maintain one's integrity, and grown almost self-satisfied (and yes self-hating) so that I probably appear to be a moody contentious egomaniac to most of the people I know. Whether sanely or madly I continue to believe that Jewboys artificial and real are the sand in the lubricated imagination of contemporary America and that which keeps it from dreaming visions of a simpler world than ever was or will be and trying to make it so with guns. So people like Irving Howe are correct in thinking that persons of my persuasion do not any longer believe in literature the way they do, but they are wrong in making us out to be cartoon figures and hypocrites, just as I was uncharitable about those people in Amherst, and fools to think they can keep running that same old number. If they think we are going to let the idea of literacy die out, they have not been paying attention. For the larger cultural despair that underlies my obvious confusion, though, I have, like the proverbial Jew, no answers, only questions.

As for the next generation, I hope when I come to it I will be modest in my sense of what my experience has to offer them. Something definite ended back in there somewhere, probably when my family moved to the suburbs, although it has taken me over twenty years to figure it out. The very fact that ethnic and regional identity is now permissible in mass culture is the surest sign that it has become almost totally devoid of substance. For in spite of the fact that I am able to extemporize and abstract the question as no one else in my family ever has — no, *because* I am able to do that, having been like so many others of my generation the first in its history to obtain a college education — a link with the past has been irretrievably snapped. I am not to the past of my people as my father is. I am not even of my people in any real sense. If one of my own sons happens to read this essay fifteen years from now, it will be as if written by a stranger. My oldest son, Gavin, who is five, speaks with a pronounced Southern accent which he will probably lose when he gets a bit older and realizes the associations it has. He refers to "All in the Family," which he has seen a few times, as "The Man Like Grandpa Show," based upon his perception that even a caricature like Archie Bunker has a certain basis in reality.

What stories of the clan I will tell them I have no idea. Maneuvering the Dean into a bureaucratic sandwich where he was forced to allow my tenure recommendation to pass has not the drama of playing fullback with a dislocated shoulder. Writing is not fighting. Not in any way I can communicate to children, anyway. So what images my boys will use to form themselves I have not yet at hand. They will have to reject something. But bookish old me? The farther I live from it, the more I am conscious of the dominant shaping of an historic past, those places and that unknown heritage that lies inarticulate beneath my father's anger and his sadness and my mother's mute dread. But like ex-Jewboy Portnoy I cannot help being what I am not, and if one has difficulty pretending, it is not always easy.

In the meantime I must report that I have a renewed interest in *shicksa* pussy. Not long ago I had in my office a young thing called, of all the alliterative banalities in the world, Wendy Wilson, one of those absolutely flawless Cybill Shepherd — Thereal McCoy types that teases your hope that there is somewhere in this world a life as simple and blissfully lovely as they are. The kind of girl who, when I was at Chatham High, could make me feel like a clot of dried mud by saying that she had plans to wash her hair for the next eleven Friday evenings, but how sweet you were to ask. Palms sweating, I am explaining dangling modifiers or somesuch, while my dangling immodifier is counseling lust, wanting to rest my hand on hers and tell her that all she need do is smile and forget the sick broodings of Conrad, Dostoyevsky, and Lyons and the world will be hers. But she has, I imagine, enough trouble getting people to take her seriously, looking as she does, and I am a good husband and father like all Jewboys, so I keep it to myself. Halfway through the discussion I notice her hands shaking and I begin to get the point. She is scared to death of me, but I suspect she is also intrigued. The metamorphosis is complete. ✡

ON BECOMING JEWISH

ANDREW POTOK AND ANITA LANDA

Andrew Potok's most recent book, My Life with Goya, *was published by Arbor House Publishing Co. in 1986.*

Anita Landa teaches Human Development at Goddard College, Plainfield, Vermont.

Last February, we decided to go back to Poland where we were born. We both live in Vermont now. One of us is a writer and the other teaches human development at a small college. We live with our own families on opposite sides of the Winooski River, and when either of us walks along our lovely back roads, we invariably come to one of Vermont's beautiful old cemeteries. For years, we have read the names of our neighbors—the Batchelders, Holts and Bartletts—on the granite tombstones and, as we grow older, our desire to know our own family has increased. We would like to place flowers now and then by the graves of our grandparents, but even to us, their names—Theophilia, Leon, Paulina, Solomon—have become foreign.

Though we've been in America forty years and speak English without accents, we're still outsiders to our Vermont neighbors. Perhaps they don't know we were born in Warsaw or that we're Jews, but they do know we read the New York *Times* on Sunday and that our children, who once boarded the yellow school bus daily along with their neighbors, are now away at private schools and colleges. By Vermonters, we are easily identified as foreigners, but it's harder for us to identify ourselves. We're Polish Jews who have become Americans, but all those words carry an abstract quality, like having type B positive blood. They're facts, they may some day be important, but they exist below the surface of everyday life. We don't belong to a synagogue, we're not Zionists. We're aware, as I.F. Stone has pointed out, that the fate of Jews everywhere is tied to Israeli politics, but Israel is as much a foreign country to us as China. We've visited both countries as informed and interested guests rather than as seekers after ethnic roots.

We both seem to have missed the traditional adolescent identity crisis. Without much trouble, we built self-images which rested on our personal interests and attainments. We attended good schools and did well. We make modest but respectable contributions to our professional fields. We've been politically active since the presidential election of 1948, when we campaigned for Henry Wallace, and if our left-wing activities haven't produced the desired effect of significant social change, they've earned us the usual honors of tapped phones and bulging FBI files. We can identify ourselves as radical intellectuals, but it now seems important for us to seek a broader identity. As our children leave home, as we begin to count up time left, we have each come to want some larger sense of belonging. It seems clear that what stands between us and the sense of a group identity is the war, the bombs and death camps, a wall of fire which separates us from our childhood and our heritage. It occurs to us that now, forty years after our escape from Poland, we can perhaps reach back beyond the Holocaust.

Why haven't we gone back sooner? Partly, we'd come to feel that the past was taboo, something you were supposed to forget. Growing up, as we came home for vacations from boarding schools in Connecticut and Massachusetts, we asked for facts about our early childhood, for news of family left behind, for details of our history in Poland which we knew went back several hundred years. But having escaped the war, the pogroms and gas chambers, our parents and their friends were determined not to remember. Not going back to Poland was part of their strategy for forgetting. When our father was alive, he traveled to Western Europe and to Russia, but he avoided Poland as though it were plague-ridden. Our mother, Anna, lives in New York City, and, at eighty-two, she walks daily to work at Maximilian Furs, the family business, reestablished when we arrived in the States in 1940. Small, elegant, firm-featured, she's a courageous woman. Neither hard work nor death frighten her, but she hasn't dared go back, either.

When we travel down to the city to tell her we want to go to Poland and ask her to come with us, she is shocked. "It's a graveyard," she tells us. "What will you find there? Anti-Semitism? Death? You don't need it."

But we do. Whatever we're going to find there, we need it. We need to know who we are, to understand what we sprang from and what displaced us.

"We'll start in Wieliszew. We'll spend time in Warsaw. We'll follow our escape route through Lublin, Wilno, Riga . . ."

"Boring places," Anna assures us. "Ugly." She sweeps her hand across the table. "If you need a vacation, go to Switzerland. It's beautiful and the air is good."

In 1938 our family had built a summer home in Wieliszew so we could all breathe good air in a beautiful place, just 40 kilometers from Warsaw. In September 1939, the war found us there. And Wieliszew is the first place we visit on our return to Poland.

The Polish friend who accompanies us stops at farmsteads asking for people who might remember where our house was. "Where did the furriers from Warsaw live?" he asks over and over. Finally, an old woman holding a scythe points the way. "You mean the Jews," she says. "Over there. That's the only place where Jews lived."

It's a shock to be identified as Jews. We'd come to consider ourselves voluntary Jews, acknowledging Jewishness as we might acknowledge socialism or feminism. But the old lady in her farm apron has left us no choice. For Polish Jews, there never was a choice, long before the Germans came. "We were progressive and cultured, we had so much to offer them," Anna told us once, "but they turned their backs on us."

Our family had been assimilated for generations. They had gone to Polish schools, had spoken Polish, not Yiddish, in their houses. Our uncles had been lawyers, doctors, engineers; Polish musicians and writers were our parents' friends and Polish aristocrats their customers. But to the Poles, they were only Jews. And here we stand in our walking shoes from L. L. Bean's, canvas tote bags slung over our shoulders, struggling unsuccessfully to accept our involuntary Jewishness.

Following the directions we've been given, we drive through a scrubby pine forest, planted years after the remains of our forest were cleared away. And here, where the road opens onto a sloping field—which might be the field where we flew kites and learned to ride bikes—is the foundation of what was probably our house. It is half buried under fallen earth and obscured by burnt branches. Nothing here suggests the pleasures of our last peacetime summer, the horror of the first morning of war.

The early morning of September first was clear and wet from an all-night storm, and we'd gone out to ride our bikes on the slippery grass. The hum of planes mixed with the receding thunder. Then we saw them flying over the tree tops, so low that we could make out the pilots' faces. Polish insignia shone on the silver wings and we jumped with excitement. But they were German planes. Moments later, the air whistled and exploding bombs shook the ground. We ran screaming into the woods.

That day, the gardener dug a shelter, covering it with pine boughs. When the planes returned, we crouched there, our parents trying to quiet us with words and caresses and, finally, with drops of valerian. Between raids, they huddled around the radio, waiting for declarations of war from England and France. When at the end of the second day, no help came, they decided to return to Warsaw.

Whatever we had known of ease and security ended that day. The summer house had been ample and orderly, preserves gleaming purple and crimson on sway-bottomed shelves in the pantry. Through rows of wide French doors we could look past the stone terrace to the little fountain splashing in the garden. Each of us has tried to recreate that amplitude and security in our adult lives. We've put in asparagus beds and planted fruit trees around our commodious Vermont houses, but in our hearts we know nothing is permanent.

Back in Warsaw now, we realize how badly we had wanted the summer house to be there. We had hoped to meet ourselves as children, to erase forty years of history, to pick up our lives where they'd been broken off. Like ghosts, we wander through Warsaw's lovely parks, looking for the past. Lazienki, where we used to play as children, surprises us by its strangeness. Its shadows are darker, its spaces divided into smaller parcels than we had remembered. But in the Saski gardens, we come upon children sailing their boats, as we used to, on the familiar willow pond. For a moment we watch them as one might watch a home movie of one's childhood. Soon our governess will come into the picture and warn us to keep our toes out of the pool, the narrow leaves will fall from the willow branches and cover the pond's surface like little fish and we'll grow up like anyone else. Then a breezy young woman in spike-heeled sandals whisks the children away, and we sit on the bench like middle-aged child-watchers the world over, smiling foolishly at the empty water's edge.

Nowhere else in Warsaw are we able to catch that magical glimpse of urban landscape, the one which connects to a fragment of memory and unlocks the secrets of the past. During the second battle of Warsaw in 1944, the Germans dynamited the city, building by building. At war's end, there was nothing left but rubble. Rubble is the first new word we learn on arriving. "There weren't any buildings," we're told, "you couldn't arrange to meet a friend at the corner of Marszalkowska and Moniuszki because there weren't any streets. There was just a sea of rubble."

Our apartment house, Moniuszki number 4, no longer exists. Nor does the building on Marszalkowska where the family business was housed. Standing on the reconstructed corner of these streets, we remember having crossed them, holding our governess's hands, to be shown to our parents' favorite customers who sat in Louis XV fitting rooms surrounded by mink and sable. At home in the States, Anna has kept our student sketchbooks which are filled with floor plans of our apartment and drawings of the lovely, quiet neighborhood with its gray Mansarded houses, shrubs and flowers growing on balconies along arched and shuttered facades. These pictures are closer by far to our prewar lives than the wide modern streets, the already shabby post-war buildings, the hectic traffic of contemporary Warsaw.

Still, as we learn to ride the busses, cancelling our tickets in the little punch boxes along with the other citizens, we begin to feel at home. Polish is spoken all around us, and we happily find ourselves becoming fluent in our native language. We are meeting people—journalists, university professors, an engineer, a translator, some old family friends who tell stories about our parents and grandparents predating our own births. Like ourselves, everyone we speak to—Poles and Jews alike—has lost family and property. When we ask a taxi driver to point out Aleja Szucha, where we sometimes came on Sundays to eat dinner with our Aunt Eva, he tells us that is where Gestapo headquarters had been. He'd lost his father there. "Blood ran in the street," he tells us, "no one came back alive." Everywhere on the reconstructed buildings we find plaques commemorating the war dead: forty were shot down here, there a hundred. No one has been spared, and no one has forgotten. We are finally surrounded by a nation of our own kind: survivors of the war who welcome us among their ranks. Gratefully, we accept the comradeship.

We come to feel we could have lived here. We imagine ourselves students at the University of Warsaw, drinking beer with comrades in the student cafes on Nowy Swiat instead of at Morey's or the White Horse or the Dôme, which were in fact our youthful haunts. We imagine ourselves participating in the Poznan uprising of 1956, serving on the editorial board of the underground newspaper which is currently circulated in Warsaw by dissidents. Like everyone else, we learn to stand on the endless queues at food stores, banks and railroad stations with the proper mixture of irritation and resignation. But, in fact, we are not like everyone else. As the woman with the scythe in Wieliszew was quick to remind us, we are Jews. We spin out our fantasies about living in Warsaw to each other, and each arrives at the same dead end, the wall of the Ghetto, the gates of the death camps. We are statistical anomalies. Of three and a half million Jews, after German extermination, Polish pogroms and forced emigration, there are six thousand left in Poland. For the Poles, the Jewish question is long settled. For us, it is just beginning.

Like ferrets, we begin hunting down our Jewish heritage. We spend a morning with the lively, intelligent editor of *Folk-Sztyme*, the Yiddish paper which, like us, is an anachronism. In this city, a third of whose population was once Jewish, *Folk-Sztyme* claims two thousand subscribers. Patiently, the editor explains the post-war emigrations, precipitated by the government's identification of Jews first with Stalinism, then with Zionism. He continues putting out the paper to serve the few Jews who remain, and assures us he intends to serve the remnant even if there are only ten left. We're moved by his dedication, but we understand, with an anguish which is difficult to express, that in fact a day will come when there are no more Jews in Poland at all.

At the poverty-stricken Institute of Jewish History, where we are the only visitors, we come to realize that the Jewish heritage is faring no better than the few remaining Jews. Scholars cannot be found to translate and catalog the documents in the archives; funds are lacking to acquire books for the library; membership is down to ninety. At the Institute, we can read the sepia-inked cards tacked next to the familiar photographs of the destruction of the Jews of Poland. To rubble, we add the words for martyrdom and despair. One set of photographs has particular meaning for us—portraits of the Jewish Resistance Fighters, the young people who took up arms against their murderers. "We do not fight for our lives," one of them wrote, "none of us will survive. We fight for human dignity." We add dignity to our vocabulary.

But it is hard for us to relate to the extinct people whose once diverse culture, rich in scholarship and spiritual longing, is so tenuously preserved here. We had never even seen the Warsaw Ghetto; no one we ever knew owned a prayer shawl or studied the Torah. If we knew how to say Kaddish, we might recite it as we leave the Institute, but neither of us can pray in Hebrew.

Finally, we go to the Jewish cemetery. It is huge and unkempt. The Holts and Batchelders would be ashamed of it. The only living person here is an old women who serves as our Virgil. She knows everyone and tells us their stories. She comes every day to tend the graves of her own family: they died in the Ghetto, in Treblinka, on the streets of Warsaw, pried out of hiding by informers. As we follow her along narrow paths through acres of undergrowth, we understand that this is the only Jewish community left in Poland.

Preparing to leave Warsaw, we realize that nothing has come clear for us. As in Vermont, we're still neither Jews nor Poles, the strands of our heritage won't knit together. We've been excited and saddened by Warsaw, but most of all, we experience a sense of loss. It's hard to define what we've lost—the million dead who lay under the rubble? The murdered Jews we can't relate to? The illusion that visiting our birthplace would illuminate our lives? The feeling of loss is strong for both of us, but there's some compensation for it: we've come closer to one another than we've been since childhood. It's a long time since we've experienced the same feelings and been able to share them so directly. Whatever we've lost, we've gained an old sense of intimacy, much like the closeness we felt when we were leaving Warsaw the first time.

When we left Warsaw in 1939, the city was in flames. We had come back from Wieliszew at night to find the dimly lit streets clogged with milling people and the church opposite our apartment house collapsed in its own cobbled courtyard. Our spacious apartment was filled with relatives from Bedzin, Krakow and Lwow. All through the night, while we stuffed underwear and favorite toys into our suitcases, these relatives sat around the huge dining table with our parents, smoking, shouting, drinking tea from glasses, trying to decide who would stay, who would go, and where.

We left Warsaw early in the morning, before the day's bombings started. Of those who had sat up through the night, only our immediate family had decided to go. Our suitcases and a few valuables were packed into the Citroen van which belonged to the family business, and Aunt Eva, dressed in black, stooped on the sidewalk to kiss each of us goodbye, her tears hot on our faces. Then we joined the slow-moving caravan of wagons, cars and trucks heading southeast towards Lublin. We hoped to find a convoy which was rumored to be bound for Rumania, but by the time we reached Lublin, the roads south had been destroyed and the Russian army stood poised to occupy Lublin itself.

We turned north, groping our way along a narrow unoccupied corridor, the Germans pushing from the west, the Russians from the east. We traded a sapphire ring for bread, a mink coat for a tank of gasoline. All along the way, the endless procession of refugees was bombed and strafed. When each raid ended, those left alive got out of roadside ditches, pushed disabled vehicles out of the way, and continued. The first time, our parents tried to hide the dead from us by covering our eyes, but we were curious and, after a time, indifferent.

Low flying aircraft still alarm us; we have to stifle the impulse to hide. But, like most survivors of disaster, we're careless of personal safety, we have a sense of living charmed lives. Only our nightmares remain ominous. The details of our dreams are personal to each of us, but the themes are the same: we are being pursued by deadly enemies, we are guilty of an unnamed crime, the landscape is devastated, there is no place to find shelter.

Driving through Poland now, we take several detours before beginning to retrace our escape route. We go to Bedzin in Silesia where the Potok side of the family lived for generations. There, we find the remains of the vegetable oil refinery which our great-grandfather built in the 1860s. Only the new section, added by grandfather Solomon in 1914, still stands intact. As we circle it in hopes of finding evidence of family ownership, an old man in T-shirt and suspenders approaches us. We ask if he knew our family.

"Knew them? I played with all of Solomon's sons, my father sold them milk. I will show you everything."

We walk up a dreary street in an industrial suburb, and the old man points: "This is where the railroad came with the coconuts, the corn and peanuts. And here the wagon with sunflower seeds. Over there was the waterfall that powered our generator, and over here a restaurant. Twenty-five buildings, for canning and bottling, pressing and refining. Here a machine shop and a blacksmith . . . we had everything."

"And where did they live?"

"Right there, in that house."

The large stucco building, painted two shades of pink, is now the regional planning commission. Our guide fetches the caretaker, and the four of us go in. Again, we are told what used to be: the curving staircase has been removed, the balcony cut off, these partitions added. "But here," says the caretaker, opening the door into a room which to us looks like all the others, "you can still see how it used to be." She draws our attention to the floor. It is as intricately inlaid as the parquet in the throne room of the Hermitage; eight varieties of wood were used in each square, some of the carefully fitted pieces no wider than a birch twig.

"This is where Solomon received people," the man in suspenders tells us. "If your cow died, you could come to him and he'd buy you a new one. They were rich and generous. They were good little yids. Everyone on the street will tell you—good little yids."

He uses the word *zydki*, which we've never heard before, but we know its meaning as if we'd been born knowing it. We look closely at his face: it is suffused with nostalgia and good will, there is not a trace of malice. And our own feelings? Something less definite than indignation or outrage, something more dangerous than shame: the beginning of acknowledgment. We accept the epithet as belonging to us.

Before leaving Bedzin, we ask if anyone knows what became of the family, how they died. Our guide doesn't know about the others, but Solomon was shot down in the street by the Gestapo. He had been hidden in the cellar for a while, but he wouldn't remain there. He'd refused to give up his right to fresh air. Solomon was generous and proud, and we are proud to have gained knowledge of his life and his end.

A few miles from Bedzin, in the ancient Jewish cemetery of Krakow, amid great spreading trees and tangles of wild ferns, we discover more family history. We find graves of Solomon's wife's family, the tombstones predating by centuries those of our Vermont neighbors. It's raining when we read these tombstones, engraved in Polish and Hebrew. The caretaker has lent us an umbrella, but we're too excited to shelter under it, and the rain splashes over our happy faces. We've finally reached back beyond the war to those who died of natural causes. This is what we've come for, this simple assurance that in our family history there are those who died in their beds surrounded by grieving children, that their graves can be visited four or five centuries later.

It's the only satisfaction we're to have for some time. As we drive through the heart of Poland, following our escape route towards Wilno, Latvia and Sweden, death camps lie on every side. The Germans administered 5877 prisons and camps on Polish soil and even though only a few are preserved as memorials, it is not easy to avoid them. In fact, after long debate, we've agreed not to avoid them. After all, we assure each other, what surprises can these places with their awesome names—Auschwitz, Majdanek, Treblinka—still hold for us?

These:

At Auschwitz, the blown-up i.d. photos of thousands of murdered inmates which line the walls of the dormitories remind us of our father, of Aunt Eva, of the kids we played with in the Saski Gardens, of ourselves. We look at the shaven heads, the terrified eyes, the occasional grotesque attempt at a smile, and we see family portraits.

At Majdanek, as at Auschwitz, the weird beauty of the instruments of death astounds us. The iron locks on the massive metal doors of the gas chambers still fit perfectly, though a million hands have scratched and pulled at them. The ovens are expertly crafted, their custom-made angle irons neatly tying the fire brick in place, the masonry skillfully laid. Tracks are sunk into the concrete floor in front of the oven doors, and the wheels of the metal carts which brought bodies from the gas chambers thirty-five years ago still run smoothly on them.

On our way from Majdanek to Treblinka, we start an argument which lasts several hours. It's about the nature of art, and we haven't had such a fight since college. We argue about abstraction, accessibility, the legitimacy of various art forms. We yell, wanting to hurt somebody, we hurl quotes from Conrad and Heidegger. It's a wonderful fight, it takes us away from Poland, ourselves, death; its form and content are familiar and comforting.

On the high crest of this discourse, having almost missed it in its woodsy seclusion, we stumble onto Treblinka. We remember our father, driving desperately along a rutted track somewhere in these woods, squinting through the bullet-shattered windshield of the Citroen, his thick spectacles askew on his face. "We're in the frying pan," he'd said bitterly. "No food, no gas, and now I can't see a goddamn thing."

He'd driven like this all the way to Kaunas, in the same light summer suit, his fine-woven straw hat crammed on the back of his head. Accustomed as he was to a luxurious life, he had dealt on that trip with deprivation, hardship, countless near disasters. He had made one correct decision after another, and gotten us out of Europe. If not for his energy and determination, we might well have ended our lives here, at Treblinka.

The camp no longer exists. There is nothing here but stones and granite slabs set into several vast meadows. The stones, put here in memoriam to the lives of 800,000 Jews, stretch to the horizon. We stand among the endless markers, we hold one another and, for the first time in forty years, we cry.

The next day, we continue to Wilno. When we reached it in 1939, Wilno was a Polish city. It is now called Vilnius, capital of the Lithuanian Soviet Socialist Republic. Soviet regulations forbid us to drive there, and we cross the border by train. In 1939, we were among thousands of cars trying to cross, inching forward, desperate to make it through before the border closed. We remember the masses of retreating Polish soldiers, rainsoaked, their weapons abandoned. Anna has often repeated a snatch of conversation she heard that night: "We may have lost Poland," one soldier said to another, "but at least we'll be rid of our Jews."

At 2 A.M. we're awakened in our train by a Soviet customs inspector and a large officer in a beige uniform. They take our passports and visas and begin to search our luggage. Ignoring the gifts we've bought for our families, the customs inspector pulls out all the printed materials we carry. "What," he asks, "are these?" displaying in turn our copy of *Folk-Sztyme*, the literature we picked up at the Institute of Jewish History, several books and pamphlets from Auschwitz, a Jewish history book in Hebrew which we're bringing to friends in the Soviet Union. "Jews," the customs inspector tells his colleague, "yids." The words are close enough to Polish so there's no mistaking them. Our U. S. passports aren't marked with Stars of David, but they are taken away with the books and papers which confirm our crime: we are Jews, enemies of the state.

The train stands endlessly in the station. In our dim compartment we try to open a window, but it's sealed shut, as are the hall windows and the lavatory door. Border guards patrol the platform outside.

We urge each other not to panic. "What can happen to us? We haven't done anything." But neither had those other Jews done anything, the ones whose pictures we saw at Auschwitz and among whose stones we walked at Treblinka. We're Americans, we assure ourselves. But in fact, we've never felt less American in our lives. We are Jews, and as Jews we feel imperiled. Gently, we try to keep each other from overdramatizing, but in our hearts we feel Anna was right. We don't need this. We shouldn't have come.

The sun rises, and we peer out into the countryside we'd driven through in our battered van forty years before. The wheat has been harvested and stands in the fields in small conical stacks, like witches' hats. Then, without warning, the train lurches forward. Our compartment door slides open and our documents and books are thrown in to us.

We're tired and ashamed. We feel

On Becoming Jewish

cowardly. In our fantasies, we were Resistance fighters, like those brave men and women whose pathetic dispatch cases and frail guns we'd seen with so much pride in the museum in Warsaw. We'd always assumed that the Germans couldn't have taken us away without a struggle. We would have fought tooth and nail. Now we're not so sure.

We come home from Europe through New York and stop at Anna's for the weekend. She's enormously relieved to see us; she wants to know everything. She feeds us smoked salmon and cold chicken and plies us with questions. We interrupt each other answering: the house at Wieliszew was destroyed; Warsaw is rebuilt and looks different; we went to the factory in Bedzin; we found graves in Krakow.

"And what did you learn?" she asks finally, as she used to ask when we came home from school.

"We learned about being Jewish."

"You needed to go all the way to Poland to learn about being Jewish?" She is genuinely astounded.

We are surprised, too, We did not expect to be drawn to the hearts of ancestors we never knew. We were claimed as kinsfolk by the dead and the living. And we acknowledged the claim. Gladly. ✡

Part II

The American Jewish Experience: Threads and Themes

ANTI-SEMITISM, MALIGNANT OBSESSION

HAROLD SCHULWEIS

Harold Schulweis is the founding Chairman of the Foundation to Sustain Righteous Christians, Rabbi of Valley Beth Shalom in Encino, CA, author of Evil and the Morality of God, *and a contributing editor of* Moment.

Anti-Semitism informs our lives. In its multiple forms—verbal, economic, social, political, racial—it clings to our being. It is the dominant psychic reality for most Jews, transcending religious and secular differences as nothing else does. If "we are one," it is not in the commonality of our beliefs or religious practices or language or mastery of texts, but in the sharing of our common traumas. And so, when all else fails, the specter of anti-Semitism provides the ultimate rationale for Jewish identity, fidelity and philanthropy. Nothing can mobilize Jews quicker than an anti-Semitic graffito smeared on the synagogue walls or a hurled "hymie" epithet.

Fear of anti-Semitism is a powerful emotion. Abba bar Kahanna, a third century Palestinian rabbi, observed that the bestowal of Ahasuerus's ring, conferring power upon Haman, did more to effect the piety of the Jews in Shushan than did all the chastisements and pleas of the 56 Jewish prophets and prophetesses (*Megillah* 14a). In an age of inattention, fear of anti-Semitism shakes Jews by the shoulders: "Pay attention, we are an endangered species." When their co-religionists grow complacent, some Jews even covet crises to rouse the apathetic from their somnolence. After all, they think, "It is the pogroms that have kept us alive."

Fear works—but it exacts a fearsome price. The phobia of anti-Semitism has ravaged our inner lives. It affects our morale, our morality and our statesmanship. Anti-Semitism has become our dybbuk, shaping our character, forming our judgment, planning our future. Anti-Semitism must be attended to. But we have to pay attention to what anti-Semitism is doing to our inner life and to our children's. What does anti-Semitism as the prime motivator for Jewish identity, education and charity do to our understanding of our Jewish selves and of the character of Judaism?

Anti-Semitism is not treated as a matter of historical record; it has become the centerpiece of Jewish metaphysics. Anti-Semitism explains Jewish history; history cannot explain anti-Semitism. Anti-Semitism has been raised to a mystique attached to the essence of Judaism. The metaphysics of anti-Semitism spawns a profoundly dualistic outlook. History is perceived as hopelessly divided: on the one side, Sinai; on the other, *Sinah* (hatred). The human genus is split into two primordial and eternally antagonistic species: the seed of Jacob, the perennial pariah, and the seed of Esau, the perennial persecutor. This primitive antagonism is seen not as an accident of history; it becomes the very essence of Jewish destiny. Anti-Semitism does not refer to Pharaoh, Antiochus, Haman, Torquemada, Hitler, Stalin, Khomeini alone. It spells a curse co-extensive with Judaism and the Jewish people. "In *each* and *every* generation they rise to destroy us." There are no exceptions. Until the coming of the Messiah, to be a Jew is to suffer the fate of the victim. The hateful imprecation of John of Chrysostom, "You are hated," has been internalized and accepted. We are hated. The whole world seeks our destruction, not once but always. The anti-Semitic circle of repetition envelops our lives: What was, will be; what will be, already was. We are forever "children of the martyr'd race."

The metaphysics of anti-Semitism gives forth a spiritual biologism. There is something inherited in our chosenness and in our rejection that is larger than our putative choices. There is something in the spiritual genes and chromosomes of individuals and peoples that no naturalistic account can explain. Shneur Zalman, the revered founder of the Chabad Chassidic sect and the author of the *Tanya*, explains the basic grounds for the rupture between Jews and non-Jews. In the opening chapters of the *Tanya*, he cites Genesis 2:7, "And He breathed into his nostrils the breath of life," not as referring to the birth of the soul of Adam, the generic human being, but exclusively to the Jewish soul. The souls of Jews, even those that originate from evil "husks," contain the good characteristics found in the innate nature of all Israel. "The souls of the nations of the world, however, emanate from the other, unclean *klipot* (husks), which contain no good whatever . . . for all the good that nations do is done for selfish motives."

In a similar vein, Michael Wyschogrod, a graduate of Yeshiva University and a professor of philosophy, in his new book *The Body of Faith*, describes the Jews as "a biological people who remains elect even when it sins." The Jews are God's favorites "irrespective of what [they] believe or what virtue they have." God's loving choice is not equally distributed and it is no surprise that those not elected might be hurt that they are not "the seed of Abraham whom God loves above all others." They and we have to accept the scandal of Israel's "carnal election" transmitted through the body, not through character or purely spiritual criteria. Much as the Israeli Jewish thinker Yeshayahu Leibowitz considers morality "an atheist category," Wyschogrod argues that ethics is the "Judaism of the assimilated." Such biological chosenness is a far cry from the chosenness of a moral noblesse oblige, the burdensome privilege tied to moral causes, Israel as a "light to the nations." All that is necessary to accept is that Israel is God's favorite. Period.

This kind of spiritual biologistic thinking attached to a metaphysics of anti-Semitism gives rise to a validation of chauvinistic morality. Its antecedents lie in the writings of Yehuda Halevi and the Maharal of Prague, among others. That genre of dualistic metaphysics emerges anew in the current debate over "Who is thy neighbor?" which inevitably touches the heated controversy of "Who is a Jew?" In the debate, the celebrated biblical verse "Love thy neighbor as thyself" (Leviticus 19:18) is interpreted by a number of Jewish intellectuals in a highly restrictive sense (*Modern Jewish Ethics*, edited by Marvin Fox). "Thy neighbor" means *b'nai amecha*, "thy people's children," i.e., Jews. Such an exclusivist interpretation is supported by the Rashbam, Maimonides and Moses of Coucy. If, wherever "neighbor" is used, only Jewish neighbors are meant, then Jews would, for example, have no legal obligation to return lost articles of gentiles, or to violate the Sabbath to save non-Jewish lives or to be subject to the proscription not to stand idly by the blood of thy neighbor. Rabbinic authorities such as the 12th-century Rashbam (Rabbi Samuel ben Meir) further qualified "Love thy neighbor" to mean, "If he is truly your neighbor," i.e., if he is good. But if he is wicked, then fulfill the verse (Proverbs 8:13), "The fear of the Lord is to hate evil." Maimonides restricts love of neighbor to Jews who observe the commandments and devote themselves to the study of Torah. The circle of neighbors is narrowed to those who believe and act as I do. Professor Harold Fisch of the Hebrew University in Jerusalem argues, without any intended humor, that it is burdensome enough to love thy Jewish neighbor. To include non-Jews as neighbors to be loved "is to expect the impossible."

The belief in the universality and omnipresence of anti-Semitism has filtered down into popular sensibility. An Israeli song, made popular after the 1967 war, lyricizes: "The whole world is against us. This is the ancient tale told by our forefathers. Well, if the whole world is against us, we don't give a damn. If the whole world is against us, to hell with the world." The metaphysics of anti-Semitism is transformed into folk dogma. The character of Judaism turns increasingly insular, isolationist and suspect of "the world."

All this has Jewish conscience against it. "To hell with the world" is a blasphemy mocking the essential Jewish mandate to mend the shattered world. It betrays the basic liturgical formula that blesses God, not as Lord of the heavens but as "Lord of the Universe." This universe which He Himself formed and made, He "created not in vain, but formed to be inhabited" (Isaiah 45:18).

When a tortured Rabbi Ishmael screamed his pain heavenwards, a heavenly echo cried out: "Ishmael, one more cry from you and I will turn this world to ash and water." Ishmael bit his tongue and silenced the voice of his pain. He would not cry, "To hell with the world." To retreat within so as to abandon the world without is to mock our own protestations against the calloused who sang hymns and Gregorian chants that drowned out the screams of the tortured; against those who protected the domain of their own ecclesiology by shutting up their windows, doors and mouths. For Jews to imitate the corporate selfishness of church and state is surely to learn the wrong lesson from the Holocaust.

Behind the resolute slogan "never again" lies the contradictory presupposition "ever again." Anti-Semitism is endowed with an awesome immortality. But if fear is used to motivate Jewish loyalty and constancy, the result is a demoralized and demoralizing pedagogy. Our children will not be scared into life or tied to us by threats. To cast Jews into the hated leprous circle is more likely to produce either a paralysis of the will to live or a desperate desire to escape. Catastrophic thinking robs us and our children of basic trust, that vitality requisite for activistic statesmanship. To bathe our children in the tears of *leidensgeschichte,* stories of suffering, and then dry them off with the cry of Nachman of Bratslav's *"Yidden, zeit zich nisht miyaesh"* (Jews, don't despair!) is tragi-comic. Why, if the whole world hated, hates and will hate us, should we not despair?

Today, we need to be concerned with Jewish morale with the same wisdom with which our sages confronted the destruction of the Temple. They knew how to struggle against a people's despair. Our liturgists cautioned the people to remember the light in the darkness; our Massoretes arranged the synagogue readings of the Torah so that they did not conclude in despair; our Talmud sages fought against the melancholy that leads to cynicism and resignation. They rejected Balaam's blessing-curse, "This is a solitary people, not reckoned among the nations of the world." Against this alleged benediction, they imagined the prophet Amos rising to protest, "Cease, I beseech you. How should Jacob live alone?" And the Lord repented and declared, "This shall not be" (*Makkot* 24a). We and our children are not fated to be the hated victims of history. We must not allow the darkness and oppression of the past to eclipse the light and freedom of the present and the hope of the future.

But instead, a mind-set of basic distrust greets every act of goodness with indiscriminate suspicion, as if fortune for Jews is a Trojan horse carrying disaster within. A fixated negativism is allowed to embitter Jewish joy and turn our thanksgiving sour. It robs us of celebration and appreciation. Consider the recent magnificent airlift of thousands of Ethiopian Jews from Sudan, an operation planned, directed and engineered by the agencies of the United States government, by the State Department, the CIA, the American Embassy in Khartoum, Vice-President Bush and President Reagan. "Operation Moses" was master-minded by the United States—not a Christian country, but not a Jewish country either. Consider, as well, the U.S. trade agreement with Israel that eliminates all tariffs between the two countries, the first such U.S. arrangement with any nation. Consider the voting behavior of Americans who send Jewish senators to Washington from Pennsylvania, Michigan, Ohio, New Jersey—and from Nevada, New Hampshire, Minnesota and Nebraska.

These are phenomena of our times that must not be discounted. They ought to be raised up, but they are strangely repressed. The White House was not bombarded with congratulatory telegrams and letters in appreciation of this country's extraordinary intervention on behalf of Ethiopian Jews, an intervention that risked the ire of the Arab countries and that was pursued with competence and modesty. Is our inhibition to praise related to the reinforced perception that we are friendless and alone? What do we tell our children about the decencies in this pock-marked world? Are they taught about the decency of the House of Representatives in 1911 when it voted to abrogate the commercial treaty with Czarist Russia because of its inhumane treatment of Jews, or of the consistent posture of our presidents and Congress vis-à-vis Soviet Jewish refuseniks? Are our children taught about the moral behavior of the Bulgarian Orthodox Church and the Sobranie (Bulgarian parliament), which were responsible for resisting the Nazi order to deport Bulgarian Jews to the camps? Do our children know the names of the Italian Army's General Roatta and General Robatta who saved the lives of thousands of Croatian Jews from the murderous grip of the Nazis? Do Jewish schools teach about André Trocmé and the citizens of Le Chambon in Nazi-occupied France, responsible for the sheltering and protection of 5,000 Jews?

Teach our children of the terror and bestiality of the world—of course they must know these things—but do not allow the sparks to be buried. Instead, the spiritual biologism that condemns wholesale the souls of the nations of the world seems embarrassed that among the sparks are gentile souls. And so every virtue of non-Jews is rationalized away so as to deprive it of any authentic altruistic claim. But is it history or metaphysical obsession that determines such a negative perception? A wiser Jewish tradition that knew how massive evil often is knew as well to stress the singular power of the few, assigning disproportionate significance to the saving of one single life. A tradition that knew the overwhelming evil of Sodom and Gomorrah held on to the saving power of ten who could redeem whole cities from destruction. A tradition that knew the multitude of wickedness raised to high honor the few, the 36, without whom the heavens would fall.

We transmit more than events to our children. We transmit a moral Geiger counter, a way to register and give weight to deeds, a way to appreciate not only what is threatening but what is life-affirming in the world. How and what our selective principle of significance works affects the morale of our children, the hope and meaning in Jewish living. Whether they are raised to think that being Jewish is a hopeless malediction of the genes, or a sacred opportunity for new initiatives to lift the scattered sparks, affects their spirit.

It is one thing to remain vigilant against the real threat of anti-Semitism. It is another to be overwhelmed by an *idée fixe,* an imperative idea that sweeps away any evidence contrary to the invincible assumption that we are doomed to martyrdom. It is one thing to be alert to Jew-hatred and another to live fearful of good news and suspect of good people. Of course we should not live naively, with indiscriminate trust, but neither ought we view the world with the paranoia of basic distrust.

For the sake of Jewish morale and Jewish statesmanship the metaphysics of anti-Semitism that bifurcates the world, converting non-Jews into real or potential foes, must be overcome. To live with obsessive fear of the non-Jewish world is to be condemned to live a thousand deaths, to be paralyzed, unable to initiate new paths for change. The spell of fatalistic metaphysics and catastrophic thinking must be broken. We need to return to a Jewish theology of faith, hope and decision that respects the openness of the future and the possibilities of new beginnings. There are allies to be won among non-Jews. There are millions of real and potential friends among the nations of the world whose souls are not damned with irredeemable contamination, just as we ourselves are not immune to the illness that is callousness. There are sparks of divinity among them, as among us, that must be patiently and lovingly raised and praised and freed. There are signs and signals of good news and good people that must not be trivialized. Jewish motivation, morale and morality must be drawn from Jewish affirmation, Jewish love, joy and idealism. We owe our children more than withdrawal from the general society, more than an expectation of suffering, more than a victim heritage. We owe them a rationale for Jewish living, not out of spite or fear of the other, but out of respect for ourselves and basic trust in our capacity to change our imputed lot. For if we cannot change our lot, what does it mean to remember that we crossed the sea from slavery into freedom? ✸

ARE GOOD

WILLIAM NOVAK

Suzanne, a close friend of my wife, has just turned thirty. She's smart, funny, friendly, generous—and very attractive. Suzanne enjoys a fine career as a social worker, and heads a major department at a Jewish communal agency. Last year she was involved briefly with a lawyer who worked for consumer rights, but they decided to break it off when it was clear to both of them that the relationship was just not working out. This year Suzanne has no social life to speak of. "I'm not talking about meeting my prince," she jokes. "I can't even get a date with a guy I *wouldn't* go out with!"

Suzanne's complaint is hardly unique. Everywhere I look these days I see terrific young women who are, as it's called, "looking." Some of them are my friends, or friends of

---

William Novak is the author of several books, including The Great American Man Shortage and Other Roadblocks to Romance. *He is also the co-author of* The Big Book of Jewish Humor *and the memoirs of Lee Iacocca,* The Mayflower Madam, *and Former House Speaker Tip O'Neill.*

---

my wife, or *their* friends. Others I meet at parties, or in publishing houses, or in the bookstores I frequent, or the salad restaurant I go to for lunch. Sometimes I talk to these women and, perhaps because I'm married, and certainly because I'm inquisitive, they tell me things I didn't hear when I was single. Most of them, I find, describe variations on a single theme: There just don't seem to be many good, available men around with whom to have a relationship.

Of course not all single women are interested in meeting men, and not all single women find it difficult to do so. But many, many women are in this situation, and the man shortage is doing strange things to them. It undermines their self-confidence, affects their emotional stability, and, worst of all, it causes them to blame themselves for a situation that is mostly beyond their control.

"Is there something wrong with me?" many of these women wonder privately. "After all, if I really am attractive and appealing and intelligent, then why am I not meeting anybody? It doesn't make sense that all the good men are married or gay.

Maybe I'm doing something wrong. Maybe my standards are too high. Or maybe, as my mother keeps telling me, I'm just not doing enough to meet men."

I'm not sure exactly how I became aware of the problem. Certainly it's not new. "It starts in high school," my friend Ann explained. "The girls were always complaining that there weren't enough boys at parties, and that the boys who did come weren't mature." Ann's recollection made me think of the old joke about the two Jewish ladies at a resort hotel. "The food is terrible," one says to the other. "It's like poison." "I absolutely agree," her friend replies. "And such small portions!"

So when I first started hearing these complaints from women I knew, I didn't pay too much attention, and dismissed them as the predictable and self-indulgent laments of women who would rather be married than single. So what else is new? But as the stories began to pile up, and as I was able, temporarily, to set aside my traditional male biases and my male pride, a different picture emerged. With few exceptions, the women who were tell-

A VANISH

JEWISH MEN

ing me these stories were impressive and desirable. By no stretch of the imagination could they be considered "losers"—although, in truth, some were beginning to feel this way. Could it be that what they were telling me was objectively true? And, if it was, why was nobody else talking about it?

I decided to check with my male friends who were single, the counterparts to all these women, and the first thing I discovered is that I didn't have very many. This got me to wondering if the women weren't more right than I realized. The men I know who aren't gay or married tend to be single only in the literal sense of the word: many are in a solid relationship with a woman, while the rest have no trouble meeting good, available women—even if they haven't yet found the right one.

The women, I was starting to understand, were describing a real situation which has generally gone unrecognized in our society, even though it's a terribly important fact in the lives of millions of Americans. As Suzanne likes to put it, there is an elephant in the room and nobody is talking about it.

Well, not nobody, exactly.

Whenever I get into one of these discussions with single women, the first thing that becomes clear is that the elephant is actually talked about all the time and in great detail—among these women and their various single women friends. As often as possible, they joke about it, but very often they can't. "You talk about it with very close friends and you get each other depressed," says Ellen, 29, a graduate student in history. "The idea that you might not have it someday—it's terrifying, a bit like thinking about death."

When these women are not laughing or getting depressed, they try to understand how things got this way, how the elephant ended up in the room in the first place. While they usually don't come up with many satisfying answers, these discussions do serve an important purpose: They reinforce the idea that there really *is* an elephant in the room, even if the rest of the world is convinced that there isn't.

I think it's important that somebody who isn't a single women comes forward to testify that he, too, can make out the wrinkled, bloated form of a large, grey, four-legged mammal. I realize that this testimony may be depressing to those women who still hold out the hope that what they think they are seeing is merely the zoological equivalent of a flying saucer, a mirage made out of their own unhappiness. On the other hand, perhaps this statement can be useful. "I really hope you write about this," one woman told me, "so I can send it to my mother with a note saying, 'see, it isn't just *me*.'"

I'm also naive enough to believe that talking about the elephant might also benefit men. Strictly speaking, this article is not really about men, but about women's perceptions of men. And so in an objective sense, what I report about men is unfair to them, as they have no chance to reply to the women, and worse, they have no opportunity to emerge here as individuals. So this does not represent the whole story, but merely one aspect of it.

How can I risk being unfair to men? While part of me still believes that I'm just one more footsoldier slogging it out in the endless war between the sexes, and that my saying these things somehow constitutes an act of extreme disloyalty

ING BREED?

Moment/61

to my side, I also know that at this point in my life my chief concern is no longer with the members of my own sex, but rather my age group—my generation. And a lot of women in my generation are getting a raw deal.

Let me spell out the problem in more detail: Among educated people now in their late twenties or in their thirties, the people who used to constitute the sixties generation, there are many who are single and who would prefer to be married—or at least to be in a committed relationship. Within this group, women are at a significant disadvantage in two major respects.

The first part of the problem has to do with numbers, and the numbers it has to do with are startling. Very simply, roughly 20 percent of all young Jewish women are not going to marry a Jewish man because there just isn't one available.

Here's why: First, in the 20-34 age bracket, there are 92 Jewish males for every 100 Jewish females. That's just a four percent difference, but then we have to take account of the intermarriage statistics. Out of every 92 male Jews who marry, roughly 24 are going to marry "out," a choice which only 12 out of every 100 Jewish women will make. And that reduces the number of Jewish males who are available as husbands from 92 to 68, as against 88 Jewish women who are available as wives. Sixty-eight men, 88 women, or 20 women who are a kind of remainder; 20 out of every 100.

These numbers are rough estimates. Maybe they're off, maybe the figure is not 20 percent, but only 15 percent. Still, there is a very large group of Jewish women who are, for all practical purposes, stuck. They could intermarry, of course, but they don't. It's not clear why they don't; perhaps they agree with my friend who says, "I sometimes think I could marry a Buddhist, if he were a genuinely nice person, but that's only a passing thought. I'm so socialized against marrying somebody who isn't Jewish that I really can't take my desperate thought seriously. I refuse to imagine Shabbas as a solo affair, or one which my sweet Buddhist will indulge me."

There are, in short, not enough men to go around. When all the sorting is done, some women are going to be left over, and they will most likely blame themselves, because nobody has bothered to tell them the harsh statistical truth.

A truth which gets worse: According to Noreen Goldman, a population researcher at Princeton University's Woodrow Wilson School, there are several other factors involved. Let's consider the case of a woman born in 1947—we'll call her Fran—who will turn 33 in 1980. If Fran is single, and if she ever wants to have children, she had better find a man pretty soon—unless, of course, she decides to have children outside of marriage. But even then, Fran understands that she must act relatively soon. At her age, if she waits too much longer, there may be real and significant pregnancy risks.

But even if Fran doesn't want to have children, she is still, like other women, statistically likely to marry a man who is older than she is. Noreen Goldman calls this "societal pressure," but whether or not it's perceived in these terms, it's a fact of life that the overwhelming majority of women marry men who are older than they are. In Fran's case, she is most likely looking for a man who was born before 1947. And here comes the crunch: Because she was born near the beginning of the baby boom, Fran is going to have a hard time finding such a man. There were, it turns out, more than 400,000 fewer babies born in 1946 than in 1947, the year of Fran's birth, and there were more than *half a million* fewer babies born in 1945 than in 1946. And so, by definition, the men that Fran would find appropriate are in short supply and, being slightly older, many are already married. And so Fran finds herself in what is called a "marriage squeeze."

Under these trying circumstances, you might expect that Jewish women would be so desperate that they'd settle for just about anybody. But they don't, and they won't. And that's the heart of the story, the part that doesn't show up in the charts and the tables. That's the part that has to do with women's evolving expectations, with the shortage not of men but of *mentschen*. The men who *are* around, if they're not married, gay, or otherwise unavailable, are often disappointing as people. However successful they may be in their working lives, they seem (to these women, at least) to be lacking in the personal realm. Their range of interests is often narrow; more important, there seems to be something missing. Their emotional resources and supportiveness, their willingness and ability to enter into a committed relationship—these all seem underdeveloped. What's missing, in short, is a set of qualities which women find so readily in other women.

At this point I can hear some readers muttering that the scapegoat—or the criminal, depending upon one's point of view—is the women's movement. Both sides are right; the women's movement *is* at the heart of this new situation. Now that some of the dust has settled, we can pause for a moment to consider the effects of one of the fastest, most sweeping revolutions in modern history. The women's movement has achieved many important gains, but in the interests of truth it must be pointed out that these gains have not come free of cost. There has been a stiff price to pay and a series of hidden injuries to both men and women that have yet to be acknowledged. And the current situation of single women in America—the very people who have also benefited the most from the women's movement—is perhaps the most obvious casualty.

It would be difficult to exaggerate the tremendous effects of feminism during the 1970s, even—or perhaps especially—on those women who have never seen themselves as "members" of the movement, but rather as fellow-travelers, a phenomenon which *Ms.* Magazine recently called the "I'm not a feminist—*but*" syndrome.

A decade ago, when feminism moved from rhetoric to real action, one of its chief goals was to promote a kind of remedial effort among women. If men had good jobs, the high salaries, the positions of power, the political clout, the sexual freedom, the seemingly interesting lives, then the suitable response, in addition to pointing out these inequalities, was for women to pursue these goals in the same way that men did: by insisting on their rights, by attending professional and graduate schools, by learning to be ambitious and aggressive, by working hard, and all the rest. "All the rest," it turns out, was no less important than the first part of the injunction, and it included such diverse tactics as becoming more worldly, participating more in the national culture, and in general paying more attention to the external world.

At the same time, however, and to its credit, feminism did not find it necessary to break or to weaken the connection of women to their own *internal* worlds of who they were and how they felt. On the contrary: The women's movement built upon that very base and actually strengthened the internal worlds of many women through a variety of means including, above all, consciousness-raising groups, as well as psychotherapy, the reading and writing of feminist literature, the development of feminist history, music, art, cinema and theater, the keeping of journals, the general value placed on personal sharing and the broad, common concerns of sisterhood—and above all the accurate perception that political change arises directly out of the heartfelt truth of individual, personal experience. The women's movement, in other words, was among other things a political legitimization of what women always knew about themselves and each other: that despite their denigrated positions in the external world, they possessed large and important internal resources which could be the basis for a strong and powerful movement.

It was taken for granted, then, that in order to catch up to men, women had to work on these two different fronts: external and internal. But while this was going on, it turns out that there was very little to catch up *to*. While feminism was giving women higher expectations about themselves, nothing of the sort was taking place among men. So instead of narrowing the gap between men and women, the movement, in some ways inadvertently, actually widened it. Or, as Suzanne explains: "By now, women have mastered the so-called masculine skills of how to succeed in a profession. And we've had the emotional skills drummed into us from birth. Well, it turns out that any idiot can learn how to achieve, but it is apparently less easy for men to learn how to love, and how to be emotionally supportive—especially if they're not even trying!"

If the aim of the women's movement was to make women subjectively equal to men, it could have stopped long ago. Women no longer need men to provide them with status, money, or physical security; they can get these things on their own. What women are now asking for are the harder things. Unfortunately, although men did (and still do) enjoy better jobs and more money, many men achieved their success precisely by giving up on their development as people. It is somewhat of an overstatement, but it is as though millions of women had trained earnestly for a race that most men never took seriously. Having won easily, the women now stand around the finish line, awkward and disappointed, looking in vain for suitable men to run not against—but *with*. But the men are nowhere in sight.

Some men, of course, *have* changed as a result of feminism, but this occurs most often by their being in an intimate relationship with a woman. And unless that relationship ends, those men are unavailable anyway. "But what about men's liberation?" several women asked me during the course of our interviews. "Well, what about it?" I responded, and I would be told about a conference in Denver last October, or a mimeographed magazine coming out of San Francisco. Everything I know about the rather small "men's movement" in this country I have learned from women, who in general are more informed about it than most men. And there you have the the problem in a nutshell.

What has happened, then, to the men? Some really *are* gay, of course. Many women believe that there are more gay men than gay women, but there are no reliable statistics on the subject. "You have no idea what a drag it is," says Marlene, a physical therapist, "to have a sparkling conversation at a dinner party with a man who's really stylish, handsome and warm, only to be interrupted by his male lover who's come to take him dancing." It is particularly painful for single women to discover that gay men exist in larger numbers than they ever imagined — especially in New York. And although this has become a cultural stereotype, women often find that these gay men seem to be among the most talented, most sensitive and most emotionally responsive men they have ever met.

Another large group of otherwise available men got married during the 1970s—often to younger women. And many women believe that this group includes some of the more emotionally stable and secure men. There are, it turns out, some fairly alarming statistics about the differences between single and married men in our culture. One writer, George Gilder, has written an entire book on the subject called *Naked Nomads*, in which he cites one of the more disturbing figures: Apparently, single men are six times as likely as married men to die as a result of "accidental falls."

While George Gilder is known as a conservative, a similar point is made by Dr. Hugh Drummond, who writes a column on psychiatry for *Mother Jones*, the radical monthly magazine published in California.

Quoting a popular adage that "good women marry late; good men marry early," Drummond observes that "marriage seems to be good for men and bad for women." The obvious conclusion, he quips, is that men should marry other men and leave women alone.

Even those women who are eager to be married are often ambivalent. Sandy, 31, is a research scientist. "To give up being single," she says, "is to give up a great deal. I couldn't imagine doing it lightly. It used to be that single women couldn't wait to escape their fate. I wish I had another twenty years of being 31 and single, now that I've finally gotten good at it."

Not long ago, when Terry was having lunch with two friends, both single and thirty, the three of them had their nineteen thousandth discussion about the men they were meeting—and not meeting. They started talking about their "lists," and each of them decided to write down what was especially important to her in a man. By and large, the lists were similar: Each woman wanted the man she would meet to have an interesting job, to be assertive and aggressive when necessary, and so on. What was particularly interesting was that heading each list was the same criterion, in slightly different words: "He should be emotionally generous, with the capacity to give and to be supportive."

While women these days have various complaints about men, calling them self-centered, narcissistic, indecisive, afraid of making commitments, and all the rest, the word "emotional" invariably turns up during the first thirty seconds. The most common complaint is that a man is "emotionally immature," and from there the responses go out along a spectrum: emotionally underdeveloped, emotionally retarded, emotionally crippled—all the way to "emotional eunuch." Ironically, many women have begun psychotherapy or psychoanalysis because they have assumed that their not meeting men was their own fault—and in some cases, of course, they were right. But as a result, these women generally emerge from therapy or analysis with deeper insights into their emotional lives. And that, in turn, raises their standards when it comes to the men they are meeting, which makes the whole process even more difficult.

"You meet a 35-year-old man," Judy asserts, "and you assume you're meeting a man. But very often it's just an adult body with a little boy hiding inside it, saying 'me, me, me.' He doesn't know who he is, and he doesn't know what he wants. Can you imagine what it's like trying to give your love to such a man? And that's what really hurts: Maybe I'm wrong, but I think of myself as somebody with a lot of love to give, somebody who could really be good at loving—and I can't find anybody to give it to. I feel like I'm being wasted."

And Lois adds, "I hate stereotypes, but I can't stop feeling that maybe the stuff about the Jewish mother is right. *So* many of the men I meet are impossibly spoiled, and their success in their careers simply confirms what they've been taught to believe about themselves—that they are prizes. I know that somewhere under those layers of arrogance, there must be some fears, some areas of softness, the things that make a person human. Why is it so damned hard to get to them? I don't want to marry a career; I want to marry a person."

Are non-Jews any different? I ask. "Yes and no. They don't seem nearly as achievement-oriented, they don't seem to be constantly trying to prove something or to satisfy somebody else's expectations of them. But the differences turn out to be superficial. It just takes longer to find out that they're as shallow and as boring as everybody else."

Lois isn't an observant Jew, or especially involved in Jewish life. For those of my friends who are, the problems are still further compounded. One single women, active in a havurah, observes that she and her friends "all know the same nine bachelors." Another, dead serious, tells me that every night she says the Sh'ma—and then adds a prayer that men will change. The special problems of those for whom the holidays matter, for whom the substance of Jewish life is a major concern, are very real. For them, the harrowing question is whether they are going to have to trade off, to sacrifice their beliefs and their concerns in order to marry. They attend the weddings of their friends—painful enough as it is—and then are subjected to the unintended cruelty of the well-wishers who greet them with, "*Im yirtzeh HaShem*—God willing—soon by you!" Often, these are women who have been prepared ever since birth for marriage and for having children. Sometimes deeply affected by the women's movement, sometimes untouched by it, they still see themselves as stunted; without marriage, and with the prospect that they may never marry beginning to haunt them, they live on the edge of panic. There's not much else they can do; as one said to me, "I want to meet a good man, but I'm not about to jump under the *chuppah* with the first guy I find."

What these various complaints boil down to is that women today believe that a relationship can no longer get by on the traditional specialization, with men required to carry all the financial burdens of the relationship while women take responsibility for the emotional side. It's as simple as that.

When I started really listening to the complaints of single women, I kept hearing comments like these:
—The men I meet are selfish, they're princes. They want everything to revolve around them. They want you to be attractive, interesting, and entertaining, but if *you* have problems, they don't want to hear them.
—He was a terrific man: successful, nice, handsome and kind, but emotionally he was about 12 years old. He couldn't listen to my problems, and I would have had to spend all our time together listening to his.
—Men just want to be entertained. They want their egos bolstered. They want to take rather than to give. I'm reaching out and they're not there.

At this point I want to make clear that, surprising as it may seem in light of these comments, most of them are made without anger. All the women I spoke with were eager to be proved wrong in their perceptions of men. There was nothing ideological in their complaints about the opposite sex. True, I found plenty of disappointment and sadness and a certain amount of resignation. But conspicuously absent were the offensive man-hating and casual denigrating of men that were so common five and ten years ago—what David calls the "men are shmucks" point of view.

A sense of humor is essential in this area. Carol, 31, an office worker, wants to market a bumper sticker: "MEN ARE BEASTS"—and then, in smaller print, "Hug a Beast Today." "There are four types of men I keep meeting," Carol says. "First there is the nebbish, the poor guy with no real strength or personality. Then there is his opposite number, the macho man who thinks he's God's gift to women. Then comes the immature man, who can't stand to be alone and who sometimes still lives with his parents. Finally, there is the 'crazy,' who is apt to be flighty, unrealistic and self-centered."

Within this motley crew it isn't difficult to guess who represents the most acceptable prospect: At least the "crazy" provides some hope. Carol told me about an episode on *Taxi* she had seen recently in which a woman cabbie picks up a fare who turns out to be an interesting and exciting man. During their long drive they get into an extended conversation, and she feels herself falling for him. Arriving at his destination, she finally blurts out, "You must be married, gay, or crazy." And then, muttering to herself, "Come *on, crazy!*" He is, and she is delighted.

"You should really talk to men," I was repeatedly told, but very few women could think of any I should talk to. One woman who was not interviewed heard about the article and called me to insist that I talk to her friend, who had this wonderful divorce lawyer with his own views on the matter. I tracked him down: A Harvard man in his mid-forties, married with a family, clearly thoughtful and sensitive, who proceeded to tell me about his clients. His own views, it turns out, coincided with everything else I was hearing, but his different perspective was useful. "The women I see are together and attractive," he told me, "while the men are into a different scene every week. Men are on a wholesale retreat from intimacy. Women are always asking me if I know anyone. If you find a man who's willing to talk about his feeling and his problems, and if he's also willing to listen, he'll be adored by women—and quickly snapped up."

He continued: "Riding into town each morning on the train, there are pockets of working men and women, and I sometimes listen to their conversation. The women talk about their lives, or other people, or families, relationships, personal experiences—things with emotional content. Men sometimes talk about their work, and occasionally about women, but most often they're talking about the Red Sox, the Patriots or the Bruins, or whatever team is currently breaking their hearts."

Breaking their hearts. The phrase made me think that somebody ought to look into the ways in which many men use sports, not only as a shield against intimacy, but perhaps as a way of engaging those very same qualities—like love, loyalty, companionship and above all *involvement*—which might play a role in their relationships with men.

The various changes which occurred during the 1970s with regard to men and women have not yet led to a new reality, but only to a new sense of frustration. It is clear that some things have changed—but not for everybody. For example, it wasn't so long ago that most women who were single just wanted to be married; it didn't matter so much how, or to whom. But now that women demand higher standards in the rest of their lives, it is only natural that they should be more selective when it comes to men.

The problems begin when a woman who has changed meets a man who hasn't. "It used to be so easy," recalls Suzanne. "If you were pretty and well-behaved and if you asked a man about his interests, you'd do fine. A friend of mine went out for dinner the other night with a guy who turned out to be a real jerk. He didn't shut up for a minute, and was interested only in himself. She said nothing at all for two hours, and three days later he called her again for another date! Has this guy been living on the moon, or what?"

These days, nobody seems to know what the rules are any more. Take the myth of initiating women. While it's true that some women are far more aggressive in the sexual marketplace than they used to be, in the overwhelming majority of cases it is still the man who makes the first phone call, who initiates the social overture. (The media like to suggest that this is no longer true, but for the most part it still is. How else, for example, do we account for that annoying series of television commercials for Harveys Bristol Cream in which a sexy but very proper woman, upon inviting herself to a man's house, hastens to assure us that it's really fine for her to act this way because she is bringing a bottle of Harveys, which makes the whole thing respectable, or, as she puts it, "downright upright.")

But for most women it's downright difficult to take the first step in social intercourse with men. The men, meanwhile, knowing that the women at least *have* this new option, and believing what they are told—that women are using it—have in many cases abdicated their traditional roles of initiation without adopting any new postures, thereby leading to an uncomfortable vacuum, a lack of momentum and energy. Women are afraid to call men, afraid to looking foolish or needy. And men, for their part, are afraid of being rejected, or increasingly, of being *intimidated* by the New Woman they've heard so much about.

Like many women these days,

Are Good Jewish Men a Vanishing Breed?

Barbara, a thirty-two-year-old teacher, is badgered by a mother who is convinced that her daughter isn't doing enough to meet men, that she isn't taking advantage of every conceivable opportunity. "Join the ACLU," Barbara's mother tells her every three weeks. "Once, thirty-five years ago," Barbara told me, "a man asked my mother to marry him. She turned him down. 'In that case,' he told her, 'I know somebody you'd like.' And that turned out to be my father. How would you like to grow up with that story?"

One of Barbara's mother's rules—and it isn't just Barbara's mother who says this—is that if you're a single woman, and a man asks you to go out, and you already have plans with another woman, you cancel those plans without a second thought. Today, most women will have none of that, although this doesn't mean they're not unconflicted. "A guy called me a few weeks back," says Barbara, "and I told him I was busy Thursday night, having dinner with my roommate from college. And he wouldn't believe me. '*Seriously*?' he asked. 'Then change your plans.' Of course I didn't, but now I'm getting lonely and a little apprehensive about the future, and there's always that nagging thought that perhaps my mother was right."

One of the few bright spots in this whole picture, at least from the women's point of view, is that a few more men are now appearing on the scene as a result of divorce, or, as Suzanne calls it, "recycling." While most women are understandably cautious about recently divorced men, who often turn out to be totally uninterested in a stable, serious relationship, those who have been on their own for a couple of years or more are judged innocent until proven guilty. "You assume they've learned something from the trauma they went through," says Tina.

"When I'm at the beach," Carol says, "I keep an eye out for young children—accompanied by men who seem slightly lost." Carol has had bad experiences with newly divorced men, but she also feels that she doesn't have the luxury of waiting for the men to be ready to enter a new commitment; by that time they are invariably involved with somebody else. "Really," she says, "it's worse than looking for an apartment in Manhattan, where people read the obituaries to get a head start on the competition. Given how bad things are, you have to wonder if it isn't fair to intervene slowly in a bad marriage, once you know they're going to break up anyway."

But by and large it's a bleak picture for many women with a lot of love to give and nowhere to give it. While they're waiting for a solution to the problem, they give each other advice: "Be open to everything but don't appear to be looking too hard." "You've got to initiate; don't let a potential prospect get away. If he doesn't like the fact that you called him, you don't want him anyway." And "have a sense of humor about it all and cultivate your own life; don't be too down on yourself about something you can't control."

A cynic might point out that the solution may be for women to lower their expectations, to give up on the idea that men are going to turn up who will change their lives. The best response to that comes from Diane White, a columnist for the *Boston Globe,* who wrote: "We persist because we are women. We are romantic. We want to fall in love. We want to get married. We are embarrassed to admit these things, but they're true. We are supposed to want to be independent and self-sufficient and successful. We want all these things and we want a man too. It's the heartbreak of heterosexuality."

It is true, of course, that men also have their problems, their anxieties, and their complaints around this issue. Certainly it does not take a woman to say, as one told me recently, "Can you imagine what it's like to light the Shabbas candles every Friday night and then, when you turn around, to see that there's nobody there with you?" I have not been writing here about men, but about something different: women's perceptions of men. The loneliness and vulnerability of single men is an important story, but it's not this story. *This* story is about women who are looking for men — and for *mentschlichkeit,* both of which they find in short supply.

Nor is this the whole story. Some women, undoubtedly, choose to blame the shortage and the inadequacies of men rather than facing their own problems. Some women who think they want to get married are actually ambivalent in ways they don't recognize. And some women set such impossibly high standards that no man has a chance to live up to them. There are, in short, many individual exceptions to the general picture I have described here. But even when all these exceptions are accounted for and deducted from the total, there is still a major problem left.

Perhaps there are large numbers of Jewish women who prefer the single life, or who are terrified by the prospects of marriage. I did not find them, and I suspect that they do not exist in such large numbers as the media would have us believe. I found, instead, a profound moral yearning, a strong fear of being passed over, a fervent commitment to intimacy—and to family. And I found all of these emotions expressed more in sorrow than in anger, and, generally, with hope rather than resignation.

Given the numbers of people involved, and their quality, we're not talking here about a private problem. It would be painful enough if that were so. But some of the best young people that the Jewish community has produced are not getting married—although they very much want to. They feel strong pressures against intermarriage, but they also don't want to end up alone. They want, many of them, to bear children, and they watch the passing years with growing fear that they may not. What happens to these women—or what fails to happen—will matter significantly not only to their own lives, but to the future of American Judaism. ✻

IT MATTERS HOW THE DEAD ARE BURIED

ROBERT KANIGEL

Robert Kanigel's book, Apprentice to Genius: The Making of a Scientific Dynasty, *was published by MacMillan in 1986. He is a freelance writer who has received the Smolar Award and the Simon Rockover Award, and he has been published in the* New York Times *and* Science '86.

It matters how the dead are buried. And it matters how they're mourned. A state funeral full of pomp and ceremony stirs in us one set of feelings, the sight of naked bodies piled atop mass graves another. An Irish wake.... A burial at sea.... An elaborately choreographed graveside service of "dignity and simple beauty...." The living weep, or shudder, or remain numbly unmoved. But somehow the dead must be buried and the living must mark their passing. And it matters *how*. Whether it matters to the dead themselves may be a theological question; but it certainly matters to the living left behind.

In Washington, D.C., the members of a Conservative congregation, Tifereth Israel, have joined to change the way their dead are buried and mourned. They have reclaimed for themselves an area of communal life for decades the almost exclusive province of commercial funeral homes. They have dusted off religious practices centuries of Jewish tradition deem a good and decent way to deal with death but which, among American Jews, have been forsaken by all but the Orthodox.

And the change they've made has made a difference. "It works," says a woman whose father's burial was handled in this new, old way. "It does what it's supposed to do."

For years Louis Charnow had lived in Hollywood, Florida, running his own real estate agency—busy, active, vital. Then came the series of strokes and heart attack that left him no longer able to live on his own. He moved to Chevy Chase, Maryland, a suburb of Washington, D.C., to live with his daughter, her husband, and their two small children.

Pearl Schainker and her husband didn't know how long her father might live; they knew only they wanted to make whatever time he had left as comfortable as possible. That wasn't easy. Mentally, he was as sharp as ever. But the stroke had impaired his sense of balance; he needed a walker to get around the house. It had also left him deaf; communicating with him meant writing notes. "We used up reams of paper," recalls Pearl, a 36-year-old social worker. What was more, that stroke had caused a condition known as tinnitis, a persistent roaring sensation in the ears which left him almost unable to concentrate. They'd hoped he might learn sign language. He wouldn't, or couldn't. Lip reading? No, he wasn't interested. Nor was he overly interested in people visiting him, nor in visiting others, nor in physical therapy.

The man his daughter remembers as "a very outgoing kind of guy" had become, in short, profoundly depressed. "He never got out of mourning for his own lost health," is the way Pearl's husband Lawrence sums it up. Only cuddling the children—especially their year-and-a-half-old girl—seemed to give him any pleasure.

That's how it went on for month after month. "It was difficult," says Pearl. "It was hell," says her husband. "It required a tremendous amount of emotional energy. It was continually frustrating." Pearl had dimly hoped that, as an example for the children, her father would "set a model for one with declining powers." He didn't. And this, she admits, "produced some anger in me."

By October 1977, a year after moving from Florida, Louis Charnow had virtually stopped eating. He'd lost a lot of weight. And now, in the early hours of a Friday morning as Pearl lay in bed half asleep, she could hear his racked coughing; on top of everything else, he had a cold. The day before, he'd been well enough to get around the house on his own. He'd even asked someone to fetch him a corned beef sandwich; but then, when it arrived, he couldn't eat it. "That night when we put him to bed," says Pearl, "I think I knew what was going on...."

Now all at once she became aware of a silence in the house; she couldn't hear the coughing. She rushed downstairs. "He took a few more gasps," she says, and died.

It was into this emotion-wrought setting, the product of a year of growing frustration, filled with every sort of confused and unresolved feeling, of grief and loss and anger and desperate, grim fatigue, that the Jewish community of Congregation Tifereth Israel of Washington, in the person of two representatives of its funeral practices committee, stepped into the lives of Pearl and Lawrence Schainker.

The death of a loved one poses an array of common problems for those left behind to mourn—and to cope. Typically, the bereaved are intensely vulnerable—perhaps overcome with grief, or racked with guilt for emotional "business" left unresolved, or divided, one from the other, by internal family tensions.

And yet the deceased must be buried, the mourning and recovery process must be set on its way, and much needs doing. Relatives must be summoned. The body must be prepared for burial, and brought to the cemetery. A ceremony to mark the occasion must be held. And to perform these larger tasks, a thousand dreary details need tending. All at a time when those best equipped by their relationship to the deceased to deal with them may be least equipped emotionally.

In the American system, human needs inevitably find profit-making enterprises ready to step in and meet them. Death is no exception. Most of the time today, the details of death are handled by commercial funeral homes, which function more or less efficiently, with more or less sensitivity to their customers, and with more or less fevered preoccupation with their profit-and-loss statements.

It has not always been thus, especially among Jews. Once, in the cities and shtetls of Europe, every Jewish community had its *chevra kadisha*—literally, "sacred society"—whose workings collide brutally, in almost every respect, with their modern American counterparts. There, a Jewish burial was handled according to Jewish law, and was seen as the responsibility of the entire Jewish community. What Tifereth Israel has done, making it among the first non-Orthodox congregations in the nation to do so, is to take on that ancient responsibility as its own, to make the death of one of its members the "business" of all of them.

The first thing Pearl Schainker did when her father died was call her sister in Boston. The next thing she did was call Carol Hausman, whose name was listed in the Congregation's bulletin, along with several others, as one to be notified in the event of a death.

It was early Friday morning, maybe two or three a.m., when the call went out. But Carol Hausman didn't wait until "business hours" to show up at the Schainker house in Chevy Chase, nor even until dawn. Along with Harris Weinstein—like her, a key figure in the evolution of the Congregation's funeral practices—she was there in less than an hour, and immediately set to work. Recalls Pearl Schainker: "They kind of organized us."

The kids—they were Pearl's first concern. Should they be awakened and told their grandfather was dead? Or should the body already be gone from the house by the time they were up? Weinstein and Hausman were there to lend an ear and offer advice. (What they settled on was to let the children sleep, then tell them the moment they awoke.)

Weinstein and Hausman helped the family say the appropriate prayers, in Hebrew and English. They asked if the Schainkers were going to want *minyans* at the house for saying *kaddish* during *shivah,* the seven-day mourning period following burial. They asked which family members should be notified. When they sensed it appropriate, they broached the burial options available, including the synagogue's own traditional one. Weinstein called the funeral home. Hausman arranged to call and explain why Mrs. Schainker wouldn't be able to keep an appointment.

Pearl, raised in a generally observant home, recalled the tradition of *shomrim*—people to remain with the body, chanting psalms, until it was interred. But how, she wondered, do you *get a shomer?* Weinstein and Hausman knew. The congregation maintained a registry of volunteers, and Weinstein saw to it that the first *shomer* was at the funeral home by the time the body arrived there. Weinstein also called the man who would, with another, perform the *taharah,* or ritual cleansing of the body, before it left Washington.

The body was to be taken to New York for burial. First indications were that, to cross state lines, it would have to be embalmed—in violation of Jewish law. Pearl was at first resigned. "If someone tells you it's state law, well. . . ." But "we had someone here to take care of it for us," and discovered that it was not required after all.

"Everything was taken care of," says Pearl, "usually before we'd even thought of it." And yet, the blind, take-charge authoritarianism that sometimes replaces impotent passivity at times of stress, says Pearl, was wholly absent. "There was none of that 'We've arranged everything, and you can't change it' kind of attitude."

As they take turns recalling the events of two years past, Pearl and Lawrence Schainker make no effort to mask the warmth and gratitude they feel toward all those who helped them. As we sat and talked in the large conference room of the Washington medical center at which her husband works, Pearl is the more voluble of the two. But it is Lawrence, a calm, precise-spoken 39-year-old physician, who says it straight out. "It was," he says, "one of the most touching expressions of loving kindness I've ever experienced."

When Harris Weinstein and Carol Hausman drove up to the Schainker house early that October morning in 1977, they did not do so unprepared. She is a therapist, he is a greying, 44-year-old lawyer with a large Washington firm. Neither, in any professional sense, qualified as a "bereavement counselor" or any such thing. Still, he says, "It isn't as though we walked in cold. We had trained ourselves." They'd been immersing themselves in the whole subject for two years.

It had all started at a Congregational retreat in 1975. *What are the obligations and responsibilities of a community to its members?* was the theme as it evolved. Before long, it was zeroing in on death and bereavement. Those attending, including Weinstein and Hausman, decided to set up a committee through which to educate themselves and perhaps formulate a policy.

The committee looked into how Jewish funeral homes in Washington worked. They went into the economics of the business, determined the wholesale and retail costs of caskets and shrouds, studied the merits of, and need for, embalming, even pinned down figures on overhead expenses. They re-opened the long-closed book on traditional Jewish funeral practices, and began to study it with fresh eyes. And by the spring of the following year, they were able to report to the congregation that they were ready, at the least, to offer bereavement counseling to Congregation members.

At the least—for they were not yet through. Their research, their knowledge of the Congregation and its members, their evolving sense of Jewish tradition, and their preoccupation with that original retreat topic—the responsibility of a community to its members—were all drawing them to a radical conclusion. And that was, says Weinstein, uttering the words as if they truly were in italics, *"to make funerals for members and their legal dependents a congregational responsibility."*

Shades of an earlier time and a distant place, of shtetls and the *chevra kadisha.*

A Jewish Funeral Practices Committee of Greater Washington was set up with representatives from Tifereth Israel along with those from other Washington congregations. Its aim? In part it was to negotiate with the established Jewish-owned funeral homes in the area to make simple, traditional Jewish funerals available, at a fair price, to all who sought them.

Neither Weinstein nor Tifereth Israel Rabbi A. Nathan Abramowitz feels overly comfortable talking about the impasse they reached with Washington's Jewish funeral Establishment. Potential legal hassles. . . . Recent FTC hearings into the industry. . . . Weinstein, plainly bitter, won't talk for the record at all. Rabbi Abramowitz, for his part, is content to point to "the broad absence of traditional practices in what Jews had thought were 'Jewish' funeral homes," and to how Jews were being routinely misled to think they were being offered "one of several acceptable Jewish practices."

Jack Zeller, a Washington pathologist and chairman of the Congregation committee responsible for ritual cleansings of the body, is not so shy. It was, he goes so far as to say, "the petty thievery of the funeral homes that caused us," in part, "to seek alternatives" to them. Unless a bereaved family specifically identified itself as Orthodox, he says, it was invariably led into extravagant funerals. He claims an accountant with whom the Tifereth Israel group worked told him he'd "never seen a bill for less than $2000." At casket selection time, the bereaved family would be "led into one room after another, each bigger and more luxurious than the next." One funeral home boasted a salesman "so smooth he could sell you down the river and have you shake hands with him for it."

Taking potshots at funeral homes, of course, hardly rates as sport anymore. When it comes right down to it, Harris Weinstein, for one, says he has no qualms with the principle of making a fair profit from providing funeral services. Indeed, it was to the city's Jewish-owned funeral homes that the synagogue's funeral practices group first turned. But their apparent unwillingness to grant the Congregation any role in setting funeral practices for its members was, he claims, the sticking point in the negotiations. The ticklish issue of price was scarcely even broached.

Feeling spurned by the Jewish-owned homes, the Committee turned to a Gentile one, named Chambers. And out of the ensuing negotiations came a "letter of understanding" by which Chambers agreed to provide at a fixed cost—recently, about $500—a specified basic funeral. It would pick up the body, obtain death certificates; provide a plain, all-wood coffin, furnish facilities for ritual washing of bodies, transport the body to the cemetery, and so on. This agreement in no way limited Congregation members to the simple funeral; but it did make one easily and routinely available to them.

There was one other stipulation in that standard agreement: Chambers would not try to "sell the bereaved any goods or services not included above without approval of the designated congregational contact or Rabbi." Not only was this a Spartan funeral, lacking in all frills; it closed the door to frills. It was, in effect, a take-it-or-leave-it funeral.

By design. "A bereaved family is very conscious of wanting the community's recognition of the respect and affection they had for the deceased," declares Harris Weinstein. He states this baldly, categorically. There is no hint of a veiled snigger in the observation, no suggestion of character weakness on the part of the bereaved. No, he states it as if he were a scientist who, after years of research, were reporting a universal law of nature.

And it is this apparent "truth"—whether rooted in human nature, cultural conditioning, whatever—that has made the funeral industry what it is. "People *like* to spend money," on the funerals for their loved ones, is how Rabbi Abramowitz characterizes the rationale of funeral home owners. And if, after all, it's "community recognition" the bereaved want, how better to get it than via a copper-lined casket stuffed with fluffy satin pillows?

There's nothing new in this of

course. The Talmud speaks of the rich being brought for burial "on a tall state bed, ornamented and covered with coverlets," while the poor were reduced to a plain bier. It was the recognition of this apparent human tendency that led, the Talmud tells us, to the insistence on democratically equal funerals in the first place. Part of Tifereth Israel's avowed purpose, says Harris Weinstein, is to "try to make socially acceptable [once again] this traditional and simple funeral."

Everything in the traditional Jewish approach to death, burial, and bereavement speaks to the same principles of simplicity and respect for the deceased. *Taharah,* the ritual cleansing of the body. *Tachrichim,* the simplest of white shrouds. *Shomrim,* or guards to watch over the body until interment. The simple pine box. The closed casket. The speedy burial. The *halachic* or traditional justifications for each, says Rabbi Abramowitz, are normally couched in terms of the needs of the deceased. The idea behind *taharah,* for example, is that "the deceased is entitled to personal honor and concern." It is not, says the Rabbi, something done by "hired hands, mechanically, but carefully and personally, by human beings reciting prayers."

But do the dead really care?

That's not really the point, Rabbi Abramowitz broadly hints. "The fact that the law states it that way"—as done out of respect for the dead—"doesn't mean the law is blind to the circumstances in which it is used.... The religion is fully aware of the implications for the living." Thus *taharah,* in this sense, becomes "a way for the bereaved to feel he is personally attending to the loved one." Indeed, bereaved families tell him, he reports, of their "enormous relief and appreciation" for it.

Those "implications for the living" don't stop with the bereaved themselves. In an ABC documentary about Adath Jeshurun Congregation's similar program in Minneapolis, one man tells about performing his first *taharah.* "After I touched him the first time, all concern and fear just vanished," he says. "By having to move the body in certain ways, you almost embrace it.... It's an intimate relationship, and you're confronted with the ultimate reality [that] you yourself will be there sometime." All in all, he says, "it was not a bad experience. In fact it was relatively exhilarating when it was all done." Tifereth Israel's Jack Zeller, one of those who performed the *taharah* for Louis Charnow, says much the same. "There's nothing spooky, nothing squeamish, nothing superstitious about it," he says. "It's an extremely touching thing. It's an awesome experience."

Over and over, traditional Jewish burial and bereavement practice seems to work this way—that the observance, whatever its theological basis, is fairly drenched in psychologically sound and spiritually rewarding significance for the living. Somehow, it comforts the living to know that the body of his loved one is not stuck off alone somewhere, but is being "guarded" by *shomrim.* *Kriah,* the rending of the garment, and *shivah,* the strict seven-day mourning period, though formulated as commandments, are really, says Rabbi Abramowitz, "not obligations, but *limitations,* because people often want to punish themselves out of guilt, or feelings of abandonment." Similarly, the imperative of a plain wood casket and simple white shroud relieves the bereaved of any potential embarrassment for insufficiently lavish caskets or burial garb.

Thus, the traditional practices toward which Tifereth Israel has returned, far from a retreat into ritualistic mumbo-jumbo, amount to an exercise in profound realism. Here, midst the most emotionally wrought of life's events, in an area shrouded in mystery, cloaked in superstition, and grist for grade B horror movies, Jewish tradition steps in with the most mundanely unemotional prescription: This life is gone, these practices collectively say. A body remains. It will not be here for long, but while it's here, respect it enough not to pump it full of eosin dye to give it the false pretense of life. Instead, merely wash it—carefully, consciously, lovingly. Let the bereaved rest assured that it is not alone. Place the body into the simplest of shrouds and thence into the plainest of coffins, one that least pretends it is destined for anything but dust. The dead are dead. The living live. Grieve for your loved ones—but only so much and only for so long....

What a marvelous piece of hidden wisdom in this seemingly unexceptional set of practices—that these ritualized limitations on grief, this demystification of death, should give so much comfort to the living. "There was something that happened in all that," says Pearl Schainker, reliving the days and weeks after her father's death. "It was a defusing, a kind of winding down of pent-up emotions." The period just before his father-in-law's death, says her husband, was one of "a lot of mixed feelings, including those of intense anger." The period that followed, eased by the aid and comfort granted by the Tifereth Israel approach, gave it, he says, "a format for mending."

It's all well and good to speak of simple funerals and congregational responsibility for them; it's quite another to attend to the welter of details that goes with that responsibility.

"There are so many little things you have to do," says Harris Weinstein, who ought to know. Is there an adequate supply of *yarmulkes* on hand? Is that briefcase stuffed with prayer shawls and prayer books readily available? What about the black ribbon for *kriah*? And the equipment for *taharah*? And is there a place to store each? What of simply getting into the synagogue for, say, a late Sunday afternoon funeral service; where are the keys? At the very first funeral for which the Congregation took responsibility, the service was held in the synagogue itself. But what route ought the coffin take through the synagogue? How should it come in, and go out? Such things had to be decided; in that instance, they hadn't been—and so had to be settled right on the spot.

At first blush, these must seem merely tiresome chores, demeaning to a lawyer, or a physician, or high government worker—and so, yes, maybe better left to hired hands. Yet Tifereth Israel relies on its own hands—to serve as *shomrim,* to counsel the bereaved, to perform *taharah,* to make sure there are enough *yarmulkes.* "We've never," Harris Weinstein reports, "had a problem with too few people." And the surprising thing is, in attending to these sometimes grubby details, there's been a hidden payoff for the Congregation as a whole.

A clue: In the three years since adoption of its reformed funeral practices, the Congregation has suffered about a dozen deaths; about half the bereaved families have opted for the Congregation's package. Who has and who hasn't? Well, reports Rabbi Abramowitz, those who, through old family ties, sentimentally "belong" to one of the Jewish-owned funeral homes, by and large stick with them; while Congregation members new to Washington, or otherwise less firmly rooted in the city's soil, tend "to go with synagogue."

Plainly, its funeral program is a boon for those it directly serves. But in so squarely assuming responsibility for the funerals of its members—including, formally, financial responsibility—Tifereth Israel has also helped fashion a genuine community out of a northwest Washington district more than usually torn up by residential rootlessness. In this respect, says Harris Weinstein, "the congregation fulfills the role that in other communities and other times would have been filled by relatives and family."

In a real sense, one of the most fundamental lessons from the self-sufficiency movement of the Sixties, its co-ops and community organizations and collective child care centers, has been relearned: That somehow, when people *do for themselves* instead of relying on the impersonal money system to do for them, a sense of community can most organically emerge. At Tifereth Israel, the dreary and mundane details of death have been almost alchemically transmuted into community bonds that bring the living closer together.

"People did not know us, yet they did all that for us," says Pearl Schainker, still in wonder of it all two years later. People took time out from work to help them, to pray with them. "For all the people involved," she says, "I still have a special feeling." At synagogue, people *still* ask about her sister, who'd come from Boston after her father's death. And the Schainkers reciprocate. When the wife of one man who attended *minyans* for them died, they were present at the services during the shiva period. Lawrence now works on synagogue committees, has helped research traditional Jewish views on autopsy.

A sense of community "doesn't happen so readily when you're spread out geographically," Lawrence points out. He and his wife tend to be home-bodies. "We live on a street, in a town, but it often feels as though we're not part of a community there." But through their ties to the synagogue after her father's death, they "sort of precipitously established relationships with other congregation members. . . . It was a starting point. . . . And people *need* that feeling of extended family."

If he and his wife didn't have it before Louis Charnow's death, they've come far toward it since. It was, through the congregation's rediscovery of old values and old ways, his farewell gift to them both. ✱

It Matters How the Dead Are Burried

PES

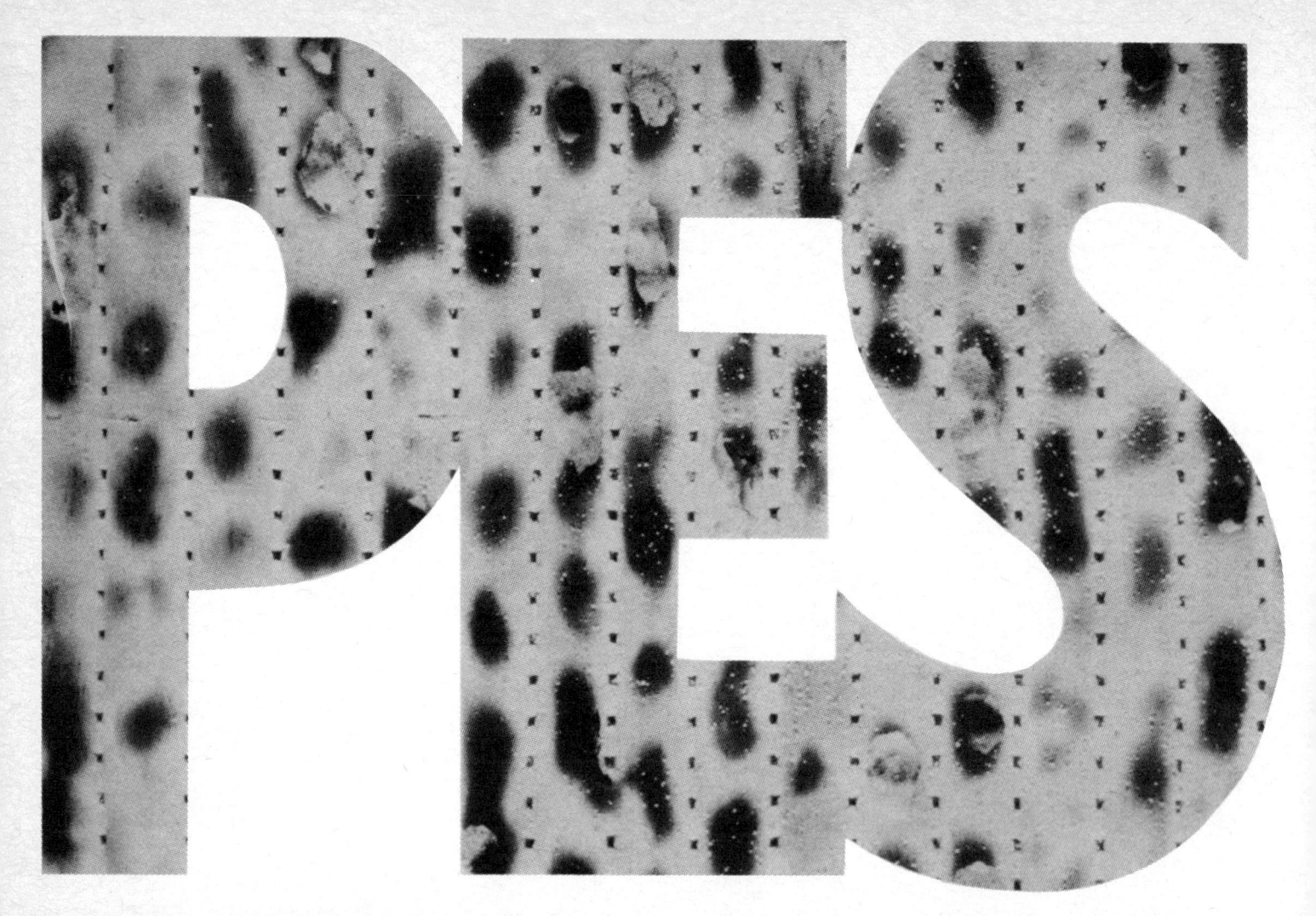

MY FATHER'S RITUAL
DANNY SIEGEL

Danny Siegel is a freelance author, lecturer, and poet living in Rockville, MD. He has published more than a dozen books of poetry, midrash *translations, humor, essays, and a book on* tzedakah *and Jewish values. He also gives readings from his works. His prose career began when* Moment, *of which he is a contributing editor, published his first article on* tzedakah— *"Gym Shoes and Irises."*

Passover in my father's household has always been a celebration of freedom and equality. Two nights a year twenty to thirty people would sit around our table and join my father in the recitation of the tale of the Jews leaving their bondage in the Land of Egypt.

From the first Seder-nights I can recall, our guests were our closest friends, plus soldiers (there was World War II, and Korea, and they were far away from home), and students at universities in the area who could not afford to go back to Missouri or Illinois or California for the holiday.... And a special element, as if Chagall or Dali or Kafka designed the scenery and script: a month before the onset of Passover, my mother would call local institutions for brain-damaged children. She would ask to come down to acquaint herself with six or seven of the children, to talk with them, to bring them things, and to tell them Passover was coming. And then, the afternoon before the first Seder, my brother and sister and I would set the tables as my parents took both cars to the institutions to bring the children back in preparation for the evening in our home.

Besides the regular guests, there were always some new faces—a rotation of doctors, a new patient of my father's who had not seen a Seder-ritual in years, perhaps the parents of a child my father had delivered in their home years before. My grandfather was there, of course, and my grandmother, until she died while I was still a teen-ager, an aunt and some cousins, a friend or two of mine, and the six or seven children.

You will say their noises disturbed the recitations. That is true.

You will say my mother was burdened enough cleaning house and

72/Moment

ACH

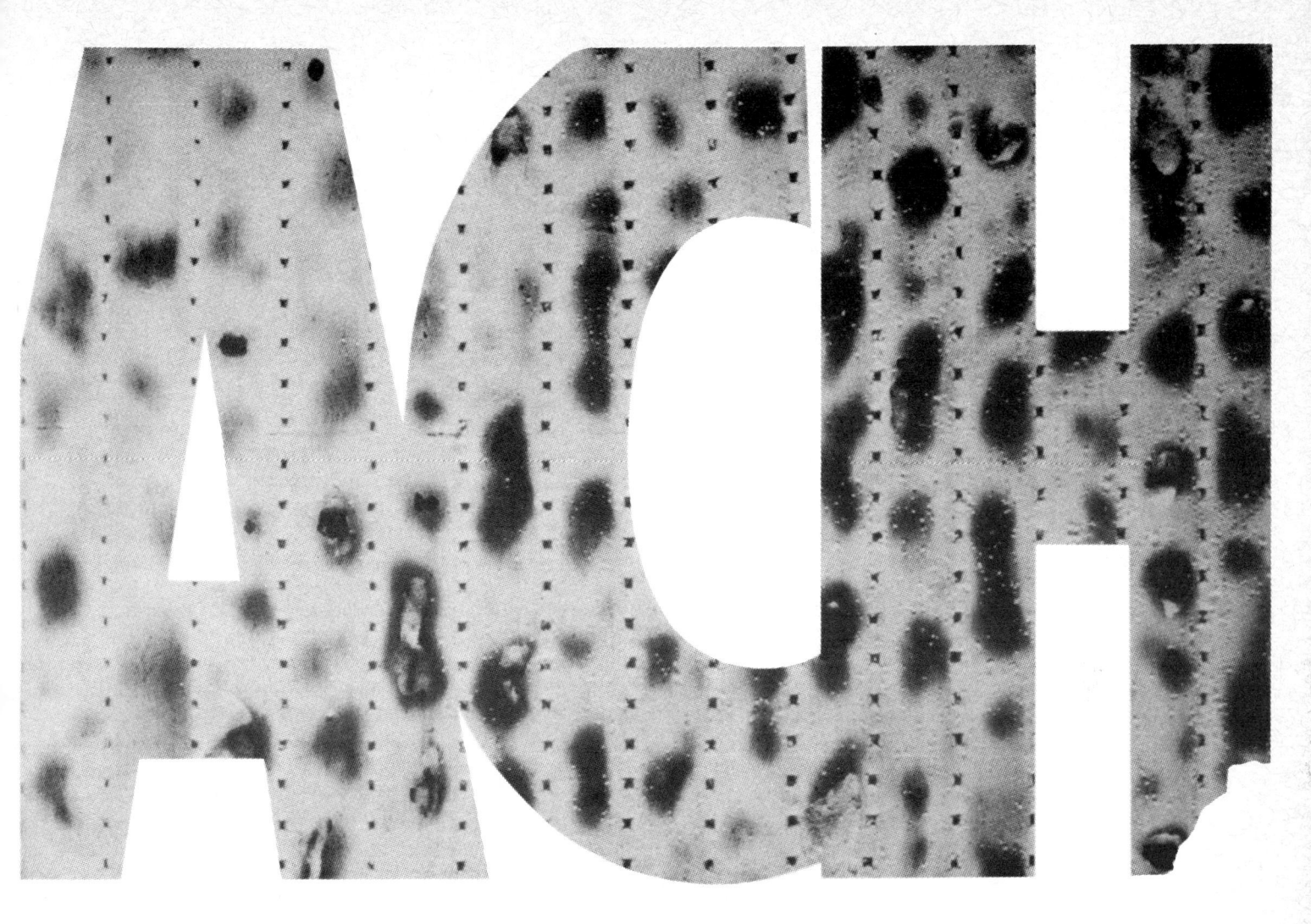

cooking the week through for fifty or sixty people. That is true.

You will say the children needed watching every minute: they would spill things, they would throw up, they might start to shout, and that, too, is true.

But next to each member of my family and in between other couples was one of these children, and each of us was charged with caring for the child, watching over all of them and treating them as best as Moses might have treated them among the masses being taken from Pharaoh's slavery—for we must assume that there were palsied and polioed children three or four thousand years ago, too. Each of us was to bring the message, however dimly perceived, to these children.

And when it came time to eat the meal itself, my father would rise in his white robe, having tasted of the food as prescribed by Jewish law, and would go from seat to seat, cutting the lamb or roast beef and spoonfeeding whoever needed to be fed in such fashion, and joking with each.

The meals would last long past midnight. The mishaps were many, and the fulfillment of the dictum "He who is hungry shall come in to eat" went slowly, for each had his own needs and peculiarities. Yet each was to be fed with the utmost care.

In our household on Passover nights, everyone felt at home, everyone was comfortable. No one winced, no one sat in silence while my father's personal ritual was performed, no one ignored or paid extra attention to what was taking place. Our guests-of-many-years knew what was to happen, and the newcomers soon learned, became momentarily uneasy, then leaned back against their pillows (as free men must have pillows on Passover night), and partook of the wonders of freedom.

The following afternoon each disease was explained to me. The names were impressive in their Latin and Greek configurations, but the symptoms and the sufferings were a terror to conceive, a travesty of creation. Nevertheless, at our table they were—these children cast off by their families—an integral part of our People, of our Greater Family, no more or less normal for their chromosomal defects and their birth-traumas, the disorders of their nervous systems and their Mongoloid features, than the doctor who fed them, their Father.

Those nights, the feeding done, the thanks recited, the singing would begin. It was a dissonant chorus resembling in my early imagination a choir of Heavenly Hosts, but with flesh and blood instead of halos, twisted words and sounds of human beings in place of the perfect harmonies of angels who need neither food nor drink, nor the affection of my father.

That is why it is better to be a human being than an angel.

A WALNU

PHYLLIS ROSE EISENBERG

Prologue

He told me later that during the ceremony he had felt handsome and free and glowing as though the sun had been shining especially for him.

I told him later that the ceremony had been just as special, just as beautiful as our traditional one of 30 years ago. I told him that 30 years ago I did not, could not comprehend what sharing a life with him could be like, and now that I did know, I felt deeply privileged.

He told me that on our wedding day everything had looked bright and clear to him and that the day had been filled with a richness and a mystery, and that he felt it all over again during *this* ceremony, this ceremony under the walnut tree in our back yard, this ceremony with no one but the two of us, and with just the sounds of squirrels crunching walnuts, and of crows cawing, and even with the thunderous zooms of motorcycles whizzing down our street, he felt it all over again—that very same richness and that very same mystery.

Once, a dozen years ago or so, during a fight concerning our only child, he raised his hand to slap me and I pushed my face deliberately close to his hand and challenged him to go ahead and hit me, half hoping he would so he'd feel guilty and I could feel self-righteous. He lowered his hand then (reluctantly, it seemed to me) but we both screamed hateful things that slapped each other's beings harder than any hand ever could. And the air between us was charged with electric barriers that stayed and stayed, for almost a week, I believe it was.

Once, long ago, he had a bad cold, or maybe it was a touch or two of flu. At the same time my pregnant friend had hurt her back and couldn't take care of her two young children and couldn't drive herself to the doctor. And so with a quick good-bye, I flew to my friend and got her to the doctor and took care of her children and made them all dinner.

When I got home, he hated me for nursing my friend and neglecting him and I hated him for his self-pity and uncharitableness and we concentrated very, very hard on our hatred. He buried his head inside of the Kleenex box and wouldn't look at me and I buried mine inside of the typewriter and wouldn't look at him. Then he blew his nose extra loud and made disgusting little moaning sounds to show how sick he was and I typed two thousand words a minute to appear properly unconcerned.

I could not say, "I thought of you today," and he could not say, "I needed you today," because we were so intent on wallowing in our martyrdom. I think that we wallowed all of that evening and maybe the next morning, too.

Once, on our honeymoon, we had ordered through room service: I, a non-drinker, had two mint juleps and he, an occasional social sipper,

---

In addition to two published books for children, A Mitzvah Is Something Special *(Harper and Row) and* Don't Tell Me A Ghost Story *(Harcourt Brace Jovanovich), Phyllis Rose Eisenberg has published many stories, poems, and essays for adults both in this country and abroad. Her work has been anthologized in the U.S. and Canada. She has developed a writing program for children that she has presented in 50 schools.*

T TREE,

had three. In the morning we found clothes on the floor near the bed and in the bathroom and the dressing room and when we looked at each other and recalled most of the delights of our joyous and rowdy stripping, we laughed so long we were much too weak to eat breakfast. (And so later we ate a lot, quite a lot, for lunch.)

About a month before our 30th anniversary, while musing over the possibility of buying new wedding bands, I said that I might not replace my old one after all and that maybe the money for buying a new one could be used for something else—for something far more practical. And he had nodded agreeably.

A day or two later I told him that I had given the subject deep thought and I confessed I had no real sentimental feelings about my old ring and that perhaps I would just put it away and wear no wedding ring at all. And again he had nodded agreeably, this time saying, "Why not?" He was so congenial that I found it unsettling and we hadn't had an argument in an awfully long time anyhow. And so I said, "Why do I need a wedding ring? I know I'm married—if I don't know it now, I'll never know it and—" He interrupted with a smile so wide and so warm and with eyes so twinkling that I could only respond with love, a rush of love that made me so breathless I even forgave him for depriving me of giving a compelling lecture on symbols, commitment, monogomy, polygamy, and family customs since Neanderthal man.

So the next day I tried on three hours' worth of rings at five differ*ent stores until I felt that the one I selected was worthy of our union.*

Once, when he was out of work far too long for anyone to be out of work and keep his sanity, he told me when he'd come home from still another fruitless job interview that he felt like killing himself. I could not cry and I could not think and I'm sure I did not breathe.

In all of those nights without days, he had never voiced this feeling aloud and now the words hung like black icicles all around us. In a while, a long while, he said, "They've all decided I'm too old. Did you know that 49 is old?" He stared down at the rug and put his head in his hands. He was being penalized for living, I thought, for to live is to grow older.

He stayed alone with his words and I stayed alone with them, too, for a hollow eternity of several minutes. Then our fingers touched lightly and his thumb nail began to lightly trace a back and forth pattern of life on my wrist—on my wrist exactly where a mosquito had bitten it the evening before. "Thanks, that feels good," I said. "You're scratching my itch—scratch harder." And he did.

But we both learned that although he had enough strength to soothe the places where mosquitoes had been, he did not have the strength for laughter, because the world had sucked that strength out of him and had left an itch that no amount of scratching could soothe for a very long time.

Once, when our son was three years old, he was sick and completely lost his appetite. He even refused his favorite of all foods, chocolate pudding, which he called "poodink."

On Wednesday the doctor had said that unless he started to eat by Friday, he would need to be hospitalized. All of that day he sat on a chair, looking frail and sad, and he could not eat and he could not smile. I reminded him often that there was lots of chocolate pudding, but he just shook his head. We read him his favorite books and told him funny stories, but he didn't seem to hear. That night we told him to be sure to call us if he got hungry, and then we stayed awake listening, listening to the silence.

On Thursday he was too weak to sit up and had to be in bed. We bought him a puppet, a funny, smiling clown puppet that held an accordian. The puppet played a tune when you wound him up and we showed our little boy how to do it. But he just looked through us as though we were not there.

On Thursday night we again told him to be sure to call us if he got hungry, and again we stayed awake listening for his call. Finally, we began to face the bleak practicalities of hospital arrangements, discussing the calls we'd need to make in the morning and deciding on the best route there, when we heard his thin voice say, "Can I have some poodink?" We raced down the hall to the kitchen and brought him two dishes of pudding, and watched him eat every last drop.

Then he said, "Can I see that puppet?" and we got it and he wound it up and then watched in amazement as we danced around his room wearing expressions that matched the clown's. He laughed so

A GLASS

hard and he laughed so long that he soon laughed himself to sleep. We watched him a while, then kissed his pale face and then kissed each other.

We took the puppet into the living room and danced until we were very tired. And then he said, "Do you know what would be an appropriate celebration?"

And I said, "Yes, but do you know it's 4 o'clock in the morning?"

He said, "I know."

So we each ate a serving of poodink and then we each ate another and nothing that we have eaten since then has tasted so sublimely delicious nor has looked so joyfully festive.

Once, some years ago, he sulked on the sofa for what seemed like hours after an argument that had all of the grimness of a life-death crisis, but probably concerned lost theater tickets or no gas in the car because a few weeks later we couldn't remember the cause of it at all.

When I talked to him, he didn't respond and he looked through me like a piece of cellophane. And when I asked him specific questions, he answered in monosyllables that seemed to be arising out of some distant Egyptian sphinx. And I began to feel very sad and very far away from him and very guilty for making him feel so weak he could barely make an understandable sound.

But later, when he perked up and talked of routine things, I focused all of my attention on the walls and light fixtures and dishes to prove to us both I was blotting him out of my consciousness. I noticed (out of the corner of my eye) that he looked very sad and very far away from me and very guilty.

That night he whispered in a hug, "I'm sorry," but I wasn't sure who the victim was so I said, "What did *you* do? Why do *you* need to be sorry?" But he could not speak, so we moved our bodies closer together. The warmth of him made me sure that *he* was the victim so I said, "I'm the one who's sorry."

"What did you do?" he asked. "Why do *you* need to be sorry?" But I could not speak.

Slowly, magically, rhythmically, the sweetness of kisses and the perfect fit of us absorbed all of the harshness of the day's suffering.

In the morning, as I made the bed, I reminded myself that incidents like yesterday's might happen again, since no marriage is without discord, but since we cared for one another so deeply, never, never ever again, need future tiffs (I called yesterday's battle-in-a-tomb, a "tiff") be so devastating. I smiled as I thought that and reminded myself that I must remember it forever. But the sun was shining and the birds were chirping and I still felt warmed by his body, and so by the very next day I completely forgot what it was that I had decided to remember forever.

A few days before our 30th anniversary, we planned to have our ceremony in the yard immediately after Saturday's breakfast. For a year now, each Saturday and Sunday, we have had onion bagels and cream cheese and coffee on a card table in our back yard. It is a time we look forward to. We read the paper or watch a hummingbird (if we're lucky) or we sit dreamily in happy silence. And so, for a special treat to mark this occasion, I had bought a surprise: four slices of lox. (At $7.00 a pound, that amount just fit our purse.)

When Saturday came, there was such excitement over the piece de resistance (which we hadn't had in years and so now tasted ultra-exotic) that we didn't even remember we'd forgotten the ceremony until the next morning.

The next morning the aroma of heated bagels and fresh coffee and the sight of rich cream cheese made him remember Saturday's treat and he said that he now felt totally addicted to it and was suffering such horrendous withdrawal symptoms that he was finding it extremely difficult to digest this sub-standard meal. This announcement precipitated a decidedly fast-paced discussion on feelings of deprivation in certain eccentric individuals.

The topic was so provocative, we forgot all about the ceremony once again . . . until that afternoon.

That afternoon, we made long and exquisite and exciting love and we felt very new and very young and so we knew then that our ceremony would be quite soon. We showered and dressed in our ceremony clothes—he in a yellow sport shirt and green pants and sneakers and I in a green blouse and tan skirt and sandals. We looked at one another admiringly for we knew that we saw that we were both shining, as though these everyday clothes had been chosen and custom made months and months ago, waiting for this very moment.

During the little walk from our back door to the walnut tree, I noticed that he was carrying a single glass of wine. "Where's mine?" I

OF WINE,

said, ready to be slighted. He shook his head, just the tiniest bit and I was relieved that I understood the unspoken message, lest the ceremony be postponed once again due to a tiff born of my greed. One glass of wine to share, his almost imperceptible nod had said. One glass to share as we have shared serenity and chaos, joy and pain, love and hate. One glass for the two of us, of course.

Once, on a weekend vacation, our idle conversation began to focus on puns—not just any puns, but those words specifically referring to vegetables. It began innocently at lunchtime with "You're zo keeny," and "I carrot for you," and moved through the lazy afternoon to "Don't turnup your nose at this one" and "the water is cold as rice." At dinner we almost choked over "Peas pass the butter" and in the middle of the night it was vital to shake him awake with "Lettuce have another go at it." He proved his allegiance with a sleepy but cheery, "I corn hardly wait."

Within seconds our guffaws caused our neighbor to shrilly suggest that we "knock it off" and "lay off the booze" and "fercrysakes lemme sleep." We stayed silent for almost a minute until he said, in an admirably moderate tone, "I yam tired of this whole thing." For the rest of the night no vegetable or fruit, no cereal or meat, no fish or fowl or condiment or sweet was exempt from our word degradation and in between snorts to steady our hysteria and stuffing sheets into our mouths in deference to our insomniac neighbor, we flew to the bathroom and urinated with such force and with such frequency, that if it were not for our total dedication to sound health habits, our dehydration and fatigue might have left us too weak for breakfast.

Once, when his mother had been a living corpse for 63 weeks, we wept in her empty apartment for the injustice of life, because his mother had been devout and cheerful and had cared for the sick and had obeyed all of His laws. And now for her there was only pain; only pain and pain and pain.

We walked into the kitchen where she had cooked countless meals and we sat on her sofa and touched the doilies she had crocheted. And he began to sob, softly at first, then louder and louder, because the mother that he knew was now someone else, a suffering ghost who begged for peace and was denied it.

We prayed silently together for the cessation of her pain and we prayed silently for the continuance of our strength so we could comfort her in whatever small ways and could comfort each other in ways very big. After we prayed and after we embraced our tears seemed to flow from one pair of eyes.

Once, not long ago, the newspaper announced that the community was invited to join college students on a desert nature walk. We accepted the invitation and learned that we alone were the entire community.

The students were bright eyed and fresh faced and dressed in sandy jeans and sandy sweat shirts and sandy desert boots and they were up to their chins in zoology books and pressed leaves and pressed flowers and portfolios.

The community had on their new matching plaid jackets (devoid of any desert color) and a baseball hat (full of character) to protect his mole-prone scalp and a pure silk handkerchief to protect her just-set hair. They carried binoculars (to outsmart sneaky mirages) and cameras (because the National Geographic couldn't know *everything*) and a huge straw bag, bursting with miscellaneous that included all of her charge plates, because who knew what department stores might be lurking behind some high-rise tumbleweed.

"Notice the leaves on the Hesperocallis Unduleta," said the bright eyed, fresh faced, desert-clad professor, as he squatted down near some Hesperocallis Unduleta.

"Oh, wow! Hesperocallis Unduleta!" exclaimed the class, examining them carefully and taking notes and drawing drawings at a feverish pace.

"What's all the fuss?" I whispered to the community. "All I see are four itsy yellow flowers."

He crouched down with the others. "Five," he said smugly.

"And over here," said the professor, "are Rafinesquia Californica—illustrated on page 572."

"Oh! Rafinesquia Californica!" said the class, buzzing like 1000 queen bees at a coronation.

"All I see are six itsy pinkish flowers," I said to the community.

"Six is right," he said quickly, because it was safer to agree than to join the class again and risk a charlie horse.

Later, when the class moved on to some thriving Argemone Platyceras, we moved on to the shade of a deformed yucca tree.

Walnut Tree, A Glass of Wine, and Thou

AND THOU

"I don't think I learned anything," I said. "Did you learn anything?"

"Yes," he said. "I learned that five itsy yellow flowers and six itsy pinkish ones are native to this desert. Also, I noticed two itsy baby blue ones behind a rock, but I refrained from announcing it so as not to usurp the professor's position."

"I admire your humility."

"Me, too. Furthermore, I learned that community spirit is a beautiful thing."

"Hey, let's drink to that," I said, taking warm beer out of the bag, "and eat to that, too." And we had turkey sandwiches, swiss cheese, sweet pickles, lots of macadamia nuts and only one nectarine each because we were counting calories.

Once, when I had an eye injury, a sudden stab of pain made me scream out in the middle of the night. And then, just as suddenly, he began to shout that I had chosen the wrong doctor and that I always did things like that and what was wrong with me anyhow?

I ran from the room sobbing, and long, long after the physical pain had left and he had gone to work, I clutched the pain of his words to me and wouldn't let go of them all day so that my contempt would slice him into a trillion shreds when he came home.

When he came home, he knelt by the bedside and in a strained, halting way, as though each word pierced his throat, he told me that my screams had terrified him beyond reason. I quickly added, "Beyond *any* reason," to emphasize that there could never be pardoning from this crime. He lowered his eyes. "I felt so helpless," he said, "so frightened for you—it even flashed through my mind that you might lose your sight and that I couldn't do anything to help you . . . do you understand?"

"No," I said. "It hurt too much to understand, and I *still* don't understand."

His strained tone became an almost raspy whisper. "It was easier for me to be angry than to tell you . . . I was afraid." He reached for me and kissed my lips, my cheeks, and then tenderly, oh so tenderly, he kissed the brow just above my injured eye. And I began to weep. I wept for myself and I wept for him and finally I wept for all of the people in the world who are unable to respond humanly, lest they be accused of being human.

On the afternoon of our ceremony, underneath the walnut tree, we stood together ready to recite our unwritten vows. But despite all of our planning and despite the absence of any guests, save the squirrels and the crows, and despite our long years of knowledge of one another, we became suddenly self-conscious, so when he spoke, he mimicked an actor he was expert at mimicking. But then I guess my look revealed that I needed him and so he became himself and said something about the year ahead, and I don't remember what he said but it didn't matter because his eyes and his gentle mouth told me, in an indelible shock of recognition, what commitment really was, and I felt it in the center of me—I felt it like a rainbow almost too beautiful to view. And then my shoulders began to sob and the rest of me did, too, because I was only prepared for a pleasant experience out there under the tree, just a gentle little ritual to remind us of a day long ago. I was not prepared for breathtaking rainbows—not prepared at all.

When he finished his part of the ceremony, I buried my head in his shirt and cried that I didn't know what to say and I was ashamed. He gently pulled me away from him and said softly, so that only I could hear, "Just keep it simple." And so I did. I kept it very simple.

Then we put the rings on one another's fingers and sipped the wine until the glass was drained. And then we went into the house because it was getting on towards dinner and we were hungry—very hungry because strange as it seems, we had forgotten to eat lunch. ✦

ANNETTE HENKIN LANDAU

"YOUR MOTHER," THE SOCIAL WORKER SAYS, "IS HAVING SOME TROUBLE ADJUSTING."

The nurse telephones. She has fallen out of bed again, my imperious mother. "I can't manage her no more, mizz," the nurse says, forgetting my name as she always does. "She gettin' too heavy for me, I got to get a policeman heist her back." Her voice sighs professionally. She is not really a nurse, Social Service sends her.

Poor Lily, flopping out of her nightgown in front of a strange policeman, she must have hated that.

Someone has to talk to her, she cannot stay in her apartment any more. Social Service says that she has exhausted the skills of domestic aides. She should be in a nursing home.

The words shock me. I think of her still as competent, demanding, her walk brusque, her voice authoritative. We have an extra room, I say tentatively.

Social Service frowns. I have a teenage daughter. She has friends, a stereo, they smoke pot. You think your mother could handle that? Could your daughter?

I am thinking about it.

I have a job, I worked hard to get it, a master's degree, three credits at a time, ninety dollars a point. You want to give up your job to take care of your mother, is that what you really want?

To race up the stairs at Lily's command, carrying bedpans, wringing my hands raw, screaming at my husband, blaming my child. Is that what I really want? Yes.

Annette Henkin Landau is a reference librarian and freelance writer, whose work last appeared in Commentary, *February 1977.*

Guilt, says Social Service, shaking her head in reproof. My mother is senile. Incontinent.

I don't believe it. Such a literary word, incontinent. It makes me think of Lily's life, her drive, her pushy ways, her obsession with the school. The gutsiness of her, a bookkeeper with a high school diploma, she made herself into an authority. A pioneer in early childhood education. Her school one of the first in the city, still cited in the literature. She saw the need for it. Also the money.

And Sidney, my father, the school set him free to find his fortune in a multitude of imaginative businesses, chocolate covered popcorn, synthetic heels that explode in the summer heat, every gamble beginning with high enthusiasm (the chance of a lifetime!) and ending in disillusion (the partner turned out to be a bastard). Lily kept the school money separate from my father's business, a point of bitterness between them.

A pioneer without credentials, the State Education Department is always after her. A professional director has to front for her. But Lily is the personage, the one the parents trust. She fills up on books and articles, writes papers for conferences, reads them before professionals in her brash downtown accent. Lily is the one who never hears me, she is so busy worrying about other people's children.

She sends me to college to get the credentials. With a B.A. from Barnard and a Master's from Teachers I can keep the director's salary in the family. I will always be there to front for her, she never has to give up the school. A practical plan.

I betray her. I don't take education courses. Secretly I major in French, by the time Lily finds out it is too late. She wants to kill me. Raging through the upstairs of our house (downstairs the school is going on), her wrath is ungovernable. She berates me, insults me, calls me her enemy, calls me a bum, vows to throw me out into the street, hits me across the face.

Incontinent. Senile. Magic words to make you vanish.... They really mean peeing.

I visit Lily's doctor. I want to do the right thing, I say. Tell me what to do.

The doctor is an Israeli. He wears sharp denim leisure suits, his mouth turns down at the corners. "Do," he says. "Who knows the right thing to do? To die in your own house, that's the right thing to do. Who accomplishes this? Sometimes a daughter she takes care of the mother, she drives herself crazy, also the husband. The mother dies she feels better, she did the right thing. *Meshuggenah* daughters."

Double messages.

I don't need his Israeli irony. He doesn't need my American ambivalence.

I call my brother in Chicago. First he tells me his troubles. His ex-wife, my ex-sister-in-law, has been bothering him. She wants to send the four children to camp so she can have the summer free. She is studying bio-rhythms. My present sister-in-law's ex-husband is also bothering him. He wants my brother to be a better male image for his two sons. The youngest

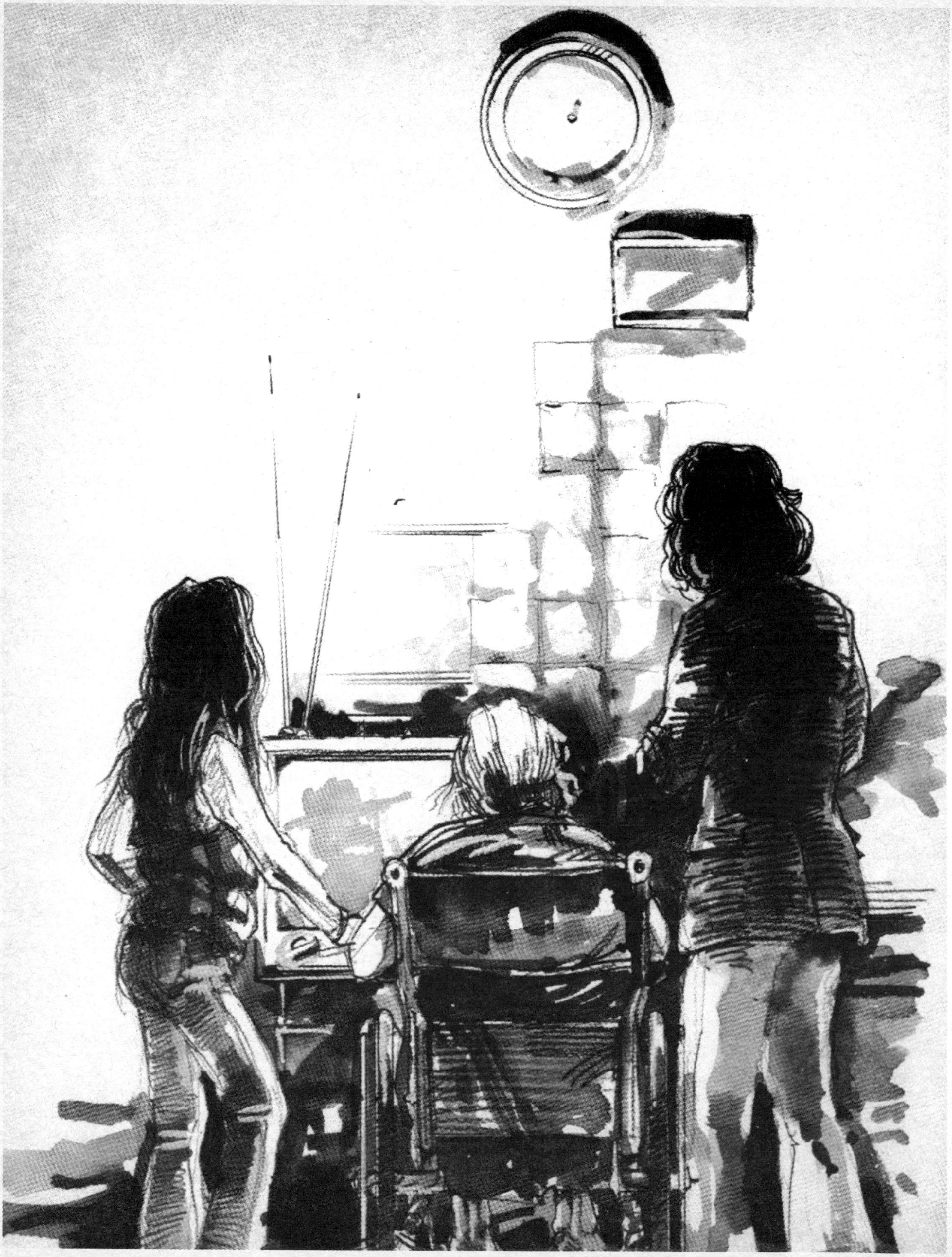

child, the one they have between them, is asthmatic. "What should we do about Lily," I say.

Through the telephone he shrugs. "Baby, do what you want," he says. "I can't spare any money for private nurses, I got alimony, child support, doctor's bills. I'm up to my butt in psychiatrists."

You could come and tell her she has to be in a nursing home. She would take it better from you.

No go. He gives me to understand that I am trying to fob my obligations off on him. Angry, I hang up. Now he is having trouble with me.

In the end the dirty job falls to my husband. It is easier for him, he is less involved. In later years she thinks better of him, she forgives him for marrying me. Whatever is past is past, she says.

She will not forgive him any more.

We visit the geriatric center, the best in the country, they tell us. It is on the grounds of a famous Jewish hospital. Once it was the Home of the Children of Abraham on Eastern Parkway in Brooklyn, now it has a secular name. All the venerable Children, they packed them up one day and moved them to the suburbs. The building is massive, stressed concrete, bulging and curving and rippling into balconies, shadowy gray glass slitting dense walls. No expense has been spared, the building has won an award. In the lobby a marble plaque honors the donors. All important people, I recognize the names.

The Supervisor gives the tour at a measured pace, stopping nowhere, drawing attention with discreet social worker gestures to the muted lighting, thick carpets, wide corridors, gliding elevators. The occupants are invisible, it is rest time, but each room has a balcony and a private bath. Here is the occupational therapy room, does Mother like to crochet? And this is the auditorium where we have many programs for Friends of the Center, we hope you will join.

On the bulletin board is a notice. A famous sex therapist is giving a lecture on Thursday evening: Beyond Sensuality.

At the rear of the lobby is a place where the architect has solved a problem in aesthetics. What to do with the accumulation of bronze memorial plaques that were gathered from the walls and doors and beds of the home on Eastern Parkway. The architect has fastened them to rods and hung them at different heights from the ceiling, sharp, spiky, unreadable as stalactites. A holocaust landscape. Fortunately, it is dark and nobody goes in there.

Lily is in the geriatric center three hours and she is giving orders to take her home. She has not forgotten how to give orders, but she does not know what to do when nobody takes them. They smile and humor her. Later, later, mama, she is told.

Her eyes are wild, she rages at me. "Why are you letting them do this," she says. "To take me out of my beautiful apartment and put me in a place like this?"

"It's a nice room, Mom." My voice chokes.

A sweeping contemptuous arm is my answer.

"It's a nice room. It has a balcony, a *loggia* like in *The Magic Mountain,* you remember?"

I hate myself. I am humoring her too.

She spits at me. "You think I don't know what you're doing," she says in her old principal's voice. "At my funeral you want them to say what a wonderful daughter you were you put me in a place like this."

Angry tears sting my eyes. I go into the corridor. Six television sets are on, two have no sound and one is flopping. The wheelchairs are drawn up in front of them, heads are sunk on chests. Only the young black aides watch the programs, interrupting their gossip to cheer as a contestant races down the aisle to claim a refrigerator. An old man plucks at me and grimaces like a conspirator. *"Tochter,"* he whispers hoarsely, "help me, get me out of here." I run down the corridor. In the distance I see two aides in white uniforms. One of them is trying on a blonde wig, the other is screaming with laughter.

I return to Lily's room. I am still angry with her. Lily is dying and I am still angry with her. Her eyes gleam shrewdly, she has a trump card. "Sidney wants me to come home," she says, "he can't manage without me."

My father. He made her a widow at fifty. Now, in her age, he has become the prince of her dreams.

They assign a Social Worker. To Help Me Deal With The Trauma. She is a middle-aged woman back in the job market, like myself. She is pretty, her dark eyes brim with sympathy, her head nods in perpetual acquiescence. "Tell me about Mother," she says.

It is not easy. I open my mouth hopefully and something comes out. When my mother was fourteen, I tell her, she won first prize in an essay contest for all the children of the City of New York. The subject was Citizenship. And the First Prize goes to—Lily Gottlieb, Washington Irving High School. The Mayor of New York himself hung the medal around her neck to thunderous applause.

My Lily was the smartest girl in New York, said my grandmother as she lay dying. The Mayor of New York wanted to marry her, but she didn't love him. She loved instead an Italian on the boat coming over, for three weeks throwing up in his lap.

Lily, sitting beside her mother's hospital bed, laughs tearfully. "Make me a promise," she says to me. "Don't let me get crazy like this. Shoot me first."

I stare at my mother. Can I make such a promise? I am only fifteen. She puts her head down on the hospital bed, her tears fall on my grandmother's hand. "What are you crying," says my grandmother, "I lived enough already."

"I'm not crying for you, Ma," says Lily.

"Your mother," the Social Worker says, "is having some difficulty adjusting. Tell me what she liked to do before she came here."

I don't know what to say. They're going to give her a school to run, accounts to go over, parents to consult with? She held on to the school too long, then she sold it. There was nothing else to do, I had surrendered my birthright. When she retired she read a lot of novels she had missed, but she didn't like them. She traveled and met somebody who wanted to marry her, but she scoffed at the idea. What did she like to do? Sometimes she liked to listen to music, thinking of the time she had an opera subscription. "Oh fine," says the Social Worker, relieved that I have remembered something.

They wheel her chair into a large open area, soft blue carpet, dusky lights. A white haired woman with a Viennese accent is playing an accordion and singing into a microphone. She sings "I'm Just Wild About Harry" and "The World Is Waiting for the Sunrise." All together now, she says, efferybody join in. She sings "Bei Mir Bist Du Scheyn." Some of the wheelchair audience are obedient, they wave handkerchiefs. The rest pay no attention.

Junk, says my mother as they wheel her away, junk.

There is a Family Conference for the children of the residents. We meet with the Staff in the Board Room, around a rosewood directors' table. Coffee is served in styrofoam cups. We are encouraged to say what is on our minds, the Staff appreciates our difficulties. I look around the table. We have the eyes of cancer patients. Stricken people.

A tall man speaks. He has a small distinguished paunch, he looks like a lawyer. "All I can say," he begins in a tight, cultivated voice, "is that I brought my father here a fine, alert gentleman. He liked a little brandy, a good book, a card game. The only problem was his legs, he couldn't get around. And now. And now."

His voice gives way and his face collapses into his hands. He shakes his head, he doesn't want to go on.

A thin blonde woman says in a worried voice that she can't understand why everything is so dim. Maybe a little color, a few posters? To cheer things up.

The Supervisor is pleased to explain that point. Research has demonstrated that older people prefer muted colors.

On the way down in the elevator I stand near the man who broke down. Our eyes meet. My mother, I start to say, but the elevator doors open and he leaves.

My mother was a woman of accomplishment, I was going to say.

How does Lily look, her few old friends whisper. Frail and fearful, they do not dare to visit her. How does she look? I do not dare to tell them. She looks furious, her eyes glare with helpless anger. She tells the aides who she is, what she wants them to do, how they are to run the school. The sweet ones smile at her, the careless ones ignore her. She is not in charge. She is fighting on unknown terrain. She has no credentials. She is losing.

She wants to go to the bathroom. I ring for the aide. Nobody comes. She becomes desperate and I try to help her off the bed. She is too heavy for me, her fat old legs don't work any more. "Hurry," she gasps. I rush to the bathroom, find the bedpan and try to put it beneath her. I am too late. Water is running down between her legs. The bed is wet.

The aide comes in and stares at the wet bed with flat expressionless eyes. Out of the generations a word comes to Lily, crossing the ocean, fighting through thickets of English. It has a history, this word. *"Schmeer,"* croaks Lily frantically, *schmeer.*

I search my pocketbook and find a five dollar bill. I push it into the hand of the aide. She takes a folded sheet and wedges it under Lily. "Goin' home now," she says, "she do it on the next shift."

I complain of this in Family Conference. The Social Worker scolds me. "You must not bribe," she says. "If you bribe you start a situation that we cannot control."

I complain of the quality of the aides. Black teenagers racing through the halls, laughing raucously, treating their patients with indifference or contempt. We are turning our parents over to their enemies, I cry bitterly, stung as I am by the charges of bribery.

The Supervisor looks at me coldly. For a moment I think she is going to lose her professional decorum. Jewish teenagers don't seem to want these jobs, she says at last, with a minimum of irony.

I yell at my daughter. "Go visit your grandmother. How can you be so selfish?" Her lip trembles. "What are you yelling at me for? She doesn't remember me. Last time I went she thought I was someone named Margo."

Margo. The director who fronted for her.

We cry in each other's arms. My daughter strokes my shoulder awkwardly. I apologize to her. My most feeling, tender-hearted child.

I need her, so she comes with me. We find Lily in the corridor, tied into her wheelchair in front of the television set, her head slumped on her chest. Somebody has tried to pin her hair flat, but it frizzes wildly, gray and kinky, with its own stubborn will. Years ago she used to have it straightened.

"Grandma," says my gentle daughter, touching Lily's hair. Lily will not raise her head.

We sit in front of the television set. The sound is off. Two old movie stars, wetlipped and openmouthed, are embracing. One died of a brain tumor. The other O.D.'d. Finis. "Grandma," says my daughter, leaning over the wheelchair, the movie is over.

Troubled eyes in Lily's young face, taffy colored hair in a splendid Jewish Afro. Lily in a photograph, her chin high, white pleated skirt blowing across slim ankles, on the handsome granite steps of Pennsylvania Station. She is laughing, her arm raised to keep her straw hat from blowing away, the smartest girl in the City of New York, starting on her honeymoon.

Make me a promise. ◆

JACOB SCHIFF AND MY UNCLE BEN DAYNOVSKY

Calvin Trillin

"The silk-hat banker Jacob Schiff, concerned about the conditions on the East Side of New York (and embarrassed by the image it created for New York's German Jews), pledged half a million dollars in 1906 to the Galveston Project, which helped direct more than ten thousand East European migrants through Galveston into the South and Southeast."

. . . *The Provincials:
A History of Jews in the South,*
by Eli N. Evans

Calvin Trillin is a staff writer at THE NEW YORKER, *where he writes a series of reporting pieces called "U.S. Journal." His most recent book is* AMERICAN FRIED, *published by Doubleday.*

And who is Jacob Schiff that he should be embarrassed by my Uncle Ben Daynovsky? My father's family certainly came to Missouri from Eastern Europe around 1908 via the port of Galveston, and, I'll admit, that route struck me as rather odd every time we read in history class about how all the tired, poor, huddled masses swarmed into this country through Ellis Island. It never occured to me, though, to explain it all by assuming that Jacob Schiff found my family not only tired and poor and huddled but also embarrassing. I always considered the Galveston passage to be one of those eccentricities of ancestral history that require no explanation — the kind of incident we hear about so often from people who have family trees concocted for themselves by wily English genealogists ("For some reason, the old boy showed up late for the Battle of Hastings and therefore survived to father the first Duke, and that's why we're here to tell the tale.") I have always been content — pleased, really — to say simply that my grandfather (Uncle Ben's brother-in-law) happened to land in Galveston and thus made his way up the river (more or less) to St. Joseph, Missouri, leaving only sixty miles or so for my father to travel in order to complete what I had always assumed to be one of the few Kiev–Galveston–St. Jo–Kansas City immigration patterns in the Greater Kansas City area.

To be absolutely truthful, it occured to me more than once that my grandfather and Uncle Ben might have caught the wrong boat. I have never heard my mother's views on the subject, but I have always assumed that she would believe that the use by my father's family of a port no one else seemed to be using had something to do with the stubborness for which they retain a local renown in St. Jo. As I imagine my mother's imagining it, my grandfather would have fallen into an argument with some other resident of Kiev (or *near* Kiev, as it was always described to me, leading me to believe as a child that they came from the suburbs) about where immigrants land in the United States. The other man said Ellis Island; my grandfather said Texas. When the time came to emigrate, my grandfather went fifteen hundred miles out of his way in order to avoid admitting that he was wrong. My grandfather died before I was born, but my Uncle Ben is still living in St. Jo; he has lived there for sixty or seventy years now, without, I hasten to say, a hint of scandal. Stubborn, O.K. But I simply can't understand how anyone could consider him embarrassing.

"Who is Jacob Schiff that he should be embarrassed by my Uncle Ben Daynovsky?" I said to my wife when I read about the Galveston Project in *The Provincials*.

"You shouldn't take it personally," my wife said.

"I'm not taking it personally; I'm taking it for my Uncle Ben," I said. "Unless you think that Jacob Schiff's descendants are embarrassed by my moving to New York instead of staying in our assigned area."

"I'm sure Jacob Schiff's descendants don't know anything about this," my wife said.

.... that he should be embarrassed by my Uncle Ben Daynovsky (left)?"

"And who are they that they should be embarrassed by my Uncle Ben Daynovsky?" I said. "A bunch of stockbrokers."

"I think the Schiffs are investment bankers," my wife said.

"You can say what you want to about my Uncle Ben," I said, "but he never made his living as a moneylender."

I'm not quite sure how my Uncle Ben did make his living; I always thought of him as retired. As a child, I often saw him during Sunday trips to St. Jo — trips so monopolized by visits to my father's relatives that I always assumed St. Jo was known for being populated almost entirely by Eastern European immigrants, although I have since learned that it had a collateral fame as the home of the Pony Express.

Until a few years ago, Uncle Ben was known for the tomatoes he grew in his backyard and pickled, but I'm certain he never produced them commercially. A few years ago, when he was already in his eighties and definitely retired, Uncle Ben was in his backyard planting tomatoes when a woman lost control of her car a couple of blocks behind his house. The car went down a hill, through a stop sign, over a meridian strip, through a hedge, and into a backyard two houses down from Uncle Ben's house. Then it took a sharp right turn, crossed the two backyards, and knocked down my Uncle Ben. It took Uncle Ben several weeks to recover from his physical injuries, and even then, I think, he continued to be troubled by the implications of that sharp right turn. One of his sons, my cousin Iz, brought Uncle Ben back from the hospital and said, "Pop, do me a favor: next time you're in the backyard planting tomatoes, keep an eye out for the traffic."

"First that car makes a mysterious right turn and now he's being attacked by a gang of stockbrokers," I said. "It hardly seems fair."

"There's something very interesting about the Schiffs listed in *Who's Who*," I said to my wife not long after our first conversation about the Galveston Project.

"I think you'd better find yourself a hobby," she said.

"As a matter of fact, I'm thinking about taking up genealogy," I said. "But listen to what's very interesting about the Schiffs listed in *Who's Who*: the Schiffs who sound as if they're

I always considered the Galveston passage to be one of those eccentricities of ancestral history ... It never occurred to me, though, to explain it all by assuming that Jacob Schiff found my family not only tired and poor and huddled but also embarrassing.

descendants of Jacob Schiff seem to be outnumbered by some Schiffs who were born in Lithuania and now manufacture shoes in Cleveland."

"What's so interesting about that?"

"Well, if Jacob Schiff thought people from Kiev were embarrassing, you can imagine how embarrassed he must have been by people from Lithuania."

"What's the matter with people from Lithuania?" she said.

"I'm not sure, but my mother's mother was from Lithuania and my father always implied that it was nothing to be proud of," I said. "He always said she had an odd accent in Yiddish. I'm sure he must have been right, because she had an odd accent in English. Anyway, *Who's Who* has more Lithuanian Schiffs than German Schiffs, even if you count Dorothy Schiff."

"Why shouldn't you count Dorothy Schiff?" my wife said. "Isn't she the publisher of the New York *Post?*"

"Yes, but why is it that she is publisher of the New York *Post?*"

"Well, I suppose for the same reason anybody is the publisher of any paper," my wife said. "She had enough money to buy it."

"Only partly true," I said. "She is the publisher of the New York *Post* because several years ago, during one of the big newspaper strikes, she

84/Moment

Jewish Possibilities: The Best of Moment

When I told her that Schiff used to charge people who made telephone calls from his mansion—local calls; I wouldn't argue about long distance—she said that rich people were bound to be sensitive about being taken advantage of.

finked on the other publishers in the New York Publishers Association, settled with the union separately, and therefore saw to it that the *Post* survived, giving her something to be publisher of."

"Since when did you become such a big defender of the New York Publishers Association?" my wife said.

"My Uncle Ben Daynovsky never finked on anybody," I said.

"Maybe that passage in *The Provincials* was wrong," my wife said when she came into the living room one evening and found me reading intently. "Maybe Schiff gave the money to the Galveston Project just because he wanted to help people like your grandfather get settled."

"I'm glad you brought that up, because I happen to be consulting another source," I said, holding up the book I was reading so that she could see it was *Our Crowd*, which I had checked out of the library that day with the thought of finding some dirt on Jacob Schiff. "Here's an interesting passage in this book about some of the German-Jewish charity on the Lower East Side: 'Money was given largely but grudgingly, not out of the great religious principle of *tz'dakah*, or charity on its highest plane, given out of pure loving kindness, but out of a hard, bitter sense of resentment, and embarrassment and worry over what the neighbors would think.'"

"I don't see what you hope to gain by finding out unpleasant things about Jacob Schiff," she said.

"Historical perspective," I said, continuing to flip back and forth between the Jacob Schiff entry in the index and the pages indicated. "Did you know, by the way, that Schiff had a heavy German accent? I suppose when it came time to deal with the threat of my Uncle Ben, he said something like, 'Zend him to Galveston. Zum of dese foreigners iss embarrassink.'"

"I never heard you make fun of anybody's accent before," my wife said.

"They started it."

"My Uncle Ben never associated with robber barons like Gould and Harriman," I said to my wife a few days later. "When it comes to nineteenth century rapacious capitalism, my family's hands are clean."

My wife didn't say anything. I had begun thinking that it was important that she share my views of Jacob Schiff, but she was hard to convince. She didn't seem shocked at all when I informed her, from my research in *Our Crowd*, that Schiff had a private Pullman car, something that anyone in my family would have considered ostentatious. When I told her that Schiff used to charge people who made telephone calls from his mansion — local calls; I wouldn't argue about long distance — she said that rich people were bound to be sensitive about being taken advantage of. "One time, he was called upon to give a toast to the Emperor of Japan, and he said, 'First in war, first in peace, first in the hearts of his countrymen,'" I said.

"It's always hard to know what to say to foreigners," she said.

"What about the checks?" I said one evening.

"What checks?" she said.

"The checks Schiff had framed on the wall of his office," I said.

"I can't believe he had checks

Photo/ N. Y. Public Library

"And who is Jacob Schiff.... (above)

framed on the wall of his office," my wife said.

"I refer you to page one hundred fifty-nine of *Our Crowd*," I said. "Schiff had made two particularly large advances to the Pennsylvania Railroad, and he had the cancelled checks framed on his wall."

"Did he really?" she said, showing some interest.

"One of them was for $49,098,000," I said.

"That is kind of crude," she said.

"Not as crude as the other one," I said. "It was for $62,075,000."

"I think that's rather embarrassing," she said.

"I would say so," I said, putting away the book. "I just hope that no one in St. Jo hears about it. My Uncle Ben would be mortified." ✦

Jacob Schiff and My Uncle Ben Daynovsky

PERSPECTIVE

AN EXTRA PAIR OF T'FILLIN

JOEL GROSSMAN

It was a *bris* (circumcision) in Fargo that first brought Reb Itzikel to the Jorgensens. He had been sitting in his tiny synagogue checking a pair of *t'fillin* when Charlie Cohen rushed in breathlessly: "It's a boy!" shouted Charlie, whose wife had been expecting any day now for weeks. Reb Itzikel spoke only two words to Charlie: *"Mazel tov."* To his wife he spoke only one: "Pack!"

While his wife was preparing food and clothing for the trip to Fargo, Reb Itzikel quickly finished checking the *t'fillin*. Convinced of their purity, he threw them and several other pairs into the saddlebags. It had taken Charlie three days to reach Grand Forks, and if the *bris* was to be performed on the eighth day they would have to hurry. Reb Itzikel opened his file box of maps and began to pore over one with Talmudic intensity.

"Look Charlie," he said, pointing. "If we cut through this farm here we can save maybe two days."

"But Rebbe," Charlie answered, "I thought you liked staying only by Jews. To go this way we'd have to stay by Jorgensen."

Reb Itzikel thought. As a circuit-riding rabbi he had done much traveling. His territory covered both the Dakotas and a good hunk of Canada. He completed the circuit at least once a year. In addition there were special trips: a funeral here, a wedding there, and once in a while Reb Itzikel's favorite: a *bris*. Nothing excited him more than, as he put it, "turning a little boy into a little Jew with one quick stroke."

A wedding could be planned, but a *bris* was something else. Eight days from birth and no more. The rebbe needed to take the quickest route to Fargo, even if it meant staying with non-Jews.

Whenever he traveled Reb Itzikel liked to stay with Jews for three reasons: first, he could get kosher food. Second, he could do his job—after all he was a rabbi and without Jews to teach, to comfort or to slaughter meat for, he wasn't working. Finally, this was after all 1875, and the Dakotas were not exactly barren of anti-Semitism. Reb Itzikel had heard stories of traveling Jews murdered in their sleep by outwardly friendly farmers. When staying with non-Jews he was always nervous. To say he slept with one eye open would be only half true.

Under the circumstances, however, he had no choice. Unless they took the shortcut through the Jorgensen farm they might arrive on the ninth, even the tenth day.

"Charlie," the rebbe asked, "Do you know these Jorgensens?"

"Yes, Rebbe," Charlie answered, "Nice people. Norwegians. As far as I know not anti-Semites."

"Let's hope," said Reb Itzikel. But he spent an especially long time reciting the Traveler's Prayer.

Reb Itzikel and Charlie Cohen saddled up and set out for Fargo. They spent the first night of the journey at Moses and Sarah Blumenthal's, where they feasted on stuffed cabbage and fresh chicken, slaughtered by the rabbi himself. Before leaving the next morning, the rabbi remembered where he would be spending his second night, and he asked them about the Jorgensens.

"Good people, Rebbe, very good," said Moses Blumenthal. "They sent us soup last winter when Sarah was sick."

"Good soup," said Sarah, while her husband kicked her under the table. *"Treife,* but good." The rabbi joined Sarah's hearty laughter. After all, who was he to judge?

In spite of the good opinions of Charlie and the Blumenthals, it was with some trepidation that Reb Itzikel knocked on Tom and Inga Jorgensen's door late that afternoon. After all, who knows what false friends these anti-Semites can be. Pharoah too pretended to love the Jews.

The woman who opened the door was the healthiest woman Reb Itzikel had ever seen. Tall, muscular, blonde, blue-eyed; she made him think of a Norse goddess. He reminded himself that many of our enemies had been fair of face but evil-hearted, and he resolved to keep his guard up. "Ya?" said Inga Jorgensen, smiling broadly.

Charlie did the talking. He and the rabbi needed a place to spend the night. They also wished to purchase a chicken and have Mrs. Jorgensen cook it, though the rabbi would slaughter it. Also, they wished to supervise her while she cooked it, to be certain she used only specified ingredients.

Mrs. Jorgensen, fascinated, immediately agreed to these rather bizarre requests. After all, who was she to judge the strange ways of these wanderers. Some Americans thought her people strange as well. The dinner was delicious, and the conversation delightful. The travelers and their hosts spoke avidly about their crops, the weather, philosophy and religion. After dinner there was more talk and much laughter. Reb Itzikel and Charlie were offered the warmest spot in the house, next to the fireplace. They slept soundly.

In the morning Reb Itzikel put on his *t'fillin* and recited the morning prayers, to the amazement of Tom and Inga. They all shared a big breakfast and, after warm farewells, Charlie and the rebbe set out for Fargo. They arrived early in the morning on the eighth day of Tom Cohen's life.

So it began. So thoroughly did Reb Itzikel like the Jorgensens, and so thoroughly did they like him, that he began to take the "Jorgensen

---

Joel Grossman is an attorney who lives in Seattle. The story he tells is true; the names of its people and places have been changed.

short-cut" whenever he went to Fargo. Inga and Tom began to look forward to these visits. Each time the rebbe came he taught them something new about his strange religion. He showed them his collection of ritual knives—some for kosher slaughtering, some for circumcisions. The rabbi was embarrassed as Inga demanded a full, clinical account of the latter, but he gave it to her. Another time he explained in detail the laws of *kashrut*. After that discussion the rabbi never worried about eating at the Jorgensens. Inga and Tom were so full of thoughtful, probing questions and so eager to learn that they reminded Reb Itzikel of the Wise Son at the Passover Seder.

Never, though, did they ask about his *t'fillin*. Tom had told Inga that it was rude to ask a man what he said when he prayed, and just as rude to ask him about what he wore when he prayed. When Inga asked Tom how wearing leather straps could help the rabbi talk to God, Tom shrugged and told her, "That's between the two of them." Inga's curiosity was not satisfied, but she listened to her husband.

At the end of every visit the rabbi would offer to pay for his lodging. The Jorgensens would never accept, saying it was a sin to take money from a holy man. They would repeat this discussion each time the rabbi said goodbye. Like good actors, they recited their lines time after time with great sincerity.

It had gone on this way, year in and year out, for thirteen years. Now Reb Itzikel was growing old and he would soon retire. He decided that his next trip to Fargo— for Tom Cohen's bar mitzvah— would be his last. As always, he stopped at the Jorgensens on his way. Over dinner he told them that this would be his last trip to Fargo, and the last time he would stay with them.

"But Rebbe," Inga cried out (by now she used the Yiddish version of his title) "You have so much more to teach us. There's so much more I need to know."

"I know, Inga, but I'm tired and now I must rest. A new rabbi will be sent to take my place and I'll tell him to stay with you whenever he travels to Fargo." "Ya, but it wouldn't be the same, Rebbe," Inga replied. Reb Itzikel could only shake his head. She was right. It wouldn't.

In the morning he woke up a little later than usual. He lingered in bed, trying to delay his departure as long as possible. Finally he rose and dressed and donned his *t'fillin*. He walked into the yard to pray.

Inga followed. After thirteen years of silence she had decided it was now or never.

"Rebbe, forgive me, but I must know. Those straps and boxes you put on each morning, what are they for?"

Reb Itzikel hesitated. If he told her the truth—that Jews were commanded to make a sign on their arms and place frontlets between their eyes—she might not understand. He was tired, and it was already late, and he didn't want to make a long explanation. Forgive me God, he said silently, but I'm in no mood to teach this morning.

"These things," he told Inga, "are for arthritis." She smiled and went to cook breakfast.

A short time later the rabbi was prepared to go. He quickly recited his traditional offer of payment; after thirteen years, a mere formality. Inga surprised him.

"Yes, Rebbe," she said, "you can pay me for your lodging."

Both Reb Itzikel and Tom Jorgensen were stunned. Inga went on:

"Not money, of course, we'd never take your money. But you see Rebbe, I too have arthritis. Please leave me a pair of your arthritis boxes. I know you always carry extras."

Reb Itzikel blanched. How could he give this woman a pair of kosher *t'fillin*? There were, after all, Jews in the world who needed them. The extra pair in his saddlebags was to be Tom Cohen's bar mitzvah present. On the other hand, he reasoned, how could he refuse? Had not this woman fed him and sheltered him off and on for thirteen years? Surely he could find another pair for Tom. Besides, who would ever know? "Of course, Inga, it's the least I can do. Take them, with my blessing." Silently he said, "God forgive me," and handed her the *t'fillin*. He embraced Inga and Tom and rode away.

The Cohen bar mitzvah was a huge success, but all the singing and dancing confirmed Reb Itzikel's feelings that he was, indeed, too old to continue. When he returned to Grand Forks he announced his retirement. He wired the yeshiva to send a replacement, and a young graduate was quickly dispatched.

Reb Itzikel spent many hours helping his replacement, Reb Daniel, learn the ins and outs of his circuit. He explained his filing system, his catalogue of births and deaths, his collection of maps and his sacred knives. He also told Reb Daniel about all the congregants, the good and the bad. Finally, he told Reb Daniel about the "Jorgensen short-cut," and the splendid people Daniel might stay with on his way to Fargo.

It was not too long before Reb Daniel made use of this advice. Tom Cohen's oldest sister, Becky, was to be married in Fargo. As Becky was due to give birth at any moment, time was of the essence and Reb Daniel needed to take the quickest route to Fargo. He put aside his plans for a leisurely trip around the circuit and resolved to take the "Jorgensen short-cut."

Reb Daniel's first night at the Jorgensens was as pleasant as Reb Itzikel had promised. To Daniel's amazement, Inga presented him with a live chicken and asked that he slaughter it properly. She advised him that she was thoroughly aware of what ingredients she could use to cook the chicken, and showed him her special pots and pans which she kept just for Reb Itzikel's meat meals, and her special set for Reb Itzikel's dairy meals (Reb Itzikel had never been with her for Passover).

Reb Daniel ate well and slept soundly. In the morning he lingered in bed, a little worried. He had never been seen by non-Jews in his *t'fillin*. Would they laugh at him? Worse

An Extra Pair of T'fillin

yet, would they think he was some kind of demon communicating with the dead? Then Daniel remembered that his predecessor, Reb Itzikel, had spent many nights with the Jorgensens. Surely they had seen him in his *t'fillin*. Comforted by this thought, he quickly dressed and donned his *t'fillin*. As he walked out of the room he thought to himself, knowing Reb Itzikel, he's probably explained to them what *t'fillin* are for.

Then he saw her. Seated at the kitchen table, a benign smile on her face while she peeled potatoes, was Inga Jorgensen wearing *t'fillin*. Reb Daniel was so stunned that he could not speak. Never, ever, had he seen a *woman* wearing t'fillin, let alone a blonde, blue-eyed *shiksa* in the middle of North Dakota! He stared at her for several moments, but still he could not speak. Inga looked up from her potatoes and turned to Reb Daniel with a look of deep sympathy in her eyes. "You poor man," she said kindly. "So young to have arthritis."

Shortly after Becky Cohen's wedding Reb Daniel rode out of Fargo heading East. At the first town with a train station, he sold his horse and bought a ticket for New York. He was often asked in later years why he left his circuit-riding congregation so soon after arriving. His answer was always the same: "Where the shiksas wear *t'fillin*, who needs a rabbi?"

WANTED DEAD OR ALIVE

JACOB NEUSNER

One of my sons, when he wants to know how things were when I was his age, asks, "What were things like when you were alive?" Just as the young cannot imagine that their parents enjoy, or even know about, sex, so they cannot comprehend that their parents are alive in the same way in which they are alive.

About sex, they are wrong. About being alive, they have a point.

My generation—the third generation of American Jewry—began somewhere, cared and dreamed and worried about some things, and is now finished. By and large, the things we wanted to make happen have happened, and the young see us as finished. And I think they are right.

I grew up in West Hartford, Connecticut, a suburb of Hartford, when only a few Jews lived there. I remember, about being Jewish, only two things: first, I thought it was something to do only in private; and second, I wondered whether it would be done at all for very much longer.

I came, please understand, from a very Jewish—though not at all Judaic—family, so I was one of those who cared about being Jewish. I was, for example, one of the only people I knew who voted for Roosevelt in 1944 (as a sixth grader), which was a very Jewish thing to do in West Hartford (except when it was a very Irish thing to do). And I was one of the only people I knew who was aware that something of great importance was happening in 1948. Most of the Jewish kids I knew were not much interested in being Jewish and did a very good job of adjusting their appearance and behavior to match their lack of interest. My mother, a matriarch of the second generation, was proud of not having been born in "Europe," which was less a place than a state of mind. (In our house, everything vulgar and tasteless was "European.") She called me Jackie, until my voice deepened and she switched to Jack. But it was only when I turned twenty-one and applied for my first passport that I discovered that my name, my only name, the name bestowed upon me at birth and hidden from me for more than two decades, was not Jackie, was not Jack, was, in fact, Jacob.

Those few of us who thought about being Jewish, who were part of the generation that was too young for the Second World War, too old for Vietnam, that missed Korea by virtue of student deferments, that seemed stuck in the cracks between great historical events, we worried about the Jewish future. We knew how few we were, and we knew how different we were from our grandparents, how far removed from the manifest wellsprings of faith and commitment and culture, and we could not imagine what a Jewish future might be built upon, from what new springs it would draw its strength.

Specifically, we could not know and did not guess that most of our friends, the ones who did not know and did not care, the ones who were busy "waspifying" themselves, would one day marry Jews and join synagogues and temples and choose to live near other Jews and care about Israel and all the rest: that they would want to be Jews.

The mystery of the third generation: Jewish but not too Jewish. Not so Jewish that you stop being an American. We knew about that from our grandparents, who had remained too European ever to become Americans. Our parents tried to overcome the alienness, and succeeded. They became undifferentiated Americans, to everyone except themselves. And we, in our turn, became for a time what

Jacob Neusner is University Professor and Ungerleider Distinguished Scholar of Judaic Studies at Brown University.

our parents wanted us to be—undifferentiated Americans, to everyone, ourselves included.

Those of us who knew from early on that the Jews were supposed to last, who wanted the Jewish connection to survive, were, as I have said, few in number. I recall that one day, when I was in the ninth grade, I was walking along Farmington Avenue when a terrible thought occurred to me. A time would come, I realized, when the rabbi of our (Reform) temple would be dead, and my father, too, would die. And then I would be the last Jew on earth—or, at least, on Farmington Avenue in West Hartford. That was the day I decided to become a rabbi, a decision I promptly shared with the whole world. Years later, it is what those who knew me then most remember: "He was the one who wanted to become a rabbi!"

What I really wanted to be and to become, of course, was a Jew. But I must have sensed that for our generation, being Jewish would require a special kind of effort and commitment. It had to become a vocation, because, left to flourish in a less explicit environment, it would not flourish at all. There being no longer a sustaining environment, it would wither. One had to set out to discover Judaism and self-consciously to make a Jew of oneself, because we had neither encountered it nor been invited, nor, perhaps, even permitted to encounter it as we grew up.

The thing we wanted most was to be part of a community that would share our concern for "being Jewish," whatever that might mean. In our day, that meant finding others who shared that most peculiar wish—in seminaries, in youth movements, in a few other scattered places. And when we found those places, we used them to try to expand the Jewish possibility, to make the entire community a congenial place for our Jewish aspirations.

And that is why the work of my generation is now over. We won the fight.

Think about it: if there was an "organized Jewish community" back when I was growing up, it was so remote that we never heard about it. In towns such as ours, federations did not yet exist or, if they did, scarcely thought of themselves as anything more than welfare agencies for the distressed. The Jewish community center was inaccessible, had no program that I can remember hearing of. There were few camps of Jewish content (though I went to a camp where everyone was Jewish), no youth movements to speak of (except for misfits). I never knew about the shabbat; I never saw a sukkah. I remember how shocked I was, when I came to Oxford, to meet young Jews of intellectual distinction who knew the grace after meals—yes, the *birkat hamazon*—and said it. When I was at Harvard, the few observant Jews, almost all the sons of rabbis, were curiosities.

A Jewish community? To be built from what? Where were the people; where were the models? That is what we wanted to know, and there was no answer save as we ourselves, we few, were ready to be the people, to provide the models.

But to make that work, to make it last, to make it possible for our children to step easily into a living community, we had to develop a public agenda as well. We had to force the Jewish community to resolve its own ambivalence in order, I suppose, so that we could resolve ours. Either become Jewish, really Jewish, whatever that might come to mean, be made to mean, or stop bothering, stop insisting on the difference, stop insisting even on survival.

Accordingly, we approached the community back in the late 1940's and early 1950's with a very peculiar set of demands. I remember, for instance, my earliest writings on the budgets of Jewish federations, published in my father's newspaper (the *Connecticut Jewish Ledger,* which we subsequently sold). I analyzed the budgets of the Federation from year to year, and wondered in print what was Jewish about them or it. Later on, our group—for we

became a kind of group—we few—went on to ask what was Jewish about Jewish community centers, and again, we found remarkably few answers. We wanted more attention to be paid the State of Israel than was paid back then, before the earthquakes and revolutions that transfixed the entire community. Ah, there was so much that we wanted!

And we got it. We got it all.

We were right to want it; we were right to get it. For the third generation, for the generation that married Jewish but did not know why, that wanted Jewish but did not know how, we provided the structure of organizations and the intellectual underpinnings which today serve as the foundation of organized Jewry in this country. My own three "projects" were the reform of federations, the formation of *havurot* and the development of Jewish studies in universities. The federations have now become principal vehicles of Jewish expression and continuity; *havurot* multiply and are fruitful; and Jewish studies in universities, both quantitatively and qualitatively, have achieved distinction.

But what we wanted and needed and achieved, we wanted and needed for ourselves, not for those to come. What we accomplished was in response to our own agenda, an agenda that grew out of our own distinctive experience as the third generation. The world of our children is paradoxically different from our own. For them, being Jewish is much less a given, a fixed condition, than it was to us, just as it was less a given to us than it had been for our parents, less to our parents than to our grandparents. But at the very same time, the *crafting* of Jewish lives, of a Jewish life, is no longer the laborious, idiosyncratic effort it was for us. They have available to them a Jewish education far richer than we had. Schools, summer camps, youth programs, and, of course, the State of Israel—a set of educational resources that is rich beyond any-

What we should have known all along, but are only now coming to see, is that neither money nor organization can secure our future.

thing we dreamed of. As well as an intermarriage rate larger than we imagined we could bear. As well as a growing number of converts to Judaism. Paradoxes all the time.

Paradoxes that will not be resolved until the fourth generation matures. I am inclined to be hopeful, for that is my nature, but I am also mindful of Arthur Hertzberg's warning: "There is more passion for Jerusalem and more loyalty to Judaism in the American Jewish community today than we shall have in a decade, *if we do not do some radical things now.*"

I agree with Hertzberg, but I also think that we, who are no longer alive, are not the ones to do the things that now want doing or even to say very much about what those things might be. It is for the living to name those things and to do them, because the things that are to be done, whatever they are, will have to respond to the agenda of need of a generation that was framed by different experiences from our own and is defined by different needs. I do not see that there is much for "the organized Jewish community" to do these days except not to block or to blight the things that still-unheard-of-names will soon be proposing, perhaps even demanding.

So here I am, about to pass the torch. But first, as they say, a word of advice, from the rocking chair to the runner.

Don't make the mistakes that I, or others like me, made.

We all got sucked into the value system of the organized community, as it existed in our day. We took seriously what we were not and apologized for what we were. We pretended to think, and some of us even came to think, that there is something more important than ideas. We, who spend our lives in classrooms and in libraries, in studies, pulpits, editorial offices, the places where intellectuals do their work, learned a whole new vocabulary, chose to play on alien turf. We were intellectuals out to reshape the world we loved, the Jewish world, but we neglected our own gifts of intellect and heart, our own vocabulary. Instead, we raised issues of material and mass, issues to which we had nothing special to contribute.

What, after all, were the foci of the reforms we proposed and effected? They had to do with the spending of money, the building of institutions, the ordering of priorities. We wanted the federations to spend their money on consequential things, Jewish things. So they did.

And now we have learned that money is not the answer.

We wanted the synagogues to organize themselves in ways that related to the individual and his needs, in this time, in this place, to permit the formation of groups where people would not feel lost. So they did.

And now we have learned that organizing an institution in one way rather than in another is not the answer.

We wanted the community to focus its attention on the great cultural resource represented by the State of Israel, to pay attention, as it had not adequately in the 1940's and 1950's, to the political requirements of Zionism. So it did.

And now we have learned that our salvation does not lie in the East.

The important thing to remember is that we were not frustrated in the pursuit of our goals. Our disappointments derive from other sources, not from our failure but from our success.

How is it that we were so very successful? Chiefly, we came to the community with what it already was coming to know. We were just a bit early on the scene. Even without us, the passionate reformers of the 1950's and 1960's, the things that we like to think we had a hand in making happen would have happened. They might have taken a bit longer, but they would have happened. The community is in the hands of practical and effective and intelligent people, both lay and professional. They had as much good will as we and as much constructive purpose. They, too, understood what needed to be done, and they did it. They drew on what they had: money and organizational skill.

What we should have known all along, but are only now coming to see, is that neither money nor organization can secure our future. And when we chose to play on alien turf, we added only another layer of veneer to the House of Israel in America, a house that has still no solid foundation.

I am not saying that we were wrong to make the choices that we made. I am saying only that those choices are no longer the choices that need making, and it is disheartening to encounter so many, third and fourth generation alike, who persist in fighting yesterday's wars. Our victory in those wars makes possible a new war. And to win that war, too, intellectuals will have to stick to their lasts.

The new war is to shape an idea, not a shared consensus, but a consensus worth sharing. There is simply no corpus of intellectually consequential ideas about what it means to be a Jew, here and now, in this time and in this place, to which Jewry today has access. The ideas the rabbis preach must come from somewhere; the policies expressed in federation meetings have to begin with someone. If theology and ideology for contemporary Jewry were merely what people pretend—a conventional apologetic, a ritual of excuses—it might not matter. But ideas do move people; without ideas, people will not move. They will merely twitch, pretending life.

What people think really matters. How embarrassing to have to write these words. Yet the words are no longer obvious. They are not obvious to the formers and shapers of Jewry because we, who formed the corpus of ideas, of theology and ideology, over the last thirty years, behaved as if they were secondary, and actions primary. As, perhaps they were—for a time. We did not invite the shapers and movers to our turf; we eagerly invaded theirs. We led them to believe that in their distance from the life of the Jewish intellect, from Jewish ideas, in their remove from the soul of Judaism, they could and should do those things that would secure a worthy Jewish present and a viable vision of a Jewish future. They looked to us for ideas. And we talked to them of money and how to spend it.

They had power, and we imagined ourselves impotent. So when they invited us to join them, that is exactly what we did, forgetting that if all we had to offer was a pale imitation of the resources they already had, they would not have wanted or needed to invite us. They did not know how to ask the question, and we did not hear the question they did not ask, the only question we might have been able to answer with some authority. We were too enamored with the trappings. So we lost our voice; we answered other questions, questions whose answers were already known, questions that mattered but that did not require us to answer them. We behaved like directors of agencies: asked for money, competed for money. And offered nothing of what we knew. Pretended to sophistication. Lost our nerve, our sense of self.

Ideas come first. Vision takes precedence. The educated heart is what creates and shapes our energies to act. Did not the State of Israel begin in the minds of dissatisfied intellectuals? Was it not born as an idea? Was it not shaped by first class minds? Long before there was a Jewish state, there was the idea of a Jewish state, and there would never have been a Jewish state without that idea. An idea: mostly talk—but what a conversation, and what an impact!

So it is with the great movements of every age. They start in our minds, not in our bellies (*pace* the Communists and the federations alike), not in our bank accounts. And when intellectuals are responsible for events, it is because they develop ideas that are compelling, not because they aspire to positions of power. The seductive attraction of high office subverts the far greater power that intellectuals who do not deny themselves might exercise.

So there is the advice. Do not be other than what you are. In this context, let those with ideas remain true to their hearts, their minds, their intellects. We are a people to whom a book is an event, a rare insight, an occasion for celebration. I think, for example, of Abraham Heschel, who in the late 1950's laid forth an intellectual heritage still not adequately interpreted or understood. His monumental intellectual achievements of that period received no hearing either then or later. It was during the 1960's that he became a public figure and gained a vast and impressive hearing—but that was not for his distinctive intellectual contribution. I cannot blame him, but I think we would be better off today had he pursued, in his last years, those lines of thought and modes of reflection which in a few brief years yielded *Man Is Not Alone* and *God in Search of Man*. Heschel's public power was vastly greater in the 1960's than it had been in the 1950's. But it was a different kind of power, and it yielded different products, and all of them have now evaporated.

The plain fact is that the future of American Jewry will not be decided by the synagogues, the federations, the centers, the day schools, the hospitals, the American Jewish Committees and the Anti-Defamation Leagues. Nor will it be settled by raising another billion dollars for the State of Israel, nor even a billion for Jewish education and culture. The future of American Jewry will be decided, for better or worse, by the ideas that American Jews have and come to have regarding their future. It will be settled by what the fourth generation manages to achieve by way of a set of ideas. We of the third generation built a building, and that was an important thing to do. It is time now to place a foundation under that building. That has yet to be done. And that foundation does not take dollars. It takes words, and ideas. ✦

Part III
Israel

DUAL CITIZENSHIP

Nancy Datan

Nancy Datan, who died as this book was going to press, was, most recently, Professor of Human Development and Chairman of the Department of Women's Studies at the University of Wisconsin in Green Bay.

This is the fourth war in Israel, and people abroad are growing tired of them, or so one of my colleagues suggests at lunch: "That's the craziest place in the whole frigging world. They ought to fence it off and let them kill each other off." I have no ready response to this, he is not a man with much international feeling anyhow, and I doubt if he would have donated the price of a lamb chop to Biafra. What is more, I am privately wondering how widespread his feelings are, at universities like this one and elsewhere across the United States. And still more privately, I am wondering whether I might have felt anything similar if I had not, ten years ago, become a (legally) permanent resident of Israel.

Others among my colleagues view the war as one might a football match. "I like the way the Israelis go to war," says one, "it's just like a game of *Go:* they capture territory and to hell with the men." I have not yet seen the newspapers with their black-bordered names of the dead, but I remember searching in 1967 for the names I knew and finding tears, suddenly, for a stranger.

Meanwhile among my Jewish colleagues there is some concern that it doesn't look good for the Israelis to be bombing Damascus. I am close to inquiring whether it would look better if the Syrians bombed Jerusalem. Indeed, if I let that out it will not be long before I am asking whether it didn't look best when the Jews were being shoveled wholesale into furnaces: but I do not trust myself to say anything at all, and over the days of the fighting I have been silent. Or at least I suppose myself to have been silent: something has escaped me, for when I came late to a class, one of my students looked at me gently and said, "We thought you'd enlisted." But for the most part, I pay the price of dual citizenship as quietly as I can, waiting by my mailbox . . .

. . . although when the letter does come, it takes me wholly by surprise; I am packed and ready to leave for the airport for a conference and badly in need of a week of comic relief, glad to hear from Aaron, my co-author, colleague, and friend, and I open the airletter with pleasure, and I had always wondered how I would behave at a moment like this — "I thought you should know . . . David Katz was killed . . . It is unimaginable, but it is evidently true . . . What is there to do but weep?" but I had discovered that for myself before I was able to read that far.

And meanwhile the suitcases stand by the door, the ticket to Miami Beach is in my purse, and my children's babysitter is due to drive me to the airport within the hour. It is not only a matter of schedules that have been set but of obligations as well: my department is planning a spring conference, and I am to speak to potential participants. I can hardly speak to my own children, who ask me what is wrong; I cannot decide whether it would be easier to face my students here or my colleagues in Miami Beach. In the end, the habit of meeting obligations, which tends to become stronger in me when the world becomes uncertain, tips the balance; and I practice a bland face on the babysitter, who tells me warmly to have a good time, and I step giddily onto the plane which takes me to my connecting flight in Pittsburgh.

In the Pittsburgh airport I have a three-hour wait. Either the airport is chilly or I am. I spend the time writing letters to a very carefully chosen assortment of friends. One is an Israeli Arab, a close friend to me and to David, and I wonder as I write if the dislocations in daily life in Jerusalem may mean that mine is the letter which gives him this news: for, I am told, there has not yet been official publication of the names of the dead. Subhi called him "Reb Dovid," a form of respectful address used by speakers of Yiddish; and, so finely honed was Subhi's sense of irony that it applied only to himself, while his Arabic-accented Yiddish conveyed nothing but affection.

For what seems to me to be the very first time, I am able to understand something of minority-group status, which has been Subhi's since 1948, when he became a citizen of Israel; which was mine although I did not care to know it and migrated from the United States to Israel in order to avoid discovering it. Minority status is not only a function of numbers, I write Subhi: it is an affliction, it is the forced understanding of all points of view, even, God help me, that of my colleague who thinks the Middle East should be sealed and its inhabitants allowed to kill each other off.

And it is eternal dissonance: while the goyim drink in airport bars, the Jews wait for the names of the dead. The flight for Miami is boarding: presently I am seated, directly in front of a loud omniscient woman who shares her knowledge with her flight companions non-stop. She takes about forty-five minutes to complete the transition from Florida real estate to the politics of the Middle East: "Now I feel really terrible about the war, I just really do. Why should the Syrians and the Jews fight each other? They look alike, you can't tell a Syrian and a Jew apart, why, they're brothers! Now, take me, I'm not Jewish" — that's something, at least — "but I'm pro-Israel, and I say, why should the Egyptians and the Jews fight?" — his unit was at the Suez Canal, on routine reserve duty, before Yom Kippur, and they were overrun by the Egyptians on the first day of the war, the letter said — "The Jews and the Egyptians and the Syrians are all brothers, they have no reason to fight!" My own seat-mate turns to me and murmurs, "Did it ever occur to her that maybe they hate each other?" I have been maintaining a feverish gaiety throughout this flight and I am not about to let it crack: "It's very complicated," I tell him, and run to the bathroom.

At last my plane reaches Miami, I have arrived, checked in, and I make my way to the opening recep-

> We are clumsy imperialists: the Athenians taxed their subject territories, we tax ourselves.

tion, for I am badly in need of familiar faces. My own face, unfortunately, is permeable to grief, and within two minutes I have met a friend and he has asked me what is wrong and I have told him. The telling does not ease me, in moments I am asked by someone else who knows my face well, and I have told her, and I am beginning to tremble.

We move outside to the reception and there is an Israeli colleague, but it is easier to tell him: Hebrew is remarkably well-suited for the sharing of pain. I must know half-a-dozen words for "dead in combat." And in the notices, after the names of the dead, the several ways the Jews say "Rest in Peace" — *on him be peace*, for instance; or *blessed be his memory;* or sometimes, for those who fall under fire, as it was said of the eleven dead at the Munich Olympics, *may God revenge his blood.* David would not want that said of him, the closest he ever came to rage was indignation, and that generally in someone else's cause; indeed, though I have seen him in uniform when he was on leave from reserves, I cannot imagine him going to war. Meanwhile, in Miami Beach, in the absolute privacy ensured by speaking Hebrew, I am told: "Twelve of my family are in uniform. We are calling the Embassy all the time. But, thank God, all are well so far." The tide of friendly colleagues separates us and the night hides our faces. And there is evening and there is morning: the first day.

I have a small flock of graduate students to tend, who are arriving by automobile, and who had been looking forward to a week's frivolity with me. By morning I am beginning to grow anxious about them; but at the same time I am not looking forward to the extra effort it will require to maintain a convention façade. After lunch they turn up, having driven all night, weary but safe, and I make my recommendations for interesting panels and point out some famous names. We part, with reunion scheduled for the evening's round of parties; and I spend the afternoon pursuing participants for my own spring conference.

At the first party of the evening, drinks are for sale rather than for free: I am asked what I would like, and I tell my host that an ice cube would do, to wear rather than to consume. This remark will pursue me for twenty-four hours. I move on to the next party, at which drinks are free, and obtain some ginger ale and reconnoiter with my students. But I have hardly begun the business of introductions to significant persons when I am interrupted by a colleague, who draws me aside to meet another Israeli, with whom I achieve the instant intimacy of exiles. Around us eddies of flirtations, political maneuvering, camaraderie: and in Hebrew he tells me, "One thousand eight hundred and fifty-four killed. One thousand eight hundred and fifty-four." And the casualty lists are still unpublished, and all I can think is, my God, I only know one name so far. He is to leave in the morning, in the middle of the evening's hilarity our embrace passes unnoticed. And there is evening and there is morning: the second day.

At breakfast I seek out my Israeli colleagues: first, a farewell to the one departing for Israel; and after he has left for his taxi, coffee with the other and a brief sanctuary from my own unending efforts to smile at everyone. But he turns to me with a face too carefully controlled, and tells me: "Something made me want to call home this morning. My brother told me one of our family has been taken prisoner," and, after a moment, "but at least he is not dead," and, pausing, adds, "They are getting tired of our little wars, Nancy. They have grown tired of us."

Yes, that is what I have been thinking myself, people are tired of the Israelis, certain that they will win, indifferent to the price. But it is silly to suppose that Israel will win: even before this war, which is demonstrating that desperation alone is not enough, a casual study of the history of the Jews would have shown that victory for Israel is not only not inevitable but has, in fact, been very rare. We have a better-than-human-frailty percentage of military losses recorded over the centuries. Hath not a Jew eyes, hands? When you prick him, does he not bleed? Indeed he does, copiously, more often than many peoples, and perhaps too shrilly for some. Twentieth-century Israel is so often compared to the warring Spartans: but it was golden, legendary Athens which held an empire, as Israel is now supposed to be doing — I think of my taxes, building hospitals in the West Bank and connecting Gaza to the electric grid, and I think also of the West Bank Arabs, giving blood for the Israeli Army, though they do not love their occupiers, nor would I. We are clumsy imperialists, the Athenians taxed their subject territories, we tax ourselves. We know defeat more intimately than victory: yet even Athens fell once, nations fall and so might we. Jerusalem has fallen often. To my Israeli colleague, whose face shows that he does not need to be reminded of the history of the Jews, I say nothing at all; we abandon our coffee and pursue our separate duties for the day.

Day passes and evening comes. At the student party inhibitions vanish: in some this is precipitated by a drink or two, in others by conference-satiation, in me by exhaustion. My host of the preceding night's party turns to me with mischief in his eyes and an ice cube in his hand and approaches me slowly, dramatically. My own students are called as witnesses; one is doing a paper on formal and informal dimensions of socialization at academic conventions. I have my self-respect to maintain: under these circumstances by retaining my composure, which is easy enough, since in me affection for the man and amusement at the action mingle with a bleak indifference which has leached the color from everything. As sometimes happens, anticipation exceeds the act itself, and the ice cube's brief travel down my shirt is actually missed by my own student, and has to be repeated.

I am not contented with my passive role in this transaction, the more so since my assailant is not only senior to me but also older and considerably taller. These factors converge in me after a while and induce recklessness: with a melodrama exceeding his, I stalk him, cold sober, hoping as I think of it that no one else is. Deliberately and grandly I push his tie aside, and pop two ice cubes into his trousers.

He watches rather admiringly: "I thought you'd lose your nerve."

"Certainly not."

"I've discovered something about your character, Nancy: you'll never back down on a dare," and I think to myself, that is true, and what is more, it explains not only my present behavior but even perhaps, my migrations of the past ten years. It is a component, surely, of the conscientiousness with which I meet my obligations. My students are watching, some seeking knowledge of social processes and others seeking knowledge of the private selves of their educators. But I, who teach them, have learnt more than they will. And there is evening and there is morning: the third day.

The fourth day of the conference is a day of escape for me: some friends have rented a car and invite me to join them on an excursion to the Florida Keys. But among my friends the careful mask of hilarity drops from me, and, in a car full of good will and affection, I sink at last into the privacy of my own pain, wishing I had not come, afraid to be among strangers, afraid to be among friends, and afraid to be alone. At Marathon we stop for lunch, and I look forward to stone crab, until it arrives, and suddenly I discover — I, who had not known that the Jews kept meat and milk separate when I immigrated to Israel in 1963 — that I have no stomach for *treif* food.

When lunch is ended we move on, and in the late afternoon discover a small key with an isolated beach. The peace I could not find in the company of friends I achieve at last on the silent white sand, listening to the waves and not to my own thoughts. But it is a short-lived peace; we must return to Miami Beach, I have a banquet to attend and the last of my speakers to contact; and then, my obligations met, the week's fatigue overwhelms me and sleep finds me. And there is evening and there is morning: the fourth day.

On the fifth and final morning, I drink my coffee with the melancholy relish that comes to me when I anticipate the ordeal of airports and connecting flights; and, leaving the hotel for the last time, I take leave also of the few colleagues with whom I had been able to share pain; and soon my plane is leaving Miami Beach behind, and then we have come to Pittsburgh, and I have boarded the last plane of this journey.

Aboard the brief commuter flight which will take me home, I discover myself to be sick to my stomach: the eight-seater Beechcraft is being tossed all over the skies, and in and out of intermittent snow flurries, and at first I suppose myself to be airsick. But no, I have never suffered any form of motion sickness in my life, this is an existential sickness, I should like to vomit up the whole of the past week, the polystyrene hotels of Miami Beach and the endless unsuccessful efforts at concealment. The week gave me nothing of the interlude I need for mourning, I am afraid to pick up my accumulated mail; and I perceive at last that it is not the indifference of my colleagues that I am dreading. Toward indifference or antagonism I can turn an impassive face, and maintain it indefinitely: it is kindness which causes me to crumble.

I shall discover my colleagues, who were untouched by the six o'clock news, to be touched by my own visible pain, and yes, it is just this which I fear. I will insulate myself deep in the pile of obligations waiting for me, until my colleagues learn that I have ceased to eat lunch, ask me how I am feeling, suggest that I take a day off. This pain is full of private ironies for me, I would like to shield it and myself, but it translates the announcement of "over eighteen hundred dead" of the news broadcasts into one thousand eight hundred fifty-four persons, for those who are unfamiliar with the wars of Israel and Israeli grief.

The plane, which had not risen much above the clouds for its twenty-minute flight, begins to descend; and I find that the hills of West Virginia, which had borne the last traces of autumn color when I departed, have become bare and brown in my five days' absence. The plane's approach follows the valley of the Monongahela River, and on the river I can see two coal barges, moving slowly, laden for the cold winter ahead. ♦

WE THE HOMEBORN

"There was the rebirth of the language and there was the 'Hebrew plow' and the 'Hebrew sword' to complete the 'holy trinity' of the Second Aliyah, and there was the perpetual pathos of tomorrow."

HAIM GOURI

Notes from the chaos and dread of the foreseeable future: André Malraux wrote in the late 1950s: "The Israelis are no continuation of the Jews; they're a transformation of them."

Malraux's use in French of a verb form of "metamorphosis" was intended to indicate an existence quite at variance with what came before. And we the homeborn believed in it; it was our great expectation as natives of this country.

We knew, of course, who our fathers were and where they had come from and what we owed them and the whole history we were continuing. We did not accept, most of us, Yonatan Ratosh, the "Canaanite," who called on us to cut the "Gordian knot" and wage a spiritual and political war of annihilation on Judaism, the sworn and eternal enemy of the reviving Hebraism. The somersault, which he thought a life-saving leap, to the antique past of Qedem, to the rebirth of paganism in the Land of Prat, seemed to us a chimera from the beginning.

But we were, emphatically, offspring of the Zionist revolution, in all its ardor and gravity and its wish to effect here the national renaissance that would include so fundamental a renewal and transfiguration that our life would be a polar opposite of the Diaspora.

Natan Alterman spoke of "Tomorrow's Shulamit," of the nation taking shape here, "between Sidon and Philistia," which combined all the generations. Yet in the gathering conflict underway here between the returning folk and its land, in this collision that alters the features of both, something is happening that is reminiscent of the powerful primordial sagas.

A potent new beauty is shaped in cruel combat with the enemy. The hammerblow of the enemy is what gives this potent beauty its form, it's in this struggle with the burning topography and with the hatred of opponents that the renaissance takes place; the return to Zion that creates the Hebrew human being, "Tomorrow's Shulamit," comparable in her strength to the emergence of Noah's sons, of Shem and Ham and Yafet in ancient days.

We the homeborn saw how Tchernichovsky repudiated all Jewish history except for "the wilderness generation," with which he identified in his *oeuvre*–it was only the biblical renaissance he cared for–in the name of "the blood of those who took Canaan by storm. . . ." Not the blood of the Maccabees and not the blood of the martyrs. Utter repudiation of an entire history in the name of the return to the nation's origins. No revolution ever raised its banners without an antithesis, without an angry "against," for the sake of a new truth.

It's all quite understandable: There was an urgent need to abandon the Diaspora and to create something else here. There was the rebirth of the language and there was the "Hebrew plow" and the "Hebrew sword" to complete the "holy trinity" of the Second Aliyah, and there was the splendid pathos of tomorrow.

There was an immense hunger for renewal and return to the symbols and the rituals of a people living in its own land, of celebration of the bringing of the first fruits and peasant and shepherd dances and the 15th of Av and that yearning for "the day made tangible by hand, the day solid, hot, strong . . . here on our own land!"

We the homeborn knew this biblical frenzy, the encounter between Hebrew literature and the Hebrew land, the marvelous vitality revealed here, the grand dream of building a new society and an indigenous culture that would encompass the best of the values the people brought with them, alongside the transforming experience of the Land. There was recognition of a genuine wish to create the *"Eretzyisraeli,"* the Land-of-Israel human being, in whom would be evident the here-and-now rootedness of a glorious human creativity.

It was a spiritual-political enterprise rich in contradictions and

Haim Gouri is an Israeli poet, writer and journalist.

Adapted from his article, "Anachnu Hamikomi'im," Davar, July 13, 1984. Translated from Hebrew by Stanley F. Chyet.

contrarieties that fashioned the Hebrew Land-of-Israel ethos, and we took our shape from it and ourselves gave it shape, with the contention of adversaries and with the sense of motherland as one love, complete. For us there was no "How many lands we've traversed"—we knew no anguish of two motherlands, like the "birds torn between earth and sky" of Leah Goldberg's poem.

Obviously, the cost was steep, but there was no alternative and it had to be paid to the last penny. So, the children of Martin-Buberite parents were conceived and born here and when they emerged from the womb, their mother was dismayed to see them clutching a revolver in their hands. Later Professor Roth said, "They're acquainted with only two philosophical concepts: the machine gun and the tractor."

Arthur Koestler, in the 30s, saw in them "Tarzans from the Galilean hills," saw their young women as bosomy and heavy-hipped and so on, saw in all the natives a complete contrast to their refined, sensitive forebears, the intellectuals who'd grown up in the crosscurrents of European culture, in those spired cities. Long live the newspaper stereotype!

The *Eretzyisraeli* was immeasurably diverse, but what was born and grew here and took shape here expressed a national revolution, secular at its core, though it suffered no alienation from Jewish tradition and even drew considerable strength from an entire history. The feeling of real landedness was not for the homeborn a matter of narcissism or Levantine decadence. S. Yizhar was right when he said of Yigal Allon and Moshe Dayan after their deaths that the Land of Israel had constituted their attachment to the Jews.

The story of the homeborn was the story of the bold effort to change self images, to create a new and renewing culture, to bring forth a society of labor and justice within the very "thorny delight" that Yosef Chaim Brenner described. True, there was nothing here of the richness of Jewish life Gnessin ascribed to the generations of the Diaspora. Here was the stone-tormented field and the "naked fire" but also the loveliness of a motherland whose son and creator you are. You uncover her antiquities, to the least of the clay fragments belonging to you. As master here, you plant the youngest of the saplings and you're a Jerusalemite in stone and memory and everything past, and also a Tel-Avivian on the shore of the sea separating you from your father, in the asphalt concrete glass city sprouting up as a new beginning.

The revival of language, plough and sword. The blows of adversaries. A story of national rebirth that created the fact and the lifestyles and the intellectual currents and the spirit here—and confronted an historic catastrophe there that destroyed the people in the lands of their dispersion. And when the waves of mass immigration subsided, the Exile endured: still the Diaspora, and now orphanhood, a people without its most natural hinterland, as well.

The ongoing struggle with the Arabs was not governed by a "we or you" attitude but by the constant surge forward in a land that wasn't empty, a hunger for a spirit of "We're your allies in the Semitic pact that will eventuate in due time." Most of us who warred with our neighbors also searched for a link with them, a togetherness. This was part of the Land-of-Israel ethos. A whole literature took it up in fiction and poetry and philosophy and science. The tension of enmity and the meeting which held the possibility of changing our *Mizrach,* the Orient that belongs to all of us! Lawrence of Arabia was right to say that Zionism would have its impact on Arab history, too, and would alter it so that one day the Arabs would thank the Zionists for the powerful transformation Zionism has wrought in them.

Most of us weren't such saints. We knew how to unsheathe a sword with the cry, "We've no choice." Still, the encounter with the Arabs wasn't solely one of sharp and desperate enmity; it included also an astonishing effort at conciliation and communication. For all that the conflict was prolonged and venomous and painful, it lacked the character of a religious war pitting Judaism against Islam and Christianity. It was a local struggle for a piece of territory that served the Jews as their "pauper's lamb" without which their continued existence would be insupportable. Our literature bears unmistakable witness to the pain of the war, the civil war between peoples who must settle their differences in this Orient of motherlands.

We did not deceive ourselves for a moment that the situation was perfectly simple. We recognized all the contradictions vibrating in ideas and actions. But in time there took shape among us a culture of life and struggle that determined the rules of the game and the values and limits giving our culture its direction.

After three or four generations of astonishing national success, the picture has become unrecognizable. I sense defeat in the air. The Land of Israel as a counter to the Diaspora and as its negator in the name of an alternative existence is far more "Jewish" today, from Agudat Yisrael with its Council of Torah Sages to Gush Emunim with the terrorist organization that has emerged from its ranks: two potent responses to the local pattern set here years ago. Hanan Porat, a leader of Gush Emunim, told me in 1979 or so: "You (Labor Zionists) have had your say. You said it powerfully, devotedly, truthfully and most effectively. Without you none of what we have here now would have come about. But now you've nothing to say. Now it's our turn to speak and act. You hate us because our way has continued on beyond the spot where your weariness overcame you, so step aside and let us speak!"

The homeborn, Hebrew, secular Land-of-Israel outlook reacts with shock and horror to the Jewish fanaticism that adds a distinct religious dimension to the bitter quarrel between us and the Arab national movement, the quarrel with all Islam. Those who want to murder Arabs as Arabs, and to blow up the Al-Aksa mosque and the Dome of the Rock in order to reestablish "the Kingdom of Israel" and rebuild the "Temple" and repair the "historic error" have created a way of life that stands in opposition to everything developed here in deed and in spirit. This is the first time there has been such a retreat from the whole system of principles and concepts and values shaped in the Land of Israel under the inspiration of the Hebrew national revolution. Such a retreat, such an explicit challenge.

Begin was the first non-secular prime minister, and his demonstrative association with the symbols and language of the tradition, together with his effort to delegitimate the labor movement, its values and its historic role in building the state and the society, created a new climate. And with that, he conferred incalculable and unprecedented political power on the Orthodox. And was the rebirth of Jewish terrorism in his days entirely a coincidence? He went back to speaking of the "Jewish soldier" and the "Jewish boy," he addressed himself to "the poor and the pious," he won them over: "They" talk, he said, about the New Hebrew–but what was wrong with the Old Jew, yes, the good Old Jew like your father, who says, "With God's help"? The conflict with the Diaspora was suspended during his time. His meetings with the Jews there, until his collapse could no longer be concealed, were an ongoing celebration of one identity and self-identification. He loved them and they saw in him a reflection of themselves, a mutuality. No Nahalal, no Ginossar, no Degania with their inevitable alienation, with their renaissance, their revolution.

After years of Israeli sovereignty the turmoil all around is terrible. We who, inspired by our Land-of-Israel Hebraism, knew who we were and what we wanted, are increasingly absorbed into a reality that suggests a genuine and quite significant counter-revolution.

Was the end of our vision already implicit in its beginning, in the unsuccessful attempt to forge another identity that would transform the Jews in their own land?

Bialik, I'm told, met with a group of *chalutzim* (pioneers) in the Jezreel Valley during the 1920s and declared that if a state arose in this land it would not be Jewish and if something Jewish arose it would not be a state–in other words, a Jewish state is a paradox.

And now who are we? Jews? Hebrews? Israelis? Eretzyisraelis? What is our border? What do we want it to be? Who are we in the struggle with and the proximity to the peoples and nations surrounding us and living in our midst? What have we to offer them? Some life-enabling common denominator?

Janus-faced, contradiction-ridden. While we cling to this motherland, the Land of Israel, the land of our ancestors, we fear the others who live in the land and are caught in it and multiply in it and fanatically and patiently and in their *tsumud*, their sense of relatedness, reinforce their Arab identity on both sides of the Green Line. Canaanism, stillborn as a national solution in the fabled Land of Prat, survives as a literary orientation, as a "spirit," as a bacillus found in varying degrees in the homeborn. More than a desire for amalgamation with the nations and tribes of Qedem in a covenant of ancient Hebrew identity, it represented a withdrawal from our Jewish identity. But it pursues us and imposes a dreadful choice on us: either unity as a state that to all intents and purposes is bi-national–with all that such a prospect implies–or the relinquishing of precious portions of our motherland. Either a return to the limits of "Jewish identity," or a prolonged war to the death that would expel most of the non-Jews from our "inheritance" as the opportunity arises. We cannot, we would not wish to accommodate such alternatives.

We prided ourselves on the humaneness and morality and decency of the Zionist revolution and always reiterated proudly that, from the outset of the modern return to Zion until the 1948 war, the Arab population tripled in the Land of Israel. Later, we boasted of our ability to create here a state of equal justice for all and a system of review securing the freedom of the citizen and a High Court of Justice standing night and day by those threatened with persecution. But of late, a new voice, in direct opposition to everything we thought and taught and believed, claims to speak for us, and it announces that Joshua was no heartless nationalist but a great statesman who understood that the only way to settle the land was through displacement of the Canaanites and subjugation of the survivors.

I remember one meeting with Rafael Eytan 10 years ago in Merom-Golan, where his advance command post was located during the War of Attrition that spring, before the Separation of Forces agreement. S. Yizhar asked him how things were shaping up in his opinion, and the general (as he was then) replied: "I've learned from the history books that disputes of this sort last on the average two to three hundred years. I'm not at all convinced that Arab antagonism has decreased since a century ago. On the contrary, it's getting stronger. If that's the situation, we have to anticipate another hundred or two hundred years of conflict. There's no space in this house for two rooms!"

He spoke of an Israeli Sparta, of a stubborn struggle and grueling labor and educating children to make the necessary sacrifices and demonstrate an uncompromising zealotry.

And he, Eytan, represented our strength–I mean he's one of the homeborn–I mean everything that sprang up here in blue-shirted, labor Eretz Yisrael. He comes from Tel Adashim in the Jezreel Valley just as Arik Sharon comes from Kfar Maalal in the Sharon Plain. They're not students of Jabotinsky; they grew up in the labor movement.

But his understanding is utterly at odds with the spirit of the labor movement, which knew how to combine historic necessity with the moral values of socialist Zionism.

All of a sudden the mosques on the Temple Mount! Where and when did we begin going wrong? And who's to blame? We didn't cry out, "Israel, trust in the Lord" (Psalms 115), we didn't hold it a commandment and an obligation and a responsibility, and we went up without it and did face-to-face battle with the well-armed foe, as Bialik might have said. How did the Rabbi Waldman-General Eytan alliance come about? Where is it heading? What has happened to messianism?

An entire way of life that lasted two or three generations and that, despite their differences, included both Allon and Dayan, has been virtually cut off these days, replaced by an alternative political culture fashioned by a different spiritual understanding.

The summer of 1984. The era of extremist choices. The homeborn in disarray. The Lebanese War aggravated the crisis to an incurable degree, but its beginning lies in the Six Day War, the war that united the Land of Israel and ripped apart her people.

Our national philosophy has been unable to formulate a system of rights and obligations governing our relations with our neighbors either internally or externally. We've gained strength militarily and become stuck politically. Even our right to take steps to defend ourselves in the north as occupants no less senior than Damascus (from the time of Hiram and Solomon) has been undermined and disputed to the point of a terrifying fiasco because of the lack of proper, bold and correct political-historical thought.

People who rushed to save the Lebanese Christians from a "holocaust," God forbid, later witnessed the theft by Jews of the bones of the Christian Tirza Angelovitz from the cemetery near Tel Aviv where she lay buried, may we be spared such scandal. The society of Hebrew labor, as a basic asset in the process of redemption, has become, in part, a society of employers. Hebrew rootedness has become Levantine decadence and many Israelis leave the country with no cry of pain. Those who dreamed of a people sustained by the labor of its own hands and exerting itself for its independence look in dismay at the black market for dollars on Lilienblum Street and at the dreadful dependence on philanthropists. Those who strove for an indigenous culture that would inherit the choice of the nation's treasures drawn from its long history now ask themselves what Israeli culture means, is coming to mean.

And so, during these fateful days, we the homeborn, the Israelis, the *Eretzyisraelis*, the Hebrews, the Jews, are called to a soul-searching. ★

BACK FROM THE FRONT

THE TRUE WIFE ADVENTURES OF A RESERVIST'S FAMILY

JUDY LABENSOHN

After six weeks of Lenny's serving in Lebanon with a crack paratroop unit of the Israel Defense Forces in June 1982, I sought a consultation with one of Jerusalem's wise old women about my smoldering breakdown. The symptoms: in a fit of rage at my neighbor, I uprooted all the geraniums in the roof garden and threw them at him; I bawled like a baby whenever my two-month-old son wanted to nurse; every time the two older children (ages four and seven) asked to be taken to the swimming pool, I exploded like a mine.

Phone calls made my blood pressure soar. Was he in Damour? Beirut? Had he been shot in Sidon by a 12-year-old sniper? Were they calling from Rambam Hospital in Haifa to let me know his injuries were considered "medium," crippled only from the waist down? Had his armored troop carrier, affectionately called "Zelda," fallen over a cliff into a cedar-lined ravine? Was he burning alive?

"Oh, I see you don't have much experience with wars, my dear," the Algerian-born consultant said in English with a heavy French accent. Sitting in a straight-backed mahogany chair with rococo angels fluttering around her shoulders, she flung her confident head back in a regal gesture. The magenta cushions and gray pillows, encompassing her like a cocoon, supported her flabby arms.

"What do you think it was like in Europe? For six years we lived with war, never knowing when it would end. But we coped, because we had to survive."

Realizing I had chosen the wrong address for an abreaction, I took my leave of the grande dame of Jerusalem's finest meditators, wondering why I should feel so shaky over a little war that had been going on for only 42 days. 1939-45, 1914-18, 1860-65, the Thirty Years' War. These were episodes that elicited legitimate breakdowns from over-burdened housewives. How dare I, a simple mother of three young children with no close relations this side of the Mediterranean, fall apart after a mere skirmish in Lebanon?

"Your *abba* is somewhere up north making the world safe for democracy," I shouted at the four-year-old upon my return home, when she asked why Daddy couldn't take her bike-riding.

"Your *abba* is somewhere in Lebanon making the Galilee safe for swimming," I ranted at the seven-year-old when he asked why no one ever took him rollerskating.

"You should be proud and stop kvetching," I added, as we all slammed our respective doors. "Write him a letter telling him how much you miss him," I suggested from behind my fortifications.

The infant, pushed into a world at war by no choice of his own, complained bitterly about the sudden switch from breast milk to frozen pizza, but, like all sabras, accepted his bitter fate with heroic fatalism.

Annual reserve duty with the Israel Defense Forces for men who have completed their compulsory service is called *miluim* in Hebrew. This is the plural form of *milui*, which can mean fulfillment, as in fulfillment of a duty. Lenny's *miluim* were not always as problematic for me as was his sudden call-up in June '82. In fact, before the Lebanese War, I had come to look upon *miluim* as a welcome respite from the roller coaster we call marriage. *Miluim* afforded a legitimate interlude, a relapse into singledom at best, and a taste of single parenting at worst. Everybody's needs were served by the annual army reserve duty—the army's, which depends on its civilian soldiers until the age of 55; the husband's, who is always grateful to leave the headaches of work and the hassles of family life; the wife's, who longs to listen to Mozart rather than watch "Dallas" on Monday nights.

"How long did it take you to get used to your husband going off to the army every year?" my American cousins, staying at the King David Hotel during their UJA reconnaissance missions, would ask.

"Only six years," I replied, feigning the staunch, heroic posture of those mythical Israeli women who are sanctified at Women's Division fundraising luncheons when the coffee and tea are being served.

The IDF entered our marriage during the Yom Kippur War. Lenny, a *chalutz* (pioneer) from Montreal born 50 years after his spirituo-ideological time and, therefore, unable to drain the swamps and folkdance his way across the Jezreel Valley under a full moon, volunteered to serve as a driver in a paratroop unit. This, after he had done only the standard five-week military training course for aging new immigrants, which qualified him to examine ladies' purses at the entrance to movie theaters.

He had learned how to clean a latrine, which was to come in handy after I read Betty Friedan, and dismantle a World War II "Czechi" rifle, an equally important skill. Barely understanding the IDF jargon, a foreign

---

Judy Labensohn lives in Minneapolis with her husband and three children. Her articles have appeared in Moment, Present Tense, Hadassah, *and* The Cleveland Jewish News. *She also writes a humorous column, "Mum's the Word," which appears in* The Jerusalem Post.

language in itself, comprised mostly of Hebrew acronyms and deciphered only by veteran soldiers who have done the normal three-year compulsory service, Lenny found himself holding the eastern front with little more than the equipment he had been trained to handle.

When he and his buddies succeeded in their mission, following Hussein's decision to stay put, they finally caught up with some action in northern Sinai. Then, they chased after more in the Golan Heights. After the ceasefire, they were shipped out to "Africa" to hold the line. During that winter of '73-'74, Lenny managed to finagle leaves of absence every few weeks. He would trudge into the house with Sinai sand in his boots and smells of Goshen in his newly sprouted beard. I would *kvell* with pride over my soldier-husband, who, weeks earlier, had been sitting behind a civilian desk, and now was besieging the entire Egyptian Third Army.

No one would have guessed that I had once marched in anti-war picket lines on Pennsylvania Avenue until my feet got blisters.

In March 1974, Lenny was released back into the civilian rat race. He had served his country well. His officers had taken note of his loyalty and perseverance and so promoted him from private to corporal. We hung the Egyptian bayonet, taken off a dead soldier rotting in Sinai, in the entrance hall to our apartment. Better it be used for decoration than for immolation, we mused. Slowly, we learned how to be married again, after the six-month tour of duty. We had even been enjoying each other's company for several consecutive months when a malicious little brown envelope from the IDF appeared in our mailbox.

As I fingered the call-up notice, my stomach gurgled. The fetus inside kicked. Though the envelope wasn't addressed to me, I opened the flap. My hands trembled as my eyes homed in on the rectangles in which the dates of the reserve duty are neatly written. I calculated the length of his forced absence and called Lenny at work.

"Five weeks in green coming up. Over," I communicated to my hero, with the disingenuous resolve befitting a corporal's wife.

It was during the ensuing years of Lenny's army reserve stints that I discovered how a five-week *miluim* could consume 15 weeks of our married lives. They fell into a pattern with its own dynamic, consisting of three phases:
- Phase I: Preparation for Separation (the six weeks from the time of receipt of the call-up notice until the date of departure)
- Phase II: Revolving Door Syndrome (the *miluim* itself, with its unannounced home visits)
- Phase III: Whatever Happened to Home Sweet Home? (the month following re-entry into civilization)

Each phase also had its own internal dynamic. Once these processes were recognized, defined, discussed with other wives of *miluimnikim* and accepted as the norm, *miluim* became a pleasant interlude—up until the summer of '82. As mentioned earlier, this healthy attitude took a mere six years to evolve, but this is probably due to my own inability to overcome separation anxieties experienced in the late 1940s when my father was a traveling salesman. I have known women who adjusted to their husbands' *miluim* in as little as four years' time. But, then again, their mothers live right around the corner from them. . . .

For the benefit of those women still in the throes of marital stress due to *miluim,* and for those women contemplating immigration to Israel with a fit, able-bodied male under the age of 55, I offer the following analysis.

Phase I—Preparation for Separation:

Legally, the civilian soldier must be notified of his reserve duty at least six weeks before his date of departure. This waiting period enables the married couple to work through the anxiety surrounding the impending separation. In our case, the subject would not be discussed for four weeks after receipt of the little brown envelope. Then, a surprise attack.

"Why don't you take down last week's garbage already? The place smells like a pig sty."

"Why don't you bring vegetables home from the market every Thursday, like Shoshana's husband?"

"Why don't you ever change a diaper?"

The entire division of labor of our household was suddenly called into question—the volcano erupting exactly two weeks before the scheduled departure. The attack and counterattack usually lasted until Lenny boarded the bus for his base. By this time I was relieved to get rid of him. But by 11 o'clock that night, I was wallowing in guilt for having made his last two weeks at home so miserable.

While Lenny was somewhere adjusting to army beds, food and boredom, my gut feelings emerged in full force and clarity: I was angry at him for going off with the boys and leaving me behind to mind the store. "Keep the home fires burning," he had shouted as he boarded the bus. It was absolutely archaic—sending the men off to defend us vulnerable womenfolk, who would have to learn to rub the stones together all by ourselves, while nursing the babies. Not to mention the hunting and tool making.

I, like so many of my female friends, wanted a vacation too, a paid vacation forced upon me by the state. So what if it meant sleeping in a dusty tent with no privacy, fighting mosquitoes and the occasional scorpion? So what if it meant endless hours of doing nothing, small talk, senseless missions or even dangerous escapades? Didn't I deserve a break, too, from the routine rigors of family life?

But the IDF was not interested in me. In fact, it had released me from any commitment whatsoever at the age of 22, indicating that I was already over the hill. I was never to learn which end of an Uzi shoots, never to experience the thrill of seduction by the batallion commander. The army's priorities were clear: I was designed for nursing babies and Lenny was just right for driving armored troop carriers over treacherous terrain for endless hours.

Eventually, my jealousy subsided as I realized I had the better deal. Then I was able to make Phase I pass harmoniously. I would bake Lenny's favorite chocolate cake on the Shabbat before departure and chuck out the spoiled baked potato rotting on the bottom shelf of the fridge. I would buy a new negligee. Little things that conveyed the message: Be strong and of good courage. I'll hold this fort. You hold yours.

Phase II—Revolving Door Syndrome:

No sooner had my lips dried from our good-bye kiss and I was enjoying my freedom by serving shnitzel for lunch rather than dinner than mate would turn up for a surprise visit.

"Hi, pumpkin," he would call out, trailing sand into the front hall. "I managed to get a 36-hour furlough. What's to eat?"

It was at this point during those early years that I would be transformed into a witch, wielding a broomstick as threatening as an M-16. The children would hide in their bunkers.

"Whaddya mean what's to eat? Look at this dirt you're trailing in here. Take the broom!"

Lenny was dumbfounded, of course, to be confronted with a barrage more devastating than a katyusha salvo.

"Help your son with his math. He's threatening to quit school and he's only five."

"Call the garage. We owe the cheats 50,000 shekels and the damn thing still jiggles in second."

"Yogurt's for dinner. If you don't like the menu, you can go back to the boys."

The ensuing 35 hours felt like a game of bumper cars. At the end of his leave, Lenny would depart, wondering why he had even come home in the first place. I would weep into the baby's bib. Why couldn't I be warm and loving like the army wives in Hollywood?

But, just as I had mastered Phase I, so too was I able eventually to overcome the irrational feelings that led to my bungling Phase II. After six years of experience, I got the hang of shifting gears between independence and interdependence, freedom and compromise, being alone and being together. My emotional gearshift became as agile as a Corvette's. As my rage subsided, tenderness emerged. I would rush to the kitchen as soon as I heard Lenny's boots on the stairs and quickly prepare his favorite chicken soup. I would wear the new negligee and whisk the children off to a babysitter. Little things that conveyed the message: I'll be waiting for you here at the cave. Be strong and of good courage.

Phase III—Whatever Happened to Home Sweet Home?

Seated on a normal toilet after five weeks of latrines and sand dunes, Lenny would give me a rundown of the sexual escapades of his buddies, and of the greasy food that had constipated him, as soon as he returned home from *miluim*. I was not exactly listening with my third ear, for I had three nagging children tied to my apron, each pulling in a different direction. At the dinner table, when Lenny started playing sergeant with me (he had been promoted again), all hell would break loose.

"You know, I function very well without you. I can finagle the bank manager to increase our overdraft. I can kick the washing machine into doing a rinse. I can take the puppy to the vet with all three kids and no crying and I can even convince the crooks at the garage that consumer awareness has hit Israel. So where do you get off telling me to blend the chicken soup so the progeny will eat their celery?"

Lenny knew he had re-entered civilization by the feel of the *mandlen* bullets.

Eventually, I also learned to cope with Phase III. With time, I switched from *mandlen* to soft *knaidlach,* and then, I would just throw kisses. By the time *miluim* was no more than an ambivalent memory, life returned to normal: shnitzel at dinnertime and "Dallas" on Mondays. Little things that conveyed the message: You have repossessed your territory.

So, this became the scenario, the norm. The separations of *miluim* were accepted in their proper perspective. Lenny went to the army and came home and then went to the army again. It had a rhythm like the seasons.

Unfortunately, the war called "Peace for Galilee" shattered my *modus vivendi*. No longer was *miluim* a piece of time with a guaranteed return home at the end. Black humor was now needed to cope with the overwhelming anxiety when Lenny received a second and then a third and fourth call-up notice to serve in the Land of the Cedars, where children handle guns and missiles with the nonchalance of an American kid playing video games.

"Shall I sit *shiva* now so you can see who comes?" I asked one night. We were watching the bloody scenes from Beirut on Israeli television. The fighting was followed by a funeral with the inevitable screaming mother and numb wife.

In my imagination, I heard doorbells ringing.

"Are you Judy?"

"Yes. What's the matter?"

"The Israel Defense Forces regrets to inform you that your husband. . . ."

"No, I don't need any Valium, thank you," I practiced saying to the young, embarrassed soldiers from the Rehabilitation Unit standing at the cave's entrance.

A foolish traffic accident. A mine. A sniper sporting an RPG. It didn't matter how. The time for heroism was over. Now there were only victims.

As long as Israel remains embroiled in Lebanon, the dreaded encounter with death, which pervades Israeli society—thrusting it into the everpresent Now with a vengeance—snickers from every little brown envelope. Like thousands of other Israeli women, I will hope that the IDF can find work for my soldier-husband elsewhere.

But if he should be called back to serve in the land of anarchy, terrorism and blood rivalries, I know he will go dutifully. Then, I will return to biting my nails feverishly and hanging on to each newscast. The fantasy of seeing his face staring out at me from a photograph surrounded by a thick black frame will return. The fear of calling our children "war orphans" will jolt me from my sleep.

Each time he returns to the cave, I will kiss his tired face gently, close my eyes and give thanks to the One God who guided him home. ★

UNOFFICIAL RUMORS OF THE WAR

MATTHEW NESVISKY

We're sitting on the terrace of a café overlooking Beirut and we're sipping coffee and watching the war; journalists are barred by the Israel Defense Forces from entering downtown Beirut today. The reason given is concern for our safety, and that reason will do. It's the last week of July, and we don't know it yet but it's the beginning of the end. Israel has just commenced the heaviest bombardment so far of the western sector of the city. According to one published estimate Israel will fire more shells during just this 24-hour period than it did on all fronts throughout the entire Six Day War. In its next issue, *Time* will headline the statement: "Beirut Goes Up in Flames." That's premature and inaccurate, but Israeli wars are usually calculated in hours and days and so are always hard to handle on a weekly printing schedule. Still, I'm not thinking about that now. I'm just sipping my coffee, legs crossed, notebook on my knee, and watching the war.

I won't need time later to reflect in tranquility on what is happening today. I can tell it's bad. The once-pristine city by the bay is shrouded in the smog of war. Skyhawks, shrieking horrendously, rend the sky over the Green Line that divides Christian East Beirut from the Moslem western half. On the opposite hill artillery snaps out a semaphore like flashbulbs at a Hollywood premiere; the result is that deep in the warrens of the PLO strongholds, chunks of apartment buildings—as well as the roof of West Beirut's last remaining synagogue—go spinning into the streets like so many whittled chips.

The rattle of 50-caliber machine gun fire suddenly starts up, seemingly from right below our terrace. My photographer sweeps up his equipment and scoots his chair behind a pillar, cradling his cameras in his lap. Our IDF escort officer—without one no journalist is allowed to travel from Israel to Lebanon—mutters something about the flak jackets we've left in the car. I notice that we're now the only ones on the terrace. The residents of this lovely mountain suburb of Beirut, who have long since become accustomed to sitting here and watching the war down below each afternoon, have all moved inside the café. No question, it's very bad down there today.

Urged by my companions to get the hell out of there, I finish my tiny cup of coffee and take a sip of the accompanying glass of cold water. I stand and make an elaborate business of gathering my things. This is not a show of bravado for the coffee drinkers watching us from inside the café, although it is partly that; it is more an attempt to demonstrate my disdain for the war. For I am disgusted. I actually liked this war at the outset; I am disgusted by it now. Paradoxically, I could handle it much better when I was in uniform. Now, sitting in a café and watching others getting shot at causes a vague but palpable nausea. It's a true existential nausea brought on by the absurdity of taking notes on an urban free-fire zone while drinking coffee and smoking tax-free English cigarettes purchased right here in this pleasant resort village. I'm sickened by the obscenely absurd destruction below, and I'm sickened by the obscenely absurd role I am playing here.

As a measure of just how absurd the situation is, I have in my notebook the West Beirut telephone number of Yassir Arafat (302432). I also have the phone number of the PLO's chief spokesman, Mahmoud Labadi (312198). I actually came into this café in search of a phone. But that was before the bombardment began. And the phone wasn't working here anyway.

The proprietor of the café, who was apologetic for his phone being out of order, now refuses our money for the coffee. He pumps our hands, heaping praise on Israel, and this is absurd, too. "Your bill is taken care of," he says. We feel embarrassed, flattered, foolish and somewhat seduced. For the first time I wonder what a woman feels when a barman delivers her a scotch "compliments of the gentleman at the corner table." Like maybe somebody's out to screw me. This is, after all, wily, anarchic Lebanon.

The ground shakes such speculation from my mind. On the slope below the café a volley of Katyusha rockets has set an olive grove ablaze. We go back to the car.

"There will be heavy civilian casualties today," our IDF escort officer says. Such editorializing exceeds his mandate; he is simply supposed to answer our questions and to guide us where we want to go. At the same time we are not permitted to endanger him, and so he is authorized to supervise our itinerary so that we don't get our asses shot off. We could disobey him or even give him the slip, but then we'd be denied permission to enter Lebanon again. Our relationship is good, however, certainly better than if we were not Israeli journalists, and so his free commentary on the action is accepted. Accepted and gratuitous, because we know without being told that civilian casualties will be heavy today.

Civilian casualties of course have been the hottest issue of this most unusual of Israeli wars. The issue will eventually be resolved, after the bodies are counted and the moral assessments are duly placed on the scales. Other issues, I think, will resonate longer, such as the morale and peformance of the troops, the wisdom and ultimate effectivenes of air strikes, the political gains and losses of the war. But for the time being, while the machine gunners are still pissing on their gun barrels to keep them from melting, we are obsessed with the matter of casualties, and that is as it should be.

Yet even as we spin down the mountainside from Aley and reach the crossroads at Damour, I'm not thinking about civilian casualties. This is something of an achievement, if you will, for Damour is a refugee camp that has been reduced almost to powder by strafing, artillery, rockets and bombs. It stands just off the coastal highway not far from Beirut's international airport, and so bears mute witness to everyone who travels up from Israel to Beirut. And everyone I've talked to, including correspondents who have seen it all in Vietnam and Northern Ireland and Somalia and Nicaragua, is stunned by the destruction of Damour. Havoc was wrought there in the late 1970s in a war of all

---

Matthew Nesvisky, a Moment *contributing editor, lives in Jerusalem and is an editor at the* Jerusalem Post.
All photos by Karen Benzian.

against all, and what was left the Israelis smashed apart this summer in their drive on the headquarter of the PLO.

Yet even now I'm not mourning the slain civilians of Damour or Beirut. I'm thinking instead of only one casualty. For days now I've been contemplating what a British correspondent in the Crimean War called the First Casualty in every armed conflict. All reporters worth their salt know the axiom: The First Casualty in any war is Truth.

Getting to the truth about Operation Peace for Galilee is also going to be one of the abiding issues that will resonate for years to come. For this is the first Israeli war that caused widespread doubt and questioning. Was the war necessary, as all previous wars were perceived to be, for the survival of the State? Why did the announced objective of the war change in mid-battle? Did the Defense Minister mislead the cabinet? Did the government mislead the people? Why were soldiers on leave protesting the war? Why was the foreign press so hostile to Israel? Why was the Israeli press so inadequate? Why couldn't we determine if that one infant did or did not have its arms blown off?

Talk to me about casualties and I'll talk to you about the First Casualty. That is the chief reason why, despite my keeping copious notes for the 11 weeks of the war, I was determined early on not to write anything about it. Silence in the face of uncertainty seemed the wisest course. Why add to the cacophony of description, analysis and evaluation that was already taking place? Why drive yet another nail into the coffin of the First Casualty?

One example. In my very first paragraph here I wrote: "According to one published estimate Israel will fire more shells during just this 24-hour period than it did on all fronts throughout the entire Six Day War." Notice how I reinforced the credibility of the statement with the phrase "published estimate." We like to think that if it's published, it's true. But we know better than that, don't we? Still, *is* the statement true? Perhaps, but what matters more is that it is impressive—to a layman. Military men know that Israel employed very little artillery in the Six Day War: air power conquered the Sinai, infantry and armor took the Golan, paratroopers captured Jerusalem.

Little wonder then that, like Pilate, I preferred to wash my hands. Yet eventually I realized that withholding even what I knew was only my *perception* of the truth was merely an excuse to avoid addressing my feelings about the war. Suspending judgment, like postponing protests until the war is over—another hotly debated issue in Israel—is very circumspect but not, I think, especially moral. An old Yiddish proverb says, "Tell the truth—and run."

In short, I didn't want to write about the war because I didn't think I could get it right. Now I don't think it's possible to get it wrong. Or put it another way: A few days ago I was editing a piece of news copy and came across this felicitous phrase: "Unofficial rumors yesterday indicated . . . ."

I liked that enormously. *Unofficial rumors.* Let's call this "unofficial rumors of the war." Thrown in the hopper with all the other reportage and duly weighed and fondled by time, what is written here just might contribute to some unofficial truths.

It was the same, but different. Those of us called up on the first day of the war reported to our assembly point somewhere in the north of the country just as we always had in our practice mobilizations. We gathered at our emergency supply depots, greeting each newly-arriving reservist with the sort of grins and jokes you get at alumni get-togethers. But this time we didn't just check our equipment, down our coffee, cheese sandwiches and apples, and head for home. In the dead of night we were rolling out our armored personnel carriers, loading ammunition and swapping trousers and shirts in hopes of getting at least one uniform that fit.

Still, if the long-rumored Israeli incursion into southern Lebanon was about to take place, my unit didn't really believe it would be called in. We considered ourselves a third-line outfit. Most of us were family men in our 40s, with our combat days long behind us. The world press makes much of Israel's vaunted "civilian army." But we knew that the strike force of the IDF is the small but superb regular army and its crack reserve units like the Golani Brigade. We might be called on later to hold positions, as we were in the Yom Kippur War, but certainly not to go in the first day. Unless this was something much bigger than the Litani Operation. Unless some sort of all-out mass invasion were planned.

So we rumbled out and camped in a Jewish National Fund forest and settled down to wait, and so far it was just like bivouac on our annual maneuvers. It was Sunday, June 6, and we figured we'd be back home the next day, Tuesday at the latest, no question of not being home for Shabbat. So the homecoming weekend atmosphere prevailed.

Except among Yoav and Itzik and Davidi and the other men from Kiryat Shmoneh. They were silent, seemed angry. We soon found out why:

"You guys from Haifa and Netanya and Jerusalem, you don't live on the border. Katyushas blew the balconies off our flats yesterday. This morning we had to leave our wives and kids in the shelters. We don't know what the hell's going on there now."

That sobered us. So did seeing our officers remove their insignia. A few minutes later we were throwing away our loose change. Much to our surprise, we were being sent in.

None of the men in my company was enthusiastic for war. None was reluctant. And no one, I am certain, was frightened. When you are part of a vast army column of well-oiled and well-armed vehicles stretching for miles before and behind you, you feel perfectly secure. And the ranks of cheering civilians make you feel morally self-assured. As we ground through northern settlements, beaming women, children and old men lined the roads, tossing us cigarettes, candies, popsicles, books. So it had been in every previous Israeli war. The troops had a job to do, and we were determined to do it as an unhappy but necessary duty. That belief was underscored by the support of the civilian population, which after all was us.

Our mood was further reinforced by our reception on the other side of the border. Residents of the predominantly Christian villages of southern Lebanon also lined their streets and verandas and applauded and cheered as our column rolled by. Each house had at least one white flag showing, which led cynics to remark that the villagers would cheer any army that rumbled over their territory. But I believed their welcome was genuine. Old women conveyed it clearly in sign language, eyes rolled heavenward, hands alternately pressed in thanksgiving and outstretched toward us in gratitude. Men fisted and showed biceps to signal, "Go get 'em." Whenever the column halted, which was often, urchins scampered gaily among our tracked vehicles taking orders for Cokes and Marlboros from the village grocery stores. Already on the first day of the war the Israeli shekel was accepted currency in Lebanon, four to the Lebanese pound.

Less demonstrative but still clearly showing approval were Shia Moslem households, identified by their Amal militia insignia and the ubiquitous pictures of their spiritual leader, the Imam Mussa Sadr, believed kidnapped by Muammar El-Qaddafi's agents some years before. Also giving us the high-sign were youths in battered Mercedes sedans that flew the flag of Major Sa'ad Haddad's Free Lebanese Forces. Even drivers of UN vehicles, crawling out of our path like bugs, waved in resigned acknowledgment and flashed us acquiescent smiles.

The reason for this reception was clear to all of us. Up on the horizon, looming on the highest ridge and hunkered like a cancerous growth on the neck of the entire body politic, was the Beaufort Castle, the massive Crusader fortress from which the PLO for years had ruled—and frequently rained arbitrary death—over much of south Lebanon, over these welcoming people.

Up ahead, too, something was delaying our column again and again. As we inched our way out into open country, we learned what it was. The crack IDF brigades, the real fighters, were clearing the way for us. Our holiday mood abruptly changed as evening came on. The sounds of shelling, tank fire and air strikes increased. Helicopters clattered overhead. Fire rolled with a ghostly glow over hillsides. We drove into valleys dotted with smashed and burning half-tracks and crisp bundles of black that had once been men. It was a scene from *Apocalypse Now*. Only it was more than that.

Toward the end of the war all eyes appear to be on Philip Habib as he negotiates the final details of the PLO evacuation of Beirut. But there are other developments that mean more to some people in the area than any superpower machinations.

This day, for example, I discover that the IDF command staff in Sidon, the capital of southern Lebanon, is near-frantic about a rumor that threatens to sweep the Shia population. The rumor is that the revered Imam Mussa Sadr is *not* in fact being held captive in Libya, but was recently found by the Israelis when they overran the PLO stronghold in the Rashadiya refugee camp. The aged Imam, so the story goes, has been taken to an Israeli military hospital, where he is slowly recovering from his long ordeal in captivity.

The IDF is distressed because if the story takes hold among the Shias, Israel will be expected to produce the Imam. And Israel cannot do that; according to our intelligence, the holy man has long been dead and buried beneath Libyan sands. Yet if the Shias, who often bear photos of the Imam on their rifle butts, believe that Israel is holding Mussa Sadr, it could cause great tension. The Shias are already delicately balanced between appreciation for Israel's smashing of the PLO and their sympathies for the Khomeini regime in Iran.

The IDF has traced the rumor to two Beirut newspapers that often serve the interests of the Palestinians. Israel believes the story was planted by the PLO as a diabolical piece of disinformation—an official rumor, if you will—to undermine the Israeli position in Lebanon. The story threatens to spread like wildfire, and the IDF is urgently attempting to stamp it out. They are doing this in a low-key manner, however, fearful that vociferous public denials will only fuel the flames. So they are making discreet approaches to Shia leaders, and in particular to the Imam's sister, who is venerated by the masses.

My paper thinks this is a fascinating story. We're also intrigued by the question of whether the military censors will allow us to publish it. We write it up and duly submit it. The censor apparently is fascinated by the story as well. "Nothing here is censorable," he tells us laconically on the phone. "But we certainly don't think it'll do the country much good if you print it. The decision is yours."

That's a curious response. The censor's job is to cut or not to cut, not to provide advice. Normally I have few problems living with the censor; since it is well known that our enemies carefully comb Israeli newspapers looking for details about troop movements, references to military equipment and so on, it seems reasonable that the military should review material that could be useful to the other side. (The story and photographs you are holding now have been submitted to the censor, which may explain certain vagaries in detail here and there.) And because this is the Middle East, or perhaps because we are Jews, a certain amount of dickering goes on. You can bargain, *shuk*-like, with the censor if the need arises, and you win a few points and you lose some. The censors are neither rigid nor capricious; they are fair-minded and they are human.

Yet during the Peace for Galilee Operation the censorship comes under heavy attack. Foreign news services, though apparently content to subsist on official daily war communiqués handed them in Teheran and Baghdad, are outraged when Jerusalem wants to review their copy. But even local newsmen claim that in no other war in

Israel's history has the amount of permitted information been so sparse. The state-controlled radio and television, especially in the first weeks of the war, are widely criticized by the public as inadequate. A scandal brews about a purge of "leftists" at the Army radio station.

I don't envy the job of the censor, and I would never be one myself, but I, too, am very dissatisfied with the situation during the war. Happy reports, such as the Beaufort Castle being captured without the loss of a single Israeli life (this turns out to be untrue), are given wide currency. Unhappy reports, such as hospitals being shelled, have less chance of publication. One story I was editing about an IDF patrol that ran into an ambush described the survivors feeling "numbed and depressed." The story came back from the censor with the words "and depressed" excised. Conceivably, publication of those two words would have a negative effect on troops still in battle, not to mention the population at large. They might even give aid and comfort to the enemy. But it seems moot. Anyone who would not expect troops to be depressed after taking heavy casualties in an ambush is simply playing footloose with the truth—the First Casualty in any war.

Eli Geva, the officer who asked to be relieved of his command because he couldn't continue shelling Beirut, declines to be interviewed by the press. But I get a minor scoop for my notebook when I pick up a hitchhiking soldier one day and he turns out to have served under Geva.

"Sure," he says, "I can tell you why Eli packed it in. Our spotter gives us coordinates and we fire and the target's still there. We get coordinates and we fire again and the target's still there. We get coordinates and we fire so much we can't even *tell* if the target's still there. And that's what they call pinpoint bombardment. Don't ask me if Eli was right to get out. I can't judge. I didn't have the responsibility he had. *L'azazel*, to hell with it."

To me there has never been any great mystery about why men agree to go to war. For all its constant discomforts, occasional dangers and vast stretches of boredom, men like it. For one thing, many restraints are suspended during wartime. You can spit and curse and belch and break wind with abandon. You can skip washing and shaving and you can squat around the campfire and eat with your fingers and then wipe them on your clothes—and you must not minimize how much this means to the little boys within us all. And the more you do it the more natural it seems.

War affords other forms of license as well: Bursting across a border without the formalities of passports or other permission provides a genuine ripple of pleasure. "Penetration!" I thought as we barreled into Lebanon, our gun barrels and cannons bristling symbolically at all and sundry. And then, of course, you get to use those guns that all through training you are drilled never to point at anyone.

There are other attractive aspects to a combat situation: Peer pressure keeps you from performing badly, with the result that you are subsequently self-congratulatory about your behavior. At the same time your comrades, who are essentially strangers, are linked to your welfare and destiny, and you to them, in a manner that is evident nowhere else in society. The interdependence is reassuring and gratifying. In this uniformed herd you feel capable of accomplishing much; you can test yourself; you feel younger and more fit than you really are; you feel extended; you feel responsible to the rest of the herd and protected by it because you feel it cares about and relies on you to do your share.

But there is pop psychology and there is political reality. By the third day of the war I have recorded in my diary: "This war will resolve nothing; no good can come of it." Yet I know that this is just for the record. What I was really thinking was: "God damn, but this is a good little war."

The Beaufort has fallen. The Syrian missiles in the Bekaa Valley have been obliterated. So many MIGs have been shot out of the sky that we were joking: "The Russians show the Syrians how to put the planes up, and we show the Syrians how to bring them down." Best of all, the bulk of the terrorists have fled, and we are just mopping up and securing the area.

By the end of the first week of Operation Peace For Galilee, however, war's true face was becoming starkly evident. I'll give you three faces—perhaps out of them we can form a composite of what I have so grandly called the true face of war.

The first was the face of the dead solider we discovered on the previous night's patrol. Our searchlight picked out some movement. We halted and saw the bloated corpse of a man in uniform about 20 yards off the road. A skinny dog was chewing a flap of the soldier's scalp. We approached only close enough to determine if the soldier's uniform was Israeli. It was not. So we kept our distance. We had been lectured about booby-trapped cigarette packs, radios, doorways, bodies. We could leave the corpse there in good conscience, just report its position at the end of the patrol and let some burial detail worry about it. Still, even if that were a PLO body out there we didn't feel right about letting a mongrel eat its brains. We held a short conference. It was decided that our corporal would shoot the dog. He fired his Galil and hit the corpse in the groin, causing it to buck obscenely. The dog scampered away. Now, unfortunately, we had an even better view of the soldier's face. The top of his head was gone but the lower part looked smooth, healthy, even jaunty with its carefully groomed mustache. The dog returned; it was hungry. The second shot tore off the dog's head.

A second face: At dawn this morning I was crouched on a rooftop overlooking the checkpost where we were turning back virtually all traffic heading into Nabatiya. Far up the highway I could see a solitary figure walking our way. It was a Bedouin woman, barefoot and balancing an impossibly large bundle on her head—mint, as I eventually made out, or possibly some other greenery she had gathered. With a sinking feeling I watched her as she walked down that long road toward our roadblock. From my position, there was no way I could signal her to go back. After 15 minutes, she finally arrived below where I was watching from the roof. My comrades on the pavement explained that searches were under way in Nabatiya and that no one was allowed in or out of the town that day. Words like military government or travel document must have meant nothing to her. Yet only a momentary flicker of disappointment or confusion showed on her round, brown face. She did not know why she was barred from going to the market, as she likely had been accustomed to doing for years. She knew only that uniformed men said it was forbidden. And she stoically accepted it.

Menashe, sitting next to me, said the people here must be used to it, as the PLO and the Phalange and the Free Lebanese Forces had all at one time or another operated their roadblocks here. I couldn't understand how anyone could get used to it. In the meantime, the barefoot woman, her face a study in passivity, turned and began plodding back up the highway. It must have been ten miles or more to the next village.

A third face, that of Gregor, twisted and flaming with animal fury: That afternoon we had been sweeping up suspected terrorists, either flushed out of orchards and caves or picked up at roadblocks. Each was bound and blindfolded and trucked to a collection point for questioning. Some had been captured after firefights in the hills. Others had been plucked out of automobiles at checkpoints because they had no papers, or because their documents were inadequate or suspicious. Which is to say some of our prisoners were surely terrorists, some were probably just unfortunate day laborers on their way to their jobs in Nabatiya who didn't realize they needed proper identification. In either case there was no excuse for Gregor, a new immigrant from Leningrad and a follower of Rabbi Meir Kahane, to be hurling bound and blindfolded men and boys off the back of our half-track. Until we restrained him, he was even kicking them in the spine and thumping them with his rifle butt. I could not recall ever seeing such blind rage in a human face before.

Somewhere among these three faces, I think, is the true face of the war. In any event, before the second week was out I had learned that this was no longer a "good little war," and had noted in my diary: "I hope I don't come home from this like those Vietnam vets, viewed as having done something dishonorable." And this was long before Operation Peace for Galilee turned into Operation Hell for Beirut.

Dr. Clinton Bailey is senior lecturer in Middle Eastern Studies at Tel Aviv University, an expert on Bedouin poetry and well known in Israel as an outspoken advocate of the rights of Israel's Bedouin in the face of the government's often cavalier attitude toward their tribal grazing lands. Like all Israelis, Bailey wears more than one hat, and when he was called up for the war he was appointed advisor to the IDF unit for aid to Lebanese civilians, headquartered first in Nabatiya and later in Sidon. I ended up serving 41 days and was glad to get out when I did. Bailey felt he had so much to do he actually requested to be kept on beyond his release date.

I admired Bailey's civil rights activities as a civilian and I find much to respect in his military role. He is already famous in the area for racing about unescorted in a jeep anywhere and everywhere he might be required—to remote villages, to the depths of Sidon's Casbah, to the heart of Palestinian refugee camps. He sleeps in his office in the Sidon municipality building, and rises each day to solve bureaucratic problems, calm fears, investigate complaints, deal with parents whose sons have disappeared or are being detained.

I'm lucky to catch him in his office. And I'm surprised by what he has to tell me.

"I'll admit, frankly," he says, "that when this war began I was totally opposed to it. I saw it as solving nothing—and worse, I saw it creating a whole new set of problems for us. But after these few weeks, I've changed my mind completely. I've done a complete 180-degree turn."

I ask him why and he responds briskly. "Because of what we've learned about the reign of terror the PLO perpetrated on southern Lebanon these past seven years. We obviously haven't solved the Palestinian problem, and we may not even have secured peace for Galilee. But believe me, just getting the terrorists off the backs of the Lebanese is a mitzvah."

But, I interject, was it *our* mitzvah to perform?

Bailey shrugs. "A mitzvah is a mitzvah and no one else was going to perform it. We've been gathering such horror stories—they would curl anybody's hair. Rape, butchery, extortion, the stealing of children. We have teams out collecting and documenting. In the Nabatiya area alone we gathered 5,000 reports of atrocities, just in the first few weeks. Even if you accept only a fraction of these reports. . . ."

But that's just the problem, isn't it? Beyond the notorious Arab penchant for fantasy, isn't it natural for an occupied people to tell horror tales about the previous occupier, to win sympathy as victim, to demonstrate innocence, to curry favor with the new power? In an effort to show loyalty and appreciation to whoever might rule there next, would not some south Lebanese slander the Israelis?

"All right," Bailey says, finishing his can of pineapple juice. "Don't take my word for it. Just wait here." He pops out of the office and returns a moment later with a thin, neatly-dressed gentleman in tow. Bailey introduces the man as a well-known local poet and professor of Arabic literature at the Sidon campus of Beirut University. He is a Maronite Christian, and agrees to speak only after I promise not to publish his name.

"It's lucky I just happened to see Dr. _____ out in the hallway," Bailey says. He turns to the professor. "Just tell him what you were telling me the other day about life at the university."

It takes a considerable amount of prodding—to be fair, the professor's English is not good—but he eventually tells his story. "We have 6,000 students at the university," he says. "About 2,000 of them are Palestinians. They could make life hell for the others. They alone ruled student political life. They either recruited for the terrorists or extorted money for their cause. Even worse, they terrorized their teachers. Just before final examinations were scheduled in May, they came to professors' homes at night and at gunpoint demanded the questions in advance. No, they didn't come to my house. But there were reports. . . ."

The professor doesn't have much else to say, except that he is grateful that Israel invaded. And he concludes: "Lebanon is a narrow little country between the desert and the sea. To us the desert means Islam and the repression of the Middle Ages. Thus we must look to the sea, to the Christian west, to the light of democracy."

Bailey escorts the professor out. Everything he said may be true, but I still don't like the smell of it. I don't like how he was "produced" here at the Israeli military headquarters to perform for the press. Did the PLO students terrorize teachers? "There were reports." Did it happen often, once, or not at all? For that matter, why extract only exam questions at gunpoint? Why not go whole hog and demand advanced degrees and department chairmanships?

Bailey returns and acknowledges that the professor sounded unconvincing. "But the other day, when he spoke freely with me in Arabic, when there was no reporter here—it would have curled your hair."

I believe Bailey is sincere. I am just unprepared for the hawkish attitudes he has been expressing. But then I've been going through some changes myself since this war started. That's the kind of war it is. You keep stumbling over what may be the corpse of that First Casualty.

The most exhausting duty we had was conducting searches through orchards, sweltering in the July heat under our helmets, packs and flak jackets. The most insane activity we had was clearing canyons and wadis, performing what in Vietnam was called "reconnaissance by fire," that is, blasting away at caves and groves of trees to see if they shoot back. The most boring job we pulled was manning roadblocks and guard posts, especially in the dead of night. But the most unsavory assignment we had was house-to-house searches.

At first I thought it was just my Anglo-Saxon hang-up about the sanctity of private property that made breaking down doors so distasteful. Later I wasn't so sure. It is one thing to hunt for terrorists or weapons or documents; it is another to root through cabinets and closets, photo albums and school bags, sewing baskets and family Korans.

I nominated myself to stand guard outside while such searches were conducted, and no one criticized me for this. But I couldn't fool myself; I was taking part. I would glance in the doorway and see my sergeant chopping open a locked attaché case with a pickax, and I couldn't pretend that I wasn't helping him. And if I saw men liberating souvenirs—an interesting poster, a penknife, some condoms—I kept my mouth shut. I didn't witness any out-and-out looting, but I still had the gut feeling that what we were doing was morally impermissible.

Earlier in the war, when we came upon a PLO mountain redoubt that had been abandoned so quickly that knives and forks were still lying on tin dishes around the cookfire, we cheerfully pocketed Paco Rabanne after-shave and packs of Marlboros and Winstons; we even gathered up their foam rubber mattresses. But that was different. Now we were dealing with civilians.

And within a few weeks, in fact, five men in my unit would be in jail awaiting charges of robbing Lebanese citizens. This happened to be an extraordinarily high number for one outfit, and it earned all of us the sobriquet as the *ganavim*, the thieves. We were all shocked and depressed by the thefts, and resentful of our bad reputation. And we all agreed this war was going on much longer than we had ever dreamed possible.

Rina is rapidly becoming a legend among the foreign press corps. An Israeli photographer working for an overseas news agency, Rina is fearless to the point of insanity. While we huddle with our IDF escort officers behind buildings that are slowly being chipped away by machine gun fire and rocket-propelled grenades, Rina is out there edging along the Green Line in a military low-crawl, snapping pictures of terrorists in West Beirut. Bullets are stripping the pink blossoms off the Persian lilac trees and Rina just keeps pulling herself forward on her elbows and taking pictures. "That woman is simply not to be believed," Neil Johnston, a veteran of two years as a war correspondent in Southeast Asia, says admiringly.

My admiration for Rina is mixed with despair. What is the point of becoming a casualty yourself in pursuit of that First Casualty? And I wonder why I was so much more sanguine about bullets when I was in uniform.

The whole business of the media coverage of the war interested me only after I was out of uniform. Israelis were outraged by the foreign press and TV reportage of Operation Peace for Galilee, and so were American Jews. I shrugged the matter off, ascribing hostility toward the press to the desire to slay the bearer of ill tidings. In any case, there seemed little to be done about it. As one IDF escort officer told me: "I've tried again and again to explain Israel's case to foreign journalists. But when I do, they invariably open up their newspapers and refuse to listen."

But I don't know what an IDF spokesman could say that would alter the view anyone gets traveling up the coastal road from Rosh Hanikra to Beirut. Chris Buckland, a British newsman who covered the battles in Belfast for seven years, said: "I've never seen anything like it. The firepower that was unleashed, the wholesale destruction. There wasn't an apartment house that wasn't shot up, not a shop or garage that wasn't blitzed, a hundred miles of it. I know the villains were holed up in private homes and all that. But this Israeli assault was just awesome."

Buckland is telling me this over a gin and tonic at the Gesher Haziv guest house where the journalists assemble for their run up to Beirut each morning and where they stagger back for their booze each night. Chris is amiable, intelligent and, from what I gather, fair-minded. I have little reason to believe that the majority of the press corps here is any different. That is, until I pick up a paper like London's *Daily Mirror* of August 3 and read an unsigned story that begins:

Israel is ruthlessly destroying Beirut, street by street, block by block, and killing or wounding thousands of innocent civilians as it does so.

The bombardment of the Lebanese capital has been so brutal, so sustained and so devastating as to be a crime against humanity.

Maybe it's schizophrenic to oppose

the war and to be appalled by such reporting at the same time. If so, I wouldn't be the first to be driven round the bend by a war.

Half an hour later I find myself arguing with the noted leftist journalist and former Knesset member Uri Avnery. We begin by agreeing that the war is awful. We agree that the siege of Beirut has become an unintended propaganda prize for the PLO. But then Avnery raps *The Jerusalem Post* for invariably referring to all the PLO as terrorists.

"Take Farouk Kaddoumi," he says. "The man is in charge of the PLO political department. He's a diplomat. Yet you always call him a terrorist. But as the Americans say, if it walks like a duck and talks like a duck and looks like a duck, well, it must be a duck. Kaddoumi's a diplomat."

"I don't know, Uri," I reply. "Remember how the Shah of Iran dressed like a statesman and talked like a statesman and everyone treated him like a statesman? But we found out he wasn't a statesman. He was a tyrant and a thug."

Avnery laughs and crams more Flying Dutchman into his pipe and says nothing. I congratulate myself for scoring points. Then I immediately wonder what I'm congratulating myself for.

If the truth be told—and that is what this essay is about—there were some sweet moments back there in the war. I'll always remember how my buddies were scrupulously fair in sharing out battle rations, never forgetting to set aside an ample portion for whoever happened to be on guard duty at mealtime. I was impressed by the ease with which our Arabic speakers won the trust of the Lebanese, how they were vigilant in showing courtesy and respect for the local population. I was touched by the comradeship amid hardship, as when we created a Sabbath Eve celebration for each other even as our minds were on our families back home. I remember how we ran to gather up each other's damp uniforms when a helicopter began to churn a huge cloud of dust in the direction of our laundry line. I recall how everyone who went on leave unfailingly telephoned reassurances to families of comrades, and invariably came back with enough homemade cakes for all. I'm proud of our rushing a wounded PLO man to a military hospital, a lost child to a local police station, a water tanker to a cut-off village. The endless political debates; the bitter condemnation of those few black sheep who had been caught thieving; the warm feeling of being invited onto a Lebanese citizen's veranda to watch the World Cup soccer playoffs on TV together; the respect the secular soldiers had for the religious men among us; how the mood abruptly changed after June 15 when the siege of Beirut began; these were all heartening things. I remember, too, how Moshe, in civilian life a member of a poor Moroccan poultry-growing moshav in Western Galilee, sat by my little radio and listened through to the end as an exquisitely ordered and harmonious Telemann quartet was broadcast. When it was concluded he asked me what it was and said: "That was really beautiful. You know, I wish this war was done with."

All of the above is true. It is also sentimental claptrap, but true for all that. The good Lord, who knew that men would go to war, who on occasion even instructed men to make war, built the human mind so that good things would be remembered and bad things would be repressed. To keep men sane.

So I did my 41 days of army duty, and for the next 40 days or so I worked overtime as a newsman, running up to Beirut several times and filling slots for colleagues who were called up after I was released. Finally, as the first PLO contingents were about to set sail for Tunis aboard the *Sol Georgios*, I decided a little holiday was due. My wife needed it, too. The past months had not been easy on her either.

We were lured northwards, where the hotels and guest houses were offering generous discounts in an attempt to rebuild the tourism that had suffered so from the periodic shelling before Operation Peace for Galilee.

We had a nice weekend, thank you. We swam in the Kinneret and went to the Mount of the Beatitudes. We drove along the beautiful and solitary northern road and rode the cable car to the grotto at Rosh Hanikra. On Saturday night we dined at a Chinese restaurant in Nahariya and joined the crowds strolling that little resort town's main drag, and later ate ice cream at the popular Penguin Café.

Spending Saturday night in Nahariya was a buoyant experience. The streets were packed with young mothers pushing baby buggies, old *yekke* couples strolling arm-in-arm, soldiers on leave, UN personnel on the prowl, giggling teenagers, honeymooners, tourists. There was folk dancing in the park and the little rowboat concession at the end of the town's canal was doing a roaring trade. The eucalyptus trees were strung with colored lights, and the town's famous horse-drawn carriages were everywhere, adding to the festive atmosphere.

Peace for Galilee. Nahariya took more than its share of Katyushas over the years, suffered abundantly from terrorists landing on its beach in rubber boats in the dark of night. You could say the war was fought so that mums could push their strollers without fear. So that tourists could crunch eggrolls at Nahariya's Singapore Restaurant. You could say that sounds maudlin or banal or even absurd. You could also say it is the truth.

The next morning we drove a few kilometers down the highway from Nahariya to Kibbutz Lochamei Hageta'ot. I had never before visited the Holocaust Museum there. Just last May, however, a month before Israel decided to invade Lebanon, I visited Dachau. On the wall of the crematorium there I noted that someone had scratched the slogan "Never Again" and that someone else had tried to scratch the slogan out, and I heard myself say aloud that I was glad I lived in Israel.

Among the exhibits at the kibbutz Holocaust Museum are an exact-scale model of a concentration camp, built by a carpenter who had been a prisoner there, and a street-by-street miniature replica of the Warsaw Ghetto. I've long felt we Jews have a proclivity for remembering our blackest hours, our most ignominious defeats. To be sure, General Stroop was accurate when he crowed: "The Warsaw Ghetto is no more!" But the siege of the ghetto has become an immortal moment in the history of the Jews.

As I studied that model I couldn't help thinking that some Palestinian some day, somewhere, will construct a little replica of West Beirut to celebrate a glorious moment in Palestinian history. General Sharon says that all his aims have been achieved in the war, and that the PLO has been dealt a mortal blow. But the PLO claims it fought a much mightier power to a standstill, and its survivors are greeted as heroes in their latest temporary havens.

Can everybody win? Can everyone be right? Apparently the truth is just a rumor—and you choose your truth and run with it.

I've told a part of the truth here, a fraction of what I've seen and heard, a bit of journalism, which Arnold defined as literature in a hurry. Others are already assembling their books on Operation Peace for Galilee. Good luck to them. May they not become casualties. ✡

THE KAHANE CONTROVERSY

According to Israel's Attorney-General, "Kahanism, which has become a synonym for racism, is a shameful, loathsome and dangerous phenomenon." How one MK challenges Israel's democratic tradition.

WALTER REICH

Umm al-Fahm, an Arab village in northern Israel, is built on hills overlooking the Wadi Ara road. More than 3,000 years ago, before the children of Israel entered the Promised Land, that road was an already-ancient mountain pass that carried armies from Egypt toward Mesopotamia and back. Over the millennia it was the site of numerous battles and ambushes, with forces occupying the heights above usually destroying the invaders below. Sometimes, by stealth and daring, the invaders surprised their foes and routed them in battles of biblical dimension.

Last summer, Meir Kahane, just elected to the Israeli Knesset, vowed to become the road's newest invader. His goal, he said, was to open an Arab emigration office in Umm al-Fahm. The villagers, all citizens of Israel, vowed, for their part, to stop him. The confrontation promised to be the most dramatic challenge yet to the integrity and survival of Israeli democracy.

I had come to Israel shortly after Kahane's election to try to understand the meaning of his unexpected success. For many of Kahane's critics, he was just a "stray weed" in Israeli politics, a racist extremist who represented no more than the 26,000 Israelis who had endorsed him—merely 1.3 percent of the electorate, just over the minimum one percent required to win a Knesset seat. But even those voters, his critics added, had given Kahane their support primarily to send a message of angry rejection to the country's established politicians. The majority of them, these critics explained, did not agree with Kahane's calls for the expulsion of Israel's Arabs, just as they did not agree with his calls for laws against sexual relations between Arabs and Jews or the establishment of a theocracy based on his fundamentalist version of Jewish law.

Other Israelis, however, feared that Kahane's election was in fact an accurate, and ominous sign of a serious deterioration in the health of Israeli democracy. He was, they said, no stray weed. The decades of unrelenting Arab hostility and the country's increasing international isolation were, they argued, beginning to fray the fabric of Israel's national democratic consensus. Internal divisions, which had always existed, were growing sharper. Differences between many Jewish groups—between religious Jews and non-religious Jews, between those of Oriental, or Sephardi, origin and those of Western, or Ashkenazi, origin, and between those on the political left and those on the right—were taking on the character of strife rather than healthy debate. As the country's economy has worsened, as foreign criticism has increased, and as other pressures have grown, intolerance has become more prominent, and those whose views are different from one's own have been seen increasingly as enemies, even traitors, rather than as participants in the national political discussion. Kahane's railings against the Arabs, the Israeli left, non-religious Jews and Western values were attracting a genuine, if still small, following among the most polarized and frustrated sectors of the population. And, these apprehensive Israelis warned, if that following continued to grow, and if many other Israelis joined the flight into extremisms of one sort or another, then Israel's political life would lose its broad center, the country would become radicalized, the trust necessary to maintain civil compromise would be damaged, and the democratic traditions and institutions in which Israelis have for so long prided themselves would be threatened.

And, more than that, the country's very existence would be threatened. If it lost its character as a democratic state, these Israelis predicted, it would probably also lose its main friend in the international arena, the United States, whose government and people have long supported it and wished it well because the democratic values to which it subscribed were the same as theirs, and because those values made it a stable and reliable ally in an otherwise unpredictable and autocratic corner of the world. With all that at stake, these Israelis concluded, Kahane's sudden and striking electoral success betokened something very ominous indeed for the future of the Jewish state. Small wonder, they added wryly, that Kahane had received more than a few votes among the country's Arab population.

That Kahane chose to invade Umm al-Fahm—where he would, as he put it, "make the Arabs an offer to leave the country they couldn't refuse"—was no accident.

First of all, the village had been, for more than a decade, the main center for some of the most radical Arab groups in the country. One such group, the Ibn al-Balad, or Sons of the Village, has repeatedly held strikes to protest Israeli policies. And other groups, operating secretly and re-

---

Walter Reich is Senior Research Associate at the Woodrow Wilson International Center for Scholars in Washington, D.C.

Waiting for Kahane: the scene at Umm al-Fahm

The Kahane Controversy

portedly linked to the PLO, have been subjected to crackdowns and arrests for storing caches of weapons to be used in terrorist attacks.

But there was another and far more important reason that Kahane chose Umm al-Fahm as the target of his post-election invasion. In 1949, when the village became part of the newly created Jewish state, it had a population of 3,200. In the 36 years since then, the figure has grown to 24,000. This enormous jump—a nearly sevenfold increase—has been seen by some Israeli Jews as emblematic of the population explosion that has been experienced by Israel's Arab minority. Numbering only 156,000 in 1949, that minority now totals 700,000, with the increase due almost solely to the Arabs' high fertility rate. Given the fact that their fertility rate is nearly double that of the Jews, it appears, according to some Israeli demographers, that the Arabs, who are now about 17 percent of the country's population of 4.2 million, may, in 30 years, be 24 percent.

According to Kahane, however, that estimate is low. He insists that, by the middle of the next century, the percentage of Israelis who are Arabs will be much higher than the experts predict. By then, he says, the Arabs will be unified, control a plurality if not a majority of the vote, and use the power of the ballot to dismantle the underpinnings of the Jewish state—especially the Law of Return, passed by the Knesset in 1950, five years after the Holocaust, which gives every Jew everywhere the right to automatic haven in Israel. With their votes, the Israeli Arabs could revoke that law, revise the Declaration of Independence, which identifies Israel as a Jewish state, and even change the name of the country to Palestine. In this process, carried out solely through democratic means, Israel would cease to exist, the Jews would no longer have a national home, and Jews being persecuted in other countries would once again have nowhere to flee.

But as unsettling as this demographic nightmare is to many Israeli Jews, Kahane adds a coda designed to unsettle them even more. The Arabs of the West Bank and Gaza, he says,

The newly-elected member of Knesset, in front of Jerusalem's Plaza Hotel.

who now number 1.2 million, must also be included in these calculations. Though not citizens of Israel now, they could become citizens if those territories, occupied by Israel since the 1967 Six Day War, are, as he and other Israelis believe they should be, annexed. Should that happen, then Israel's Arab population would suddenly constitute about 35 percent of the total, and, within just 30 years, according to the predictions of even the most conservative demographers, it would amount to well over half. If these Arabs, too, are given citizenship, they could, even more quickly than the current Israeli Arabs acting alone, dismantle the Jewish state.

What Kahane concludes from this demographic nightmare is that Israel cannot be both a democratic and a Jewish state. If it remains democratic, and Arabs can vote, then it will eventually stop being Jewish. Since for him the Jewish nature of the state is more important than its democratic nature, the latter must be abandoned in favor of the former. The Arabs, he argues, must be "transferred" from the country, both from Israel proper and from the occupied territories. They must be encouraged to leave through financial incentives and other means, including intimidation; and those who choose to stay must no longer have the right to vote.

On the morning that Kahane announced he would invade Umm al-Fahm, thousands of angry Arab residents were waiting to confront him in the village. Nor were they alone.

The previous night, several hundred Israeli Jews had arrived to give the village their moral support; and, that morning, a dozen members of the 120-member Knesset, most of them Jews, had arrived to do the same thing. Hundreds more Israeli Jews had come that morning to give their support, but, unlike the Knesset members, were not allowed entry into the village. The police, a thousand strong, considered the situation extremely dangerous. Unable to stop Kahane because of his newly-won shield of parliamentary immunity, they expected the worst, and had orders to keep all outsiders, whether supporters of the villagers or of Kahane, out. The Wadi Ara road below the village soon filled with Jews, many wearing facsimiles of the yellow Star of David that the Nazis had forced Jews to wear in European ghettos and concentration camps, each star inscribed, in Hebrew, with the words, "We Will Not Let Racism Pass."

Trying to enter Umm al-Fahm that morning as well, I approached the police officer on the road, asking to be allowed into the village. He refused. After I pressed him again, he grew agitated, warning that anything could happen, that tempers were so high an explosion might take place, that no more persons could be let in, even journalists, and that if I pressed him any further, and distracted him from the task of keeping order, he would be forced to arrest me. Suddenly, down the road, I saw a group of Jews bolt across a field and up a hillside. I followed, quickly climbing the hills above the ancient pass. Soon dozens more were climbing, pulling themselves up by the rocks and scrub. We reached the other side, climbed still more hills, and found ourselves, finally, on a bluff overlooking the village entrance below.

Kahane had promised to arrive in Umm al-Fahm at 10 a.m. Three nights before, emigration forms had been placed in the village square together with leaflets saying that Israel was the land of the Jews and that, in order to avoid conflict, the Arabs had to leave. Arabs willing to emigrate to Western countries, the leaflets added, would receive visas, housing and jobs.

Numerous Israelis, from the left of the political spectrum to the right, as well as newspapers and organizations, urged the Interior Minister, Yosef Burg, who was in charge of the police, to bar Kahane's entry into the village. Burg, however, argued that the principle of parliamentary immunity is an important one and should not be suspended arbitrarily. Victor Shemtov, a Knesset member and the leader of the left-wing Mapam Party, then a partner in Shimon Peres's Labor Alignment, sent Burg a telegram asking him to prevent the visit, which, he warned, was "of a provocative nature," and "apt to lead to serious incidents"; allowing Kahane's followers into the town, he warned, might start "things that no one knows how they will end." Burg held firm. A local police commander warned the Umm al-Fahm council that "if one stone is thrown at Kahane, the entire council will be held responsible." Earlier that month, the head of the council, Hashem Mahamid, predicted that, were Kahane to be allowed into Umm al-Fahm, the residents of the village would respond by stoning him. On the day before the visit Mahamid added that, if any violence were to take place, it would be Burg, not the council, who would be responsible.

On the Wadi Ara road that morning, the commander of the northern police district, Rahamim Hadad, a Jew of Oriental origin, had a telephone line open to the Israeli Police Inspector-General, Arye Ivtzan, who was, in turn, in touch with Burg. Within the village itself, the tension mounted. Residents and their Jewish supporters, facing a barricade of policemen, chanted "Jewish-Arab brotherhood!" and "Fascism won't pass!" Above them, on a barren hillside, many more watched, climbing up and down, as if aimlessly, with an increasing frequency that matched their increasing tension. Suddenly, just before 1:00 in the afternoon, as the police commander drove in from the Wadi Ara road, rumors spread that it was Kahane. Screaming "With our blood and spirit we will redeem you, Umm al-Fahm!" the Arabs surrounding me on the hillside, with whom I had just been talking, youths as well as grown men, hurled stones at the car and the police. The police, in turn, shot volleys of tear gas. We ran further up the hill, our skin burning, enveloped in the acrid, burning smoke. Children passed me sections of onion, which they said would counteract the effects of the gas. An Arab family, seeing me coughing, ushered me into the refuge of its modest house. A woman inside gave me water, and told me she was ready to crush Kahane's skull.

Only later did the villagers learn that, before noon, Kahane had been stopped on the Wadi Ara road just a mile from the village, and that, soon after, he had been forbidden entry into it. The police told Kahane that they would be unable to guarantee his safety. And, they told the press, the situation was by then so dangerous that it threatened state security. Under the circumstances, parliamentary immunity could not be maintained. The police commander's arrival in the village, which had precipitated the first volley of stones, had in fact been for the purpose of informing the villagers that Kahane would not come.

Interviewing the chairman of Umm al-Fahm's village council later that day, I learned that the villagers saw the event as a victory. "A great thing happened today," Hashem Mahamid told me exultantly. "We achieved a unity of Jews and Arabs working together. The first victims of Kahane would be the Arabs, and the next might be the leftists. This is the first line of the history that will be written about the cooperation of Arabs and Jews in fighting such phenomena."

But if the Arabs of Umm al-Fahm saw the day as a victory of Israel's democracy over the efforts by Kahane to destroy it, many anti-Kahanist Israeli Jews saw it in far less hopeful terms. For them, the battle of Umm al-Fahm was not yet over, and was in fact only part of a much greater battle within Israel—a battle not only between Arabs and Jews but, even more powerfully, between Jews and Jews: a battle about the role of religion, about relations between different Jewish ethnic and political groups, and ultimately, about democracy and the future of the Jewish state.

Who is Meir Kahane? How has he come to be able to frighten not only the Arabs of Israel but also the Jews?

The archives of newspapers, both in Israel and the United States, contain volumes of clippings documenting his exploits; their indices are full of references to his clashes with Jews and

Hashem Mahamid (right), with other village council members and Noam Tzion of Netivot Shalom (left), outside the council's meeting room.

Arabs, blacks and whites, Jerusalem police and New York police, Soviet officials and Israeli ones. No one considers Kahane an ordinary man, least of all Kahane himself.

Now 52, Kahane grew up in the Flatbush section of Brooklyn—in the streets, as he put it, learning to live in a rough world in which young Jews with yarmulkes were often beaten and robbed. Bloodied more than once, he learned to fight back, and then to live with—even, he says, to drink beer with—his former tormentors; as soon as the bullies saw he would not be bullied, he believes, they came to respect him.

Kahane's father was an admirer of Vladimir Jabotinsky, the Russian Zionist Revisionist and mentor of Menachem Begin. Kahane's first arrest, in 1947, when he was 15, took place, he recalls, when he helped smash the car of Ernest Bevin as it was coming down the Queen Mary's gangplank in New York; as the British foreign secretary, Bevin had been blocking attempts by Jewish survivors of the Holocaust to enter Palestine, and Kahane considered him an enemy of the Jewish people.

Following his graduation from the Brooklyn Talmudical Academy in 1949, and then Brooklyn College, Kahane studied law and international relations at New York University and obtained rabbinical ordination from the Mirer Yeshiva in New York. After an unsuccessful attempt to settle in Israel, he returned to the United States, was fired from his position as the rabbi of a synagogue in Queens, and became a journalist, first for the *Brooklyn Daily* and then the Orthodox *Jewish Press*.

While at the latter newspaper, during the mid-60s, Kahane began to lead, as Sol Stern put it in the October 2, 1984, issue of the *Village Voice,* "a double life." Using the name Michael King, he rented an apartment on Manhattan's East Side, spent many nights there while his wife and four children remained in Queens, began to attend parties, and left the impression that he was a representative of a foreign wire service, well-connected with the U.S. intelligence apparatus, and, by some accounts, a bachelor and a Christian. It was during this time, in 1966, that the 33-year-old Kahane, according to Michael Kaufman and Richard Severo, two reporters for the New York *Times* who later investigated his past, apparently had a brief affair with Estelle Donna Evans, a 21-year-old Christian woman; soon after Kahane broke off the relationship, Evans jumped off New York City's Queensborough Bridge, was rescued, and died two days later. Sol Stern, in his *Village Voice* article, argues that, despite Kahane's frequent subsequent denials, that affair really did take place, had a profound impact on him, and played both a tragic and ironic role in the life of a married rabbi who would later press for an Israeli law banning sexual relations between Jews and non-Jews. Curiously, in a 1972 *Playboy* interview, Kahane claimed that he had assumed the name Michael King, and had led his double life, as part of an arrangement he had with the FBI to do research on the American radical right.

Later, in 1968, this time as Meir Kahane, he founded the Jewish Defense League. His aim, he maintained, was not only to protect the lives of Jews in a period of rising anti-Semitism, but also to change their image from craven victims to self-sufficient equals. In the process, he and his young followers clashed with the city's blacks, whom they accused of preying on helpless, especially elderly, Jews; and, as the Jewish emigration movement grew in the Soviet Union, he added, as targets of his attacks, Soviet officials and property in the United States, as well as Americans doing business with the Soviet Union.

In 1972 Kahane moved his operations to an Israel reluctant to receive him, still shuttling back and forth between the two countries. In 1974 he founded his militant Kach movement in Israel, whose name, meaning "thus," was taken from the motto of the Jewish underground, the Irgun Tz' vai Le' umi, that, under Menachem Begin's leadership, had fought the British in Palestine, sometimes with terrorist tactics: "*Rak kach!*—Only thus!" Running for the Knesset in several elections, Kach failed to win the one percent minimum required for a seat—failed, that is, until the vote last July.

Altogether, Kahane estimates that he has been arrested "hundreds of times," both in the United States and Israel, and that he has spent more than a month in prison after at least 20 of those arrests. Some of the arrests were for violating probation; some for arms smuggling; some for incitement; and some for entering areas, usually Arab towns and villages, from which he had been banned. The Israeli prisons, he recalls, were always tougher than the American; in America, in fact, where he served a sentence for being involved in a conspiracy to manufacture a bomb, he was able to obtain special treatment and kosher food, while in Israel he was often subjected to harsh conditions. As a result of his election to the Knesset, he won not only a seat but also protection from the police under Israel's laws of parliamentary immunity. Those immunity laws are probably the most far-

Dede Ben-Shitrit

reaching in the world; they were originally passed to ensure Israeli democracy by guaranteeing that no dissident Knesset member would be restricted in his freedom of speech or action by the power of an arbitrary government.

I met with Kahane, three weeks after his election, in a catering hall of the Plaza Hotel in West Jerusalem. The hall had recently been used, was in disarray, almost totally dark, and, with its air conditioning off, very warm. A small ceiling light barely illuminated the corner table at which we sat.

"I'm convinced," Kahane told me, glancing around the large, empty room, "that there are any number of people in this country who, because of the last two-and-a-half weeks of nonstop hatred and lies, may feel that it's their patriotic duty to assassinate me."

Sitting forward in his chair, the collar of his white shirt spread over the lapels of his suit jacket, Kahane characterized the unremitting post-election attacks on him by a broad spectrum of Israelis—ranging, as it happens, from former Prime Minister Menachem Begin ("I totally reject everything he says") to Jerusalem mayor Teddy Kollek ("a stain on Israeli democracy")—as a kind of McCarthyism typical of liberals: "There is no greater defamer or basic fascist than the liberal, who has an arrogance that transcends his ignorance—the arrogance of assuming that anyone who doesn't agree with him has to be an evil person." But all that criticism, he said—as well as the unprecedented refusal of Israel's President to consult him in the process of attempting to form a government, and the orders given to the staff of the state broadcasting service not to report on him—only serve his ends. "What they're doing for me," he explained, "is what they did for Begin: They're creating in the minds of the underdogs of Israel a champion who is himself an underdog."

Kahane laughed: "Of course that helps me. Of course that helps me." He predicted that, in a new election, people who had not voted for him in previous elections out of the fear that they would be wasting their vote on someone who could not win would finally do so: "I'd get four or five seats without the *slightest* problem. The future *is* mine!" And that future, he added, would be all the more his the more the Israeli media ignored his popularity among the Sephardi Jews and among the young. "They can't stop me and they know it," he went on. "This whole election was a miracle of God. I walked between the raindrops. The only answer is God." It must have been God, Kahane insisted, who saw to it that the effort to remove his party from the ballot was stopped by the Israeli Supreme Court, and it must have been God who saw to it that the effort to censor his election commercials served, instead, to provoke sympathy for his cause. One television commercial that was not censored referred to Jews he said had been murdered by Arabs, and showed drops of blood dripping onto a tiled floor, with a cross-armed Kahane, Jerusalem's Temple Mount behind him, saying, "Give me the power and I'll take care of them."

I asked Kahane what he meant by "I'll take care of them."

"I'll take care of them. What's so difficult about understanding that? I have a program in which I call for the transfer of Arabs out of Israel. Give me the power and I'll take care of them by transferring them out of Israel."

"Transferring them—which is another way of saying expulsion?"

"It's another word for throwing them out, it's another word for paying them money—it's for transferring them out of the country any way that they will go. In 1945 the Poles and the Czechs transferred—expelled, threw out—12 million ethnic Germans from Silesia, the Sudetenland, Danzig and so on. It was ratified at Potsdam; it's part of international law today. Truman, Attlee, Stalin—nobody said anything about that. I have no intention of losing my country to Arab bullets or Arab babies."

Kahane insisted that Peace Now and other Israeli peace groups had arisen in the country only because of Jewish guilt over the dispossession of Arabs as a result of the creation of Israel; and he insisted that the Israelis in those movements, as well as other Israelis on the left, hate him because he makes them feel their guilt all the more by reminding them of a contradiction inherent in their idea of Israel. "Secular, political Zionism," he explained, "came into being to create a Jewish state. A Jewish state means, at the least, a state with a majority of Jews. [The founders of the state] certainly didn't want to create another Brooklyn! On the other hand, the same Zionists babble about democracy. Well, democracy finds it irrelevant whether you're a Jew or not a Jew. So the [Israeli] Declaration of Independence, which is a model of schizophrenia—it's just a magnificent model of it, as were Herzl and Ben-Gurion—says that Israel is a Jewish state with equal political rights for all its citizens. Well," Kahane sneered, "you can't have a *democratic* Jewish state! You can have a democratic state or you can have an Jewish state or you can have an Arab state, but you can't have a *democratic* Jewish state. And I get up and say that and they go

Uriel Simon

crazy because I've touched the most horrible of all sores. They've got to choose: Am I a Western democrat or am I a Zionist?"

Kahane is convinced that, in 50 years, the Israeli Arabs will reach majority status in the country as a result of their high birth rate and the rising emigration rate of the Jews. And, if the West Bank and Gaza were annexed, then the Arabs would become a majority population much sooner than that. "That's why," Kahane explained, "I want these people out."

Kahane went on to explain why he is hated by so many Israelis. The right-wing parties hate him, he said, because he threatens to take votes from them. And the left hates him because he makes them face the reality they prefer not to see. The *Jerusalem Post,* he said, as well as the rest of the left-leaning Israeli press, repeatedly misquotes and excoriates him because what he says reveals the untenability of their beliefs: "What bothers the *Post* is that I challenge them to answer the question, 'Do the Arabs have a right to be the majority in this country?' That's what kills them."

Finally, Kahane dismissed my warning that, were Israel to try to carry out his program—the part of it involving the "transfer" of the Arabs or the denial to them of citizenship in Israel should they wish to remain there—then other nations might react harshly, with disastrous results: "What in the world makes you think there was no outside world in the time of Joshua? What in the world makes you think that the Canaanites didn't have a lot of cousins, and angry cousins, outside of Canaan? What in the world makes you think that somehow in those days there was no outside world that cared? But also my whole program is based on the assumption that God is stronger than Ronald Reagan. If God isn't stronger than Ronald Reagan, I'm in the wrong business. I'm in the wrong faith, the wrong people. I should go back and bury myself in Brooklyn. I believe that when God says in the Torah, 'They are a people that dwells alone, and is not counted among the nations,' that it means something. It

Yeshayahu Leibowitz

either means something or it means nothing. We're a people, a people with a faith. What does it mean that we're Jews? It's not that we eat kosher. It's that we believe that if we do what He wants that He will save us."

During my stay in Israel, other Jews told me, some desperately, that what they wanted most want to be saved from is Meir Kahane. That he is dangerous for Israel, and wrong about Judaism, they had no doubt; the main disagreement among them was about the extent of the support he enjoys in the country.

Some insisted that he is just an aberration—that every society has its fringes and its outcasts, and that Kahane and his Kach followers are nothing more than that. The fact that he attracted 1.3 percent of the voters was, they thought, not very significant. What percentage of American voters, they asked, is ready to vote for the Ku Klux Klan or the American Nazi Party or other far-right or far-left fringe groups? Probably far higher than that. And equally extremist and racist parties regularly run for election, and regularly attract a far higher percentage of votes, in other democracies, without it being said of those countries that they are themselves racist or extremist; in fact, the successes of those parties, if noticed at all, are cited as testaments to the democracies that permit them.

Other Israelis, however, told me they fear Kahane is in fact an extreme expression of an increasingly-powerful sentiment among Israeli Jews. One such Israeli, Yehoshafat Harkabi, a professor of international relations at the Hebrew University and formerly chief of Israeli military intelligence, pointed out that, like every religion, especially every religion with ancient roots, Judaism contains many elements, some of them harsh and inconsistent not only with modernity but also with other of its elements. It's possible, he said to me (as, indeed, he argued in the pages of MOMENT in November, 1984), to point to one or another religious source and justify any action against the Arabs, especially in the light of the fact that Arabs have themselves preached, and even carried out, far more severe actions against the Jews during the centuries when Jews lived under their control—and particularly in the light of the unremitting hostility still focused by most of the Arab world on Israel, as well as the denial by so many Arabs, including Palestinians, of Israel's right to exist. Under these circumstances, it might be understandable that, now that Jews have sovereignty and power in their own land, some of them might be attracted to an ideology that gives expression to some of their frustrations and resentments.

But that ideology, Harkabi said, is not only wrong; it is a path toward national suicide—especially the part of the ideology that calls for the annexation of the West Bank and Gaza on the grounds that it is the Jews' God-given patrimony. It is that call, he said, that, for obvious demographic reasons, makes Kahane's program for the expulsion of the Arabs seem necessary to some Jews, and it is that

Avi Ravitzky

call that has given rise to the Jewish terrorist underground now on trial in Israel. This is, Harkabi told me, at its root a religious problem; its solution depends on the willingness of Jewish religious leaders in Israel to face, and dissociate from modern applicability, those elements in ancient scripture that have been resurrected and inaccurately cited, with a vicious and anti-humanist vengeance, by such demagogues as Meir Kahane.

As it happens, some religious Israeli Jews have already taken up theological arms against Kahane and other manifestations of the religious right. Allying themselves to varying degrees with secular Israeli peace movements such as Peace Now, these Jews have, in the past decade, and especially in the last few years, argued energetically that neither Kahane nor the Gush Emunim—the "Bloc of the Faithful" committed to settling the West Bank—can justify their activities on religious grounds. For every quotation from the Bible or the Talmud that Kahane or the Gush have cited to support their respective (and very different) efforts, they have cited others more consistent with the humanist ethos that yearns for peace and harmony between Jews and Arabs; they have insisted that the traditions of Jewish law and learning are overwhelmingly on their side, and against Kahane.

One such group, called Oz VeShalom—Strength and Peace—maintains that the spiritual values that are at the heart of Judaism are more important than any claim to land, however justified historically, and that such a claim cannot be pursued if it damages those values. Yehezkel Landau, the information secretary of the organization—an immigrant from the United States and a former student of psychology and theology at the Harvard Divinity School—told me that his group believes that no theological claim can justify damage done to another people. He believes that the kind of messianism exemplified by Kahane and the Gush Emunim has severely wounded the Jews in the past; that no one can say with any authority or knowledge what God wants or doesn't want in this or any generation; that Judaism views all human beings, including Arabs, as worthy of dignity and respect; that the ancient precepts in Joshua and Numbers regarding the conquest of the Land of Israel have no bearing on modern realities in the area; and that what Israeli Jews must do is seek a political compromise with their Palestinian brothers for sovereignty in the land that is dear to, and home to, them both.

Other members of Oz VeShalom and an allied religious organization, Netivot Shalom (Paths of Peace), expressed similar views in my meetings with them. One, Uriel Simon, a professor of Bible at the Hebrew University, believes that the Jewish religious tradition is above all a tradition of justice and humaneness, that Israel must not inflict on Arabs the kind of indignities that have been inflicted on Jews, and that, for the sake of peace and justice, Israel should permit Palestinian self-determination in the West Bank and Gaza. Another professor, Avi Ravitsky, in a televised debate, challenged Moshe Levinger, the Gush Emunim leader in Hebron who had already criticized Kahane for calling secular Jews *mityavnim*, or assimilated Hellenists, to dissociate himself fully from Kahane, and argued that it was precisely the narrow religious and nationalistic ideologies of Levinger and other Jewish settlers that had fostered the kind of extremism that was finally being exemplified by Kahane and the Jewish terrorist underground.

Still another religious peace activist, Jeremy Milgrom, went even further. A Conservative rabbi in his early 30s—an immigrant from the United States who was ordained by the Jewish Theological Seminary in New York—Milgrom has devoted most of his life to improving Arab-Jewish relations in Israel. Exquisitely pained by any injustice, especially injustice by Jews toward Arabs, he does everything he can to foster understanding between the two communities. At Umm al-Fahm on the day that Kahane had pledged to come, he was arrested after attempting to separate the Arabs and the police. Intently, almost plaintively, he told me that he wants to help right the wrongs that he feels Arabs have suffered at the hands of Jews, even if they have been suffered in the process of Arab efforts to deny the Jews what the Arabs themselves now want—national self-determination.

Other religious Jews I interviewed, including some religious authorities, strenuously rejected Kahane's conviction that all religious Jews would prefer to live in a theocratic rather than a secular state. One, the 81-year-old Yeshayahu Leibowitz—a physician and former professor of biochemistry at the Hebrew University, now a professor of philosophy there and the author of numerous articles and books on Jewish law and belief—thundered his insistence that the state was, by its nature, a secular construct, and should in no way be allowed to take on a religious character or function. And still others insisted that Kahane's repeated assertions that his positions and beliefs are grounded in Jewish law are simply, and mendaciously, wrong.

But my talks with Israelis revealed sharp repudiations of Kahane by members of yet other segments of the population on whose allegiance he and less extreme nationalists have laid claim. While most of Kahane's support has indeed come from the Oriental Jewish community, especially those from Morocco, many of the Sephardi Jews I interviewed were appalled by his beliefs, and insulted that Jews outside Israel, and within it, automatically associate their communities with Kahanist sympathies. One, Shlomo Elbaz, a professor of French literature at the Hebrew University, had helped found HaMizrach el HaShalom, East for Peace, which advocates a Peace Now position but with a special Oriental Jewish perspective. A Moroccan-born Jew himself, Elbaz told me that Israelis will have to find their place in the Middle East by being more like the Arabs; with the Oriental Jewish community now a majority in the country, and with Oriental-Western intermarriage now at a level of perhaps 20 percent, Israeli Jews are creating a culture that lies between East and West, one that will hold on to its humanism while retaining the rhythms and texture of life in the Levant. For him, Kahane is not only a stray weed among the Jews, but Kahanism is a stray weed among the Orientals—stray and without a real future.

Yet another Moroccan-born Israeli I interviewed, Dede Ben-Shitrit—not a light-skinned, refined professor like Elbaz but a dark Moroccan Jew of lower-class origins who had become a member of the Jerusalem Municipal Council because of his organizing activities at the neighborhood level—indicated that the poor Oriental Jews are not, at heart, fertile soil for the kind of vegetation that Kahane's ideas represent, and are perhaps more ready for accommodation with the Arabs, and less fearful of them, than are their Ashkenazi counterparts.

And, in the Knesset itself, efforts are being made to curb, and even stop, Kahane. During a November debate, one parliamentarian, a Liberal Party member in the right-wing Likud coalition, called Kahane "a cancer in the body politic," and proposed that the Kach Party, "and any party that strikes at the foundations of the state's existence," be outlawed. Another member of the Likud, belonging to Menachem Begin's Herut Party, denounced as racist, and similar to Hitler's Nuremberg Laws, two bills Kahane had circulated that would make it a criminal offense for Jews to have sexual relations with non-Jews, that would forbid non-Jews from living within the boundaries of Jerusalem, and that would provide for separate schools, summer camps and beaches for Jews and Arabs. Later, Israel's Attorney General, Yitzhak Zamir, attacked Kahanism as a shameful, loathsome and dangerous phenomenon that is opposed to Jewish tradition, international law and the principles of Zionism, and is more dangerous for Israel's Jews than for its Arabs. Zamir made public two Knesset proposals. One was to establish a Basic Law that would bar from a general election any party that opposes the existence of Israel as a state, that opposes its democratic system of government or that supports racism. Another was to authorize the police, for a period of a year, to prevent Kahane from entering any Arab settlement, or any factory that employs a majority of Arab workers, if he announces such an intention in advance.

On December 25th, by a secret vote of 58 to 36, the Knesset did indeed limit Kahane's parliamentary immunity by barring his entry into Israeli Arab villages such as Umm al-Fahm. The split vote does not necessarily reflect the full extent of opposition to Kahane within the Knesset itself. Despite their strong anti-Kahane sentiments, some Knesset members, like many Israelis, oppose the efforts to limit Kahane's immunity or to pass other laws aimed at restricting his freedom of action; they fear that such restrictions could create dangerous, anti-democratic precedents that might later be applied to others with unpopular views. But they, and many other Israelis, have repeatedly taken to the streets against Kahane, with one Tel Aviv demonstration in November drawing several thousand Israeli youth. Yet despite the split vote on the anti-Kahane resolution, there was in the Knesset a unity of sentiment against Kahane that is rarely evident in that very contentious body. In presenting the resolution, the chairman of the Knesset committee that had drafted and passed it, Micha Reiser, a Likud Party member, said he knew of no other issue that had so coalesced the Knesset: "No political party, from Techiya [on the right] to the Communists, has concealed its dissociation from, and even disgust" with Kahane's words and deeds.

Certainly, the fact that extremists like Kahane can attract any support at all should be troubling to anyone who admires the ability Israel has shown until now to maintain its institutions of democratic governance despite the circumstances in which it finds itself. That it has been able to do so, after all, is something extraordinary, even unique. Ever since its creation, Israel has been surrounded by states that, with the recent exception of Egypt,

Yehezkel Landau

have refused to recognize, and on several occasions have tried to erase, its existence. At the same time, it has absorbed a large and expanding population of Arabs who were deeply wounded by its creation and has given them political rights—more rights, ironically, than are enjoyed by most Arabs living in Arab lands. Also at the same time, it has absorbed a still larger population of Jewish refugees who fled from Arab countries and who are very different, in their traditions and outlook, from the Western Jews who were once its majority. And, finally, it has identified itself as the unique haven for persecuted Jews—as a Jewish state—but also as a state devoted to the Western ideals of humaneness, tolerance, social justice and political equality for *all* persons, regardless of race, religion and national origin.

Whether Israel's democracy will survive will depend on its ability to continue to overcome, and successfully transform, the internal contradictions, both demographic and conceptual, that its people and institutions have faced as a result of these circumstances.

For it *is* inconsistent, in some pure and ideal sense, for a country to be a Jewish state as well as one that gives full political equality to all its citizens, including those who are not Jews. And it *is* inconsistent for that country to maintain a state of unblinking vigilance agaisnt efforts by the Arabs surrounding it to destroy it, and yet insist that the kinsmen of those Arabs within Israel—who believe their people to have been dispossessed by the establishment of the country, and who are increasingly nationalistic in outlook and goals—are loyal citizens of that country and can be safely entrusted to share in its governance if not in its defense. It is precisely these inconsistencies and challenges that Kahane uses to taunt his liberal critics and fellow Jews and that represent the greatest, and truest, danger to Israel's democracy—not Kahane's demagogic, religiously exclusivist and racially offensive utterances.

In the end, it will be reality, not only generous intention, that will determine whether Israel will be able to overcome these inconsistencies and challenges. Certainly, if it remains militarily capable of staving off the external Arab threat, then the power of the internal one will remain, in realistic terms, inconsequential. And if the main groups of clashing Israeli Jews sense the increasingly destructive consequences of their clashes—and the growing possibility that those clashes may, in the worst case, precipitate, for the first time in the history of the modern state, sustained incidents of Jewish civil strife—then they may be willing to pull back from the precipice of confrontation over which they could well hurl not only themselves, but also their society as a whole. There are reasons to believe that the majority of Israel's religious Jews have come to view the activities of the tiny minority among them who yearn for a theocratic state, and who seek to "hasten the coming of the Messiah" by such actions as the destruction of the Al Aqsa Mosque, to be dangerous for the country—far more dangerous, perhaps, than any realistic Arab threat. And there are reasons to believe that the majority of Oriental Jews, having finally gained positions of real political power, may recognize that the country as a whole does not have an endless capacity to withstand civil confrontation, and that such confrontation must be restrained as the dangers inherent in it become more apparent.

But what about the demographic threat that Kahane so regularly exploits with such a stinging and racial thrust? Will the Arabs ever be numerous enough to undermine Israel's Jewish identity and national existence by democratic means?

Within Israel's pre-1967 borders, most Israeli demographers believe, probably not. The high birth rate of Israeli Arabs is falling as their income and educational levels are rising, and, barring a substantial rise in Jewish emigration, will probably not result in a population that could vote out the Jewish state, at least in the foreseeable future.

The much more serious and acute demographic question relates to the West Bank and Gaza. If the territorial compromise plan favored by the Labor Party—which favors the retention of relatively unpopulated but strategically important parts of the West Bank, and the return to Jordan of the heavily populated parts—is not realized, and if the West Bank and Gaza are eventually annexed, the possibilities narrow considerably. If the Arabs within the West Bank and Gaza are granted citizenship, and choose to exercise it, Israel will be, very quickly, a binational rather than a Jewish state; if the Arabs are not granted citizenship, Israel will no longer be a democratic state.

It seems unlikely, therefore, that such an annexation will be favored by a majority of Israelis; rather it seems reasonable to expect that ways will continue to be sought, despite the enormous impediments on both the Israeli and Arab sides, for some kind of compromise that will yield both peace and security for Israel and national rights for the Palestinian people.

The stakes for Israel are too high for it to allow its democracy, and its commitment to Western values, to be swallowed up by nationalist yearnings and civil despair. After nineteen centuries of exile, Jews have finally established a state in which they have achieved, as the early political Zionists had hoped, both social justice and a measure of national normality. Part of such normality, unfortunately, is the stress of internal strife and the potential for self-dissolution. Such a potential exists everywhere, but in few places with greater closeness than under the circumstances of siege and internal pressure that beset Israel. Yet the achievement of the country has so far been enormous, and has been made possible by the sacrifices it has made during the first three-and-a-half decades of its existence and by the unspeakable European tragedy that made that existence come to life. It has been a successful experiment in democratic rule, worthy of a great and creative people. The future success of the experiment depends on Israel's continuing adherence to democratic principles, as well as on its persistent devotion to the nobility and highest traditions of the people that has brought it, with such determination, so far.

★

HEBRON THE ROOTS OF JEWISH TERROR

Hebron is the root, to which the severed cling. Here Adam and Eve sought refuge in their exile from innocence. Here Abraham, uprooted from his father's house and sent wandering after uncharted stars, found his first dwelling place in the Land of Canaan. "And Abram moved his tent, and dwelt by the terebinths of Mamre, which are in Hebron." Later, following his self-inflicted circumcision, Abraham returned to Hebron, to heal, perhaps from an intimation of the suffering he had just released into the world. Isaac, too, came to Hebron to recover, immediately after his reprieve from the altar, stunned into becoming the most ethereal of the fathers, withdrawn and morose.

When the spies were sent into the desert to survey the Land, they came to Hebron, and there found the last refuge of the anakim, *primordial giants, the earliest human form which emerged, grotesque, from the exuberance of Creation. "And they ascended into the Negev, and came to Hebron, where Ahiman, Sheshay and Talmay, the children of Anak, were." The* anakim *inhabited fortresses like towers of Babel; their grapes were the size of boulders. Terrified, the spies resolved to warn the Israelites: Moses has led us from the haven of Egypt to a grave.*

Yet Hebron contained not only giants barring entry to the Land but also the Cave of Machpelah, burial place of the Patriarchs and Matriarchs, receptacle of the promise of triumphant Jewish settlement. And so to the Cave fled Caleb ben Yefunah, spy from the tribe of Judah, seeking assurance that this first glimmer of permanent exile was deceptive, and the wandering Israelites would find refuge in the Land.

When the spies returned to the desert, they declared: "The cities are great and fortified up to heaven; we were in our own sight as grasshoppers, and so we were in their sight." And then spoke Caleb, as emboldened by Hebron as his comrades were cowed by it: "Let us go up at once, and possess it, for we are well able to overcome." And the City of the Fathers fell to Caleb as an inheritance, for he had sought comfort from evil counsel among the ancestors in Hebron.

YOSSI KLEIN HALEVI

*Be not ashamed or confused
Why are you downcast, why do you grieve?
The wounded of my people will find refuge in you
The city rebuilt on its ancient site.*
–From *Lecha Dodi,* a prayer of welcome to the Sabbath

It is the night after Simchat Torah, the festival of rejoicing, when the Torah scrolls are wound back to their point of origin and rings of dancing Jews simulate its circular movement. On the hilly roads from desert settlements to the south, on unlit new highways from nascent Samarian cities to the north, on the narrow, climbing road from Jerusalem to the west, where cars with yellow Israeli license plates are often stoned and an Egged bus was recently ambushed by gunfire, chartered buses are bringing Jews to Hebron, to prolong the festival of dancing.

Army roadblocks outside the city detour traffic to a back road that passes the white apartment blocs of Kiryat Arba, Hebron's Jewish suburb, and leads into a vacant lot near the Cave of Machpelah. The buses empty their passengers into the darkness: yeshiva high school girls in braids and knee socks and parkas with epaulets, tall and wiry bearded men with intense eyes and few words, fat men with handlebar mustaches and pistols without holsters jammed into the waists of their pants, women with stoic faces, no makeup, whose only whim is the carefully measured hair protruding from the kerchief line drawn just above their foreheads, teenage boys whose yarmulkes slip to the sides of their heads like bandages, their jackets open against the cold autumn night.

The crowds move past barricades like passport controls segmenting the narrow streets into separate domains. A soldier wearing the pine-green uniform of the Border Patrol, a small plastic blue-and-white flag pinned to his chest like a rose, raises his fist in greeting, as though he were guarding a border of time, welcoming the Jews to their most distant past. "*Juden verboten!*" says an American celebrant, laughing.

From stone alleys whose darkness is relieved only by the distant lights of Arab villas on the surrounding hills, groups of Jews appear. When they recognize among one another's shadows the bright round knitted *kippot*, their pace quickens, they nearly leap with the joy of sudden release as they realize that tonight only Jews are on the streets, as though the Arabs have all been evacuated. Tonight no Arabs will stare at a returning Jew as though he were an amnesiac absurdly confusing this place, this time, for his home. The very Arab presence reminds these Jews of the massacres that have happened here: the recent murders of two yeshivas students, Aharon Gross, stabbed on a July afternoon while waiting for a hitch, and Yehoshua Salome, shot in the marketplace while buying fruits for Tu b'Shvat, the festival of planting; the Beit Hadassah Six, ambushed in 1980 while on their way home from Friday night prayers at the Cave of Machpelah; Esther Ohana, killed by a stone fired from a slingshot; and worst of all, the destruction in 1929 of the ancient Jewish Quarter, the longest continuous Jewish settlement in the Land, 63 passive Orthodox Jews stabbed and burned to death, the mutilated survivors banished to Jerusalem.

The Arabs have fled to their villas, the aqua doors of their stores are padlocked, the curved letters of their signs scattering in panic before the arrival of the Jews. Someone begins to sing, "*V'shavu banim ligvulam,*" the sons will return to their borders, and hundreds of others join in the words of prophesy whose vindication they are: the generation that should have been the last of the Jews, recoiling from its violation full circle back to this place of innocence. They sing loudly, almost shouting the words through the silent side streets, so that the Arabs will know that nothing can defeat this nation in its joy.

"I heard there's a curfew tonight for them."

"Just like *we* couldn't pray at the Cave of Machpelah when *they* were the big shots here."

"Till the seventh step: from there Jews could peek inside."

"And that's when they were being *good* to us."

"*Yimach shemam*–May their names be blotted out."

The crowds emerge into Hebron's main street, a narrow road without storefronts or sidewalks that was not built for lingering. They fill the area where the road bulges on either side into open space: Aharon Gross Square to its right, not a square at all but a shapeless paved emptiness ending at the low stone walls of the Moslem cemetery and named for the yeshiva student killed on this spot; and to its left, the now-deserted lot where wholesale vegetables are loaded from concrete platforms, behind which, terraced on a hill, are the grey stone shells of the Old Jewish Quarter, their facades torn off like an unhinged door revealing an unbearable intimacy: ghost-blue walls and rusted random pipes and half-moon windows without glass and domed ceilings hunched beneath their own weight, peeling entire chunks of plaster and stone, the shame of unburied death.

Within this space, the crowds form dancing circles. Above them crisscross strings of bulbs frosted purple and yellow, dark blue and bright orange, as though a flame has been sifted and subdued into its component colors, the night fading in and out of the alternately brooding and radiant lights. A clarinet and organ play chassidic songs over loudspeakers, the frenetic pace of the mournful music simulating joy. Teenage girls forming rings of pressed fingertips bounce three steps forward, turn their heads, hop and kick, the last *hora* enthusiasts. The boys grip one another's shoulders and spin, encircling their friends who rapidly wave large Israeli

---

Yossi Klein Halevi, *a contributing editor of* Moment, *lives and writes in Jerusalem. This is a draft of an essay that appears in "Contemporary Jewish Religious Thought," edited by Arthur A. Cohen and Paul Mendes-Flohr.*

Photographs by Michael Fein.

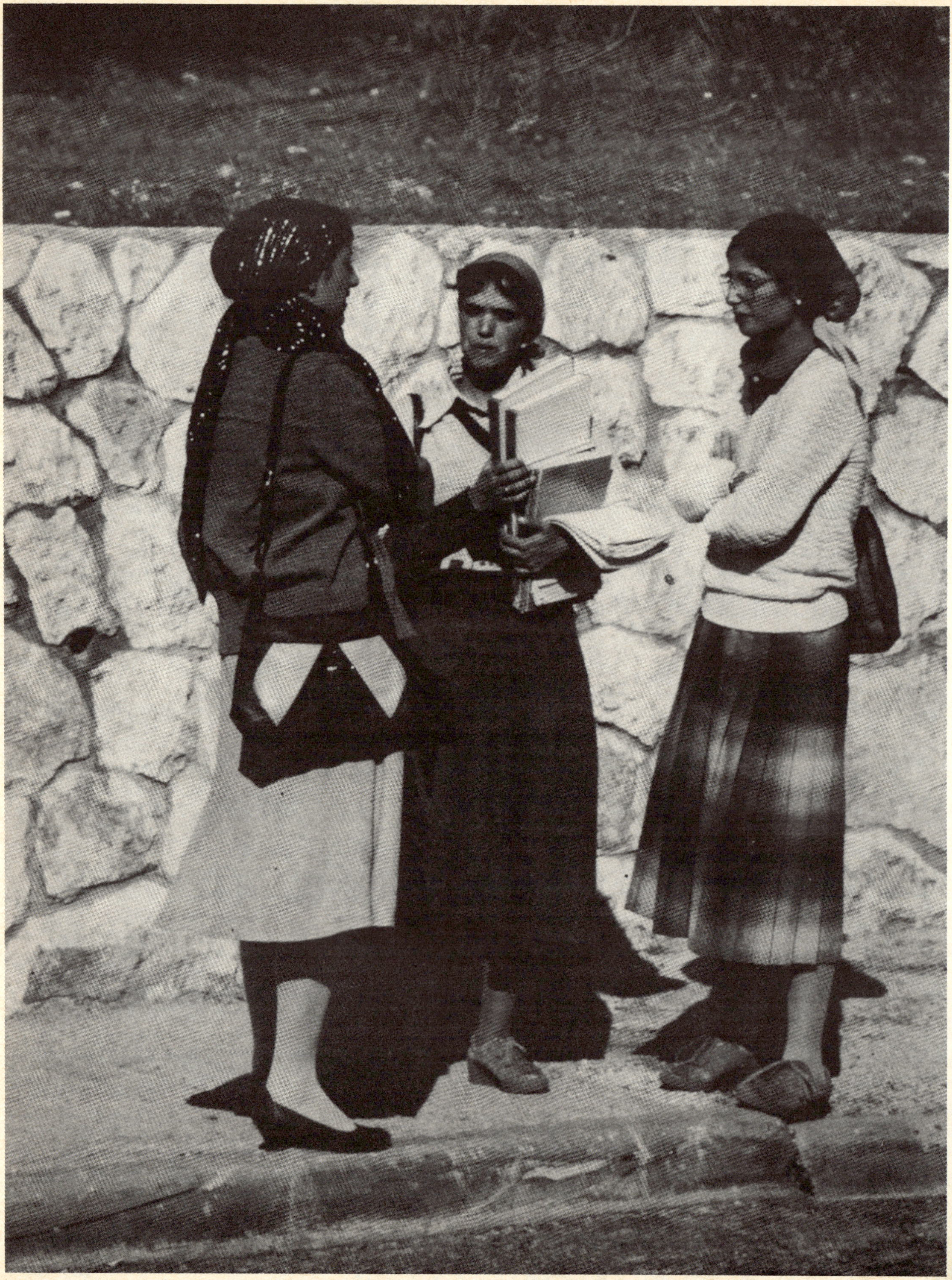

flags, blue and white smoke rings, mimicking the circles below.

Hovering above one circle, hoisted on shoulders, are the leaders of Gush Emunim, sponsors of tonight's celebration. They hold each other's hands, a circle in air. Hebron, starting point for Jewish settlement in *Eretz Yisrael,* is Gush Emunim's spiritual home. Here Abraham purchased the first piece of Jewish land, paying four hundred shekels of silver for the Cave of Machpelah; here the first Jews are buried, imprinting with death the Jewish right to the Land; here Caleb dissented from the defeatism of the spies and urged the invasion of Canaan; here David first founded his kingdom, not yet strong enough to conquer Jerusalem.

And here began the Israeli settlement of Judea and Samaria. During Passover 1968, 10 families led by Rabbi Moshe Levinger and claiming to be Swiss tourists checked into the Park Hotel. When Passover ended, they revealed themselves as settlers and refused to leave. The ruling Labor Party moved them to the compound of Hebron's military administration while it debated what to do; in 1970, it built Kiryat Arba, the first Israeli town in the territories, on a hill outside the city, the squatters compromising their demand to settle within Hebron itself.

Ten years later, a group of Kiryat Arba women occupied Beit Hadassah, a Jewish-owned building on Hebron's main street abandoned in the 1929 pogrom. Only after six Jews were ambushed and killed outside Beit Hadassah in 1980 did a reluctant Likud government agree to a limited Jewish return to Hebron, its ancient Jewish community destroyed and born again in blood.

The several thousand people here tonight have come to celebrate Hebron the pioneer, this time as the first Arab-populated West Bank city successfully penetrated by Jews. The Jewish presence has expanded from Beit Hadassah to sites throughout the downtown area: crumbling stone buildings with large domed ceilings and damp walls, protected by soldiers in wood towers and sandbag boxes; trailers parked behind the wholesale vegetable market, just beneath the gutted Jewish Quarter; and near the old Jewish cemetery, wanderers seeking permanency, only to find it in ruin and death.

Rather than harbinger of renewed vibrancy, the randomly dispersed houses and caravans seem like skeletal remains, clinging to the fading memory of intactness, utterly peripheral to the self-absorbed Arab life going on about them. The inner city through which most of the Jewish dwellings are scattered is meant only for shopping. Few of its signs are in English, almost none in Hebrew. The faded blue-green stores on the short, twisting side streets that surround and conceal the *shuk* offer burlap sacks of spices and trays of diagonally-cut pastries and bowls with sheeps' heads floating in their own blood to the constantly moving crowds of Arab women in uniform grey housecoats. The city is so muted that the plastic strips of glitter displayed by one store suggest not gaiety but hysteria. But for occasional political graffiti, the stone walls are empty, without even the elsewhere common, brightly-painted Mid-East movie posters. The most Islamic of West Bank cities, Hebron resists all penetration.

The music pauses. But the circles, as though programmed, continue to spin, the dancers singing so loudly they fail to notice the band has stopped playing. The loudspeakers plead for order and, when most of the circles have finally unwound, announce that the children of Rav Dan Be'eri will be honored with carrying the large Sephardi Torahs, whose cone containers resemble shell casings. The crowd responds with the song of Exile, *"Tzion halo tishali l'shlom assirayich,* Zion, won't you ask about the well-being of your prisoners." Rav Be'eri, a French convert to Judaism, is founder of Kiryat Arba's renowned yeshiva elementary school, Talmud Torah Hebron, whose integrated curriculum is based entirely on the Bible. They are honoring Rav Be'eri tonight, however, for his imprisonment with the other members of the settlers' underground, now on trial for the car bomb attacks on West Bank Arab mayors, the killing of three students in Hebron's Islamic College and the mining of six Arab buses ferrying worshipers to the Dome of the Rock.

"Will the brother-in-law of Menachem Livni come forth and take a Torah," and the crowd cheers the name of the leader of the underground. One by one, relatives of the arrested men are summoned to a flatbed truck and handed Torahs. Posters supporting the underground members and bearing rows of their snapshots–fat and jovial and mustached, lean and bearded and intense–hang on the stone walls of the Moslem cemetery, and, nearby, on the high circular railing surrounding the six-pointed marble memorial to Aharon Gross.

By linking Hebron's Jewish renewal with the underground, Gush Emunim has implicitly acknowledged the charge of its opponents: that forcing a few dozen armed settlers into an Arab-populated city must end in Arab terror and Jewish counter-terror. More Jews have been killed in Hebron than anywhere else in Judea and Samaria; in Hebron, the settlers' underground was born. The attack on the Arab mayors was in retaliation for the murder of six Jews at Beit Hadassah; the attack on Hebron's Islamic College followed the stabbing of Aharon Gross. Indeed, the leader of the underground, Menachem Livni, was also chairman of the Committee for the Renewal of Hebron's Jewish Quarter.

Nearly half the underground's members are from the Quarter or from Kiryat Arba, or helped establish the Jewish presence here before moving elsewhere to further the settlement effort. They include the sons-in-law of two of Hebron's leading rabbis, Moshe Levinger, founder of Kiryat Arba, and Eliezer Waldman, head of its military yeshiva; two former chairmen of the Kiryat Arba municipal council; members of the original "Swiss tourists" group; the elite of Hebron Jewry.

But this night remains, above all, a celebration, not just of Simchat Torah and of reborn Jewish Hebron, but of Gush Emunim itself. Ten years ago tonight, Gush Emunim staged its single most successful event, Operation *Hakafot,* Operation Dancing, sending thousands of protesters to prospective settlement sites throughout Judea and Samaria. Tonight is a time of reunion for those who participated in Operation *Hakafot* and now live in thriving settlements built on those empty hills, a night of rejoicing in the extraordinary success of Gush Emunim.

If Gush Emunim grew from protest to established settlement movement, it was because many Israelis saw it as a counterweight to the post-Yom Kippur War defeatism, a defiant response to the oil-induced pressures for Israeli concessions and to the diplomatic marginality of the Jewish state. But perhaps the main attraction of Gush Emunim was its ability, as much by default as by intention, to lay claim to the pioneering past abandoned by a depleted secular Zionism, its young religious settlers in sandals and workshirts restoring Zionism's youth and claiming the legitimacy of its precious symbols.

But now, some of Gush Emunim's leading activists are in an Israeli jail. And tonight, demonstrating its support for the underground, Gush Emunim has exchanged its claim to the *chalutzic*, the pioneering, tradition for a sectarian marginality, theirs no longer a struggle *for* utopia but *against* extinction. Worse, the underground members being celebrated in Hebron were arrested by Israel's most hawkish government, led by Yitzhak Shamir and others who had joined Gush Emunim against Begin on the Sinai withdrawal; and they are being tried by a judge who wears a *kippah* and whose sons live on Gush Emunim settlements and study in its yeshivot. For the first time, Gush Emunim is in danger of becoming peripheral even among its supporters.

Knesset member Meir Kahane appears. Kahane, who once lived in Kiryat Arba, has returned to the people who in the last elections gave him the largest percentage of votes of any town in Israel. The deafening music prevents him from speaking with the many well-wishers who crowd around him, laughing as they pat his back. Kahane, black beard grey at the tip, laughs too, bent as though overcome with merriment. The lowered corner of his right eye nearly touches the rising corner of his mouth, as if winking, sharing a private joke with the boys: "Can you believe we convinced them a bunch of yeshiva guys like us could be dangerous?"

Kahane is pushed to the head of a row of teenagers lined one behind the other, clutching the shoulders and waists before them as they shuffle through the crowd, colliding with the dancing circles like a chain belt cut loose and wildly swinging through the otherwise perfectly synchronized cogs; pulling bystanders into their snake dance, pace quickening, until they no longer dance but run, laughing, stumbling teenagers trying to catch onto the racing bodies before them.

Kahane is raised atop sturdy shoulders and handed a giant Israeli flag on a pole, and laughs as he points the flag forward, leading the charge. When he is lowered back to the ground, he is taken to Rabbi Moshe Levinger. Levinger, taut face sunburned as though singed by his bristling red beard, spaces between his protruding teeth, confronts his old enemy. As the founder of Kiryat Arba, mingling with the highest government officials, Levinger had barred the disreputable Kahane from Gush Emunim circles, had even convinced the Likud government to dismantle Kahane's settlement, El Nakam, God of Vengeance, in the Hebron Hills. Kahane had denounced Levinger as a traitor, and sent his Kach followers into Levinger's living room, fistfighting with Levinger's wife, Miriam. Now, Kahane is a Knesset member and Levinger is leading the campaign for the settlers' underground. They hold each other's hands and dance in the center of a clapping circle.

The dancing continues for hours. Even after the band and the man selling cotton candy have all gone home, and departing chartered buses have thinned the crowd to a few hundred; huddled in tight spinning rings blurring their own gradual displacement from the center of a thriving crowd to a corner of Arab Hebron, reasserting now its proper dimensions as Jewish Hebron again becomes memory; the dance of the Jews of Hebron, rejoicing in their farthest return, only to find there the circle's end.

David Rubin has the face of a man prematurely stunned into old age and of a teenager struggling against the persistent traces of childhood. His blond hair and full beard are greying, his cheeks are round and red: a face waiting for its components to agree on a common identity. Covering most of his head, bowl-like, is a large knitted white *kippah* without embroidery on its rim, like those worn by Islamic mystics. David is friendly, empathic, the corners of his mouth awaiting a smile. He speaks with measured passion, as though constantly examining his words and forcing from them new depths of honesty:

"I'm living in Kiryat Arba since 1977. Before that, it's a bit of a story. In 1970, I was shot six times by the Milwaukee police in a firebombing attempt against a couple of buildings. My companion was killed. It was an anti-Vietnam protest, but that's all I'd prefer to say about it.

"What happened next was that I was recuperating on bail in my parents' house. My lawyers were kind of telling me, 'We know where *you'll* be for the next fifteen years.' The political climate was not good for my future well-being. It was the height of the Nixon years. The government was able to do anything it pleased, including gunning down its own citizens in the street. So I had a friend quietly contact foreign embassies, to inquire what if I happened to show up in their country and ask for asylum. He checked out Cuba, the Scandinavian countries, a whole bunch of places, and they all basically said, 'Hey, don't bother us, it's a criminal case; if he shows up, we'll extradite.'

"Finally, my friend contacted the Israeli Embassy. The absolute last place in the world I wanted to go to was Israel. I was a leftist; I bought the whole line. But the reaction of the Israelis stunned me. Their basic attitude was, 'Hey, if you make it into Palestine, you're in.' The old *Aliyah Bet*, illegal immigration, mentality. That impressed me; I couldn't put it aside. No country in the world was willing to take me in, except Israel. I was asking for help and they were willing to give it to me just because I was a Jew.

"Meanwhile, my prospects for the trial began looking better, and I dropped the idea of fleeing abroad. It turned out that the police had acted illegally in shooting me six times and killing my friend. They knew in advance of our plans; they could have arrested us instead of laying an ambush. They also had information we weren't armed, but they shot us anyway.

"The trial began, and it was very controversial. Lots of media coverage. Because my name was Rubin, and because this was Milwaukee, I began getting all kinds of hate mail: 'You Jew,' this and that. I thought, Why are people making this distinction? I did what I did for the good of *all* Americans! You know. So I began to think a Jew is never going to fit in here; we're never going to be white enough.

"What finally happened was that the court had mercy on me and let me go with a heavy fine. They figured I'd suffered enough. In 1972 I married Rivka, who wasn't Jewish at the time. Of course, my attitude towards Israel had changed, and now I knew a lot more about anti-Semitism. But being Jewish still didn't affect my personal life. I had gone to Sunday school and got the requisite bar mitzvah, but after eight years of that I didn't know what *tefillin* [phylacteries] were. I can't even remember the Six Day War; it just passed me by.

"Then my wife got pregnant. Somehow I knew enough to know that if the mother isn't Jewish, the child isn't either. That bothered me. I thought, Hey, my child isn't going to be a part of my people? What if some day *he* needed a place to run to—and Israel would be closed to him?

"My wife and I both began reading. We started with the Bible. That got us interested. It was a long process. When Rivka converted, we decided to move to Israel. Sometimes you see everything at once: If we're Jews, shouldn't we live in the Jewish state? We went to see a representative at the Israel immigration office, and he was very wary. He said to us, 'Why don't you go first for a visit?' We told him, 'We've got just enough money for these tickets; if we go for a visit, who knows when we'll go back to live.'

"In December 1976, we made *aliyah*. It was a real shock. We arrived at night; it was pouring rain, our child was cranky, and this lorry from the absorption center picks us up and drives us through Lod, past these little felafel stands, mud running through the streets. . . . I thought, My God, what have I done?

"What finally happened was that a friend in the absorption center took us to Kiryat Arba for a Shabbat. The people were unusually warm and it looked like a terrific place to raise a family: quiet, healthy air, beautiful hills, lots of kids. We were open politically; we didn't know much about what was going on. But we felt Jews should have the right to live in the West Bank—the territories, we called it.

"I've had no regrets since. I love it out here. I'm not saying there are no problems. I carry a gun when I go into Hebron. I'm not proud of carrying it, I don't get pleasure out of it. I don't enjoy bullying people. I know what a gun can do to someone. But I don't have a choice.

"Some people here have the attitude that it's okay to kill Arabs. 'They kill us so we should be allowed to kill them.' That's crap. I've drunk coffee in Arab homes and held their kids in my lap. If I put a bomb on an Arab bus, I couldn't very well say then, 'Hey, you can't put a bomb on *my* bus, you can't kill *my* wife and children.'

"I see an incredible amount of arrogance developing in Gush Emunim: 'We're on the one true righteous holy path and we can do anything we want.' That mentality didn't begin with the underground. What do you think Yamit was about? 'Hey, it's okay to fight the Israeli army.'

"People here ask each other what will be if the government gives up the territories. Some people talk about a Yamit-type last stand, only much more serious. I say I'll take my family and move back across the 'green line.' I came to live in a Jewish state, and if its government makes what I consider to be a stupid mistake, it's still my government; I have to obey it. I'm not about to fight the Jewish people.

"But I don't for a minute believe it'll come to that. We're not sitting here for our own sake; Kiryat Arba is protecting Jerusalem, not the other way around. There's a national consensus for our being here. Who built this place if not Labor? Yigal Allon, author of the famous peace plan.

"What do I think will happen here? *Eretz Yisrael* is definitely a one-day-at-a-time place. I don't, however, foresee it getting a lot better with the Arabs. Our situation is very complex. If we go back to those eight-mile-wide borders, there's no way the Arabs will resist trying to cut us in half. Everyone in Israel knows that; only some of us are too exhausted to admit it.

"But the peace movement is also right: We can't absorb a million Arabs.

"So what do we do: if we have to keep the West Bank but, for the same reason, survival, we can't absorb the Arabs living there, that leaves, as I see it, only one solution. It's not a very popular solution, but I'm forced to agree with Kahane: sooner or later, we're going to have to expel the Arabs. I'm not saying it's the most just solution. I'm not deliriously happy about it: Hey, great, I'm taking that guy's house, his rug.

"Look, I know from my own life how things are done. The state has an obligation to democracy—until the state decides it has to act for self-preservation. Then, a democratic government can shoot its own citizens in the street. Look what America did to its Japanese citizens—and I'm not defending that. They didn't do it to the German-Americans—just another case of American racism. The Japanese-Americans were no threat; they were loyal citizens. If that's what America did to *them*, what would it do in *our* place, with Arabs who *are* a very real threat?

"If anyone has a better plan, I'm willing to listen. I'm not happy with expulsion, but I think it's not only for our own good, but ultimately also for the good of the Palestinians. They deserve their own state. But not here. They have Jordan, which is historically part of Palestine. Look, there are 22 Arab states. There's only one Israel. For me, justice is to make sure the single Jewish state survives, not to create Arab state number 23. Where do we go after here? This is our absolute last stop."

On the border between the Judean farmland and desert rise the Hebron Hills, their slopes terraced with low stone walls, each patch of alternately green and exhausted earth continually reapportioned. Spread comfortably through the hills, settled on the ground or balanced on thin pillars like stilts, are single-story, white stone Arab houses, angular but softened by arched windows, over which weave metal trellises, not for protection but whim. Low mats of grape vines surround the houses, and squat olive trees, their branches bending toward the earth.

Kiryat Arba rises suddenly. Its four-story buildings appear to house giants, alert, sleepless. A barbed wire fence rings the area, as though it were quarantined. A single road circles the huddled buildings like a moat, an army jeep always on patrol.

Kiryat Arba faces outward with small windows, squinting, attempting to see only the outline of rolling hills and deny the details upon them: the Arab houses taunting the compressed Jews with their agility on the Land, sidling close to Kiryat Arba, as though on a dare, their crops ending at the fence.

In 1967, these hills were bare. Only once the Jews built here, three years later, did Arabs do the same, extending Hebron's borders to the edge of Kiryat Arba. Elsewhere in Judea and Samaria, that process might be offered by settlers as proof of the prosperity brought by Israeli occupation. Here, settlers attribute it to Arab provocation, a plot to uproot the Jews or at least hem them in, create a stone and vegetable barrier as the Arab equivalent of the barbed wire fence; their villas inching toward Kiryat Arba, rows of cabbage like mines with which to cramp the movement of the Jews.

Yet this is not paranoia; it is, in fact, happening. Separated only by a fence from Kiryat Arba's modest industrial area, is a new mosque, financed by the Saudis, that resembles a missile launcher: its circular base is several stories high, its pink stone spire triumphant over the buildings of the Jews. A new landscape rises here, competing towers of Babel, lookout posts not to the heavens but toward one another.

Severed from the surrounding hills, Kiryat Arba relaxes into itself. Rolling lawns and flower beds separate the white stone buildings, still new in the sun, rising and falling upon the slopes. There is always a breeze here, even in the middle of summer. Few cars disturb the unusual quiet. Even the barbed wire fence becomes unobtrusive from within, concealed in the modest valley that surrounds Kiryat Arba. Close to 5,000 people live here; yet it remains intimate. Kiryat Arba recalls the post-1967 neighborhoods built to broaden Jerusalem, as though it too were one of those neighborhoods suddenly cut adrift, extending Jerusalem's boundaries too far before realizing the rest of the city hasn't followed.

Near the gate's entrance, which is unguarded except at night, is a small commercial strip, its only frivolity a fast-foods café, concession to the many soldiers passing through. There is no movie theater here, no public entertainment without higher purpose: a visit by a pro-settlement politician, a circumcision, a wedding. At such times, Kiryat Arba reveals that, despite its public sobriety, it is not withdrawn but poised for joy. Often, on an ordinary week night, dancing crowds will fill the circular street, escorting a groom to his bride, or a Torah scroll written for four fallen soldiers to the yeshiva in which they studied.

When one's gaze remains inward, Kiryat Arba becomes the most tolerant Orthodox community in Israel. Secularists are welcomed; unlike other Orthodox areas, no roadblocks deter Shabbat drivers here. Kiryat Arba encourages no internal barriers of any kind. It offers haven to those uneasy elsewhere, just as in biblical times, when Hebron was a "city of refuge" to which an accidental murderer could flee the avenging family of his victim. The late Rav Zvi Yehudah Kook, spiritual leader of Gush Emunim, wrote: "Hebron, as a city of refuge, awakens within us feelings of responsibility and concern for every soul in Israel, even a soul as dishonored as the unintentional murderer. In that spirit must we rebuild the City of the Fathers."

Settlers living elsewhere in the territories jokingly delineate four areas of Gush Emunim settlement: Judea, Samaria, Gaza–and Kiryat Arba. Kiryat Arba is perhaps the most eclectic Orthodox community anywhere, embracing converts sent by the Chief Rabbinate, which knows that only here are they assured a warm welcome: the son of a German Supreme Court judge, a Frenchwoman who spent 15 years as a missionary in the Congo, the nephew of the former Arab mayor of Hebron; black Jews from Ethiopia, sent by the government because here their presence is not simply tolerated but requested; Soviet Jews, including Trotsky's grandson, fleeing a dissipating universalism to a Jewish nationalism that strains against its self-imposed limitations and so sees in its own liberation a cosmic messianic process; apocalyptic pessimists for whom the root is the safest underground shelter in the coming fire; apocalyptic optimists who have glimpsed a vision beyond destruction but who remain apocalyptic because they cannot transcend their own personal traumas; Sephardim looking for cheap apartments, and finding in Kiryat Arba an Ashkenazi respect for their culture; a city of refuge for the "new Israel," itself a coalition of marginal Jewish groups who now find themselves, by default, at the center.

Throughout apartment building halls in Kiryat Arba, beside pictures of Galilee and Negev scenery meant to dispel the fear of severance from the rest of Israel, hang photographs of Jews murdered while shopping or praying in Hebron below. Here, anxiety is focused outward, toward the avenger waiting by the fence for a hint of weakness, an incautious moment. Perhaps it is this sense of hopeless siege that accounts for Kiryat Arba's internal tolerance. And who, besides, would care to judge his neighbor in a city of refuge?

When Avraham Nahliel was an orphan in Morocco, wandering from city to city, no place able to hold him, he dreamed of being a Torah scholar in Jerusalem. Just as Maimonides imagined messianic times: simply to be left alone by the *goyim* and allowed to learn in peace. When he let his mind roam further, he would review all the *mitzvot* a Jew could only learn about in the Diaspora but which he could actually perform in *Eretz Yisrael*: the pilgrimage to Jerusalem, the Temple sacrifices, the land left fallow every seventh year. The Torah was not meant for Exile but for *Eretz Yisrael;* only there could its ways be perfected.

Avraham Nahliel is short, brown eyes wide, tight curls grey. His shoulders hunch, perhaps from his recent heart operation, which has left him hollow-cheeked and shaking, or from his years working as a carpenter, or the long nights bent over a holy book. Or perhaps it is the impressed stoop of a Diaspora Jew, unobtrusive, the young Avraham suppressing any gesture likely to draw attention: a careless expression that could be mistaken for mockery, a sure gait confused with strutting; eying the street to anticipate the footpaths of Moslem passersby and prepared at a moment's notice to leap out of their way; and refraining, of course, from any sin that would force God to use a Moslem as a punishing rod against him.

But no matter how hard Avraham tried to disappear into himself, still they abused him. Once, a group of Moslems put a knife to his throat. Another time, they tied him up and took him to the shore and, had Jews not intervened, they would have thrown him into the sea, rehearsing their design on the future Jewish state.

"*Reshaim gedolim,*" Avraham says of the Moroccans, very evil men, the concept so foreign to him it is as though he were describing mythical characters. "*Yimach shemam,*" he adds for emphasis, may their names be blotted out, pronouncing the Hebrew guttural "*chet*" like a breath, "*het,*" as though trying, on second thought, to soften his harsh words.

The young orphan found refuge in Torah, learning till midnight after a long day of labor at odd jobs. When he says the word, "Torah," he laughs, stretching its latter vowel into an exclamation of delight. "Everything comes from Torah and everything returns to Torah." No point is made without the approval of a biblical passage or rabbinic saying. "This is very important," he says, and, though he otherwise has trouble standing, rises in a single movement to retrieve one of the holy books that fill the shelves from floor to ceiling in the spare living room, until the table, too, is covered with books, their spinal titles erased from constant bending. "Books are a great thing!" he says, laughing, his mouth open, its scattered, yellow teeth dancing.

Torah was Avraham's father and mother, teaching him respect for others and for himself, and also self-control, so that he could avoid the company of other orphans begging in the streets or, *chas v'shalom,* God forbid, sinning. Torah taught him a parent's love, God's love for the Jewish people, and also sibling love, *ahavat Yisrael,* the love of Jew for fellow Jew. "The Jewish people is one body. Why do I pray for all the exiles to come home, if I myself am already in the Land? Because until all of the Jewish people is home, I still have one foot in Exile."

When the State of Israel was declared, Avraham, married now with young children, rushed with his family to the first available boat. "What greater joy is there in the world," he says, raising his eyes. He arrived on the eleventh of Elul, a new date added to his sacred calendar. But the joy is great, perhaps, only in retrospect. Though the eleventh of Elul was a Shabbat, the Moroccan Jews on the boat took their belongings and followed the officials into lorries, convinced that the holy custodians of the Land would not dare ask other Jews to desecrate Shabbat unless it was absolutely necessary, a national emergency perhaps, and surely sanctioned by rabbinic decree. Avraham knew that the officials were lying when they told him that the Law was meant only for the Diaspora, that here, in the Land, it could be violated; he remained on board with his family till sundown, watching the shore, the Land of Israel just beyond reach.

Avraham speaks little of what followed. He will not repeat the sin of the spies, besmirching the good land to which he was brought. But hints of the rage he will not admit to himself involuntarily seep into his conversation, as when he recalls the two *lirah* each immigrant was handed, like a beggar, in place of a word of welcome or a smile from a fellow Jew; or the way they were packed onto trucks like prisoners, the dour faces of the officials not bothering to conceal their ambivalence towards the human material entering the Land.

Many Moroccan immigrants never overcame the shock of that moment when, their arms open for embrace, they were met instead with officious distance, so that the immigrants themselves became distant from their fellow Jews, and even, some of them, from the Land itself. Avraham never, *chas v'shalom,* joined those Moroccans longing for the Exile like the tribes in the desert dreaming of Egypt. Where others lost their love for the Land because they could no longer yearn for it, Avraham waited for the real *Eretz Yisrael* to reveal itself.

Avraham wandered from moshav to town, trying to feed his children, and to keep words of the Torah in their mouths, so that they would remain as Jewish in the Land as they would have been in Morocco; to prevent from happening to them what was happening to other Moroccan children, as though, coming into the Land, an entire generation had suddenly become orphaned.

In June 1967, like a submerged continent whose discovery forces an instant deepening of history, *Eretz Yisrael* surfaced. Days after the reunification of Jerusalem, Avraham wrote a letter to President Shazar: *Adoni,* sir, I am a simple Jew, all my life dreaming of ascending to Jerusalem; I hereby offer myself, my wife and my nine children as pioneers to resettle the holy Old City. Shazar wrote a polite reply, stating that the time had not yet come for Jews to move into Arab-populated areas.

A year later, Avraham heard a radio interview with Rabbi Moshe Levinger, leader of the "Swiss tourists" squatting in Hebron. Avraham wrote Levinger the same letter he had written Shazar, substituting Hebron for Jerusalem. When that went unanswered, he wrote again, and yet a third time, until, finally, Levinger responded, and invited Avraham to Hebron for Shabbat. Avraham went the very next Shabbat to the Hebron military compound where the government had temporarily settled the squatters. There, he saw the pristine holiness of Hebron, wedded to the State. He made immediate plans for his permanent return.

"My neighbors said, 'You've become crazy? Taking your family to the wilderness?' But I said to them, 'I've had hard times before and God always took care of me. He'll take care of me in the holy city of Hebron.'"

The family moved in late 1968, and adopted the name Nahliel, from the verse "*Zeh nahalat El*–This is the inheritance of the Lord." Here, among the religious pioneers of Hebron, Avraham inherited the Land. From his living room Avraham can see Yeshivat Nir, the military yeshiva that is the center of Kiryat Arba's religious and social life. "You see those windows?" he says, pointing to the yeshiva and laughing. "I installed them!" The miracle of life in *Eretz Yisrael*: even one's physical labor is part of the work of Torah.

Here, in *Eretz Yisrael*, Avraham is a *ba'al habayit*, a "lord of the house." "In Morocco, I had no Arab friends. But now, yes. I drink tea with Arabs in Hebron; I go everywhere to visit. And why? Because here I am a *ba'al habayit*."

No vengeance: a *ba'al habayit* can afford magnanimity. When Avraham goes to Hebron he never carries a weapon. "*Chas v'shalom*, heaven forbid! I show every human being a pleasant face. Once, I was driving with someone to Hebron. When we got there, I told him, '*Adoni*, sir, if you don't put away that weapon I'm not getting out of the car.' I follow the Torah: 'Its ways are the ways of pleasantness, and all its paths are peace.' Those who do violence against the Arabs, who want to throw the Arabs out from here, are sinning. *Chas v'shalom!* God doesn't want that. They live here. But they have to accept reality. We, not they, are the *ba'alei bayit* here."

In the hall outside Avraham's apartment, a neighbor has posted a typed sheet in support of the settlers' underground: "THE ARABS ARE OUR ENEMY! The enemy chooses the time, the place, and the means–AND ATTACKS!"

Avraham opposes the underground. "*Adoni*, what they did was forbidden by Torah. But we also have to try to understand them. 'Don't judge your friend until you stand in his place.' *Ahavat Yisrael* is for every Jew. They weren't maniacs, these boys. Every morning I *davened* in the Cave of Machpelah with Uzi Sharabaf, Rav Levinger's son-in-law. A very significant Jew, Uzi Sharabaf. But what? Aharon Gross was his study partner. Every person has his limits. When Aharon Gross was killed in the middle of the day in front of hundreds of Arabs, Uzi lost his head and went into the Islamic College.

"In Torah, we have the city of refuge. Why does the murderer have to run there? Because the *go'el hadam*, the avenger of blood, is chasing him. Why? '*Ki cham libo.*' Because his heart is hot. You see? It's not a simple thing."

When reminded that in the Torah the *go'el hadam* is permitted to pursue only the actual murderer, and that those killed at the Islamic College were not responsible for Aharon Gross's death, Avraham nods his head: "Absolutely forbidden. 'No person sins except that a spirit of folly enters him.' So why should he be punished? He couldn't help himself! The rabbis answer: A person has to stand strong, even against a spirit of folly.

"When I heard that Uzi was the one who had done it, I couldn't believe it. Uzi? The world is hell, exactly hell."

The Arabs wanted to be *ba'alei bayit* everywhere, even here, in *Eretz Yisrael*, and their greed had forced religious Jews to sin. The Jews lived in Morocco for thousands of years, but they never forgot they were guests, deferential to their brutal hosts. Here, the Arabs only had to stay peaceful and they would live like kings. The Jews would not treat them the way they had treated the Jews. But when they threw rocks, even murdered? And then that terrible comment by Labor Party leader Bar-Lev after the ambush at Beit Hadassah: "If they hadn't been there, they wouldn't have been killed." As if the Law had been suddenly reversed and one could be murdered simply for living in a city of refuge . . . .

But, says Avraham, laughing, the Messiah is coming. To restore us to the farthest root, beyond even Abraham: back to the Garden. Why did Abraham choose as his burial place the Cave of Machpelah? Because he saw a divine light radiating from its entrance. Inside, he discovered the graves of Adam and Eve, and, just beneath them, the opening to the Garden. So that when the Messiah comes, he will appear first here, to reveal to the world the Garden of Eden, buried, for safekeeping, in the holy city of Hebron.

Return us to You
and we will return.
Renew our days
as of old.
–Lamentations

Upon the subterranean Cave of Machpelah rises a massive stone fortress without windows, as though the rectangular structure, the color of sand, were itself buried underground, none but those already within permitted to enter. Its side entrance is narrow, surreptitious, the building's only flair the rounded turrets that fail to dispel its prison-like facade.

The foundations of the fortress were laid by Herod. Later, Byzantine conquerors built a church upon Herod's incomplete structure, suppressing the old Israel beneath its weight. Finally, Moslem conquerors converted the church into the mosque that stands today, imprinting themselves here so totally a visitor would assume the Patriarchs had been princes of Islam; the disinherited heirs of Abraham become not merely the spiritual but the physical Israel, usurping the Jews at the source.

The fortress opens into an unpainted hall, whose stone walls are peeling into chalk, cracks like tangled roots breaking through the damp stone floor. The hall winds into a sunny courtyard, where soldiers lounging on folding chairs, their guns laid across their laps, and old Arab men, wearing pinstriped jackets and clashing pinstriped shirts, watch the tourists rush from room to room, in clusters, as though afraid to be alone.

To the right of the courtyard is the room devoted to Abraham and Sarah. Its dimensions are untenable: a small square base supporting a towering vaulted ceiling. The ceiling is painted like a beach umbrella in stripes of yellow, red, green, colors chosen for their gaiety, but faded now, as though bleached in the sun, the room rejecting all false vigor imposed upon its years.

On either side of the room, locked behind a bronze gate whose bars curl into Islamic crescents, a part of the wall has been hollowed to accommodate a large empty mausoleum. Each chest-shaped stone, approximating the burial spot of Abraham and Sarah in the Cave below, is covered with a green Persian carpet, its patterns obscured, inlaid with dust.

Tiny, round Sephardi women enter the room, kissing their fingers and then waving in all directions, singing "*Avraham avinu, Sarah imenu,*" Abraham our father, Sarah our mother. They rush back and forth between the opposite gates, as if continually recalling something they forgot to say, their outstretched palms quivering up and down, slowly, like an uncertain scale.

One of the women, wearing a faded floral dress and floral kerchief tied like a bonnet beneath her throat, approaches a young man praying quietly in a corner. He wears a white shirt, indifferent polyester pants, sandals unstrapped like houseslippers. His *uzi* rests beside him like a staff. Only the settlers come here alone, unafraid, *ba'alei bayit*. He barely moves his lips as he prays, not swaying or moaning, as though he were not praying at all but answering a prayer, his very presence here its fulfillment.

"Make for us a *mi sheberach*," the old woman says to the young man, demanding the prayer often said for the healing of the sick. "What is the name of the sick person?" he asks. "There is no sick person," she says, annoyed. "Just make a *mi sheberach* for all our boys, they should come home safe."

He begins: "*Mi sheberach avoteinu, Avraham, Yitzchak, Yaakov,*" He who blessed our fathers, Abraham, Isaac, Jacob. The women gather around and repeat with him each name, conjured by a Jew fifty, a hundred times a day, no petition offered without first invoking the merit of the fathers, whose sleep is continually disturbed by a cacophony of pleading accents, orphans repeating familial names to ward off drift.

When the prayer is over, the women distribute damp and fragrant myrtle branches from immense plastic bags to tourists who shout at one another, "Which one's Abraham?" as they aim their cameras and videos at the sites they will notice only later, spies gathering masses of random information whose relative importance they cannot determine. One of the Sephardi women announces to the tourists: "I saw him like I'm seeing you. On Chanukah it happened. *Eliyahu Hanavi,* Elijah the prophet: the Angel of Chanukah. He said to me: 'The gates of peace are opening.' That's what he said: 'The gates of peace are opening.'"

The room of Abraham and Sarah leads, like an antechamber, into the vast hall of Isaac and Rebecca, its domed ceiling likewise painted in faded colors. Two empty crypts, festive in red and white stripes, sit like crates in the middle of the hall, each capped with a blue pyramid from whose peak extends a gold scepter, small gold circle on its tip, the quarter moon of Islam in full blossom.

Dozens of Chassidim crowd near Isaac's uninhabited stone hut, which marks his burial spot in the Cave below. Though there is room for them to spread comfortably around the large crypt, the Chassidim remain huddled along one side, several layers removed, restless eyes darting as though attempting to stroke the stones their tangled arms cannot reach. The large brims of their round black hats overlap as they press against one another, no intimacy too intense, always prepared for a spatial contraction and fearing only a sudden opening in which one might become irretrievably severed.

The Chassidim are on a day-long tour of Judean and Samarian grave sites that has already taken them to Rachel's lonely tomb in Bethlehem. On other days they have travelled to Galilee, to the tombs of the obscure, kept alive only in the infallible memories of the Chassidim; and to the tombs of the famous, like Rabbi Akiva, whose flesh was torn by the Romans with giant iron combs, and like Rabbi Shimon bar Yochai, still performing miracles, vibrant from beyond the grave.

Were it not for these tours, they would never see the Israel beyond their self-contained neighborhoods. The Chassidim have become guardians of the graves, their link to the Land confined to those buried within it, an entire community turned into a *chevre kaddisha,* a burial society. Even their political struggles revolve around the real or imagined violation of bones, the desecrations of secular Israel culminating in a literal trampling on the ancestral graves; a Chassidic war to the death in which no tactics are too desperate or insane: some fasting in sackcloth and even painting swastikas on Israeli flags and desecrating the parental graves of archaeologists in retaliation for their stirring up the sleeping bones of the fathers.

They are the first Jews without ancestral graves. European Jews programmed for continuity, they find themselves now on the wrong side of a void so total it has erased even the markings of death. And so they prowl the Land in search of the elusive burial site of *mameh* and *tateh,* and arrive, finally, here, at the deepest family grave. All ancestral graves are interchangeable now, because the layered stones upon which succeeding generations built have been shattered and scrambled, the face of the first father merged into the face of the last. And they, children, the passive recipients of a world which then vanished, are left alone to mimic every remembered detail: habits and beliefs, superstition and wisdom, all the inherited traditions of equal worth. Frozen in that moment between continuity and rupture, they cannot even embellish the tradition as their own fathers and grandfathers had done, lest an essential detail be irrevocably obscured. The commentaries have already been written; all they can do is preserve that Judaism perfected in Exile, so holy it dissolved into air.

"*Mincha!*" The men instantly sway, furiously, as though attempting to flee their bodies, thrusting backward and forward, but in vain, their bodies clinging to their coattails, anticipating even the most desperate sudden lurch. The words of the afternoon prayer speed from their pressed lips as though on a higher vibration, or else simply a mumbling buzz, nonsense syllables which once formed words whose meanings explained everything, but are now welded together, one indiscernable from the next, Hebrew reduced to a single emanation.

They call to the Fathers in their Yiddish names, rouse them in the Hungarian accents to which their ears would be most accustomed: *Avrom Yitzchok Yankev! Not a dot from your Torah have we changed, even your clothes we still wear, your black silk bekechers, your swirling fur streimls which you wore every Shabbos . . .*

But the biblical shrine offers no mirror returning their own image. Instead, the red-and-white stripes of the crypt mock their austere dress, the gold-lettered verses of the Koran etched along the walls confound them like an unknown ancient dialect, and the barefoot Arabs crosslegged on rugs as though natural sons in their parents' home recall the *goyim* who seized their own homes and businesses the morning after deportation.

The Chassidim press against the crypt, peaked with the strange pyramid as if here lay not an ancestor of the slaves but their oppressor. Those closest reach out to touch the stone house, but it is empty, deserted, not a tomb at all but a reminder of the elusiveness of family graves. They cannot sprawl upon their parents' stone, whose coldness would stroke their damp foreheads, its roughness a fatherly pinch on the cheek; they cannot pour out their constricted hearts: *How is it we live in such perfect continuity and still feel so fragmented . . . .*

When *mincha* ends, the Chassidim rush from the crypt, their feet barely touching the ground, an interlocking mass of black choking all space within itself and propelled forward as though pushed or pursued. The black mass comes to a full jerking stop before a clover-shaped, padlocked manhole, beneath which is the inaccessible staircase leading down to the Cave. The men squat close to the ground, spread their black coats like parachutes, and peer through the tiny apertures of the bronze manhole, squinting at the pinpricks of light below, inverted stars. The men take turns peering into the holes as though at a planetarium, the manhole a telescope through which one can attempt to count the infinite lights. And they gaze below into the beginnings of the Jewish group soul, shimmering in and out of the deep. And they spread themselves upon the manhole as though trying to squirm through, cringing from the cavernous expanse of the room, the intolerable heights of the vaulted ceiling, its mad profusion of colored stripes. And they clutch the rounded sides of the manhole, huddle into one another as they realize, too late, that they are separating through a widening sieve, all they once remembered loosening, the solidity containing the holes dissolving, and they feel themselves drifting away.

In the northwest corner of Ethiopia, perched between Christian and Moslem tribes, in mud-walled and grass-coned villages hidden in steep mountain refuges remote from any road, lived the biblical Jews. The Ethiopians called them *Falasha*, strangers. They called themselves *Beta Yisrael*, the House of Israel. They had been separated from the Land since the First Temple, and preserved the literal Judaism of that time of origins, when the people held to the bare letters of the Torah, avoiding the spaces between them like an abyss which, only later, could be filled with commentaries and interpretations, Mishna and Talmud; the Jews of the First Temple still close enough to the Revelation of Sinai to be intimidated into silence by the spoken word of God.

According to one *Beta Yisrael* legend, their ancestors had left the Land while the First Temple still stood, to escort Menelik, son of Solomon and the Queen of Sheba, back to his mother's kingdom in Ethiopia. Because they had left the Land willingly, the *Beta Yisrael* were punished with exile. An eye for an eye: they had turned their gaze to an alien place, and now they would be kept from the Land which, like Moses on Mount Nebo, they strained, once a year, to see: the white-robed pilgrims following the chanting priests bearing Torah parchments and ascending Mount Sigd, slowly, like old men, up the well-trod path to the top of the mountain, facing Jerusalem, not even its outline visible, only a haze in the farthest distance rising like smoke from the ruins.

If the *Beta Yisrael* continued their penitence of yearning, they would some day prove to God their worthiness to return to the Land. Until that time, they sharpened their memories on the black letters clear against the haze of yellow parchment, and kept the blank margins freed from new ideas that might obscure a precious detail and thereby sever their link with the Land. In the mountains of Ethiopia, white-turbaned priests slaughtered sheep on Passover eve and smeared the blood on doorposts. Families built their huts near a river to allow for ritual bathing, so frequent the Ethiopians could tell a *Beta Yisrael* by the smell of water on his body. They wrenched time from its crazed deviations and steadied it for all generations to the First Temple, when the Land and its people were merged, so that when the *Beta Yisrael* would finally be returned, the Land would recognize them, embrace them as Jacob did Joseph.

So faithfully did the *Beta Yisrael* conjure the forms of the Land, signalling to God their preparedness to return to it, that they recreated the kingdom of David and Solomon. For four hundred years the *Beta Yisrael* fought to preserve their kingdom, their armies equipped with weapons made by their own blacksmiths, the finest in Ethiopia. They were led by powerful rulers, like Queen Yehudit, who rose against the Christians trying to forcibly convert her people, and captured the holy city of Axum, the New Jerusalem of the Copts, burning its churches and massacring its ruling family and filling its wells with sand. Queen Yehudit was finally defeated by a Christian-Moslem alliance; and though her kingdom gradually was constricted to the highest mountains, it endured. Not until the 16th century, when the Portuguese explorers came and sold guns to the Christians, were the *Beta Yisrael* soldiers, armed with spears and swords, driven onto cliffs, slitting one another's throats rather than surrender into slavery.

Measure for measure: their ancestors had chosen exile and now exile had rejected them. They were forbidden to own land in the country they once ruled, serfs harvesting the corn and grain of absentee Christian masters, uprooted like the grass on the roofs of their huts. To their Christian neighbors they were demons, learning their blacksmithing skills in the region of fire, where they had fashioned the nails to crucify Jesus; at night they turned themselves into scavenging hyenas and kidnapped Christian babies and drank their blood. In the mountain enclaves to which they had fled, the *Beta Yisrael* were hunted like rare animals, sold as slaves as if there had been no Exodus, their children abducted into monasteries. Many became hidden Jews and tried to maintain a kingdom of memory; but its territory gradually dissolved into isolated, indefensible fragments.

For those who remained *Beta Yisrael*, redemption depended on the intensity of their alienation from Exile. And so they reciprocated the revulsion of their neighbors, confirming themselves as Ethiopia's untouchables. When a *Beta Yisrael* went to the market to sell straw baskets, he took with him a wooden bowl, in which a Christian would deposit payment without violating the *Beta Yisrael* with his touch; if a *Beta Yisrael* had physical contact with a stranger, he would immerse in water and remain outside his village till sunset. The *Beta Yisrael* believed they were the only Jews in the world, the Covenant depending on them alone. And so no other Diaspora, however ghettoized or fenced within rabbinic law, so isolated itself as the black Jews of Ethiopia.

In the 19th century, the white *Beta Yisrael* appeared. They spoke of endless Diasporas like mythical kingdoms, of expansive legal and philosophical systems, embroidered rituals around the letters of the Torah. The *Beta Yisrael* were confronted with cosmic vastness. They were not the center of divine attention but its periphery; a senile man who could recall the intimate details of his most distant past but of the present knew nothing.

The white Jews promised help, and over the years, sent some money and books. A few *Beta Yisrael* were even taken to Europe for enlightenment; and to the villages came European Jews passionate for the black Jews who recalled the time of Israel's innocence. But the *Beta Yisrael,* who once were said to number a million, continued to lose their people to disease, attacks and now to new Christian missionaries from the West, whose aid was often more substantial than that of the white Jews.

In the late 1940s, word spread in the villages: The Jewish kingdom had arisen in the Land and defeated seven Arab armies. Israeli planes were flying to remote lands and ferrying Jews home; Israeli emissaries were ferreting out Jewish children hidden in Polish monasteries, Afghani Moslem tribesmen rumored to possess Torah scrolls, prowling the most hidden corners so that no Jew would be excluded from the great ingathering. But no planes came to the mountains of Ethiopia. Perhaps in their excitement the white *Beta Yisrael* had forgotten them. Perhaps the planes had approached but could not land.

The *Beta Yisrael* waited. Patiently: they would not repeat the tragedy of a hundred years before, when the villages emptied and barefoot *Beta Yisrael* had followed a mad messiah and died by the thousands on a futile exodus to the Red Sea. The messiah had promised that the Red Sea would part, and thereby redress a *Beta Yisrael* legend that claimed their ancestors had been Israelites who arrived at the Red Sea shore too late, after it had already opened and sealed, watching their brothers on the other shore proceed to the Land while they remained in Exile forever.

Some villagers, restless, trekked to the Israeli Embassy in Addis Ababa, hoping for visas to the Land. They were told by Israeli officials to go home; there were no visas available, not even for tourists. But Christian pilgrims requesting visas were welcomed and processed. It had to be a bureaucratic mistake; it was not possible that the Christians would triumph even here, in the building that flew the blue-and-white banner of the Land. To thwart the officials, who surely would be punished when the leaders of the Land discovered what was happening, *Beta Yisrael* youth began appearing in the embassy wearing large wooden crosses around their necks; and only when they came to the Land did they remove the crosses and ask for asylum under the Law of Return.

But the Law of Return, which offered refuge to every Jew in the world, did not include the *Beta Yisrael*. Even here, they were *Falasha,* strangers; the Land, amnesiac, claimed never to have known them. The government and the rabbinate didn't recognize these Jews who had never heard of the Talmud. It had to be a misunderstanding, not at all malicious: just as the *Beta Yisrael* had not at first believed there could be a white *Beta Yisrael,* perhaps the government had not yet adjusted to *their* existence. Perhaps the rabbis could be forgiven their suspicion of *Beta Yisrael* origins; the *Beta Yisrael* themselves had a dozen contradictory legends about their ancestry. Surely this was God's final test of their worthiness to enter the Land, one last measure of their patience and will.

And, in fact, emissaries from the Land did appear in the villages, bringing with them maps and songs and legends of great battles. Some village children were even sent to the Land, for study; but when their study was completed, they were returned to Ethiopia, forbidden to remain. Patience, said the emissaries; your problem is being dealt with. And the *Beta Yisrael* were patient.

In 1972, the Israeli rabbinate recognized the *Beta Yisrael* as the lost tribe of Dan; three years later, the government embraced them in the Law of Return. Some *Beta Yisrael,* hearing the news, sold their possessions and came down from the villages and waited in the towns for planes. But still the planes didn't come. Perhaps the pilots hadn't heard the government's decision. Perhaps the leaders of the Land didn't know they were waiting.

In 1977, the monarchy was overthrown by a pro-Soviet revolution. In the resulting chaos, *Beta Yisrael* were slaughtered by right-wing gangs and left-wing gangs, for supporting the revolution, for supporting the monarchy, for Zionism, for sorcery, for turning Christian corpses into mules, for Queen Yehudit who had burned the churches a thousand years before. The slave trade in *Beta Yisrael* resumed. Still the planes didn't come. The only Jewish community in the world facing physical extinction was the only one denied Zionism's promise of refuge. Letters in fractured Hebrew began arriving in Israel from Ethiopia: "We are still waiting with much patience and hopes to our salvation by the Israeli nation in our holy country for which we are dreaming. . . . We are asking you to do anything in any way in your possibility to save our lives, without any doubt we will not be in life very soon and the action anyway will come to stand still when our life will be over. . . . I cannot find words to express or stress the terrible situation of all the Jews here. Just to say that they all about to die. And this thing is very much sorry, that it occurs when the State of Israel is already existing. . . ."

Falashas fled their villages and crossed the border to Sudanese camps crowded with starving refugees from the revolution. Others gathered in the Ethiopian town of Gondar, scanning the skies. Perhaps this was the final uprooting for the sake of ingathering, the apocalypse before redemption.

Conditions in Ethiopia, and perhaps, too, an embarrassing public campaign against the Israeli failure to rescue Ethiopian Jews, persuaded the government to move. Several thousand *Beta Yisrael* were brought to Israel by the government of Menachem Begin, the first Israeli prime minister to meet with Ethiopian immigrants and take personal control over rescue operations.

In autumn, 1984, the Ethiopian famine worsening, Prime Minister Shimon Peres initiated the massive rescue airlift known as "Operation Moses." Israelis, reminded of the purpose for their economic and military troubles, embraced the barefoot refugees who had trekked hundreds of miles, some of them carrying dying relatives on their backs. Clothing depots were set up throughout the country. Building contractors volunteered to renovate homes for the new immigrants. Dentists offered free treatment. One young nurse at Shaare Zedek Hospital, where entire wards were filled with Ethiopian children, said: "I always felt a mixture of guilt and envy that I wasn't born when the great waves of immigrants came, and there were real sacrifices to make. Now I will have something to tell my children, too."

But when the euphoria settled, the *Beta Yisrael* realized they were not yet fully home. Israel's rabbinate decided the Ethiopians must first undergo "symbolic conversion" to reaffirm their Jewishness, since they had for so long been severed from the Jewish people and had not followed talmudic law. For the women, this meant immersion into a ritual bath; for the men, a new circumcision. Couples, including the elderly, were told their marriages were invalid and required a new ceremony.

At a meeting between Israel's chief rabbis and immigrant leaders, one *Beta Yisrael* elder said: "Through all the generations of our persecution, our worst enemies never imagined a way to hurt us the way we have been hurt by our own brethren." Another said: "For thousands of years we suffered for the Torah. We never dreamed that we would come back here, only to be told we weren't really Jews. When will you let us feel we are really home?"

Other Israeli realities marred the homecoming of the *Beta Yisrael*. Racial jokes were told loudly in their presence; unemployed workers accused them of taking their jobs. Mayors of several hard-pressed towns publicly told the Ethiopian immigrants to stay away; one mayor went so far as to promise he would personally load Ethiopians onto trucks and drive them out of his town.

Government officials calmed the Ethiopians: All immigrants have had similar difficulties. But for the *Beta Yisrael*, every insult was magnified by their knowledge of their country's reluctance to admit them; no other community had to fight the government of Israel for its right to *aliyah*.

One town in Israel requested the honor of receiving *Beta Yisrael* immigrants: the City of the Fathers, Kiryat Arba. Here, in the burial place of those Jews who lived not only before the Talmud but before Torah, the *Beta Yisrael* were embraced.

Over 300 *Beta Yisrael* now live in Kiryat Arba. They are everywhere: their children playing with Kiryat Arba's children in the numerous little playgrounds that fill the town's empty spaces, the women in bright bulbous kerchiefs and white sheets over long embroidered dresses, teenage boys in jeans and t-shirts and tiny knitted *kippot* pinned flat against their tight round hair, old men with wooly white beards, the rims of their dusty fedoras entirely lowered or raised.

The *Beta Yisrael* are concentrated in three buildings, below the circular road and outside the ring of Kiryat Arba, part of the town's expansion into the valley along the security fence. In the middle building live Yaakov and Sarah Kasa and their five children. Though the Kasa family has been here a year, the apartment looks as if its occupants are just now moving in, waiting for the things that fill these rooms to animate and reveal their purpose. Except for a flat straw basket covered with swirls and a broken imitation cuckoo clock, the white walls are bare, smudged as if with the groping fingerprints of a blind man. A glass-encased breakfront is empty, awaiting the porcelain dogs and gondolas with which Israelis fill their living room displays.

Yaakov Kasa sits on the edge of the couch, utterly still, as though afraid to provoke the pink floral bedsheet thrown over the cushions that has already decided to move half-way to the floor. He is goateed, tiny, so thin that one imagines his heart visible beneath his shirt, caught between his ribs. Sarah hovers over her husband, cheeks pinched, her arms tightly crossed at her breasts as if to steady herself in this wavering box perched upon other boxes, testing man's vertical limits, so precarious that she has more than once felt the rooms swaying in the Hebron winds, and only by miracle did they not topple and crush the children playing in the dirt lot below.

"We are worried about our families," Yaakov Kasa says, looking down, his body frozen. "They are in refugee camps. In the Sudan. We hope the Israeli government will bring them to us soon. It is very dangerous for a Jew in the Sudan."

Yaakov says the people of Kiryat Arba have made him feel at home. "Just like by *abba* and *imma*. Everyone is good to us. If not for people here, we would have no shoes."

Yaakov points to his 10-year-old daughter, who is wearing second-hand clothes, proof of Kiryat Arba's generosity: high heels several sizes too big, a grey maxi skirt hanging perilously low on her hips, a matching grey t-shirt with the number "22" on its chest, a string of greyish imitation pearls at her neck.

Every night, says Yaakov, there are classes here in Jewish history and ritual, all that has happened between the First Temple and the *Beta Yisrael* return to the Land. For Sarah, there are classes in modern life, like how to make vegetables emerge from the frozen blocks sold in colored boxes; as if the white *Beta Yisrael*, too long in exile from the Land, had forgotten that vegetables are grown on soil, which they cover here with concrete as though to deny it, only the Arabs across the fence recalling how to treat the earth.

"We are grateful to everyone here," says Yaakov. "But it is very hard."

Yaakov has found only part-time work in Kiryat Arba's small industrial zone. Sarah works a few hours a day sweeping the town's immigrant absorption center. "If not for the people here, we would not have food to eat," he says.

In Ashkelon, in Afula, other *Beta Yisrael* have settled and found full-time work. Yaakov says maybe he should move there too. He knows those places are not like Kiryat Arba; the people aren't so good as they are here. But what can he do? He has to feed his family.

But Yaakov cannot leave Kiryat Arba. He spreads his hands apart, slowly, the most vigorous gesture he can muster. "I can't. I *can't*." The government gives an immigrant his apartment, and then he must fend for himself. How can Yaakov afford to buy elsewhere without selling his apartment here? And who will buy an apartment in a *Falasha* building in Kiryat Arba?

Yaakov sits, unmoving, palms pressed together, as if cementing the two sides of his body. All his worries merge into the vertical lines rising from his slender nose into his forehead, the only wrinkles on his taut face; all the questions he cannot yet articulate and that jumble together, one contradicting the other: how it was possible for the Israeli government to know what was happening to the *Beta Yisrael* and wait for so long to bring them to the Land; how, having been rescued, he and his family could find their refuge turned into a prison; and, when he looks at his children in their strange costumes, wondering, perhaps, how it is possible that the biblical Jews could be returned to the Land, to Hebron itself, only to be transformed into something unrecognizable.

The Talmud Torah Hebron, Elementary School for Boys, faces the empty hills behind Kiryat Arba, away from Hebron, where no Arab villas confound the biblical view. On its freshly-painted, bright orange walls hang cut-outs of animals mentioned in the Bible, lions and leopards and elephants who once roamed these hills, and pictures of biblical trees and plants that once covered the landscape but now grow scattered. On classroom walls hang posters that urge, "And you shall settle the Land," as if that commandment were itself sufficient, embracing all others. The classroom windows are unusually large for any school, and inconceivable for a yeshiva, as if deliberately inviting the students to daydream into the landscape.

In a classroom over whose blackboard hangs a map of the ancient borders of Israel, stretching to Tyre and Damascus in the north and past the Jordan River to the east, and segmented into plots possessed by the 12 tribes, a black-bearded young rabbi paces the aisles, adjusting the fingers of his students to the proper place in their large-type Bibles, like the print used in books for the visually impaired. The rabbi waves his hands and nearly shouts his singsong questions and answers, as though he were addressing not 30 squirming first graders but an army about to march to its greatest victory.

"What is Abraham missing? Only one thing. What? He has all the money he needs, all the sheep; he has *Eretz Yisrael*. God has given him *everything*–and why? So the nations will fear the God Abraham serves. But who will Abraham leave it all to? To whom? To whom? To whom! God gives me money; what is it worth? God gives me *Eretz Yisrael;* what can I do with it if I don't have–what? If I don't have a son! A son! A son!"

The rabbi sings a biblical verse, and the students, screeching, repeat the chant, each word of more than one syllable rising and falling in a happy key: "And there came one that had escaped and told Abraham the Hebrew; now he dwelt by the terebinths of Mamre. And when Abraham heard that his brother Lot was taken captive, he led forth his trained men, born in his house, three hundred and eighteen, and pursued as far as Dan. And he divided against them by night, he and his servants, and smote them, and pursued them unto Hobah, which is on the left of Damascus."

The children wear large *kippot* clipped to their hair, the bright swirling stitches, tightly knit, covering their heads like a helmet; unlike the flimsy black cloth *kippah* of the Diaspora, unpinned and vulnerable to a sudden wind, its wearer restricted from vigorous movements. The thin braided *tzitzit* along the sides of their pants don't dangle in mid-air, candlewicks waiting to be burned, but reach down like roots. Their *payot* flow from headfuls of hair, not like the chassidic *payot*, stranded at the temples of a shaved head, reminders of loss, the youthful exuberance sheared like an enervated Samson.

Many of the children wear t-shirts imprinted with the names of Israel's nationalist parties, Likud, Morasha, Techiya. One student wears the yellow t-shirt of Meir Kahane's Kach, its emblem a Star of David squeezed from within by a fist. Some wear the old t-shirt of the Yamit squatters, its slogan, "Stop the Withdrawal from Sinai," imposed upon a black map of Israel segmented into white diagonal stripes that mark the stages of Sinai retreat, the stripes proceeding into the Negev, the central plain, Galilee, until all of Israel is severed into fragments: the fear of losing the Land on which converge nature, history, vigor.

Affirming *Eretz Yisrael*, Talmud Torah Hebron restores to Judaism the physicality it had once, before Diaspora, celebrated: a tangible holiness, a religion whose protagonist is a people interacting with its land; its calendar the seasonal cycle, its holidays historical triumphs, its vigorous saints improving the world measurably, through *mitzvot*. Exiled from the temporal, ghetto Orthodoxy subverted Judaism to its opposite purpose, not the perfection of physicality but its neutralization, disembodying nature by observing in strange climates the seasonal rhythms of the Land, turning history into metaphor for an individual's spiritual struggles, banishing the impact of *mitzvot* to unseen realms: a vicarious religion exchanging for physicality the memory of physicality, a poltergeist clinging to the cherished place it could no longer inhabit.

The Orthodox Jew became stranger even to his own body, mistaking that ultimate exile for spiritual perfection. Orthodoxy divided into rival camps of chassidim and *mitnagdim,* advocates of the soul and of the intellect, as though, too long in proximity to Christianity, Judaism had abandoned its mediation between spirit and matter and accepted the Christian despair of the world. As etherealness became timidity, the Orthodox Jew forgot how to survive. And so, when Zionism offered to turn the yearnings for Zion into concrete refuge, among its greatest Jewish opponents were the Orthodox, resisting any encroachment of the real upon their metaphorical Judaism; and when the Nazis came, those least able or willing to fight were the Orthodox.

After the Holocaust, many Orthodox Jews accepted the conversion of their world into air as the final verdict on the nature of the Jew. Some of the surviving chassidim and *mitnagdim* formed in Israel a new grouping, *charedim,* those who fear God, blurring the old distinction between soul and mind and creating instead a new demarcation within Orthodoxy: those who fear not only God, but all of His creation; and those without fear, the Orthodox Zionists who, like blind men given sight, exult in the world, in their own materialization. *Charedim* are the only Jews in Israel who don't serve in the army and who can't handle a gun; the Gush Emunim settlers–the Zionist Orthodox–are the only Israelis who always carry a gun.

Alone among yeshivot, Talmud Torah Hebron draws its entire curriculum from the Bible, chronicle of Jewish intactness, Israel in its youth, at once physically rooted and divinely linked. In Talmud Torah Hebron, all subjects are derived from the Bible. From the paschal sacrifice, reenacted in the ritual slaughter of a sheep, students learn anatomy; from the Tower of Babel, ancient civilizations; from the verse, "Now Abraham and Sarah had grown very old, and Sarah was past the age of child-bearing," sexual reproduction.

For *charedi* yeshivot, the Bible is a children's primer, dispensed with as soon as the student is strong enough to carry a volume of Talmud. The Bible is embarrassing; too much needs to be explained: The generation of the Exodus, so worthy that all subsequent generations have been on a steady spiritual decline as though slinking away in shame, prostrate before the Golden Calf; the great *tzaddikim* who spoke with God, judges, prophets, kings, compared to whom we are like grasshoppers, married to pagan women. The Talmud is relief: There, finally, is the familiar Judaism, rational, refined, no unrestrained pagan urges, the completion of the transition only tentatively begun in the Bible: from animal to Jew.

In Talmud Torah Hebron, the Talmud is deferred to its not-yet-established high school. Even among Zionist yeshivot, this is a radical departure. Yet the school's founders are not the anti-religious biblicists of early Zionism, leaping over the culture of the Diaspora to suppress all reminders of its trauma. Like the *charedim,* they are committed to preserving rabbinic Judaism, the rhythms and rituals of a lost Diaspora. For *charedim,* however, no trauma must be overcome, because their destroyed world persists, its constricted model a perfect reproduction; whereas for the Orthodox Zionists of Talmud Torah Hebron, only a return of the Diaspora to its biblical youth can redeem the rituals sullied with the martyrdom that belied their power. Back to that time when the sound of the *shofar* could topple walls, the mere sight of the Ark scatter Israel's enemies in flight; back to when the symbols of Torah were transmitters of Divine intervention, receptacles of visible energy; when the Jew spoke to God and God answered, in clear, unmistakable words, nothing less compensating for centuries of divine silence.

In Talmud Torah Hebron's administrative office, director Aharon Toledano pauses from his workload, unusually heavy these last weeks, to explain to a visiting journalist the school's philosophy. "We are a school for the children of *Eretz Yisrael* in *Eretz Yisrael*. Our curriculum is based on the Bible because that is how Jews studied when they inhabited the Land. Everything is taught here in a living context, not isolated in artificial categories: A history class, a geography class, a grammar class: Why? Why give the children a separate grammar class so that for the rest of their lives they should hate grammar? Let it emerge *naturally,* from the text itself. Our job is to create an authentic *Eretz Yisrael* education, not to borrow the ideas and methods of *Galut,* of Exile. Did we come to *Eretz Yisrael* to recreate the German *gymnasia?*"

Toledano laughs at his mention of the *gymnasia,* the educational system popular in the early years of the *Yishuv.* But there is no maliciousness in his laughter, only amazement at imposing such a confining model on the children of *Eretz Yisrael*.

"Look around you," he says. "Does this feel like a *Galut* yeshiva? Large windows. Light: no gloom. You should see our gym."

"We had once a saying in Israel:

'The best to the air force.' Now the saying must be, 'The best to education.' Why can't we create here the finest educational system in the world? Who else if not the Jews? But first we have to break from the ideas of *Galut*. Maybe for *Galut* it was fine to take second-rate teachers for the *cheder*, those who couldn't find jobs anywhere else. Or Talmud: no one will argue its importance. But to study Talmud at such an early age? Why burden the children with difficult and abstract concepts?

"Our goal is to produce religious doctors, leaders, engineers, army officers. Not just rabbis. Every Jew should be knowledgeable enough to make his own *halachic* decisions, without having to run always to a rabbi. And the rabbis who will, God willing, emerge from here will be *leaders,* guides for life's *important* questions. Our rabbis today can tell you how to steep tea on Shabbat. But for the larger questions, they can't help you. That, too, is a curse of *Galut*."

Toledano is continually interrupted by teachers and secretaries. He shrugs and smiles to the journalist. "With Rav Dan away . . . ."

Rav Dan Be'eri, founder and principal of Talmud Torah Hebron, is away in jail, a member of the settlers' underground. The journalist asks Toledano if he is concerned about the effect of Rav Dan's arrest on the students.

"Not at all. Our students are taught to be loyal citizens. Rav Dan wrote them an open letter explaining that what he did was only because of unusual circumstances; it is not to be considered the norm. We have a government and we have to respect its laws, even when we don't agree with them.

"But," adds Toledano, "there are times when a loyal citizen must violate the law. Pinchas also took the law into his own hands."

Pinchas: the Israelite who, seeing a prince of the tribe of Simeon bring a Midianite woman to his tent, slew the couple with his spear. Moses, wrote the rabbis, was so disturbed by this act of recklessness, and so concerned that Pinchas would be taken as a model for zealotry, that he planned to excommunicate him; and only when God assured Moses that Pinchas had acted with Divine guidance was the verdict stayed. Nothing less than the spoken word of God, imply the rabbis, can sanction the behavior of a Pinchas.

But it is precisely the boldness of his action, not the cautious afterthought of the Rabbis, that moves Toledano to invoke Pinchas. Yet Toledano is a rabbinic Jew; the smallest details of his life are governed by rabbinic principles. He knows the secular Zionists failed to create an enduring biblical culture because one cannot profess loyalty to distant ancestors and deny one's father and grandfather; that, paradoxically, only those Jews dedicated to rabbinic Judaism are best equipped to return to the Bible.

But that paradox ultimately undermines the Orthodox Zionist, because the rabbinic Judaism he seeks to preserve neutralizes the biblical vigor meant to infuse it. And so he makes this compromise: He will consult the rabbis on how long to steep tea on Shabbat, but on the larger questions of life and death he refuses to be burdened by their abstract concepts; twice before in this century, on Zionism and on Nazism, those abstractions failed him. Even a loyal Orthodox Jew must sometimes violate the Law.

Toledano would be appalled at the suggestion that the underground and its supporters were rebelling against rabbinic authority, or that Talmud Torah Hebron's policy of deferring Talmud study to an as-yet-non-existent high school expresses an unacknowledged urge to be freed from the Talmud completely. An Orthodox Jew, Toledano seeks validation for his break with rabbinic authority and finds it in the Bible, in Pinchas: murdering without due process and ignoring Moses and the Elders, who might have displayed the caution of the rabbis, who branded as cruel a court that once in 70 years condemned a man to death. An eye for an eye: not, as the rabbis explained it, monetary compensation for the bodily wound, but as it is written, as it was meant by a vigorous, natural people to be practiced.

Toledano says: "These boys from the underground, you think they're killers? They enjoy killing? It's fun? Do you know who those mayors were? Every one a PLO leader. And the Hebron 'College': People hear the word 'college' and think, a college. Like that 'college' in Shechem where the army found thousands of manuals on how to make bombs. If you're not a member of the PLO, you can't even get in there. If you're for Arafat, you're a moderate. A college.

"Do you know what it's like to travel the roads here? To have your wife and children take a bus to Jerusalem and not know if they're going to come home in one piece? You think it's a joke, stones. A stone is a weapon, just like a grenade. A three-year-old girl here in Kiryat Arba nearly died from a slingshot wound that just missed her brain. Esther Ohana already died from a stone. A yeshiva boy from Brooklyn is still a vegetable after seven years, from a stone.

"What is this, stones? Children throw stones at stray cats. Are we animals that they throw stones on us? Do they think they can do to us here what they did to us in *Galut*? Maybe for Peace Now, it's normal for Arabs to throw stones on Jews. Only when Jews fight back it's not normal. Then it's terrorism. What do they want us to do, sit on our hands like ghetto Jews?"

Perhaps the stonings, mocking the Jews in their biblical pretense, are even worse than terrorist attacks. Was a biblical hero ever stoned? With each new humiliation, the foundation of rebuilt Hebron is threatened, as though it were being dismantled, stone by stone.

But more terrible still is the memory of 1929, not the massacre itself but the passivity of its victims, the young Talmud students and frail rabbis so used to deferring to the Arabs that they had rejected the protection of the Haganah. No Jewish community in the *Yishuv* had suffered such a pogrom; none had died so easily.

In Toledano's office are stacks of Talmud Torah Hebron's glossy promotion brochure. It opens to a picture not of its airy new building with the large windows and gym, nor to an explanation of its unique philosophy and curriculum, but to a picture of a

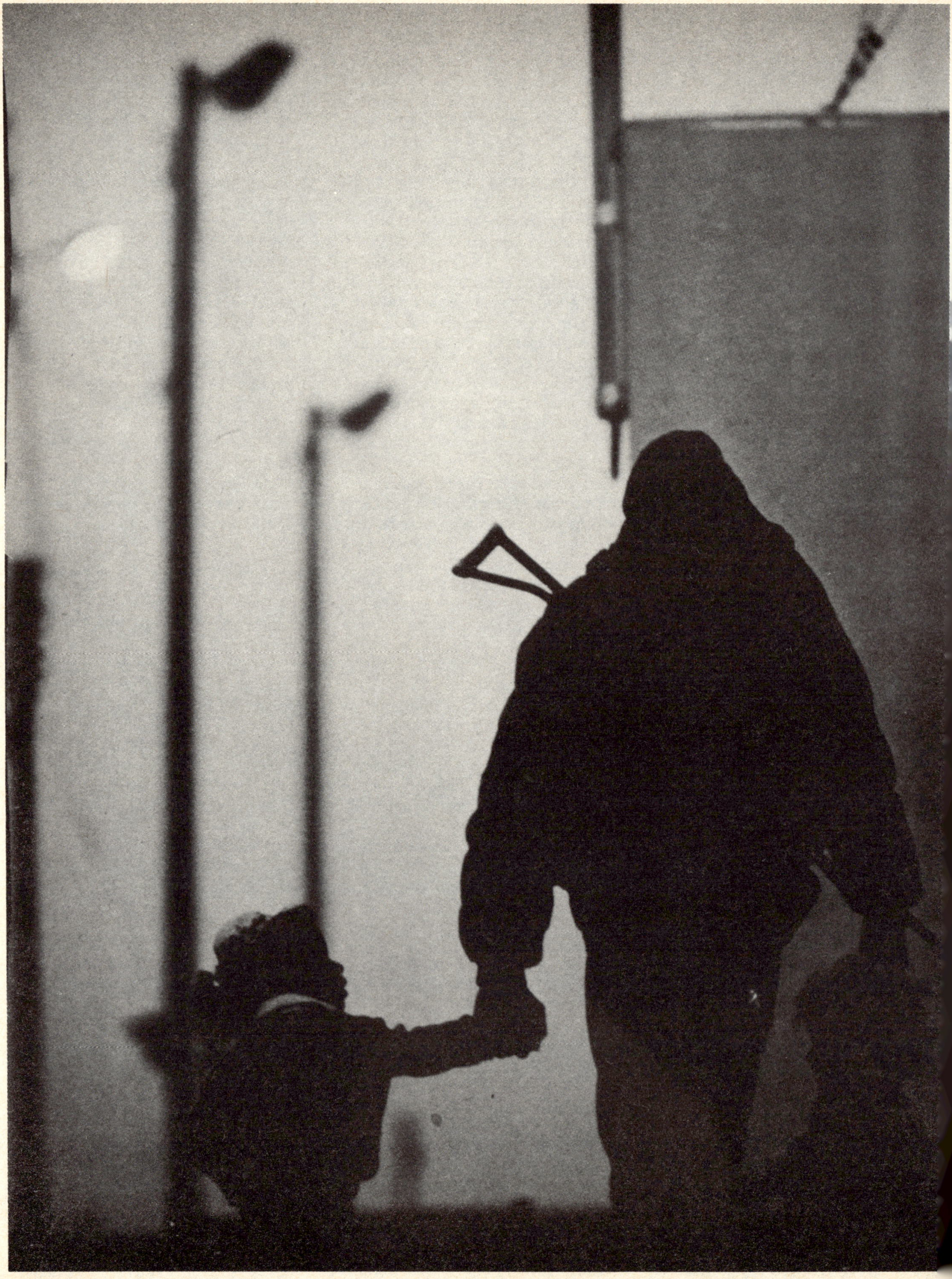

bruised child, orphaned in the massacre, eyes wide, and what appear to be white hairs wild on his balding scalp. Beside it is a picture of torn and singed Torah scrolls. Every child in Talmud Torah Hebron can recite the details of the massacre, knows of every Jewish symbol sullied here as brutally as anywhere in the Diaspora: the cemetery stones dug up and replaced with a tomato patch; the Avraham Avinu synagogue turned into a public latrine; the Jewish houses sacked, hollowed, their stone doorposts chiselled away to erase the indentations where the *mezzuzot* had been ripped out, denying even the memory of desecration.

For the Hebron Jew, history now begins in 1929. Much as he tries, he can flee no further back. Fixed at the center of his consciousness is the passivity of the ghetto, demanding of his every action its own negation. And despite his acts of random rage, he cannot defeat those who wish to exile him again from here, because in the end it is Hebron itself he must defeat. For though Hebron confirms the Jewish right to *Eretz Yisrael* and the tenacity of Jewish settlement, it is now also proof of our transience on the Land, of the ghetto's endless reach, extending retroactively, poisoning the root.

In homes and buildings throughout Kiryat Arba hang identical framed photographs of an old Chassidic Jew, gazing straight ahead, almost severe in his steadiness. Abraham Isaac Kook, Chief Rabbi of Palestine at the time of the *chalutzim*, the pioneers, and theologian of the religious Zionist synthesis, is beloved in Kiryat Arba for his ecstatic vision of Jewish renewal, his glorification of the Jew and the Land.

Rav Kook, however, understood Jewish separateness as a prelude to the coming messianic consciousness, in which the borders between Jew and gentile, even between human and animal, would be transcended. History was not circular, striving backward to a lost golden age, but progressive, an irreversible process toward interdependency of all life. Darwinism, wrote Rav Kook, was an apt scientific description of this spiritual reality, the infinite evolution of the collective soul.

An Orthodox Jew, Rav Kook believed the Temple would be rebuilt and its animal sacrifices resumed. But Rav Kook, evolutionist and vegetarian, saw that not as the goal but as the initial stage of the messianic process. We return to the exact place of our yearning, he believed, only to be taught that we have outgrown the forms adequate for our ancestors. With our longing for the past at once fulfilled and frustrated, we can then resume our spiritual ascent. The animal sacrifices will be replaced with grains and fruits, followed by levels of refinement which even Rav Kook could not envision.

Rav Kook died in 1935. He did not live to see the revelation of evil that has stunned his followers back into a biblical literalness. Evolution reverses before the abyss; only the past seems to offer perfection.

Were he alive today, would Rav Kook see in the Jewish return to Hebron a blessing? With the thwarting of the expectations Jews bring to Hebron may come the realization that the past offers no permanent refuge: whether it is the former leftist convinced that the Arabs like the Canaanites must be expelled, but whose conscience shrinks from brutality; or the Moroccan Jew who desires the completeness of Torah in the Land and finds instead a wildness that undermines its laws; or those seeking a Diaspora that has vanished, or a biblical past obscured by the intervening Diaspora.

Indeed, Rav Kook might see in Hebron Jewry a new people trying to be born. In its ingathering of Diaspora fragments, mirroring human diversity, Kiryat Arba implicitly concedes the universalism that the Jewish people, according to Rav Kook, by nature embodies. The astonishing number of converts here is, perhaps, yet another step in Hebron's evolution: Not yet ready to embrace the world, Hebron is instead infiltrated from without.

Even in Jewish-Arab relations, Rav Kook might find consolation. For here, in Israel's potential Belfast, is the only shrine shared by Jew and Moslem: the Cave of Machpelah, where Isaac and Ishmael together buried their father, Abraham. Perhaps the Jews and Moslems who worship here are praying for each other's disappearance; but nowhere else do Hebrew and Arabic prayers commingle. Here, in the root which has not yet been branched, rabbis and kadis together preside over the Cave, offering a model for joint rule of the Jews' Judea and Samaria and the Arabs' West Bank, the only solution befitting holy land.

Or perhaps this is all illusion. Hebron is not only birthplace but burial ground. The last refuge of the *anakim*, Hebron is primordial earth, untamed.

Hebron is the source of both coexistence and strife. When Abraham came to purchase the Cave of Machpelah, the people of Hebron so welcomed him that they offered the burial site as a gift; only when he insisted did they accept payment. But when the children of Jacob came to bury their father in the Cave, Esau blocked their way; and only when Chushan ben Dan drew his sword and severed Esau's head could Jacob be buried among his fathers. Hebron, the root, contains all possibilities.

The Mishna *Yoma* says: When the priests prepared the morning sacrifice, a messenger was sent to see if the dawn had come. Mattitya ben Shmuel says: The entire eastern sky must be lit, all the way to Hebron. For Hebron's mountains are higher than Jerusalem's, obscuring the dawn. But if light has appeared even over Hebron, then surely the time for Temple service has come. ★

THE ENDS AND MEANS OF ZIONISM

"Israel is the only truly modern society, knowing both annihilation and redemption."

YOSSI KLEIN HALEVI

Yossi Klein Halevi, a contributing editor of Moment, *lives and writes in Jerusalem.*

I.

In 1945, the Jewish people abandoned its historic strategy for survival. Until then, within Jews, disaster summoned perseverance, gradual painstaking rebuilding. But when, after decades of infighting and ambivalence, a majority of Jewry embraced the idea of return to Zion, it determined that, for the first time, group survival now depended on a leap into metahistory. While most Jews, perhaps, would have denied their Zionism to be anything more than a political strategy for survival, they were nevertheless conceding that survival was now possible only through the realization of the central event in Judaism's eschatology—the return of the exiles to Eretz Yisrael, metaphor as well as catalyst for the return of an exiled world to its source.

Yet if, for post-Holocaust Jews, survival had become inseparable from redemption, this differed from previous Jewish perception only in its immediacy. For Jews never saw their survival as perpetuation for its own sake. Alone among peoples, the Jews justified their existence by a goal, however distant or deferred: the gathering of the nations in worship at Mt. Zion, a Divine redemption confined not to the souls of the spiritually gifted but amplified publicly, embracing all humanity.

To effect this universalist vision, the Jewish people was, paradoxically, set apart, as a testing ground for the possibility of redemptive interaction between humanity and God. For, as a people, the Jews are a random cross-section of humanity in microcosm. And if this people could be transformed into an instrument for Divine intimacy, then the hope of transcendence could be extended, eventually, to all peoples.

The Jewish people was inducted into its task in a mass exodus and revelation, imprinting on its soul a vision of egalitarian redemption. A handmaiden at the Red Sea, says the *midrash*, experienced greater revelation than did Ezekiel in his vision of the chariot. The Jewish calendar reinforced this message by celebrating the collective past rather than the miracles of individual saints. And to impress upon Jews the redemptive capacity of the world, they were given *mitzvot*, commandments, which manifest the potential holiness in everything material.

Finally, the Jews were sent into history—to accumulate the wisdom and practical experience that would some day enable them to release the plan locked within the seeming randomness of human events. And so each new disaster, rather than invalidating history as the arena for redemption, reinforced Jewish experience and merit. And the goal toward which Jewish survival aspired was brought one step closer.

II.

The Nazi assault on Jewry was, in essence, an attempt to defeat the egalitarian messianic vision. For Hitler, that vision threatened to enervate man's ability to survive in nature. In seeking to free the world of Jewish messianism and replace it with a radical social Darwinism, Nazism defined its own role as messianic. The Final Solution, in Nazi eyes, was no mere scapegoating of a helpless minority, but the apocalyptic endwar between evenly matched protagonists. "The mightiest counterpart to the Aryan," wrote Hitler, "is the Jew." And the outcome of their struggle, he concluded, would determine the fate of the world: "If the Jew is victorious, his crown will be the funeral wreath of humanity, and this planet will, as it did thousands of years ago, move through the ether devoid of men."

To defeat the Jewish messianic threat required the discrediting of history as sacred process. The Jews had had the profound audacity to offer their own tortured history as proof of this world's promise, a challenge that the Nazis accepted. If Jewish history could be aborted, then Marxists and liberal democrats and all other adherents of Judaic ideological derivatives whom Hitler so despised would not again dare to imagine a just culmination to history.

Parodying God, the Nazis chose the Jewish people as their testing ground, to prove the absence of an historical plan. "Where is your God now?" SS officers taunted Jews before the mass graves.

The rhetorical question was directed not only to Orthodox believers but to all of European Jewry. No Jewry at any time ever devised so many varied and practical strategies for hastening redemption as did the Jewish communities of Europe. Jewish Marxists, Zionists and Reform rabbis all agreed on one point: Theirs was the time of messianic fulfillment. Hitler feared the Jews of Europe, their messianic restlessness, attributing to them the most awesome conspiracies for world domination—justifiable in the sense that Europe's Jews were actively conspiring to remake the world in their image. By revealing the impotence of Israel's God, the Nazis were really striking at the Redeemer of history in all His modern guises.

Because Nazism was antithetical to the religion of redemption, it often deliberately timed its attacks on Jewish holidays, celebrations of sacred history. The final destruction of the Warsaw Ghetto began on the first night of Passover, 1943. On Purim, 1942, 10 Jews were hung in Zdunska-Volya to avenge the hanging of Haman's 10 sons, a retroactive undoing of the Purim miracle. The following year in Zdunska-Volya, another 10 Jews were hung, on Shavuot, festival of Sinai, in revenge for the Ten Commandments.

Unconsciously, perhaps, but no less precisely, the Nazis subverted the traditional prophetic imagery of redemption. The Prophets had envisioned an ingathering of scattered exiles, and the Nazis ingathered, from Tunisia to the Ukraine. The Prophets had promised that the gentiles would acknowledge Jewish chosenness and centrality in history, and Nazi ideology obliged. The Prophets had imagined a rational heaven on earth, and the Nazis created death camps that were a perfectly rationalized hell.

After the Holocaust, most Jews instinctively realized that if this time, yet again, they repeated the classic Jewish pattern of survival, rebuilding the ruins and accepting history's slow progression toward redemption, Jewry would not long endure. For by actualizing, in reverse, the myth of redemption, the Nazis had poisoned the very motive for Jewish survival. If the Jews failed now to emulate the Nazis and impose *their* vision on history, if they failed to summon a Divine revelation as awesome as Auschwitz, they would concede redemption to the demonic. Most Jews, already removed from tradition, would then find the notion of sacred history and, consequently, of a positive Jewish identity, unbearable irony. Surely some Jews would maintain the faith. But their impetus would no longer be vision but spite, or inertia; and only by exiling Judaism into otherworldliness could they uphold a religion whose antagonist had been far more successful, however perversely, at implementing the messianic vision.

By ingathering the exiles into Eretz Yisrael and restoring the redemptive direction of history, Zionism re-appropriated messianic imagery and could therefore challenge, if not negate, the Nazi counter-redemption. Those religious Jews who, even after the Holocaust, remained unmoved by Zionism became proponents of an untenable paradox, a Judaism that deferred redemption into oblivion. Europe's decimated yeshiva and chassidic worlds heroically transplanted and rebuilt their ruins; but by retaining their pre-war hostility to Zionism, isolated themselves from the Jewish consensus that demanded a post-Holocaust departure from mere reconstruction. In rejecting Zionism, fundamentalist Orthodoxy denied the dialectic upon which post-Holocaust Jewry was founded: that modernity, having created literal hell, had now become the arena of myth fulfillment, thereby making redemption, too, for the first time possible.

III.

Auschwitz is the rationale for the nuclear age. If man at his most civilized can now effect the global Final Solution, that expertise was acquired in the planned, dispassionate genocide of the Holocaust. The Nazis appropriated rationalism, the foundation of civilization, as the functional basis for mass murder. Turned against itself, civilization flirts with suicide.

Gradually, the nuclear world awakens to the same choice that faced the Jews in 1945: transcend or perish. Old patterns of survival have become untenable. If the nations continue to stagger from conflict to conflict, they must one day blunder into self-annihilation. World survival now depends on transcendence, the nations reconciled to their commonality by the vision of extinction.

The nuclear world needs the state of Israel not only because its mere existence is proof that modernity can yield redemption, but because Israel, whose society has ingathered the most concentrated microcosm of the nations, is the incubator for a new world consciousness. Israel is the world's only truly modern society, its people having tasted modernity's potential for both annihilation and redemption. And it is when, in moments of extremity, Israeli society has laid aside its multiple differences, that humanity has glimpsed the possibility of its own survival through transcendence.

Describing the Jews assembled before Sinai, the Torah says, "And there Israel camped." The singular form, notes Rashi, describes the unity of the tribes, "as one man, as one heart." Only when they had merged their separate selves and achieved a monotheism of peoplehood could the Jews connect with the One. Thirty-five hundred years later, during the Six Day War, the Jewish people re-enacted that unity, perhaps not since Sinai so focused on a single event and emotion—culminating in the revelation of return to Jerusalem.

Since 1967, however, Israel's competing ideologies have become increasingly alienated from one another, each fearing in the triumph of its opponent a threat to the very survival of the state. Once the basis of national unity, concern for survival has now become the pretext for dissipation.

Yet Israel's political and religious problems persist without solution. If Israel's ideological factions have stalemated one another, it is because each has appropriated a particular truth, a fear or hope, that does not negate the truth of its opponent. The responsibility of Israel's vying groups is not to triumph over rivals but to create a new politics and culture of synthesis, gathering truths from across the ideological spectrum. Israeli society needs synthesis not only for its own survival—though that will surely depend on its ability to constrain ideological rivals from destroying the country in their mutual frustration—but for the sake of creating a model of human coexistence.

Christianity and Islam each proclaimed the Jewish vision of human solidarity and then turned against the Jews for persisting in their separateness. Yet the Jews refused to relinquish either their pre-messianic exclusivity or their universalist vision, deferring a resolution of the paradox to a distant future.

With the onset of the Enlightenment, however, the ability to sustain that paradox collapsed, and the Jewish people divided into rival camps of particularists and universalists. Artificially severed from one another, means and end became distorted. Particularists saw in redemption a private Jewish affair, and universalists grew impatient with the requirements of self-preservation.

But with the creation of Israel in the nuclear era, both camps must know they are working toward the same goal, because Jewish cohesion is now a universalist imperative. The Jewish people will become a model for world harmony when its particularists concede that Jewish survival is ultimately for the sake of all humanity, and when its universalists perceive in unity among Jews the most hopeful first step toward world reconciliation. When Jewish cohesion is no longer the passing response to crisis but the basis of national existence, the Jews will be positioned for a revelation of Oneness, toward which all spiritual striving aspires. The Prophets linked the return to Zion with world redemption, and only now is a possible connection between the two discernable. Camped as one, the Jewish people will beckon to the nations to join it in prayer on the mountain of God. ✯

HERE WE BEAT OUR RUGS OUT THE WINDOW

And other revelations of a night guard at Haifa University

WENDY LEIBOWITZ

Wendy Leibowitz graduated from Oberlin College and moved to Israel in 1982. While working in a health project in Arab villages in the Galilee for two years and studying at Haifa University, she wrote extensively on the everyday lives of ordinary Israelis in extraordinary circumstances. She has recently completed a graduate program in journalism at Columbia University.

"Remember—don't just check the bags, check the *people*," the head of security at Haifa University told me. "Look them straight in the eye as you feel around the bag and watch their reaction. *Shmirah tovah*—Have a good watch."

I took my seat by the main entrance to the university. This is part of my Israeli education, I suppose. Already I'd learned that I couldn't take exams unless I completed three hours of guard duty. What I hadn't learned was to report early to the security office to pick out a quiet, deserted building, preferably one that closed early. Instead, I innocently reported later than everyone else for my post and got stuck with the Main Entrance, Evening Watch. Two years in Israel and I'm still a step behind.

Haifa University, a 29-floor skyscraper sticking straight up like a bookend on top of Mount Carmel, commands a spectacular view during the daytime: The glistening bay and the sight of Akko shining white in the distance are quite distracting during class. But it was dark and foggy now; the evening mist was turning to drizzle. In an effort to cut utility costs, the building was too dimly lit even to read. There was nothing to do but sit and think. Three hours.

An Arab student drifted in, automatically opening his briefcase for me to glance curiously inside: notebooks, a Hebrew textbook, clipboard, pens, sandwich. "Thank you," I said. Do guards say "thank you"?

After a few more people crossed my path (knapsacks, Army duffels, elegant purses, Sportsacs, briefcases, one paper bag), I had mastered the three ways to check a bag: squeeze it from the bottom for heavy items that don't feel like books, peek inside to spy anything suspicious (what do suspicious things look like?) or just glance at the bag and trust that a dangerous person looks like a dangerous person and would be deterred by my mere presence by the door. This last approach, recommended by the head of security, did seem to be the most effortless and efficient. Besides, looking inside people's bags isn't that interesting: People basically carry the same equipment with only minor variations, such as the professor who happened to have packed his laundry (blue underwear) in his briefcase.

My presence seemed symbolic at best. If anything happened I'd be the first person to run. What was I doing here? Three damn hours. I was exhausted. Today I'd spent one hour cleaning the three-room apartment I call "home." My Israeli flatmate, Danny, insists that we beat the rugs out the window every week. This is very Middle Eastern and picturesque and he even has a rug beater (like an enormous fly swatter) for the purpose, but beating rugs is very physical work. The rugs are heavy and I always manage to drop one, and then have to descend four flights of stairs to the courtyard, in full view of the neighbors, to pick it up out of the bushes, dusty and grassy. This is not at all picturesque. Then we have to put all the rugs back again, under the furniture and lamps, and I'm sure something will break soon.

"You know, Danny," I told him today, "in the United States we don't beat our rugs out the window."

"Then how do you clean them?"

I couldn't remember. This always happens when I talk to Danny. He asks me about pop stars, salaries, car mileages—in vain. America has faded from my conscious memory. I know that in the States we have wall-to-wall carpeting that can't be beaten out the window very easily, because our windows are too small.

"I'm too tired to remember. We just don't beat our rugs out the window."

"That's why you're no good at it, then. Americans must have filthy rugs."

Sitting by the door staring at the rain, I tried desperately not to fall asleep by concentrating on how we cleaned rugs in America. Two students came through the door, lifting their sopping knapsacks for me to look at. They were talking politics.

"If we pull out of Lebanon too quickly the Syrians will roll in right behind us, to fill the vacuum."

Of course! A vacuum cleaner! I gave them a warm smile and felt a new burst of energy. Now, how do you say "vacuum cleaner" in Hebrew? My English has deteriorated to the point where it is at least one-fourth Hebrew, and my Hebrew is still poor enough so that something foreign like a vacuum cleaner, which does not exist in my Israeli reality, does not exist in my vocabulary.

A flash of lightning illuminated an ancient man wearing a black scullcap, stooped under the weight of his umbrella as he crossed the street. A Moroccan once told me of a long drought in Morocco, during which Jews fervently prayed for rain. The drought continued despite their prayers. Their great tzaddik, Rabbi Chaim, passed away, and his congregation was convinced that the instant Rabbi Chaim reached Paradise he would be able to use his influence to bring rain. Months passed, but not a drop fell. Finally, one Friday night, it started to rain. The cantor stopped services and announced, "Praise God! Rabbi Chaim has just arrived."

Rabbi Chaim hurried through the door past me, shaking the rain off his umbrella and scowling. What was Rabbi Chaim doing at the university at this hour? Several students rushed in, some opening their dripping bags for my inspection, others just waving as they rushed by. "Where's Yeshayahu Leibowitz speaking?" one asked me in passing.

"I don't know." They walked away with disgusted "Why-don't-guards-ever-know-anything" expressions–an expression I had often worn myself.

Was Rabbi Chaim actually Yeshayahu Leibowitz, the illustrious left-wing Orthodox philosopher? "He went that way," I called to them. I wished I could hear him speak. It's not fair. Two and a half more hours.

"Excuse me–you can't take your weapon into the building," I said apologetically to a young, bespectacled, soaking wet soldier carrying a Galil machine gun.

"I came to hear Leibowitz. Don't I know you? Do you folkdance at the Technion?"

"Yes!" Anyone who folkdances can come into the building carrying all kinds of explosives and suspicious objects while I'm on duty. "Tell me what he says," I say wistfully.

Could I have kept the soldier out of the building if I'd wanted to? How silly. Yet for a brief moment the capricious exercise of power beckoned. It would be a way to get back at all the bureaucrats and administrators who say "It can't be done" whenever they feel like it. They make Israel so hard to love sometimes. Today in the library, for example. I've been looking for a book in the reserve section for two weeks. There is only one book for a class of 75 students and exams are approaching. The book is never on the shelf.

"Excuse me," I said to the lady at the information desk, "but I think there's a problem with Friedman's statistics book, Number QA276.54F. It's forbidden to take the book out of the library, it's not on the shelf, no one is using it. I've been looking for it for two weeks."

"What do you want me to do about it?" the lady said without looking up from her newspaper.

"Well, I think it may have been stolen."

"In that case, it's not in the library."

"Is there any way to find out if one of the employees has seen it lately, or reshelved it–"

"Look, the book must be in the library. If *you* can't find it, why do you think *I* can?" She turned the page of the newspaper triumphantly. I retreated, feeling as if I'd been socked in the stomach.

If that lady shows up at this door, soaking wet and shivering with cold, she will only get in over my dead body.

I hope all of the Israeli bank tellers who have treated me in a similar fashion will appear at my door, desperate to get inside. Especially Bracha, who today refused to cash a traveler's check. "You know how much money you lose on the exchange, Wendy?" She shook her head and clucked disdainfully at the check. "Why don't you deposit the check in an open account and withdraw money from your closed account?"

"I'm about to get interest on my closed account and if I withdraw any money I forfeit the interest. Just cash the check, please?"

"You don't know how much money you're losing. You lose on bank charges, a bad rate of exchange–much more than any interest you'd get. Why don't you want to listen to me?"

"I just want to cash a traveler's check!"

"I'M TRYING TO HELP YOU!"

"Don't yell at me!" I yelled. Why does everything have to be a fight?

In the end, as always, I had to do it her way, withdrawing money from a closed account and forfeiting the interest. I never win at the bank.

No, Bracha and her ilk would not gain entry to this building during my watch.

I suffer from an American assumption that the system is supposed to work *for* you; in Israel operations seem structured to *fight* you. They say Russians and people from totalitarian countries are able to adjust to that aspect of Israel because they assume that the system, if it can't be avoided, is an opponent that must be wrestled. Certainly a woman at an information desk is by no means obligated to help you, or even be sympathetic; a bank teller, lacking a certain form, will force you to handle your money in a way that is convenient to her: Life is a contest between you and them. So tiring, this constant wrangling. So tiring. . . .

"Sleeping on guard duty, eh?" I started awake, to find Yeshayahu Leibowitz and a group of his admirers smiling at me in amused understanding. "Good night–*chalomot paz*," Leibowitz wished me, passing through the door into the night. Is there any other spot on earth where Rabbi Chaim would wish a night guard "pleasant dreams" on duty?

Their footsteps faded away and I sat in the dim light, listening to the rain, thinking of home. No sign of anyone. I was all alone. Are guards supposed to be this scared?

One more hour. ★

Part IV

The Pursuit of Religious Meaning

Gym Shoes and Irises
DANIEL M. SIEGEL

We know Ralph Nader and the Lubavitcher Rebbe are out there fighting for us and God and Truth and Right. We know they're doing big things, battling City Hall and beyond, up to the Highest of High Courts. But what about all of them? The Mitchell-Momzers and General Browns, the Men with the Petrodollars, the large-, medium-, and small-scale Destroyers? Players with the nation's railroads (Penn-Central), diplomats trading off this for that, the any-and-every size Mafiosi stuffing Mankind down a umongous drain. Paranoics of the World, we are outnumbered! Chip chip, gnaw, crunch, the newspaper-thoughts chew away hope, affirmation, the will-to-try. The little guy, statusless, getting dumped on everywhere, trying to do his bit to sew, therapeut, and carpenter the ailings and shambles of All Mankind. Teensy-klayna Yidden, unite!

illustration/Phyllis Lerner

Where, Why, and How the Revelation Belted Me

Last fall friends and acquaintances began gathering for Israel; crisis, again, as usual, was hanging in the air. It seemed apparent that millions of new pages would be written in papers and analyses about whatever chunk of History was going to come crashing down on the Holy Land, any day. For myself, the Urge began to chomp away at me, the Psalm-craving to go back to *Aretz*, though I had just fin-

Danny Siegel is a freelance author, lecturer, and poet living in Rockville, MD. He has published more than a dozen books of poetry, midrash *translations, humor, essays, and a book on* tzedakah *and Jewish values. He also gives readings from his works. His prose career began when* Moment, *of which he is a contributing editor, published this, his first article on* tzedakah.

ished a year in Jerusalem that previous August. I would go, I decided, *stam* — just because I wanted to go (or had to, or should go, or whatever). To me this was Kosher Jewish thinking . . . the more reasons given for the trip, the less chance of gathering the aromas and sounds and stirrings of Holiness waiting to be ingested in the Holy Land.

My tenth trip. You know how you feel when people tell you, "Oh, I've been there 18 times. Just last year I was over for Sukkot, Purim and the summer. Ho, hmmm, hum." It is the Repetition Syndrome which teachers, assembly-line workers, and secretaries suffer from (to say nothing of occasional neurosurgeons, Professional Fundraisers, and other assorted busy individuals). What I would do while in Israel was unclear to me, though a month in Jerusalem, if correctly unplanned, could be awesome,

Moment/151

> Part-time I-caring is astronomically effective. Even in the most discriminating retrospect, it is impossible to grasp fully the ad infinitum extent of what you have done to move human hearts through a single gesture. Faith, innocence, and the Yes come streaming out at us through these acts with the force and mystery of a laser.

enjoyable, or at the least, fun.

As was my custom, I visited my well-wishers, telling them to "Give me a buck for Tz'dakah." I would give it out *somewhere* as the occasion presented itself *somewhere* in Israel. Apparently some friends adjusted their palms to the cost-of-living index, as $5's and $10's and $20's and $25's began inundating my pushka. I usually consider $10 a nice sum to take with me, but by the time this occurred to me for Trip #10, I was rated by Dun & Bradstreet at well over $150. So I decided to steamroll a little, making the rounds of aunts, cousins, parents, in-laws, friends, and passers-by, saying, "I'd really like a thousand."

I left with $900-plus, and counting what arrived while I was there, we reached $955, or 5730 Israeli pounds.

Except for three people who specified where I should give their money, I was on my own, the Chevrah's *Shaliach* (messenger) to the Holy Land.

I assured them I would stretch every bill and coin. I would sanctify their money by giving exclusively to those who were reliable, hated bureaucracy, and could use it as directly as possible to bring some assistance, joy, and the sense of *Mah Rabbu Ma'asecha*, How great are Your Creations, O Lord, to the recipients.

No one I asked felt that he was being "hit." Each considered it a privilege to take part in the Mitzvah with me. No receipts, no questions of income-tax deductions, no hesitations like "Well, I already hit my 10-20 per cent for the year."

A family of eight in Oklahoma spent the better part of a late evening working out how much they could send me.

Some never let me finish my description of "The Plan." My wallet fattened before I could say, "I'll send you a report."

O there might have been one or two who play-grumbled. But I assured them (taking the last $7 from their hand) that even the most grumbly giver with the most obnoxious intent is moving Heaven and Earth. And I threw in a quote and some trumped-up page number from the Talmud to bolster my argument.

Reviewing my preparations, I see that the friends and relatives and strangers created a *Mitzvah-Chevrah* that would go wherever I would go, speak with me, and give me some insight into the work at hand.

So it was me, Dan Quixote, the 35 or so of them, and a few others against the Montefiore Windmills. The "few others" included my rabbi, my forebears, and some Russian Jews.

My rabbi: When he was in love and had found the woman with whom he chose to live his life, my rabbi gave $1000 to Israel in place of buying his fiancée an engagement ring. I think it was in the late '40's. He told me that story, I think. (I was, fifteen years ago, his favorite, his hope, his most intimate prayer to God.) I remember that: his ring of love was a gift to Israel.

My forebears: Sometime in the last century, Usher Zelig Siegel took to wife a certain Sarah Golda, whose family name is forgotten. They begot a multitude of children, among them Zeev David, called Velvel, my Zeyde. I pilgrimaged to Keansburgh, N.J., to supplement the old pictures and conversations with my father and aunts and cousins. His drygoods store is now a gun and ammunition shop, but the cop who grew up with my father said, "He would take a nickel on a pair of gloves, and let them pay the rest whenever they could. He was a kind man." I remember that.

His son, my Abba, has carried on where Velvel left off. It is fit and proper to praise his generosity. Now that I am past the age of rebellion and crankiness towards my parents, we can sit and recall and work out insights into Tz'dakah, because he is my Rebbe-Master in this domain of *Mentschlichkeit*. I am his child and again and again return to childhood when I wonder how his vision and foresight have been acted out by me, whether I am worthy of him and his parents and grandparents, all the way back to Abraham. When I bring to mind my years of knowing him, a constant flow of Tz'dakah acts-and-intimations gushes forth.

Some Russian Jews: Crossing into Russia from Finland, the border guards took half, more than half, of our Siddurim and calendars and M'zuzot, and Magen Davids. They were entitled to them — they are Russians and we are Jews, 64 Jews with a pittance of thing-gifts for our friends in the Soviet Jewish Community. Stripped to the bare heart. I remember that feeling of being scared: 20 Yiddish phrases and a few tchatchkes to give. Over There, you give someone a $3 prayerbook, and your thanks are in tears. Whoever gave me a $3 gift that moved me so much? *That* question has stuck in my kishkes.

At select times in life, simplistic thinking is profound, and miracle-working. At those times, Big Think Metaphysics should be crated and stored in the garage, and bullheaded, one-sided Mitzvah-doing fully activated to achieve wonders that will make the splitting of the Red Sea look like pulling a rabbit out of a hat.

These thoughts and questions are everyone's, I thought.

I thought, as the plane approached Lod, *Ki tireh arom v'chisito*! When you see the naked, clothe them! Isaiah, I hear you, we hear you. The thousand one-shot Tz'dakah-slams that had whipped my BigThink brain over 30 years were waiting to explode.

Being a *Shaliach* is an ego-safeguard. Wherever you go and however you choose to distribute your funds, you are constantly aware of the fact that you are just the representative of those who sent you. When speaking to the recipients, you simply say, "It's my friends."

What Happened to the Gelt

It immediately became clear to me that there are two distinct psychologies of giving out Tz'dakah money: Big-Gelt and SmallGelt. If you have $500,000 to distribute, you go to different places, talk to different people and give out different proportions and quantities than if you have $955. You are constantly aware of the fact that $50 too much here means next week there may not be anything left to give, just when you are discovering that the next week's encounter is the one that needs the $50 the most. As a result, I determined to watch carefully each grush, and to proceed with a sharpened sense of spontaneity vs. overprudence.

Just as I had chosen to collect the money through straightforward, friendly means, so, also, I decided to search out the people and places of my mission through my friends, by word-of-mouth and suggestions from whomever I knew or got to know well enough to be touched by his grasp of what I was about.

I started with flowers at Life Line for the Old. Life Line (*Yad LaKashish*) was discovered by my mother about five years ago. During one of my previous visits, she, the Mitzvah-Searcher-Outer *par excellence*, put her JewishMotherly foot down and declared that I *must* go — in the tone of voice of "No questions, no wise remarks, kiddo!"

"Tell Mrs. Mendelow I sent you," she said.

Life Line is workshops for the elderly. It is food for invalid-old people who are unable to get out. It is a choir and tree-planting, and a Chevrah of Dignity. None of the pathetic foolishness of basketweaving is to be found in its precincts, and, indeed, the handiwork that they produce has won awards in various countries, not because a bunch of doddering old fools made them, but because they are joy-forever things of beauty. The American custom of stashing away aging parents in (ugh) Convalescent Homes to let them die out-of-the-way, stripped of their well-deserved majesty and treated like infants—all this is foreign to Mrs. Mendelow. He who would wish to learn what *Mentschlichkeit* is would do well to visit her and the young Old People of Life Line.

My Shabbas tablecloths are from their workshops, as are my sweaters, and a few of my toys.

So me and my friend, see, we marches in with a flower for each one to take home for Shabbas.

Big man, you say! A flower! Tzaddik (righteous one)! Ten lousy bucks and he thinks he's turned the world on its ear! One lousy rose or chrysanthemum or iris per person. Whoopie-do!

And to spite my cynic-self, the next day (Friday; Thursday at Life Line . . . closed Friday) I did the same for my Chevrah at Hadassah. There is a certain woman on the staff of Life Line who for the last seven years has made the rounds of the soldiers at the hospital, bringing fruit and cigarettes and candy and other things for anyone there from the Israeli Army. After being introduced to the people in the Military Office and obtaining a list of who was in what ward, the lady, my friend, and I, bundled in flowers, began to walk the corridors.

It couldn't hurt, could it, fellas? I know they're soldierboys, and tough, and Israelis, and this is sort of twinkie, but the lady said, "Don't worry. It's all right."

Big Man — Tzaddik, with a wad in his pocket, doing cheap-ticket-to-Paradise Mitzvahs. Flowers for everyone!

Until you talk to the boy (that's all he is, a boy) in the eye clinic, with a bandage, and he tells you he writes and you say, I write, too. And he tells you he wrote a story about a soldier who was badly wounded, the only survivor in his tank, and his girlfriend comes to see him in the hospital. But he dies. And she never makes peace with it all. And cracks.

And then he says, "It's the other way around. My girlfriend died in a car crash, and I don't know what to do."

Big Man!

Gym Shoes and Irises

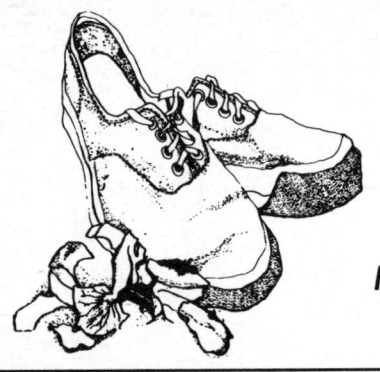

By being a Mentsch with all that it suggests—kindness, sympathy through weeping, feeling and giving, uprightness, and a touch of human nobility we may be momentarily united with the Almighty, fulfilling the vision of Mentschlichkeit we preserve so deep within our Selves . . . and ignore, or forget, or let slip by.

And the mother, who is all War Mothers, standing over her son (the one with the head wound, the paralyzed one), trying to feed him.

Here.

Here are some flowers for your son.

See, Shimon, she says, they brought you flowers (who? oh just some friends from America). See, Shimon, say thank you.

Is there anything we can do?

Pray.

Tears.

Hers, I think.

Big Man. A dime's worth of flowers!

I decided then not to do any more of these Mitzvahs alone. I wanted others, preferably three or four others, standing with me, because I am not so sure I can stretch that far — even for the Chevrah.

By Sunday I had called my friends and flipped through the note cards of Recommended Tzaddikim, adding here and there a few names suggested by my people in Jerusalem. Spontaneously (I would try spontaneity again and see how far it would go) I picked Mrs. Eva Michaelis. It was a name my mother had given me, because she knew she was *edel* — refined, devoted, kindly, a decades-long crusader for the retarded. Her most recent project is *Magen*, making a home for older retarded people whose parents are too old and too ill to take care of their children. I began to like one-way conversations: "Speak to me, Mrs. Michaelis. Say anything." And she would take up her evangelical theme, displaying verbally her struggles with the government and Welfare Department to get the proper funds, then passing to some miracles, saving children from the Nazis at the outbreak of the War, meeting Eichmann (you mean Eichmann's henchmen? No, Eichmann.), and stepping out to get me coffee and cookies.

"I cannot give to your building fund," I explained. "My Chevrah wants more direct, more immediate results, and they want the funds to be under your personal control." We gave her 250 pounds for anything she liked, like cab fare for Irena Gaster, 77, who is a little shaky on her legs. Nevertheless, she personally went to interview the 40 candidates for *Magen*.

Ms. Gaster: founder of almost everything in Israel having to do with the retarded, denouncer of psychiatrists who are too quick to label, thereby condemning someone to retardation, anathema-hurler at agencies and institutions-gone-bad, Lover of Children Class-A with four Oak Leaf Clusters. When a child would be sent to her who could not learn to feed himself, more likely than not she taught the child to feed himself. If the child was a bed-wetter at age 10 (and therefore disturbed), she stopped the bed-wetting. More miracles, s.v.p., G'veret Gaster. Oh, here's another one, and another, and another (with absolute humility and a tinge of modest pride). And I never took a penny from anyone. And this is all I own (hand sweeps the air around the apartment on Ramban St.). And Miss (Henrietta) Szold said I would never get anywhere — that was when I first arrived. And now we have this *Magen* (take some more tea) project.

I was doing well. In the course of less than one Jerusalem-week I had discovered three of the 36 Righteous People. If I could just find another two or three, I would have fulfilled my mission. I had seen with my own eyes and the eyes of the Chevrah the all-the-time Holy People, rubbed my hands in theirs, and felt warmth and hope and the mysterious glory of what it is to be a Creature of God. There were two kinds: the quiet, softspoken, unannounced Tzaddik, and the other — overpowering, energetic-to-exhaustion, piling adrenalin on adrenalin, fighting and shouting where necessary to actualize their vision, not shying away from the Obstreperous of the Earth, convinced and justified in their Rightness, because it was for the sake of others. They are formidable, and for the unprepared, more difficult to be with, these Tzaddikim, because they are so right. You wonder how you ever thought of the million million wrong ways to do this thing, Living. And *they* know they are converting you to *Mentschlichkeit,* and that you might not be able to keep up their pace. But they also know you will make something of the encounter, and that is enough for them. They are reliable, trustable individuals, and you become willing and inspired to give them anything they want, even if they won't tell you what they will do with your gift. Their wisdom and understanding of what is happening in the hearts of men is sufficient. And since they have revealed themselves to you entirely and unabashedly, there is, thank God, never any room for doubt.

Back to the stories. I will skip around, including and selecting and excluding, since there are too many,

The singularity of split-second Mitzvah-events is enough, for it carries over into however long our futures will be, reminding us that we are never alone because we have broken through to others who also felt, at some time, that they were alone.

and not every one involves a Tzaddik. I planted trees, eight of them, for births and deaths and friends and my 82-year-old Zeyde Shmuel who last planted one for his 80th birthday, when I prayed I would do the same on my 80th. There was also a *bris* my friend Mickey said would be nice, but there would only be cookies and juice and soda and some wine, though a bottle or two of schnapps would go really well. So 50 Israeli pounds became some fancy-schmancy schnapps, though I don't know whose *bris* it was, and the parents certainly never heard of the family in Oklahoma.

I also Tz'dakah-alchemized 100 pounds into gasoline. Boris is my only friend in Jerusalem who has a car. I said, "Here's 100 pounds for benzine — put yourself at Bracha Kapach's disposal till the gelt runs out." Rebbetzin Kapach (or as the Sefardim would say, *HaRabbanit*) is the Utmost Yemenite, the woman I was looking for but didn't know was true until I saw her and watched her walk around Jerusalem doing her acts of gentlelovingkindness. Four of the Chevrah had asked me to find someone to whom they could send clothes, so this was a priority. This Rabbanit-Rebbetzin gives clothes, Shabbas food, love, weddings, a jar of hotsauce and Yemenite bread, books, or whatever is needed all over Jerusalem and into the boondocks on the Hillsides of Judea . . . the most extensive far-stretching private Mitzvah-Matchmaker I was to meet, coordinating the Givers and the Receivers with enthusiasm and uplift as I had never seen before. Mickey and I went Shabbas-flowering with her, into the homes of large-families-in-two-rooms that are around, if you look for them. On the way back to her house she saw some children she knew who should have been in school. Why not? she asked. No gym shoes, the two girls said. I don't know if they needed gym shoes for gym class or whether it was teen-age fashionable to wear the casual style and, therefore, embarrassing to come to school in some other shoe. Either way, the 25 newly-arrived dollars were searing the seams of my pockets, and I understand that within a day, as if by magic, they were transformed into sneakers for the girls.

I didn't see, but I heard about a person she found who goes with an elderly blind lady to the hairdresser on Fridays, to fulfill the Old Woman's wish of being presentable to the Sabbath Queen.

Through another lead I entered the bowels of Israeli bureaucracy (just once, to see what it was like): The Department of Welfare. The assistant director, Aharon Langermann, understood me and the Chevrah immediately, and with 350 pounds from the fund assured me that it would be used individually, directly, and personally for anything that comes to him that will not be taken care of by the Red Tape Machine.

A widow needed a loan. OK. The money will be re-cycled when she has finished with it.

Sara Pearl, Mother of the Soldiers all over Galilee. I couldn't get to Safed, but I called and told her husband the Chevrah believes in her. The check is for whatever she wants.

Hadassah Levi's day-care center for young retarded people in Ramat Gan. Swings for them. Let me call her The Most Loving Person in the World. Take my word for it.

Ya'akov Maimon, inventor of Hebrew shorthand, recorder for the Knesset, 72½, short, dressed like out of a movie, rumpled hat, thick glasses, shlepping me up and down and up and down steps visiting families (Iranian, Indian, Algerian, Moroccan) to whom he brings tutors in English for the children. For over 20 years he has been doing this, bringing truckloads from the University and other parts of town, dropping them off, picking them up, remembering each name and making sure each one is working well, becoming a part of the family. I would have wished him "*ad meah v'esrim* — may you continue your work till you are 120—" but it seemed a shade insulting. He will no doubt do this much longer, with the same vigor and grandheartedness.

Mickey's cousin, Rabbi Mordechai Gimpel HaKohen Wolk, scion of great rabbinic houses, devoted to children, particularly of large families, placing them in good yeshivas, throwing weddings and simchas and worrying for their welfare. He is the full embodiment of the Life of Torah. Listening to his tales, his quotes, following his hands, you understand a hint of Hillel.

The list is longer. This is not a lyrical exposition or high falootin' dissertation. If you want more, you'll ask, or you'll go.

Getting Your Jollies and Shaking Your Kishkes

Everyone should be a Shaliach-

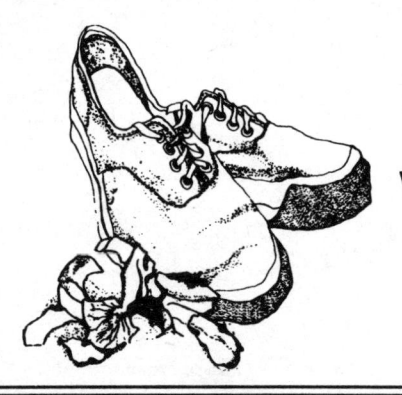

> When He spoke at Sinai and proclaimed Tz'dakah as a just way of life, (I believe) the lowliest desert bushes brought forth flowers, and the assembled multitudes heaved the ultimate sigh of relief—men, women, children and livestock alike.

Messenger sometime. Even if you will be in Israel only a week. Even if you won't be in Israel for a while but want to do it in Minneapolis, L.A., or Aberdeen, S.D. The moral insight and imaginative investment will be proportional in at least a 100 to 1 ratio to the quantum of money put in the pot. By giving your own money, you treat yourself to the feeling that you are not as tight-fisted as you thought you were, Recession or no Recession. You will become more aware of the privilege of Mitzvah-doing and of allowing others to join you. As the Talmud informs us: He who encourages others is even greater than he who does it himself.

So you will say: Well, I'm not all that good. I'm only part time, and Wolk and Kapach and Maimon and Levi and Gaster and Michaelis are too much . . . I'm not those people. Which is exactly right, and exactly the point. Part time is good enough.

You can play disguises: in one place you can assume such-and-such a name, and in another (wearing a different hat, sunglasses, and shirt) you can be someone else from Norman, Oklahoma, instead of Chicago. It is a Purim-play of the highest order. Your bravado, naiveté, and flair for romance that lie latent can come out to your heart's desire, and you can swagger and swashbuckle your way into a Grand Old Time of It for the Sake of Heaven. It is a real zetz in your soul, a kick in your spiritual life, and you are entitled to feel good about it.

And you may never consider despair again.

The next step is to do BigGelt projects. To raise $1,000,000 to be put at your disposal, all you have to do is convince 200 people to throw a $5,000 wedding for their kids, instead of a $10,000 jobbie, or 400 people to throw a $2,500 bar mitzvah instead of a whopper for five grand. With the remaining money, you take them, their wives, their sons and daughters, and all their dear ones to Israel for a Tz'dakah-junket, a spree of Tzaddik-touching.

Next: find yourself a local millionaire and surprise him with a $10 proposal. Tell him you are not a foundation, institution, or home for anything, but on the contrary, think you can get a lot of Mitzvah-mileage out of $10. If you get $1,000, don't panic. Just check your Matchmaking files and start asking more friends about more people.

Heavy Conclusions

The risk and emotional drain are immense. You are in unaccustomed touch with those who suffer from circumstance, misfortune, or the Will of God in its less pleasant manifestations —and with those whose lives are hour-by-hour tied to these people. Spiritual exhaustion is a possibility to be considered. So, too, are the dangers of surprise. In distributing irises and gym shoes, you are never certain who will be there to meet you in the next house, or corridor, or on the park bench.

For nine trips I loved wandering the streets and alleys of Jerusalem. I used to watch the sun throw different shadows and light-cartoons on the buildings and street corners and trees. I believe I saw an entirely different city on this visit, shimmering with an extraordinary glow of Holiness I had missed without the Chevrah's help.

When we at long last re-curriculum our Sunday schools and Hebrew schools and day schools, we must include — aside from courses on risk, joy, fear, loss, uncertainty, failure, BigThink, and death — lectures and labs on *Mentschlichkeit* and Tz'-dakah. By the very fact of having reached bar or bat mitzvah, a Jewish child becomes obligated to fulfill the Mitzvah of Tz'dakah. Why should we spiritually orphan our children, sending them insensitive as the cattle of Nineveh into the world, only to have them discover at age 25 or 33 or 41 that they have missed out on this most unique privilege for years? Let them begin with their 10-20 per cent from the earliest age, and let us teach them the ins-and-outs of finding the Righteous Ones and the creativity of giving. Too few people consider that a hat, a hand gripped firmly on someone's arm, or a cheap $3 prayerbook can give a sense of startling and sublime joy to another person. *Mentschlichkeit* should be a word in every Jewish child's vocabulary.

According to the Torah, each Jew is required to write his own Torah. By doing these acts, by conscientious and energy-charged consideration of the swirl of people around us, we can do just that. By being a Shaliach-Messenger or Mitzvah-doer or just plain old part-time giver.

And of course, by re-telling the signs and wonders of the people we meet along the way. ✡

AN I FOR AN I

On Rosh Hashanah last, the congregants of Temple Valley Beth Shalom in Encino, California, found a small booklet on their seats, on its cover the word "Passport." Rabbi Harold Schulweis—a contributing editor of this magazine—devoted his sermon to an explanation of the booklet and its purpose. We think his message deserves a much wider audience, and we therefore reprint it—adapted to the printed page—here.

HAROLD SCHULWEIS

Harold Schulweis is the founding Chairman of the Foundation to Sustain Righteous Christians, Rabbi of Valley Beth Shalom in Encino, CA, author of Evil and the Morality of God, *and a contributing editor of* Moment.

Seeing their nakedness, Adam and Eve fled from before the presence of the Lord.

When Jonah heard the voice telling him to go forth and to prophesy to the people of Nineveh, he hid himself in the gray womb of the whale.

The Rizhiner Rebbe, when he came home one day, noted the fact that his little boy was crying. He asked his son why, and the boy answered, "Because I have been playing hide-and-seek." "But that's no reason to cry," said the Rebbe. "It is, Papa. I was hiding, but nobody was seeking."

So it is, said the Rizhiner, with the soul of man, that it hides, and nobody seeks.

A midrash: when the angels heard that God was going to create the image of His own being, and breathe the breath of His life into it, the angels conspired with each other to hide the image of Divinity. One angel proposed to put it on the top of the mountain. A second proposed to hide it at the bottom of the sea. But the wiliest angel of all said, "Let us hide it by putting it in man and woman, because that is the last place anyone will look for it."

Our tradition talks a great deal about the fact that human beings are hiders and gravediggers and concealers. We're always looking for getaways, whether through work or through leisure, in health or in sickness. There are appointments to be kept, and there are patients, and there are clients, and there are customers and there are investments; there's jogging and there's dieting and there's bleaching and there's dyeing. There are mountains and seashores and cathedrals and museums, all to get away to. And there are committees. And all these are ways for us to hide from the very first question that is posed in the Bible: *Ayeka*? Where art thou?

We hide so cleverly that when we hear that question, we think it is the bank teller who is asking. So we produce our wallet, and our social security number, or our driver's license, or our credit card. (When I show my American Express card, they will know who I am.) We confuse identity with identification.

The ultimate question—the question of identity, the question of where we are, of who we are—that question gets drowned in small talk, or in doubts, or in quarrels, or in drink, or in infidelity. Most of all, people hide the question behind a complaint: "I am bored." People tell me that they are bored, and I ask them how they can be bored, observing that they have everything to live for. Nevertheless, they tell me, they are bored. What is it that they want, I ask. And they tell me they do not know what they want; all they know is that they are bored.

Once in a while, in a crisis situation, when one has to face the gray walls of a hospital or a mortuary or a divorce court, the boredom ends, the strategies of evasion crumble, and the question comes out in the form of a scream: Where is the life I have lost while living?

Mi ani: Mah ani? L'mi ani amel? Mah yeshuati? Mah g'vurati? Mah kochi? Who am I? What am I? What do I stand for? What shall I say before myself? What does life demand of me—or is there absolutely nothing demanded of me?

These are terribly uncomfortable questions, and I know that people don't like them. These are spiritual, metaphysical, philosophical, theological questions, questions of purpose, and such questions make us very uncomfortable because we are, all of us, very practical people, and we live in a marvelously technological society, and technocrats never ask questions like "What for?" They ask, "How much?" or "How" or "When?" They say, "I will get you there faster, I'll get you there more efficiently, but once you get there, I have nothing to say to you. That's not my job."

Ours is a society that is concerned with means, with instruments, with gadgets not with ends. Ends petrify us. It makes us terribly uncomfortable to be asked,

"What for?"

We prefer to live out Kafka's parable of the messenger, he who traverses long distances until finally, exhausted, he arrives at the palace of the king—and has forgotten the message.

Now comes Rosh Hashanah. Rosh Hashanah can be treated as we treat any other holiday, or it can be treated with a radical uniqueness, because there is no other time like the time from this day through Yom Kippur. On every other Festival we can hide behind the skirts of the community. We can hide behind historical events, we can have our own lives swept up by history: On Pesach we were redeemed, and on Sukkot we wandered in the desert, and on Shavuot we received the Revelation, and on Tisha B'Av we suffered the destruction of the Temple, and on Chanukah the Temple was rededicated, and on Purim we won a great victory over the enemy, and on Yom Hashoah we suffered the loss of 6,000,000, and on Yom Atzmaut we witnessed the establishment of the State of Israel.

But Rosh Hashanah has nothing to do with community and nothing to do with history. There is no real "we" on Rosh Hashanah and Yom Kippur; there is only the first person singular. And the commandment, which is a commandment for each of us during these days, is "*Mibsarcho lo titalem*"—"You shall not hide from your own flesh."

That is why I want to ask that we now strip aside all kinds of small questions, and have the courage to ask ourselves the big questions, the hard question, the scary questions that suit this day. Let us set aside, for a time, Judaism as a system of means, or of ceremonies, and even the Judaism that is going to redeem the world or redeem the Jewish people or keep the family intact, and focus instead on the holy self-centered Judaism that has to do with finding *my* meaning, *my* self, *my* esteem. Is there anything that I can do with myself in confronting the ultimate that will enable me to live out my life *b'chol l'vavi uv'chol nafshi u'vchol moadi*—with all my heart and with all my soul and with all my might. Without hiding place, without retreat.

When talk about Judaism on this day, I am not talking about it in the usual way, the way you are used to hearing it talked about. I want to talk about it in the unusual and uncomfortable way: What does Judaism tell me about the way that I am supposed to live my life?

When we look at the texts or listen to the preachers, the answer is plain: "Study." Learn, attend a school, become a master of the text. Which other people holds that the House of Prayer is holier than the House of Study? A church is called a church, a mosque is called a mosque, but we call a synagogue, a "shul"—which comes from the word *schola*, and means school. And we believe in the power of learning. That is why 85 percent of our youngsters who are eligible are in college, 400,000 in all, that is why 10 percent of the college faculty members in this country, and 20 percent in the elite institutions, are Jews.

But that is not what the rabbis had in mind by study. The great rabbis also asked, "*tachlit*?" (what for?). And that is why we are taught, "The function of wisdom is to do repentance and to do good deeds so that a man should not study Torah and Mishnah and Gemorrah and then kick his father and his mother and his teacher." Beware, you who are given to cerebral conceits, say the rabbis, beware of your boasting of the *yiddisher kop*, because the *yiddisher kop*—a Jewish brain—can kill the *yiddisher hartz*—the Jewish heart—and that is why the rabbis of the Gemorrah say "He who studies Torah, Torah, Torah, only Torah and has no other considerations is considered as if he does not believe in God."

Or; "If somebody studies not for the purpose of doing something, it would be better if he were not born." Why? Is this not strange for a people with such an intellectual history as ours? Yet the sin of Adam is that he eats of the tree of knowledge. If we are punished for eating of the tree of knowledge, that means that knowledge is not the end.

Knowledge is not the end? How can that be so? Just two weeks ago I met with a rabbinic colleague who is a Jewish historian of some note. He had contracted a disease that involved the wearing out of the fatty substance at the end of the nerves. So he was told that he should see a neurologist, which he did. And the neurologist had to perform a very painful procedure, electrical conduction on the nerves. And because it was painful, the doctor said to my friend, perhaps to take his mind off the procedure, "That's a Mengele machine." "What did you say?" "That's a Mengele machine." It developed that my friend the Jewish historian was being treated on a machine perfected by that sadistic monster, Dr. Joseph Mengele, during the course of his experiments to determine whether there was sensation in the vagina, a curiosity he satisfied by placing electrodes in the vaginas of Jewish women, most of whom died in excruciating pain.

And my friend and I, when he told me this story, talked for a while about the idolatry of the brain. Mengele was a very bright man, and he had a PhD, and he was a great scientist. Hitler's doctors and Hitler's lawyers and Hitler's scientists had wall-to-wall degrees, they were very bright people, and so were the engineers of IG Farben and Krupp, those who invented Zyklon B gas.

Adam's transgression was that he chose to eat from the Tree of Knowledge and not from the Tree of Life. Yet when we put the Torah—which is wisdom—back, we don't sing, "*etz da'at hi lamachazikim bah*"—"it is a tree of knowledge to them that cling fast to it"—we say "*etz chaim hi*"—"it is a tree of life." While we revere the Torah and recite blessings over it, the Jewish moral sense teaches and Jewish law holds that if you need money to redeem hostages, you sell the Torah. If you know of a poor orphan girl who needs money for her dowry, you sell the Torah. The function of the Torah is not to be owned, or to be quoted, but to be *used*, to be used as a tree of life.

To *be* the truth is more important than to *know* the truth. When the yeshiva bocher came to his rebbe and boasted that he had gone through the Talmud five times, the rebbe asked him, "And how many times has the Talmud gone through you, my son?"

No, the intellect is not going to answer the ultimate question whose answer we seek today.

Maybe the answer lies in prayer.

How about prayer, about the tallis and the tefilin, the liturgical life, the yearning to be part of a spiritual community? But the problem is that if you know Judaism in depth, you understand that the purpose of prayer is not to pray. The purpose of prayer is to pray into your hands. We don't come from a baby religion that makes of prayer a kind of magic, that makes of prayer a substitute for being oneself. Prayer begins with the trembling of the lips, but it has to end in the movement of the legs. Do you know what kind of a tradition we have? Twenty-eight centuries ago, there was a prophet by the name Isaiah, in the time of the First Temple, the time of sacrifices and priests, who said these words: "In the name of God, when you spread out your palms, I, God, will close my eyes to you; even though you utter many prayers, I will not listen. Wash yourselves clean; remove your evil acts from my sight; cease to do evil; seek justice; aid the oppressed; uphold the right of the orphan; defend the cause of the widow." In the eighth century before the Common Era! Do you know what kind of people we come from?

The radical character of Judaism's teaching is that holiness has to do with morality. That revolution has still not been absorbed by the world, not even by the Jewish people.

One of my favorite teachers is Israel Salanter. He was the founder of the Musar movement, a movement of ethical revival. He was a man of vast ethical concern, and also fastidiously observant. Yet he found time to be disgusted with the swaying, the "shokling" of davening, of intense prayer. He was suspicious of public piety. And he wrote, "Even when you are in intense movement, and you are doing things for the glorious God, and you are praying with such avidity, make sure that you do not trample the foot of your neighbor. Make sure that when you take your tallit, you don't slap the face of your neighbor with its fringes."

No, it's not prayer that is the end. And it's not study. So what is it that's left?

How about kashrut, about yom tov, about ritual observance in general? Who can deny these? Well, if you have the courage of Rosh Hashanah, and you know the tradition, you can. For here is what the oldest midrash of all says, the midrash on Genesis from the sixth century of the Common Era: "What difference does it make to God whether you kill the animal by the throat or by the nape of the neck? Is God helped by the one way, or frustrated by the other? Rather, the function of the mitzvot is to sensitize the character of the human being." Ritual is a means, and to make a means into an end is to engage in idolatry.

Israel Salanter said it very well. He was a man of absolutely impeccable credentials. Citing the law that it is prohibited to eat an egg in which you find a speck of blood, he said, "And if you take money in which there is blood, the blood of exploitation, you think that is kosher?" And then, "It is prohibited to swallow an insect alive. And if you eat up another human being with your eyes, in envy, in jealousy, in corruption, you think that is not tref?" Salanger was suspicious of people who were very pious. He was suspicious of people who were oh so scrupulous and diligent in their observance. In those days, before the *motzi,* everybody used to take a large jug of water and pour it over his hands up to the wrists. But Yisrael Salanter used to take just a few drops of water and put them on the tips of his fingers. When he was asked why, he would answer, "Did you see that maidservant over there? She carries from the well on her back a yoke and on the yoke two large jugs of water, and I don't want to earn mitzvot, credit, on her shoulders."

So what is the end, what is the "what for?"

The answer is the cultivation of a *yiddishe neshomo,* a soul and a character of *rachmanut,* of *erlichkeit,* of *edelkeit*; of sensitivity, of dignity, of care, of compassion. Otherwise every one of our wonderful symbols becomes nothing but dead wood. What good is it that we kindle the Sabbath lights, if we extinguish those lights with the breath of quarrelsomeness in our home? When we shout at each other, we make dark our home. I have children in large numbers from this congregation who speak to me of their pain and their sadness at such darkness. What meaning has the sweetness of the kiddush wine? It sours at a table that is full of accusation and fault-finding. What good is the soft challah when life has become so hard and judgmental? What good is the Grace after Meals when we are so graceless during our meals?

From Proverbs: "Better a dry morsel—and quiet therewith—than a house that is full of meat and sacrifices—with strife." What good is fasting, whose purpose is to make our heart soft, when the home is full of testing and labeling and stigmatizing?

From Isaiah: "You fast in strife and you fast in contention and you smite each other with the fist of wickedness." If there is no capacity in our life, growing out of our character, to relate to other people, the house can be kosher, but it is tref.

I can hear you thinking, "I always said that. The rabbi is saying that it's not important to observe ritual or to go to shul." But that is also a way of evading the question. The question is not whether you believe in morality *or* you believe in ritual, the question is not whether you believe in ethics *or* you believe in kashrut, the question is not either-or, but the question is whether you understand the end, the purpose, the meaning, the thrust. Because if you do, you will daven, but differently, you'll keep kosher, but differently, you'll come to the synagogue, but differently, you will even say the blessings differently: "Blessed art thou O Lord our God who has commanded us by Thy commandments and has made us *sanctified*." I am a sanctifying power, a hallowing power. There is holiness in me because I can be moved to tears, I can be stirred into action when I see bitterness, helplessness—that is my pride, and that is the answer to the question, "Who are you?"

No pitch today. I don't want your money, and I don't want your checks or your credit cards or your cash. Because you can't answer today's question with a check, and I want you to answer it. How can I permit myself to talk that way? Because I know the Jewish tradition in depth. If you look at the Gemorrah Sukkah, the rabbis asked, "What's the most important thing in life? Is it tz'dakah?" The answer was no, because though tz'dakah is important, the highest and most important thing is *gmilut chassadim,* an act of love which is performed without money—not only for the poor, not only for the living. *Gmilut chassadim* means comforting the bereaved, making records for the blind, settling the stranger in our midst, writing a letter to a Russian family. *Gmilut chassadim* heals, but it heals not only the object of its goodness, not just the recipient. And I'm not even interested in the recipients just now. I am interested in holy selfishness, a holy and divine self-centeredness. I am interested in the giver, who pledges not his money but his soul, who when he engages in *gmilut chassadim,* transforms not only the external situation, but also his own character.

No checks. Checks are for alimony Jews, Jews who are ready to pay for Judaism but who are not ready to live with it. I want something else. Last night, when I spoke about this to a group of young people, a young man came over and I asked him whether he was going to tithe his time and his energy, and he said to me, "I don't have to do it, my daddy is going to do it." But I don't want your father and I don't want your mother and I don't want your brother and I don't want your sister and I don't want your wife and I don't want your husband to do this. I want you! And I want you to do it not for anybody else, but for your own *neshomo,* for your own calloused and incarcerated soul. If you are old enough to be able to sit in this sanctuary, you are old enough to do something.

For God's sake, what do you want? There are poor people in the world. Do you want to wait for the elections to feed them? Should we tell them not to be hungry until November? And there are bored people in the world, in this sanctuary. Should we tell them to wait for their next vacation? I know there is more to us than hedonism and materialism. We have a *neshomo,* and we can find it by linking it to the world out there that has to be saved. There is something, no matter how small, that every one of us can do, something we can do with our very being, and not with anything else.

There is no blessing for *gmilut chassadim*. There are blessings for apples and pears and for cucumbers and for lightning bolts, but there's no blessing for *gmilut chassadim*. There are two reasons for that: First, the act itself is a blessing; second, nothing should interrupt the act. So take the pledge card; take it for yourself, not for your son or your daughter. Take it, and do it, for God's sake, for your own sake. Take it as the way to answer the gnawing question, "Who am I?" I am a human being who can develop in himself a character of sanctifying power. I have a *neshomo*. I care. I can heal, and in healing, I can heal myself.

This day, this act, is only a beginning. So was the first act: *B'reshit bara Elohim*—it is only with a beginning that God creates the universe. ✡

At the conclusion of the service, 600 people turned in their "pledge cards," with the tabs they had selected turned down. Two weeks later, 300 of these came to a special meeting to get started with the fulfillment of their pledges. We wish them well; we applaud their action and their example.

What help can there be when you have just been told that your child has cancer?

LOVING KINDNESS IN NEW JERSEY

DEVRA WEINGART

Devra Weingart is a freelance writer who is a regular contributor to the Suburban News, *a New Jersey weekly. An article written for that newspaper about the history and significance of Chanukah received an award from the New Jersey Press Club.*

Last month, we published an interview with Harold Kushner, author of When Bad Things Happen to Good People. *There, Rabbi Kushner dealt mainly with the personal crisis we confront when we encounter tragedy. The bad things that happen to good people raise problems not only for the good people, but also for their neighbors—that is, for the communities of which they are a part. Below, the story of how one such community, following an ancient tradition, reaches out in times of need.*

What help can there be when you have just been told that your child has cancer? What words are there? How do you learn to switch abruptly from the small time stuff of bruises, colds and chicken pox to the big time? And how do you span the two worlds in which your several children are living, the one of health and the one of illness, so that no one is left physically unattended or emotionally starved?

These were the questions we faced on November 23, 1979, when we learned the results of our eight-year-old child's surgery; Jennifer's malaise, pain, and body malfunctions had been caused by the growth of a malignant tumor in her pelvis.

A month went by before we left the hospital, a month of pain, fear, and desperate attempts to grasp at threads of hope. During this month, family and friends cared for our two younger children, Caren and Amy, at home. Leaving them without preparation or precedent, I lived at the hospital with Jennifer while my husband divided his time between hospital and home, trying to sustain both his legal practice and his fragmented family.

Finally the day came when we were allowed to leave the hospital. Jennifer, unable to walk since the operation, came home in a wheel chair, surrounded by ominous looking medical supplies. But neither the wheelchair nor the medicines diminished the joy we felt as we visualized ourselves as a family at home together once again. The combined joys of Jennifer's homecoming, Shabbat, and the first night of Chanukah enveloped us in an oasis of happiness.

The oasis lasted briefly. Cancer does not wait for its victims to gain the strength and the knowledge with which to cope—nor do the needs of small children.

. . . by Torah . . .

We had to face the reality of everyday life. Jennifer, formerly independent and helpful, had become physically almost totally dependent. Each day began with time-consuming rituals. Four or five times a week we made the trek to the hospital in New York City for chemotherapy and radiation, often returning late in the afternoon. Although caring for Jennifer was of primary importance, we wanted to restore as much normal routine and loving care as possible to Caren and Amy, ages six and three. The mundane chores of home and family still had to be done. The need to cook, clean and wash clothes never disappears or diminishes in deference to emergencies. The level of demands was so high that even with the devoted group of people who had helped thus far, we could not manage everything.

We were distraught, unnerved, unsure of what steps to take first. And it was then that the Mitzvah Corps of our Synagogue, Temple Beth Tikvah in Wayne, New Jersey, joined with us. It helped us take those first steps, it became an integral part of our family, it continued to tread the way throughout the long difficult days that followed.

The Mitzvah Corps had been organized five years earlier by a Sisterhood president who wanted to encourage warmth and closeness among the members of our growing congregation. Her hope was that mutual help and emotional support of one another would foster such feelings.

There is an historic precedent from Talmudic times for the Mitzvah Corps. *G'milut hassadim,* the bestowal of loving-kindness, was considered by the rabbis to be even more important than *tz'dakah,* charity. Manifest through personal service, or giving of oneself, it is mentioned in the Mishnah as one of the three things that sustain the world: "The world is sustained by three things: by the Torah, by worship, and by loving deeds." (Avot: 1:2) *G'milut hassadim* is unlimited quantitatively, whereas when giving charity "one should not 'squander' more than a fifth of one's possessions on good works." All-encompassing by definition, it could be given by and to rich and poor alike.

During the Middle Ages in Europe groups called *bikkur cholim holim* developed. Following in the tradition of *g'milut hassadim,* members of these groups visited and cared for sick people. These communal associations were centered around the synagogue. When there was a emergency in the shtetl, an announcement was made in shul after the Torah was read. People were then able to organize themselves to help one another.

The Mitzvah Corps of Temple Beth Tikvah began with a volunteer committee of four women. They decided to make themselves available to any Temple member who needed help and to do whatever was most needed. They made specific plans for situations they thought would be likely to arise. They expected, for example, that they could help out when illness made it difficult for a homemaker to shop and cook for the family. They therefore established a system for providing meals. They also planned to visit the sick, telling people through word and deed that there were others who cared.

Soon after the committee formulated its plans, a congregant was hospitalized with a viral infection and high fever. The Mitzvah Corps cooked meals and brought them to her family. They also brought the flowers that had decorated the *bima* during Shabbat to her hospital room. Another woman became incapacitated after breaking her leg. Women from the Mitzvah Corps visited her and brought meals to her

> "The world is sustained by three things . . .

162/Moment

Jewish Possibilities: The Best of Moment

... by worship ...

home. Money was allocated to reimburse anyone who could cook but who could not afford the added expense.

These first loving deeds were carried out by the original committee of just four women. As people were helped, they became eager in turn to give help. In this way, the list of volunteers grew. With time, the needs grew as well.

The rabbi's secretary, a Temple member, became seriously ill and was put on a dialysis three times a week. For each treatment she had to be taken to a hospital in a nearby town and picked up several hours later. The volunteers relieved the woman's husband, making these trips for two years.

A social service worker contacted the Mitzvah Corps on behalf of a man in a nursing home. He was recuperating from a stroke and was alone. Mitzvah Corps volunteers brought him Passover and Shabbat meals—and companionship as well.

When we returned home from the hospital, the help the Mitzvah Corps gave was varied and unlimited. People rallied in ways and to a degree we could not have imagined. Our family and closest friends, the people the younger children felt most secure with, were always willing to care for Caren and Amy, but we needed people outside this immediate circle to help in other ways.

As in the days of the shtetl, the president of the congregation made an announcement during Shabbat, explaining the need for a person to accompany us on our trips to the hospital and outlining the time commitment involved. Volunteers signed sheets indicating days on which they would be available. From these names, the Mitzvah Corps chairperson organized a daily schedule, notifying each person, who in turn called us to make arrangements to meet at the appropriate time on a given day. That person became the pair of extra hands that was essential, parking the car, pushing the wheelchair, supplying tissues or adjusting blankets during the tedious drive home following chemotherapy. She stayed with us throughout the day, a friend offering conversation, diversion, encouragement and sympathetic understanding.

Another kind person brought a cooked meal to our home whenever we were scheduled to spend the day at the hospital. Caring even to note the children's tastes in food, "meals on wheels" kept arriving in disposable aluminum containers, often warm and ready to serve. There were days when we did not even know who had brought the food, so unobstrusive were the people who came to our home. Thoughtful planning, shopping, preparing, all taken over by someone else.

If we did not always know who had brought our dinner, we did know that there were strong, loving hands reaching out to us. If we felt that we were submerged in a sea of unbelievable, unrelenting problems, we also felt that there was a circle of warmth surrounding us. How moved we were by the outpouring of support.

Nothing could change Jennifer's fate; she died on November 5, 1980, nearly a year after her illness was diagnosed. But I am happy to know that she was able to experience the goodness of people and to know how much they cared during her short life.

Similarly, nothing can change our feelings of loss and grief. But we, too, know that people care, and that has been a sustaining factor during this time in which we have been and still are trying to recover. We will never be the same people we were before, most of all because of the loss of our beloved Jennifer—but also because of what we have seen in people, what we have learned of the power and beauty of *g'milut hassadim*. ✡

... and by acts of loving-kindness."

Loving Kindness in New Jersey

BROTHER CAN YOU SPARE A DIME?

I can't read much Hebrew, I can't read much Aramaic, I never went to yeshiva, But I study Talmud every chance I get. The treatment of beggars according to Jewish tradition.

ARTHUR KURZWEIL

In my neighborhood in Manhattan there is hardly a day when I am not approached by an individual who asks me for spare change, a quarter or a subway token. These individuals (whom I will call "beggars" from this point on, though I am aware that this label is narrow and therefore unfair) come in various forms: some are bag ladies, some are "street people," some are alcoholics—and so forth.

Although the organized Jewish community has honed the mitzvah of giving tz'dakah down to a virtual science, and though I have been a member of an alternative form of giving tz'dakah for four years, (a "tz'dakah collective"; see *The Third Jewish Catalog,* p. 31, Jewish Publication Society, 1980), I was confused as to what I should do about the beggars I meet almost daily.

My habit regarding beggars was inconsistent:

1. Sometimes I gave nothing for a day or, occasionally, for blocks of time.
2. Sometimes I'd get into a giving mood and give to beggars in a flurry over a period of time.
3. Sometimes I'd get into an angry mood over the issue and never give a penny, thinking that "they ought to get a job" or "ought to go on welfare."
4. Sometimes I'd give consistently though selectively to people I "decided" were worthy recipients.
5. Sometimes I'd give enthusiastically to a familiar beggar, only to ignore him or her the next day or week.

There were other inconsistencies as well, but these five are enough to indicate that my thinking on the subject was, as I have said, confused. But more than confused, I was troubled: what *should* my attitude toward beggars be? And does the Jewish tradition have anything to say to me on the subject?

The following are the results of my exploration of these two questions. I would like to make a few things clear regarding my research:

1. I am not a Talmudic scholar.
2. I do not have a working knowledge of Hebrew or Aramaic, so all the sources I have consulted are in English.
3. Every source quoted comes from my home library.

This third point is made for two reasons. First, I want to stress that the sources I have checked are limited. But second, I want to indicate that quite a bit of productive research can be conducted by using readily available sources—again—in English. (I will detail my research methodology later.)

My approach to the question of "What should my attitude towards beggars be?" was first to sit down and list all of my personal questions and dilemmas in regard to the subject. I came up with 15:

1. Do Jews give to beggars? (Is there precedent for my giving to beggars—as a Jew who wants to fulfill the mitzvah of tz'dakah?)
2. What if they are fakes or frauds? (How many times I have wondered whether they are making more than I!)
3. What if they are nasty or otherwise offensive in looks, smell, etc.?
4. What if I feel I simply can't afford to give to beggars?
5. Aren't there better causes to give to than these people?
6. Shouldn't these beggars be supported by official or organized agencies?
7. Shouldn't I just ignore these people?
8. What if I am in a rush?
9. What if they aren't Jewish? (Should my tz'dakah priorities go to worthy Jewish causes exclusively?)
10. What if I have no money with me, or no spare change?
11. If I do give, how should I treat these people? What should I say to them?
12. What if I see the same people every day? (They'll get to know me

Arthur Kurzweil is the author of From Generation to Generation: How to Trace Your Jewish Genealogy and Personal History *(Schocken Books). He is Editorial Vice President of Jason Aronson Publishers and Editor-in-chief of the B'nai B'rith Jewish Book Club.*

as an easy sucker.)

13. What if I've given to a few beggars in one day? (Is there a limit to this?)

14. If they ask for money, perhaps I should go buy them a cup of coffee instead. After all, they will probably spend it on booze anyway!

15. Finally, if I do give to beggars, how much should I give?

These fifteen questions seemed to cover just about every possible question or issue regarding beggars. The first 10 raised objections to giving to beggars, while the last five seemed to admit defeat, wondering just how and what to give if I must. In all, my questions reflected a resistance to giving to beggars—while my eagerness to do research on the subject balanced that resistance.

Joshua ben Perahyah says: Provide thyself with a teacher.
                    Pirke Avot, Mishnah 6

No research skill, however creative, can endure without being directed by a teacher, and I provided myself with the finest. Danny Siegel, teacher, poet, scholar and friend, guided me, on a weekly basis (a few hours each) for two years through the great works of our tradition. While we now live in different cities, hardly a week goes by when I am not on the phone to him, asking him for an explanation, a source, or simply a "talking out" of some Talmudic question.

So, principle number one for the kind of research that I am about to explain in detail, is, in the words of the Talmud: provide thyself with a teacher. You may not have the opportunity to sit with a teacher on a regular basis, but even to have a knowledgeable person who can get you out of some muddy water is important.

Fortunately most of the books I used—including the Soncino edition of the Talmud (18 volumes)—have an index. So, my first question when looking for an insight into the Jewish view of beggars was to figure out what key words would help me to "dig out" the material. With some creativity and a lot of trial and error I found that beggars would appear under the following topics: beggars, poor, charity.

I spent a frantic and exciting few days with my books, grabbing those I thought might have items under these three headings. In many cases I was quite successful. I read an enormous amount, copying lines, passages, quotes, and paragraphs. If a secondary source (such as a Jewish quotation dictionary) gave me a Talmudic passage, I was able to go to the Talmud itself—in English of course—and see it in context. Often by going to the "original" I was able to find more material on the subject that the secondary source left out. I was also able to compare translations (and when there were significant conflicts between translations I'd be on the phone to Danny Siegel once again for a glimpse—through his eyes—at the *original* original!)

After going through every book in my home library, I put each source I found on a separate note card. By the end I had about 60 cards! That is, 60 different times, one of my sources added to my knowledge of how Jewish tradition views beggars. In the process, I read a great deal, learned more than I ever hoped to, and, most remarkably, I felt that I had a significant insight into the subject at hand.

Perhaps the most amazing result of my research on this subject (which might come as a surprise to some and none at all to others) is that each of my 15 questions about beggars was dealt with by one or more of the sources I discovered. Our tradition is amazing: what I would have thought was a quite contemporary question—what, for example, do you do if you think the beggar is a fake?—is dealt with in ancient texts. The following is the result of my exploration.

1. Do Jews Give To Beggars?

Our Rabbis taught: If an orphan boy and an orphan girl applied for maintenance, the girl orphan is to be maintained first and the boy orphan afterwards, because it is not unusual for a man to go begging, but it is unusual for a woman to do so.
                    Ketubot 67a

Already there are two things to note. One is that the passage is a bit sexist—reflecting the times in which it was written, of course. But I put it here, and put it first to indicate that it is sometimes difficult to "swallow" everything one comes across in the texts.

The second thing of note is: what does "Ketubot 67a" mean? "Ketubot" is the name of a section of the Talmud. "67a" is the page number. Every page of Talmud is numbered—but rather than each side getting a number, each leaf gets a number, with a side "a" and a side "b."

R. Abun said: The poor man stands at your door, and the Holy One, blessed be He, stands at his right hand. If you give unto him, He who stands at his right hand will bless you, but if not, He will exact punishment from you, as it is said, "Because He standeth at the right hand of the needy." (Psalm 109, 31)
                    Midrash Ruth V-9

R. Isaac said, "He who gives a coin to a poor man is rewarded with six blessings. But he who encourages him with friendly words is rewarded with eleven."
                    Baba Bathra 9a

(The "R." before a persons name denotes "Rabbi.")

Question #1 is therefore answered. There is no doubt that it is within the Jewish tradition to give to beggars. But we have 14 questions remaining, each of which tries to obtain a better understanding of the complexities of the whole issue.

2. What If They Are Fakes Or Frauds?

Our Rabbis taught: If a man pretends to have a blind eye, a swollen belly or a shrunken leg, he will not pass out from this world before actually coming into such a condition. If a man accepts charity and is not in need of it, his end will be that he will not pass out of the world before he comes to such a condition.

Ketubah 68a

If anyone is not in need of relief and yet receives it by deceiving the public he will not die of old age before becoming a public charge. Such a person is included in the Biblical utterance: "A curse on him who relies on man." (Jer. 17:5)
Rambam, *Mishneh Torah* "Gifts to the poor" 10:19

These items agree and the message is clear, but it still doesn't help us. Should we give to the fakers? All we know so far is that they'll be punished for faking. Onward:

R. Eleazar said: Come let us be grateful to the rogues for were it not for them we (who do not always respond to every appeal for charity) would have been sinning every day.

Ketubot 68a

In other words, the fakers keep us in the habit of giving.

A beggar once came to the city of Kovna and collected a large sum of money from the residents. The people of the town soon found out that he was an imposter; he really was a wealthy man. The city council wanted to make an ordinance prohibiting beggars from coming to Kovna to collect money. When R. Yitzchok Elchonon Specter, the Rabbi of Kovna heard about the proposed ordinance, he came before the council and requested permission to speak. He told then that although he sympathized with them, he had an objection to raise. "Who deceived you, a needy person or a wealthy person? It was a wealthy person feigning poverty. If you want to make an ordinance, it should be to ban wealthy persons from collecting alms. But why make a ban against needy beggars?"
Ethics from Sinai, III, p. 121.

Rabbi Chayim of Sanz had this to say about fraudulent charity collectors: "The merit of charity is so great that I am happy to give to 100 beggars even if only one might actually be needy. Some people, however, act as if they are exempt from giving charity to 100 beggars in the event that one might be a fraud."
Darkai Chayim (1962), p. 137

This last quote, from the Sanzer Rebbe Chayim Halberstam, who was the teacher of my great-great-great grandfather, Chayim Joseph Gottlieb, the Stropkover Rebbe, seems to sum up question #2 clearly: Don't let the frauds stop you from giving. And, as earlier sources quoted point out: the frauds will get theirs!

3. What If They Are Nasty Or Otherwise Offensive?

The Chofetz Chayim's son wrote that his father was particularly careful not to hurt the feelings of beggars, although sometimes these unfortunate people say things that could arouse one's anger.
Michtevai Chofetz Chayim (1953) Dugmah Midarkai Avi, p. 38

Rabbi Shmelke of Nicholsburg said, "When a poor man asks you for aid, do not use his faults as an excuse for not helping him. For then God will look for your offenses, and He is sure to find many of them. Keep in mind that the poor man's transgressions have been atoned for by his poverty while yours still remain with you.
Fun Unzer Alter Otzer, II, p. 9

This last quote, coupled with the first one, is somewhat helpful when dealing with the question of the alcoholic who asks for money. In some ways, the suffering he is undergoing is "punishment" enough. My denying him money "because he'd only use it for booze" is not helping anyone.

4. What If I Feel I Simply Can't Afford To Give To Beggars?

To him who has the means and refuses the needy, the Holy One says: Bear in mind, fortune is a wheel!
Nahman, *Tanhuma*, Mishpatim #8

Even a poor man, a subject of charity, should give charity.
Gitten 7b

5. Aren't There Any Better Causes To Give To Than To These People?

While it is commendable to aid students of the Torah more than commoners, the Jewish law knows no such distinction. The latter must also be aided.
Nachman of Bratzlav quoted in *Hasidic Anthology*

This "excuse" is a familiar one to me. How often I have passed by a beggar thinking: I gave to Oxfam International—The World Hunger Organization. The irony is too obvious to explain!

6. Shouldn't These Beggars Be Supported By Official Or Organized Agencies?

In answer to an enquiry from a community, overburdened with beggars, Solomon b. Adret ruled that although, "the poor are everywhere supported from the communal chest, if they wish in addition to beg from door to door they may do so, and each should give according to his understanding and desire."
Responsa, pt. 3, #380

7. Shouldn't I Just Ignore These People?

R. Joshua b. Korha said, "Anyone who shuts his eye against charity is like one who worships idols."
Ketubot 68a also TJ, Peah 4.20

R. Joshua b. Korha said, "He who closes his eyes to a request for charity is considered as one who worships idols."
Baba Bathra 10a

The same person with the same thought, in two different locations in the Talmud.

Rabbi Itzikel of Kalish was known

for his kindness for everyone. Once a non-Jewish beggar asked the Rabbi's wife for some bread. At the moment she had only a full loaf, newly baked, and she disliked cutting it lest it become dry. But the Rabbi enjoined her to give the beggar a portion of this bread. A few years later, the Rabbi was traveling through the Carpathian Mountains toward Hungary. On the way brigands captured him and his companions, and brought them to their chieftain. The latter recognized the Rabbi as his benefactor when he came begging at his door. He freed Rabbi Itzikel and restored to him his possessions.
  Or ha-Meir (Lemberg, 1926), p.15

The above is a strange story for a few reasons. First, the lesson is clearly not: give to beggars because they might become crooks and rob you. Second, like too many stories, the hero is the Rabbi, while the insensitive one is the wife. Third, the beggar/thief is a non-Jew. Despite all this, the moral message still manages to sneak through: don't ignore beggars.

Rabbi Aharon Kotler once gave alms twice to the same beggar, upon entering and leaving a synagogue. He was afraid that someone noticing him pass the second time without giving might assume that he had reason not to give to this particular beggar.
  R. Shaul Kagan in *Jewish Observer*

8. What If I Am In A Rush?

The following story, from the Talmud, is one of the most vivid and powerful I've ever encountered. Every detail is radically unsettling.

It is related of Nahum of Gamzu that he was blind in both his eyes, his two hands and legs were amputated, and his whole body was covered with boils and he was lying in a dilapidated house on a bed the feet of which were standing in bowls of water in order to prevent the ants from crawling on to him. On one occasion his disciples desired to remove the bed and then clear the things out of the house, but he said to them, "My children, first clear out the things from the house and then remove my bed for I am confident that so long as I am in the house it will not collapse." They first cleared out the things and then removed the bed and the house immediately collapsed. Thereupon his disciples said to him, "Master, since you are wholly righteous, why has all this befallen you?" and he replied, "I have brought it all upon myself. Once I was journeying on the road and was making for the house of my father-in-law and I had with me three asses, one laiden with food, one with drink, and one with all kinds of dainties, when a poor man met me and stopped me on the road and said to me, 'Master, give me something to eat.' I replied to him, 'Wait until I have unloaded something from the ass;' I had hardly managed to unload something from the ass when the man died (from hunger). I then went and laid myself on him and exclaimed, 'May my eyes which had no pity upon your eyes become blind, any my hands which had no pity upon your hands be cut off, may my legs which had no pity upon your legs be amputated,' and my mind was not at rest until I added, 'may my whole body be covered with boils.'" Thereupon his pupils exclaimed, "Alas, that we see you in such a sore plight." To this he replied. "Woe would it be to me did you not see me in such a plight."
  Ta'anith 21a

9. What If They Aren't Jewish?

The irony of this question is that when I was in Israel and when I met poor Jewish beggars in Eastern Europe, I never questioned the idea of giving to them. My own prejudices become crystal-clear with this question!

The non-Jewish poor should be maintained and clothed along with the Jewish poor for the sake of peaceful relations.
  Rambam, *Mishneh Torah* "Gifts to the Poor" 7:7

Poor Gentiles should be supported along with poor Jews; the Gentile sick should be visited along with the Jewish sick; and their dead should be buried along with the Jewish dead, in order to further peaceful relations.
  Gitten 61a

These last two items reflect a limitation on my part. From my reading, I know that there are long discussions as to the true meaning and nature of the phrase "peaceful relations." On the surface it sounds as if we must do it not because it's right but for peace. The matter is much more complicated than that and is one that I do not have the ability to examine at this point. This is clearly one of the drawbacks of my own limited background.

10. What If I Have No Money On Me Or No Spare Change?

If a poor man requests money from you and you have nothing to give him, speak to him consolingly.
  Rambam, *Mishneh Torah* "Gifts to the Poor" 10:5

If the poor man stretches out his hand and he has nothing to give him, he should not scold and raise his voice to him, but he should speak gently to him and show him his goodness of heart; namely that he wishes to give him something but cannot.
  Shulchan Aruch, 249:3-5

11. If I Do Give, How Should I Treat These People? What Should I Say? How Should I Approach Them?

Rabbi Chana bar Chanila. . . would leave his hand in his pocket so that (by the immediacy and naturalness of handing him money) a poor person who came to ask would not feel humiliated.
  Brachos 58b

Anyone who gives tz'dakah in a surly manner and with a gloomy face completely nullifies the merit of his own deed, even if he gives him a thousand gold pieces. He should rather give him cheerfully and gladly, while sympathizing with him who is in trouble, as it is written: "Did I not weep for him whose day was hard? Was not my soul grieved for the poor? (Job 30:25)

Rambam, *Mishneh Torah* "Gifts to the Poor" 10:4

12. What If I See The Same People Every Day? Won't They Get To Know The Sucker?

Though you may have given already, give yet again even a hundred times, for it says, "Give, yea, give thou shalt . . ." (Deut. 15:10-11)

Sifre Deut., Re'eh, 116

13. What If I Already Gave To A Few Beggars In One Day?

If you have given a "perutah" to a man in the morning, and there comes to you in the evening another poor man asking for alms, give to him also...

Avos d'R. Nathan 19b

14. If They Ask For Money, Perhaps I Should Buy Them A Cup Of Coffee Instead?

Nehemiah of Sihin met a man in Jerusalem who said to him, "Give me that chicken you are carrying." Nehemiah said, "Here is its value in money." The man went and bought some meat and ate it and died. Then Nehemiah said, "Come and bemoan the man whom Nehemiah has killed."

T.J. Pe'ah, VIII 9, 21b

In this example, the case is reversed: the person wants an item of food rather than money. But the point is the same: don't decide what is best for the beggar.

15. How Much Should I Give?

A pauper who begs from house to house should be given only a small sum.

Shulchan Aruch, 250, 1-5

It is forbidden to turn away a poor man entirely empty-handed. Let him give something, if only a fig, for it is written, "Oh, let not the oppressed return ashamed." (Psalm 74:21)

M. Isserles, note on *Shulchan Aruch* 249:3-5

Just as in a garment every thread unites with the rest to form a whole garment, so every penny given to charity unites with the rest to form a large sum.

Baba Bathra 9b

The message seems clear: don't ignore the beggar, don't treat him or her with anything but kindness, don't find excuses as to why not to give. Rather, give to everyone, regardless of who he or she is—but just give a little.

Each person's relationship to these texts is different. For me, the texts represent an ideal, and one, I confess, I do not live up to regularly. Yet this research was not just an academic exercise for me. I certainly learned more than that the classical texts (and others) of our tradition have much to say—in very contemporary terms—about the matter at hand. I certainly learned that I *am* able to explore the texts with a minimum of background and knowledge. But most important, the exploration of the text moved me—literally—to avoid passing up the opportunity of observing the mitzvah of tz'dakah each day in my neighborhood. I often fail at seizing each opportunity offered to me, but I struggle to come closer to the ideal—and that is, in my opinion, the purpose of the teachings.

Bibliography

If an item has an asterisk (*) in front of it, it means that it is of extraordinary quality. If you are using this bibliography to aid in your purchase of books for your home library, it is these items that I would most strongly recommend. If an item has an (o.p.) in front of it, it means that it is "out of print" and therefore no longer available from the publisher. Nevertheless I suggest you examine these books if your libraries have them—and keep an eye out for them in good used bookstores.

Classical Texts

(*) *The Torah; The Five Books of Moses.* Jewish Publication Society, Philadelphia, 1962.
(*) *The Babylonian Talmud.* The Soncino Press, London. (18 volumes)
(*) *The Midrash Rabbah.* The Soncino Press, London. (5 volumes)
(*) *The Minor Tractates of the Talmud.* The Soncino Press, London. (2 volumes)

Basic Reference Sources

(*) *Encylopaedia Judaica.* Keter Publishing House, Jerusalem, 1972. (16 volumes)
(*) Birnbaum, Philip. *Encylopaedia of Jewish Concepts.* Hebrew Publishing Co., New York, 1980. (paperback)

Quotations, Compilations, Selections, Etc.

Alcalay, Reuben. *A Basic Encyclopedia of Jewish Proverbs, Quotations, and Folk Wisdom.* Hartmore House, Bridgeport, CT, 1973.
(o.p.) Baron, Joseph L. *A Treasury of Jewish Quotations.* Yoseloff, South Brunswick, NJ, 1965.
Cohen, Dr. A., *Everyman's Talmud.* E.P. Dutton, New York, 1949.
Feinsilver, Rabbi Alexander. *The Talmud For Today.* St. Martin's Press, New York, 1980.
(*) Klagsbrun, Francine. *Voices of Wisdom; Jewish Ideals and Ethics for Everyday Living.* Pantheon Books, New York, 1980.
Meiseles, Meir. *Judaism: Thought and Legend; an anthology on ethics and philosophy throughout the ages.* Feldheim Publishers, New York, 1964 (paperback)
(*) Montefiore, C.G. and Loewe, H. *A Rabbinic Anthology,* Schocken Books, New York, 1974. (paperback)
(*) Rosten, Leo. *Leo Rosten's Treasury of Jewish Quotations.* Bantam Books, New York, 1977. (paperback)

Introductions To Talmud

(o.p.) Bokser, Rabbi Ben Zion. *Wisdom of the Talmud,* The Citadel Press, New York, 1962.
(*) Steinsaltz, Adin. *The Essential Talmud.* Bantam Books, New York, 1976. (paperback)

Miscellaneous Sources

(*) Newman, Louis I. *Hasidic Anthology; Tales and Teachings of the Hasidim.* Schocken Books, New York. 1963. (paperback)
Pliskin Zelig. *Love Your Neighbor; You and Your Fellow Man in Light of the Torah.* Aish HaTorah Publications, Brooklyn, 1977.
Twersky, Isadore. *A Maimonides Reader.* Behrman House, New York, 1972 (paperback)
(*) Steinberg, Milton. *As A Driven Leaf.* Behrman House, New York. (paperback). (Note: This is a *novel* that takes place in Talmudic times; no source material here, but a wonderful introduction to the Talmud and its major personalities.)

COMING OF AGE AT 66
A MOST UNFORGETTABLE BAR MITZVAH

LINDA KERBER

Linda K. Kerber is the May Brodbeck Professor of Liberal Arts at the University of Iowa, where she teaches American Women's History. Her books include Women of the Republic: Intellect and Ideology in Revolutionary America *(1980) and* Women's America: Refocusing the Past — An Anthology *(edited with Jane Dehart-Mathews, 1982, 2nd ed. 1987).*

I baked a cake of course. In our small academic community of 150 Jewish families, we always bring food for a bar mitzvah Oneg Shabbat. But what gift do you bring for a 66-year-old bar mitzvah? And what do you say when the 66-year-old bar mitzvah "boy" is mentally handicapped?

We went to Bill's bar mitzvah thinking we were doing Bill a favor. As it turned out, he did us one.

Bill's story is tied up with the larger immigrant experience. As Barry Morrow has reconstructed it, Bill was the child of Russian-Jewish parents who emigrated to Minneapolis at the turn of the century. Bill was born in 1913; his mother was widowed six years later. Social agencies diagnosed the child as "subnormal" and "feebleminded" in the language of the day, and the desperately impoverished mother was persuaded to commit her son to the Faribault State School for the Feebleminded and Epileptic. It is now agreed that Bill may have been less severely retarded than he now seems to be, but the prejudices and assumptions of the time, along with the language difficulties, made it easy to label him. Institutionalized, and treated since childhood as seriously retarded, he failed to develop normally.

During the 44 years that Bill was in institutions, his religious background was obscured. He went to Jewish and Christian services indiscriminately, responding to the music and the ritual, as he still does. In 1964, when work-release programs were opening locked doors of institutions, Bill was placed in a boarding home in Minneapolis. He was working as a handyman in a country club when Bev and Barry Morrow met him. It was the Morrows who managed to have the old records scrutinized. They confirmed Bill's Jewish identity.

Bev and Barry Morrow arranged for Bill to come to Iowa City when they moved here several years ago. He boards with a kind woman, Mae Driscoll, who helps him keep his things in order and prepares his lunch. Bill keeps his pet bird Chubby in his room, feeding and caring for it. "I found a good home," says Bill, "and I've been home ever since."

Every morning Bill boards the city bus and heads for his job. The University of Iowa School of Social Work may be the only school in the country with a mentally handicapped staff member. Bill's title is formidable: Special Developmental Disabilities Consultant. He putters around the lounge, making fresh coffee, sanding furniture, straightening up, chatting with children who wander up from the Early Childhood Development Center, ready to pass the time of day with anyone who happens by. "Shabbat Shalom," he says cheerfully to everyone, any day of the week. Someone has put up a sign: "Wild Bill's Bar and Grill."

"It started as a generous gesture on our part," observes Barry Morrow. "But Bill is a major educational resource. He offers friendship, warmth and music. On a lazy afternoon, Bill is as good a person to spend time with as anyone I know. Over a cup of coffee, he teaches social work students the very essence of their profession."

As befits a member of a distinguished faculty, Bill can list honors and awards on his vita. He has a bronze plaque naming him "Handicapped Iowan of the Year—1976" that was presented to him by the Governor at a formal banquet. He has an award from the American Academy for Cerebral Palsy and Developmental Medicine. But perhaps his greatest achievement is that he holds no bitterness. He remembers being badly treated at Faribault, but of those days he will say only, "That was bad."

"He's not trapped by his past," observes Jim Cosper, who loves to spend time with Bill. "What some would take as a sign of retardation,

I think may be a sign of advancement."

It was Saturday afternoon, and the sun was setting. At the Hillel sanctuary the folding doors were opened, the chairs moved out of the way, an improvised Bimah set up in the center of the floor.

"We wanted something informal," Rabbi Jeffrey Portman observed later, "and Havdalah seemed just right. We also wanted to arrange it in the round, to increase access to the Torah, since that is the part of the service Bill likes best."

The familiar words of the Mincha/Ma'ariv service began, and we shuffled, awkwardly, into a vague circle. Gathered were well over a hundred people, children and adults, Jewish and non-Jewish. Familiar faces from the congregation, from the faculty, staff and students of the School of Social Work. Our ceremony would be a formal welcome into the Jewish community of a man who had been institutionalized as feebleminded sixty years before.

The Torah service began. Rabbi Portman handed the Torah to Bill, who wrapped his arms around it. The usual verses were too complex a musical line, but Bill knows and loves Hine-ma-tov, so we sang that, over and over again as Bill carried the Torah slowly around our circle, making sure that everyone, including children, got to touch it. "Hine-ma-tov, Hine-ma-tov," hummed Bill. "Behold it is good."

"Y'a'mod Simcha Ben Abraham, ha bar mitzvah." Jonathan Goldstein, the professor of ancient history who regularly reads our Torah, called Bill by the Hebrew name that Rabbi Portman had devised for him: Simcha for happiness. They said the words of the aliyah together: Rabbi Portman loud and clear; Bill echoing along in his own Hebrew.

The president of the synagogue made the same speech he makes to every bar and bat mitzvah, presenting a certificate testifying to the successful completion of Hebrew preparation. Martha Lubaroff, the president of the Sisterhood, presented a tallis. Bill's parents are long since dead, but his court-appointed conservator, Barry Morrow, was there.

"There have been many occasions like this when I've stood beside you, Bill, but somehow tonight seems like the most important. I know you missed many things when you were growing up—your bar mitzvah was one. Tonight you have been reunited with your religious heritage and the faith of your parents."

It was time for the bar mitzvah to make a speech. Bill moved to the Bimah. "Thanks to all my friends for coming. God bless you. Thank you very much." Pausing a moment, he reached for his harmonica, and, facing the Torah, for all the world like the Fool in the Isaac Bashevis Singer story, Bill Sackter played his harmonica before the Lord.

Bill's bar mitzvah has come to be a mythological event for the synogogue of Agudas Achim. "Let us tell you about Bill's bar mitzvah," we tell anyone who will listen. It taught us that the form of all ceremonies need not be precisely the same, that the rules can be broken yet the essentials kept.

It is important to say bluntly that Bill's was not a second-class ceremony, a pathetic gesture for a retarded patient. Though Bill could not understand the words, he understood the essentials. He understands that he has a lot of friends who had gathered to welcome him. He is proud of his bar mitzvah certificate, which hangs framed on his wall. He is proud of his tallis, which he wears as often as he can. He feels a legitimate part of the community; "I had a bar mitzvah," he tells visitors cheerfully.

Every Friday night and Saturday morning, Rabbi Portman or another friend stops by to bring Bill to services. He loves the music and the ritual; it is very important to him to have a friend keep him on the correct page.

"He is the most consistent shul-goer in the community," observes Debbie Cosper. "If I don't go, Bill will worry that I'm sick, and I worry that no one will help Bill find his place. So I go, and then Jim goes, and that makes three."

Bill watches Rabbi Portman count the adults, and he is as pleased to be needed for the minyan as we are to have him there. He has a good ear, and his approximation of the aliyah has come a lot closer over the years. Nearly every Saturday Bill carries the Torah. And after services Bill's harmonica is a joyous celebration of the Sabbath.

Iowa City is a university town, and ours is a homogenous community. Most of us are middle-aged, in our thirties and forties. We tend to be highly educated; many of us teach at the University. We are doctors, lawyers, writers. We are vulnerable to the sin of pride in our intellectual accomplishments; "What do you *do?*" we demand of the stranger at the Oneg.

But we cannot demand of Bill, "What do you do?" We have to find something else to say. He has a wonderful ability to disarm the pompous. "I think he's the easiest person to talk to because he accepts you right away," says Debbie Cosper. "He doesn't care what your status is. Getting to know him means getting to know a *person*, rather than a doctor, a lawyer...." She pauses, gropes for the right phrase. "I watch new people who haven't met him before. The encounter is a test of whether you are a *mensch*."

Our encounter with Bill has been profound. We have not been used to thinking of mentally handicapped people as assertive or aggressive, but we have learned from Bill that they can be. No one pushes Bill around; he goes where he chooses.

Bill gives our congregation depth of age. He gives us our minyan. He gives us music. He has instructed us in encountering another human being directly, without the trappings of status or ascribed roles. And he teaches us philosophy.

"The Lord," says Bill, "helps those who *can't* help themselves." ✡

Bill with Zoeanne Morrow, Bev and Barry's daughter.

Bill and Chubby.
Left: After his bar mitzvah, Bill celebrating with Bev Morrow on his left, Barry Morrow on his right, and other well-wishers.

IF ORTHODOXY IS THE ANSWER,

Look around... look at the astonishing capacity of people who have explicitly entered—and conquered—the most modern precincts of the modern world, and who continue to celebrate the ancient tradition... and look also at the degree to which the rest of us have become defensive in the presence of the Orthodox.

We have shown the world that the Torah's NO is NO. Now it is time to show that the Torah's YES is YES. It is not enough to generate from within Jewish law ingenious emergency responses to new situations. We must generate from within Jewish law the kinds of moral initiatives which would serve each new situation and liberate its spark of holiness.

WHAT IS THE QUESTION?

A SPECIAL SECTION

How unassailably secure one's fortress feels if questions about family planning, the use of heroic life-sustaining measures, or the limits of waging justified warfare can all be answered with the same dualistic "kosher or trefe" with which a "cooking spoon" question is answered!

Except for the handful able to adopt the Orthodox way of life in all details and assimilated into Orthodox circles, Orthodoxy has nothing but ugly and unfriendly words. Orthodoxy does not love the Jewish people—unless they are Orthodox.

Maybe I don't look down my nose at people who aren't observant, but once I've come to the decision that what I'm doing is right, then it follows that the people who don't do it are wrong. It is the best way. And if it is the best way, it is the only way.

PROLOGUE

One of the central puzzlements of recent American Jewish history is the growing strength of Orthodox Judaism. Who would have supposed, back in the 1950's, that Orthodoxy was here not only to stay, but to grow? A generation ago, the assumption of the rest of us—insofar as we ever bothered to think about the matter at all—was that Orthodoxy was a quaint vestige of earlier times. Wishing it no harm, we nonetheless supposed that it would bow before the strength of modernity. Had our grandparents not also been Orthodox (although they did not use the word)? And were we, their descendents, not what we were—secular, Reform, Conservative—but surely not Orthodox? The process of history, we concluded from our own biography, was inexorable: the tradition would weaken, crumble, change. Orthodox Judaism was doomed.

Look around. Look at the Lubavitch movement. More important, look at the modern Orthodox congregations, the ones with substantial numbers of members who teach physics at distinguished institutions, who are psychiatrists, corporate lawyers, business tycoons. Look at the Talmud classes attended by government officials. Look at the astonishing capacity of people who have explicitly entered—and conquered—the most modern precincts of the modern world, and who continue to celebrate the ancient tradition.

And look also at the degree to which the rest of us have become defensive in the presence of the Orthodox.

For now that we see that Orthodoxy cannot only make its peace with modernity, but actually thrive in the modern world, we are bound to confront the obvious question: is not the Orthodox way the authentic way? And, if it is, is not every other way less authentic, which means, fundamentally inauthentic?

When we believed that Orthodoxy was not viable, when we believed that the compromises which modernity so obviously demanded would ennervate Orthodoxy, when we believed that our survival as a religious civilization required of us radical adaptation of the ancient tradition, when we believed that Orthodoxy in America was exotic and impractical, we did not have to face the question of authenticity. But now? How can we continue to evade the question?

Yet how can we ask it, we non-believers, weak-believers, confused-believers, ambivalent believers? The dominant faith of American Jews—as shown in survey after survey—remains, whatever the distribution of denominational affiliation, agnosticism. We are Jews by desire, Jews by instinct, Jews by habit, Jews by passion—but hardly Jews by faith. For at least ten years now—since the Six Day War—Zionism has been the collective religion of the Jews, and the needs of Israel rather than the demands of the halachah have provided the norms for communal behavior. Among mainstream Jews, it is the performance of Israel-related tasks rather than of traditional mitzvot that provides the measure of authenticity. And when there is deference displayed to the ways of the tradition, it is prompted by sentiment or by courtesy rather than by conviction.

Accordingly, it might be thought that the non-Orthodox have no need to confront the challenge which Orthodoxy raises. To each his own authenticity: to the one, halachah; to the other, devotion to Israel.

Yet the Orthodox challenge remains. In the popular perception, Orthodox is at least "more," perhaps also "better." The Orthodox, it is supposed, know what they believe, and what they believe is what Jews are, in some sense, supposed to believe. If the rest of us do not believe it, it is not because we are smarter, or because we believe more important things; it is because we are lapsed, or because we are lazy. Orthodoxy is normative Judaism; it provides the standard from which all else is a deviation.

For decades, aggregations of

deviants have struggled to articulate coherent and compelling alternatives to the Orthodox vision. But the folk, although it has eagerly adopted such alternatives, has known them for what they are: compromises, adaptations, facsimilies. Shadows. For one reason or another, most of us have preferred to live in the shadows. Sometimes we have explained our choice on the grounds of intellectual conviction, sometimes by pointing to the irrelevance of the Orthodox way, or to its costs. We have resented the Orthodox for reminding us of our weakness, and we have resented them for their pettiness, and we have resented them for their apparent certainty. But we have secretly envied them for their stubbornness, and for their ability to believe, and for their fidelity to a constitution and a covenant which are our own as well. We have known that without that fidelity, we would not be, hence we have been grateful to them for preserving the faith. We who have preferred the shadows are thankful that there are those who have chosen the sun, with all its discomforts. Nor do they sweat, nor do they evidence the discomfort. What is it that they know that we do not?

The question now presses more insistently, as we become aware that they do not wilt or wither. It presses as we begin to restore the customs and ceremonies of yore, even as we continue to resist the convictions. It presses as we pursue our own search for meaning, for the persistence of the Orthodox way suggests that meaning may be nearer at hand than we have wanted to believe.

The question presses because now we see the Orthodox. Even Chassidism is no longer merely exotic, not since the Lubavitch have mounted their mitzvah-mobiles, opened their Chabad houses on a dozen campuses, and provided the only systematic Jewish response to the soulsnatching cults of our time. But Chassidism, at least, is so very far from where most of us are, or want to be, or can imagine ourselves being, it is so outlandish, that it offers no direct challenge to our self-perception. The challenge is more from the traditional Jew in Brooks Brothers clothing than from his beshtreimeled colleague. For it is not just his clothing that is our clothing. His language is our language, his neighborhood our neighborhood, his occupation ours as well. And secretly we wonder: Does his belief insulate him from the tribulations we experience? How does he manage to sustain his belief, and where does he derive the energy to pursue his way, and is he as complacent as he often seems, and is the smugness we see a reflection of our own defensiveness or is it the natural consequence of a certainty we cannot imagine?

All these questions, because it has now become clear: If Orthodoxy is an anachronism, as we have been pleased to suppose for so many decades, it just may be the healthiest anachronism going. Save your kipot; the Tradition will rise again. Who can any longer claim with confidence that fifty or a hundred years from now it will not be the way of the Orthodox that will have become the normal way for us all?

A difficult question, because it is asked by people who cannot easily answer a much simpler question: Would you want your daughter to marry one? Not one of the kicky kind, the kind who dabbles in the aesthetic of the tradition, but a real one, one of those we see as humorless and musty. A nice place to visit, but would you really want to live there?

I speak, of course, from outside the Orthodox movement, with all my confusions intact. I am neither proud nor embarrassed to be what I am, and what I am, most of the time, is a Jew who takes Jewish religious metaphor very, very seriously but who cannot (or will not) move beyond religion-as-metaphor. I find the metaphor aesthetically pleasing, culturally invigorating, morally enriching. But I do not *believe* it. And that means that I

> We have resented the Orthodox for reminding us of our weakness ... but we have secretly envied them for their stubbornness. What is it that they know that we do not?

must will myself into a religious sensibility. The commandments become options, the Commander becomes just an idea, the whole system—as I suppose the Orthodox understand the system—is subverted.

Does that make me an incomplete Jew? (I cannot abide the notion of a "good" Jew.) Of course it does. And it is not the only thing that does. And I am not the only one who is. The uncertainties I here announce are not personal idiosyncrasies; one way or another, they affect most of us, including, I imagine, a goodly number of those who call themselves Orthodox.

I have some resources with which to compensate. They are in the form of consoling formulas, such as these: lacking faith, I can still be faithful, lacking belief, I can still will myself into a metaphoric framework that connects me to my brother the believer and to my ancestors the immersed. Although I do not accept that there was a revelation at Sinai (which, according to the Talmud, means that I have lost the world to come), I accept entirely the tradition which teaches that all the Jews—the dead, the living, the as-yet unborn, were present at the Revelation. It did not happen; I was there. (Which at least gives me a firm grasp on the world that is.) I long ago proposed, and still believe, that even the Jewish atheist knows full well what the God in whom he does not believe expects of him.

Formulas? Alibis? The yoke of the commandments replaced by glib—but empty—sentiment? Who can say?

On a lazy day, no problem. The Orthodox themselves solve the problem for me, for in their institutional behavior (of course I know the exceptions) they continue to offend. The lead article in a recent issue of *The Jewish Observer,* the publication of the Agudath Israel of America, quotes with smug satisfaction a critique of Judaic Studies programs on college campuses, and then adds, "This is not in the least surprising, for most of the teachers of Judaic Studies courses are Conservative and Reform rabbis, or others of marginal commitment." So much for *ahavat Yisrael,* love for one's fellow Jews. Another recent issue of the same publication takes the Reform movement to task for its commitment to social action, which "rests on dubious moral foundations" and which "can do untold harm to Jewish interests—witness the terrible backlash suffered by Jewish merchants in the Deep South as a result of conspicuous Jewish participation in the civil rights movement." So much for *tikun olam*—the repair of the universe.

But that is all on a lazy day. The real question, I think, is not the Orthodox, but what Orthodoxy claims to stand for. What else is there to stand for? There is the defense of Jewish interests, of course, and there is Israel, to be sure, and there is nostalgic chic. But that which makes the interests worth defending and Israel worth protecting and the memories worth preserving is what we stand for. And what is it that we can be said to stand for more centrally than a system of belief? And who is it that cares the most about that system, and, manners aside, takes the greatest care to sustain it?

My Reform and Conservative friends will object. They will claim that they believe no less profoundly, and much more plausibly. The best of them will argue that Orthodoxy provides a framework, but that the framework must be subjected to review and renewal by each generation of Jews. I like what they have to say; it suits me. There are times I imagine the House of Israel to be an ongoing constitutional convention, the Orthodox resisting casual amendment, the Reform only now beginning to understand the critical difference between constitutional law and statutory law, the Conservative taking a judicious middle course, taking the constitution seriously but not passively. At such times, I can live comfortably with the debate, knowing that the distinction is not between one interpretation and another, but rather between believers and non-believers. But most often I remain troubled that, at least so far as the folk (rather than the rabbis, the theologians) are concerned, the distinction is not what we believe, but in how certainly and how coherently we believe.

More important, ever so much more important, the issue of Orthodoxy forces us to ask what it means to be Jewish. Whether the answer is to be found within Orthodoxy as an idea, or among the Orthodox, as a movement, I do not know. I would prefer to think there are answers to be found in other and more congenial places, although the answers I sometimes stumble upon strike me as rather cumbersome, considerably more complex even if more palatable than the Orthodox answers. Nonetheless, I am happy to have the questions forced. Most of all, I am happy to have the following question forced: What shall I tell my children about why they should care?

A tough question. The burdensome agenda of Jewish interests makes it easy to avoid. Who has time for philosophy when there are Jews in distress? But somewhere, in the back of my head, I know that I would not be the Jew I am had my grandfather the Rav not been the Jew he was. And if that be the case, what can I say of my children's children? What is it that they will have to remember and to be nourished by? Will they have the metaphor still, or will the distance between metaphor and meaning have become so vast as to make the metaphor entirely alien? And what, in the meantime, do I tell myself, do we tell ourselves? Issues of belief are much easier to avoid than to confront, at least for those of us to whom belief does not come naturally. And that is why I am unable to do more than let the questions dangle, turning to others to propose answers.

From diverse perspectives, those others address themselves to one part of the question: What does it mean to be Orthodox in America today, to be a part of the community of believers? —L.F.

FAITH AND FEAR
MOSHE ADLER

Being an Orthodox Jew in an assimilatory world is something like trying to celebrate Shabbat in a house where it's Saturday. People bustling about, skirting your Shabbat table, often resent your being in the way, sometimes tolerate you, maybe even distantly respect you; but they hardly ever understand you, and rarely if ever do they realize that the table is set not just for you. It is also set for them.

The proper thing to do, you would suppose, would be to sing the Shabbat songs with greater sweetness and devotion than ever, so that (if and) when one of the bustlers stops and asks you to hum him a few bars to carry away, you can draw up a chair for him, pour him some wine, teach him the melodies, and watch him discover that he has time to celebrate Shabbat after all. That is, of course, what our master, Hillel the Elder, would probably have done. It's risky and takes lots of patience.

But you know the disciplined attention to detail that has gone into making Shabbat out of this day. Indeed, you know that this day is itself but a glimpse into a higher world of eternal beauty and mystery. Rejoicing with the Lord is serious business, not some kind of "glorious cultural heritage." How, after all, can you represent the Shabbat by humming a few bars of its melody? How can you teach someone the whole Torah while he stands on one foot?

So you push the bustler away, back into Saturday. Hillel was saintly but Shammai was right, you tell yourself, and it's enough to be right; we can't all be saintly. Indeed, it might just be easier to move the whole Shabbat table into a private room and lock the door. So you do. "Now," you sigh, "I can celebrate my Shabbat. *My* Shabbat. If they want to share it, they know which door to knock on. Of course, I have the key...."

When Shabbat became Saturday—when a secularized world decided to label the Biblical-Talmudic tradition "Orthodoxy" and lock it away with other medieval anachronisms—Jews who still revered that tradition as the living word of God accepted the label—and the locking away. We did it to preserve our vision of the whole, to keep alive our sense that "the awe of God is pure, abiding forever" (Psalms 19:10). Any who desire Torah know where to find it, we told each other. Of course, we have the key....

In some measure, our resistance to outside influence paid off. But in larger measure it has worked against us. Some who sought certainty in an age of uncertainty have found it with us; many have found only smugness. Some who sought clear direction in an age of religious and moral relativism have found it with us; many have found only stagnation. For some we became a home in the universe, but for many we became instead a maintenance crew preserving the Biblical-Talmudic tradition alive within a fortress so that they might borrow elements of it to use on the outside.

But suppose that we were to draw up chairs for would-be tradition-borrowers, to offer to teach them not just a few bars but all the melodies, and then watch them discover that they have world enough, and time, after all? Wouldn't they then buy into the whole system?

Sometimes, but not usually. Bright, devout seekers from without have found the living word of God in so much of the tradition that they desire to find it throughout. But when they look to us, keepers of His word, to show the way, all too often they find that long years of living inside the fortress walls have made our vision too narrow to encompass the whole, made our fear too mean to be called "the awe of God." Yet still we persist in equating our vision with the whole itself, and our fear of initiative with the awe of God. So they, the seekers, may grant that we have *a* key—but not *the* key. And they take away what they can, and continue their search for God's word in non-traditional systems.

Let us make no mistake. We are not dealing here with a pedagogic question: How can we make Yiddishkeit more attractive? We are dealing with several substantive questions: Does Jewish law, purporting to be the norm-creating process of a divine Torah, really reflect the justice and compassion of God, or is it just and compassionate (merely) by definition? Will an observer of Jewish law acquire heightened spiritual awareness and reflect justice and compassion in the way he lives, or is Orthodox piety a form of scoring celestial brownie-points? Is the way we understand halachic categories open to insight gained from new kinds of experience and new kinds of consciousness about the world, or did God give us a time-flawed system and command us not to notice the cracks? Can the very Torah, including the Bible, withstand the test of historical and critical analysis and emerge the stronger and the more enduring for it, or are we secretly afraid that if we examine it too closely, we will discover ourselves living inside a movie that ends with our

Moshe Adler teaches Bible at the Talmud Torah of Minneapolis and is on the faculty of the Minneapolis Community School of Adult Jewish Studies. He is active in the movement for unity among American Jewish religious groups, in Oz ve-Shalom—an Israeli-based Orthodox peace movement, and in Jewish/Christian dialogue. He continues to lecture, write, and teach on the applicability of Jewish tradition to contemporary issues.

discovery?

With rare exceptions, modern Orthodoxy has refused to address these questions on their own terms, but has instead worked up an elaborate apologetic to assure itself that the questions are not questions. What started out as a legitimate defense of the faith has become a circular rhetoric which convinces no one who does not already profess that faith. We have reached the point where an Orthodox Jew who does not subscribe to the apologetic, who instead takes a fresh look into the system to find new answers, will have his Orthodox credentials seriously challenged. The very suggestion that the questions are real, let alone in need of a new approach, has become for much of the Orthodox community a "Conservative" or "Reform" thing to do. If exponents of non-Orthodox movements have made "the need for change" their watchword, and in its name have abolished or watered down much of Jewish observance, then words like "change," "new," and even "interpret" become for a defensive Orthodoxy a vocabulary of heresy. If non-Orthodox Jews subject Jewish law to the arbitration of conscience (with non-observance being the frequent result) then "conscience" becomes for a defensive Orthodoxy synonymous with "doing whatever you want and calling it Judaism." Such a stance not only closes off meaningful communication between Orthodox and non-Orthodox Jews. It also closes off the possibility that Orthodoxy will ever deal honestly with the questions raised, questions which genuine seekers necessarily ask. And so the circle closes: fear of dangerous ideas leads to fear of dangerous words, which in turn leads to a refusal to acknowledge that the questions are questions, let alone that they may have exciting and enriching answers.

Where does this Orwellian cycle lead? It leads to what the late Professor Heschel, of blessed memory, called pan-halachism: the notion that all Jewish religious questions are reducible to disinterested halachic questions. In the pan-halachic universe, Jewish law is nothing more than a vast storage-and-retrieval system, operating on the one unchanging program fed into it when it was first plugged in. The halachist is a master key-punch operator who feeds raw data into the system, punches the right keys, and invariably gets the right answers—one and only one per question. Subjective considerations, such as the halachist's personal outlook and experiences and the unique ways these shape his vision of the whole, cannot be permitted to enter the operation, for they would undermine the system's divine perfection—which is to say, its total objectivity.

When Jewish law becomes a storage-and-retrieval system and the halachist a master retriever, and when each question is susceptible of one and only one answer, people expect that the single admissible answer to each halachic question must invariably be dualistic: kosher or trefe, permitted or forbidden, mandated or exempt. There can be no room for multiple solution models like, "The range of halachically acceptable or desirable options in this particular situation is a, b, c, and d." Though such models are precisely the kind required by the complex social issues which characterize this age of unprecedentedly rapid social change, they are the kind offered least frequently by today's jurists of Jewish law. Why is this so?

Pan-halachism leads to dualism—everything is reducible to yes or no, good or bad. This dualistic approach leads in turn to authoritarianism. The authoritarian mind fears the freedom to make moral decisions, especially where right and wrong choices are so sharply marked, the more so where the context is a law purporting to be divine. There is simply too much personal responsibility in making such decisions. Of course, some degree of trepidation is in order if one is not to make moral decisions in a cavalier manner. Moreover, the Jew who keeps Shabbat in a world where it's always Saturday knows only too well how fatally tempting it is to tolerate greater and greater ambiguity—and error—until one becomes a *vochedike* person, celebrating a Shabbat that is not Shabbat, losing touch, thereby, with the ground of Jewish being. How unassailably secure one's fortress feels if, instead, questions about family planning, the use of heroic life-sustaining measures, or the limits of waging justified warfare can all be answered with the same dualistic "kosher or trefe" with which a "cooking spoon" question is answered! The surrender of one's personal moral autonomy becomes, for many, a fair price to pay for this feeling. Some, in fact, deem it a duty to ask a rebbe or a yeshiva dean to make all major personal decisions for them—from whether and whom to marry, to whether or not to go ahead with an operation, to how to feel about affirmative action.

When authoritarianism becomes the dominant mood of Orthodox Judaism, everyone, including the leading jurists of Jewish law, feels compelled to move a step to the right. It is hard to resist the compulsion: one doesn't wish to find oneself suddenly on the outside. The situation is sometimes described as follows: A little old winemaker in Meah Shearim is the world's supreme arbiter of Jewish law. Why? The Haredim community of Meah Shearim and New York would like to be just a little more liberal, but they're afraid he won't think they are religious enough. Rabbi X, a leading right-wing jurist of Jewish law, would like to be a little more liberal, but he's afraid the Haredim won't think he is religious enough. Rabbi Y, a leading left-wing jurist of Jewish law, would like to be a little more liberal, but he's afraid Rabbi X won't.... Like most such fables, this one is exaggerated, but not by much. Orthodox Jews go on querying and jurists of Jewish law go on responding, as should be the case, yet two things most urgently needed are lacking: The first is an open climate of inquiry, in which all questions—even those whose answers have long been considered foregone—are addressed on their internal merits and not on their political overtones. And the second is the generation of multiplistic halachic models for responding to complex social questions.

But the authoritarian spirit carries over from halachah into theology, so that, whereas the tradition offers varying doctrinal languages for articulating Jewish faith, modern Orthodoxy holds fast to one language and roundly rejects all others. This narrowed agadic perspective in turn reinforces the pan-halachic, authoritarian climate of Jewish law, thereby rendering ever less likely the possibility of a more open climate. Healthy reverence for our illustrious forebears, the prophets and sages, has become a dogma of regression: every generation further from Sinai is assumed to be roughly one more light-year away from moral worth and intellectual certitude, and our generation (whichever it may be) is the lowest yet. We can no longer innovate, we can but restate and refine. Attempts at innovation, particularly when they involve the appropriation of a rejected or untried doctrinal language, render one's Orthodox credentials suspect. Orthodox Jews, it is maintained, all affirm their faith the same way, and have always done so. A person affirming Orthodox faith in an unconventional doctrinal language isn't really Orthodox, though he may style himself so. (Why anyone but a believer would want to style himself Orthodox in a world where it's so much more advantageous to be styled something else is never explained.) And how does one prove that an unconventional form of faith-affirmation is unacceptable? The very fact that it is unconventional is all the proof that is required.

Authoritarianism ultimately leads to (and is reinforced by) a basic distrust of the self. The individual is viewed as inherently so vicious that, were he not reined in by God's law, he would sooner or later rape his neighbor's wife in the Temple on Yom Kippur that falls on Shabbat. If a spoonful of medicine is good for you, a bottleful is marvelous. So bring on the restrictions: where the Torah or the sages left some openings, fill them in not with moral options but with prohibitions. Perhaps our righteous ancestors (that is, anyone who lived at least one generation before us) could have exercised moral options, but we degenerates cannot. All authority resides in someone else, and that person is either dead or out of town. In such a universe, *na'aseh* (we shall do, obey) is not, as we are taught, the prerequisite for *nishma* (we shall hear, understand) but rather its antithesis; one's deepest moral and religious impulses are disguised lusts; conscience is expediency; and multiplistic halachic models and doctrinal languages are tricks of Satan.

The painful "chad gadya" I have been rehearsing here is my attempt to describe from within how Orthodox Judaism, in an effort to save the last Shabbat table left in a world of Saturday, has turned itself gradually into a garrison state. I am angry enough to want Orthodoxy to find its way out again, and confident enough in the self-regenerating power of God's Torah and in the decency of Orthodox Jewry to believe we can find that way. But to be motivated to look for the way, we need a powerful catalyst.

I contend that we have such a catalyst in the questions raised by Jewish feminism. At present, Orthodox Judaism resists dealing with these questions, perhaps more than with any others. Yet, precisely because the halachic, agadic, and theological implications of these questions are so radical and far-reaching, our ability to deal with them adequately will be a measure of the truth of our claim that "the Torah of the Lord is perfect, renewing life" (Psalms 19:8).

Dealing honestly with the feminist questions means confronting our own fears and stereotypes and getting past them before we are entitled to invoke a single halachic category. For we are, in this area, dealing with an interplay of unstated, perhaps unrealized, fears: those associated with ordinary feminism, as well as special fears like these: Since Jewish law and myth, starting with the Bible, are male-centered, won't the pursuit of these questions lead from doubt to heresy, from heresy to overthrow of the system? (It isn't just a fear that men will lose their privileged status; it's a dread that Judaism itself simply cannot become egalitarian and still remain Judaism.) Is it even meaningful to speak of separating Judaism from patriarchalism? Isn't that like separating the statue from the marble—possible in philosophy but not in sculpture? If it is meaningful to speak of separating Judaism from patriarchalism, how would we go about doing it? How far could we go in reinterpreting halachah before we'd find ourselves smack-up against some locked doors? What could we do when we got there? Would we be willing to make those changes now that are possible under our present understanding of halachah, and would we be willing to back them up?

We have shown the world that the Torah's NO is NO, because that is what we felt we had to do. Now it is time to show that the Torah's YES is YES. It is not enough to generate from within Jewish law ingenious emergency responses to new situations. We must generate from within Jewish law the kinds of moral initiatives which would seize each new situation and liberate its inner spark of holiness. Indeed, the very effort of doing this would call forth our strongest faith, our finest religious sensibilities, our loftiest prayer. Our table would again become the source of light and music, bread and wine for a dark and troubled world—not just for those of us who already cherish its delights. For it is in choosing to keep God's law that we learn who God is—and it is in the exercising of conscience within the framework of God's law that we learn who we are.

THUMBS AND EGGS
DAVID SINGER

David Singer is Director of Information and Research Services at the American Jewish Committee and the editor of the AJC's American Jewish Year Book.

Why was this Passover different from every other Passover? Because along with large numbers of other Orthodox laymen, I had access to Rabbi Shimon Eider's *A Summary of Halachos (Laws) of Pesach*. More precisely, we pored over two installments of his study; installments dealing with forbidden and permissible products, and with the requirements of the seder. Next year, when Rabbi Eider presents his final installment, taking up matters relating to the disposal of hametz and the kashering of utensils, he will have said just about everything that can be said about Passover from a halachic perspective. He will have also—and Rabbi Eider may not be fully aware of this—driven the last nail into the coffin of Orthodox folk religion. Let me explain.

Sociologists distinguish between elite and folk religion. Elite religion, as Charles Liebman has expressed it, consists of the "ritual, belief, and doctrine which the acknowledged religious leaders teach to be the religion." Elite religion is fully self-conscious, well defined, and anchored in an authoritative interpretation of sacred texts. Folk religion, on the other hand, is the popular religious culture. It is expressed primarily through ritual and symbol, rather than precise doctrinal formulation, and is rooted in tradition and custom. In terms of Orthodox Judaism, elite religion is best represented by the circles of rabbinic scholars, while folk religion finds a place for itself mainly among the unlettered masses.

In a very real sense, the story of Orthodox Judaism in America is a tale of the triumph of elite over folk religion. While in Europe both variants of Orthodoxy always existed side by side, in the United States, prior to World War II, it was the folk type that was completely dominant. This is attributable to the fact that the rabbinic scholars and their followers refused to emigrate to a *trefa* land. Orthodox Jewry, at that point in time, constituted, with but few exceptions, a community of *am haratzim*. Small wonder then, that Jewish education was woefully neglected, that religious observance was notoriously lax, and that so many nominally Orthodox Jews drifted into the Conservative movement.

With the Second World War, however, a radical change came about. For the first time, large numbers of Jews, deeply committed to elite Orthodoxy, and most particularly to its emphasis on *lernen*, i.e., intensive Torah study, came to the United States. At their head were the talmudic scholars who had held sway in the great East European yeshivot; men who were determined to recreate in the United States the pattern of life they had known in the Old World. Before long, academies for advanced Talmud study were founded, tight-knit communities were established, and elite Orthodox patterns of thought and behavior began to make themselves felt in the Orthodox community as a whole. The much talked about Orthodox "move to the right"—a phenomenon which has been apparent for the past twenty-five years, and which continues unabated today—is directly attributable to the influence of the elite Orthodox cadres.

Until fairly recently, the message of elite Orthodoxy was conveyed by men who spoke only Yiddish—a factor which hindered the full dissemination of elite ideas and perspectives among the highly Americanized "modern" element of the Orthodox community. Now, however, a large body of English language material has made its appearance, including several works by Rabbi Eider. Indeed, Rabbi Eider, in addition to authoring volumes dealing with the laws of the Sabbath, Succot, and Passover, has prepared tape cassettes covering the same topics. If *A Summary of Halachos of Pesach* stands out among this material, it is because it underscores especially well the demise of folk Orthodoxy.

By its very nature—i.e., because

of the complexity of its laws, and because it brings to the fore powerful oral anxieties and cleanliness concerns—Passover provides a golden opportunity for folk religion to manifest itself. To be sure, the exact ritual requirements of the holiday are laid out in the corpus of rabbinic writings. The point, however, is that the masses of Jews, throughout Jewish history, never (either because of a lack of ability or a lack of concern) consulted these works. What they did do, in the classic fashion of folk religion, was to take note of the practices that prevailed at home and in the community. Sometimes—as with the laws pertaining to the seder ritual—these practices did not measure up to the standards of elite Orthodoxy. In other instances—as in the case of the laws concerning prohibited foods—they went far beyond the demands of the halachah. While the rabbinic leadership was well aware of this situation, it did little about it, in part because it lacked an effective communications system, and in part because it felt little compulsion to act. After all, folk Orthodoxy was the "law" as far as the masses were concerned, and could anything better be expected of *amcha*?

Rabbi Eider will have none of this. Reflecting the aggressive mood of contemporary elite Orthodoxy—an Orthodoxy cut off from its roots in Europe, and thus from any organic ties to the folk religion of the masses—he wants to make *every* Jew aware of the *exact* requirements of the halachah. Hence his use of English, and his preparation of tape cassettes; hence also his explanation of the logic behind the laws, and his careful citation of sources. To anyone raised in a folk Orthodox environment, *A Summary of Halachos of Pesach* is an amazing eye opener. It turns out that perfume, hair spray and roll-on deodorant are hametz and are not permitted on Passover; that milk, sugar, coffee, and concentrated frozen juice, if purchased before the holiday, may be used on Passover, even though they don't have Kosher for Pesach labels; that rice, corn, and legumes may be owned and displayed (though not eaten) during the holiday; that there are specific points in the seder ritual when it is obligatory to recline, and that reclining is always on the left side; that romaine lettuce rather than horseradish is the preferred bitter herb; that the haroset is shaken off the bitter herb before the latter is eaten; that it is not permissible to point to the shankbone on the seder plate; that virtually all of the laws relating to the seder are binding on women as well as men; that a portion of the Haggadah has to be read in the vernacular if the seder participants do not understand Hebrew; and, that under certain circumstances, it is possible to fulfill the commandment of the four cups by drinking coffee rather than wine.

Which brings me to the thumbs and eggs. Every Orthodox Jew is aware that it is obligatory to eat an olive-size piece of matzah at the seder. Rabbi Eider and the elite Orthodox possess the additional knowledge that the same measure applies to the bitter herb, the korech (the matzah and bitter herb sandwich) and the afikomen that are consumed. More remarkably, though, they also know that "olive-size" has nothing to do with the run-of-the-mill olive, and that, in fact, it represents, in terms of the *realia* of the seder, pieces of matzah 6¼ x 7 inches, portions of romaine lettuce leaves covering an area 8 x 10 inches, and servings of horseradish sufficient to fill three tablespoons. How is this possible? As Rabbi Eider explains it, it has its source in the fact that the Talmud mentions two ways of determining the proper measure; one involving the use of thumbs, the other of eggs. When Rabbi Ezekiel Landau, a noted 18th century scholar, compared the two methods, he discovered to his dismay that they did not square. Since, he reasoned, the size of the human thumb had not doubled since talmudic times, it had to be that the typical egg is only half the size of the one the Talmud had in mind. Hence his advocacy of doubling the egg measure; hence—since an olive is considered to be half the size of an egg—elite Orthodoxy's super king-size olive.

It takes some doing for the folk Orthodox to adjust to elite standards. In Stamford, Connecticut, where I live, there was palpable tension in the air prior to Passover, as people fretted whether they would be able to "do it right on seder night." Eating large amounts of matzah and bitter herb is no small trick, especially when you are trying to consume the individual portions in less than two minutes each, and when you have been drinking cups containing 3.3 ounces of wine. Of course, the mandatory silence during this part of the seder helps; it makes it easier to concentrate on the task of eating. And there is a bonus for the women: after all the matzah and bitter herb, who has room for a multi-course festive meal?

It is difficult to imagine a set of circumstances arising that would make for a revitalization of Orthodox folk religion on the American scene. The victory of elite Orthodoxy is nearly complete and probably final. One looks forward, therefore, to a spate of publications by Rabbi Eider and other elite spokesmen covering the full range of the halachah, ethics as well as ritual. This year Passover, next year gossip and business ethics.

ARROGANCE AND AUTHENTICITY
JACOB NEUSNER

Jacob Neusner is University Professor and Ungerleider Distinguished Scholar of Judaic Studies at Brown University.

When you consider the power of Judaism, realized most fully and profoundly in Orthodoxy, you must wonder why every Jew should not be Orthodox and Judaic—not merely Jewish.

The grandeur of the Judaic perspective on humanity, the extraordinary relevance of that perspective to everyday practice, the ineffable beauty of the consequent way of living, a holy way of living, separate and distinct, in full measure congruent with the profound meaning of our mortality and our human striving—what is life without that vision? And how can people turn their backs upon it?

Who are we when we do not live up to that image which is God's and ours? And what can we be when we fully reckon with that image? This, to me, is what shapes the transcendent and compelling call to Orthodoxy, the true Judaic way of life.

And yet. And yet, the great majority of North American Jews who choose to be religious also choose not to be Orthodox, and a near majority of them choose not to be religious at all.

So there is the paradox: the power and mystery of Judaism on the one hand, the indifference of the Jews to Judaism on the other. Since, we must all agree, Orthodoxy is the fullest expression of Judaism, we surely have the right to turn to Orthodoxy for some insight into the current paradox.

Nor should we underestimate the force of that paradox. When young Jews wish to resume the holy way given up by their parents or grandparents—when they become *ba'alei t'shuvah,* "reverters" to Judaism—what is it to which they revert? It is the Orthodox way. That fact accounts for the growing traditionalism of Jewish Theological Seminary and Conservative Judaism, and even for the kosher eating facilities at Hebrew Union College.

People perceive, and I think rightly, that Orthodoxy keeps the grail (to use an inappropriate but weighty metaphor) of the holy way of life called Judaism. So when they return, they take for granted that it must be to Orthodoxy. And many others will concur that Orthodoxy is the standard by which all Judaism is measured.

And so it is—alas!

For if we claim that the keepers of the grail have allowed it to become tarnished, who can differ? Surely that grand perspective of who we are and what we may become, of ourselves in God's likeness and in accord with God's image, is lost. Are we not told by students of every cult and crackpot outfit, from Jews for Jesus to Reverend Moon, that Jews make up not three or four percent of their followers but sixteen to sixty percent? (Moon tells us the Jews must be a very holy people, they produce so many members for his church.) And sociologists tell us again and again that the young Jews (among others) in these cults go there for something they do not find at home, for a vivid life of the soul, a seeking after God and holiness that they cannot perceive in Judaism!

Still, why draw evidence from marginal people ("apostates")? And why indict the keepers of the grail for conditions so far beyond their control? There is better proof, nearer to the center of things, that greatness is gone from Orthodoxy, therefore from Judaism: There is evidence not only of omission—to which, after all, Orthodoxy can plausibly plead extenuating circumstances. There is evidence of commission as well. When an Orthodox Jew says, "He is very religious," what follows—that "he is a person who fears God," or "who loves his fellow man?" No. More likely, "He waits seven hours between milk and meat." "He eats only *glatt kosher.*" "He won't even eat a hard boiled egg in the home of a Conservative rabbi."

Everyone knows the measure of religiosity, and it is not ever by a standard of religious practice of other than ritualistic character. It is as if Orthodoxy wishes to prove right every piece of garbage about ritualism and self-righteousness which the enemies of Judaism have swept up to throw against Judaism for four centuries, since Luther.

It would be unfair to invoke, in this context, the names of Orthodox rabbis who were tried and convicted of exploitation of old and sick people. Nor are we interested in the many examples of a certain Orthodox indifference to ethics when "outsiders" are concerned. These are not the issues. The issue is how we may describe the face of Orthodoxy to the Jewish world itself, to Reform and Conservative Jews, and to the "non-religious?"

Does Orthodoxy approach that world with love and affection? Is its message one of the sanctification of all Israel, of the precious worth and holy meaning of every Jewish soul? Does Orthodoxy rejoice in the (admittedly imperfect) efforts of the non-Orthodox religious Jew to keep the faith and practice it?

Faced with its greatest opportunity in nearly two hundred years to regain the attention of the Jewish people, confronted by a generation of reversion to Judaism, Orthodoxy's face is frowning, not smiling. Its message is a tale of contempt to the non-Orthodox religious Jews. Except for the handful able to adopt the Orthodox way of life in all details and assimilate into Orthodox circles, Orthodoxy has nothing but ugly and unfriendly words. Orthodoxy does not love the Jewish people—unless they are Orthodox.

It did not have to be this way. There were great Orthodox rabbis who came to Westernized Jews with messages of love, with hope for a return (which finally has come about, but not under Orthodox auspices in the main). Israel Salanter in the 19th century, the great Palestinian chief rabbi, Rav Kook in the 20th—these are only two names revered by all Jews. When Jewry was unready, Orthodoxy sent forth leaders of good sense and good will. Now that the Jews are ready, ready to hear the authentic message of holiness and Torah as spoken by Orthodox voices, Orthodoxy—with only a few exceptions—speaks gibberish—and with a grimace to boot.

What, after all, is the human message of Orthodoxy? Out of the chosenness of Israel and the holiness of the Land of Israel, Orthodoxy in the State of Israel (with powerful support from North America) has made an irredentist and militarist, pseudo-Messianic ideal of keeping everything we can and throwing out the rest. True, there was Joshua. But there was also Isaiah.

Out of the holy way of life, a mode of living meant to sanctify each gesture and each moment, a way of life supposed to open our hearts to God and our minds to Torah, Orthodoxy has created a pattern of petty and trivial nonsense, a set of contemptible and humanly irrelevant gestures, practiced in a spirit of punctilious pride.

Out of the holy Torah, an intellectual tradition of amazing brilliance and continuing power, Orthodoxy has fashioned a set of propositions of dubious truth and little fact. A once reasonable tradition of religious learning now requires the denial of facts in the name of faith. It is only an accident that some *rav* has not yet declared a fundamental article of faith to be belief that the world is flat. Yeshivot, for their part, treat learning as pure ritual, so that merely repeating words, without understanding what they mean, is taken as a holy act.

And when we turn to the "modern Orthodox" and ask them for a Jewish message, what is it that we hear? We hear politics, polemic and right-wingism (especially where the State of Israel is concerned), diatribes against Conservative and Reform Judaism. Parades of words, spoken without passion and conceived without anguish, words which say absolutely nothing—and do so insultingly.

In a different context, Ray Sokolov recently had this to say about Robert Gordis' new book on Judaism and sex: "The real problem with this book is that it cannot hope to persuade thousands of apostate Jews of anything except that they were right to abandon formal Jewish observance—not so much because of the rigid views of the rabbinate, but because of the irrelevant and empty language that 'modern' leaders ... spew out in a simplistic and vacant attempt to win young people back to the fold. ... Such rhetoric says nothing and makes the skeptic yawn. Such mindless sermonizing is exactly what has driven many modern Jews into secular forms of Jewish life."

The critique is even more appropriate when applied to the Orthodox. It is simply not the case, as "outsiders" sometimes imagine, that Orthodoxy—unlike the Reform and Conservative movements—speaks clearly and decisively. The difference is that it hides its confusion behind a mask of authenticity. It is Orthodoxy that claims—and I think fairly and rightly—to be authentic and (in its vulgar and embarrassing phrase) "Torah-true." But precisely because its claim is fair and right, its expression of that claim is tragic, its arrogant demeanor an offense. "Authenticity" is no substitute for thought or for manners. It does not excuse either self-righteousness or the affectation of certainty.

For beyond and above Orthodoxy, organized and unorganized, lies the Judaism that is still best preserved in its richness and its mystery by—Orthodoxy itself. We cannot forget, after all, that the Torah studied by Orthodoxy and in mindless yeshivot is still the Hebrew Bible and the Talmud. The Pentateuch and the prophets are read fully and accurately in Orthodox synagogues. The works of the great rationalists, like Maimonides, the great mystics, like the Besht, still are opened and taken seriously—for more than a fifty-minute classroom lecture—by the Orthodox. When Jews want to live by the teachings of the great souls and minds of a tradition of four thousand years, they rightly turn to Orthodoxy. And that is precisely why we have a right to ask of Orthodoxy, for its part, that it take seriously the methods and meanings of those teachings.

DOING AND BELIEVING A ROUND-TABLE DISCUSSION

Myer (Mike) Weiner, dentist, Professor at Tufts University, Medford

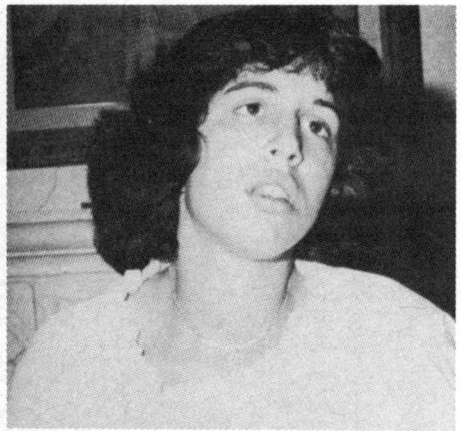

Miriam Isserow, Feldman Hebrew High, New York

Judah (Yudi) Stone, lawyer, Boston

Saul Isserow, metallurgist for US Army, Watertown

Faye Isserow, incoming freshman, Princeton University.

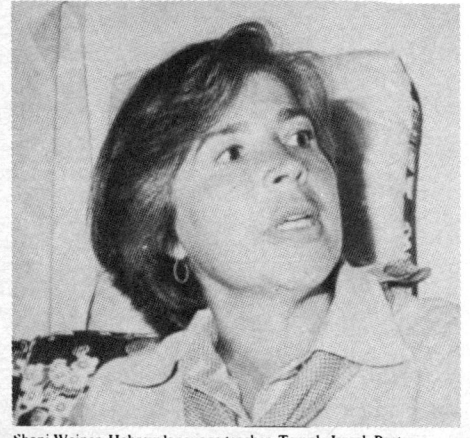

Shani Weiner, Hebrew language teacher, Temple Israel, Boston

Burton Rabinowitz, cardiologist, St. Vincent's Hospital, Boston

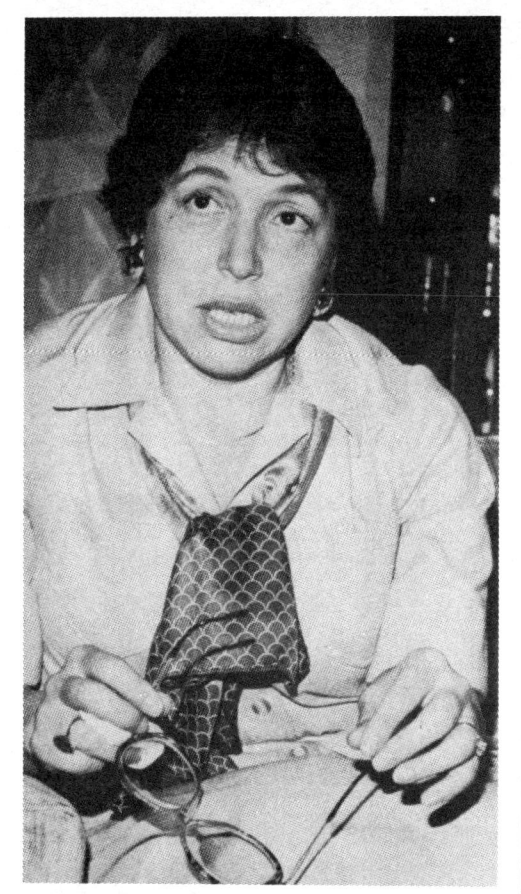

Rochelle Isserow, speech therapist, Winchester Public Schools

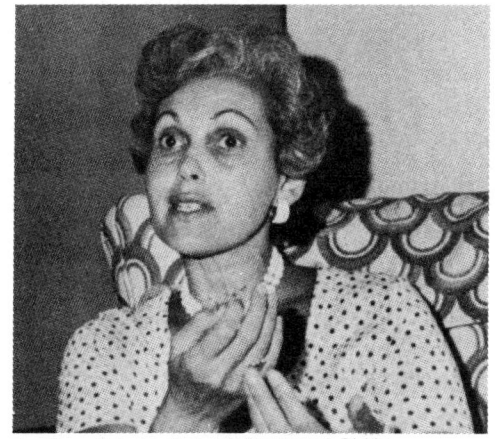

Carol Stone, Campaign Chairman of the Women's Division, Combined Jewish Philanthropies, Boston

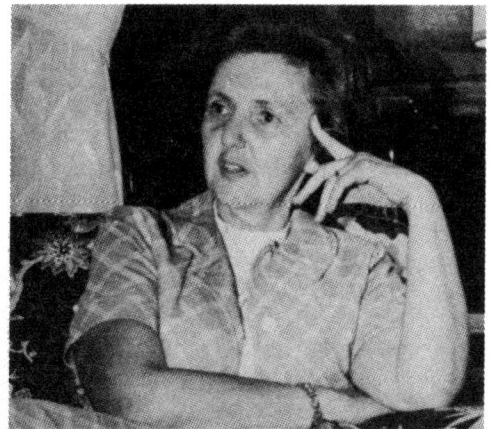

Surri Rabinovici, English teacher, Hebrew day school

Last month, MOMENT's editors spent an evening with eleven Orthodox Jews, members of Brookline's Young Israel congregation. The conversation—which just skimmed the surface—dealt with what it means to be an Orthodox Jew in America today.

Moment: Is it hard work to be Orthodox?
Morry: Not if you feel that's what you want to do. If you pulled someone off the street and said to him, "Poof! You're Orthodox," that might be tough on him. But I enjoy it; it's the way I live.
Surri: The acceptance of ethnicity these days makes it easier. I went to a high school where 90 percent of the students were Jewish, but only a very small number were observant. We were very conscious back then of how our being observant made us different from the other kids. There was real insecurity and embarrassment about it. Now, there's so much greater tolerance for difference that you're no longer considered an oddball if you have particular dietary restrictions, or if you wear a kippah. When my brother was growing up, he and all his friends wore baseball caps all the time, so they could meet the halachic requirement to keep their heads covered without calling special attention to themselves. Now no one looks twice at a kippah.
Faye: It is easier, or more convenient, now. But the tolerance itself can sometimes be offensive. Kids will say to me, "Wow, you're into kosher," or "Your thing is Shabbos," as if we're all freaks together—one person mediating, another one davvening, one person shaving his head, another wearing a kippah. It makes me a little sick to have halachic Judaism reduced to a fad, a shtick.
Rochelle: I find being observant a real hassle, largely because I work full time and have to make Shabbos. Even non-working women find preparing for Shabbos a chore. And when it comes to the holidays, it's even harder. This fall I'll be missing the students I see only on Mondays and Tuesdays for three weeks in a row, and that's a pretty hard thing to explain or to deal with. And then, of course, there's the problem of my Jewish colleagues. The non-Jews accept my kosher food, accept the fact that I won't eat in their homes. But the other Jews make a big deal out of it. One day, at the lunchroom table, I said the word "mikva," and there were peals of laughter. If I were to explain mikva to an Irish friend, I'm sure she'd understand it and respect it. But a young Jewish woman who had grown up in Brooklyn simply couldn't believe that people were still doing it. She found the word a source of merriment. So I do think that being Orthodox makes you self-conscious, and you've got to decide for yourself whether it's worth the hassle.
M: Just at the mechanical level, doesn't the attention to detail take up a great deal of your time?
Mike: It's a way of life. How can a way of life be time-consuming? Living this way simply provides a structure to the time.
Rochelle: I couldn't live without Shabbos. I just couldn't. Look, I'm sure I could enjoy a shrimp cocktail, and if shrimp ever becomes kosher, I'll indulge. But I don't want to live without Shabbos. And I don't want to live without the other things. We don't have to build a Succah; we want to.

M: Can we talk for a bit about belief?
Saul: It's interesting that when an outsider talks or thinks about Orthodoxy, he tends to emphasize belief. But from the inside, we are more concerned with practice. I don't even know whether my wife and I agree on belief.
Rochelle: I don't think I've ever asked anyone in this room about belief.
Faye: Kids talk about it all the time. After all, being observant is a hassle, and there are so many tempting things going on in this world. If you don't believe, why should you practice? Even the sense of community doesn't justify it.

A Symposium on Orthodoxy

Miriam: (to her parents) If you didn't believe it, why did you bring us up this way? It may have been fun for you, but why impose it on me?

Saul: We never taught you that you were supposed to believe this or that. We taught you what to do.

Miriam: But you must have taught us something about God when we were little; it's absurd to do it the other way around.

Shanni: When I was growing up, I didn't know there was any other kind of life. I had no idea that there were other ways of being Jewish, that there was a Jewish life outside of Borough Park. It never occurred to me to ask myself whether I believed in what I was doing. If that ever happened, it happened when I started studying philosophy and ethics. And the fact is that we have done the same thing with our own children. We have given them the chance to grow up in a particular life-style. We don't talk about belief; we live. And the children seem happy and well-adjusted. Now that I think of it, it's hard to imagine that we've never really talked about belief, but we haven't.

Carol: I come at this from a somewhat different perspective, because everyone here grew up as part of an Orthodox milieu, but I didn't. Yudi and I really had to sit down and make a decision as to whether or not we wanted this hassle, and that meant that we had to ask ourselves what we believe. And we spent some pretty sleepless nights discussing where we were coming from and where we were going, what we wanted to do with our children and with ourselves. It wasn't an easy decision; it involves changing your whole life-style. And when we started talking about it and thinking about it, the most important thing was continuity. I had to ask myself what my responsibility is. Could I really tell my children to light the Shabbos candles because their grandmother had done it? I wanted my parents to be Jewish and my kids to be Jewish but where did I belong?

M: To a non-Orthodox Jew, it sometimes seems that Orthodox Jews know things—or think they know things—the rest of us don't know. Do you?

Mike: Orthodox Jews do things. That is, there are many questions you can ask yourself before you do anything, and for us, the halachic framework tells us many of the answers. It tells us when to do, where to do, how to do, and so forth. "Why?" is the very last question to be asked. In the course of answering the when, where and how, you gradually absorb the why. If you start with the why, you'll never do anything, you'll never get anywhere.

Miriam: No. First you have to come to the why. And the answer to the why is that what we have is the truth. Then everything else falls into place. If we don't feel that what we are doing is right, then Orthodoxy is meaningless.

Burt: I come from a house where questions were never asked, where it was taken for granted that I would follow a traditional way of life. And I think what you are asking is why, if I believe, do I need all the external structure of Orthodox Judaism? I've been through this in my own life; I've spent a great deal of time thinking about it. And what I've come up with by way of an answer is that by structuring your life, you may, on occasion, derive some of the real meaning that religion has. I've found that if I do away with some of the structural aspects of religion I lose touch completely with what religion has to say to me. That doesn't mean that every time you perform a religious act you really bring home the feeling of religion. But without such acts, you never have that feeling. Religious life is founded on action, even if one cannot always fathom the purpose of the action.

I happen to work in a Catholic hospital. I answer my phone on Shabbos, and I work on Shabbos. That creates real difficulties for me. Almost every time I violate the Shabbos, I ask myself whether I am doing the right thing, whether I should be doing it, what effect it will have on the general condition of religion.

Mike: That's the point. Every time an Orthodox Jew does do something, he is forced to think in religious terms. When the phone rings on Saturday, you have to think "Should I pick it up or shouldn't I," "Is this a life-involving call that I should answer?" When you choose a box of cookies, you read the label. Whatever action you take in life, you take with your religion in mind. You are reminded of it who knows how many times each day.

Judah: My secretary, who is Catholic, once said to me, "You know, Mr. Stone, I go to Mass every Sunday, and that's when I think about being Catholic, but you are Jewish all day long." And I think she hit something there. Even though most Orthodox Jews spend almost all of their social time with other Orthodox Jews, their professional lives are spent in very mixed settings. That's true for me. But I think Jewishly all day long.

It's not really a question of belief. My belief really derives from an historical analysis of Jewish survival. We, the people sitting here, and our children, are the last generation of Galut—of Exile. Something that hasn't been given to any other generation, something for which Jews have prayed for centuries, was given to our generation. And I really feel this in a religious sense. Now, with that privilege goes a responsibility. And the responsibility is to keep the chain going. So my decision was to be a part of that chain. I think that Orthodox Judaism is the best means of preserving the next generation, as well as of promoting good.

Rochelle: It takes unacceptable pride to say, "With me the chain is over, with me it ends, because I'm going to intermarry, or I'm going to drop out of Orthodoxy." You can't deny the facts: Judaism survives on maximalism.

I can't really talk about belief. Take *Torah miSinai*, Revelation. Do I know what form that took? Does Rabbi Soloveitchik? Did Maimonides? I think there was a

huge discrepancy among the sages throughout the centuries. Am I going to be a fundamentalist, and believe that each letter matters? When I was in my twenties, I used to talk about these things. But now my answer is that I believe in the halachic process—with reservations. Of course, there's a problem: If I believe in the halachic process, what am I doing here barelegged and with my head uncovered? What gives me the right to be the kind of "relaxed" Orthodox person I am? And the way I cope with all of that is to practice Judaism to the very best of my ability, which obviously means that I fail in any number of ways. Still, I'm very self-conscious as a Jew, and I like that. It's neurotic, but I like it. I feel comfortable with it.
Burt: Still, you're drawing lines. You feel yourself to be part of the chain, but you're making personal decisions about what matters and what doesn't. How do you do that? Is it an intellectual decision, or is it based on convenience?
Rochelle: A great deal of it is tradition. A great deal of it is trying to be as consistent as possible for my children, and as open as possible about my failings. And a great deal of it is the result of a long, heavy, hard intellectual battle, which I fought mostly when I was in my twenties. And yes, a great deal of it does have to do with comfort and convenience.
Saul: My father was a hardbitten *misnaged,* and he once told me a wonderful story about the Hassidic rebbe who could never davven. Why? Because when he got up in the morning and started with the *Modeh Ani L'fanecha* he would get bogged down on each word. What does it mean to say *"modeh,"* to be grateful? And what about *"ani,"* I? And so forth, and by the time he was finished with his thinking it was too late to davven. That's what happens when you put belief before practice. The real question for us is whether Judaism can survive in the diaspora without Orthodoxy, without observance? And there is just no evidence that it can. Observance is what keeps us together and keeps us going. Now, if you want to ask why we should want to keep going, that's a different question. And somewhere, in answering that question, God comes into the picture. Maybe He has some purpose in mind for us. So that's why we stay committed. And commitment means covenant and commandment.

M: But commitment and covenant mean different things to different Orthodox people. Is it the case that "more" is always "better"? Do you think you are, in some sense, better than Reform Jews, and, if you do, that Agudah Orthodoxy is better than your version of Orthodoxy?
Mike: No, we need the right wing. It keeps modern Orthodoxy closer to the line.

M: Let's put that question into a different form. My own family is Reform; in our own way, we think of ourselves as observant. Halachically, we're no place. But I don't think that being Jewish is less important to us than it is to any of you, and when we talk about it, we use the same words. I've talked to my children about our being links in a chain on many occasions. How do you perceive me? How do you feel about me?
Saul: I wish you luck, but I think your chances are slim. How do you transmit historical continuity? How many of the original Reform families have survived as Jews? I'm not even sure that Conservative Judaism has demonstrated its capacity to survive and to insure Jewish continuity.
Faye: Besides, until a hundred years ago or so, Judaism was halachic Judaism. I haven't worked it out how after a couple of thousand years people can just announce that suddenly there's a new strain, a new version.
Mike: The point is that you still have your parents and grandparents to fall back on, to transmit to you. Who will transmit to your children?

M: I transmit to my children.
Mike: Fine, then if they continue to transmit to their children, the continuity is protected.
Burt: But that is where the structure comes in. That's how things get transmitted.

M: I don't want to be on trial here. The question is how you feel about Jews like me?
Rochelle: I don't feel about you. I don't even think about you. I hate to be mean, but when I stop and think about it, I say you must have a hell of a problem. I've got it made. I don't know what's going to happen when Faye goes to Princeton or when Miriam goes to whatever school she'll go to. They may or may not continue in this way. But I think I've done as much as I can to have them go into the mold. And when I look at our Orthodox community in Brookline, I see that we haven't yet lost one person. Not one kid has rebelled or opted out.
Shanni: The question of how we perceive each other goes both ways. I teach at a Reform temple, and I feel as though I'm on trial there. They watch every move I make. I love the experience, I love the children, and yet I have to answer for my religious outlook. Maybe it's just curiosity, but I feel that they are looking for horns when they look at me. It's better than it used to be, but they still don't understand our world and our ways.
Mike: We are trying to blend the best part of the Jewish world and the best part of Western society. And we are doing that with our children growing up in the outside world, exposed to all the dangers and the attractions and the temptations. And we want simply to give them the best background we can so that they can face up to it.

M: What I heard you say in response to the earlier question is that you recognize and appreciate other forms of commitment to Judaism, but you think that they are likely to be ineffective. One can't be an active, practicing Jew if what one practices is something other than traditional Judaism. Is that a fair summary?
Surri: I don't like all these judg-

ments about other people. I don't make judgments about the relative rightness of my way compared to someone else's way. I am not the one to say what is THE way. The key to all of Jewish life is that every individual makes his own commitment in the way that he feels is most satisfying to him. And what I do is what feels right for me.
Burt: So that brings us right back to the question of how you decide where to draw the line. Yes to keeping the Shabbos, no to wearing a sheitel? How do you decide? The ultra-Orthodox see us as violating the law, and we ourselves are aware that our decisions regarding the drawing of the line may determine whether our children stay with us or not. How do you decide?
Rochelle: I'm not a philosopher, I'm a pragmatist. I don't go around checking tsitsis, and if a person tells me he is Orthodox and his home is kosher, I believe that and accept it. If I were to start judging, and deciding that such and such a person isn't kosher enough, I might drive him out of kashrut entirely.

My father once said about the ultra-Orthodox, "They can say whatever they want, but in Vilna or in Lodz, none of them would have been considered Orthodox." We all synthesize.

M: So once again we're back to the question. How do you synthesize? Doesn't it all become merely a matter of taste, opinion and convenience—a long cry from commandment?
Rochelle: I try to follow the halachic line.
Mike: That's the point. The halachah is the basic outfit, the dress and the shoes. Then, once you've got that, you can decide for yourself what other decorations you want.

M: But one person's basic outfit is another person's decoration, isn't it?
Judah: I'd like to go back to the earlier discussion about how we feel towards the non-observant Jew. Basically, I feel a camaraderie with him, since I come from the same background, but I also feel badly, because he is missing so much.
Faye: That's something people often ignore. They tend to think we are pedantic and stuffy, but when I look around this room, every family here has at one time or another had a boarder, a kid from the local day school who couldn't attend unless he lived nearby. Every family here always has a full house on Shabbos. People just call up and say, "I'm here for a week, make my bed." People really take their Judaism seriously. It's not just about davvening in the morning and getting it over with. People here have a strong sense of reaching out to the community at large.

M: If all that is so, how come the enormous gap between the Orthodox community and the rest of the community?
Carol: I work in the total community, with all its elements. And I don't consider the non-Orthodox ignorant, nor do I want them to consider me haughty. I don't want to sit in judgment on anyone. Nor do I like it when people say to me, "Oh, you're kosher," as if I had a disease. I do think a lot about this, because I am in the world. I realize that I am just window dressing for the Federation, and I realized before I accepted my position that I was going to represent all of Orthodoxy to the women I'd be working with. For many years, the Orthodox community was excluded from the Federation world, because their affairs were not kosher. I've tried to close that gap. I've argued that if you ask someone to come to your home, you don't only invite him to the living room. You also have to be able to ask him into your dining room, to offer him something to eat. That is simple courtesy and common respect.

The gap has narrowed, but it's still there. So we have to try to bridge it, beginning with a basic respect for each other as human beings. Now it's true that sometimes, because of halachah, we have to build a fence around ourselves in order to prevent a falling away. People sometimes don't understand that. But what's really been interesting to me is how many women who have said to me, "If I had it to do over, I'd do it your way." Especially about the kids, about how to raise your children. They say; "I envy your Shabbos."

Burt: Sure, there are Orthodox groups that look down on us. I think they are wrong, that they are out of touch with modernity. But I have to admit that we do want to isolate and insulate ourselves. We want to perpetuate this thing, and you can't perpetuate it if you actively associate with people who are uncommitted. The intercourse of ideas does lead to degeneration. And so we tend not to associate or to identify ourselves with others, and there are even laws that proscribe such association. And because of that, one feels there are barriers. And a lack of dialogue. Still, I think that the more comfortable you are with what you have chosen to do, the more apt you are to relate to anyone who wants to identify himself as a Jew.
Miriam: Maybe I'm young or naive, but I think the adults have been too apologetic. I feel that I believe, and if you believe then you think that what you are doing is right. It is the best way. And if it is the best way, it is the only way. Maybe I don't look down my nose at people who aren't observant, but once I've come to the decision that what I'm doing is right, then it follows that the people who don't do it are wrong. I'm sorry to say that, but if it is right to fulfill the mitzvot it's wrong not to. So I think that mine is the one right way.
Rochelle: I hope that's not the last word.

M: It appears, then, to be a question of normative Judaism. What seems monolithic when you're standing outside of it has as much uncertainty as anything else when you've come up close. And it is the coming close, the creation of dialogue, that maintains the questioning process.

★

THE SHATTERED TABLETS

How the process of living the Law came apart— and how it can be rediscovered

Gerson Cohen has retired as Chancellor of the Jewish Theological Seminary of America. He is Jacob Schiff Distinguished Service Professor of Jewish History and Chancellor Emeritus of the Jewish Theological Seminary of America.

This article is adapted from a speech he delivered at the 92nd Street Y in a series entitled "The Shattered Tablets: Jewish Spiritual Struggles with Modernity," presented jointly by the 92nd Street Y and the Radius Institute in January and February, 1984.

GERSON COHEN

In 1871 Rabbi Isaac Hirsch Weiss issued, in Vienna, the first of his five-volume history of rabbinic tradition, *Dor Dor v'Dorshav*. I have called it a history of rabbinic tradition, but more precisely the work is a history of the exegesis of Scripture and Talmud from their origins to the beginning of the 16th century. The underlying assumption of Weiss's work—and indeed of all rabbinics since the *Ethics of the Fathers*—is that when Moses was alone with God, enveloped in a cloud on Mt. Sinai for forty days and forty nights, he was given not only the Tablets and the law by which the people of Israel were to live for all time; he was also given the rules for the process by which Torah was to be interpreted and applied in every generation.

We call this application of the Torah to life, and the process, *the midrashic process*.

Thus, in classical Jewish perception, the history of the Torah is the history of midrash—the history of the interpretation of Torah *and* its application to life. We may even go one step further: The history of all Jewish culture, at least from the days of Ezra in the fifth century BCE until the secular rebellions of modern times, can be seen in terms of this process of interpretation and application. All Jewish legal, artistic, literary, philosophical and musical expression—all the myriad Jewish responses to the challenges and needs of different times and places—were, until recently, formulated by the canons of the midrashic process.

Since the rules for the interpretation of Scripture in the view of classical Judaism were themselves part of the revelation vouchsafed to Moses, they are, accordingly, as much Torah as the Torah itself. Hence, if we are to understand how the Torah was interpreted and applied through the ages, we must understand the rules and principles of the process that Moses was given, or that classical Judaism said he was given, on Mt. Sinai. For although we say that the Tablets were shattered in and by the confrontation with modernity, I maintain that it is not so much that the Tablets themselves have been shattered, as that the process and its continued relevance to our lives seem to have been irretrievably lost. That is, while many of us still accept the Ten Commandments and, indeed, even much of the law that was appended to them, we find the authority, the method and the principles of midrash alien and unacceptable. And even if the Tablets truly have been shattered for many others, more so, I believe, it has been the ongoing process that was a part of the Tablets that has been destroyed.

Isaac Hirsch Weiss spent 20 years writing his history of the rabbinic tradition in the hope that he could release it both from the deep freeze into which he felt Orthodoxy had thrust it and and from the grave in which he felt Reform had buried it. The process, he claimed, was neither what Orthodoxy said it was, nor what Marxism and modern Christian anti-Judaism said it was; the process, the authentic process, could be set in motion again. Weiss denied categorically that Judaism had ever been static, or that the Tablets had ever been fossilized, until recently in our history. The Torah, he said, was viable; the source of our collective life for centuries, it could become that again if we but had the courage and the knowledge to revive it.

To Weiss, as to many modern scholars, one of the major determinants of Jewish survival has been the remarkable capacity of the Jews to translate and apply the Tablets afresh, again and again, according to the principles of a living process. In short, every great cultural development in Judaism was a manifestation of the process of interpretation.

I will cite only a few illustrations.

MOMENT/189

As early as the third century before the Common Era, Jewish scholars from the Holy Land went to Egypt and translated the Torah into Greek, the reigning language in Egypt at that time. Moreover, every subsequent Jewish community has translated the Bible into the dominant tongue of the culture in whose midst it lived. Thus Saadia Gaon, the head of the Babylonian academy of Sura, translated the Bible into Arabic, even as centuries earlier the Jews translated the Bible into Aramaic and made its reading in Hebrew *and* Aramaic mandatory for every Jew every week of the year.

Or, to take examples of translations in a different mode: the teachings of the rabbinic schools of Hillel and Shammai and of Rabbi Akiba and Rabbi Ishmael were, in essence, attempts by these groups to apply Scripture and the traditions they had received to the very different worlds in which they found themselves. All were part of the living process. After the Arabs had conquered the Near East and Islam had become the dominant culture there, the heads of the academies of Babylonia, the *geonim*, as they were called, attempted to apply the Judaism *they* had received to *their* world. What they had received, of course, and what underlay all of their legal and theological thinking, was nothing less than the Babylonian Talmud, at that point the most recent compilation of Jewish law and midrash—a compendium of the ancient steps of the process derived from the living Tablets themselves. Yet, in spite of having the newly compiled Talmud at hand, the *geonim* went on to issue their own updated codes in Arabic, Aramaic and Hebrew; their achievements in developing new forms of Judaism have been beautifully celebrated in a number of great works of scholarship recently issued by Harry Austryn Wolfson, Moses Zucker and S.D. Goitein. It was in the geonic period that Saadia Gaon introduced philosophy into rabbinic Judaism by making the Kalam, the regnant Arabic rationalist thought, the dominant method of rationalizing Judaism and squaring it with the canons of critical thinking of his day. Later, in the 12th century, Maimonides would do the same by bringing Judaism into harmony with Neo-Platonic Aristotelianism.

Judaism, in other words, has always been a variation on a theme. The constants have been the people of Israel bound to God by the Covenant, the Torah, the Sabbath, circumcision, the dietary laws, marital laws, the centrality of the Holy Land and of the Temple for certain aspects of observance, and above all, the centrality of the Holy Land as the land of promise for ultimate redemption. But when the Torah speaks, for example, of torts and damages in terms of "the goring ox," it doesn't mean to restrict itself to the ox; it means to regulate torts with regard to the Jaguar, too. For, as the rabbis say, *"Dibrah Torah bahoveh, dibru chachamim bahoveh,"* "The Torah speaks in the language of its contemporary world, and the sages speak in the language of their contemporary world."

Moreover, the process of interpretation and adaptation—the process by which the Torah was continually made the rule of life—made the Tablets yield not only law, but also faith and canons of taste; in other words, the entire *Weltanschauung* that is expressed by the categorical rabbinic term *aggadah*. *Aggadah* includes not only legend, but homily and philosophy. It tells us how the Torah should be applied to one's heart and mind. As early as the first century of our era a Jew who left a permanent imprint on Jewish thought recognized that the Torah had to be brought into the orbit of the intellectual Greek world and made palatable to those who were schooled in Stoic morality. The great philosophical works of this Jew, Philo of Alexandria, are, basically, commentaries on the Torah that attempt to make the Torah intelligible to a person reared in the hellenistic world. Nor was it only Saadia who integrated Kalam with rabbinic philosophy. As Professor Moses Zucker has found, other *geonim*, too, wrote extensively in the idiom of Arabic Kalam philosophy. Maimonides was an avid student not only of Avicenna, but also of Averroes and of the history of philosophy generally. A century earlier, Ibn Gabirol had written a work of philosophy that was so Neo-Platonic in content that when it was translated into Latin and his name misspelled as Avicebron, people totally forgot that the real author was a Jew; Avicebron was thought to be a Christian. It was only coincidental that in the middle of the 19th century Salomon Munk discovered "Avicebron" to be a corruption of "Ibn Gabirol" and the *Fons Vitae* of Avicebron to be the work of a Jew. What I want to indicate is that although the work had no word of Christianity in it, neither did it have a word of Judaism in it. It bespoke a philosophy to which every cultivated man could subscribe in that day.

The process of interpretation and adaptation, when applied to philosophy and *aggadah*, continually updated Judaism and brought it into consonance with contemporary modes of thought. Jew and Christian—Jew and Moslem—could reject each other totally, while at the same time, thanks to the process and the faith it reflected, sharing fundamental premises. This process and this faith are best summarized in Maimonides' statement in *The Guide of the Perplexed*, Book Three, Chapter 51, where he tells us what religion is all about:

This chapter that we bring now does not include additional matter over and above what has been comprised in the other chapters of this treatise. It is only a kind of conclusion, at the same time explaining the worship as practiced by one who has apprehended the true realities peculiar only to Him after he has obtained an apprehension of what He is. . . . I shall begin the discourse in this chapter with a parable that I shall compose for you. I say then: The ruler is in his palace, and all his subjects are partly within the city and partly outside the city. Of those who are within the city, some have turned their backs upon the ruler's habitation, their faces being turned another way. Others seek to reach the ruler's habitation, turn toward it, and desire to enter it and to stand before him, but up to now they have not yet seen the wall of the habitation. Some of those who seek to reach it have come up to the habitation and walk around it searching for its gate. Some of them have entered the gate and walk about in the antechambers. Some of them have entered the inner court of the habitation and have come to be with the king, in one and the same place with him, namely, in the ruler's habitation.

What we have here is the renowned parable of the castle. There has always been a castle in Judaism, a tent of God, a holy mountain that man could ascend. The idea is already reflected in Psalm 15, verse 6, which reads, "Oh Lord, who may stay in Your tent? Who may reside on Your holy mountain?" Later, the rabbinic tract *Hechalot* purports to describe the actual dwelling place of God.

In our day, the idea of the castle inevitably brings to mind Franz Kafka. Kafka studied Maimonides and made notes on *The Guide of the Perplexed*. He must have known this parable, and I dare even suggest that he was inspired by Maimonides' treatment of this ancient theme. But whether my suggestion is historically plausible or not is really immaterial. What I believe to be undeniable is that the messages of the two parables are mutually exclusive.

Kafka's castle mirrors our Jewish condition today, the condition in which the Tablets are shattered and the process of interpretation meaningless. To Kafka there is no doubt that there is a castle up there, overlooking and determining the destinies of all of us. It haunts us, for it houses the master of our fate. In this he agrees with Maimonides. But there is one crucial difference: Maimonides does not doubt that there is a key to the castle, and that it can be found. He does not doubt that the castle can be entered by anyone who lives by the Torah and the fruits of the process. Few may ever gain access to the innermost chamber, but some have, and their example holds out promise for each of us. We, too, can hope to experience the blessing articulated in the Talmud: "May you experience eternity within your own lifetime."

Maimonides says in his code that we must not be under the illusion that the world to come is a world outside this one, a world of the future—for it is not. It is here and present, potentially available to whomever will strive to pursue it. Maimonides describes his own religious experience in his introduction to the *Guide*, leaving no doubt that he himself has passed through the outer gate of the castle. This is what he implies when he quotes Psalm 119, verse 6: *"Az lo evosh behabiti el kol mitzvotecha,"* "Only when I contemplate all your commandments can I achieve religious salvation." For Maimonides, the totality of the Torah and the performance of that totality are what gives man the promise of salvation.

Maimonides' son, Abraham, composed a book entitled *Kifayat al Abidin,* a summa on the esoteric meaning and purpose of the Torah. Abraham Maimuni had adopted many of the ways of Sufism, the dominant mystical sect of his day; he wore a hair shirt, for example. Claiming that he was fulfilling the true meaning of his father's perception of Judaism, Abraham Maimuni contended that Judaism when lived authentically was a mystical Sufi-like faith and that this authenticity was attainable only by the few who understood Torah's esoteric meaning and the process by which the Torah shapes men's souls. For him Torah was not just law and commandments, but a way of spiritual ecstasy.

In one way or another these two paths to the castle, these two orientations to faith and the religious life, continued to control the religious and intellectual leadership, the communal institutions and the life of the normal individual Jew until about 300 years ago.

Sixty years or so after the expulsion from Spain and Portugal, however, when the kabbalists of 16th-century Safed were finally able to come to terms with the shattering of the Golden Age, they evolved a different idea of man's relationship to God. They did not speak, as we do, of shattered Tablets, but, rather, of the shattered vessels of the Godhead itself. They did not lose faith either in the Tablets or in the process by which the Tablets were to be interpreted. It seemed to them that the only explanation for their fate and for the condition of the world and man in general lay in the idea that, as a result of a primeval cosmic rupture, God Himself had suffered a trauma. This situation did not make man either helpless or useless, however; on the contrary, it gave man, or, more accurately, the people of Israel, a special role vis-à-vis both the world and God.

The profoundly original concept of the kabbalists was that every *mitzvah* that is performed redeems a divine spark from the chaotic void in which it is being held captive. To put the matter in terms of the idea of process with which we are grappling, this situation gives the process, at the heart of which these scholars put kabbalah (which, for them, was a higher form of midrash), a double function: First, it is a way to achieve mystical bliss, individually, through the performance of Torah and contemplation. And second, and more important and more daring, it is a way to restore a shattered and partially exiled God to wholeness and to His original abode and to restore Creation to its pristine form and balance.

Man, the Jew, the Torah, the process, all have renewed roles in this system vis-à-vis the castle and its master. Man, indeed, becomes almost as important as God, since it is only man who can restore God to His primal place.

In our modern situation, so hauntingly portrayed for us by Kafka in his midrash on the ruler of the universe, man exists in a demonic situation in which there is no way for him to make any meaningful connection with the castle. Note that this apocalyptic vision is the very reverse of Maimonides'. From Kafka's point of view, the universe is a madhouse and can only drive the one who tries to make meaningful connections to distraction and frustration. A castle, yes, but one that will drive us berserk. That, in Kafka's eyes, is the current human condition; and according to this diagnosis, Judaism—or for that matter any institutionalized religion—is, by implication, nothing more than a dance of madmen to no avail.

Kafka bespeaks the agony and frustration of modern man, but he bespeaks particularly the agony and frustration of the modern Jew in his confrontation with his own tradition. For the Jew is confronted with still another challenge to his sanity, one that declares *his* religion more reprehensible than all others.

The modern anti-Semite accuses us of being heirs to a tradition that is legalistic, separatistic and particularistic. But we have always known that. For centuries we bore our legalism, separatism and particularism proudly; we snorted with contempt at complaints about these postures.

But in the last 180 years we have come to agree with the anti-Semite. Why? Because we have lost the one basic element that is necessary to sustain our faith in the process: our hope for redemption in the future, our belief in the promise of redemption that is inherent in the message of the Tablets. The Tablets, in the modern view, are shattered. Or, again, to put it more accurately, the process that the Tablets bespoke is utterly without relevance for most of us.

Paradoxically, the Tablets and our belief in the midrashic process have been shattered by freedom and by citizenship. As a result of the acceptance of the Jew into the family of man, we no longer see ourselves as a people apart, as the bearers of a special destiny. Moses Mendelssohn reduced Judaism to a religion, thereby attempting to relieve us of the burden of our traditional *communal* Jewish identity; but in doing so he left us, as a group, spiritually emasculated. If a religion is what we really are, we can find it elsewhere at lesser cost and, perhaps, with greater return. Indeed, religion need not itself be meaningless, but another consequence of modernity is that today religion—all religion—has lost its objective mandate. Today religion is a psychological state, not a revealed body of truths and commands; and, as a private affair, it has lost its power to weld us into a religious *Gemeinschaft,* the kind of community expressed by the Hebrew word *am,* a kinship group all of whose members are related to each other.

Yet, in spite of our repeated affirmations of the value of individual freedom, we find ourselves urgently engaged in a quest for retrieval of the Tablets and for a new way in which to incorporate them into our lives. We long to be relieved of the feeling of emptiness that seems to pervade us.

One of the causes of this sense of emptiness and loss is reflected in a change that has taken place with regard to the very meaning of the idea of process itself. In the 18th and 19th centuries, in certain intellectual circles, process began to be understood not as the means by which man should shape his patrimony, as the application of the laws by which God requires man to live, but, rather, as the operation of independent forces, the working-out of self-perpetuating historical dynamics in which man's will and intelligence play no part. Process came to mean the impersonal processes of history that determine men's lives.

Giambattista Vico is the father of this new understanding of the history of culture. Each culture goes through three stages, Vico maintained—the age of the gods, the age of heroes, and, finally, the age of man—after which it declines to the point of extinction. Anyone who has read Edmund Wilson's *To the Finland Station,* or Sir Isaiah Berlin's *Vico and Herder,* understands the influence Vico's ideas had in the course of the 19th century. The ultimate exponents of the new meaning of process were the Marxists, many of whom were religiously and ethnically disaffiliated.

But the new idea affected the Jewish intelligentsia as well, beginning in 1840 with the publication of Nachman Krochmal's *Guide for the Perplexed of Our Time.* It is likely that Krochmal was inspired by a German translation of Vico, for he, too, saw Jewish history as cyclical and as undergoing three stages in each cycle. But in Krochmal's view the unalterable culmination of Vico's cycles was suspended in the case of Israel; for him, Israel was the sole exception to Vico's idea of inevitable disintegration. Israel could not avoid cyclicality, but Israel was unique in that it alone could avoid death; it alone could enjoy continued rebirth after each cycle.

Still, the non-Jewish, non-religious view of process triumphed, and as a result our leaders lost faith in the uniqueness of our people and its culture, and in its power to transcend the laws governing all other peoples and cultures.

Consequently, in the name of the new process we fashioned new Tablets and new ideas of redemption. In the 19th century we had several such: Socialism, Zionism, religious reform. And while, for a time, these efforts did capture the imagination of the great masses of Jews, their effectiveness was short-lived. The shattering of the ideal of classical Zionism within the lifetime of the State of Israel has been especially painful for many of us, for if Zionism has been the glory of the Jewish people—if, indeed, it has been a vehicle for salvation for many of us—it has been a source of frustration and tragedy for the Jewish people as well.

Who is to blame for the shattering of these great modern Tablets? Who is to blame for the shattering of Zionism as an eschatology, as the new road to redemption? It doesn't matter. Suffice it to say that we are in a bad way. One might say that America is also in a bad way, for America, too, has lost its perception of its mission. But we Jews can less afford the loss.

Is there a ray of hope? I believe there is. But in order to profit by it we must have the courage to face reality and to diagnose our situation unequivocally. Most important, we must have faith and commitment: We must be able to stake our existence on the fact that a law has been revealed to all men for all time, to the extent that they are capable of grasping it.

No one can prove that this is true, but religious faith is not concerned with proof. Religious faith means the ultimate staking of one's existence on the proposition that if there is no God, if there is no revealed law, then there are no canons for judgment, neither for condemnation nor for praise. If the text is not rooted in authority, what is the point of midrash?

Can we mend the Tablets and restore for ourselves a process with a mission? Here the past can be instructive. Chassidism was born as a result of a deep clinical depression of the Jewish people, which the chassidic masters overcame by instilling in them a renewed sense of mission, a sense of mission that, unlike the elitist doctrines of the kabbalists, mobilized the emotion of joy in making *all* Jews partners of the Almighty. It may be that Professor Arthur Green was right in saying that Chassidism transformed theology from an objective study into a psychological state, but it was a psychological state based on a continuing affirmation of the revealed character of the Torah, and the fact of the matter is that the pyschological state was apposite and relevant to the needs of its time: Out of a state of depression grew an enormous force in Jewish life.

Moreover, in its turn Chassidism generated counterforces of intellectuality whose advocates, I regret, are not celebrated enough. The efforts of these dedicated individuals were directed at establishing still newer kinds of midrash and exegesis to express still newer theological concepts. One was Hayyim of Volozhin, a disciple of the Gaon of Vilna, who established an institution dedicated to molding the new East European Jewish gentleman. He believed that the study of Torah and its commentaries, when undertaken not only as an intellectual discipline, but as a liturgical experience as well, would lead to a higher level of spirituality than could be achieved by any Chassid. Another was Nachman Krochmal, whom I have already mentioned, who wanted to halt the tide of assimilation and growing Jewish apathy to the tradition. He felt that if he unravelled the processes of Jewish history he might be able to create a midrash that would be relevant to modern times, and thus infuse the process with renewed energy. Then there were the heroes of the Hebrew enlightenment, the Haskalah, who sought to reestablish Jewish self-esteem, in part by the appropriation and Judaization of the secular culture of the world. And there were the Socialist-Yiddishists, who gave a secularized but nonetheless collective purpose to the Jews of Eastern Europe.

In Germany Franz Rosenzweig attempted to mend the Tablets and create a new religious idiom, a new process that would motivate Jewish life afresh. Solomon Schechter in England and in this country tried to restore the Tablets of rabbinic Judaism by affirming their validity in the face of Reform Judaism, Christianity and secularism. Professor Mordecai M. Kaplan sought to restore the Tablets, too. He sought to make Judaism free of affirmations that contradicted modern science and the modern *Weltanschauung*.

If none of these attempts continues to inflame the imagination of the intellectual leadership of our country, except as bibliographical items or venerated memories, perhaps it is because they did not find the proper idiom, the proper religious way, the proper process. Or perhaps it is because of the rapid rate of today's technical, scientific and social change. In the modern world any theological system is doomed to obsolescence within a few decades unless it includes in its system an idiom for rebirth and renewal.

If Chassidism, as I have suggested, was born of collective depression, we, it seems to me, often live in a state of collective despair–and rage. Independent of any allegiance, we live in a state of extreme individualism and in a world devoid of belief in redemption. But rage and despair are counterproductive. We must reawaken in ourselves a sense of our collective election and of our collective mission, and we must recreate a process of midrash for ourselves. Clearly, we cannot resuscitate classical midrash. What we can and must do is create a modern midrash, one that will combine our scientific knowledge and our critical reconquest of the Jewish past–in all its diversity–with our present conscience and consciousness. We must create a midrash that embraces the totality of Jewish experience and distills from it religious elements that can serve as guides to contemporary life and action. It is likely that our answers to some of the sensitive problems of modern Jewish life, such as patrilinear descent, conversion, medical ethics and ritual, will arouse resistance in some who are observant as well as in some who are unobservant. But we must have the courage, nevertheless, to develop a midrash that, while growing out of the past, connects us to the present and provides us with principles that validate or invalidate our acts.

For without a midrash no text can continue to remain relevant, and without a text we can have neither roots nor process.

We cannot retrieve the Tablets in a day. We cannot create a new midrashic process in a day. These things can only be accomplished as a result of the efforts of generations of committed Jews. But one of the first things we must do is begin to believe that we, as contemporary American Jews, are not less qualified than others to undertake this task. Israel was born out of a quest for spirit on alien soil. We were born with a determination to apply our commitment to spirit, through midrash, wherever we might find ourselves. I believe that we in America above all–because of our profound experience of freedom and because of our sense of responsibility to our brethren in Israel and in other parts of the world–can and must revitalize the idea of process.

We can learn to accept that which our grandparents and great-grandparents regarded as a rule of daily life: the continuing study of our basic texts and their application to life. Surely we can somehow create an ongoing process of our own, a process that will celebrate the reestablishment of a sense of our collective belief in, and striving for, the redemption of the community as a whole. ✡

JEWS BY CHOICE A DISCUSSION WITH CONVERTS

MOMENT: Why don't we start with each of you briefly telling why you converted to Judaism, and perhaps also something about the nature of your current relationship to the Jewish community?

Susan: I converted because in all the abstract conversation my husband and I had before we were married, he said that our children would be Jewish—period. I decided that if the children were going to be Jewish, it would be important for me to convert. Otherwise they would have had to convert eventually.

Way back, my grandfather was a Mormon minister, an elder of the church, and my mother couldn't stand that. She married to get away from home and away from Mormonism, and she did her best to raise us as nothing, to teach us to be accepting of everybody. So, depending on what neighborhood we were in, that's where we went to church. My father was a teacher at a Congregational school, and he studied Christian Science for a while. And I guess that it was really very easy for me to convert. There was nothing involved in the conversion that went against anything I believed in.

As to involvement with the Jewish community, I'm deeply involved—whether I want to be or not. My husband is a cantor now—which is something he wasn't even planning when we married. So I'm in the thick of it.

Betty: My father came from Ireland—an Irish Catholic—and he married my mother, who was a Lutheran. She converted to Catholicism. And I happened to fall in love with someone who is Jewish, and I thought it was important that we be the same. Since we weren't going to be Catholic, that meant we were going to be Jewish. I converted four years ago, after we were married. We had already decided that I'd convert, but we had to wait for the classes to start, and in the meantime, we were married in a civil ceremony. After the conversion, we got married again, and we joined a temple, and now I'm a member of a chavurah.

Peggy: I was brought up as a Catholic with a parochial school education. My father converted to Catholicism before he married my mother. And my husband is a secular Jew, with no interest or involvement or affiliation or connection with any synagogue or Jewish organization. The reason that I converted was that even though he is a secular Jew, he feels that he is Jewish and he wants his children to be Jewish. And I felt that it was important that our children have a religious education, and it's the mother who supplies that. So I've gone from a non-practicing Catholic to a non-practicing Jew, with every intention, once the children are old enough, of becoming involved.

Anne: I converted four years ago, just after Frank and I were married. I had been a non-practicing Episcopalian; my parents were basically non-religious. I really stopped practicing when I was 17 and realized that I couldn't believe in the trinity.

There were three things that made it possible for me to convert. First, I felt very much at home with the values I identified with Jews; I felt them to be my own values. By that I mean a very high standard of morality, a sense of justice and compassion, a concern for social problems. And the second reason is that it was important to Frank, although he in no way demanded or even asked me to convert. And the most important reason was that I did not want my children, in shaping a sense of identity, to have any feelings of conflict. That reason alone would have been enough.

David: I was brought up as a Catholic, and I went to parochial schools—the whole route, including mass, altar boy, and so forth. I was very turned off by the nuns, who engaged in a great deal of physical abuse. But I continued until I went to college, when I stopped going to church and more or less gave up the Catholic faith. My parents were somewhat dismayed by that.

I met my wife while in college, and we dated for five years before we decided to get married. She wasn't a practicing Jew at all. She came from a small town in Maine that didn't even have its own rabbi. Her family is Jewish, but not religious. Still, when it came time to make the decision, her parents were really against our getting married, and they put us through a lot of pressure. Susan wanted to raise our children as Jews, and since I wasn't a practicing Catholic, and didn't want to put my children through what I experienced as a Catholic, that seemed very reasonable to me. Actually, I grew up in a more Jewish community than Susan, and probably knew more about Judaism than she did.

So I wanted to convert, but I didn't get around to it before our marriage. And her parents wouldn't come to the wedding, even though it was performed by a rabbi, and that hurt her very much. About six months later, I started taking classes, and I enjoyed them very much, and decided to go through with the conversion. It's been seven years now. We don't belong to a temple, although of course we go to High Holiday services. I'm kind of reluctant to get deeply involved; it reminds me of my childhood. But

Bob Atwood

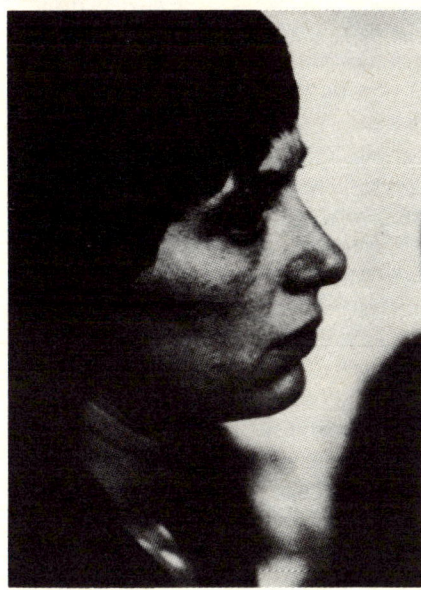

Anne Glickman

Photographs by Chris Maynard

maybe someday I'll get into it more actively.

Michael: My parents were a mixed marriage, he from a nondescript, non-religious northern Irish family, she from a devout southern Irish Catholic family. My father did convert to Catholicism. In my senior year in high school, I started having problems with some of the concepts of Catholicism—I was attending a parochial school—and for about a year and a half, I spent a lot of time talking to one of the priests, trying to resolve the things I didn't believe. I guess the real problem was that I believed what they had taught me—that if you don't believe, you're not a Catholic. So I made a very specific break from the Church, and I was quite comfortable with that.

From the time of that break until the time I met my wife, I was curious about various religions. I was very interested in examining other beliefs. Maybe I was trying to fill a gap. And when I met my wife—we decided very early in our relationship that we were going to be married—I saw a problem regarding religion. I wanted my children to be brought up in some religion, but I knew that I had no specific religion to offer. And I wanted to be absolutely sure that any differences we had weren't going to cause conflict in the family. I needed to be sure that I had no hidden hangups about Judaism, so that I wouldn't find the kids coming home from Hebrew school with something they'd been taught that would cause me to bite my tongue. So I took a conversion course, and once I resolved that I really didn't have any hangups, I dropped out until ten years later.

Over the ten years, through association with my wife's family, and with the children going to Sunday school, I realized that I was quite comfortable with Judaism, and that I had really never made any effort, and that it was time for me to resolve what I wanted to do. And so I converted. I feel very strongly that I did the right thing, and it was in no way a response to pressure. I especially appreciate the fact that there was a rabbi who was willing to marry us. That made it much more comfortable for my wife. Even though she is not heavily into Judaism, it is a gut strong belief for her, and our being married by a rabbi left the door open to us.

Because our children are required to attend at least one Friday night service a month, we go to temple, and I'm very happy about that. We're not thrilled with the temple we belong to, but the kids are getting exactly what they need.

Bob: Lynne and I have been married for about five years; I converted six years ago. My father was not religious. He and my mother were brought up as Canadian Baptists, which isn't too different from Southern Baptists, and I never found very much in that religion. When Lynne and I started dating and thinking of marriage, we talked about religion, and my feeling was that it's not so important what religion you take so long as you both have the same religion. It was important to me that the children be able to identify with a religion.

When we started dating seriously, I wasn't accepted at all. But after a year and a half or so, when it became evident that we weren't going to forget about the whole thing, Lynne's parents began to accept the idea. And I took a conversion course, even though I had made no commitment to convert. I didn't want to convert because of pressure, just for the sake of converting so that my future in-laws could say their daughter had married a Jew and everything was just fine. I wouldn't have done it under those circumstances. And finally, Lynne's parents said that if I wanted to convert, that was okay, and if I didn't, that was okay, too. It was my decision. And once I realized that it didn't matter to them, in terms of their ability to accept me, I knew the decision was mine to make freely. And then I knew that I truly wanted to convert, because I had no religion and because I saw a lot of things in Judaism that I could identify with and that made sense. It was an instantaneous decision.

We're not active in any temple or organization; that wouldn't fit our lifestyle. But I do enjoy the holidays and going to services then. I feel very much a part of Lynne's family, and I love and accept the Jewish religion. But I don't really feel like I'm a Jew;

there's something missing for me.
Peggy: The main difficulty I find is creating a lifestyle. Being Jewish is not like being Presbyterian. I have no real point of reference. I can't do what my mother-in-law does so easily, with things in the home or the celebration of holidays.
Lynne: But that's not confined to people who have converted. I'm Jewish by birth, and I have the same problem—which may be why Bob doesn't really feel Jewish. I don't know what I'm doing. The fact is that I learned more in the conversion class—we took it together—than I learned in all my lifetime before that.
Peggy: Did your mother celebrate the holidays?
Lynne: Yes, but I'd say she's more of an ethnic Jew. She doesn't know that much of the theology, the philosophy or the law—just a general working knowledge, a few traditions that she carries on, not enough for me to be able to use her as a model. And I'm at a loss, because I don't know how to be a model for someone else when I'm devoid of background myself. So, you see, it can be the same for born Jews as for converts.
Betty: I found that a problem in the beginning, too. I have two children—one four years old, the other just a year old. Until the older was a year old, we didn't do anything at home. We belonged to a temple, but we never celebrated anything. And we realized that we had better start doing something, because kids like the routine and pick it up very early—some things that happen each year, some things that happen each week.

But my husband wasn't very helpful, because he had no commitments of his own that mattered. He had said to me, "Anything you want to do is fine." So I had to make the decision, and I didn't have anyone to copy, and when I asked the people that I'd met what they did, I found that they didn't do anything either. In fact, I'm probably more Jewish than anyone else I know. I've become my own role model. And I find that the more things you celebrate, the more you can get into being Jewish. When somebody just says to you, "Now, you're Jewish," you don't feel any different; it takes a long time to become Jewish; to feel it.

Bob: When I told the rabbi who was going to marry us that I didn't know whether or not I was Jewish, he almost went through the roof. He couldn't believe that anyone who had converted could make such a statement. But I assumed that everyone felt the way I did after conversion. It's such a mixed up process, mentally and emotionally. I still don't know, and I am convinced that I won't know until I become more active. I lack the identity, the day-to-day feeling I see in Lynne's family. In my family, the only time you know what religion is is on Sunday, when you go to church, or at Christmas. But Judaism isn't like that.

Michael: I'm using my children's education as a way of educating myself. As they learn Hebrew, so do I; as they learn about a holiday, I make sure that I have all the right things—books, candles, whatever. It's really a complete educational process, and my wife is involved, too, because her learning as a child involved being dragged to school until she was twelve. Now she sees us doing it, and relating to it, in a friendly and open way. Every new step the kids take is a new motivation for us.

M: What about your old friends? Do you see them? How do you feel with them, or they with you?

Susan: I went to a wedding of a high school friend; it had been ten years since I'd seen any of the people there, and it had been a very anti-Semitic community, actually restricted until the late 1950's. But everyone there knew what my husband's job is, and knew that I was Jewish. It was a very Waspy wedding. I don't remember when I was last so uncomfortable. No food; nothing but drinking. This was the first celebration we'd been to that wasn't Jewish, and I find that I'm very uncomfortable around non-Jews now. I've made such a transition.

And it's strange, because my husband's family wouldn't have minded if I hadn't converted. We never even spoke about it. My husband's background wasn't observant; his parents had a Christmas tree. We're the ones who have added things. We keep kosher, and every time I eat a meal or cook something I'm aware that I'm very Jewish—and very different. And it's a very positive feeling. We're not doing it because of the kids; we don't have children yet. We just keep adopting more and more traditions, and the more we adopt, the more comfortable I am.

David: It would probably be a lot easier to convert to Protestantism. Here you have to find a whole new identity. Almost all of our friends are Jewish, and it's been that way ever since we started dating. I've drifted out of contact with my older friends. And even though I'm not very religious, I do feel very Jewish.

M: How do you feel at Christmas time?

David: We split the holidays; we spend Christmas with my folks. My mother does what she's always done, and I know it means a lot to her. But I also know that that part of my life is gone. I have some feelings about Christmas, but they are not religious feelings—they have to do with the closeness people feel around that time, or remembering the happiness of the season when I was growing up.

Bob: Most of our friends are mixed marriages. And it's interesting to see the way different couples handle the situation. The one that stands out in my mind is a situation where he is a Catholic and she is a Jew, and neither has accepted the other's religion in any way. I think that's unhealthy and potentially very dangerous. And if they decide to have children, the children will be brought up with nothing, and they won't know where they stand, and, eventually, they may have to choose between their parents, and I think that's totally wrong.

M: What about the marriage ceremony itself? Some of you converted before the ceremony, some after? Did it matter to you that you could be married by a rabbi? Did you resent the difficulties you encountered in finding a rabbi?

Michael: I don't think the non-Jewish spouse would resent it. But I know that my wife would have been deeply resentful if she had not been able to have a religious ceremony. We discussed the issue quite openly. She was feeling some guilt, but she also knew how strong my feelings were. It had taken me a long time to get out of one religion, and I thought it was only right that I give a great deal of consideration to the prospect of getting into another one. It isn't like going to school for a semester and taking the final in order to earn three credits. It's something—at least so far as I'm concerned—you've really got to feel. Still, she wanted a religious ceremony.

Her parents weren't pressing. When we realized it wouldn't be easy to find a rabbi, they told us not to be concerned. But we were lucky, and we did find a rabbi. And he was quite open. He told us that he wasn't really doing it for our sake, but for the sake of our children. He wanted them to have every chance for Judaism they could. And he required us to sign a paper saying that we would raise our children as Jews, and he made it clear that we were supposed to take the signing very seriously. His position was that even though you can't predict what people will do, there's at least a fifty-fifty chance that the children of a mixed marriage will be raised as Jews, and he performed intermarriages in order to improve the odds.

In my case, of course, there was no problem, since I had already gone through a process of evaluation, and I was willing to make the commitment.

But I'm sure that for many, if not most, of the couples who sign such papers, it's just a way of getting the in-laws off their backs. And I also know that for couples who have been rejected, who aren't able to have a religious ceremony, it's a real hassle—not so much for the potential convert, but for the Jew, who feels as if he's been rejected by his own community.

Susan: The rabbi who married us didn't really want to. He was the rabbi of the congregation where my husband grew up, and my husband's parents were founding members. My husband had been a junior cantor there, and certainly wasn't unknown. But the rabbi absolutely didn't want to do it, and when he did, he made it clear that it was against his better judgment. Two days before we were to be married, he called us in, together with another fifteen couples at whose weddings he was going to officiate—a really personal encounter—and we went around the room finding out the Hebrew names of everybody's parents, and when it was my turn he looked at me and said, "Oh yes, I'll talk to you later." And I felt like crawling under the rug. He made it clear he didn't want to marry us, and I was very resentful, and I still am.

Bob: I encountered some of that. The rabbi I spoke with was the rabbi in the town where I grew up, and we got to him through the minister of my church. Both men, the rabbi and the minister, were as warm and understanding as people can be; they bent over backwards to help us find some direction. But I remember the rabbi telling me that he was not going to encourage me. The most he would promise was not to discourage me. And so I got started. But it was strange not to feel any encouragement. I think the rabbi should be prepared to teach the prospective convert everything he can, and if the person wants to convert, he should be accepted—and if he doesn't want to convert, then at least he has come away with an understanding and an acceptance of Judaism, and with respect for it.

Anne: I'd like to be accepted by Jews as a Jew, and I don't think many Jews accept converts, and that troubles me. I think there are people who sincerely believe that Judaism is something you have to be born into, and that you can't convert to. And I was really disturbed when so many of our Jewish friends, when they learned that I wanted to convert, said things like, "Why do you want to do that? Are you crazy?"

M: That's a very common response. In some cases, it reflects the Jewish sense of hazard; we can't understand that anyone would willingly expose himself to the risks that go with being Jewish. And in some cases, it reflects the views of assimilated Jews, who can't imagine why anyone would choose to take seriously something they themselves have chosen to neglect. And then, of course, there's the complexity that is involved in a conversion that is specifically religious, when it is obvious that many born Jews are not believing Jews. But there's no way of formally converting to Jewish ethnicity.

Michael: Someone who converts can become very accepting and comfortable with what is considered ethnic in Judaism, and even develop a great love for it. And that may be difficult for Jews to comprehend. If you were to go to Ireland, you'd have a tough time picking up the brogue, and you might not be able to drink as much beer as a native, but you really could develop a passionate love for the country and the style—maybe even more than a native. The degree of religious observance by converts may be a way of expressing love and commitment as they go about developing a more natural ethnic style.

You see, there's a big mystery among non-Jews regarding what Judaism really is. The Jews are a very private society, and one of the hardest things is to break through and find out what is really so different and unique.

Susan: Yes, being a convert is difficult. I keep thinking I ought to have a thicker skin to deal with the remarks that Jews make about me. I've had friends, who don't know that I converted, say things like "I could never have a friend who wasn't Jewish. I don't trust them." Or people who say, "Oh, you're Jewish—that's why you're so bright." It's rough getting it from both sides, from Jews and from non-Jews. It's hard to get used to.

Betty: I'm the only convert in our chavurah. We joined about three years ago, and I had to miss the first meeting. I was hoping that my husband, who went, wouldn't say anything about me, because I didn't want to be revealed. And when I started going, it was a long while before I said anything about my background, because I wanted to feel comfortable with these people and I wanted them to feel comfortable with me. I thought if they knew about me, that might color what was said—or what was not said. It was a very personal thing.

And then, at one meeting, someone said, "Well, we probably all have similar backgrounds... eastern Europe. Why don't we just go around the room and find out?" And when it was my turn, and I said, "My father came from Ireland," that said it all. By then, we were all close enough so that they valued me because I had such a different perspective.

David: The thing I have so much difficulty with is why people are discouraged from converting. It's almost as if it were a test of your stamina, to see whether you're strong enough to become Jewish. And I think that's baloney. I don't want to be tested. If I want to be a Jew, I should have that opportunity, and not have Jews telling me I can't be until I've gone through a test. It's test enough dealing with the family problems that you've got, let alone the organized hassle. And that's really frustrating to me.

Bob: People don't understand. For example, everybody's concerned about the Jewish parents whose child is to be married to a non-Jew. What about the parents of the non-Jew? What are they going through? In most of the cases I've seen, the non-Jewish family has adapted to the thing better than the Jewish family. But somebody ought to stop and ask about them; it's not one-sided, you know.

I never asked my parents what they thought of the whole thing, I think my father was quite anti-Semitic, but his frame of mind changed quite drastically once he got to know Lynne, and realized that all Jews don't have horns; they don't all live in expensive houses. But we haven't really talked about it. We take part in the holidays with both sets of parents, and even Lynne's mother joins us at my parents' for Christmas.

Susan: My mother may have been a bit unusual. She was very pleased. When I told her that I was going to marry my husband, she smiled very complacently and said, "I didn't fail." And I didn't understand, but she explained that she had raised us not to make distinctions among people. "What's important is that you love him. So I must have done something right."

My father will never really understand. He's decided that Jews make terrific husbands, and I'll never starve—a kind of reverse anti-Semitism. When he comes to temple with us, he says, "What a nice church you have here." He still has difficulty acknowledging what I did. We've been married for ten years, and it's only the last two years that he's started sending us Chanukah presents instead of Christmas presents. But he is pleased that I'll be well taken care of, even if he doesn't understand the whole thing.

Michael: My father was against my sister's marriage, even though she was marrying a good Catholic boy who has provided well for the family; he was against my brother's marriage, fought it right through the reception after the wedding by not speaking to the bride's father, even though she was a good Catholic girl who'd gone to a good Catholic high school; he was totally against every girl that I ever brought home and pointed out several that I missed that he'd have been much happier with. He went so far as to send my intended, when we were over in Germany while I was in the service, a letter marked personal, confidential, and just scared the living daylights out of her about what a nut I was and not really a grown-up and not yet ready to take on the responsibilities of marriage. And when I brought Linda home, and he met her, and talked to her for three or four minutes, he accepted her totally. He was never so happy with anyone that he'd ever met; he was the only person in the family who sent us cards on every Jewish holiday until the day he died. I have no idea where his total and complete acceptance of her came from. It was the only smart thing I'd ever done, he thought, marrying this wonderful, wonderful woman. That total acceptance has certainly made my life easier to live. I never had another ounce of problem with my father from the day I married her—for some reason, I had grown up in his eyes by accepting her.

The only people left in my family now are my sister and my brother, and we realized when it became Christmas time—that's when the family has traditionally gotten together from all over the country—that we hadn't told anybody I'd converted. It just never entered my mind. I don't think I was blocking it out, I just didn't see it as something that involved them. They knew I wasn't Catholic; that had stopped when I was 18. And my wife was quite uneasy, "How's Jackie going to take this; the blessed virgin statue will fall

Betty Goldfarb

Mike Riley

Susan Scherr

right off the wall." My daughter solved the problem for us. As we walked in the door, she said, "My daddy converted." And everybody said, "Oh? Okay." And there was no further discussion, no discomfort. I think that's because Linda had been so totally accepted by everybody, and because it didn't really come as a surprise.

M: Then there's the reverse problem. Do any of your in-laws feel freaked out because you're "too" Jewish?

Betty: I think they're surprised, and very pleased. When it became inevitable that we were going to get married, they were not really upset. My husband was divorced, and he had married someone who was Catholic. She hadn't converted. That was not the reason for their divorce, although it probably didn't help, either. The first time around, my mother-in-law was almost ready to commit suicide, so she'd been through that, and the second time, she decided that if he'd found someone who was right, she wasn't going to get hung up about it. Now, of course, they're surprised and pleased. They're not particularly observant; and she sort of shows me off—"Oh, my daughter-in-law does this and she does that, and she reads Hebrew"—she thinks it's great.

M: I know of a situation where a converted daughter-in-law will not eat in her in-laws' home because they're not kosher enough. Can we talk a bit about whether or not the unchurched —not the intermarried—would be interested in conversion?

Bob: I think the unchurched, or people who don't have a religion, are basically lazy, and there has to be some kind of driving force for people who want to convert, whether it's to Judaism or to something else. And for all of the people I know who have converted, the driving force was marriage and the family situation. I don't think there are very many people who all of a sudden say, "I'm not happy with my religion. I think I'll go seek out Judaism, or some other religion, because I'm not satisfied." Those numbers of people are pretty small.

Betty: I would think that would be a very difficult thing to do, to just say, "I don't care very much for my religion, and Judaism looks good." I find it difficult enough identifying with being Jewish, but along with the package I got, I got a Jewish family. The person who converts strictly out of principle is going to be all alone. He doesn't have a family that he can get a sense of feeling from.

M: Yes, those of us who were born Jewish, and who think a great deal about our Jewishness, do realize that if one is at all serious about it, being Jewish is very hard. And to choose to do it out of conviction alone, perhaps you do need to be a little mad. But the reward is this extraordinary sense of community with other Jews which, on the evidence here tonight, is not all that available to people who have converted to Judaism, who are still caused to feel left out in the cold.

David: Another problem with converts is that there is no real tie between us. This is the first time since I've converted that I've been with a number of people who have converted, and we often have special problems. Most of the people around us are born Jews, and we are different. Although I feel a part of it, I am different. If something were set up where converts could meet and talk together about their feelings, particularly about not feeling really accepted, it would help them feel more at home. I know that I felt very out of things at family get-togethers for a couple of years, and I'm very outgoing, and my wife kept saying, "What's the matter with you? You're not yourself." And my in-laws were trying very hard, but I didn't feel a part of things, and I felt that they were just going through the motions. It would help to be able to talk to people who had similar experiences, to find out how they dealt with them.

Bob: I wonder how many of those problems are our own hang-ups. Maybe we make more out of it than it really is.

M: How very profound some of these feelings are. There are so many people for whom religious expression is really a peripheral part of their lives and suddenly, on the intermarriage issue, and on the getting into the family issue, you've drilled right into the nerve.

Bob: We hear them say that they won't accept us, but *why* won't they accept us? We want to accept them,

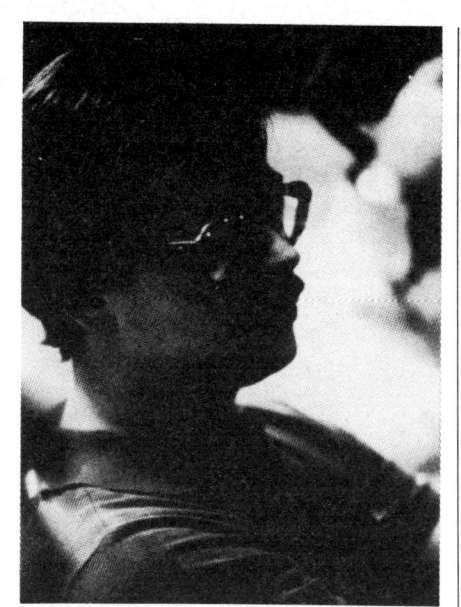

David Theriault

Peggy Baseman

and their religion, but they don't want anything to do with us.

David: My in-laws weren't religious at all, and I had the hardest time understanding. That was my first real exposure to Jewish identity. As a Catholic, I had my religion, and that was an identity in a way, but this was a whole way of life, and I just couldn't comprehend why they were so opposed to this marriage when they weren't religious at all. Then I began to hear things like, "What would the relatives say?" They'd think that my in-laws hadn't done their job properly, if their daughter didn't marry a Jew.

M: Maybe it's a terrible fear that your grandchildren are going to be anti-Semites. The hidden, primitive fear of the Jewish parent whose child is marrying a non-Jew is that the grandchildren will be raised as non-Jews. They may like their son or daughter-in-law, think they're lovely people, but the children will be raised as nothing, and a generation later, from nothing they will become Christians and from Christians become anti-Semites. I think it's a deeply ingrained fear that many people have.

Susan: I'd like to go back for a minute to the question of reaching out to the unchurched. I know how distressing it is that so many Jewish young people are being attracted to cult-type organizations, and I think one of the reasons for it is that there, they find answers. And one thing that Judaism does not do is to supply the answers. Judaism asks questions. If there is going to be an appeal and attraction to Judaism based on reason, one is going to have to seek it out.

Michael: My wife made the observation that she really envied Catholics that she knew because it was really very hard line, yes or no, black or white. You did it and it was good, or you did it and it was bad, and you knew it, and on Saturday you could go and get forgiven, and on Monday you could go out and do it again. It was a very appealing thing. I think a step that could be taken would be if there could be less of an initiation for those who come with the curiosity and the desire to hear. If it could be relaxed a little bit, and be made more open to them, and if the attitude on intermarriage could be viewed not as a rebellion, not with rejection, you would have a much, much better chance as far as the kids are concerned. And that's the key thing, the thing that everybody's worried about. And I think it would be helpful not only to the potential convert, but also to the Jews who are involved. And you can't believe it until you've heard it from people in the 25 to 35 age group. The rejection, and the unfair decisions that are placed on them make it pretty tough for them to come back into the temple when their kids are five or six years old. And you have a tough time getting them to temple in between. And the antagonism can really build.

There was something that happened when I converted that I found intriguing. It was the small matter of a ritual circumcision. I was not excited about the idea of a mohel. However, I did look around avidly for a urologist to perform a ritual circumcision. So I spoke to the rabbi, and we could find no one. And they were adamant. They would not perform a ritual circumcision. There are so many hurdles, it really seems like an initiation. That, I resent.

Peggy: That's the way I felt about the mikvah. I was terrified. I was very uncomfortable. I was quite pregnant; it was a very unattractive place, and the people were not particularly nice, and I invited no one to the ceremony. It was really my gift to my mother-in-law.

M: Obviously, we could go on all night. But we have to stop now, and I think this was marvelous. We certainly have gone all over the lot, and I'm surprised and pleased at the wide range of opinions you've offered.

Michael: That just shows you what good Jews we've all become.

"I'VE HAD NOTHING YET SO I CAN'T TAKE MORE"

When the rabbi says Jews, does he mean *all* of us? Is the Covenant meant for Jewish *women*?

RACHEL ADLER

"Take some more tea," the March Hare said to Alice very earnestly.

"I've had nothing yet," Alice replied in an offended tone: "so I can't take more."

"You mean you can't take less," said the Hatter: "it's very easy to take more than nothing."
(Lewis Carroll, *Alice's Adventures in Wonderland*)

The Mad Hatter, I have always felt, was guilty of a fallacy in the passage above. At a tea party where the rules are constant and have been assented to by all the guests, people can help themselves freely. At the Mad Hatter's sort of tea party, however, it is not so easy to take more than nothing.

Being a Jewish woman is very much like being Alice at the Hatter's tea party. We did not participate in making the rules, nor were we there at the beginning of the party. At best, a jumble of crockery is being shoved aside to clear a place for us. At worst, we are only tantalized with the tea and bread-and-butter, while being confused, shamed and reproached for our ignorance. When our external reality is absurdity and madness, it is difficult for us to retain internal coherence. We begin to ask, "Who are we, really?" We are being invited by Jewish men to re-covenant, to forge a covenant which will address the inequalities of women's position in Judaism, but we ask ourselves, "Have we ever had a covenant in the first place? Are women Jews?"

When I ask this question, it is always external to myself. I am asking, "Are women Jews in the Bible?" or "Are women Jews in rabbinic Judaism?" or "Are women named and treated as Jews in the life of the community?" I never ask myself, "Am I, Rachel Adler, a Jew?" just as I never ask myself, "Is there really a God?" These are both facts I know from my internal experience. They form the core of my selfhood. My pain and the pain of other committed Jewish women lies in the discrepancy between our internal and external realities.

Cynthia Ozick expresses this dissonance most powerfully:

"In the world at large I call myself, and am called, a Jew. But when, on the Sabbath, I sit among women in my traditional *shul* and the rabbi speaks the word 'Jew,' I can be sure that he is not referring to me. For him 'Jew' means 'male Jew.'

"When the rabbi speaks of women he uses the expression (a translation of a tender Yiddish phrase) 'Jewish daughter.' . . . 'Jew' defines a person seen in the light of a culture. 'Daughter' defines a relationship that is above all biological. 'Jew' signifies adult responsibility. 'Daughter' evokes immaturity and a dependent and subordinate connection.

"When my rabbi says, 'A Jew is called to the Torah,' he never means me or any other living Jewish woman.

"My own synagogue is the only place in the world where I am not named Jew."
("Notes Toward Finding the Right Question," Lilith, *Number 6, 1979, p. 21.)*

The feelings of alienation, otherness and exclusion described here are not peculiar to Orthodox women. Jewish women of all backgrounds experience them when they turn to the basic texts of Judaism to discover the nature of their covenant.

Imagine yourself, for example, a woman at a Shavuot service hearing the Torah reading in which the giving of the Torah is recorded. You are following the preparations for the revelation when, suddenly, you are struck in the face with, "And he said to the people, 'Be ready for the third day; do not go near a woman'" (Exodus 19:15). Clearly, "the people" does not mean you. You try to set that aside, to be caught up once more in the majesty of revelation, the thunder and lightning, the shofar, the flames, but you are jarred as the commandments are proclaimed, one after another, in the masculine singular, ending with the commandment not to covet a neighbor's property or livestock—*including his wife*. You are left standing apart

Rachel Adler is a Ph.D. candidate in Social Ethics at the University of Southern California and Hebrew Union College.

as your mothers stood under the mountain, eavesdropping on the conversation between God and man, wondering if there is anything God wants *you* to do and, if so—why doesn't He tell you so Himself?

The woman hearing the Torah reading is not there to study social organization in the ancient Middle East. If she were, she would accept as a given that, in the culture under examination, women held an inferior status. That would have nothing to do with her. But (accepting Eliade's contention that every ritual is a re-enactment of a primary event), the woman's purpose in being present this Shavuot morning must be to re-enact through this reading the first covenant of her people. And because the text has excluded her, she is excluded again in this re-enactment and will be excluded over and over, year by year, every time she rises to hear this covenant read.

Let us look for a moment at rabbinic Judaism's answer to my question, Are women Jews? Halachically, women are a unique form of property. Their acquisition is most analogous to the acquisition of Canaanite slaves. Both can be acquired through monetary purchase, through a purchase document and through a third method involving their use—for women intercourse and for slaves *chazakah,* which includes the performance of service. Both may be freed through the issuance of a document of manumission. An advantage women have is that they may be freed by the death of their husbands. An advantage Canaanite slaves have is that they may be freed if the master does them grievous physical damage (an advantage an estimated 60,000 battered wives in Israel and uncounted others in the Diaspora would be happy to enjoy).

Women and slaves are at the same level of obligation in Jewish law. The general rule is stated in *Hagigah* 4a: "Every precept which is obligatory on a woman is obligatory on a slave; every precept which is not obligatory on a woman is not obligatory on a slave." The *g'zerah shavah* to which this generalization is tied makes clear that we learn the obligations of Canaanite slaves by their comparison to women.

A Canaanite slave is, of course, a person in a peripheral status. Upon acquisition, he has had circumcision and immersion in a *mikveh* as a proselyte would, and is therefore no longer in the category of non-Jew. What distinguishes him is that he has not made an autonomous acceptance of the mitzvot. His performance of the commandments is therefore motivated by duress. Only upon his manumission does he become fully Jewish and eligible, at least theoretically, to help construct, testify concerning, or judge compliance with, the laws to which he is subject.

The commitment of the Jewish woman appears precisely parallel to that of the unfreed slave. She, too, is subject to laws from whose specification and enforcement she is barred. I would maintain that she was not considered to have covenanted.

The normative contractor of the covenant is the Jewish male. This is what is being affirmed in the oft-quoted morning blessings of the traditional prayerbook. Non-Jew, slave and woman are, in ascending order, the lower statuses of a hierarchy in which the supreme degree of Jewishness and hence of obligation, entitlement and enfranchisement belongs to the male Jew. When speaking of cultic and festival observances from which the non-Jew is by definition excluded, the tradition posits a sexual hierarchy at whose top is the male, possessor of *b'rito shel Avraham avinu*—a circumcised penis—and, in descending order, the *tumtum,* or person of undetermined sex who may possess maleness; the *androgynos,* or hermaphrodite, whose maleness is tainted by female characteristics; and, at the bottom, the woman. Whether these semi-males share masculine obligations, which in a Jewish society are equivalent to privileges, or are excluded like women is the subject of much discussion in the Talmud.

If the Jewish male is the normative participant in the covenant, the Jewish female cannot be other than a partial and diminished participant. The existence of hierarchy presupposes that the rights of individuals will be superseded by the requirements of a social organization which, not coincidentally, reinforces the privilege of those at its top while immobilizing those lower down. Otherwise, the less privileged party would move up to the more advantageous position. Saul Berman, in his excellent essay, "The Status of Women in Halakhic Judaism," explains:

"In a legal system which is contract-oriented, the basic laws are those which assure the rights of individuals. These laws are then modified or limited only to the extent necessary to secure certain basic social interests. That pattern is reversed in a status-oriented legal system where the basic laws are those which assure the social interests through status conferral. However, those laws are then modified to assure the highest possible level of individual rights achievable in consonance with the desired social goals."
(Tradition, *Number 14, Fall 1973, p. 19.*)

The social goal motivating the legislation on women, Berman suggests, is "family stability," by which he means the patriarchal system in which women are attached to male-headed families where their performance of maintenance activities enables men to be full members of the Jewish community.

My purpose here is not to do an exhaustive search of the tradition to prove whether or not women contract the covenant. Indeed, I do not think the tradition can answer such a question because it is outside the assumptions of the tradition and therefore outside its concern. It is non-data. The problem is not with the formulation of the question, nor with the inadequacies of my scholarship, although this is where the traditionalist will lay the blame. The problem is that women will never be validated as complete Jews—moral initiators independent of their fathers, brothers, husbands and brothers-in-law—by proofs from a tradition in which, as Jacob Neusner demonstrates, women's holiness is purely contextual, depending on whether they are in correct formal status vis-a-vis some man. (See Neusner's *A History of the Mishnaic Law of Women,* part 5 of *The Mishnaic System of Women,*

> A woman's questions about the case would focus on the pain, injury and terror felt by the little girl. She might ask how the man was to be held morally accountable for his behavior, and what compensation was due the child.

Leiden, 1980.)

We are confronting what Mary Daly calls methodolatry. In a methodolatrous system, the choice of problems to be addressed is determined by the method, rather than the method being shaped to address questions. Questions that do not fit the categories of the method are simply classified as non-data. Patriarchal methods, says Daly, have obliterated women's own questions about the sanctification of their experience. (See her *Beyond God the Father,* Boston, 1974, pp. 11–12.) Neusner confirms this in his essay on *Seder Nashim* in *The Mishnaic System of Women,* when he emphasizes that this code does not teach about women in general but concerns itself with "what is important about women to the framers of the Mishnah." And what is important? The orderly transfer of women and property from one patriarchal domain to another. Woman, Neusner explains, is central to the content of the code but not herself an actor in it. "She sets the stage for the processes of the sacred. It is she who can be made sacred to man. It is she who ceases to stand within a man's sacred circle. But God and man—the latter through the documentary expression of his will and intention—possess the active power of sanctification."

In the passage quoted, Neusner has made explicit the principles upon which *Seder Nashim* bases its selection of topics. Other topics concerning women's tasks and obligations will be dealt with elsewhere in the Mishnah as they pertain within the categories being treated. Once the inherent assumptions in these principles are accepted, however, the range of possible questions about women is drastically narrowed. If women are "a focus of the sacred" rather than active participants in its processes, the major question about their communal participation will be, "How do we know that they are excluded?"—the question the Gemara most frequently asks the Mishnah concerning women's participation. The questions about how women use their autonomy in harmony or disharmony with the law of God will center upon sexual behavior. This is the area where women can most easily disrupt the careful codification of God and man, by behaving as if their bodies belonged to them rather than to the appropriate representative of the patriarchy. Otherwise, since women's autonomous behavior is insignificant, it is non-data, just as women's feelings are non-data.

The categories determine the questions asked. These questions in turn beget other questions, propagations from the same family. Thus Torah, Mishnah, Gemara, codes and responsa pile up a huge body of information on some topics, while others lie invisible and silent outside the many texts. Hence, when the tradition is brought to bear on the problems of Jewish women, it prefers to address the problems on which it has the most information: namely, the status problems of marriage, desertion, divorce and *chalitzah* which the tradition itself created and from whose consequences it now seeks to "protect" women, since by its own rules they can never protect themselves.

The problem of methodolatry cannot be dismissed as an "Orthodox problem" or even as a halachic problem. It is a meta-halachic problem, touching all Jews who believe the tradition possesses some relevance to modern Jewish life. Any wedding, for example, at which the groom says, "Behold, you are sanctified to me with this ring according to the law of Moses and Israel," and any divorce issued unilaterally by the husband or by a Bet Din in accordance with the rabbinic principle, *Kol d'm'kadesh, ada'ata d'rabanan m'kadesh, v'afk'inhu rabanan l'kiddushin mineh* (Anyone who marries does so with the consent of the rabbis, and the rabbis have cancelled his *kiddushin*), is utilizing the categories of acquisition and manumission in which men are actors and women are their objects. A model of Jewish marriage and divorce in which men and women are equals could be constructed only by uprooting those entire categories of the tradition.

The struggle within the Conservative movement as to whether women may be ordained as rabbis presents similar difficulties. The question is non-data in terms of the tradition. It is most easily addressable by recourse to the *halachah*'s exclusion of women from witnessing in rituals involving status transitions such as marriage, divorce and conversion as well as in matters of civil law.

If we review the source material for the law excluding women from witnessing, we will see how the *halachah* has painted itself into a corner here. The exclusion of women from witnessing is tied by the *Sifre* to the verse, "And the two men who have the quarrel shall appear before the Lord and before the priests and magistrates" (Deuteronomy 19:17). In its plain sense (*p'shat*), the verse clearly refers to litigation. The *Sifre* takes the subject phrase "the two men" out of its context and, using a *g'zerah shavah*, links it to a phrase in Deuteronomy 19:15, "on the testimony of two witnesses." The *Sifre* uses the *g'zerah shavah* to posit that, just as the phrase in verse 15 refers to witnesses, so does the one in verse 17, and since the word "two" is in the masculine in both places, witnessing is a masculine obligation. The talmudic source, *Shevuot* 30a, already has from its Mishnah the exclusion of women and must locate the scriptural source. It, too, cites Deuteronomy 19:17. Its first step is to establish that, since the phrase "who have the quarrel" obviously refers to litigants, the phrase "the two men shall appear [lit., stand]" would be superfluous unless it referred to witnesses. This is not the case grammatically, but the Talmud is disregarding grammar as a consideration. This interpretation is reinforced by the *g'zerah shavah* utilized by the *Sifre*. The *g'zerah shavah* is then used in successive *baraitot* to dispose of the rational objections offered against the interpretation. What makes this reasoning appear circular is that for both the *Sifre* and the Talmud, the disqualification of women as witnesses in law is a foregone conclusion that is not really proven by Scriptural exegesis, but which simply expresses by means of the exegesis the overwhelming precedent in Jewish life for disqualifying women. What the exegesis accomplishes is to lock the tradition into this historically circumscribed view of women.

Thus, one Conservative rabbi, voicing his objection to the ordination of women, envisions "the creation of a 'rabbinic underclass' of female rabbis in name only," whose signatures on documents of status would be "unacceptable to the vast majority of male rabbis with whom they would be serving," and prophesies (or perhaps catastrophizes) a resultant schism within the Conservative movement. The rabbi's implicit assumption is that the preservation of a movement in which women are less than fully enfranchised Jews, and the preservation of the tradition which has immobilized them, are far higher priorities than the enfranchisement of women which threatens to blow it all to hell. This is how we all—and I do not exempt myself—conceal and excuse the weaknesses and injustices of the tradition at the expense of people and principles it violates; we ourselves are terrified by the chaos that could ensue if we questioned the tradition's methods and the categories at their very roots.

I referred earlier to the distinction between data and non-data which is brought about by methodolatry. Let us turn our attention to some cases in the tradition where there are major discrepancies between the questions answered by the tradition and the questions of concern to women. One such case is brought in Tractate *Ketubot* (11a,b) and concerns a little girl less than three years old with whom a grown man has had intercourse. The tradition's question regarding the case is whether the little girl's virginity is considered to have been destroyed, in which case the *ketubah* paid her would be only half that of a virgin. Since the assumption is that the child's hymen will grow back, the ruling is that she receives the full *ketubah* of a virgin. Raba declares, "When a grown-up man has intercourse with a little girl, it is nothing, for when the girl is less than this (i.e., three), it is as if one puts the finger into the eye." As a psychotherapist working with sexual abuse victims, I frequently see women recount, or in some way relive, their childhood sexual abuse, and I have never heard one compare the experience to putting her finger in her eye. Granted that in a culture where women were resigned to being possessed by men at will, they might not have felt the sense of outrage my clients feel; nevertheless—given the physical disparities between grown men and little girls—penetration would occasion severe pain and, frequently, injury to a child. A woman's questions about the case, then, would focus on the pain, injury and terror felt by the little girl. She might ask how the man was to be held morally accountable for his behavior, and what compensation was due the child.

But these questions are non-data.

The entire area of rape is one in which women's questions differ considerably from men's. A modern case which is particularly striking was submitted to Rabbi Ephraim Oshry after the Second World War had ended. (See Irving J. Rosenbaum, *The Holocaust and Halakha*, New York, 1976, pp. 145–7.) A man, reunited with his wife after both had been in concentration camps, discovered that she had been impressed into a Nazi army brothel. Since, if a woman has voluntarily had intercourse with another man, her husband is not permitted to live with her, the husband—inquiring whether she was presumed to have acquiesced to intercourse with Nazi soldiers during her incarceration—asked for a halachic decision. Rabbi Oshry wrote a beautiful and moving responsum in which he utilized the legal distinction between rape and seduction (a distinction that depends upon the woman's having resisted) to prove that the woman was permitted to her husband and to maintain that the woman was not to be disrespected for her victimization. He, too, however, was confined within categories which place upon women a responsibility for guarding from misappropriation the bodies that belong to their fathers and husbands. All he could do was use those categories to prove the woman's innocence. He could not and did not protest that the question itself is monstrous. No one questioned the many men who were slave laborers for the Nazi munitions plants as to whether they had participated voluntarily or had been influenced by the extra cigarette ration. No decent Jew would suggest that the many Jews who despaired or who simply chose for one reason or another not to resist violently were seduced to their deaths rather than having been murdered. It is the tradition's underlying suspicion of women's lustfulness that makes a defense such as Rabbi Oshry's necessary.

More must be said about the abundance of women's feelings and experiences which have been non-data within the tradition and which Jewish women are only now beginning to recognize and name. We have no appropriate ways of sanctifying the first menstruation of little girls or the event of childbirth for the woman who labored and bore the child. We have no models for viewing women as a sanctifying community. We have no models of friendship between women or of mother-daughter relationships. We have no conception of women's sexuality independent of men. Because we are taught to conceive of God as masculine and to pray to "Him" exclusively in the masculine, we have no instinctive sense, as men do, that we are akin to the divine. Our earliest realizations are of our otherness. All too often, in order to feel included, we must imagine ourselves to be Jewish men.

When I was young, I used to pray at a little Chassidic *shtiebl*. The rebbe himself always led the *Shacharit* service, and his voice was like the still small voice Elijah heard, a sound thin as a hair and so penetrating that it made my bones resonate. I would stand next to the high wooden wall of the women's section, hearing and not seeing, almost being at one with that prayer. For years now, I have had a recurring dream. In it I have my *tallit* over my head, and I am hearing that voice and praying with it. And I am standing in the main section of the *shtiebl* where I have in reality never set foot.

Let me explain the dilemma more clearly. My favorite of the talmudic names for God is "*HaMakom*," "The Place." God is the Place of the universe, but the universe is not God's place. That is, God is not contained within the universe. It is just the locus of our rendezvous. Just as the universe is the place where I meet God, so I am the place where God meets me. I can only talk about God and to God out of my place. That is what is so important about affirming that I am made in God's image. It establishes that I am a place where God is. I then cannot talk about God's goodness or God's holiness without talking about mine or about yours, because your face, too, is a place in the universe where I can see God.

My dilemma is that the very Judaism that gave me some names that truly reflect for me God's holiness and my own, and some frames for experience that truly reflect my spiritual experience, also can demand of me that I desert my place in order to encounter God in the place of man. When I stand to hear the Ten Commandments, when I pray for the proclamation of the fatherhood of God and the brotherhood of man, when I study cases of rape and seduction in the light of whether the woman's *ketubah* is reduced, then I must desert my place and imagine myself a man standing at Mount Sinai or studying my text. And then it is not I who am encountering God at all—it is an imaginary being, a dream person, the person who prayed in wholeness in the section of the *shtiebl* where she has in fact never set foot. And this way, madness lies.

The problems I have outlined here are huge and painful, and I do not know how they are to be solved. Although it is hard for me to remember, I remind myself that I do not have to know how to solve them alone. I did not cause these problems by being a feminist. As Susannah Heschel remarks, "The crisis has not been brought on by feminism, but feminism clearly discloses the morbid condition of Judaism that has continued untreated throughout the modern period." ("No Doors, No Guards: From Jewish Feminism to a New Judaism," *Menorah* 4, March 1983, pp. 1–2.) As Heschel demonstrates, what feminism exposes is Judaism's unfinished adjustment to the relativism and pluralism of the post-Enlightenment world. The questions, then, are the following:

1. If the process of Judaism depends upon the continuous transformation of a body of received knowledge encompassing law, narrative, ritual and imagery to render it contextually relevant, and if this body of knowledge excludes the experiences, perceptions and concerns of women, then from where are Jewish women to derive their religious understandings and behavior, and how will these be authentically Jewish?

2. What shall be our stance toward the method and categories of the tradition, seeing that they have precluded the equality of women and men? Can they be Conserved or Reformed or Reconstructed?

3. If the content of the tradition is in question, how will we retain our sense of commandedness, and how will we determine what we have been commanded?

4. How can we fashion a method that will systematically frame and name the Jewish experience of both men and women?

5. How can women be included as full and equal participants in the covenant and through what sort of ritual observance will they be brought into the covenantal community?

6. Recognizing that it is idolatrous and blasphemous to behave as if God were inherently masculine, how will we expand our God-language both for theology and for prayer so that both masculine and feminine words and metaphors will be used to *name toward* God?

Until we can answer these questions and formulate a just and consistent Judaism for our time, we must, to borrow a phrase from Adrienne Rich, "dive into the wreck." I dive into this shattered rotting hulk of the tradition which I have loved and hated, and I salvage pieces to keep: Sarah's laughter; Miriam's dancing; Deborah's song, *Mitzrayim* and *Y'tziat Mitzrayim*, matzah, the journey-bread of a traveling woman; Shabbat, my grandmother's dented candlesticks; the story of the *Shechinah*, because her experience is mine. I, too, know what it is to be in exile, a stranger, an Other, in a land not my own. I, too, feel my incompleteness and seek to be whole. I, too, bear within me a ruined Temple and am always hoping to rebuild it.

May the *Shechinah* soon be restored to her place, and I to mine. ✦

HOW DO YOU DOO?

A midrash about Adam and Amram in the Garden of Eden

MARC GELLMAN

Remember the Sabbath day and keep it holy. Six days you shall labor and do all your work, but the seventh day is a sabbath of the Lord your God: you shall not do any work—you, your son or daughter, your male or female slave, or your cattle, or the stranger who is within your settlements.
—Genesis 20:8–10

Why did God give Shabbat to the animals?

Not many people know this, but, before Eve showed up, Adam's best friend in the Garden of Eden was a donkey named Amram. Amram helped Adam do his work in the garden, which is also something not many people know. They think that life in the Garden of Eden was just one big party with a lot of bananas and coconuts. Not so! God put Adam in the garden "to till it and to tend it." (Genesis 2:15) Now the work in the Garden of Eden was not that bad. Mostly, rotten fruit and broken branches had to be shlepped away to a place near the edge of the garden where God knows what happened to them. Still, it was work and it made Adam tired. So he was happy to have a friend.

Adam and Amram had another thing in common that made them friends. They were the only two living things who liked the rooster in the Garden of Eden. It started on the first morning after the first day when every living thing had been created by God. They were all tired and sore and enjoying a good night's rest when, just as the first rays of morning light were creeping across the garden, the rooster started crowing, "Cock-a-doodle!" (Another thing not many people know is that in those days roosters only knew cock-a-doodle. Roosters are pretty dumb, and they didn't learn cock-a-doodle-doo until years later.) Anyway Adam and

---

Marc Gellman was elected to the pulpit of Temple Beth Torah, Dix Hills, New York in 1981. He had previously served congregations in Teaneck, NJ, and Highland Park, IL. He is an adjunct faculty member of the Hebrew Union College—Jewish Institute of Religion, where he teaches philosophy and theology. Rabbi Gellman has also served as contributing editor of Moment, *where his commentaries* (midrashim) *for children and adults and his essays on Jewish current affairs are a regular feature.*

Amram loved the sound of the rooster, but all the other animals wanted to wring his neck, especially the night animals like the owl, opossum, bat and raccoon, who were up all night and really needed their sleep.

Every morning of that first week, Adam and Amram would wait for the rooster's cock-a-doodle, and then start shlepping the rotten fruit and broken branches to the rotten fruit and broken branches place at the edge of the garden. Some night animals would follow, hoping that Adam and Amram would lead them to the rooster so that they could wring his neck and stop his cock-a-doodle forever. No luck! Adam and Amram would hide the rooster every morning and let him sleep next to them every night.

By the fifth day of the first week, to tell you the truth, even Adam and Amram were really tired from their work. By the morning of the sixth day, to tell you the truth, even Adam and Amram would have rather stayed asleep than listen to the rooster.

Early in the morning of the seventh day the night animals were settling down for a good day's sleep and waiting for the terrible rooster cock-a-doodle, but none came! The morning of the seventh day came and went—and no sound from the rooster. The night animals were thrilled because they figured he was dead, but when they looked around they saw him asleep between Adam and Amram, who were also asleep. This was their chance to finish him off, they thought, and so they sneaked up quietly, as only night animals know how to do, and just as they were ready to pounce, they all heard a great big "SHHHHHHHH!!!!" from God.

God's shhhhhhhh!!! even woke up Adam and Amram and the rooster, who were very surprised to be asleep so late in the morning. God then told the animals about Shabbat and about resting and about making the seventh day special and holy. God told them that if all they did was work and work and work all the time with no resting, they would all look like the rotten fruit and broken branches Adam and Amram shlepped off every day. Resting was just as important as working, God told them, and that was one of the things God made Shabbat to teach.

Adam and all the day and night animals liked the idea of Shabbat; they liked it a lot! But the night animals were still confused because they *always* rested during the day, so God told them that Shabbat would begin Friday night, not Saturday morning, so that they could have some rest too.

God even helped Adam and Amram celebrate Shabbat. On that day in the garden, not a single piece of fruit turned rotten, and not a single broken branch fell to the ground. The Garden of Eden was clean as a whistle. There was nothing to do except sit around and rest and listen to the rooster of the Garden of Eden cock-a-doodle in the middle of the afternoon. ✱

The First Rosh Hashanah

Marc Gellman

When Adam was placed in the Garden of Eden by God, he was amazed at everything. The smell of the flowers made him dance. The sound of the birds made him sing for joy. But of all the things that amazed Adam, the most amazing to him was the sun. It warmed his face without touching him, and it was the only thing in the garden he could not reach. When the wonderful sun disappeared behind the edge of the garden, Adam was really scared! He cried all night long, and he kept his eye on the exact spot where the sun had disappeared. After a long while, he felt something warm on his back. He turned around and saw the sun peeking over the other edge of the garden. Adam was happy but confused. Then God explained to him how the time from one going down of the sun to another going down of the sun was one day; the time of seven days one week; the time of four weeks one month; and the time of twelve months one year. Then God stopped telling Adam about time.

Adam began to think, "God has told me that this day will be followed by six other days to make one week, and that this week will be followed by three others to make one month, and that this month will be followed by eleven others to make one year; but, what time will come after one year? Maybe...no time! Maybe the sun will go down and

The First Rosh Hashanah

never come up again?" Adam was still amazed at things, but now he was frightened and worried. He counted the days and the weeks and the months, waiting for one year. He counted and waited and worried. By the time the twelfth month came around, Adam was fidgety and nervous and could not sleep at night. "A year is the biggest time! When the year is used up all the time will be used up. The sun will go down and never come up. I will have to live in the cold and dark where I will not be able to see the flowers or hear the birds, and I will trip over things!" said Adam. On the evening of the last day of the last week of the last month of the year, Adam did not sleep a wink. He went around the garden chewing his fingernails and saying goodbye to all the things in the garden. To each living thing Adam said, "I won't see you tomorrow. If I have hurt your feelings this year I am sorry. I hope you will forgive me. Then Adam would kiss the thing and move on around the garden. After a while, just after Adam had finished saying he was sorry to some bug, he felt something warm on his back. He whirled around and saw the sun peeping up over the edge of the garden again, just like every day of the old year. Then Adam heard God counting, "Ten years are one decade. Ten decades are one century. Ten centuries...." By this time Adam had fallen asleep. He was amazed at the bigness of time. Time was even bigger than the sun. Adam decided to remember the end of each year by apologizing to all the living things he might have hurt during that year. He felt better doing it, and he remembered how scared he had been during that first year.

When Adam awakened the next day, he smelled the flowers and heard the birds singing. ✻

Marc Gellman was elected to the pulpit of Temple Beth Torah, Dix Hills, New York in 1981. He had previously served congregations in Teaneck, NJ, and Highland Park, IL. He is an adjunct faculty member of the Hebrew Union College—Jewish Institute of Religion, where he teaches philosophy and theology. Rabbi Gellman has also served as contributing editor of Moment, *where his commentaries* (midrashim) *for children and adults and his essays on Jewish current affairs are a regular feature.*

13 THINGS KIDS DON'T KNOW ABOUT TZ'DAKAH

DANNY SIEGEL

Danny Siegel is a freelance author, lecturer, and poet living in Rockville, MD. He has published more than a dozen books of poetry, midrash *translations, humor, essays, and a book on* tzedakah *and Jewish values. He also gives readings from his works. His prose career began when Mo-*ment, *of which he is a contributing editor, published his first article on* tzedakah—*"Gym Shoes and Irises."*

I confess: about a year ago I had decided I wanted to devote all my lecture and teaching time to adults. I believe it was largely for selfish reasons—the adults could offer me more insights from their own life stories and varied fields of expertise, and I could therefore conclude a talk having been that much more personally enriched by their ideas. A store owner could tell me "the true real-life story of making a living," a doctor could bring me into the intimate realms of Life and Death, a lawyer could share his exhilaration in overseeing an estate where $100,000 was left for the Jewish deaf or a day school . . . all wonderful material for my mind and writing, rich with the strong rhythms of People and Dreams, Dignity and Hope.

On the other hand, the younger generation's frame of reference was narrower: school grades, achievement, first love and unlove, junk-food, decisions for college and graduate school. There was more, of course, but generally I demanded more, a broader vision of life, a deeper understanding of joy and tsoris, loss and redemption of the people, more than the kids could give.

Much of my material is still addressed to adults, but I have just reviewed the recent few years' discussions with the "kids"—seventh graders through college students—and I see that I have learned things I could never have discovered from the parents or grandparents. This article is only a summary of some of the negatives, the holes in one area of Jewish education: Tz'dakah—Gemillut Chassadim, how Jews give away their money, their time, their energies in acts of gentle kindness. What often happens is that I take ideas from a talk with the kids, and bring the results to the parents some other time—the questions and answers of some of the new generation, a generous but responsibility-laden gift for the adults.

The results of my review are recorded, besides, in the hope that what I have learned from the young will bring about a distinct shift in the direction of Jewish education. A good scream now and again at the Education Establishment is healthy for the community, though frankly the past has shown that educators and teachers react disappointingly slowly. The frustrations are well-known and on a grand scale. I have seen a couple of my friends leave the field and two more are about to leave, at least for now—excellent people—and I can say unequivocally that I do not blame them. (What I am really saying is that I envy them . . . and if I had some business to provide me with *parnosseh*—some livelihood other than teaching and lecturing—I would also join their ranks.)

Then let us begin this one last *shrei,* a simple non-scientific review of what I have learned from the "kids" about Tz'dakah.

1. They Do Not Know About The People For Whom They Were Named

I ask them, "How many of you know your Jewish name?" About 85–90 percent of the hands go up.

I ask, "How many of you know for whom you are named?" About 50 percent of the hands go up.

And I ask, "How many of you know anything about the person for whom you were named, how they lived, what their personalities were?" No more than one out of five responds . . . many of these indicating that all they know is that it was "some great-aunt," "a grandfather."

I believe—as an exasperated educator—that the children are being deprived of models. If they knew the grandeur of the lives of those who played a part in their lives before they were born—the kindnesses of a beloved aunt, the openheartedness of an uncle lost in the war, the generosities of a grandmother whose only legacy might otherwise be one single photograph from the Old Country—if only they knew, they might wish to assimilate those mentschlech qualities into their own lives.

Susan is named "Chaya Sara," for a great aunt who used to bake challah for the poor and leave the loaves on their doorsteps before Shabbas.

Moshe Ber from Detroit (whose American name I forgot) is named for a great uncle whose two brothers died. Each of the three brothers had three or four children—ten in all, and this Moshe Ber chose to raise all ten. So Moshe Ber told me, his face showing pride, his words coming in a rush of joy and admiration.

2. They Do Not Know What Jews Do With Unclaimed Bodies

New Jersey. A dozen kids, two doctors' children. The topic is "Introduction to Jewish Medical Ethics." We stray to the topic of the need for bodies for medical school anatomy classes. The near-unanimous opinion is that an unclaimed body should automatically be given to a medical school.

The Talmud indicates that a Met Mitzvah—an unclaimed body—is a particularly sensitive category of Mitzvah, one to be handled with specific care. Even the High Priest is obligated to handle the burial if necessary (though Kohanim are generally forbidden to come into contact with the dead—except their own close relatives). Even if he is on the way to performing the Passover sacrifice, he must delay that and bury the unclaimed body. And the body is considered so precious—so important is the dignity of a person, alive or dead—that he may be buried even in the immediate area where he is found, if that is necessary. Jewish tradition, rather than take advantage of the vulnerability of one who has died without friends or relatives, demands the utmost concern and accommodation.

I ask, "What is a Chessed Shel Emet Society?" No response.

A Chessed Shel Emet Society buries people, occupying itself with the dead to such a degree that it insures any Jew—no matter how poor, no matter how anonymous—a proper burial, with dignity, with a marker. No Jew, without his express consent, should be sent to an anatomy table, or a potter's field, a poor-man's grave.

Shirley works the switchboard at the Jewish Theological Seminary. For forty years her mother was the president of the Chessed Shel Emet Society of Yonkers, New York, collecting money from members and other people of the community to insure a proper burial for everyone. They were notified by hospitals and other agencies of a death, and if there was no one to bury the deceased, they would make all the arrangements. Shirley remembers sitting with her mother at the cemetery before the High Holidays, with a pushka, collecting coins and dollars for this Mitzvah.

3. They Do Not Know Where Their Keren Ami Hebrew School Tz'dakah Money Goes

I ask, "Where did your Keren Ami money go?" Half say, "Israel,"—maybe 65 percent. Some say, "Trees."

I ask, "Where—besides for trees—in Israel?" Most say nothing.

I think that some think that Keren Ami is really Karen Ami, some lady who has been supported in High Style through their contributions and who will some day visit their school and say, "Thank you for the Gelt."

A friend in Israel tells me that a director of a certain charitable institution bought a car from the institution's budget which is used minimally for the institution, mostly for private use.

I ask, "Would you have wanted your money to go there?" Silence.

4. They Do Not Know Jewish Tz'dakot

I ask, "Could you name for me some places where you could give your money?" "The American Cancer Society," "The Red Cross," "United Way," "Goodwill," "The Salvation Army," "Federation." At one point, eight non-Jewish charities had been named, and only one Jewish Tz'dakah. All of them, at that one study session, major organizations.

There is a group of people in Israel—ten or fifteen paratroopers whose friends were killed in the Yom Kippur War—who collect money for their friends' orphaned children, for summer camp, for bar mitzvahs, for whatever. They have no name or printed publicity for their organization, except, I suppose, "The Chevra," and word of mouth. There is a couple in Jerusalem that collects old wedding dresses that they lend to poor brides.

There is a Tzaddik in Pittsburgh who goes to mental institutions in a wide area, providing for the Jewish retarded and mental patients who need Pesach and Purim and Chanukah.

There is a man in Jerusalem—a former Clevelander—on the look-out for Mitzvot to do.

5. They Do Not Know What A Jewish Free-Loan Society Is

I ask, "What is a Jewish free-loan society?" thinking that the name itself will tell them. One out of forty or fifty has heard of one or knows of one in the local community. Once a Gemillut Chessed—Free-Loan—Society is explained, some show skepticism that anyone would do anything for anyone for free.

The Jewish Catalog, *Volume II, pages 424–25 (the Yellow Pages) lists a few of the free-loan, free-shelter, and free-clothes organizations in the American and Canadian Jewish communities.*

Dr. David Weiss, renowned Jerusalem immunologist and lecturer, informed me that there are 250–300 Gemillut Chessed Societies in Jerusalem alone. The one he works with has not had a single default in eighteen years.

I say, "Speak with your parents and

grandparents. They have heard of these things."

6. They Do Not Know Where To Find The Jewish Poor In Their Community

I ask, "Suppose you wanted to make sure some Jew living in poverty had a decent Pesach or Sukkot meal—where would you go?" Except in New York (most of the young Jews know of the 200,000–300,000 poor Jews on the Lower East Side, in Queens, in Brooklyn), the answer is occasionally, "In the old Jewish section of town. Such-and-such a street." But usually the answer is no hands raised, no words.

In the Providence, Rhode Island, area there was minimal response. I found a map, through a friend who works with the Jewish elderly, with red dots for every house where an elderly person lives who receives a government-subsidized meal (either at homes or at designated centers). Not every one lives at or below the poverty line, but that is the map with which to start.

7. They Do Not Know Jewish Retarded Adults

I ask, "How many of you have retarded relatives?" Five out of sixty hands go up; one is unsure.

I ask, "How many of you might find others, if you asked your parents about the family tree?" A couple of hands more go up as the students begin to recall stories. One raises his hand, but is confused: he is thinking of senility, an old aunt or grandmother in a convalescent home.

"How many of you have met a retarded Jewish adult, enough to have had a conversation with him?" (A Jewish day school:) Ten out of forty-five hands go up, eighth and ninth graders.

The Irene Gaster Hostel for Retarded Adults in Jerusalem is in the middle of a long struggle to find a new location. The neighbors are forcing them out. They look around and the new neighbors say, "No." Neighborhoods in the States say the same, "Property values. Zoning laws. Danger." The usual.

"Best Boy," a film by Ira Wohl, became a "sleeper" and an "event" at a Toronto film festival. A documentary of Ira's over-fifty retarded cousin Phillip, it was shown again and again at the festival and then began to move to the commercial theaters. There were staggering reviews, despite the most primitive movie equipment, including crude hand-held microphones.

"Go see it when it comes to town," I suggest.

The shock of the day school is that it is in Toronto, a place where much has been done for retarded adults by Rabbi Joseph Kelman. I was in Israel one summer and met a group of them on tour.

8. They Do Not Know The Nature And Extent Of Exorbitant Overheads, Waste, And Fraud.

I ask the students, "What percentage of your dollar goes to what the publicity says? Would you give if you knew that only 43¢ was used for what it was supposed to be used for?" An absolute "No" from everyone.

UJA fundraising expenses and overhead range from 9–11 percent, an astoundingly low figure.

Some smaller, volunteer organizations (such as the paratroopers) can function with no overhead or minimal expenses.

The December 19, 1979 New York Times, reporting an investigation of fundraising tactics of New York police associations, stated that as much as 90 percent of the money was kept by the professional fundraisers hired to solicit funds. The Metropolitan Police Conference of Eastern New York (comprising some eighty patrolman's associations) collected $676,000 in 1978, of which $436,000—64 percent—went to a private fundraiser.

TV news at Christmas time reminds people to beware.

I say to the kids, and to the adults, "Any place that doesn't send you a copy of its budget when you ask for one should not get your money. It is *your* money." And specifically to the kids, "Particularly because you may have so little to give—be careful."

Charity USA (NY Times Books, 1979), by Carl Bakal, was recently published. It is a lengthy, detailed account of just why we must be careful.

9. They Do No Know How Much They Are Supposed To Give

I ask, "How much should Jews give to Tz'dakah?" Three answers: (1) "Ten percent." (2) "As much as is necessary." (3) "As much as you want."

The Shulchan Aruch states, "One should give up to a fifth of one's possessions—that is the Mitzvah to an extraordinay degree. One tenth is considered an average percentage, and less is considered miserly."

Passionate discussion follows, sensitive insights, honest concern.

10. They Do Not Know What A Righteous Person Is, Nor Have They Met One

I ask, "How many of you have ever met a righteous person?" A group in Florida responds: three out of twenty-eight, two of whom described a person who always davened and was always at shul. In another place, another teen-ager asks, "What does 'righteous' mean?"—not asking for the connotations, but merely the dictionary definition. But they had all met brilliant people, people with straight A's on their report cards. Larger percentages had met great athletes than had met Tzaddikim.

In Utica there are Tzaddikim, I am told. In Toronto. In Sacramento, Atlanta, Chicago, Boston, New Haven, St. Louis. This is what people tell me.

11. They Do Not Know The Difference Between Tz'dakah And Fund Raising

I ask, "What Tz'dakah projects

have you been involved in?" "Walkathon," "Jogathon," "knocking on people's doors," "people knocking at our door for Girl Scouts or The Heart Fund." Often there are broader aspects to their work, youth-group projects such as entertaining at the local old age home for Purim and Chanukah or a local clothes drive, but more often than not, they describe organization or school projects: a car wash, raffle, and the like. The funds are usually turned over to some central office for distribution.

I describe friends with two separate checking accounts, one for Tz'dakah and one for daily expenses.

I mention homes with pushkas where the family sits together to decide where the money should go.

And Tz'dakah collectives: people pooling their Tz'dakah money and meeting to decide where to give.

People who make it a day-to-day activity, their Tz'dakah work.

12. They Were Not Informed That Bar Or Bat Mitzvah Time Was The Time To Begin Full-Fledged Sophisticated Tz'dakah Giving

I ask, "How many of you were told that you should have taken 10–20 percent of your bar or bat mitzvah money and given it away to Tz'dakah?" One hand in twenty, two out of fifty.

Suspecting a particular reason, I ask, "How many of you were told to put your money away for college?" Always more than half, usually more than three-quarters.

I do some Tz'dakah-mathematics with them. "Let's take an exceptional, fancy case," I say. "Let's assume the child goes to Brown or Princeton or Brandeis or Harvard. At $35,000 for this college education—and this is a conservative figure nowadays—if you take away 10 percent of $1,000 of the Bar Mitzvah gifts, that leaves $100/$35,000, or .28 of one percent.

I ask, "Why do you think the Talmud and Shulchan Aruch say that even a poor person must give Tz'dakah?" They answer, "So that they will be reminded that no matter how poor they might be, there is always someone in a worse condition." And some answer, "Giving is a sign of a Jew's self-dignity, a privilege. Everyone should have that privilege."

I ask, "Why didn't they—parents, teachers, rabbis—tell you that?" No reasonable answer other than saving for college, an Israel trip, and similar very expensive projects.

Sometimes I become Hellfire and Brimstone. "You were cheated. I was cheated. Raise hell." Often I let it pass.

13. They Do Not Discuss Tz'dakah At Home, Nor Do They Know Why It Is Not A Topic Of Discussion With Their Parents

I ask, "How many of you discuss Tz'dakah at home with your parents? Where or how they give or how much or why?" Perhaps three out of forty-five raise their hands.

"Why not?" I ask, unsure myself, surprised that my home was an exception. The answers are hazy, halting, unsure.

"Money is my parents' own business." (Justifiably so to a great extent.)

"We don't talk about anything." (Exaggerated, said humorously, typically by a teen-ager.)

"My parents are cheap." (I am astounded, and assure the student that this is certainly not the case, and that she should search for other possible reasons. Later, I am more astounded when the local Jewish professionals tell me the child was right.)

By now, it is clear I should provide some summary of this backlog of informal statistic-taking. It is obvious that the topics of Tz'dakah and Gemillut Chassadim are generally mentioned only on the most primitive levels in our Jewish schools—including the day schools and yeshivot. Rarely (except Boston, Miami, and some other scattered locales) is Tz'dakah taught as a course. There is no listing for it in the catalogue of the Jewish Theological Seminary, and I am certain that is true of other institutions for advanced Jewish study. It is almost never made a prominent part of the rabbis' speeches to the bar or bat mitzvah child. The children emerge into Jewish adulthood with a siddur or kiddush cup or Shabbat candlesticks, but no nicely-designed pushka, no list of Tz'dakot to commit themselves to. (The exception I know of—though there are more, I am sure—was a rabbi-friend who gave a pushka to each bar mitzvah or bat mitzvah child.)

A threatening, discouraging gap is created between the Hebrew School and Keren Ami days and the young Jew's emergence into the Big World where the preponderant number of young adults find themselves unaware of the privilege of giving. They do not know the most basic rules, the mechanics of Tz'dakah, nor do they have many human precedents or models. They are grossly and embarrassingly ignorant of its wonders and joys.

There is a saving grace, though—a critical one. It can be explained by the old joke, "What is the difference between ignorance and apathy?" "I don't know and I don't care." While the former may be true of the next generation, I do not believe the latter to be the case. They are definitely not apathetic to the tradition and insights of Tz'dakah. Indeed, the response, with the proper, sensitive presentation of the material, is nearly universally enthusiastic. This generation is much more involved in volunteer work, infinitely more bound to the destiny of the State of Israel, distinctly more committed to the rescue of Soviet Jews and other Jews in danger than I was at their age. If you raise the issue of Iranian Jews, they are sympathetic and willing to commit time, and money, to a solution. Mention the loneliness of the Jewish elderly in their community, the alienation of the Jewish deaf (whose intermarriage rate is very high), the needs of the Jewish retarded, and they are responsive.

Extraordinarily responsive.

Now all that we need is a sweeping, revolutionary, never-done-before re-ordering of our Jewish educational priorities: the badgering of teachers and principals and rabbis, the hell-raising with synagogues and JCC's, the battering down of old, seamy doors of the Establishment to get them to see that the alternative is a generation of bright, well-degreed, well-to-do egocentric Jews. A generation where brains mean everything, achievement per se is rewarded with high honors, and the heart is left to atrophy. The demonstrations and manifestoes, placards and marches, and sit-downs and strikes—the whole Megillah of tactics we learned in the '60s can now be put to full use L'Shem Shamayim—for the sake of heaven and for the Jews' own self-integrity and preservation. ✡

עלינו

The Riddle of The Ordinary

Cynthia Ozick

Though we all claim to be monotheists, there is one rather ordinary way in which we are all also dualists: we all divide the world into the Ordinary and the Extraordinary. This is undoubtedly the most natural division the mind is subject to—plain and fancy, simple and recondite, commonplace and awesome, usual and unusual, credible and incredible, quotidian and intrusive, natural and unnatural, regular and irregular, boring and rhapsodic, secular and sacred, profane and holy: however the distinction is characterized, there is no human being who does not, in his own everydayness, feel the difference between the Ordinary and the Extraordinary.

The Extraordinary is easy. And the

ALEINU, the title of this column, is taken from the prayer which begins with that word, and means, "it is incumbent upon us." This column is for wrestling with God and His commandments.

Cynthia Ozick, essayist, novelist, and short-story writer, received the Rea Award for the Short Story. Her new novel, The Messiah of Stockholm, *was published in March 1987.*

more extraordinary the Extraordinary is, the easier it is: "easy" in the sense that we can almost always recognize it. There is no one who does not know when something special is happening: the high, terrifying, tragic, and ecstatic moments are unmistakable in any life. Of course the Extraordinary can sometimes be a changeling, and can make its appearance in the cradle of the Ordinary; and then it is not until long afterward that we become aware of how the visitation was not, after all, an ordinary one. But by and large the difference between special times and ordinary moments is perfectly clear, and we are never in any doubt about which are the extraordinary ones.

How do we respond to the Extraordinary? This too is easy: by paying attention to it. The Extraordinary is so powerful that it commands from us a redundancy, a repetition of itself: it seizes us so undividedly, it declares itself so dazzlingly or killingly, it is so deafening with its Look! See! Notice! Pay Attention!, that the only answer we can give is to look, see, notice, and pay attention. The Extraordinary sets its own terms for its reception, and its terms are inescapable. The Extraordi-

> The Ordinary, simply by being so ordinary, tends to make us ignorant or neglectful; when something does not insist on being noticed, when we aren't grabbed by the collar or struck on the skull by a presence or an event, we take for granted the very things that most deserve our gratitude.

nary does not let you shrug your shoulders and walk away.

But the Ordinary is a much harder case. In the first place, by making itself so noticeable — it is around us all the time — the Ordinary has got itself in a bad fix with us: we hardly ever notice it. The Ordinary, simply by *being* so ordinary, tends to make us ignorant or neglectful; when something does not insist on being noticed, when we aren't grabbed by the collar or struck on the skull by a presence or an event, we take for granted the very things that most deserve our gratitude.

And this is the chief vein and deepest point concerning the Ordinary: that it *does* deserve our gratitude. The Ordinary lets us live out our humanity: it doesn't scare us, it doesn't excite us, it doesn't distract us — it brings us the safe return of the school bus every day, it lets us eat one meal after another, put one foot in front of the other; in short, it is equal to the earth's provisions, it grants us life, continuity, the leisure to recognize who and what we are, and who and what our fellows are, these creatures who live out their everydayness side by side with us in their own unextraordinary ways. Ordinariness can be defined as a breathing-space: the breathing-space between getting born and dying, perhaps; or else the breathing-space between rapture and rapture; or more usually, the breathing-space between one disaster and the next. Ordinariness is sometimes the *status quo,* sometimes the slow, unseen movement of a subtle but ineluctable cycle, like a ride on the hour hand of the clock; in any case the Ordinary is above all *what is expected*.

And what is expected is not often thought of as a gift.

The second thing that ought to be said about the Ordinary is that it is sometimes extraordinarily dangerous to notice it. And this is strange, because I have just spoken of the gratitude we owe to the unnoticed foundations of our lives, and how careless we always are about this gratitude, how unthinking we are to take for granted the humdrum dailiness that is all the luxury we are ever likely to know on this planet. There are ways to try to apprehend the nature of this luxury, but they are psychological tricks and do no good. It is pointless to contemplate, only for the sake of feeling gratitude, the bitter, vicious, crippled, drugged, diseased, deformed, despoiled, or corrupted lives that burst against their own mortality in hospitals, madhouses, prisons, all those horrendous lives chained to poverty and its variegated spawn in the long, bleak wastes on the outer margins of Ordinariness, mired in the dread of a ferocious Extraordinariness that slouches in insatiably every morning and never departs even in sleep — contemplating this, gratitude for our own Ordinariness does not come easily, and has its demeaning price. Comparison confers relief more often than gratitude, and the gratitude that comes out of reflection on the extraordinary misfortune of others is misbegotten. —You remember how in one of the Old English poets we are told how the rejoicing hosts of Heaven look down at the tortures of the damned, feeling the special pleasure of their own exemption. The consciousness of Ordinariness *is* the consciousness of exemption.

That is one way it is dangerous to take special notice of the Ordinary.

The second danger, I think, is even more terrible. But before I am ready to speak of this new, nevertheless very ancient, danger, I want to ask this question: if we are willing to see the Ordinary as a treasure and a gift, what are we to *do* about it? Or, to put it another way, what is to be gained from noticing the Ordinary? Morally and metaphysically, what are our obligations to the Ordinary? Here art and philosophy meet with a quizzical harmony unusual between contenders. "Be one of those upon whom nothing is lost," Henry James advised; and that is one answer, the answer of what would appear to be the supreme aesthetician. For the sake of the honing of consciousness, for the sake of becoming sensitive, at every moment, *to* every moment, for the sake of making life as superlatively polished as the most sublime work of art, we ought to notice the Ordinary.

No one since the Greek sculptors and artisans has expressed this sense more powerfully than Walter Pater, that eloquent Victorian whose obsession with attaining the intensest sensations possible casts a familiar light out toward the century that followed him. Pater, like Coleridge before him and James after him, like the metaphysicians of what has come to be known as the Counterculture, was after all the highs he could accumulate in a lifetime. "We are all under sentence of death," he writes, ". . . we have an interval, and then our place knows us no more. Some spend this interval in listlessness, some in high passions, the wisest . . . in art and song. For our only chance lies in expanding that interval, in getting as many pulsations as possible into the given time. Great passions may give us this quickened sense of life. . . Only be sure it is passion — that it does yield you this fruit of a quickened, multiplied consciousness . . . Of this wisdom, the poetic passion, the desire for beauty, the love of art for art's sake, has most; for art comes to you professing frankly to give nothing but the highest quality to your moments as they pass, and simply for those moments' sake." And like a Zen master who seizes on the data of life only to transcend them, he announces: "Not the fruit of experience, but experience itself, is the end."

What — in this view, which once more has the allegiance of the *Zeitgeist* — what is Art? It is first noticing, and then sanctifying, the Ordinary. It is making the Ordinary into the Extraordinary. It is the impairment of the distinction between the Ordinary and the Extraordinary.

The aestheticians — the great Experiencers — can be refuted. I bring you a Hebrew melody to refute them with. It is called "The Choice"; the poet is Yeats; since the poem is only eight lines long I would like to give over the whole of it. It begins by discriminating between life interpreted as *doing* beautiful things or *having* beautiful things:

The Choice

The intellect of man is forced to choose
Perfection of the life, or of the work,
And if it take the second must refuse
A heavenly mansion, raging in the dark.
When all that story's done, what's the news?
In luck or out the toil has left its mark:
That old perplexity an empty purse,
Or the day's vanity, the night's remorse.

Our choice, according to Yeats, is the choice between pursuing the life of Deed, where acts have consequences, where the fruit of experience is more gratifying than the experience itself, and pursuing the life of Art, which signifies the celebration of shape and mood. Art, he tells us, turns away from the divine preference, and finishes out a life in empty remorse; in the end the sum of the life of Art is nothing. —The ironies here are multitudinous, for no one ever belonged more to the mansion of Art than Yeats himself; and it might be said that in this handful of remarkable lines Yeats condemned his own passions and his own will.

But there is a way in which the Yeats poem, though it praises Deed over Image, though it sees the human being as a creature to be judged by his acts rather than how well he has made something — there is a way in which this poem is after all *not* a Hebrew melody. The Jewish perception of how the world is constituted also tells us that we are to go in the way of Commandment rather than symbol, goodness rather than sensation; but it will never declare that the price of Art, Beauty, Experience, Pleasure, Exaltation is a "raging in the dark" or a loss of the "heavenly mansion."

The Jewish understanding of the Ordinary is in some ways very close to Pater, and again very far from Yeats, who would punish the "perfection of the work" with an empty destiny.

With David the King we say: "All that is in the heaven and the earth is thine," meaning that it is all there for our wonder and our praise. "Be one of those upon whom nothing is lost" —

What is to be gained from noticing the Ordinary? Morally and metaphysically, what are our obligations to the Ordinary? Here art and philosophy meet with a quizzical harmony unusual between contenders.

For the sake of the honing of consciousness, for the sake of becoming sensitive, at every moment, to every moment, for the sake of making life as superlatively polished as the most sublime work of art, we ought to notice the Ordinary.

James's words, but the impulse that drives them is the same as the one which enjoins the observant Jew (the word "observant" is exact) to bless the moments of this world at least one hundred times a day. One hundred times: but Ordinariness is more frequent than that, Ordinariness crowds the day, we swim in the sense of our dailiness; and yet there is a blessing for every separate experience of the Ordinary.

Jewish life is crammed with such blessings — blessings that take note of every sight, sound, and smell, every rising up and lying down, every morsel brought to the mouth, every act of cleansing. Before he sits down to his meal, the Jew will speak the following: "Blessed are You, O Lord our God, Ruler of the Universe, whose Commandments hallow us, and who commands us to wash our hands." When he breaks his bread, he will bless God for having "brought forth bread from the earth." Each kind of food is similarly praised in turn, and every fruit in its season is praised for having renewed itself in the cycle of the seasons. And when the meal is done, a thanksgiving is said for the whole of it, and table-songs are sung with exultation.

The world and its provisions, in short, are *observed* — in the two meanings of "observe." Creation is both noticed and felt to be sanctified. Everything is minutely paid attention to, and then ceremoniously praised. Here is a Talmudic saying: "Whoever makes a profane use of God's gifts — which means partaking of any worldly joy without thanking God for it — commits a theft against God." And a Talmudic dispute is recorded concerning which is the more important Scriptural utterance: loving your neighbor as yourself, or the idea that we are all the children of Adam. The sage who has the final word chooses the-children-of-Adam thesis, because, he explains, our common creatureliness includes the necessity of love. But these celebrations through noticing are not self-centered and do not stop at humanity, but encompass every form of life and non-life. So there are blessings to rejoice in on smelling sweet woods or barks, fragrant plants, fruits, spices, or oils. There is a blessing on witnessing lightning, falling stars, great mountains and deserts: "Blessed are You . . . who fashioned Creation." The sound of thunder has its praise, and the sight of the sea, and a rainbow; beautiful animals are praised, and trees in their first blossoming of the year or for their beauty alone, and the new moon, and new clothing, and sexual delight. The sight of a sage brings a blessing for the creation of human wisdom, the sight of a disfigured person praises a Creator who varies the form of His creatures. From the stone to the human being, creatureliness is extolled.

This huge and unending shower of blessings on our scenes and habitations, on all the life that occupies the planet, on every plant and animal, and on every natural manifestation, serves us doubly: in the first place, what you are taught to praise you will not maim or exploit or destroy. In the second place, the categories and impulses of Art become the property of the simplest soul: because it is all the handiwork of the Creator, everything Ordinary is seen to be Extraordinary. The world, and every moment in it, is seen to be sublime, and not merely *seen to be*, but brought home to the intensest part of consciousness.

Come back with me now to Pater: "The service of philosophy," he writes, "of speculative culture, toward the human spirit is to rouse, to startle it into sharp and eager observation. Every moment some form grows perfect in hand or face; some tone on the hills or the sea is choicer than the rest; some mood of passion or insight or intellectual excitement is irresistibly real and attractive to us — for that moment only." And now here at last is Pater's most celebrated phrase, so famous that it has often been burlesqued: "To burn always with this hard, gemlike flame, to maintain this ecstasy, is success in life."

But all this is astonishing. An idolater singing a Hebrew melody? I call Pater an idolater because he is one; and so is every aesthetician who sees the work of art as an end in itself. Saying "Experience itself is the end" is the very opposite of blessing the Creator as the source of all experience.

And just here is the danger I spoke of before, the danger Yeats darkly apprehended — the deepest danger our human brains are subject to. The Jew has this in common with the artist: he means nothing to be lost on him, he brings all his mind and senses to bear on noticing the Ordinary, he is equally alert to Image and Experience, nothing that passes before him is taken for granted, everything is exalted. If we are enjoined to live in the condition of noticing all things — or, to put it more extremely but more exactly, in the condition of awe — *how can we keep ourselves from sliding off from awe at God's creation to worship of God's creation*? And does it matter if we do?

The difference, the reason it matters, is a signal and shattering one: the

The Riddle of the Ordinary

difference is what keeps us from being idolaters.

What is an idol? Anything that is allowed to come between ourselves and God. Anything that is *instead of* God. Anything that we call an end in itself, and yet is not God Himself.

The Mosaic vision concerning all this is uncompromisingly pure and impatient with self-deception; and this is the point on which Jews are famously stiffnecked — nothing but the Creator, no substitute and no mediator. The Creator is not contained in His own Creation; the Creator is incarnate in nothing, and is free of any image or imagining. God is not any part of Nature, or in any part of Nature; God is not any man, or in any man. When we praise nature or man or any experience or work of man, we are worshiping the Creator, and the Creator alone.

But there is another way of thinking which is easier, and sweeter, and does not require human beings to be so tirelessly uncompromising, and to be so cautious about holding on to the distinction between delight in the world and worship of the world.

Here is a story. A Buddhist sage once rebuked a person who excoriated an idolater: "Do you think it makes any difference to God," he asked, "whether this old woman gives reverence to a block of wood? Do you think God is incapable of taking the block of wood into Himself? Do you think God will ignore anyone's desire to find Him, no matter where, and through whatever means? All worship goes up to God, who is the source of worship."

These are important words; they offer the most significant challenge to purist monotheism that has ever been stated. They tell us that the Ordinary is not merely, when contemplated with intensity, the Extraordinary, but more, much more than that — that the Ordinary is also the divine. Now there are similar comments in Jewish sources, especially in Chassidism, which dwell compassionately on the nobility of the striving for God, no matter through what means. But the striving is always toward the Creator Himself, the struggle is always toward the winnowing-out of every mediating surrogate. The Kotzker Rebbe went so far in his own striving that he even dared to interpret the command against idols as a warning not to make an idol out of a command of God. So, in general, Jewish thought balks at taking the metaphor for the essence, at taking the block of wood as a symbol or representation or mediator for God, despite the fact that the wood and its worshiper stand for everything worthy of celebration: the tree grew in its loveliness, the carver came and fashioned it into a pleasing form, the woman is alert to holiness; the tree, the carver, the woman who is alert to holiness are all together a loveliness and a reason to rejoice in the world. But still the wood does not mean God. It is instead of God.

It is not true, as we so often hear, that Judaism is a developmental religion, that there is a progression upward from Moses to the Prophets. The Prophets enjoined backsliders to renew themselves through the Mosaic idea, and the Mosaic idea is from then to now, and has survived unmodified: "Take heed to yourselves, that your heart be not deceived, and ye turn aside, and serve other gods, and worship them." (Deut. 11:16) This perception has never been superseded. To seem to supersede it is to transgress it.

So it is dangerous to notice and to praise the Ordinariness of the world, its inhabitants and its events. We want to do it, we rejoice to do it, above all we are commanded to do it — but there is always the easy, the sweet, the beckoning, the lenient, the *interesting* lure of the *Instead Of:* the wood of the tree instead of God, the rapture-bringing horizon instead of God, the work of art instead of God, the passion for history instead of God, philosophy and history of philosophy instead of God, the State instead of God, the shrine instead of God, the sage instead of God, the order of the universe instead of God, the prophet instead of God.

There is no Instead Of. There is

God is not any part of Nature, or in any part of Nature; God is not any man, or in any man. When we praise nature or man or any experience or work of man, we are worshiping the Creator, and the Creator alone.

only the Creator. God is alone. That is what we mean when we utter the ultimate Idea which is the pinnacle of the Mosaic revolution in human perception: God is One.

The child of a friend of mine was taken to the Egyptian galleries of the museum. In a glass case stood the figure of a cat resplendent in the perfection of its artfulness — long-necked, gracile, cryptic, authoritative, beautiful, spiritual, autonomous, complete in itself. "I understand," said the child, "how they wanted to bow down to this cat. I feel the same." And then she said a Hebrew word: — אסור — forbidden — the great hallowed No which tumbles down the centuries from Sinai, the No that can be said only after the world is no longer taken for granted, the No that can rise up only out of the abundant celebrations and blessings of Yes, Yes, Yes, the shower of Yeses that praise fragrant oils, and wine, and sex, and scholars, and thunder, and new clothes, and falling stars, and washing your hands before eating. ✡

A MOMENT REPORT: WHO IS A JEW?

An old puzzle becomes an urgent political problem

It surely strikes many American Jews as strange that the issue of who is a Jew has become a political football in Israel. With all the problems the Jewish people and the Jewish state confront these days, it might appear that debating definitions is hardly a priority matter.

Yet there are certain legal areas where the matter of definition matters very much. The specific issue at hand, for example, is an amendment to Israel's Law of Return, the basic law that gives Jews the right to immigrate to Israel and to be accepted there as citizens without going through a process of naturalization. (The underlying concept, as the name of the law implies, is that a Jew coming to Israel is merely reclaiming his earlier—pre-exilic—status rather than coming to a "new" country.) The Law, in its present version, refers to "Jews" but does not define the term. Israel's Agudat Yisrael party seeks an amendment to the Law, which would insert after the word "Jew" the words "according to Halachah"—that is, according to Jewish religious law.

Jewish religious law holds that anyone born of a Jewish mother is a Jew, as well as anyone who has been converted to Judaism. It is the matter of conversion that is at the heart of the current dispute. In the traditional Orthodox view, there are very precise requirements that must be fulfilled for a valid conversion. The question in Israel today is whether that traditional view, and those precise requirements, shall become the prevailing law of the land.

American Jews, accustomed to the radical separation of church and state, may instinctively reject such a prospect. On the other hand, Israel is, formally, a Jewish state, and it is not at all clear that a Jewish state can muddle along without a definition of the word "Jew."

Prime Minister Begin, in forming his new coalition, has promised the Agudah that he will lobby for the proposed amendment; that was the price he had to pay in order to win Agudah support for his new government. But he has thus far resisted the Agudah proposal that he make support for the amendment a condition for coalition participation. There are many members of the Likud, Mr. Begin's own coalition party, who would object to such a stipulation.

The result is an uneasy compromise. The Agudah has stated that it will not live indefinitely within the coalition unless the amendment is passed.

And, in the meantime, American Jews—especially the Conservative and Reform movements—have registered their objection to the amendment in no uncertain terms. The tradition of religious pluralism that American Jewry enjoys does not readily square with the institutionalization of a particular definition, much less a particular political party's interpretation of these matters. Moreover, both the Conservative and Reform movements have sought to establish their presence in Israel, where religious pluralism is still very fragile. Adoption of the Agudah position would be seen by these movements as an insulting setback.

Because few domestic debates within Israel impinge so directly on the interests and sensibilities of American Jews, Jewish religious leaders in this country have strong views on the issue. We have spoken with three such leaders, and herewith share their views with our readers.

GERSON COHEN

Gerson Cohen has retired as Chancellor of the Jewish Theological Seminary of America. He is Jacob Schiff Distinguished Service Professor of Jewish History and Chancellor Emeritus of the Seminary.

When the Aguda demanded a change in the Law of Return, you took a very quick and sharp position. Why?
Because this was the first time that the state, as a state, had taken an act that was in violation of the spirit of Jewish law and to a considerable degree in violation of Jewish law itself. It was going to institutionalize this violation by giving a religious minority the right to define who is a Jew. Now, who is a Jew is defined by Jewish law and by Jewish tradition, and the state has operated in its history by allowing for a much broader interpretation of who is a Jew. It has never restricted the right of Halachic administration to any one group. This was going to be a departure. And this departure was fraught with terrible dangers to the solidarity of the Jewish people and to the meaning of Zionism as a whole, at least as I have understood Zionism for the last 53½ years.

One of my earliest memories is my father's promise to me that some day we would have the opportunity to live in a country in which we would speak Hebrew all day long. That was his dream. I'm glad he lived to see it and to enjoy it. But that meant a lot more to him than simply speaking Hebrew. It meant a land in which Jews could walk about in dignity. Now there is an irony here, in that a country in which the Jews found refuge and haven from persecution of all kinds is going to be the only Western democracy that imposes religious restrictions on Jews and on the administration of the Jewish religion.

For years we Conservative Jews have been harassed in the performance and in the validation of the divorces, the *gitten* that our people were issued. Sometimes our *gittin* were actually torn up in the face of the people who brought them to Israeli courts. But ultimately the state could claim, as it did, that these were local acts of local *batei din,* local courts, and if a person whose divorce was questioned had patience he could fight it through the local level to the Ministry of Religions, and then even to the Supreme Court. But here is an attempt to simply institutionalize a "deal," in the crassest sense of the term. You are going to sell the authority for the administration of Jewish law in return for political support. That, I think, is an affront to the Jewish people and a violation of the whole spirit of the Talmud.

Until now we've relied on the inherent vagueness of the Law of Return to get by, and in a few cases the Supreme Court has had to deal with it—the Brother Daniel case, for example—but the vagueness was functional. What is the argument against the American system, which simply severs governmental involvement entirely?
The argument against that is the dilemma that we have to face up to and that I don't think we are ready to solve. I would rather stay with the dilemma, which is this: We worked, all of us, for the establishment of a Jewish state. Now, this has meant to me, as it has meant to many Jews, a state in which the majority would be Jews, and a state governed by overriding Jewish principles, at the heart of which would be a concern for democracy, freedom, and social justice as well as the revitalization of cornerstones of our historic culture. We have recovered lost periods of Jewish history, we are also uncovering, from known periods of Jewish history, aspects of Jewish society that we never knew. And all of this is being blended afresh.

We are an ancient people, committed to ancient ideals, at the heart of which stands the Torah—Revelation—the doctrine of election and the cardinal tenets of Jewish faith.

I believe very firmly in the election of Israel, but I am also committed to critical scholarship, to scientific investigation, to pluralism and to redefinition in the light of conscience. I no longer believe that the Almighty reveals Himself only to the Jewish people and certainly not only to one party within the Jewish people. And the dilemma of what Jewishness means is something I think had best not be solved right now, because it can only be solved radically. By that I mean either secularly or in Orthodox fashion—both of which would mean, as far as I'm concerned, the demise of the dream of revitalization and of Zionism, which is one of the major symbols of rebirth and revitalization. If

Photograph by John H. Popper

we abandon religious idealism, there is no raison d'etre for being Jewish. But if we seize the Orthodox rationale, or version, of Jewish history, that would be a form of near idolatry.

Would you expand on that?
The Orthodox are giving finality to one perception of Jewish law or to a limited number of such perceptions. They venerate only one version, whether it's the Shulchan Aruch or some other book, and they claim that that is the ultimate revelation. To give finality to any one version is to deify it — and to me that's bibliolatry, which is awfully close to idolatry.

There is a great miracle that I enjoy, living in America: for the first time Jewish theology is on the agenda of every respectable theological institution in the United States, Jewish and non-Jewish. They are listening to us. They are listening to us theologically, they are asking what Martin Buber has to say, what Heschel has to say, what Herberg has to say, they've been interested in Rabbi Kook and Eliezer Berkovitz. That is one of the great pluses of America.

Is Heschel read in Israel?
Yes, as a matter of fact. His *Torah Min Hashamayim* — his two volumes on revelation — have had a wide readership there. Ultimately, that's one of my chief goals in terms of the current debate. We have been making enormous inroads — quietly — into the secular community of Israel by enabling the secular kibbutzim to give the religious tradition a hearing. And we've gotten them to give it a hearing because we've been able to overcome the *zelbsthaas,* the self-hate, which 19th century secularism and "higher anti-Semitism," as Solomon Schechter used to call it, had infused into the Jewish community. Today, the kibbutzim are withdrawing from the Jewish revolt. They are at least eager to hear what the rabbis have to say. As soon as you get a group that is going to say, "none of your conversions, none of your divorces, none of yours, only ours," you're going to drive them right back into secularism, and it may be with that as the alternative, that secularism is a far more religious position than that of the Agudah.

Yet there is a widespread disposition on the part of Jews to impute authenticity on a kind of vertical scale, whereby the Reform are least authentic, the Conservative next, and only the Orthodox are genuinely authentic. The most secularized Jews in America will defer to the Orthodox and praise not only their tenacity but also their authenticity.
I have two observations on that. First, a majority of Jews, including the Jews of Israel, know very little Jewish history, particularly Jewish religious history. And one current myth with no foundations is that Judaism is always preserved by the most fanatical elements in the community. That is untrue. Judaism, as far back as the Maccabees, was preserved by those who were willing to acculturate. I have written a piece about the blessings of assimilation in Jewish history. It is the blessing of the Jewish people that it was able to transcend the obstinacy of the Accadian priests who would worship only in Accadian. We were willing to translate our Scriptures into Greek, into Aramaic, and to say that a man prays in any language that he understands. Our ability to legitimize and accept prayer and the study of Scripture in every language has been one of the forces for the preservation of Hebrew — because Hebrew assumed an aristocratic force, while Hebrew concepts are transmittable through other vehicles. And that is why we have been able to cross borders. It is simply not true that fanaticism has kept Judaism alive. Fanaticism has kept ghettoization alive, has kept certain fossils alive, but I don't believe that Judaism has been kept alive that way. Judaism was kept alive in the 19th century precisely by Reform, Conservatism, and Neo-Orthodoxy — which is a form of Reform. These were our ways of accommodation to the modern world; acculturation, accommodation, and response to contemporaneity in any age is really the force that kept us alive. Now let's face it: to most people, that's not what religion is. Religion is a form of magic, and they want it vicariously fulfilled by their shamans. Their shaman can be a rebbe, or can be a priest, or can even be a Conservative or Reform rabbi, or sometimes a UJA leader.

The quality of vituperation in Orthodox rhetoric seems to have increased quite dramatically in the last few years. What do you think accounts for this?
There are several factors. First, affluence. The neo-Orthodox community now includes people who come out of Harvard, Columbia, Princeton, Yale, Berkeley, and they have with them a kind of radical chic that they can attach to their yarmulkes. That's abysmal. Frequently, they have also been successful in going through doctoral programs in mathematics and the sciences, totally insulated from the humanities and from the requirement of any form of critical thought. They've not studied comparative culture or religion or philosophy. They have also ridden on the crest of anti-discrimination in the United States, which enabled them to get very good jobs and to attain positions of so-called power and respect in the community. That has discharged a wave of hate that they have been harboring within themselves for I don't know how long. The hate reflects a bankruptcy in their capacity to deal with the genuine challenge of modernity. The only way they can deal with it is by a barrage of hatred, aggressiveness and vituperation. I am affronted that Orthodox religious leaders are speaking openly, shamelessly, about the need to capture the reins of power within the Jewish community and within the federations. They have not been talking about leading, about persuading, about responding theologically; they've been talking about where the power is. Now if that's what religion is, alas, we are in for a theocratic struggle that I deplore.

Is it not, as well, that the Orthodox have defied the predictions of just a few decades back that time was against them, that they would simply peter out? Perhaps with the conviction that they are now the wave of the Jewish future, there comes a kind of arrogance?
I make a profession of studying the

past, not of predicting the future. But if the past is any indicator, if Orthodoxy were so strong, the Jewish community would never have gone secular in the 19th century. If it were so attractive, and had such a hold on the minds of people, they would not have sold out. The Jewish community of Israel was built out of a revolt against religion. It was built *despite* the Orthodox, who then decided to join up, to seize upon Jewish sentiments and Jewish loyalty. One of our scholars here, Jack Wertheimer, has a book coming out shortly in which he has shown that for all the resentment of German Jews towards East European Jews, the German Jews fought for keeping the doors of Germany open to East European immigration. The German Jews never used the word *"ostjude"* about East European Jews. And though American Jews resented East European Jews, they fought against immigration restrictions. We can have our sectionalism, Litvaks can dislike Galitizianers, but when the chips are down, we are one people. Now, all of a sudden, we find that there is a kind of "we are the wave of the future." I'll tell you why they think they're the wave of the future—it's because they now have homes in Fieldston, and Shaker Heights, and in the better suburbs. But their children, I'm afraid, are going to encounter the same processes of attraction that Orthodoxy found and encountered 50 and 100 years ago. There is a great world out there, and our Orthodox children are simply unequipped and unprepared to cope with modernity.

The conventional argument is that it is the Orthodox monopoly on Jewish religious life in Israel that has so alienated the bulk of young Israelis and driven them to radical secularism.
I think that's a rationalization. I think they come predisposed to secularism as a result of the Diaspora revolt, as a result of the schools, and there's a polarization in Israel that one encounters everywhere. It's a rationalization to say that *we* can't be religious because *they're* authoritarian; that's post hoc, but it is also, unfortunately, self-fulfilling. The polarization antedates that.

Doesn't whatever religious alternative to Orthodoxy that develops in Israel have to be indigenous to the country? Isn't Conservatism essentially an American response to an American condition?
Conservatism is not an American phenomenon. Conservatism has been a powerful force in every country in which there is a sizable population of Jews. But each form of Conservatism is dialectically different. German Liberal Judaism was far closer to Conservatism than it was to Reform. Leo Baeck was a far more observant Jew than are Reform rabbis, generally, in the United States. He was what we would call a liberal Conservative Jew. Now, German Conservatism was closer to what we would call left-wing Orthodoxy, neo-Orthodoxy. I think that Israeli Conservatism will have to develop its own dialectic, its own dialect, its own form—based on the principle of continued exegesis and new midrash in response to particular social challenges, theological challenges and general weltanschauung. It is that method of approach to the text and to the past that is Conservatism.

I don't find every form of Conservative Judaism in American attractive to me. We need to define Conservatism here, too. I hope that Conservative Judaism here has not been fixed. I certainly see changes in Reform, as I have been noticing changes in Orthodoxy. And I do see changes in Conservatism as well. I hope sincerely that Israeli Conservative Judaism will not be simply in the American style, that it will be Israeli. But I expect that however it develops, when I visit Israel, I will feel more at home there, simply because it is open to the past and to the present, and therefore, gives more options for the future than Orthodoxy in any form does.

That's an interesting view in light of the frequent criticism of the Seminary that it spends much of its time looking over its right shoulder to see how the Orthodox will react, that the Orthodox reaction is still normative for the Seminary.
I have enough trouble with my trifocals looking straight ahead, and I want to boast that for the last ten years, this administration has been trying to look straight ahead. I am not concerned with the sides. Even when I look straight ahead, I find many different groups in my plane of vision—but not over my right shoulder. I do not look to the Reform, and I want to say very strongly that I have not looked to Orthodoxy. I have been willing to sustain defeat—not gladly, by the way. I was defeated on the question of the ordination of women for the rabbinate. I have instituted egalitarian services of a kind—not all my faculty approve. My job is to be the spokesman for and coordinator of a variety of people who are affiliated with the Conservative movement. I'm certainly not worried about what other people are going to say about it. I have become firmly convinced that, as one Orthodox leader put it, "no matter what you do, I will denounce you for 50 years—and then follow suit." That's a verbatim quote—and it's true. I take confidence from the fact that we have been producing scholarship and reproducing ourselves. I'm not by any means satisfied by the amount of scholarship or the level of theological thought; we have to aspire ever higher. But the right wing is not my measure of Jewish authenticity.

ALEXANDER SCHINDLER

What prompted your response to the Agudah demands for changes in the Law of Return?

My own reaction was not so much out of genuine concern as it was an effort to create a political counterpressure, to help Begin be true to what he once promised me. Namely, that no issue like this, anything remotely connected with the Law of Return, would ever be a matter of party discipline, that he would leave it to the free choice of the indivduals within the Knesset. And while he has some strong feelings on the subject — of course he shows his limited knowledge, he feels that one ought to, in order to be converted, have milah, and he can't understand why this is not so — he certainly insists that it should never be subject to party discipline and party negotiations. It must be a matter of conscience. But before I left Israel, knowing of the pressures which were building up, I called him again and I spent about an hour with him, and I said, "Please don't sell us down the river," and he promised that he wouldn't, that he would abide by his promise, so when I sent the telegram, I was doing it to create a public counterpressure that would enable him to fulfill his promise. So far, I'm satisifed, but I don't know what's going to happen in the course of the negotiations.

This is a symptom of a more general problem which has been of concern to you, namely the status and role of the Reform movement in Israel. What are some other manifestations of the discrimination against Reform Judaism in Israel?

Essentially, they deal with the rabbinate. Reform rabbis are not allowed to officiate at marriages, to bury their congregants, or to officiate at conversions. And some of the grants that are given by the Ministry of Religions to Orthodox synagogues are not given in proportional measure to liberal synagogues. That's the essence of it. It's not only an Israeli Jewish problem, but also a world Jewish problem.

Alexander Schindler is President of the Union of American Hebrew Congregations. He is a past Chairman of the Conference of Presidents of Major Jewish Organizations.

Some of these attitudes affect the performance of people in their official duties, people in the Jewish Agency and in other agencies who assume something they have no right to assume and that isn't even rooted in Israeli law. I received a call from a Reform rabbi whose brother and sister-in-law are immigrating to the United States from Hungary. His sister-in-law was born a non-Jew and was converted by the Neologue Rabbi of Hungary — the term is new to me, and is, apparently, a kind of cross between Conservative and Liberal Judaism — she was converted by one rabbi, they were married by another rabbi, non-Orthodox, and the HIAS official who was dealing with their immigration said "I'm sorry, I can't help you, I question the validity of that conversion, I have to investigate it thoroughly. You're a Reform rabbi, why don't you take care of it yourself and leave HIAS out of it?" Now she had no right to assume this, and no right to say this, no right to question this. So you see how these Israeli attitudes have their impact on the American scene as well.

There are more devastating problems. If such an amendment to the Law of Return should ever be effected, there would be a major altercation between Orthodoxy and Reform on the American scene.

The Orthodox seem to be primed for just such an altercation.

Well, they would be making a serious mistake. I've tried to tell that to some of my more liberal Orthodox friends. I think that it would do them a great deal of damage without doing them any good whatsoever. How is the halachah served, and the principle of the halachah, if it is to be given validation by a Knesset vote? Sanctity is not enhanced by Parliamentary disposition; the halachah does not gain compelling power because it enjoys a majority vote in the Knesset — anything that can be voted up by a Knesset can be voted down by a future Knesset, so it seems to me that to seek such a vote would be absurd from an Orthodox point of view. Even on the question of *taharat hamishpachah* (family purity), which is of concern to them, we've had 30 years of the status quo, so if there's any mixing that is thought to be a danger to us, it's already been done. So what are they talking about? What are they preserving?

Finally, it would hurt them politically and financially on the American scene. Very, very seriously. Many American Jews might have compunctions, and we, the leadership of Reform and Conservative Judaism, have always restrained them, about expressing their dismay in financial terms, in terms of Israel. They'll say, "Well, we have to help the people no matter what absurd laws the government of Israel passes under the duress of an adverse political situation," but I don't think that they will be at all upset about withdrawing funds from Orthodox institutions here in the United States. Only yesterday, I spoke to one of the most prominent fund-raisers in the American Jewish community, who is categorically refusing any kind of donation to the Lubavitcher, because he learned that much of the pressure for amending the law is coming from them. Now there are throughout the country many Orthodox day schools that are receiving Federation funds; I don't think that Reform and Conservative leadership will have any compunction about cutting these funds out, and so on the one hand, there is nothing to gain from a religious point of view, there's a great danger from a financial point of view, and they would be well-advised to drop the whole thing.

How do you react to those people in your own movement who regard Orthodoxy as authentic?
That obtains, but it can quickly change. The man I've just told you about used to say about the Orthodox, "Isn't it wonderful how steadfast they are?" He now says, "What do we need them for?" I don't need them to raise a generation of young Jews who will read me out of the Jewish people and read my relatives out of the Jewish people. I don't need it, I don't want it. I already referred to the generosity of spirit towards Israel which has impelled the leadership of the Reform and Conservative movements to eschew the financial recourse we have as a form of pressure on Israel, but maybe it's time for us to change. I would certainly have no compunctions about it on the domestic scene, and I might be willing even to carry this out vis-à-vis Israel too, if I had assurance that those same funds would go to Israel for causes that are closer to us.

What of the substance of the view that Orthodoxy is the authentic way?
Obviously it's not; you know what you can expect to hear from me on that score. Orthodoxy is not more authentic Judaism, as far as I am concerned and as far as Reform Judaism is concerned and as far as Conservative Judaism is concerned. What divides us is not the intensity of belief nor even necessarily the quantity of observance; what divides us is principle, the answer to the question "what is Torah?," Torah in the restricted sense of the first five books of Moses; those who believe that it is divine revelation given to Moses by God on Sinai are Orthodox Jews. Those who do not, who believe that there is a progressive strain in the history of Jews, are liberal Jews. This is the principle that divides us, not the intensity of belief, not the authenticity of belief. Our authenticity as Jews cannot, must not, be questioned.

Though it sometimes seems that Reform, quite apart from the integrity of its beliefs and the seriousness of its purpose as a movement, is a home for lazier Jews.
That's a failing that we have and there is no excuse for it. Sometimes when you assume the right to make a choice in terms of, say, ritual observance, you assume that the right to choose gives you the right to be indolent, but that is a violation of the principles of Reform and makes you a non-observant Reform Jew, even as there are — quite likely a majority — non-observant Orthodox Jews. We are wrong in this. I am appalled by what goes on in our congregations.

If religious pluralism does come to Israel, must it not be indigenous? Reform is fundamentally alien, is it not? Take the issue of prayer in the vernacular, so important an innovation of Reform, but absolutely irrelevant in Israel.
First of all, I agree that there is a manifest need for an indigenous movement. I don't think a movement can flourish if it is only an immigrant movement, and is not in some manner naturalized. This was the history of Reform here in America. The early Reform Jews were all German and they prayed in German, they wrote in German, and it wasn't until an American Judaism developed that you had true burgeoning and growth of Reform Judaism. This was the greatness of Isaac Mayer Wise, that he saw the need for that on the American scene. It was his dream to have an American-born Reform rabbinate, which is rather odd because just now, the Presidents of the Hebrew Union College, of the Central Conference of American Rabbis, and of the Union of American Hebrew Congregations are all German-born Jews — but I guess that a hundred years later, you can afford to have an import at the head of the movement. Obviously, it is an indigenous movement. And this will have to take place in Israel. The beginnings of an indigenous movement are visible, and as the most dramatic case in point we have now ordained three Reform rabbis who were born in Israel and fully trained in Israel and ordained in Israel as Reform rabbis. Two of the three were youngsters who had come to the United States as part of our high school exchange program and there familiarized themselves with the movement and then went back to devote their lives to the growth and development of Reform Judaism in Israel because they deemed this to be necessary for Israeli society as a whole.

To all of this I would add — and this begins to approach our last question — that the synagogue form is not necessarily the only form that Reform Judaism will have to develop as part of its movement in Israel. As a matter of fact, in setting the foundations of the movement, we are not focussing on synagogues, not exclusively. We do have some 15 synagogues throughout the country, but we have other efforts as well. We have contact through schools, the Leo Baeck school in Haifa and the Ben

Shemen Youth Village, where some sort of Reform identity is being developed. We have established a youth movement, totally unlike the pattern of NFTY here in the United States, which is essentially a synagogue youth movement. In Israel it is not; it follows the Israeli pattern of having youth organized in movements like the scouts. We have a very successful youth movement, which again is led by someone who is a shaliach from the kibbutz movement who came here, worked with our congregations, was totally converted to the idea and the principles of Reform, and came back to Israel determined to build the Reform movement in Israel and chose this way. We have established contact with the kibbutz movement and have introduced, with their help, courses in Reform Judaism in their kibbutz teacher training seminars. And, of course, we've established kibbutzim, which gets me to the main point—the distinctive element of Reform will obviously not be the vernacular—the vernacular is Hebrew—the distinctive element will be *in primus,* to go back to elements: the full equality of men and women in religious life, which is absent from Orthodox; liturgical innovation, and there we have done entirely too little; and an emphasis on the ethical element, both from a personal standpoint and from the point of view of Israeli society, as a component which is at least equal to the religious observance as a matter of importance to Judaism. I think this is what attracted the kibbutz leadership intellectually to Reform Judaism.

When you talk about religious pluralism in Israel, do you imply the American model of radical separation between church and state?
We might be approaching that as the only way of achieving the equality that we seek. I think that most American Jews are concerned about the principle of equality and their Jewish status. They will suffer no diminution of that status. They are not going to be read out of the Jewish people. They don't want to be beggars at Jerusalem's gates. They don't want to be second-class Jewish citizens when Israel was established in order to eliminate the second-class status of Jewish citizens in lands all over the world. They see the absurdity of a land that grants freedom of religion to every conceivable expression of religion in the entire universe and fails to grant it to non-Orthodox Judaism. Their demand is for equality, and they don't care how they get to it. I think that, born and bred as we were spiritually, ideologically, in societies where we have achieved our greatest safety because of the separation-of-church-and-state principle, we come to that as the only way of achieving that equality for which we strive and which we demand as our birthright.

Of course, it's a very dangerous slogan these days—a secular democratic state.
Yes, it is dangerous, and, to some extent, not a fulfillment of our dream for a fuller Jewish expression which gives a dominant force to the religious component of Judaism.

I'm sure you've noticed over the past several years an increasing level of vituperation on the part of the American Orthodox in talking about Reform and Conservative Jews. What do you think accounts for it?
I see it as a sign of weakness, frankly. I don't see it as a sign of growing strength. It's a sign of despair, not a sign of confidence. People who are confident are open; they have enough confidence in the integrity of their beliefs and practices to accept anyone and everyone, to treat other people as human beings and as fully equal partners. When you see yourself as crumbling, when you perceive yourself as fraying at the edges, you tend to draw inward and to be more exclusive, and I see it as such. I'm not a Jewish social scientist, I'm certainly not a demographer, so I have to rely on demographers to tell me what the real facts on the American scene are, but if you take the studies of even the Orthodox demographers the estimate is that by the year 1990 the Orthodox religious community will be no larger than five percent of the American Jewish community. That's a crumbling. Charles Liebman's analysis was that Orthodoxy in America as a synagogue movement was essentially a first generation phenomenon and Conservative Judaism gives every indication of being a second generation phenomenon and that the future, at least demographically, belongs to Reform. That's his analysis of the situation. In any event, Orthodoxy must know that it's declining. There's a certain growth here or there, in some movements, but it's interesting that those are the movements that have the greatest inner strength and that grow when they are open. The Lubavitch movement certainly was open, and it succeeded, at least in some measure, because of that openness. You have a congregation like Shlomo Riskin's, which is flourishing, because he doesn't read anybody out, he doesn't say that anybody who is intermarried has no business there, whether it be the Jewish partner or the non-Jewish partner, as did the Rabbinical Council some months ago. He says to anybody, "Come in." And, as a result, his synagogue is filled to the overflowing. I'm sure there are other factors, but I think that the openness is one of the factors that is operative, an indispensible prerequisite of growth. Both of these movements are essentially self-confident movements. I see this exclusivity, this reading out, as an expression of a great inner weakness.

LEVI HOROWITZ

Photograph by Joel Orent

Until now there has been a working compromise regarding the definition of who is a Jew, a kind of tacit agreement to leave the definition vague. Now, rather suddenly, it has become a matter of high priority to the traditional community, which seeks a precise and rigorous definition. Why the change?

To us, the definition of who is Jewish goes to the heart of all that Judaism is. It provides us a basic understanding of how we guide ourselves towards a non-Jew who enters the Jewish faith. The traditional community feels that when the law states that a person, for whatever purposes, has to be Jewish, then he has to be Jewish; there aren't two definitions of what it means to be Jewish. We never expected that the definition would be compromised by any movement; how could they do it? The question was just too serious.

But as time went on, things changed. When people started coming to Israel from Vienna, from Rome, where blank checks were given to those who said they were Jews, without any type of investigation, at times even with the knowledge that the people were not, in fact, Jewish—but happened to be spouses of Jews, or children, or friends—we became concerned. We couldn't rely any longer on those who administered the law to administer it properly.

It was then, and then only, that the traditional community realized that we couldn't continue to assume that the definition that had applied for thousands of years was still accepted. The concept that we had lived with, that we had understood to be true, was fast disappearing because of the laxity of the people involved.

The issue then was not Reform or Conservative; the issue was Jew or non-Jew. As a progress—or regression—took place, and we tried to define who is truly a Jew, the other movements began to take our stand as a personal attack on their approach to Judaism. Mind you, neither the Moetzes Gedolei HaTorah (the Council of Torah Sages), nor any *frum* (ob-

---

Rabbi Levi Horowitz, the Bostoner Rebbe, is a member of the World Executve Committee of the Agudat Yisrael.

servant) Jew in Israel or in the Diaspora is out to stop the non-practicing Jew from continuing in his way. There's a Talmudic saying, for example, that a person who desecrates the Shabbos is as if he had desecrated the entire Torah. This could be a very serious issue. But we see a distinction between Shabbos and kashrus, on the one hand, and the "who is a Jew?" matter on the other. The fact that the Conservative movement has instituted things like riding to shul on Shabbos pains us very much, but we didn't launch a campaign against it, because it's a very personal issue. As much as a Jew is a part of the whole House of Israel, as much as we're all connected, people have privacy, their own personal interaction with their religion, and we don't interfere. We plead, but we don't interfere.

But the issue of who is a Jew is a different story. I face the problem at least weekly. When young people come to see me regarding their identity as Jews, wanting to know more about Judaism, the greatest fear I have, the greatest problem I face, is being confronted with a young person who suddenly, at age 24 or 26, discovers that he or she is considered a *mamzer*—illegitimate—according to Jewish law.

Mamzerus (illegitimacy) is not a term that applies to children born out of wedlock. The term applies where there hasn't been a Jewish divorce. A woman who hasn't had a Jewish divorce and then remarries commits an adulterous act, and children born as a result are *mamzerim*.

These youngsters don't ask "How come the Jewish religion is taking it out on us?" They understand better. They understand that when there is a gene of insanity in a member of a family, that gene may be carried through to the next generation, and therefore people who have the gene should be careful. They ask the question, "How could our parents not understand what they're doing to the future generations, to us? How could they ignore the possibility that we might not be Reform Jews, Conservative Jews, irreligious Jews, Jews for J.? They ignored our existence."

When confronted with this problem, I'm petrified, because lives are literally at stake. Can they or can they not marry a Jewess? What is that status? And the problem is due to the fact that these people who, 20, 30 years back, when they had the opportunity to tell the parents that the divorce they were issuing or the marriage they were performing might create problems for the children, that the children would suffer in case they wanted to become Orthodox, didn't tell.

It's not only our problem. The Conservative movement requires a *get* (a bill of religious divorce); the Reform movement does not. When a Reform rabbi allows a couple to be separated without a Jewish divorce, that Reform rabbi ignores the future relationship of the family with their Conservative brethren. Ignoring it causes disaster.

Marriage, divorce, and especially conversion, affect the future generations. We cannot take the liberty of saying, "I don't care about the future generations, I don't care about how others are going to view my Jewishness." You cannot insist that the Jewish community accept your own private definition about what it means to be a Jew. And this brings us to the crux of the issue.

What makes a Jew a Jew? With regard to conversion, the tradition is absolutely clear. There are three things: The most important is *kabolas ol mitzvos* (acceptance of the yoke of the commandments)—understanding *mitzvos* and accepting them. You cannot become a citizen of the United States unless you promise to abide by the Constitution of the United States. That's the oath you take when you become a citizen. And you cannot have any mental reservations, you cannot say "I don't agree to the 12th amendment." If you have any type of reservation, you will not be granted citizenship. Acceptance of the yoke of commandment means a true understanding and acceptance of what *mitzvos* are.

Then there has to be *t'viloh* (ritual immersion) for both male and female, and for the male there's also circumcision, or, if he's already circumcized, *hatofas dom bris*—the taking of a drop of blood.

How shall the whole House of Israel, k'lal Yisroel, guide itself in accepting a person who was not born Jewish? From our point of view, the issue is similar to a problem that may be confronted by a Conservative or Reform rabbi. Take a family whose children have become observant, and are getting married, and they want to have a kosher wedding. The parents come to their spiritual leader to complain. They don't want a kosher wedding; they think their children have gone crazy. Obviously, any reasonable Conservative or Reform rabbi would say to them, "A *treifer yid* (a Jew who does not observe kashrut) can eat kosher; a kosher *yid* cannot eat *treif*. Your wedding should satisfy all the participants." Even though the people who are giving the advice may not care about *kashrus*, they would understand that when it affects other people, you go along.

Now the question is: who is a Jew, what should be the criterion for being a Jew? Should we accept the halachic (traditional legal) point of view regarding who is a Jew, the traditional point of view that we have lived with for 2000 years? It's not an "Orthodox" point of view; it was the universal Jewish point of view, with no disagreement, for 2000 years. Or shall we accept the Conservative idea that Judaism can be done in a more relaxed way? I don't know what that means. What does *kabolas ol mitzvos* mean then? What does it mean when a person is about to become Jewish and you know that the person is not going to do anything more Jewish the day after his conversion than he did the day before? What kiind of acceptance of *mitzvos* is that?

The second problem is the *mikvah*, the ritual immersion. It has to be done by a *bes din* (a religious court). You can't pick three people off the street as witnesses, and say to them, "Hey, come in, you'll be a *bes din* to the *mikvah*." A *bes din* has to be a *bes din*. Here's a person who is about to change completely, to become a new person. That's a very serious thing. I'll tell you how serious it is: I had a call from Pittsburg the other day from a woman who converted to Judaism. She has a ten-year-old son who converted with her. And she wanted to know what her relationship to her son was because the Talmud says that a convert is a new person. "Is my son still actually my son?" she wanted to know. "When my son grows up, can I kiss him, can I hug him, or is he considered, since we're both new people, no different from another male, from a stranger?"

So since the change is so fundamental, we need three people at the *mikvah* to be a *bes din*. Now what constitutes a *bes din*? Should the people on the *bes din* be asking the convert questions about things they themselves don't care about? How can you ask the convert to have an understanding of the concept of Shabbos when you yourself are out on the golf course on Shabbos? If the rabbi does that, it's a farce. So you need a rabbi who is not only an understanding person, but also a *shomer Shabbos* (a Sabbath observer).

So a person is converted, and the *bes din* signs the papers. How do we know who the *bes din* is? How do we know that it's any different from three people off the street? Can we sanction that as a halachic conversion to be accepted by the Jewish community? Should we imply that it is a good conversion when we know that it's not a good conversion, that we're only complying because we're all part of one community, and we feel that there's no alternative, that we can't do anything about it?

What do we do when there's a Jewish divorce somewhere in Nebraska? Do we accept just a piece of paper? No, we'll fly to Chicago, we'll meet the people, we'll do the thing right. You can't compromise just because you're afraid you'll hurt somebody's feelings. We're dealing with generations; it's got to be done the right way.

What does a Conservative rabbi do with the conversion of a Reform rabbi, one who comes to him and says "Hey Buddy, they've just gone through a conversion, I want you to marry them off"? So the Conservative rabbi says, "A conversion?" And the Reform rabbi answers, "Yeah, they came in, and they attended classes, and then they went before the *oron kodesh* (the Ark) and took an oath, and said they're Jews." No circumcision, no *mikvah*, no *kabolas ol mitzvos*. Would the Conservative

> Here in the United States you can't force the issue. In Eretz Yisroel it's a *mechayeh*.

movement compromise on that and say, "We accept this idea of conversion"? If they would, we'd end up with a mishmash of people claiming to be Jewish because they did one little thing or another little thing.

Here in America, there is no organized institution. Each shul is by itself, each temple is by itself: you don't like one, you go to another. You don't like the other, you go to a Justice of the Peace. But in Eretz Yisroel, there is a way to define who is a member of our community. And it's not just a matter of Orthodoxy. In Israel, they won't accept the conversion of just any Orthodox rabbi. It's not a question of Conservative or Reform or Orthodox, it's a question of a qualified rabbi doing a qualified conversion, one that would satisfy the future generations.

But isn't it the case that no Conservative or Reform rabbi would be regarded as qualified?
If the Conservative rabbi has *smicha* (ordination), that's okay. It would depend on what kind of *smicha* it is. If he has a qualified *smicha* . . .

But by definition, the *smicha* provided by the Jewish Theological Seminary is not a qualified *smicha*.
That's true, because their criterion for *smicha* is not the one that has been the accepted norm. The *smicha* is a compromise *smicha*, just as much as with the other institution, the Reform one. Inside, the JTS has a *mechitzah* (a partition in the synagogue separating men and women); outside, the Conservative movement compromises.

Now, if a person comes in, and that person has *smicha*, and he believes in *Torah min Hashomayim* (divine revelation), in the 13 Articles of Faith of the Rambam, if he lives a *mitzvah* life, the question of whether he considers himself Conservative is not crucial. If the rabbinate in Israel has a convert who has children, and the children want to marry a Kohen, whether they can or not depends on whether the mother's conversion was kosher. (A convert herself cannot marry a Kohen; the child of a "valid" convert can.) So if you go back to find out whether the original conversion was valid, and you discover that the rabbi who did the conversion was a Conservative rabbi, what would be the question? The question would be, is he a Conservative rabbi with a qualified *smicha*, is he a *shomer Shabbos*, what happened that he became a Conservative rabbi? Maybe he was out of a job, he took a job with a Conservative congregation because there was an opening and he needed a job? There would be a different approach, because we want to work it out, we have no quarrel with him. The issue is what the Conservative and Reform movements themselves declare. The Conservative movement declares its *smicha* to be a watered-down version. They would never argue that it's the same *smicha* their parents and grandparents received; it isn't. Genuine *smicha* requires that you know your halachah very thoroughly, that you go through a very rigid test on it.

If all this is so very important, how can the Knesset determine? Does the Knesset—the inherently political parliament of Israel—have the authority to make definitions here?
Absolutely not. When you have a couple that is getting a divorce, and wants to make the break religiously, just as they were married religiously, and one of the parties involved is stubborn, and refuses to do it, or demands a ransom for doing it, here in the United States you can't force the issue. You can't ask the courts to intervene and to require a religious divorce. Our hands are tied, because of the separation of church and state.

Of course we'd prefer a system, the way it was once, where the Jewish community is in control of its own. Then you take the stubborn fellow in and you lay him down on a table, give him a few slaps, tell him he has to free the woman, and that's it. But we don't have that control. So we try to get binding arbitration and that way, through the side door, receive some sort of support from the government.

In Eretz Yisroel it's a *mechayeh* (delight). Divorce falls within the jurisdiction of a *bes din*. The *bes din* consists of reasonable people, they come up with a reasonable settlement, and if people don't live up to it, they go to jail. Now you can ask whether the Knesset, the established government, shall employ the police to enforce a Jewish divorce. We would rather have our own judges and our own ways of enforcing the law, but we don't. So we turn to the institution that can help us enforce reasonable standards of living. If the government in Israel would define a Jew differently from the way we define it, we'd be in the same position we're in here in the United States. Here we have no recourse. But in Eretz Yisroel, we have a recourse. We hope to be able to talk to the government and say to them, "Help us. A person married religiously should be divorced religiously."

There's so much more expected of a convert than of a person born a Jew.
I'll tell you what my analogy is. I'm confronted with all kinds of problems, among them parents who want my help in getting their children into college. So, let's say I have a parent who calls and says, "Get my kid into Tufts Dental School, or B.U. Medical School. His grades are weak, but maybe you could help." And sometimes, I'm able to convince the school to give the student a chance, and they put him on hold, and then, after a while, he gets in, weak grades and all. Now he got in only because of pull. But if you have a student who is already in Tufts Dental or in B.U. Medical, one who got in with the best grades, and he's doing very badly, he's really in academic trouble, they won't throw him out. At worst, they'll give him a warning.

A Jew born a Jew is always a Jew, no matter how low his grades are. But of someone who wants to become a Jew, we have serious criteria for admission. If he comes to us with the best of intentions of observing Judaism, and a month later he announces that he can't, there'll be no gendarmes, no police to say that he's not Jewish any longer. So there has to be an understanding that the person knows what the responsibilities are.

The Agudah was described in this morning's New York Times as an anti-Zionist party. Would you commment on that?
The notion that we are anti-Zionist has its roots in the idea that *frume yidn,* observant Jews, did not want a secular state. The state we hoped for would be governed by Torah — not clerically, we never had clerics, we never had ayatollahs. We simply wanted a Jewish state. A secular state was not our aim. But once the state was established, we immediately joined. We signed on the Declaration of Independence, which disproves the contention that we are anti-Zionist. We joined the first government as a party; Reb Yitzchak Meir Levin was the Minister of Social Welfare, and throughout Israel's history, we've been very involved in every aspect of government.

As far as recognizing the State of Israel as *the* state that we were hoping for, absolutely not.

The Labor party would surely agree with that. Would you say something about the quality of vituperation that has entered the ongoing debate between the Orthodox community and the other movements.
I plead, in the name of Orthodoxy, of the Agudah, innocent to that charge. I don't think we have ever instituted an attack against the so-called opposition. It always came when the opposition forced their views, attempted to change the status quo. I have here a few letters on the "who is a Jew" question that have appeared in the New York *Times.* "We in the Conservative movement," one reads, "have undertaken to interpret Jewish law in the spirit and mode of the tradition in order to respond to ongoing daily issues."

I wonder how. By sanctioning a *bes din* that's not observant, even according to *their* laws? Would they sanction Reform conversions? "The assumption by Orthodox religious bodies of exclusive validity on their point of view represents spiritual arrogance." Are they saying that the Rambam is arrogant? OK, we're in good company. Is the Chofetz Chaim, or the Vilna Gaon, arrogant? We want the Shulchan Aruch. Is that arrogant? Who is arrogant, those who live by the law, by the Constitution of the United States, or those who say that this amendment or that doesn't mean anything? I don't see the desire to live up to the law as being arrogant. "They have no monopoly on the interpretation of Jewish law." But we don't interpret Jewish law; we haven't made any new interpretations. *They* are the only ones who interpret Jewish law. We don't interpret; we just take out the books that appeared in print 50 years ago, 100 years ago, 200 years ago. My heart bleeds when I confront a human problem and the law cannot be bent. But the law is the law.

How do you explain all the innovations that Orthodoxy has introduced for handling a whole host of problems that didn't confront the writers of those books?
We don't interpret. We apply, within the halachic structure. If anybody could come up with an interpretation that would permit us to make a Jew who is a *mamzer* into a non-*mamzer,* we'd jump for it. Do you think we want that people should have to live with the stigma of *mamzerus?* Reb Moshe Feinstein, the leader of the Council of Torah Sages in America, would use every type of logic that's used in the halachah to come up with a way of doing that — but he would never do it by saying "Take my word for it, it's ok." Ten Reb Moshes would not be able to do that. They have to bring the fine print, the source for their decision. It can be done with a *dreidel* (a twist), but it has to be part of the structure. Never can you find authority in the texts for converting a non-Jew without a *mikvah,* without *t'viloh,* without immersion. Now, how can we ever sanction the conversion of a Reform Jew? It's not possible. You can say, "Look, let's relax, let's twist a little here, a little there," but that would be corrupt, that would be doing that which is opposite of the law.

There are limits. If someone comes and says that the mikvah that he used was in Tulsa, and that mikvah was founded in 1935, and we heard that in 1945 it had some problems, and the conversion happened later — well, maybe you can make it all right. Maybe, if an observant Jew — that's what you need to be a *mohel,* to do the ritual circumcision — if such a person forgot to say the *brocho,* maybe you can find a technicality in the halachah

If you need a brain tumor operated on, you need a brain surgeon.

which will still make the conversion valid. But it's got to be within the framework of the halachah.

And this is where the other world just doesn't understand us. They think that a Shabbos elevator is a way of getting around the halachah. It's not; every detail of it is studied, and is within the halachah.

I'm sure that if the other movements would sit down with Reb Moshe Feinstein, and would say, "What are the minimum standards that we have to comply with to make a conversion kosher, so that it would be recognized?", I'm sure that it could be worked out.

But the answer would inevitably strike at the self-respect of those movements, wouldn't it?
Who is at fault? A Conservative rabbi would not say to a Reform rabbi, "You're qualified," so we're not alone in our approach. The Reform movement can have its self-respect for other reasons. Reform rabbis can deliver good sermons, maybe better ones than Orthodox rabbis. But the fact of the matter is that any person can get up on the pulpit and deliver a sermon. The problem is not what the Conservative or Reform rabbi is individually. The heart surgeon might be a great heart surgeon, but if you need a brain tumor operated on, that's not for him to do; for that you need a brain surgeon.

What would be so terrible if the other movement told people, "Look, we don't believe in this, but if you want to make sure, just in case 50 years from now your child is going to become *meshugge* and *frum,* you ought to go to the Orthodox rabbi." Why can't there be an agreement among rabbis? Why should each movement be tied to its whims, and more than that, to the whims of each rabbi?

The fact is that the image that is represented of us in the press isn't accurate. They make it seem as if the Council of Torah Sages consisted of 15 ayatollahs. But these people have compassion, they are the finest people, they know the *tzores* (troubles) of *k'lal Yisroel,* of our people, they carry those *tzores* on their shoulders, and they are the first ones to bend backwards. If you would consult them with a personal problem, on conversion or anything else, they would be the first ones to crusade and see to it that if it's at all possible, something would be done to help. But to open up the doors to Israel to a convert who wasn't converted halachically?

As a matter of fact, I'm not even happy with the term "conversion according to halachah," because halachah itself is a vague term today. What would happen if the Conservatives came and said, "Look, we'll show you right here, after the conference of our halachic authorities, aliyahs can be given to women"— boom, finished. What are we supposed to do? The term "halachah" doesn't cover what we need. It must be done according to the Shulchan Aruch, as it's been done for generations and generations, or else we'll get into a hassle in interpreting what halachah really means. ✡

Part V

Interviews

MARIE SYRKIN AND TRUDE WEISS-ROSMARIN

MOMENT meets with two *grandames* of Jewish life and journalism—commentators and movers through a turbulent half century

A MOMENT INTERVIEW

Marie Syrkin, left, and Trude Weiss-Rosmarin

Photos by Bill Aron

You both made quite atypical choices regarding what to do with your lives, and you both achieved quite a bit at a time when "achievement" was not the norm for women. How conscious were you, in the early years, of how unusual you were, and of skeptical reaction by the male community?

Syrkin: As far as I'm concerned, not at all. There was one exception. At the time, in the 20s, when I would have considered getting a PhD, which back then was essential for an academic career, my feeling was that I would not be able to pursue that kind of career with a baby. So I abandoned my thoughts of a PhD. Still, subsequently I managed the academic career anyway.

I don't think I came to any specific political awareness of women's rights, because I was born into what was called a "radical environment." Women's rights? When I think of how I was raised, of how acute was the notion of total erasure of male-female difference... My mother herself was advanced. She and my father met at a Zionist Congress in Switzerland, where both of them were studying medicine. This already gives you some idea of how far my mother was emancipated. And while I was being raised, the notion that there was any important sexual differentiation was taboo. That led to some trouble later, as when, when I was 16 and my father said to me, "You're not to go out with this boy," I would say, "But what is the difference between boys and girls?"

There were, then, certain paradoxes in this kind of upbringing. But by and large I came to the notion that the goals of male and female should be equal quite naturally. I may not have achieved that equality, but personally I felt no discrimination.

You mean the Zionist movement, in which you were so active, was that far advanced?

Syrkin: I noticed it not with regard to myself, because I was never in a role of such magnitude. But when I became interested in writing about Golda, an idea I had in the 50s, when she was Minister of Labor, before she became famous—that's my pride, that I didn't wait until she became the ultimate celebrity—I went to various individuals, and I noticed there was a real male feeling about the idea. Sharett was distinctly negative. Ben-Gurion not, I'll say that for him. But even with so relatively minor a person as Haim Greenberg, who was, mind you, Golda's friend; I talked with him about how when Sharett had been arrested by the British she'd taken over, and Greenberg's reply was, "Golda? Very fine speaker, lovely woman." And that was that, so far as he was concerned.

But with regard to myself, I never encountered such a reaction.

Weiss-Rosmarin: I had more or less

Marie Syrkin, born in 1899, has long been the dean of American Labor Zionism. For more than 50 years, she was the editor or a member of the editorial board of *The Jewish Frontier*. There she published memorable articles on a wide variety of subjects, including the Moscow trials of 1937, Arnold Toynbee and the Jews, Hannah Arendt, and, again and again, the meaning of Zionism in our time.

She came by her Zionism quite naturally. Her father was Nachman Syrkin (1867–1924), a founding leader and theoretician of Labor Zionism. She was, as well, one of Golda Meir's closest friends. Her books include a biography of Golda, as well as *Blessed is the Match*, an account of Jewish resistance, and, among others, *Gleanings*, a book of poems.

Miss Syrkin taught in the English Department of Brandeis University, and now lives in Santa Monica, California.

Trude Weiss-Rosmarin, born in 1904, is the editor of *The Jewish Spectator*, which she founded in 1935. Dr. Weiss-Rosmarin is a distinguished scholar, whose articles and editorials have dealt with a staggeringly diverse range of subjects, from Masada to the Jewish Agency, from the status of Jewish women to the role of Jewish literature. Her writings and frequent lectures around the country have stimulated communal debate for many decades.

Dr. Weiss-Rosmarin earned her doctorate at the age of 22; she has been called "the most Jewishly learned woman in the world." She is a link to the famed Freie Jüdische Lehrhaus of Frankfurt, founded by Franz Rosenzweig, with whom she studied; her own School of the Jewish Woman, which she founded in New York City in 1932, was modeled after the original Lehrhaus.

Dr. Weiss-Rosmarin lives in Santa Monica, California, and continues to travel extensively in connection with her work.

the same experience, even though I grew up in an entirely different environment. It was in Frankfurt-am-Main, and I became Jewishly aware when I joined Blau-Weiss, a Zionist youth movement. I was nine years old then, and I came into Blau-Weiss the way people today are coming into the cults. There was an afternoon meeting at the home of one of my friends, who invited me to join and come—they used to talk about "spearing" new members—and I came, and there was hora dancing which I'd never seen before, and singing of Zionist songs, boys and girls together. And then, shortly after, I started going to Hebrew school, which was also with boys and girls together, and I had a wonderful teacher, Yosef Yoel Rivlin, who encouraged us and was a motivating teacher. And I was a good pupil, so I didn't feel any discrimination.

Where I did feel discriminated against was in the synagogue. In the synagogue where my parents went, there was, of course, a women's gallery. A very civilized, luxurious women's gallery, with a dressing room to leave your coat and a beadle in a splendid uniform. However, Rabbi Nehemiah Noble, a very charismatic personality, who was the teacher of Rosenzweig and of Ernst Simon, when he would give the sermon, which I was too young to understand—I understood the choir, with enthusiasm—and I wanted to get a view of him, I would go down to the first row, and invariably the beadle would yank me back. And I knew that if I were a boy, I'd have been downstairs, and perhaps even been able to shake the rabbi's hand.

Syrkin: I'd like to add something. Despite my early conviction that there is no difference, I find contemporary feminism absurd in its extremes. In its denial that biological differences— which are obvious, which I don't have to specify—fail to affect psychology, there seems to me a complete and deliberate ignoring of basic human situations. To suggest that environment is significant, but to consider that the really organic environment, which is what you are yourself in your body, is not significant in the differences it may make in your reactions, is such a folly. And it's a dangerous folly, which women will regret. The obvious consequences include, for example, the notion that child-bearing should be relegated to a minor role, rather than seeing it as the most significant biological role. The attempt to ignore the connection between biology and psychology is a falsification of something very profound and very basic. And that is to me a tragedy in the women's movement.

The thing has gone to such extremes—the notion, for example, that lesbianism is not merely a possible life-style, but is actually perhaps even a desirable life-style.

Are you being fair? Can't any revolutionary social movement be caricatured by focusing on its extremes?

Syrkin: That's true, but those are the dangers. When I argue with my friends, I tell them, "You don't have to tell me to keep my family name; I kept my name before I knew that was the thing to do. I've always used my name, through several marriages, strange as that may appear. And you don't have to tell me that a woman has to be independent, I was always independent, and very energetically so." Not necessarily always to my advantage. But at the same time, I remember that when I was pregnant with my first child—I don't know whether this is too personal, but it seems to me pertinent—I didn't know whether to be ashamed in front of my advanced friends. Might they not say, "What kind of an intellectual are you, that you want a baby?" And to my own surprise, almost, I discovered that I wanted a baby very much.

And then I became a little dubious as to whether I had a right to this pleasure. But in subsequent years, when I matured, and as an old woman, I think it's a tragedy what's taking place with these young women, who are ignoring not merely urges, but—I don't think every woman necessarily has to have children, and there are obviously women who shouldn't have children, who don't want them—but to make a mockery of it? To relegate love of a man or love of a child to a minor role?

That such love may be less important than, say, becoming a stenographer? That's an absurdity.

Above all, it's dishonest to refuse to face organic differences that are also psychic differences. That seems to me a very tragic development of the women's movement.

Weiss-Rosmarin: I agree with you, but the difficulty is that ever so many people base value judgments on physiological differences. Freud, for example, coined the phrase, "Biology is destiny"; other psychologists as well, to this day, place value judgments on the physiological differences. While I perfectly agree that physiological differences imply psychological differences, they are hardly "destiny."

Syrkin: Yes, they *are* destiny; that's the problem, and it doesn't imply a value judgment. Why can't one simply say, "This is one kind of destiny, that is another"?

Weiss-Rosmarin: I perfectly agree, so long as the judgment is kept out of it. After all, being pregnant, and giving birth, and raising a child—all that takes so many years out of a person—*if* one doesn't know how to handle it. I have only one son—and being pregnant and giving birth to him, I didn't permit myself to interrupt my professional schedule. After he was born, there was of course the problem of who was going to take care of him. This was back in '38, and my husband of those years didn't feel like it. Also he didn't make enough. So I really worked in order to support a maid and a nursemaid. I literally had only two dresses, because all that I earned went to provide proper care for the kid. It was a wonderful investment. However, if I had taken off four or five years to take care of him myself, I would really have suffered major professional damage.

Syrkin: I was not able to take off four or five years, because of the circumstances of my life, but in retrospect, I would say that a woman owes four or five years to her child. I'm very dubious as to how that can be arranged, but I mean that one can't have everything. It's curious: In practice, I can't imagine anyone who has followed a more consistent feminist pattern than I have. But in theory, in evaluating the results of it all, if a young woman who wants a child were to ask me for advice, were to ask whether she should rush right out and have it, I'd say, "Good, have it when you're young, don't wait until you're 30 because you probably won't get pregnant right away, and who knows what kind of a child you'll produce if you wait until you're 40." And then I'd add, "If you want the delight of having a child, don't assume that you can do it cheaply. It merits a few years of your life."

Back in 1936, wasn't it, Dr. Weiss-Rosmarin, when you wrote your first article on women . . .

Weiss-Rosmarin: It wasn't exactly on women. I established the School of the Jewish Woman in New York, which was modeled—a poor model, of course—on Rosenzweig's Freie Jüdische Lehrhaus. I did that because of the problem that Jewish women were being shortchanged by not getting a substantial Jewish education, and I wanted to remedy that on the adult level. And that school did pretty well for about as long as the Lehrhaus had done well. The Lehrhaus began in 1920 and it closed in 1926. Rosenzweig wasn't surprised. He knew that these efforts, which are not really consonant with the temper of the community, usually don't last. The School of the Jewish Woman started with a bang. There were fine lecturers, etc., etc. But I, in those days, approached the problem from the point of view of education. I said to myself that just as I had had to get a good Jewish education, with Gemara and Rashi and everything, so should other Jewish women get the same thing. My feminism in those days was intellectually oriented.

I suppose that everyone would agree, however, that whatever one has contributed, a child is the best contribution.

Syrkin: I don't know about that. I'm not prepared to say that at all.

Weiss-Rosmarin: My son is ultra-Orthodox; he's a *rosh yeshiva* in Israel, he's writing a commentary on the Babylonian Talmud.

Syrkin: My son is a physicist.

My son the *rosh yeshiva?*

Weiss-Rosmarin: My son and I disagree, but we tolerate each other's views. A child is a wonderful thing, but one should not sacrifice . . .

Syrkin: You *have to* sacrifice . . .

Weiss-Rosmarin: Yes, sacrifice, but a man won't give up his essential personality for the sake of his child . . .

Syrkin: That's true, and that's a very basic difference. He doesn't get pregnant, he doesn't have to nurse. Biology *is* destiny.

Let's shift. You came to this country in what year?

Weiss-Rosmarin: In 1931.

Syrkin: I came in 1908, at the age of nine, so I was really raised here. I was born into Socialist Zionism—the emphasis as much on the socialism as on the Zionism. According to the Zionism in which I was brought up, this was going to be an ideal world for all mankind in which the Jews would play a leading role, because—from my father I had the notion—it is their function, arising from the prophetic tradition, to create and help shape an ideal society. I was brought up with that almost as with the ABCs.

Again, in subsequent years, one begins to question all these things.

Weiss-Rosmarin: You were very fortunate in your upbringing. After all, to be the daughter of Nachman Syrkin . . .

Syrkin: Yes, but one thing he failed to provide me. He did not teach me Hebrew at an age when I could have learned it. It's maddening. You know, when I was a child, a teenager, he would periodically get the feeling that he was neglecting me and he would take over my instruction. The books in question were *Das Kapital* in German, Spinoza's *Ethics* in Latin—I don't know why, except that I was precocious—and the Bible, where we never got beyond the first sentence. We'd get that far, and Papa would suddenly be busy, and by the next time, I'd have forgotten what we'd done so we would start over.

So that's one thing I have against my father. At a time when I was very receptive to languages—for instance, when we travelled, when I was six, seven, eight years old, in France he taught me French, in Germany, German—Papa was always getting exiled, so we travelled a lot—in Russia I learned to read Russian. But that he didn't teach me Hebrew was a serious loss.

Weiss-Rosmarin: Couldn't you have done it on your own?

Syrkin: Yes, and in this I confess I am a sinner, I am guilty, I'm a reprobate.

Do you regret not making *aliyah*, not living in Israel?

Syrkin: "Regret" is a funny word. I don't want to use it too lightly. I'm ashamed that I didn't make *aliyah*. There are no valid excuses for it. In the years when I should have done it, when I was young, I had reasons—my child, my this, my that, my personal life was very confused. But the excuses don't excuse. They may be explantions, but they're not excuses. I've known too many people who did make *aliyah*, and under the most difficult circumstances. Take Golda, for example, a person that I admire immensely. No *chochmas*. At the age of 21 she said to the boy she lived with, "Either we go together or I go alone." And that was that. It took a different kind of character. So I consider my own a defective kind of character, that in light of my conviction I nonetheless failed to make *aliyah*. And I saw no subsequent period when it would have made sense.

I remember, for example, when I was collecting material for my book on Jewish resistance, *Blessed is the Match*, in Palestine in 1945, Golda said to me, "Why don't you stay?" And I said, "But I've got all this material, I've got to write it, there's a publisher waiting," and it seemed to me that the most urgent thing I could do was that book. And I still don't know whether staying then, and missing the opportunity to write that book would have been more productive—although it probably would have shown that I'm a nicer person.

And you, Dr. Weiss-Rosmarin?

Weiss-Rosmarin: I really wanted to make *aliyah*, so I left school when I was 15 and went to join a *hachsharah*, a training farm for agricultural life in Palestine. The farm was near Berlin, but it didn't agree with me, and I got pneumonia, which in those days was a difficult illness. So my mother came and took me home, where I stayed for six weeks. And the doctor said, "You're not physcally fit for that kind of life."

Well, in the meantime I had left school, and I had lost the year, and I had to prepare for the final examinations. And my parents didn't want to pay for the tutor I needed. So—in those days, at the age of 15 or 16, we were already responsible people, capable of doing things—I took a job in a nearby town as director of a Hebrew language school, where I was really the only faculty member as well, and earned money with which I paid for my own tutor, and I took the final exam a year ahead of my class. And, having failed in *hachsharah*, I was left out when everybody in my circle went to Palestine, to Bet Zera, a kibbutz.

And afterwards, of course, I pursued my professional studies, and became deeply involved in them. And by the time I was ready, it was really too late.

Syrkin: It's a matter of fate; either at the right time one does or one doesn't. I should have gone at 20. In subsequent periods, life for me became too complicated to manage it.

You've both been very deeply involved in Jewish life in this country, and you will both recall how recently it was that the commonly accepted wisdom was that the American Jewish community wouldn't make it, that the process of assimilation would inevitably do us

in. Are you surprised by the vitality you witness today?

Syrkin: I am very worried by the demographic data. So many of the children and grandchildren of people in my circle are marrying "out of the faith," as it is known, with the usual assurances that it won't make any difference. Sometimes a minister and a rabbi co-officiate, all kinds of monkey business. I have small faith that those individuals will remain Jews. Another generation and they will be gone.

Now if the demographic trend is projected with accuracy—I'm not a demographer myself—it's a very bleak picture. And strictly from personal observation—in which, incidentally, I put great stock—it seems quite clear that the data are correct.

At the same time, I realize that there is something else that didn't exist a while back. There's a return to tradition among the young. To me, that's very interesting. It would have seemed a very backward trend to me when I was young, something primitive. And now it seems to be charming. The values change. But I can't say that salvation lies in Williamsburg and such.

Does the change in your values regarding tradition relate at all to the point you have made, that there was a time when you imagined a brilliant socialist future, but that time has now passed?

Syrkin: Obviously, unless one is crazy, one can't look about the world today and easily imagine a socialist utopia. I am old enough to remember the excitement of 1917 with the revolution in Russia. My father was almost wild; oh, the intensity of those hopes. Look, I belonged to a childhood where, in the course of my travels, I sang the "International" in French, I sang the "International" in Russian, I sang the "International" in German, I sang it in Yiddish, in Hebrew, in practically every language of the Diaspora.

And nothing has turned out as we dreamt. Of particular pain to me of course is the situation in Israel, where the marvelous hopes—perhaps the foolishly marvelous hopes—of the pioneer generation and of those that I knew of the Second Aliyah and the Third Aliyah—that all that has come to such a very sorry pass. I mean that what we have today is a very far cry from what had been hoped and desired, and, what is worse, we see not merely failures of achievement in Israel in this regard—such failures can be explained by outward conditions—but we see a change in the desires. I can disagree with an ideological member of Gush Emunim who sees biblical patrimony that he must act on—but when I read of a real estate boom on the West Bank, fueled by speculators for no other reason than to make money, I am shocked.

When one speaks of Israel, if one is really honest, the problem is this: Look at the small group of wonderful individuals who started the American democracy. Enlightened people, full of liberal ideas—and now we have Reagan. That's certainly a monumental decline.

So the Jews are precocious, because the decline took so much less time?

Syrkin: Yes, from Ben-Gurion to Begin. It's a very sad thing. But there are in the kibbutzim, in the various peace movements, people who guard the flame, to use a trite phrase. And, whatever the difficulties that beset Israel today, I still believe that Zionism and the reality of a Jewish state are the chief forces making for Jewish spiritual and physical survival in this secular age.

We are an extraordinarily resilient people. With all the blind alleys along the way, the flame doesn't go out. Blessed is the match.

Syrkin: No, it doesn't go out. But you see, it's "blessed is the *match*." A match is such a small thing. It's when one hopes for the great fire that one is disappointed. And then one realizes that it's just a small match, here and there—and that's what it's essentially been all along in Jewish history, I suppose.

But how can I cite Jewish history in the presence of the real expert?

Weiss-Rosmarin: I would use a different image. I would say, "*Hasneh einenu uchal*"—"and the bush was not consumed." I believe very strongly in the *she'ar yashuv*, that is to say, in the abiding remnant, which is really borne out by Jewish history. And I don't share your pessimism regarding the American Jewish community or the world Jewish community. I think it depends very much on where you take your statistics. Do you take them in Scarsdale or Beverly Hills, where you will get one kind of result, or do you take them in Boro Park or Riverdale, where you will get a different result?

I maintain that Jewish demographers and sociologists have over the past 20 years not at all considered what Egon Mayer calls in his book "the new *shtetl*." There is a movement from the suburb to the *shtetl*.

I recently spent a Shabbat in Boro Park. There are about a hundred thousand Jews in Boro Park. And not a car moves there on the Shabbat. And people have as many children as God gives them. And these are not old people. Most of them are American-born, children of survivors of the Holocaust. They go about in Chassidic garb. And Boro Park has satellites, new high rise buildings in Riverdale and elsewhere that weren't there eight years ago. I see a tremendous surge in this.

And also in the secular circles. For example, we have about 300 colleges and universities that teach Judaic studies—some more, some less, some better, some worse. Or take the revival of Yiddish . . .

Syrkin: If you take it numerically, it's peanuts. And I doubt very much that it really describes the important trends of the community. Here and there, perhaps, a few thousands . . . but what does it really amount to?

You know, there was a time when if you were reading a Yiddish newspaper, you'd fold it inside your English newspaper so no one would see. Now, there's no disposition to do that. Yiddish has become fashionable, which may be the best indication of how little a threat it represents, of how tiny and weak it has become. I'm afraid that's the cause of the approbation. And I think that may be the reason, as well, that secular Jews view what's going on in Williamsburg or Boro Park with approbation. What's happening there is, at best, picturesque. But you can't escape the question of how large that is within the whole body of American Jewry. You're talking about a minimal number, and even if it's a minimal number that's on the increase, you haven't really altered the balance within the total community.

Weiss-Rosmarin: But it's not just in Boro Park. It's also in Scranton, and in Denver—and those families are having seven or eight children each.

Maybe you're right concerning Yiddish. But take the number of Jewish books being published by general publishers—and there are readers for those books. That's no longer just the Orthodox community we're talking about. There is a tremendous efflorescence of scholarship.

After all, how many Zionists were there at the time of the First Zionist Congress in 1897? It's always been a matter more of ideas than of numbers.

But now you're changing the terms of the argument.

Syrkin: It seems to me that unless one believes in miracles, or has a mystical faith in that regenerative force which does seem to be a part of Jewish history and which enables us to overcome all obstacles . . . well, the matter of numbers can't be avoided. And what I'm saying is really banal. If the demographers are right, then the future is bleak. And, as I said before, I put great stock in personal observation. And you know how it has come to be these days. One meets one's friend and says, "My grandson is getting married, and would you believe it, it's a Jewish girl!" And you find yourself congratulating him because the grandson is marrying a Jew.

Weiss-Rosmarin: But you do have to look as well at things like the havurah movement, and not just havurot in synagogues, but in all kinds of places. No, you shouldn't and can't look just at the Orthodox neighborhoods. But look at the scholarship that grows and thrives in America.

Syrkin: I have the geatest respect for it, even reverence . . .

Weiss-Rosmarin: I have no reverence for it, no feeling at all. You see, I'm not a very reverent person, an emotional, a respecting person. But I have studied Jewish history, and there is a certain lesson in Jewish history, that only those whom you and I call Orthodox are truly concerned about Jewish learning.

Syrkin: I dispute that thoroughly. My father was a very serious Jewish scholar. It would be foolish to describe him as an atheist, yet he was certainly opposed to the synagogue and to Orthodoxy.

I suspect this is one argument we shan't settle here. So if I may, you've both had long connections to Jewish magazines, and I wonder whether we might not talk about that for a bit . . .

Weiss-Rosmarin: Oh, wonderful, perhaps you can tell me how to keep an ailing magazine alive?

Syrkin: If you want to hear a story about that, I have a story for you. The *Yiddisher Kemfer* . . .

Weiss-Rosmarin: . . . which is still a very good magazine . . .

Syrkin: . . . years ago, it must have been 50 or 60 years ago, it was in a bad way, in a critical condition. And they had a Central Committee which had on it Papa and a few other such luminaries, and they had a meeting to decide what to do, how to rescue the magazine. And Papa sat at the meeting, and he looked very grave, and finally he spoke: "There is only one solution," said he; "If the *Yiddisher Kemfer* is failing as a weekly, then we must have a daily." It sounded insane, but he persuaded the unfortunate comrades that a daily was essential if Socialist Zionism and the Jews of America were to be saved. And they went out and established a daily called *Di Zeit,* which lasted maybe two years. And the passion with which these people raised funds; the *chaverim,* the Labor Zionists, of course stripped themselves. And I remember that Golda told me, not so many years ago, "I have one thing on my conscience." And it turned out that what was on her conscience was that in the days when they were collecting for *Di Zeit,* when she was 18 or 19 or 20, she went around of course with all her enthusiasm, and she explained to each comrade that he or she had to part with his or her last cent in order to save the paper. And she said, "You know, there was one tailor I approached, and I made it plain that when I asked for money I wasn't asking for five dollars, I was asking for a real sum, and he said to me, 'Well, I'm saving money to bring my wife and child out of Europe.' And I said to him, 'How can you hesitate between that and immediate salvation?' And there was no gainsaying Golda, and the tailor came across with the cost of a ticket. And Golda said to me, 50 years later, "I often wonder what happened to the *chaver* and his wife and his child."

I can tell you what happened to *Di Zeit*. We suffered terribly. Papa was a regular contributor, but within three months they stopped paying him anything for his articles, and the real problem in our lives was how to pay the rent. I used to pray for the demise of *Di Zeit,* because there was no question of Papa leaving it as long as it had a breath of life in it. So on the day when it finally expired, and Papa could go back to writing for *The Day,* which paid him $50 a week, that was a cause for celebration.

And *The Spectator?* When did that start?

Weiss-Rosmarin: In 1935. We've had quite a long life.

Syrkin: That's about the same as the *Jewish Frontier,* which we started in 1934.

And I thought MOMENT was getting on, now that we're almost nine years old.

Syrkin: To be quite serious, I don't think that a magazine can exist without a core of devotees, who give their talent and their support. Look, back in the early days of the *Frontier,* when it was a good magazine, no one was paid. I wasn't paid for the whole 35 years of my editorship. [Ed. note: #!*@#!] You need a core of devoted people to bring the magazine out, and a core of devoted readers to keep it going.

You've both been so deeply involved in Jewish life all these years. Does there seem to you to have been an attrition in quality, as is often observed? Do you sometimes have the feeling that we lose some of the best talents of our people, that there is a kind of self-hatred that depletes our strength?

Syrkin: Jewish self-hatred has reached an overwhelming degree. It takes very devious forms. And, curiously, it is sometimes totally unaware of itself. For example, I have met intelligent Jews who think that *The Little Drummer Girl,* Le Carré's new novel, is a very fair account. I read it because it is a number one best-seller, so I thought it important to read; otherwise I never read detective stories, I can't stand them. Now if ever there was a blatant piece of propaganda, very cleverly done, and in which the writer editorializes, that's this book. But the book is not the problem. The problem is that apparently perceptive Jews fall for it.

That's a very subtle form of Jewish self-hatred—the unwillingness to recognize what the enemy is doing to you, because you subscribe partially in your heart to some of the accusations that are made even when those accusations are false. I'm not even talking here about the realm of opinion; I'm talking about fairness with facts.

Weiss-Rosmarin: I would like to take issue with a bit of what Marie has said. I've not read Le Carré, but I have read the reviews, and I understand that he takes very much the case of the Palestinians. Now there are many amongst us—and, incidentally, this also goes for myself—who see that the Palestinians have a very legitimate case. I know that Golda said she had never heard of Palestinians . . .

Syrkin: I have to interrupt. I consider this one of the most serious libels on the memory of a great woman. It is true that that is what she said, but to take her words out of their historical context is unjust. Why did she say that? When she came to Palestine, she was a Palestinian. The Arabs whom she encountered did not view themselves as Palestinians. In fact they rejected the term, they insisted there was only southern Syria. Now when a woman who has spent her most active years in a struggle in which the opponent calls himself an Arab, an Arab nationalist, but rejects the definition of himself as a Palestinian, and the term is only the prerogative of the Jews she knows, she's perfectly justified in saying, "Who are these Palestinians?"

Now in later years, subsequently, she learned who the Palestinians are. I'm not going to go into that whole subject. But to attempt to make of this that she ignored reality, without taking into account how the names were used . . .

Weiss-Rosmarin: I accept that; you surely know what she meant. So let's drop the matter of names. I say only that today, they have a case.

Syrkin: I agree.

Weiss-Rosmarin: I was a member of Breira, I support Shalom Achshav [Peace Now]. If you ask me how I feel, emotionally, I would want Israel to extend from the Euphrates to the Nile. You can quote me—that's what I would want. But between what I want and what is possible, there's a vast difference. Politics is the art of the possible. And for many years now, the government of Israel—that goes for Labor as well as Likud—has been ignoring the reality of the Palestinians. We live at a time when national feelings have reached unprecedented intensity around the world, and Palestinian nationalism is part of that trend. And it seems to me that too many of us do not recognize that. My reason tells me that we must reckon with it.

Syrkin: Now I have to make a correction, because I don't want to be on record as agreeing that emotionally I want Israel to extend from the Nile to the Euphrates. I don't share that emotion. I see no point in rehashing the whole argument about the rights of the Palestinians and the rights of the Jews and how the Palestinians were abused and deliberately developed as a casus belli by the Arab states. Certainly today one has to take account of the realities of the situation. I quite agree that the demographic character of the West Bank would make its incorporation into Israel a great folly, a great injustice to Israel quite as much as to the Arabs. As so many of us say, that would totally destroy the democratic and the Jewish character of the Jewish state, so I totally oppose it.

But that doesn't mean I subscribe to every accusation the Palestinians make. And Jewish self-haters, without taking the trouble to look into Zionist history, subscribe to the most outrageous statements. I think that this willful ignorance and the readiness to accept the worst interpretation—the Jews were aggressors from the first moment, they kicked out all the Arabs, etc., etc.—the acceptance of the libels, the readiness to perceive the rights of every group except one's own, which is characteristic of a great many Jews, is a form of Jewish self-hatred.

Weiss-Rosmarin: Jewish self-hatred is a rejection of integral Jewishness. It's the sort of thing we saw in Germany when German Jews would describe themselves as "German citizens of the Mosaic persuasion." I don't believe that to espouse certain rights for the Palestinians is necessarily to engage in self-hatred.

Syrkin: I quite agree with you in that regard.

Does any of this bear on the problem of measuring Israel by a double standard?

Syrkin: We do have a problem there. There exists a peculiar form of anti-Semitism directed against the Jews and in which Jews participate, namely, a demand that the Jews be holier than any other people. I don't consider that a compliment; I consider that a form of discrimination. To demand more of a martyred people? That's to pull off their nails and then demand that they be manicured. But the poor peasant who hasn't had his nails pulled off doesn't have to be manicured. In my eyes, that's a form of discrimination under the guise of a compliment.

Isn't it so that if we stop expecting more of ourselves, we lose a very central defining characteristic of our people? Haven't we thought all along that we are special?

Syrkin: That's splendid, but it should be a dream, it should be a hope, a goal, it should not be the sine qua non by which you justify your existence, unless it becomes your existence, unless it becomes the sine qua non for every other group. To choose this little group and say that it earns its very right to exist, to be treated in the community of nations as other people are, only by virtue of some extraordinary virtue, is an extreme form of discrimination.

Weiss-Rosmarin: Yes, but unless we had thought ourselves an exceptional people, a people charged with a mission, a task, whatever you want to call it, we wouldn't be in Israel today. Where else have you seen that a nation that lost its country 2,000 years ago continued to insist over the two millenia that it is homeless, that "over there" is its home and one day we shall go there? An even more remarkable thing—where have you seen the rebirth of a language as we have seen with Hebrew?

We are this people that covenants itself to a special code of goodness or ethics, and consequently we expect of ourselves and others expect of us that we live up to the idea of being a *goy kadosh,* a special people.

Syrkin: I accept that view of Jewish history which holds that we have a mission, a purpose, and that's why we survived. We have certainly been an extraordinary people. But for Jews to be emancipated, part of what is required is for this extraordinary people to have won, among its other rights, the right to be ordinary.

I don't mind if Jews have a very exigent standard for themselves. But I resent it profoundly when Mr. Arafat offers me that standard, or some character in the government of the Soviet Union or some other equally unsavory regime. It's one thing for the Jews to say to themselves, as every human being may, that they have to be ideal, that they should be extraordinary, but they must also, among their rights, stand up for their right to be as others.

Weiss-Rosmarin: "Emancipation" to me means only to have equal civil rights. You remember Horace Kallen's concept of pluralism, the orchestra of cultures, where each instrument, each culture, contributes its own distinct melody to the orchestra, to the society. And I believe that we Jews, as citizens of an emancipated country, should contribute our own distinct melody. To me, our notes, our melody has something to do—so our history teaches, and I believe in that history—with an ongoing social revolution, with ethics and ideals that come to us from the Exodus, the first social revolution in all history.

Syrkin: I was brought up on that belief.

Is there not some kind of melody that is neither a dirge nor a march?

Syrkin: We are a people with many melodies and many instruments. And we can't always be expected to be the first violins.

I thank both of you, nonetheless, for playing with such virtuosity this morning. ✡

"When we arrived at Isaac Bashevis Singer's home on West 86th Street," Isidore Haiblum relates, "he was in the midst of a translation project with his secretary. He obviously had forgotten about the interview, but he was most gracious and ushered us into the living room, where he set us at ease. We spoke with him in Yiddish for a while, and then began the interview. 'Ask me anything you like,' Singer told us. He was enjoying himself. Our Yiddish introduction may have helped. And then, noticing the young lady in our interviewing party, he beamed: 'I will get a divorce, I will come to you, you will provide for me.'" Participating in the interview for MOMENT, along with Mr. Haiblum, who is a science fiction writer and "Yiddishophile," were Adrienne Joy Cooper, a fellow at the Max Weinreich Center for Advanced Jewish Studies, and David Neal Miller, who teaches in the Yiddish program at Queens College.

an interview with Isaac Bashevis Singer

Moment: *It was your book, The Family Moskat, which gave me my Jewish heritage, to a large extent.*

Singer: It's nice to hear, nice to hear. I do not expect to hear such things, but I keep hearing them all the time, and I'm all the time astonished, just the same. I never believed that a work of fiction could do anything. It's just made for entertainment. And now, I hear other things. Still, I think entertainment is its basic purpose. If it gives something else, it's a bonus. But if it does not entertain, if it only teaches or gives you messages, then it's not literature. You can call it by any other name—philosophy, psychology, sociology, but it's not enough to make it literature. Whatever else, it must be a gift.

For me, your writing is a gift.

Thank you. It's a gift to hear that.

I'll just say a few more words.

You can say many words. But which of you is going to do the interview?

This is the interview.

Oh. Would you like a chair or something? Are you comfortable?

Yes, I'm delighted to be here. I grew up speaking two languages.

Wait. Take this chair. Give him this chair. No, this chair, not that chair. I also know a little bit the human condition, to know when you are comfortable, and when you are not.

I was saying that I grew up speaking two languages, English and Yiddish. American heroes I knew about from movies. I read about them in books. But I didn't know what an exciting, cosmopolitan life was going on in Warsaw between the two World Wars until I read your books.

The truth is that the Jewish novel has not yet been written. Jewish life is so rich, and so adventurous, and so unbelievable, that no matter what you do you can't over-describe. These twelve million people, or whatever their number, are doing more things than twelve hundred million people. No question about it. They read all the books, they go to all the shows, they write all the shows, they write almost all the books, they travel everywhere. There is not an adventure or a *meshugas* that they don't take part. There is not a good deed that they don't contribute. There is not a nonsense that they also don't take part. To know the Jews is really to know the universe. So whatever a writer does is really almost nothing.

I was brought up in Warsaw, and there the Yiddish literature was part of the tradition: pedestrian, slow, telling stories which were obvious, you know. But I said to myself, how is this possible? How is it that this great nation is so provincial, so primitive? And I felt a kind of rebellion. When I tried to do what I thought I should do, they said I was sinning against the Yiddish tradition. The tradition was always to tell a story about a shtetl, a rich girl who fell in love with a poor boy, and she loved him so much that she married him anyhow.

The reason why Jewish literature has not developed more is because Jews live in all the languages. To know the Jews you have to know the whole earth. And since no one knows all the languages, no one can really know Jewish literature.

Haven't you also done some translations?

Yes, I have translated Thomas Mann's *Magic Mountain* and some others, but I feel I have done nothing. I didn't do them as carefully as I might have, but the Yiddish readers were so eager to get in touch with the rest of the world that a bad translation was better than none.

Did the translations help you in your writing?

I would say that everything a writer does, everything he sees, is part of his writing. You came to this interview, I see your faces, you are already a part of my impression. If I need it, I can use it.

Many of your characters spend much of their effort trying to figure out why things happen—a task which they often despair of. In one of your stories, you wrote, "The world is full of puzzles. It's possible that not even Elijah will be able to answer all of our questions when the Messiah comes. Even God in the seventh heaven may not have solved all the mysteries of His creation. This may be the reason He conceals His face."

Yes, I would say the function of literature, among other things, is to make the unbelievable believable. As a rule, people don't believe in any unusual things, except when they happen to them. For instance, if you go on the street, and you suddenly see your dead great-grandmother, or you have a dog in the house, and this dog suddenly begins to talk to you, you would not call yourself a liar, because you saw it. But if your neighbor tells it to you, you say he's a liar. People cannot believe anything except the usual things, and it's the function of literature to show that the unbelievable does not happen only to you—but to other people also.

Actually, the history of humanity is the history of unbelievable things. People are created so they don't believe in unbelievable things, because it would destroy the laws of nature and the order of society. But a real writer sees these unbelievable things, and tries to stress them. So pure realism, pure naturalism, is actually the very opposite of literature. Take a man like Solzhenitsyn. Even though he's a man with great—unbelievable—courage, his writing is believable. The things that are unbelievable in his writing are unbelievable because of Russia, not because of his writing. As a rule he has not much fantasy, not much humor. He's a reporter. But again, his courage is unbelievable. When everyone was afraid, he had no fear whatsoever, and they let him go.

Do you feel yourself part of an American or Yiddish intellectual community, or do you feel isolated?

No. Because these things really depend on fashions. Today the fashion is romanticism, the next day it's futurism. The very fact that everything becomes an "ism" means that they live according to issues. A school of thought is created, and if you dare to go against it, they punish you. This is happening right now here. When you read the book reviews of the New York *Times*, you'll see that there is a certain kind of cliché, in the broader sense of the word, going on. When they talk about the human condition, they will name Dostoevski and Kafka, as if these two were everything.

But now you're fashionable also. Does that make you feel exploited?

Well, again, I may be fashionable today, and tomorrow they may say somebody else is fashionable. I'm always prepared for these things. But actually, this is unavoidable, it's human nature. Most probably, it has to be like this. Because if every human being had his own way, there would never have been any society. It seems that a society needs people who follow a leader.

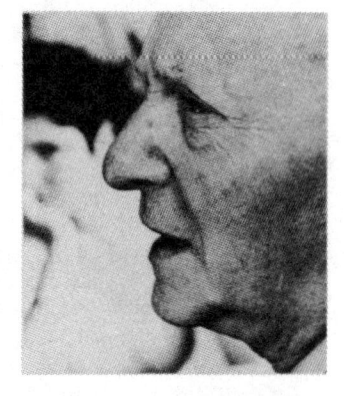

Of all your characters, it seems that your female narrators are the only ones not at a loss to explain what is going on. They grope back for some kind of folksaying and find an answer that makes sense.

This is a wonderful method to be used in writing, if the writer has a sense for language. When an old woman sits down and tells a story, she doesn't worry about style. Or repetition, or anything else except the story. My Aunt Yentl had a number of sayings that I use in my stories. Now when she would tell a story, she wouldn't worry about anything except the story. Since I rarely would write myself in such a mixed-up style, I sometimes let my aunt or some other person tell a particular story. Women are especially good at telling stories, and telling about unusual things. In other words, I would say, in literature, like in sex, the less you make an effort, the more you succeed.

You said that as a writer you felt somewhat alone in America. How about as a person? How do you feel as a person in American society?

I'll tell you. As a person I feel like every other person. Why was I born? When will I die? What will be later? This feeling of bewilderment was with me all my life. I remember myself at two years, looking around, and asking myself, not in words, actually, what's going on here? There was a pig and a dog and a sky—and I'm just as much astonished now as I was then. I don't feel I really belong to American society—I feel I belong to something which I don't understand. We are all small parts of some great machine, or whatever it is, which we shall never really know as long as we are alive. Maybe after death we will know, maybe never. It's a riddle, living in a riddle. I would say that every human being shares this, and also animals. Sometimes when I walk alone somewhere, and in a pasture I see a cow, I see it lift up its face to ask, why am I a cow? Why do I eat grass all day? What's going on here? And this is how I feel almost all the time. But since I can't go around all the time and just wonder, I do my work, whatever I have to do. I pay the taxes, I do everything which I must do.

If there had been a continuation of Jewish life and culture in Poland, do you feel you would be a different person now, writing different books for a different audience?

I don't know what I would do. The only thing I can tell you is that, even back then, I had this feeling that I didn't belong. People were all so sure of their convictions. The Zionists were sure, the Communists were sure. I was inclined more to Zionism than to Communism, there's no question about that. But again, this being sure, which is characteristic of the man of action, was never with me. And this is the reason why I never really did anything. Except scribbling, you know. I could never go into any political things, you know, like saying Carter is going to be the best President, or Reagan. I don't have, completely, any convictions, except one: since we all suffer anyhow terribly, there is no reason why we should add more suffering to other people. As much as you can, try not to add to the troubles of people. Not that I am convinced that this is the rule of the Almighty. But I think this is my own kind of conviction.

My morality, my ethics, if I have any, is based just on a feeling. Not on any philosophy. From a philosophical point of view, you cannot prove that Hitler was wrong, and Gandhi was right.

How do you feel about a revival of Yiddish, as a language?

The truth is, if we would be a normal people, I would say it's impossible. If you would say that the Germans would begin again to speak German in the United States, I would say it can't happen. Or the French. But the Jews—anything can happen. Because they are so *meshugeh*. So unusual, and so abnormal, that you cannot really predict anything. It can happen. See what happened to Hebrew. For almost two thousand years Hebrew was a dead language. Suddenly a few young people decided to go back to Israel, and a man, Ben Yehudah, decided to revive Hebrew, and it's there. So you can't predict.

All of us here decided to learn Yiddish in college.

So, you are Yiddishists. If somebody would have told me forty years ago that babies born in Brooklyn or in Queens would grow up to speak Yiddish in the 1970's, I would have said it's impossible. But here you sit and speak Yiddish. And you speak beautiful Yiddish. You were born in this country?

We were all born in this country.

So if it could happen to you, why can't it happen to others? However, I would not say yes, and I would not say no. I see it's happening in a small way, because you are really the exceptions among the exceptions. But you never know. One day you are an exception, the next day you are the rule.

Isaac Bashevis Singer

Are there any young Yiddish writers?

No.

Anyone who brings you manuscripts?

A few, but of no real significance. But about one thing I'm sure: that Yiddish literature will never be forgotten. It contains treasures, not so much of art, but treasures of information. History. Ways of life. It does not contain the great Jewish adventure, but it does contain many, many fragments of it. Yiddish books are being written in Brazil, in Argentina, in Israel—a lot of it is worthless, but still, you can always find something.

Israel, which has a Jewish culture, seems to be going in a completely different direction from the Yiddish culture which you represent.

It's another one of these paradoxes. They revived Hebrew, and went back to the land of their ancestors, which they were driven out of 2,000 years ago. They tried to skip over from the Bible to Ben Gurion and forget two thousand years of exile, which is a big *meshugas*. The political situation is such that any day there can be a new exile. They're living on a volcano. They haven't created in this new Hebrew anything of great worth. Maybe in science, which I don't know, but not in literature. Agnon is actually a Yiddish writer who writes in Hebrew; his whole vision is that of a Yiddish, not a Hebrew, writer.

As a matter of fact, I'm going to Israel in June.

Do you feel at home there?

No, I feel at home nowhere. But in Israel I have people whom I have known for many, many years. I don't think there's a single person who really feels at home anyplace. "Home" is a good word, but "at home"—this word I don't understand.

Do you think that there are certain words or feelings that are particularly communicated in Yiddish?

In my own Yiddish, I use actually three languages. Yiddish, Hebrew, and Aramaic. I use words from Talmud, *Tanach*, and words which the rabbis used. So, in a way, I bring in certain little treasures from all of these languages. And because of this it's difficult to translate my work. If you take, let's say, the language of a politician, his use of Yiddish can easily be translated into any other language. But if you have allusions to various other Jewish sources, it's much more difficult. However, I do work on the translations myself, and participate in the editing, because I have learned English, not enough, but the English which I need for my own writing. However, if a writer writes for translation, he has to be not 100 percent good, but 150 percent, to make up for what will be lost in translation. Now you have to change your tape.

No, ten more minutes.

Ten more minutes? Oh!

Do you ever go to movies?

Almost never. When I first came to this country, and I had girlfriends, they forced me to go to the movies. I was sitting there and watching gangsters shoot one another. I saw that there is no art in it, no art, no information. It was all fabrications. Most probably, there must be some good movies, but I haven't seen many. I remember one, Henry the Eighth, which was a very good movie, with this fat actor from England, I've forgotten his name.

Charles Laughton?

Yes. Neither do I go to the theater. I saw *Yentl*, of course.

Shall we talk about Yentl?

Ach, I will tell you, it was entertainment, but I haven't written it. It's taken from my story, and I had a collaborator . . . it was so far good that it did not bore me, but I heard that many people who went said it was not good.

It was interesting to watch the audience. Often they were so embarrassed they were watching the floor.

Well, I have seen plays that were so boring that I couldn't understand how the audience stayed there. The theater is in a bad way. Literature is in a bad way; it's become an industry. It was never in a good way; actually, every good word that ever appeared was a miracle. In the history of literature all the non-miracles are more or less forgotten. Can you change the tape before it runs out?

That's a good idea. . . . You once said that life is impossible without sex.

Absolutely. Well, it's possible, if you don't have it, you don't have it. Sex is one of our strongest instincts. But I'm not discovering America by saying this.

Do you think that the sexual freedom we have here is leading to trouble, or is one of the great wonders?

It can cause a lot of trouble, but it's still good. But censorship is a misfortune. No one should tell a writer—just like there shouldn't be a censor who would tell a man—speak only clever things, don't speak nonsense. If a man wants to be a fool, he will be a fool. If a man wants to use bad language, the government cannot tell him not to do it. The real writers, actually, don't use bad language. They write sexy novels, but they wouldn't use bad language. Those who use bad language do it because they have no feeling for sex. So they try to be sexy with words. But we must have literary freedom. A writer has to be free. A literature that all the time praises its people cannot exist. The Old Testament does not flatter us; it says the worst things about the Jews. I know one man who, reading the Bible for the first time, said, "I thought I was reading *Mein Kampf*." The Bible calls us thieves, murderers, lechers, on every page almost. And yet the ancient Jews made this the holy book. The modern Jew wants to be flattered. Tell him that he's good, he's wonderful, he's honest; and some Jewish writers believe that we should always show how great we are. We are great. But just because we are great, we should not all the time boast. A great person does not boast all the time.

But sometimes other people boast for a person. Rebecca West and the late Edmund Wilson nominated you for a Nobel Prize.

I never take these things seriously for a moment. No writer writes for prizes. The great writers don't always get prizes. Tolstoy was nominated for the Nobel Prize, another man got it, nobody knows who he is. Proust, Joyce, didn't get prizes. When a writer sits around and waits for a prize, it's a very miserable situation. Although I got a few prizes.

You've said that all your fiction is in some way autobiographical.

This is true about everybody. Even when you write about other people, you're writing about things that you have seen or imagined.

There seem to be a number of stories, about middle-aged Yiddish writers, that seem to invite an autobiographical interpretation. They seem like you but they're not exactly you.

Well, there's no reason why I should not combine my own experience with other things. The main thing is that there is a story, and that the writer says what he wants to say. His means and his methods can vary according to how he wants to do it. He can just as well avoid the first person. Until now, in all my novels, I never wrote in the first person. But I may do so in the future; I think it will work.

But you have done this in your Yiddish writing.

Well, I was speaking about English. My readers in Yiddish, in the *Forwards*, are at least five years in advance of my English readers.

You write most of your fiction in serial form in newspapers.

Yes, and it has both advantages and drawbacks. It's a good discipline, and you have a better sense of your audience. Dostoevski, Balzac, Dickens—they all worked this way. It would be a good idea if newspapers would once again publish fiction. It would do literature a lot of good. Also, when you write this way, you remember that there must be some tension in your work. The reader should be eager to read the next installment. One of the problems of modern literature is that the writer is so busy expressing himself that he forgets that there is a reader, that he also has to get something out of this business.

   It's all right to express yourself, but if a man comes to you and speaks about himself for five hours, you will say, "All right, it's very fine, but why should I listen to you? I also have a self—I'm interested in me." The older writers understood this. They wrote for the reader. Some of the writers today feel that the reader does not exist. And the truth is, for these people, that the reader doesn't exist, because you cannot read them!

Are you in contact with other Yiddish writers?

Sutzkever and I were both published in Israel recently, in Yiddish. There was a time when Yiddish was *treif* for them. This is itself a miracle. If Ben Yehudah would come out of his grave and see this, he would tear locks out of his bald head.

Do you have any hope for Yiddish in Israel?

More than in any other place. In spite of everything. Their enmity will disappear after a short time. The new generation is not afraid that Yiddish will take the place of Hebrew. So they are becoming more lenient from day to day. They gave me a doctor title, last year, in Jerusalem, and so on.

If my students ask me if Isaac B. Singer explained why they should be sitting in my class learning Yiddish, how should I answer them?

Answer them that a person must have roots. In the dictionary you can find "a man," just a human being, but actually, nobody is just a human being. If we are Jews, we have to have our roots; if not, we lose ourselves completely. Take an assimilated Jew. He's still a Jew. His grandparents did not come on the Mayflower. He begins to be a kind of a bastard, if he denies his ancestry. No past, no history—he becomes something from a dictionary, not from life. You need a home to be part of society. If you are a man of the Bowery, you will get very few invitations.

Should any living Yiddish writers be translated?

Some write twenty pages about the hairs on a rabbi's beard. They're boring. A real writer must know how much a reader can take. When he doesn't have a real story to tell, he keeps on describing without end.
   I would like in this interview not to mention any names.

What about writers who are no longer living?

The dead? The dead you can malign as much as you want. But then they have children....
   Yiddish literature, like all literature—as a rule, it's no good, but it has exceptions. Mostly garbage, but a few treasures. Of course, from a higher point of view, the garbage is also treasure. It contains atoms, and molecules, and what not.

Thank you.

It was my pleasure. I sometimes think I give too many interviews, but just the same, I say things that I didn't say before.

(May 10, 1976) ✦

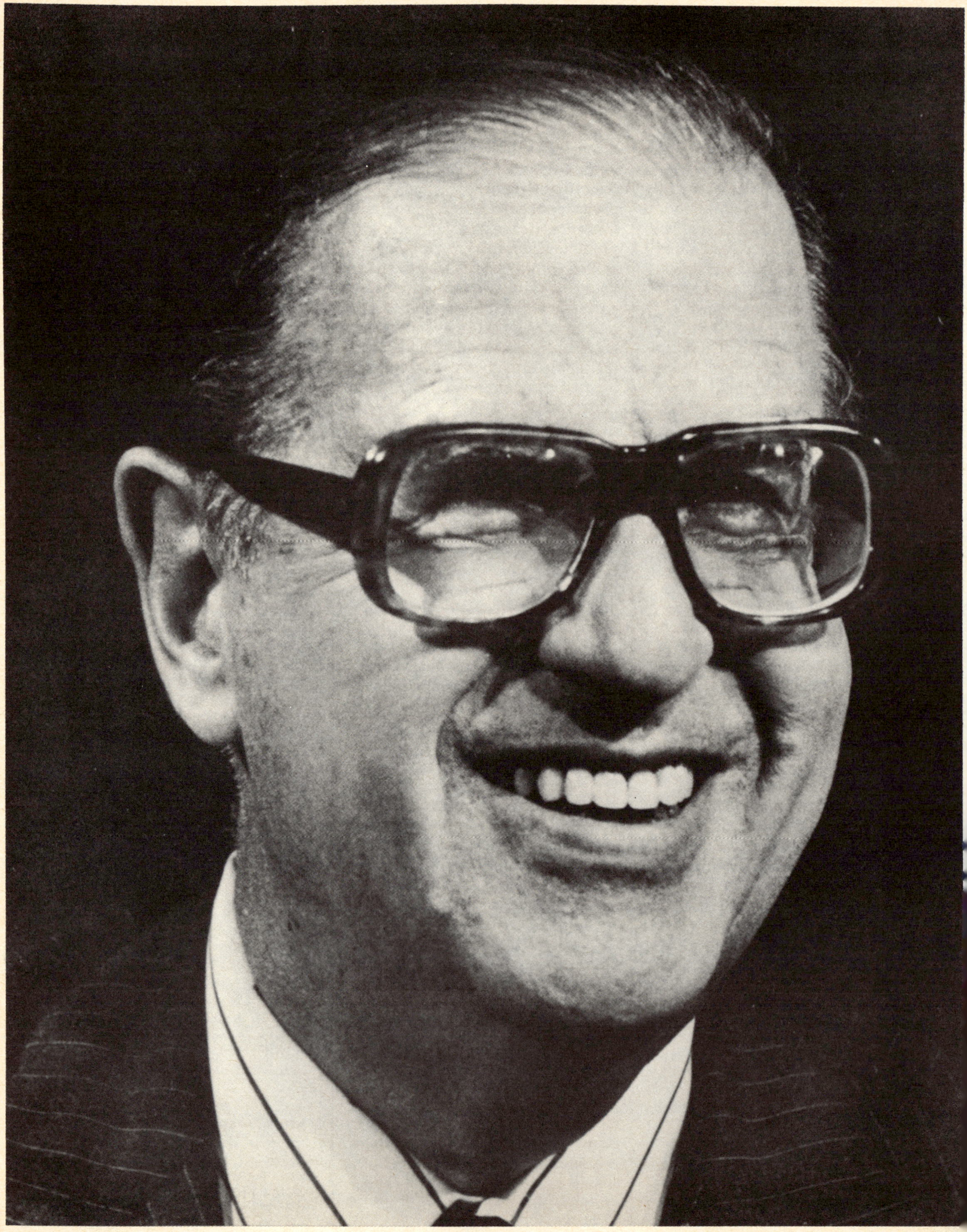

ABBA EBAN MOMENT INTERVIEW

Abba Eban, a contributing editor of this magazine, is a member of the Knesset and has served as Deputy Prime Minister, Minister of Education, and, from 1966 to 1974, as Foreign Minister of Israel.

Has Labor learned anything during its time in opposition?

It has, I think, learned the lessons that derive from separation from power. There is virtue in the rotationary principle in parliamentary life. Nobody enjoys that principle when he falls on the wrong side of it, but it does give one a chance to look at the national situation with different eyes. Those who are charged with office tend to lose touch with the popular mood. Being out of office provides an opportunity to revise platforms, thoughts, attitudes. Of course, there are some people who never lose the chance to miss an opportunity. But I think we have taken the opportunity. There is also a certain humility that goes with the absence of office that I think is very salutary. The inflated effects of public office must have had a more corrosive effect on us than we wanted to confess or than we were conscious of.

Felix Frankfurter used to tell me the story of a man who was brought up before the court because he had not paid his alimony, and he explained that he hadn't made enough money. The judge asked him what his occupation was, and he replied that he was the toilet attendant in City Hall. And the judge asked, "Why don't you get a job that pays better, so that you'll be able to pay your alimony obligations?" And the man looked at the judge sternly and said, "Your Honor, are you not underestimating the glamour of public office?"

But even beyond these general influences, among which I give precedence to the concept of humility, of having to live the life of ordinary citizens, I think our leadership has achieved a more balanced position on the most crucial issue—namely, our relations with the Arab world. I see rather less evidence of new or original thinking on the economy and the society. In those areas, I think the Labor Party has discharged its duty of criticism—and heaven knows there's been a lot to criticize—but on the question of the conditions of co-existence with the Arab world, the fact that our connections have been much less with foreign governments and much more with Social Democratic movements has had an effect on us. I think that on the whole, the Labor policy is rather nearer a moderate dovish position that it was when we left office, largely because we are without Moshe Dayan. Dayan was a very dynamic influence in formulating our proposals. In fact, many of our Party documents, such as the Galili document and the so-called Oral Law were formulated not on their merits, but as a device for assuring that Dayan would graciously consent to appear on our party list at election time. There was no international or intrinsic party motivation for having such documents at all. Therefore, his departure, with all the pain that it caused, did enable us to fix a very clear position, distinct from the right wing. Such formulations as "We do not intend to exercise permanent rule over the 1.2 million Arabs in the West Bank and Gaza" never appeared in our platform before. There used to be a vaguer formulation; we'd said that we wanted Israel to be a Jewish state. But that's a rather egocentric reason for not wanting to rule over 1.2 million Arabs. The real implication of that statement was that if we had more Jews, we wouldn't mind such a rule. But now, our reluctance to rule over 1.2 million Arabs is stated as an independent moral imperative, not only because it's useful to us in the preservation of Israel's Jewishness, but also because it is the right thing not to want to do.

Out of that premise of not wanting to rule 1.2 million Arabs there flow obvious corollary positions, such as rejection of a unitary structure for Eretz Yisrael. If you're serious about saying that you don't want permanently to rule over 1.2 million Arabs, that determines your settlement policy as well. You don't establish settlements in such a way as deliberately to break up the territorial contiguity of the Arab population.

So on the whole I would say there has never been a time when the intellectual and moral frontier

Moment/249

between us and the Likud has been as sharp as it is today. It was not sharp enough when we fought the election of '77.

But when we look at the internal coalition with Labor, that coherence is not obvious. Motta Gur, for example, has been elevated to a senior position within the Party, yet his perspective on Israel's relations with the Arabs is hardly in agreement with what you've been saying. He seems to be rather to the right of Dayan.

That's true, but he doesn't have the weight of influence that Dayan had. You're drawing accurate attention to the composite character of large political parties, each of which is a coalition. We do have hard-liners in Labor as well. But their position was easier to sustain when there was no response to the idea of peace on the Arab side. Frankly, when we were not negotiating with any Arabs, the hard-line policy didn't do much harm. It may have done us harm in terms of image, but here I come to a great dilemma as a liberal. Every Egyptian of whom I've asked the question, "Why did you change your mind?"—after all, from the annihilation of Israel to a peace treaty is a very dramatic ideological transition—every one of them, from Sadat downwards, has said, "Because of your strength." Not one of them has said "Because of your rectitude." All of them have said, in effect, that if they had been able to get their territory and their interests back without this ideological wrench they would have preferred to do so. If they could have had a Middle East without Israel, then their historic memory and imagination made that preferable. But when they became aware that that was not possible, that they could not get anything from us by violence, they went over to the idea of getting their interests back through diplomacy and conciliation—and they have been triumphantly successful. "We didn't get anything back from you by war," they've said to me, "but by peace we got back our territory, we got back the oil, we got back the Suez Canal, we got an American alliance."

Now the implications of all this should be rather grave for us. It means that the obdurate element in our policy was one of the major incentives for bringing them to the peace table. And I think we as doves ought to look at that very carefully. It means that objectives which ought to be obtained by human grace and understanding are obtained, if at all, by methods which most liberals would choose not to adopt. Therefore, if I've been reluctant to accept the dove image, it is because I cannot bring myself to eliminate the question of power from international relations. The major positive developments in modern Jewish history—the resistance to Hitlerism, the establishment of Israel's independence and the peace treaty with Egypt are all connected somehow with power, and not one of them—neither the defeat of Hitler, nor the establishment of Israel, nor peace with Egypt—would have been obtained by a policy in which some element of steel was missing.

The art of politics, of course, is how to integrate the obdurate element into a policy that is also flexible, to be tough enough to deter aggression and yet flexible enough to make negotiation viable. I would say that that is now a fair statement of the Labor position. We're not just a pushover, we're not going to give up our interests for nothing. Sadat came to Jerusalem in '77 largely because of those ten years in which we on the one hand kept the wall up and on the other hand had a door in the wall.

How does what you've been saying affect your perspective on the negotiations now under way?

Now that there is a negotiation, it's not enough to have an image. You have to make a decision. In the party, there are people like Major General Motta Gur, some people in the Kibbutz Meuchad, some of the old activists of the Achdut Avodah, some who voted against the peace treaty—in other words, some who were to the right of Begin. Now and again some of our people propose motions attacking the government for not settling enough in the Golan. To my regret, some of my colleagues signed a petition saying that the Golan is a part of the State of Israel. I don't know why Peres, Rabin and the late Allon signed that, because my belief has been that the concept of territorial compromise applies to the Golan as well. But there are attempts to draw the Labor party away from its vocation of flexibility, of reasoned flexibility, towards a nationalist consensus closer to the Likud. But my feeling is that the mainstream now has a clearly defined position in which we prefer peace to territory, in which we prefer a selective security settlement policy to the irresponsible settlement policy that has caused so much furor in the last year. And since we have a different vision of the future, and since in our vision of the future the Arabs of the West Bank and Gaza are not Israelis, therefore we could afford to interpret autonomy more liberally. For we would not have this phobia that by giving too many powers we might be laying the foundations for a separation or a secession.

Autonomy does tend to lead to secession—and we face that frankly. The predicament of Begin lies in the gulf between the policy to which he aspires and the document which he has signed. He has signed a document which definitely creates an objective gravitation towards secession—full autonomy, withdrawal and replacement of the military administration, transfer of authority—the language is rich with associations of eventual separation. But having done this at Camp David, and received the Nobel Prize, all the encomiums, he seems to have looked at the document again and said, "Oh my God! Did I really sign that?" And under the pressure of Gush Emunim and others, he has really gone back to a pre-Camp David position.

But when I say that in Labor we are more definitive than before, I must make a personal reference. I think Shimon Peres has been largely responsible for shifting us into a position different from the one with which he himself used to be associated, and quite different from the Dayan-Galili documents. I only hope that he and others will not allow themselves, in the quest for what is called "party unity," or consensus, to obscure or to blur these very sharp definitions.

One of the implications of what you've been saying is that the Labor policy might provide Hussein with the inducement to join the process which he evidently feels is lacking today. But is Labor today prepared to move beyond its insistence that only a Jordanian solution can be contemplated? Is Labor prepared to initiate a national debate on other alternatives, including, most obviously, the alternative of an independent West Bank-Gaza state?

I'd like to clarify my own thinking here. I still believe, as I did when we last spoke, that if you could reconstruct a Palestinian-Jordanian entity on both sides of the Jordan, that would be the most rational course. You'd have a state that was capable of absorbing refugees, in which the center of geographical gravity would be rather removed from Israel. I also think that there's nothing to praise in the uncontrolled proliferation of "statelets" that has marked the international system. An area that France used to govern as a single province has become twenty sovereign states in West Africa. What used to be called the West Indies under the colonial regime has become about seven or eight states, with little islands joining all the time.

But my feeling is that we can do no more than state a preference. We cannot say, on the one hand, that we plan to separate from these territories, but on the other, that we will control their constitutional future. I therefore think we should move in two installments. If a Labor government came in tomorrow, I think that next week we should send a letter to Jordan, directly or through the United States, saying that we suggest that we now negotiate a peace treaty on the basis of Resolution 242. They accepted 242; we know their interpretation of it. Although the idea of the Jordanian character of the territories has been muted by Palestinianism since then, there is some juridical legitimacy in Jordan's position in the West Bank. The residents of the West Bank are Jordanian citizens, the UN has never cancelled its resolution. I think that should be the first step. Now Begin cannot say to them, "Let's have a discussion of the basis of 242." His theory is that 242 excludes Jordan and is applicable only to withdrawal from Sinai. If, having read our platform—which we will enclose as an explanatory document, including the sentence "We do not plan to rule 1.2 million Arabs"—they would recognize its value, we would begin to negotiate with him.

I think in the second round, when Hussein said "What about the Palestinians?" we would say, in terms of Peres' statement of May '76, "we are willing to negotiate with every Palestinian representative who accepts the idea of peace with Israel." We might then create the motivation for a Jordanian-Palestinian-Israeli discussion, of which the first item would be, "Does the territory remain with Israel?" or "What are the conditions in which we could give it up?" and "What are our reservations about giving all of it up?" because the fact is that we would not give all of it up. At that point, we are involved in a real negotiation.

Now if, in the course of such a negotiation, Palestinian particularism were so strong and were so much recognized by Jordan and the world, if they were to say that whatever territory we choose to give up or we agree together you should give up will *not* be centralized under Jordan, then I would come in with my proposal for a confederative or community structure. We would say that, provided our relationship with our Eastern neighbor is based on the concept of open boundaries and accessibility and mutuality of contact and intercourse, and, of course, a due measure of demilitarization, it is for them and not for us to decide whether they want to have a Jordanian-Palestinian federation or whether the two parts of it would be confederatively linked to each other and to Israel, according to the Benelux idea. I remain convinced that the destiny of the West Bank has to be ambivalent with respect both to Jordan and to Israel— separate from Israel politically, but I hope not hermetically sealed off the way it was under the Armistice. It might now want to be separate from Jordan politically—but nobody can deny the immensity and the multiplicity of links—family, human, Arab—between them. So we have to find a formula in which the West Bank and Gaza area is separate—and not separate. And that's why the community idea ought to be explored.

Let's shift, if we may, to the world. Do you share the generally critical view regarding the quality of this generation's political leaders, around the world?

I think that's a fact, not a view. I remember sitting next to the late Haile Selassie, and not knowing what on earth to talk about. Desperately groping for something to say, I came up with "Your Majesty, that's a very interesting legend, the one about your descent from the Queen of Sheba and King Solomon," and he looked at me sternly and replied, "That isn't a legend, that's a fact."

If we take Europe first, and look at the founding fathers of the community, Churchill and Adenauer and Spaak and deGasperi—and I'd even include DeGaulle, despite his initial anti-Europeanism—that's a generation without successors. And therefore the broad sweep of the European idea, with its implications of federalism, and supernationalism, the concept of creating a power that would be equivalent at least to the Soviet Union and the United States, has been dissipated in squalid discussions about how much Mrs. Thatcher should pay and what should be the price of butter and grapefruit. It's been trivialized by a kind of provincialism and mercantilism in which only the pay-check and the prices of agricultural commodities are brought into account. And Europe as an idea, as a vision, as a will, has receded. Incidentally, I believe that's one of the reasons for Europe's very equivocal position on the Middle Eastern situation, a position dominated by fossil fuels rather than by a vision of regional stability.

Amongst the powers, I think it's true in the Great Power relationship as well. A formula as subtle and elusive as "detente" must be manipulated with some degree of intellectual vitality and resourcefulness. Instead, there's a tendency for fragmentation and pettiness in international thinking. For example, in the American-Soviet dialogue, since 1972-73, when detente reached contractual form in the Nixon-Brezhnev communiqués, there hasn't been a review of the concept itself, as a result of which there has been a series of crises, with Soviet encouragement. The fact is that detente was based on an initial ambiguity. It represented a change in the American thinking on the Soviet Union. It did not represent a change in Soviet thinking on American interests. If we take the situation since 1972, when detente was formally enacted, in 1973 the Soviet Union encouraged the Syria-Egyptian attack on Israel; in 1975, after the Paris accords, the Soviet Union incited Cubans to establish communism in Angola; in 1977, the Soviet Union encouraged a united Vietnam to attack Cambodia; in 1978, the Soviet Union encouraged South Yemen to conquer North Yemen in the communist interest; in 1979, in the Horn of Africa, the Soviet Union sponsored a takeover in Ethiopia; in 1980, you have the invasion of Afghanistan. To all this, the United States has reacted sometimes passively, sometimes with episodic indignation. But it has never said, "Shouldn't we meet together and look at the whole thing again?" What happened since 1972, to say nothing of the Helsinki agreements, in which the Soviet Union was to liberalize contact and intellectual interchange? How much Helsinki has been implemented we may see in the Sakharov imprisonment. There seems to be a reluctance to have what I would call comprehensive studies of inter-power relationships. And the same is true of the American relationship with Western Europe. To what degree does the American nuclear umbrella commit Europe to solidarity? Or to what degree do the special interests and experiences of Europe justify separate and autonomous judgment? I haven't seen the United States government enter into a conference either with Western Europe—what does the alliance mean?—or with the Soviet Union—is this really what detente is about? There seems to be a preference for individual, fragmented treatment, for crisis management, and this might be a reflection of the conceptual limitations of leaders.

Which does not appear to be on the verge of repair.

Yes. It's interesting that there hasn't been a broad international discussion in the past five or six years. The last serious attempt was the 1972 and 1973 meetings where an attempt was made to define detente. There was a rather silly meeting in Helsinki. Here I do agree with my ex-neighbor, George Kennan: when you talk to the Soviet Union, you must not talk in general terms which they and you interpret differently; you must say, "What is it that you promise to do and what is it that we promise to do?" And, "What is it that you promise not to do and what is it that we promise not to do?" Instead of which, you signed a joint declaration about the rights of man and the virtues of motherly love.

You said that here you agree with Kennan, indicating that elsewhere you disagree. I presume that the "elsewhere" has to do with Mr. Kennan's reflections on the Soviet invasion of Afghanistan.

Yes, I think he's wrong on two points. I think he has swung too far over from his own doctrine, as "Mr. X" of containment. Now he has a tendency to underestimate the gravity of Soviet expansionism. And second, I come back to what I said before: He dismissed the power-strategic element by statements like "I don't know much about it," whereas it is in fact the build-up of Soviet military power that is the starting point for consideration of detente, or, to put it in a more balanced way, for a disturbance of the equilibrium. The fact is that the Soviet Union has the capacity and the will to put power to work beyond the capacity and the will of the United States to put power to work. And I think Mr. Kennan was really caught short when in his last irascible reply to his critics he argued that we must understand the difference between a Soviet Union that works through proxies and puppets and totalitarian regimes that used to use their own armies. By the time that was published, the Soviet army was in Afghanistan. And that is why he was reduced to describing the invasion as an "essentially defensive reaction." But even defensive reactions can be dangerous. In order to defend yourself, you capture a belt of protective territory. Then, in order to protect the protective territory, you capture another belt.

That sounds rather like Israel's current settlement policy.

Yes, you have Israelis who, using that theory, can get you as far as Alexandria or the Sudan. There is a point at which the quest for unlimited defensive security becomes illegitimate, because unlimited security for you means unlimited danger for others.

No, insofar as I would advise Americans—advice, after all, is Israel's chief export . . .

And criticism is its chief import . . . .

. . . I would say that one of the problems that affects your friends everywhere in the world is not what you do to us, not American attitudes towards Israel or towards any other nation, but American attitudes towards America, which are probably just as important. I think that's true of Europe as well. They're not complaining about American attitudes to France, to Germany, to Italy, but about a lack of consistency and coherence in American policy itself. What we want from America, they are saying, is not benevolence towards us, but a shrewder concept of your own interest and responsibility. If, for example, we read that young Americans don't want even to be registered for the defense of their country, while the Soviet Union has no such inhibitions; if the United States, by its insistence on the nuclear weapon, creates a situation in which the only choices are between nuclear weapons and doing nothing, a situation which makes it clear that you'll end up doing nothing, in which, paradoxically, the nuclear obsession leads you to impotence; if the Soviets have no inhibitions about moving their ships around the Persian Gulf and the United States doesn't recognize that by the Law of the Seas you have exactly the same rights to be anywhere that they are; if by a righteous revolt against abuse you go to the extreme of undermining the presidential executive power; if you won't give yourselves a fair deal in your information policy; if there's an atmosphere in which nobody would dream of capturing a Soviet embassy but people do dream of capturing American embassies and they even carry out such dreams, then there seems to be a lack of what I would call a psychological equilibrium. I don't know whether measures like not going to the Olympic Games will get the Soviets out of Afghanistan. Going to the Olympic Games would have been disastrous, but the fundamental problem remains: how to get an operative result, and how to reconstruct Western self-respect.

Would you doff your international diplomat's hat and don your Jewish historian's hat? Scanning the troubled Jewish horizon these days, there's a very disconcerting trend.

The Soviet Union is at war with Afghanistan; both vilify Israel and the Jews. Afghanistan and Pakistan are at odds; both vilify the Jews. Pakistan and India are feuding; both vilify the Jews. Iran is at odds with everyone; it vilifies Israel. What is it that leads to this obsession with our tiny people?

There is certainly a very dark wave flowing across the world. I don't remember a time when Israel and the Jewish people were more embattled, at least on the level of international sentiment. I think that not only Israelis, but Jews everywhere should be concerned.

I think one reason for all this is psychological. The elements of our history that gave exhortation to our Jewishness are fading from memory—I mean the Holocaust and the establishment of Israel—and there is no clear image of what being Jewish means. I am thinking a good deal about that now, in connection with my work in preparing a television series that will depict the entire Jewish story, not simply in Holocaust terms, not simply the Jews as victim, but the Jews as creators, as champions of their own persistence and originality, the extraordinary paradox of resonance, of a small people whose voice ought not to be heard at all and yet which reverberates across history. There's no real reason why people should be interested in the Jews at all. After all, how many are we? Fourteen million, less than one of the smaller states of the United States. There are about a hundred bigger nations in the world, and yet we have a bigger resonance than 14 million. Why this capacity to survive and to be oneself? And to resound? All this has to be told again because the episodes which illustrate it are now in history books; they are not part of people's memory any more, in the way that they were as recently as two decades ago.

I think another reason lies in the unresolved nature of Israel's struggle. And I come back here to the crux. In a world in which there is so much suffering and anguish, you could argue that the plight of the 1.2 million Palestinians is not all that dreadful. They go about their business in serenity day by day. They're not being massacred, they're not starving. But the paradox of a Jewish state exercising jurisdiction over another nation without the premise of temporariness—that is a startling thing. There is a difference between a temporary situation in which you find yourself and in which it is clear that you want to cease this jurisdiction, if only conditions permit, and a situation where you come to regard it as fixed. Is it a part of the nature of Israel to be ruling another nation? That is such a change in the assumptions under which Israel secured legitimacy and recognition that it sends a shock reaction throughout the whole international system. It's very rare that you have a nation going back on the principle that enabled it to be born. And although I don't believe that this exonerates or excuses the exaggerated reactions of the international system, the fact is that the Israeli-Palestinian relationship is a very strong contributary cause of the development you cite.

Perhaps it's not a such a bad thing that Israel seems to be held to a very high standard of performance. It would be a defeat, would it not, for Israel to be held to the same debased standard which informs our judgment of international affairs and the behavior of nations?

That's another problem. Even a few decades ago, there were so many communities in a tutelary relationship to other communities that Israel's exercise of jurisdiction over the West Bank and Gaza would not have been very startling. But now, after the settlement in Zimbabwe—which is, incidentally, together with the Egyptian-Israeli treaty, a triumph of reconciliation—we might soon end up as being the only free country that is exercising a coercive jurisdiction over other people. The eccentricity of our position becomes marked more and more.

And the problem may also have something to do with the American

Jews, who are, after all, the dominant factor in creating the image of the Jews. American Jewry has been very effective in political pressure, in self-preservation, but has not been very successful in explaining itself in historic ideological terms.

In order to explain yourself, you first have to understand yourself.

Yes, its own cohesiveness arises more from intuitions and emotions and sentiments than out of intellectual analysis of what it is and why.

And of course, there is a continuing tendency in the Gentile world to seek an Israeli or a Jewish cause for every human affliction. Take, for example, the monstrous irrelevance of linking Israel with the Iranian and Afghan crises. You say the words "Middle East", and there's a fallacy there, since under that umbrella you have totally disparate and disconnected situations. Incidentally, the sources of instability in the Middle East have always been polycentric, with most of the focal points lying outside the Israeli context. But the Israeli episode has been so dramatic and evocative that the tendency has been to say "Middle East" and you immediately equate it with the Arab-Israeli dispute. But the Arab-Israeli dispute is one thing, the Middle East crisis is another. If you look at the sources of crisis in the Middle East, you see how few of them lie within Israel. You have the great poverty of the Asian peoples, the galvanizing and intoxicating effect of oil wealth, the torment of Moslems who want Western technology but who fear the effect of technology on their ancient sources of faith and culture, the unresolved competitive appearance of the two major powers—these are the events that are shaking Western Asia to its foundations. They have nothing to do with Israel, and you can prove that by elimination: If the Israeli-Palestinian problem were solved either by Israel subsiding into the sea, as the Palestinians would like, or by a settlement that was satisfactory to everybody, would the Soviets move out of Afghanistan? Of course not. Would Khomeini release the hostages? Of course he wouldn't. Would the price of oil be changed? Of course it wouldn't. And yet you find everybody, from Edward Heath to George Ball, writing articles in which the two appear together, in which the argument is put forward that you cannot solve the problems of Afghanistan, of Iran, of the Moslem world, unless you solve the problems of Gaza and the West Bank. Well, the problems of Gaza and the West Bank ought to be solved for their own reasons, within their own rhythm and context, but they are irrelevant to these other matters. Perhaps it has something to do with a kind of atavistic tendency towards "cherchez le Juif," whether it's the Black Plague or an economic crisis. That's a grave thing to say, but I don't understand otherwise how people of lucid intelligence like Ball and Heath can drag the Afghan-Iranian-oil problems back to Gaza. Why is Gaza any different from the Cyprus question? Of course the Cyprus question ought to be solved—but nobody says that unless you solve that, you can't solve anything else. Since the Egyptians withdrew themselves from the circle of war, my theory about the Arab-Israel dispute is that it's become provincialized. It's not all that central, it's not one of the world's major problems. It's a problem, but not one of the major ones.

That says something about Saudi policy, which I presume you mean to say.

Yes, that was proved when it came to condemning the Soviet invasion of Afghanistan. The Saudis voted in the UN with 104 others. They came to a conference of Moslem countries in Islamabad and condemned Soviet aggression. They will probably not be at the Olympic Games. And their oil policy is obviously dictated by a very shrewd economic interest. There hasn't been one occasion on which you could attribute a price increase in oil to a development in the Palestinian-Israeli context. The paradox here is that among the OPEC countries, those that have tried hardest to push for higher prices are those who have nothing against Israel at all, like Venezuela and Nigeria, and Iran under the Shah, which was the most mischievous influence in that direction.

You made a passing reference to American Jewry a few minutes ago, and I'd like to pick up on that. There's no senior Israeli who has watched American Jewry for so long a time and so intimately as you. Are the changes that we here note and celebrate obvious to you, or do we seem to you today merely a straight line projection from what we were two or three decades back?

In a sense, what we see today is a lineal descendent of the community of the late 1940s. The community today has taken over the priorities and the slogans and the solidarities of its predecessors. It seems to be much more anonymous, in the sense that its leaders, the leaders of organized Jewish life, seem to have less reverberation.

Much as the political leaders we were talking about a while back.

Yes, but perhaps we can afford it less. American Jews are a minority community, and you have to compensate for the lack of quantity by a degree of intellectual incisiveness. In general, the less power you have, the more intellect you have to display. For example, such jobs as the Pope or the Secretary General of the United Nations depend entirely on the presence or absence of intellectual vitality in the incumbent, because there's nothing else behind them. That's why Pope John or Dag Hammerskjöld were what they were. But we've had others, whose names I won't mention, whose careers prove that nature does not always abhor a vacuum. American Jewry needs to compensate for its numerical and other limitations by the vitality and intellectual resourcefulness it musters.

On the consoling side, I was much more apprehensive than events have proved warranted that young Jews, born in a generation for which the Holocaust and Israel's struggle for independence are matters of documentary history rather than personal memory, would not react in the same way as those who actually witnessed the events themselves. Yet I find that there is still an extraordinary power to react, although it is now, in a sense, a vicarious reaction. The way Jews respond to the Holocaust memory and the way that in spite of all difficulties they rally around Israel—this is comforting.

Another consoling factor, which not all my fellow-citizens would regard as consoling, is that there is now an element of criticism in the American-Jewish attitude to Israel. It's no longer "Israel right or wrong," perhaps because we are not as right as we used to be, perhaps because the leaders no longer excite the same unquestioned fidelity as the original leaders of the Ben Gurion era. I think that is a favorable development. I've written and spoken against the idea that we should deny the legitimacy of dissent on the grounds that "the goyim might be listening." If they do listen, I think they are likely to have respect for the new pluralism and diversity of expression. Under these circumstances, when we do show solidarity it will have more meaning. If we say to the Jews of America and the other Diaspora communities, "We want your money and your political pressure, but we don't want your opinions," in other words that the contribution should be political and financial but not intellectual, they would probably accept the veto and then subside into apathy, leaving Israel's cause impoverished.

Those are favorable developments. Unfavorable developments are the institutional conservatism, the total refusal to look at priorities. In 1948 what we needed most from American Jews was financial support. We didn't have a manpower problem; we had 650,000 people who came in the first two years. The danger then was that we had too much manpower and too few resources, and that we would end up in catastrophe—with famine and starvation and disease—that the Zionist adventure would collapse under the weight of its own success. And therefore there was logic in saying to you, in 1947 and 1948, that your job was resources, finance. We therefore built a pyramid of Jewish priorities with financial support at the top, political lobbying—not quite as sophisticated in its organization but still very impressive—in second place, the educational network which could be better is not negligible, third—and right down at the bottom, things like aliyah, although really what we now need from world Jewry is an increment of manpower. That pyramid doesn't make any sense. It ought to be turned upside down, with aliyah and education at the top.

Inverted pyramids have a distinguished history in Zionist theory.

Perhaps it doesn't even have to be inverted. My theory is that if you have more education, and more aliyah, financial support will also increase. It's not a zero-sum game, where if one thing goes up the other must go down. But today, there's a kind of fossilization in the priority which is given to fund-raising, and everything else becomes incidental. We also carried over from the early days, when the need for resources to go to Israel was so great, a hostile view towards the allocation of any American Jewish resources to American Jews. I now think that Israel should declare its interest in American Jews keeping a good share of their resources in America and building their schools and their centers and anything that makes for Jewish conservation—because if they're not going to be Jews, Israel is not going to benefit. The struggle against tendencies towards assimilation, abandonment of heritage, matters to us, and instead of being hostile or envious, I even think that people like myself should be asked to come here and speak on behalf of the establishment with Jewish money of Jewish institutions in Cleveland or Chicago or wherever—which is heresy today, because this is seen as a diversion.

When Israeli leaders come here and speak egocentrically only of Israel, I think we bring to light an ideological predicament that has not been solved. Israeli opinion is still based on the classic Zionist doctrine of *shlilat hagolah*—the negation of the Diaspora—the doctrine that held that if the Diaspora exists, it's an anomaly, an abnormality, it oughtn't to exist, the attitude towards it should be negative: Get what you can from it while it exists, but it has no legitimacy. My feeling is that we should abandon an ideology that has no relationship to reality, because the division of the Jewish impulse between the impulse for concentration and the impulse for dispersion—on the one hand to be yourself in your own terms, on the other hand to flow with the stream of universal culture—this duality has gone on for so long that it's time we recognize its permanence. It's gone on at least since the destruction of the first Temple. The great poet who wrote "We wept when we remembered Zion", he wept and he wrote in Babylon—and nobody knows whether he went back with the Shavei Tzion or whether he stayed on in Babylon writing distinguished poetry. I think we should take this duality as part of our historic experience and not react negatively one to the other.

Clearly, a community that has a sense of itself and of its own possibilities cannot accept as its organizing principle the doctrine of its own illegitimacy.

Exactly. You can't say that you exist, but that you ought not to exist. That reflects a negative view of yourself, in which there is no pride. You end up in the position of that person who was once compared to a mule—having neither pride of ancestry nor hope of posterity.

Which may be as good a place as any to pause for a month. Thank you. ✦

A MOMENT INTERVIEW WITH MARION PRITCHARD

Marion Pritchard, who was born and raised in Holland and now lives in New England, was designated a "Righteous Gentile" by Yad Vashem.

In pre-war Holland, was interaction between Jews and non-Jews common?

Holland prides itself on taking in refugees, whoever they are. And society was so integrated that I was not aware until during and after the war that there had been any sense of prejudice here and there. We didn't distinguish who was Jewish, who was Catholic, who was this or that. My awareness that there was any difference at all came from the fact that my father was a judge, who socialized with all the other judges, and I knew that one Jewish judge wasn't included, and I've since wondered whether that was somehow custom, or whether it was a personality thing. But basically Holland was very integrated. There was a lot of intermarriage, which became a real problem during the war. And I was very shocked when I first met up with American Army attitudes in Germany, and then later in 1947 when I came over here I was appalled.

You mean when you encountered anti-Semitism here?

Yes, and the extent of it! When my husband and I arrived—he was an American, he had been in the army—we couldn't talk about anything other than displaced persons. We had worked with them for two years, 24 hours a day, seven days a week, and we were totally imbued with it. And we found that our friends just didn't want to hear about it.

Most American Jews are not at all aware that half the people who have been honored as "Righteous Gentiles" are Dutch. And very few of us have any real sense of what it was like for non-Jews in an occupied country. How much was life disrupted?

Even for the Jewish citizens, in the beginning it was not nearly as disruptive as one might expect. Of course, there was a tremendous disruption for the first five days, when the Dutch were still trying to defend themselves, and there was fighting going on. After that, everything falls together. In order to carry out Hitler's Final Solution, obviously it's much easier if you get the local population to collaborate with you and be on your side than if you've got them working against you. So they worked very hard at being nice to us, and they did not start any measures against the Jews immediately. They did it extremely gradually, and by such seemingly small and unimportant measures that it was very hard to know where to take a stand.

If I remember correctly, the first thing that happened was that we had citizens' air raid patrols, people who went around and checked to see that you had your blackout in place and all that, and the first thing that happened was that the Jews weren't allowed to belong to that.

One of the big steps, of course, was making Jews wear yellow stars. That came after little measures like forbidding Jews from going into the park between three and five, barring them first from this profession, then from that profession, then requiring that they go to separate Jewish schools. It was all very...lulling is the word that comes to mind. A lot of people didn't realize at all what was going to happen. Because what the Germans did, very gradually, by all these little measures, was to segregate the Jews completely. They had been so completely integrated. First of all, putting stars on them immediately made them outgroupers. For the first few days, if someone with a star would come into a trolley car, a lot of people would get up and offer their seats. Then the Germans decided that Jews could only stand in the back. Then after a while, they couldn't ride in the trolley cars at all. And then they were all forced to live in certain parts of town.

And every time, people would say, "Is this bad enough to make a big fuss about?" And by doing it so very gradually, they got everybody exactly where they wanted them.

But they really didn't bother us much for the first two years. If I remember correctly, when they got tough was when they realized that there was no way they were going to make the Dutch into Nazis. They got tough in the late spring of 1942.

The deportations didn't start until later, right?

That's right. Obviously, they were getting ready for the deportations. There was a place called Westerbork.

256/Moment

That was set up in 1939, before the war started. A lot of German Jews came to Holland before the war, starting in 1933 when Hitler came to power. It seems to me that that's when the first anti-Semitism in Holland started. There was a distinction made between them and "our" Jews. There was a feeling on the part of many people that the German Jews were aggressive and pushy, and there was definitely tension between Dutch Jews and German Jews.

Most of the German Jews who came to Holland made their own arrangements. They had friends, or they had money, and they settled down among the population. But there were I don't know how many, maybe a thousand or 1,500, who didn't have any place to go, and the Dutch government built this little village, Westerbork, small houses, very simple houses, as sort of a base where they could start life in Holland. There were no gates or fences; it was in no way built as a concentration camp, but there was a collection of houses where these German Jews were living. So when the Germans decided to go full speed ahead with the deportations, they added to Westerbork, and they built fences around it, and watchtowers, and made a concentration camp out of it. Actually, it was a transit camp; there wasn't deliberate killing there.

Among your friends, was there an adjustment to the situation, to the occupation, to the treatment of the Jews? Did there come a time when it was taken for granted, and life went on more or less normally, or was the 'situation' a constant preoccupation?
You have to start with the fact that the Dutch have always liked the English and the Belgians and the Norwegians better than the Germans. And there was a tremendous amount of resentment against the occupying forces even though they were behaving politely and did let life go on to some extent.

We had a number of Jewish professors in the school of social work where I was studying by then, and they gradually disappeared, and they talked before they disappeared. Looking back now, that's really amazing, that they would talk about it in class, because there must have been some collaborators there. But what they said made us aware of the need to do something about that, and, obviously, people who were in a school of social work were disposed to respond to human need, so it was natural for us to start becoming involved.

When did you first become involved in "illegal" activities?
It's so long ago...let me remember....

My father was not a law-and-order man, but he believed very much in justice and "the law." And when the Germans said that our law, which was based on the Napoleonic Code...that the law, which my father—to say of so austere and controlled a man as my father that he worshipped the law may sound exaggerated, but he did—to him the notion that Nazi philosophy was taking the place of Dutch law was intolerable. He developed cancer and died in 1943.

In fact, the Germans came to take him hostage. One of the things the Germans did was to take prominent people as hostages, and then if the underground or anybody would do something they didn't like, they'd take out a number and shoot them, which surely helped make people think before they'd act against the Germans.

He and I used to talk about what we could do and what could be done.

My determination actually jelled in the fall of 1943 or thereabouts. I was on my way to the school of social work on my bike, and it was a nice day, and I went past a home for Jewish children and they were emptying it out. And I guess that had a considerable shock value, because the Germans, in their inimitably clever way, when they started deporting the Jews, they installed a Judenrat. Quite early on they did that, and they made the Judenrat do their dirty work.

At the beginning, they would tell the Judenrat, "We need so many people at the station at such and such a time," and a lot of people simply went. I saw the kind of announcement people got, and it read like the kind of list you give kids when they go to camp—two sheets, four blankets, a pair of workshoes, a flashlight—and a lot of people really believed it. It was so diabolical to make the Judenrat believe at first that they could help, that for them to take care of things was better than to let the SS or the Germans deal directly with the Jews. I really don't think that a lot of them knew that they were completely the instruments of the Germans.

Anyway, in those days people still took themselves to the station, climbed into the trains themselves. And then when they didn't get enough people, they began to go to their houses and collect them, but it was still all done very politely.

So I was particularly shocked that morning. I don't know whether the SS men involved were drunk, or whether they were just a particularly sadistic bunch, but the kids didn't move fast enough, so the soldiers picked them up by an arm or a leg or their hair and just threw them into the truck. And the kids were crying and screaming. It affected me fundamentally. It was eight o'clock in the morning, the street had been blocked off, and there were two other women on the street and they got so mad that they attacked the SS men, they flew at them and clawed at them and they got beaten too.

And that was when I really began to believe all the rumors that we had heard. They turned out not to be rumors—but I was only 20, what did I know, I could have been wrong. That's when I realized that they were going to systematically destroy the Jews. I didn't realize the extent to which it was an industry. It was a mass industry—and, at the same time, it was incredibly deceitful.

Photos of Marion Pritchard by Michael Peirce

That's when I decided that whatever I could do I would do.

But that's not easy. If you want to do something, you've got to find people to work with. How do you go about doing that?
Well, of course at school we talked about it. And the people who I worked with were mostly from the school of social work. And we made mistakes, too. We had to find families that would take Jews in. And the more time went on, the more clear it became that the Germans regarded that as a criminal activity, and if you were discovered you would suffer the same fate as the Jews you had hidden. So even though there were a lot of people who were willing to do it, because they thought it was the right thing to do, it's amazing how things then fell apart, disintegrated on a personal basis, for odd reasons. Here, for example, you have a family that's functioning in a certain way, and then you take in one or two or three other people who can't go outside, who are totally dependent on you, who can't make noise, because you can't risk the neighbors hearing, you have to hide them completely. And every one has different personal habits.

That kind of thing was repeated over and over and over. You see it, of course, in the Anne Frank diary. I knew Ann's older sister; she was a friend of the kid sister of a friend of mine. Anyway, often you had to try and place the same people several times.

Sometimes, in the midst of all the horror, there were amusing aspects to it. I remember, for example, that there was a group of people I worked with, artists. I had taken ballet lessons until I was about five. I knew the people involved in the Amsterdam ballet quite well. One of them—I saw him when I was there last March—went into hiding with a Dutch woman who was a painter. Karl, the dancer, was a homosexual. Now when the Germans came and raided you at night, because they'd heard that maybe Jews were being hidden somewhere—a lot of people had hiding places—it was important that there not be any empty beds. So that if you'd hear the truck coming down the road, and the Jews went to their hiding places, and the Germans came in and there were four people but six beds had been slept in, they'd be aware that there were two people missing. So always the people who were being hidden would share a bed with one of the people in the receiving family. And this Dutch paintress was going to make an enthusiastic heterosexual out of Karl. And he came to me and said, "Marion, I'd rather go to a concentration camp."

There were funny things along with the tragedy. But what Karl then insisted was that he preferred we give him a different identity. And we got him Aryan identity papers and we dyed his hair and he lived the rest of the war walking around.

When you engage in these kinds of things, are you afraid most of the time?
Before I spent six months in jail, I was theoretically afraid. I knew that I was supposed to be scared and I had some idea of what could happen to me, but I didn't have the real fear that I had later. And it's strange how it lives on. The scariest sound at night was the sound of a truck stopping in front of a house. And now I live on a dark road in Vermont, and I've only recently realized as a result of my analytic training that the reason I jump out of bed when I hear a noise is that memory. My husband says, "It's just a truck." But the fear is still with me.

Most of the people and children I dealt with I just performed occasional services for, but there were three children I took care of. One of them was a week old when I got her. When you take care of three children yourself...yes, I was very scared.

Have you seen them since?
Sure. It's a very strange business. One of them took on a gentile name after the war, and one of them works for Lufthansa in Germany. With all my analytic training, I'm at a total loss to understand that.

Their grandfather was the concertmaster of the Concertgubow Orchestra; their father was a futurologist. He wrote his PhD theses in economics and philosophy while he was in hiding, and I spent a lot of time typing them. And he would get really annoyed when I made mistakes.

Anyway, the youngest one I didn't see after the war. I didn't know then as much about early childhood as I do now. I thought, well, she's got her mother back, her father back, the family's reconstituted, fine. She wrote to me about six years ago to tell me that she had become a clinical psychologist. Nobody in her family had done that, but it's in the same ballpark as what I was doing. And in her own analysis, she had just arrived at the point where she recognized her rage at having been abandoned by her mother— me— when she was three years old. I took care of her for three years and then I walked out of her life. And she suffered some pretty serious depression.

What were the circumstances of your arrest?
That had nothing to do with my main involvement during the war, which was in trying to get people not to have to go to concentration camps. But some friends of mine put out what in the beginning was one of numerous mimeographed newspapers. We had all been required to turn in our radios. Most people kept one radio. But in order to keep the people's spirit up, these newspapers, bulletins, whatever, were produced and distributed. And my friends produced this paper in the house where they lived. If you wanted to study with other people for an exam you had to spend the night, because curfew was at eight o'clock. And one night I was studying, and somebody had betrayed them, and the Germans came and took everybody who was there.

And they kept you in jail for six months?
Yes…and one day they just let us out. They were very arbitrary.

I have to ask you "the big question." You've been in analysis, you've taught, you've reflected on these things. You did something that was very, very dangerous, something most people might have done but didn't do. Do you have any sense of what accounts for your choice?
Part of it was definitely my father— his rectitude, his sense of right and wrong. And I guess, in a funny way, being an active and communicating church member.

What's "funny" about that?
Well, if you asked me to explain every word in the liturgy, I couldn't do it. I have a son who's a historian, he has a PhD from Yale, and he's written a book about Catholicism in Elizabethan England, he can give you chapter and verse, he knows all that stuff inside out—I don't. I sat in the church, I was conditioned. With analysis and all that, I can intellectually say that it's all nonsense and that we create God to meet our own needs and so forth and so on, but there's no way that I can honestly say that I don't believe. Even though as an adolescent I would refuse to go to church, I would say it was all hogwash, the opium of the masses and all that, it never left me, and I guess at some level I knew that there was no way I could face the good Lord when I died if I didn't do the right thing.

There were times that I didn't do what I could have done, that I was too scared, times that I carried out big debates with myself and rationalized not doing something that I should have done. I'm sure that's why when the war was over, we didn't talk about it. We didn't talk about it, number one, because we'd survived and people who had done a hell of a lot more than we had had not survived…there was guilt about survival. And there was guilt about all those times I could possibly have done something and didn't.

Under those circumstances, it's got to be awfully easy to rationalize your way into doing nothing. After all, you're up against a megasystem, and the fact is that nothing you can do will defeat that system. Three people more or three people less saved— what's the difference?
That's the choice I made the first time, when I saw them load that truck. And I saw those women throw themselves against the SS. They knew it wouldn't help, but they acted. And I kept one foot on the sidewalk and watched. I remember feeling absolute rage. It was so sickening, so incredibly awful—but I didn't do anything.

And if you had done something that day, then the three children whom you later saved would have been killed.
I know. That's the obvious and simple way to look at it. But…I talked to a man whose niece lives in Vermont who was interested in what is a collaborator. To some people that seems so simple; you were either with the Germans or you were against them, there's nothing in between. But the fact is that there are lots of gray areas. What is a collaborator? The policeman who stays with the police, even though the police have to work with the Germans? Should all the police have said they won't be policemen anymore? But there were some policemen who helped, who saved Jews. And at the same time they collaborated.

The Germans were brilliant, and diabolical. They knew, the Germans, how to do the worst, how to literally make a business out of destroying people and at the same time convince them it wasn't going to happen.

In addition to the 'normal' disposition to deny, isn't the explanation that there was no precedent for what was happening—that in those days, the idea that this was what the Germans were doing was literally unthinkable?
I'm wondering about that now. I can't believe what's going on in El Salvador and a whole lot of other places. We see it on the television. We see Solidarity in Poland. We see brutality on the television. What the hell are we doing? What on earth are we doing? And so, was there *really* no precedent back then?

I remember a very critical comment that Bruno Bettelheim once made about Otto Frank. He said that Otto Frank must have known that one day the SS would find the family. And so, the normal, the logical, the rational thing to have done would have been for him to supply himself with a gun. That way, at the very least he could have killed two or three of them. But the fact is that Otto Frank survived the war, and he wouldn't have if he had had a gun. More important: Otto Frank, whatever his qualities as a human being, was trying within that insane context to preserve normalcy. It would have been abnormal for an Otto Frank to own a gun. What is your view of this?

If he had done it, of course, we know what the Germans would have done. In Westerbork, if somebody escaped—and my guess is that two or three hundred Jews escaped from Westerbork, I was involved with some of that—the punishment was that extra people got put on the Tuesday night transport to Auschwitz. It's the same thing as when they took hostages. If the Dutch resistance did anything violent, they went to the jail and took out 20, 50, whatever, innocent hostages and shot them. So Frank, if he had shot a few SS men, would have condemned 10, 20, 30, 50 other people to death.

Was there a point in your involvement in this when the rumors ceased to be rumors, when one knew, when somebody came who had information or when the hints mounted so high that one knew what was happening?

Some of us knew. You mentioned denial earlier. It was sort of too horrendous to take in.

Now, 40 years later...I've been interested in why *now* there's this great interest. I *never* talked about all this until...I guess somehow my analysis made all this come up. But since I came to this country, and had kids—why, my kids didn't know that I had anything to do with all this stuff in Holland! When, two years ago, I invited them to come to the ceremony where I was honored for these things, they said, "What?! You?" I hadn't talked about it. I didn't talk to my husband about it. I didn't talk to anybody about it.

But knowing is not the same as believing. There was no proof, and there was a huge need to deny. I think it partly was so huge because a lot of people, if they had believed, would have felt that they had to do something, or do more than they were doing.

My knowing, in a way, was born the day I saw them treat those children that way. I thought, if they can do that, they're capable of anything. So from then on I believed every rumor and every story and every report I heard. I believed it, and I thought it was worse. And my father believed it too.

And your mother?

My mother wasn't really very in touch with it. My mother was—I want to say decorative, but that's underestimating her—my mother was very cheerful, and gay, and everybody who came into contact with her loved her. She was no intellectual at all; my father was, my mother wasn't at all. My mother was all feeling and all action. And the notion that anybody would dare do anything to her just didn't occur to her. I had a terrible time persuading her to close the windows when she listened to the British radio.

Towards the end of the war, I wasn't living at home. My God—a couple of times I took people to my mother's apartment overnight because there wasn't anything else I could do. And I would say, "Mother—please—nobody must see them!" And then the next morning she'd say to the milkman, "Can I have some milk today because I've got somebody staying over." "Mother!" "Well, I can trust the milkman; I've known him for years!" "Dear Mother, you can't trust the milkman!"

During the last year of the war, she was making union jacks out of sheets and material and stuff, to hang out. That night, they came around. (I don't know why they picked it—I think maybe it was the whole apartment block that night, or whatever.) They asked her what she was doing. You know—there was material all over. And she said, "I'm making a union jack for when you beggars get out of here." And they sort of looked at her, and they left. And that was my mother.

My little brother: Here's an illustrative experience of the randomness of the brutality. My brother was walking home from school with a friend. The school is here, the SS headquarters is next, and our apartment is over there. There was this very beautiful, modern school that they took over. And my brother and his friend are making snide remarks about the Germans. And they are overheard. So they leave my brother alone, but they say to his friend, "Listen little fellow, you can't talk about us like that..." Anyway, they take him in, they call his mother, they tell her that he's being disrespectful to the occupying forces, and would she rather have her husband go to a concentration camp, or should they give her kid a good licking? Now, this woman is making lunch for her kids, right? So she chooses to have the kid given a good licking. She went and picked up the body that afternoon. The randomness of the brutality!

I sometimes wonder about the extent to which our current dehumanization is our legacy from those days. I mean, look at the statistic that five children a day get killed in the United States by their parents. That's simply a fact! That's true! Do we get excited? And for every one that dies, there are thousands who are beaten.

Tell us about the time after the war.
At the end of the war, I went to work for UNRRA (the United Nations Relief and Rehabilitation Administration), the UN agency that was working with displaced persons. For one thing, I just wanted to get out of Holland. And for another, I felt that maybe the quickest way to find out where some of my friends were was to work in a displaced persons' camp. So I did that until 1947, when I came over here.

I started out working in a Jewish camp, in Bavaria. Then they wanted to send me to another camp. But by then it was quite obvious that there were a lot of collaborators and Nazis in the DP camps. The Americans were so anti-Communist that all a foreigner had to say to an American screening team was, "I'm afraid of the Russians," and he was immediately embraced and given DP status. I was not about to spend my time working with Nazi sympathizers who pretended to be afraid of the Communists. So I spent a little bit of time then in a child search place, and then I was in another camp, where my husband was director.

During the war, my husband was commander of a field artillery battalion, and the battery he commanded ended up guarding some Polish displaced persons. He had a very high point score, and could have been discharged as soon as the war ended, but he became interested in the DPs, and so, instead of coming back to the United States, he signed up with UNRRA in Paris. I met him at an UNRRA training base, and we were married two years later.

Anyway, there were two organizations in the camp. There was the official UNRRA organization, that supposedly ran the camp—big joke!—and then of course there was the Jewish organization, which was along political lines. My husband and I became "collaborators" there, because against Third Army instructions and against UNRRA directions we did everything we could to help the Jews get out to Palestine. The camps were used as transit places for people to go to ships like the "Exodus," and the "Exodus" itself. You just get your camp organized, and you have your school going, and this, that and the other, and you wake up one morning, and most of the people are gone.

After the war, UNRRA was organized to help displaced persons go home—displaced persons being people who were forcibly brought to Germany during the war, and who couldn't get back on their own. Nice idea. After the war, some of those Jewish displaced persons who were still alive went back—on their own, or with the help of UNRRA—to Poland, and so forth and so on. But they met with more anti-Semitism than they'd left. So they had no place to go, and at the same time, the Zionists were working very hard on concentrating them all in the American zone of Germany so that the Americans would put pressure on the British to let Israel become an independent state.

My husband and I got very caught up in this. We were more Zionist than the Zionists!

I don't know if I could have taken staying with the child search team. Because some children—Jewish children who didn't look Jewish, or children who were maybe half-Jewish—were put in German families if they had blond hair and blue eyes. And so you have a baby who has been placed at six months or whatever, and then the war is over, and he's grown up with a German family who may have indoctrinated him as a little Nazi, and he has been brought up as a child in the family. And then these people come in uniform, accompanied by some strange-looking people with *payiss*, and they are the real parents, and those children screamed in terror and ran.

Obviously, when Jewish babies were born during the war, it would have been damn foolishness to register them as Jewish babies, so we used to register them as our own illegitimate children. I once had two in five months, but nobody caught on to that. I don't know what happened to two of "my" children. I don't know whether their parents survived, I don't know whether they're still walking around with my name, or whether they've changed, and their parents could still be looking for them.

We didn't keep track of anything. Maybe that's why some of it is hard to remember. Because we tried to know as little as possible so that if you were arrested—and after I'd been in jail once, I certainly was scared to go there again—what you didn't know, you couldn't betray. And the rule was: Try to keep your mouth shut for 24 hours, to give people a chance to hide or whatever. The point was to know as little as possible, so that when you'd placed a child, and done what you had to do, you didn't follow up, because you would have known something that might be better not to know.

I'll always wonder, till I die, what happened to those two. ✡

Marion Pritchard

A MOMENT INTERVIEW WITH CONGRESSMAN BARNEY FRANK

Observations on being a Jew and a liberal from the representative of Massachusetts's fourth district

Photographs by Herb Snitzer

Several weeks ago, the Jewish members of the House of Representatives—all 30 of them—were invited to a meeting with Secretary of State Shultz at the home of Representative Scheuer, and 28 of the 30 showed up. Would such a meeting have been held a decade or two ago? Maybe they just wanted to see Scheuer's house?

The fact is that since I've been in Washington—that's just a little over two years—I've been to maybe a dozen or so meetings of Jewish congressmen. Sid Yates is usually the convenor, and Sid presided that night with Shultz. We're not a formal group, but Sid is the senior member, and he also happens to have the biggest office. We met with Evron several times, and with Arens several times, and with Begin once, and then we met with the Conference of Presidents on the Soviet Jewry issue. Scheuer convened this one because he's closer to Shultz.

I'm not aware that people wouldn't have come in an earlier time. Now, Jews are statistically overrepresented in Congress, with eight senators and 30 members of the House. . . .

Do you have a hypothesis as to why this sudden surge in Jewish membership?
I think what you have to account for is why Jews were underrepresented before. The current numbers are not higher than the general presence of Jews in politics and government. The fact is that in the operation of the other branches, you might even have a higher proportion of Jews, if for no other reason than simply as a reflection of the socio-economic position of the Jews. You'd expect them to be deeply involved in politics, given their background, and they are. But until now, they've not been so involved in electoral politics. The wraps are coming off now, because Jews are more interested in it and because people are more accepting of it.

In other words, the numbers don't reflect a new interest by Jews in politics; we've always been interested in politics. The new interest is in *electoral* politics, in actually standing for office.

The surprising part is that Jews are getting elected from every kind of district; there's no longer any district that's "bad" for Jews. There are Jews who represent districts that have a lot of Jews, and there are Jews that represent districts that have no Jews. Well, you might say that you could have expected that; the problem, instead, would be with districts where there were some Jews, enough to make an issue, but not enough to carry the vote. But that turns out not to be a problem either. My district is 13 percent Jewish, and a lot of us are from districts in the eight to 15 percent range.

Another interesting development is that the Jews in Congress are from both parties.
That's true in the Senate; it's much less true in the House. In the House, there are four or five Jewish Republicans; in the Senate, there are four Jews from each party. You'll remember that the only Black in the Senate was a Republican. It may be that the Republicans are better disciplined, and can get the nomination for someone who's not a member of the dominant ethnic group.

You're saying, then, that there's no apology today for Jews in Congress, qua Jews, getting together to explore and to defend Jewish interests.
Absolutely. People are very accepting of it, comfortable with it. We kid about it, we make Jewish jokes about it. There's a kind of camaraderie. I certainly feel less constrained than I did as a member of the State legislature in Massachusetts. It's really quite ideal—the fact that we're Jews is a consideration only when we want it to be. There's never a negative to it; it's only positive, as far as I can see.

So what does happen when you get together? What, for example, took place at Scheuer's house?
It was interesting, because among ourselves, either when it's Members only or when we're meeting with Arens, Evron, and such, there's a lot more disagreement expressed. People say things like, "You've got to stop expanding the settlements"; "You can't try to take over the West Bank"; "You can't stay in Lebanon to try to make them trade with you." But there, with the Secretary, there was much more of a sense that we had a common position to present.

I feel that myself. I've got some criticisms of Israeli policy, but then you listen to others, and it's a good way to remind yourself what side you're on. That's probably a useful thing, because there's always a tendency, when you're working mostly within your own group, to overemphasize differences.

As in a family, where people may feel free to disagree vehemently with each other, but will put up a united front to outsiders?
Yes. And of course, evenings like that can be very useful. You meet people

Barney Frank

Moment/263

from the State Department, and there's a good interchange. The session was off the record, so I can't talk about it, but I can say that it's clear to me that the fear that there is a Bechtel-Shultz-Weinberger axis is unfounded. I think Shultz is a little bit embarrassed by Weinberger. I won't quote anything Shultz said about the Arabs, but I can tell you that at one point he did say, explaining an aspect of American policy, "Well, you know, I'm not in charge of everything." Whereupon Howard Wolpe said, "Why not? Your predecessor was."

An evening like that is a good opportunity for us to get across some of our concerns. Take American behavior towards the Saudis, for example. We give them everything they want. They're like Lucy with the football, and we're like Charlie Brown. You know how every year Lucy says to Charlie Brown, "This year I'll really hold the football for you," but then, at the last minute, she pulls it away and Charlie Brown falls down? Well, the football is moderation, and we keep giving them F-15s, or the AWACS, or this or that, and they never respond the way we hope they will.

We're told they're being helpful, but nobody says how. And the thing that really frosted it for me was about a year and a half ago when we met with people at the State Department on the issue of the Falashas. Now the Falashas have to be the most bedraggled, misery-infected people in the world, the worst-possible off. Now some of them are in the Sudan, and we asked why we can't get those people into Israel more quickly, and the answer, from our own State Department, is that the Sudanese don't want to offend the Saudis. I quoted that statement to Shultz, and I said, "You know, the Falashas are militarily worthless, they're going to remain objects of charity for many years to come. So what kind of hatred infects the Saudis that they nonetheless begrudge the Falashas a bit more decent life?" And he doesn't have a good answer for that one.

Let's switch to the secular side for a bit. How do you react to the term "neo-liberal"?
I'm a liberal. I think that when people say, "Don't label me," they mean, "Let me appeal to everybody." Labels aren't perfect descriptions, but they're useful indicators. The term "neo-liberal" makes me nervous, even though I think it makes less difference practically than it does rhetorically. If you look at the voting records in Congress, you can tell the liberals from the conservatives; I doubt that you could tell the neo-liberals from the liberals. Partly, I guess, I just feel that no one should be a "neo" anything. If you don't like it, don't be it. Don't try to imply that you're all of the good and none of the bad. And in the specific case of the neo-liberals, they're contributing to the myth that we've tried the liberal solutions and they didn't work. You hear that all the time, and it's usually based on an exaggeration of the amount of money that was actually spent on solving the major social problems, on an unfair denigration of what was accomplished.

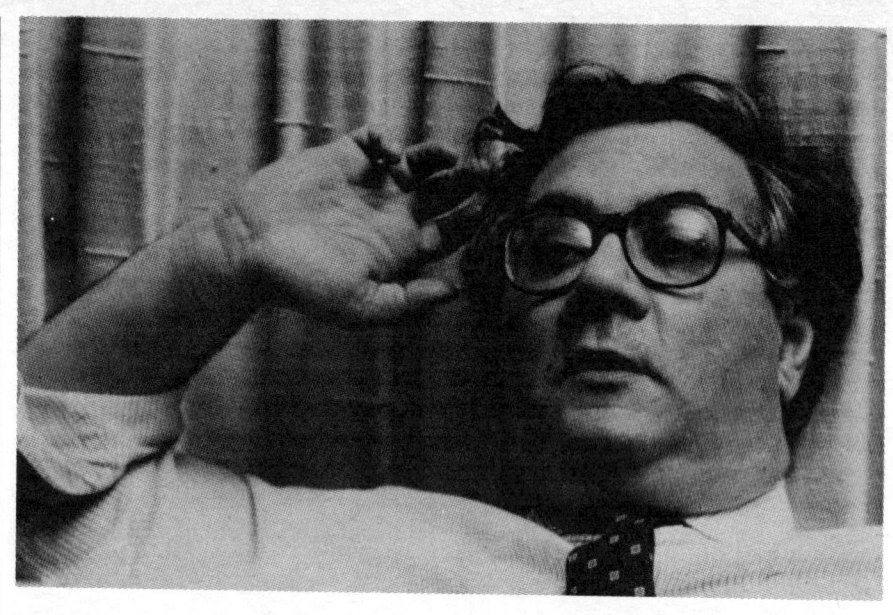

Anyway, I have no problem at all with the term "liberal." If the neo-liberals have made any contribution, it's in the area of emphasizing the implications of the international economy. A lot of liberals didn't understand the free market, and the neo-liberals have helped make it clear what the uses of the free market are, and that's useful. But I'm more comfortable with the old term.

Is there still a coherent and energetic liberalism?
Sure. I think you see that in the candidates. That doesn't mean there's been no recognition of constraints; there has been. We understand better the long-term effect of deficits, the implications of international competition and things like that. We've learned, for example, that your tax system may not be able to be quite as progressive as you'd like it to be if you're competing with countries that give subsidies to their industries.

But coming to Congress was a really exciting experience for me, after having served in the House here in Massachusetts. Here in the Massachusetts House, there are a lot of people who are Democrats, but the liberals are a very small minority. But in the House of Representatives, in Washington, the liberals are the majority, and it was a really pleasurable shock to me to find that. In area after area, I find people who think about things the way I do, people from all over the country. I'm talking about the House—you really don't get to interact much with senators. There's a very real separation between the House and the Senate, much more than in other legislative bodies.

While there's been a perceptible shift in Jewish political opinion in this country, on most issues Jews are still quite dramatically more liberal than other groups.
Oh yes. Drinan, whose district I represented after he left the House, is a good example. In 1972, and in 1974, and in 1976, his major opponent was

Jewish. And he beat them by carrying Brookline and Newton, heavily Jewish districts.

Still, there has been an attitudinal shift, and it seems to be related to a few issues that are especially compelling, issues on which liberals were either silent or wrong. Crime is a good example of that.
That's a fair point. Crime is probably the area where the liberals have been weakest. Liberals have acted as if there were something wrong with punishing criminals. Accepting a sociological explanation for crime in general doesn't provide an excuse for a particular criminal. You can believe that the underlying cause of crime is social without believing that the person who commits a crime is justified.

In fact, the only ward in the city of Newton to vote for the death penalty was Ward 8, the most Jewish ward in the city, the one that gave me my largest majority of any ward in 1980, clearly the most liberal ward in the city, and it's the only ward to vote for the death penalty. And I've heard the same thing from other places in the country. So it's pretty clear that liberals made a mistake here, that we've got to understand that there's nothing inherently wrong with punishing criminals, so long as it's done in a fair way.

Can there be a politically viable liberalism without a leader to articulate its meaning for the public?
In American politics, there usually isn't a single leader. We don't have that kind of party structure and organization. And we do have Tip O'Neill, who does a very good job of being a liberal leader. His style may be a little different from what some people would like, but he's been sticking to liberal principles right along. He's held to the view that the government has a responsibility to help people. Yeah, we've got to stimulate the economy, but we also have people—sick people, poor people, old people—and he's done a pretty creditable job of it. And there are some other people in the House who, when they speak out, get a response. Mo Udall is obviously one such person. Phil Burton, who just died, was another. Over on the Senate side, Ted Kennedy is still one of the most effective liberals, certainly one of the most articulate. Howard Metzenbaum does a lot of pace-setting on issues. In general, liberals are still in pretty good shape. Just look at the Democratic presidential candidates—that's a pretty liberal group, starting with John Glenn, who's a liberal-moderate candidate, and it moves liberalwards from there, to Mondale and Hart and Cranston.

I think it's fair to say that we now have a more unified and coherent Democratic party, around a fairly liberal position, than we've had since the New Deal. I just came from a state Democratic convention, and it's the first time I can remember where nobody got booed. Ronald Reagan has helped us get our act together, because he's brought to the fore the issues where most of us can agree.

And the excesses that sometimes marked liberals have gone away. Nobody's talking any more about excessive lenience towards criminals. With regard to defense, nobody's talking about a weak defense for America. On that issue, I often remind my constituents that the debate is about whether to increase the defense budget by eight percent or by 14 percent. Just ask yourself whether any budget at the local level is going up by eight percent these days—let alone by 14 percent. I mean, that's a pretty hefty increase; I think it's too high; it certainly can't justify accusing its supporters of being "weak" on defense.

You spoke earlier, in connection with Israel, of the difference you feel when you're talking "in the family" from the way you feel when you're talking outside. One sees that a bit with Jewish audiences, too, where quite a few Jewish leaders who might privately be highly critical of this policy or that will not voice such criticism before an audience, will, instead, imply or even explicitly state their support for those same policies.
I think that's a great mistake. I see speaking to predominantly Jewish audiences as an extension of the intra-family conversation, and I think it's essential that we talk among ourselves about American policy towards Israel—including the areas where we have differences with the Israelis. We can do two services for Israel. One is to keep working for supportive American policies that will help Israel, and the second is to point out to the Israelis what things they may be doing that will make it hard to maintain that support. That has to be done. The notion that American Jewish audiences have to somehow be sheltered from the real differences is crazy. Where does such a notion come from? Where do people get the idea that friends don't have differences? America from time to time finds itself in major disagreement with France, with England, with Canada. Why is it that nobody can contemplate that the American government, or we individually, would have differences with Israel?

Differences like that should be talked out, especially now, when they are about some pretty fundamental things. Anyway, adults shouldn't be treated like children, and it's unfair, therefore, to try to keep such things from audiences. Back during the AWACS debate, it was Richard Nixon, that great *mayvin* of moral responsibility, who suggested that Begin was interfering in American politics. Well, the proper answer would have been to say, "Of course Begin is making his views known, he's got a responsibility to do that, and if people are influenced by those views, so be it." And the same thing holds in the reverse direction.

I just don't understand where the idea of being quiet comes from. It's not one that we have in any other area, and I think if you adopt it, you weaken the relationship. If you treat the relationship as so fragile that a word of criticism will destroy it, it will become exactly that fragile.

If the Israeli government feels that the American Jewish community will monolithically support any action it chooses to take, then it's making a mistake. The American Jewish community doesn't automatically support every action the American government takes, and it shouldn't. No one should expect that it will when it comes to Israel.

How do you actually go about making your views known to the Israelis?
I've on occasion written letters or made phone calls. I've found the Israeli Embassy staff very open during the two and a half years I've been down in Washington. And then from time to time there are meetings, maybe six or so since I've been there. Of course, when, for one reason or another, there are other people there, you've got to be careful to re-emphasize the fundamentals. I may not like what Israel is doing on the West Bank, but you've got to be careful when you say something like that in front of people who don't understand your basic commitment that you make that commitment explicit.

Do you find any generational differences in Congress regarding Israel? There was a study a few years ago that found a difference between the Second World War generation and the Vietnam generation, where the older generation had a much more instinctive concern for Israel's welfare than did the younger.
The skepticism and anti-establishment views that we associate with the Vietnam generation I don't find in Congress. Still, there's no question that having lived through World War II does make a difference, having experienced that horror firsthand.

In the same vein, it used to be that one could assume that liberalism and pro-Israelism went hand-in-hand. Has that connection been broken?
There's some criticism of Israel on the left, but the reports of it seem to me to have been overdone. People say, "Well, the liberals have run out on Israel," but on the AWACS sale, it was the right wing that ran out on Israel. I worked up a list that ought to be of special interest to those who want to make a *yeshiva bocher* out of Jerry Falwell; it turns out that there are at least eight cases where Falwell-type senators replaced liberal Democrats with pro-Israel voting records, where their replacements voted with the Administration on AWACS. And Jerry Falwell didn't lift a finger to help. I know what his people can do when they really care about an issue; they didn't do it on AWACS, and the Falwellite senators just voted for the sale.

Still, there is something to it, but I think it has more to do with the changed circumstances. People who grew up in the 40s and 50s grew up with David Ben-Gurion and Golda Meir, defending what appeared to be a beleaguered Israel against unremitting Arab hostility. And the Arabs have gotten smarter. I think one thing that affected Israel somewhat negatively is, ironically, Camp David. For all that Israel did, for which it didn't get enough credit, Sadat was the first Arab who was really popular in America, and, in terms of American public relations, that helped change the overall image. Look, it's just one of the problems of democracy. Menachem Begin obviously has a great deal of appeal within Israel, but he doesn't sell well overseas.

How do you come to all this? What's your own Jewish background?
I grew up in Bayonne, New Jersey, in a very Jewish though not very religious family. Still, my bar mitzvah was in an Orthodox synagogue, and we observed the holidays. We didn't just stay home from school, we went to the synagogue, and I went to Hebrew school. We were pretty active. I remember a "BOYCOTT BRITAIN" bumper sticker on our car back in 1947, and a lot of our social life revolved around the Jewish community center, and the Center Day Camp was where we went in the summer. So being Jewish was a big thing to me.

What's it like taking Father Drinan's place in Congress?
It's really very good. First, I sort of inherited some issues. Human rights issues, mostly. I think people pay a little more attention to me on those issues because I'm Bob's successor. So that's been helpful. And I also inherited an enormous base of political support. If Bob hadn't supported me, I wouldn't have won. And I got a nationwide list of political supporters, who've been much more important than the opponents I also inherited. Bob Drinan was a very strong figure; he had a lot of fans, and a lot of detractors.

In my last election, 70 percent of the district was new, after the reapportionment, and I could tell the difference. There weren't the strong supporters; there weren't the strong enemies. What I owe to Bob Drinan mostly in straight political terms is a very good national list of supporters. In my last campaign, what I got mostly was so-called small contributions, $200 and under. We raised over a million dollars in contributions of that size; we had more than 16,000 contributors. Of course, there were other reasons we did that well, such as the circumstances of the election. The way things turned out, I was kind of the poster child for liberalism in 1982. ✴

A MOMENT INTERVIEW WITH JACOB RADER MARCUS

This spring Jacob Rader Marcus, the iconoclastic dean of American Tenth historians, will be 85, and will celebrate the completion of his sixtieth year as a teacher on the faculty of the Hebrew Union College in Cincinnati as well. He is the founder and director of the American Jewish Archives, and is Honorary President of the Central Conference of American Rabbis.

One day last summer he was interviewed by Elinor Grumet at his office in his home in Cincinnati. They talked about his boyhood in the Ohio Valley at the turn of the century, the Reform rabbinate and Dr. Marcus' latest book, on American Jewish women, which will appear this spring. Elinor Grumet is a Mellon Post-Doctoral Fellow in the Humanities at Brown University.

All photographs of Jacob Rader Marcus courtesy of the American Jewish Archives HUC-JIR Cincinnati.

What have been the major changes in Hebrew Union College since you've been there?
At one time the College had a budget of around $100,000; today it's over eight million. We began, or I began, in the original college building; it was a private home in what by the time I came to school was already a slum. The private building had once been a mansion occupied by wealthy people who probably fled. It had three or four floors. And in those days the fourth floor was not the attic; it was a dance pavillion for guests and that was turned into a chapel for us.

So the college had the whole building?
The college had the whole building. And the chapel was where people would come and talk to us back in 1911. It was there that I heard a talk by the first chairman of the Board of Governors. He had been appointed in 1875, and he was still alive. Isaac Mayer Wise probably recruited young men who would listen to him and take orders from him. This chairman of the board was Bernard Bettman. He was born in Germany, and was really a cultured, educated man—but he was reputed to have said in his heavy German gutteral, "I vant you boys to go out and to dissimilate Judaism." And the boys have been doing it ever since.

How did you get to the College?
My father was a peddler, and in 1900 we moved to a steel town called Homestead where Carnegie had mills. It was in Pennsylvania. As far as as I knew, my father was the only Jew living in this little village and he peddled out of this village as his base. Since then, a researcher has found the charter of an Orthodox congregation in the 1890s nearby. My father was one of the charter members. New Haven was a village, the base from which all the Jewish peddlers in Southwestern Pennsylvania moved into the coke ovens and the steel towns for 25 or 30 miles around to sell goods to the Slavs. My father spoke all the right languages. He spoke Russian because he had been a soldier in the Russian army for five years. He spoke a little German, he spoke Czech, and could get along with the Croatians.

Your family was Orthodox?
Oh yes. We kept strictly kosher in the house, although we weren't Shomrei Shabbas. And they had a cheder in town, but it wasn't a commercial cheder; it was a congregational cheder where you learned to read Hebrew. They were supposed to teach you more but we never got beyond learning to read Hebrew and a few stories.

How many years did you go?
Maybe two or three years there. Then we moved to Pittsburgh, and my father, being Orthodox, sent me to an Orthodox synagogue, the outstanding Orthodox synagogue in the city and the finest Sunday school, better than the Reform Sunday school of the elite Germans, because the rabbi had Vassar and Smith girls running the school and he had a man who was superintendent who was very eager to do the right thing. Everything in good English and good textbooks. And then I went to Wheeling, and I was confirmed at the Reform synagogue.

Why Reform?
I was also Orthodox; I'd become a bar mitzvah. But my father wanted me to have a good education. He was a good Jew, but he was a Litvak, and Litvaks are not fanatical.

But why suddenly Reform? Was that the better school?
Yes, although my father wouldn't go in the place. He objected to the prayer book, which he called a "consumptive" prayer book, it was so small. But there was no school at all among the Orthodox. All they had was a minyan, but no school, no cheder, nothing. Now in my days, the Reformers wouldn't even talk to the Orthodox people. I had come from the wrong side of the railroad tracks and I was never invited to a party of my colleagues in the confirmation class.

It was Harry Levy who was the

Reform rabbi, wasn't it?
It was Harry Levy who later on became one of the great liberals of New England. He was a fine gentleman, but he was of East European origin—though you wouldn't know it. He had a lovely accent, almost English, and he wrote a book on the Jew in English "Lit-er-a-tyure."

And it was he who told you that you were going to be a rabbi?
Yes. So my father wanted to be sure I was going to the right place to become a rabbi. He consulted an authority. The authority was the solicitor for the *Morgen Journal,* our Yiddish paper. He came around to collect, and my father asked him, and he said: "You send this man to Cincinnati, he will come out a *mishummed,* or apostate Jew."

Your parents read the Morgen Journal?
They read the *Morgen Journal;* they wouldn't think of reading the *Forwards,* which was socialistic. They'd want to spit when they pronounced the word *Forwards.* So, "Where shall I send my son?" said Mr. Marcus. "Send him to Schechter's school," said the solicitor. That was the only name they knew: Schechter's school. Solomon Schechter's JTS. This was in 1909. Schechter came to JTS in 1902.

So I wrote to JTS, and a young instructor by the name of Israel Davidson, who later on became one of the great scholars of America, was then the registrar. He wrote back a curt note: "We don't take freshmen in high school; write us eight years from now." JTS was only a graduate school. So, we told this to the rabbi and he said "No problem. You go to the Hebrew Union College, and when you graduate you become an Orthodox rabbi." In my day at HUC, at least half the boys, even more, were of East European origin. Native American, but of East European families. And some of them looked as if they had just come off the steamship, though they hadn't, but living in New York on the East Side, and having cultural ambition, they dressed like Yiddish intellectuals. And so when they came, I would think maybe they had just come off the ship out of the steerage. So in 1911, after two years of study and two years of high school in West Virginia, I came here. I was not prejudiced *against* Reform, or predisposed *toward* Reform. But Reform was associated in my mind with social rejection. A lot of the other boys, particularly the boys who were born in Europe, had the same idea. It didn't make as much difference to me, because I was just a kid going to school. I had no ambitions or anything, I was just like an animal hitched to a plow: Pull,—and I pulled.

So how did you evolve into a Reform Jew? Was it a violent or sudden transformation?
It took me four years to eat non-kosher meat. I was one of the few boys who kept kosher, one of the very few. And almost all the boys lived in Orthodox homes, because the Germans wouldn't take them in. There were exceptions, there were German boarding houses too, but most of the boys stayed in East European homes, where they automatically ate kosher—and where they got garlic sandwiches. And some of the boys who were embarrassed would take the sandwiches, and when they turned the corner, would throw the sandwiches into the empty lot. That's what they did, and poisoned the poor birds, and then they'd buy themselves lunches. So we were exposed to various influences in the college. Every member of the faculty, with possibly one or two exceptions, maybe one exception, had been an Orthodox Jew, but they all had different stances. Some who came from very Orthodox homes despised Orthodoxy, and they were constantly attacking it, and the attack on Orthodoxy retarded my entrée into Reform because I was fighting for my papa and my mama. When they poked fun at t'fillin they were poking fun at my old man.

Do you perceive a change in the nature of the rabbinate or its function or the kind of people it educates or accepts? Do you see a change in the profession?
What happened is that until at least World War II, and even after World War II, say to about approximately 1960, the ideal was Classical Reform. And the boys patterned themselves on that, and I guess that I have been profoundly influenced by that. My whole philosophy and theology is Classical Reform. I totally reject halachah. I maintain that peasants (and 99 percent of the people in Mesopotamia were peasants) have no right to determine what I am to think 1500 years later, and what I am to do and how I am to make my life.

What do you do about papa and mama now? What do you do about the historical connection?
You can't ever reject papa and mama. The result is you make your own Shulchan Aruch. And that is why I have never consciously eaten any pork product—even with two years in the army and bacon every morning, which made me very popular at breakfast. I have never consciously eaten shellfish, and when I discovered that Chinese eggrolls have shrimp in them—I have never forgiven the person who told me the facts about eggrolls.

The facts of life.
The facts of life. So I revered my father and because I revered my father, and because I'm conscious as an historian how Jews have died for kashrut. I observe biblical kashrut. Those are the only things that are forbidden.

Let me ask a different question altogether. What troubles you most about the contemporary Jewish situation in this country?
This is going to shock you. Nothing troubles me. Why, Dr. Marcus, why is it that nothing troubles you? The answer is because I spent several years in Germany and Germany was going through in my time what we're going through here now. And a man named Felix Theilhaber wrote a book, I think its called *Der Untergang des Yiddishchen, The Decline of the Jewish People,* and he

pointed up all the statistics, showing that intermarriage is 33 percent, which is approximately what we have today. The Jewish people are going to disappear, he said, and I believe he also said that therefore our only salvation is our homeland in Palestine. Now, I am an historian and I know the history of Jewries. All Jewries are destined to die. No Jewry is permanent. There may be fragments that remain, as in Italy, and even in Egypt, and other places, but they die. I know that all Jewries will die. Jewry is saved not by numbers but by the saving remnant. The *she'erit hapleitah*, the *sh'ar yashuv*, the percentage that's going to persist. We are not going to be helped by a country of our own. We will always be a minority group.

You're saying that American Jewry is on the way out, because it's repeating the history of German Jewry in the 20s?
I want to modify that. It's certainly declining radically in numbers through defections of all types. But German Jewry, with 560,000 or whatever it had when I was there, was in my opinion the cultural core of world Jewry. There were five million East European Jews who were doing nothing but regurgitating Talmudic passages and interpretations that go back for centuries. They were making no cultural contribution. No single book of any value, of any world-humanitarian cultural value ever came out of Poland.

What about distinguished individuals like the Vilna Gaon?
He made a critical contribution to the study of the Talmud, but no great book or anything came out of it. Everything that we know scientifically about Jewry came out of this group of half a million German Jews, and that is why in 1922 I went to see Julian Morgenstern, and I said, I'm going to Germany. It's the only place I could go. Now let me make my point in a sentence or two. Jewry will not disappear. American Jewry is destined to decline, very slowly, but it will decline. And the more it declines, the more to a certain extent you will have Jewish loyalty, and you'll have learning and scholarship and we will exercise hegemony to a great extent culturally even over world Jewry.

Isn't your understanding of history fatalistic: If there's no hope, if decline is inevitable, why bother, why be hopeful? Why found institutions if they are to decline?
You see, Jews have declined in other countries where they had no general cultural opportunities. There was no cultural opportunity for the Jew among the Poles, nor in North Africa. They *did* have this cultural opportunity in Spain from approximately 1000 to 1300 and that's why they produced a Golden Age. The important thing is that we are going to become strong culturally because we are creating a synthesis here of American culture and critical Jewish culture. And it will be limited to a relatively small group who will have tremendous influence.

I'm stuck on your parallel with Germany. You're saying then that German Jewry would have declined even without the Holocaust.
It would have. Instead of 560,000, say a generation later, you might have had 450,000, but culturally it would have been and would still be the hegemonic center of world Jewish culture. And now I'm going to give you another suggestion: From a Jewish point of view, World War I was a great misfortune. Not only because it killed a lot of East European Jews who were crushed between the oncoming East Slavic armies and the German Austria armies, but also because if Germany had won and imposed its culture on the five million Jews of Poland and the Ukraine, we would have had the greatest efflorescence of Jewish culture—Hebraism and German culture—that the world had ever dreamed of. What happened was a major calamity.

So you regret the culture of your father, too?
My father was a man who loved Jewish things. He was not a scholarly man, but from the age of six or seven till thirteen he had had no secular training, only Jewish training. He knew the Tanach fairly well. And I must say *this* to you, I love Judaism. I'm leaving out something important: Before or about the time that Harry Levy was speaking to me I was already reading Jewish books. One of the books that profoundly influenced me was Israel Abrahams' *The Jew in the Medieval Period*. And I can still see my father in a rocking chair opening Isaiah and turning to me and saying, "This is wonderful." I never forgot that influence. I wanted to be a good Jew. And my brothers were pretty good Jews too.

Do you see any further parallels between Germany in the '20s and America, say in terms of anti-Semitism? Do you think a holocaust is possible here?
I would say a holocaust is possible anywhere. The Holocaust in Germany was an accident because there was less social prejuduce, and less actual *expressed* prejudice in Germany than there was at the same time in America, and than there is today in America. I have a paperback in my library here that lists hundreds and hundreds of vandal attacks on cemeteries and synagogues in America, and acts of violence against the Jews. A hundred years from today, if God forbid there should be trouble here, people would take that book and would say that it was predestined that the Jews should be destroyed in America. Look at what's happening every day. Look at the Ku Klux Klan, look at this man in North Carolina, getting thousands and thousands of votes, look at this man in California, who got thousands and thousands of votes. And it's not at all impossible, if we have bad depressions, that we will have an anti-Semitic block in the Congress as they had in Germany since the 1880s.

Does it make a difference that between then and now there's been a fuller development of scientific anthropology? The dominant anthropology is no longer racial, so that

anti-Semitism, if it ever has political power, could not have the full authority of an academic racial ideology. The people who are going to propogate hate, the Ku Kluxers, don't know race from schmace. They are the rank and filth of society. They don't care. They are people who are illogical, inconsistent and full of hate. I'm a subscriber to *The Thunderbolt*. I get their periodical, under my name. They're glad to send it, they probably know I'm a Jew, they're probably glad to get my two or three dollars. I look through that thing. Those people believe everything and anything. So I believe that there is room for calamity here, and that's what the crowd hired by the American Jewish Committee never did. They never really, in my opinion, analyzed the psychopathology of the ignorant anti-Semite. They're at somebody like Henry Adams—cultured people. I believe that there is still room for a good book on the psychopathology of the anti-Semite, which would include also the motivations for the cemetery vandalism and its relationship to necrophilism.

Aren't the fairly enlightened mass media a major difference between our situation and that in Germany?
It doesn't mean a thing. The Jews were very powerful in the German newspapers. You can't foresee an accident. None of these arguments applies. If times are bad, really bad, and people have to have a scapegoat, nothing will deter them, particularly if there's a chance to go down and to plunder Jewish property. When the movement takes form and shape then the clever, cultured, ingenious people who want to make careers, they'll join up. They'll have no conscience.

You once spoke, I remember, of omni-territoriality.
That's my English word, which I created out of a German word.

—and what you mean by that is that the only hope for the ultimate survival of Jewry is that there should be Jews living everywhere on the globe?
Yes, and that idea is also found in the Talmud in Pesahim, page 87A or 87B, with a comment of Rashi in the margin. Rashi says the Lord dispersed us so they couldn't destroy all of us at once. The survival of the Jews lies in a minyan in Patagonia. We have to have Jews everywhere. And we should make compromises socio-economically. If we can get a minyan who will be left alone in China, we should go to China.

So galut is a good thing.
Galut is a good thing, yes.

That brings us to your feelings about Israel. Does that make Israel a bad thing? Or Zionism a bad thing?
I don't like the fact that so many people are there; three million Jews are there. And I dread and would not be shocked at the prospect of a holocaust in Israel.

You're saying that the idea of a coherent Jewish culture, on which Zionism is predicated, is fallacious?
I think so, yes. There is no such thing as a universal Jewish culture. Every Jewish culture is a dual culture, a mix between the host culture and the culture we bring with us. And Israeli culture is going to be dual culture: a blend of what the Israelis are developing and traditional Jewish culture.

So the Kingdom of David is irretrievable.
Yes. What the Israelis are doing is developing an Israeli culture that is a form of civil religion.

Don't you think a Jewish state serves the purpose of being an *ir miklat*—a place to run to?
No doubt. The reason I give to Israel, and give very generously, is that there has to be a place where the Jew can go. I have no conviction, no absolute conviction, that we will live in America eternally and ride in our 8, or 6, or even 4 cylinder Chevrolets. My only worry is that if *we* go down the drain, I think Israel will go down the drain. I think Israel, to use a Talmudic phrase, lives by the breath of the United

Jacob Rader Marcus

States. And if anytime Israel really annoys the United States, they can have resort to a device that was attempted in Eisenhower's day. We have a confidential memo in the Archives written by Admiral Lewis Strauss. He met with the National Security Council when it was proposed that the government remove the tax exemption for all American Jewish gifts to Israel. That would have meant a loss of over half a billion dollars a year. And I think, fiscally, that would destroy Israel because how many Jews, if they couldn't get tax deductions, would give money to Israel? And when Strauss objected, they not only withdrew the proposal, but they apologized to him. We have the document at the College.

Are your feelings about Israel colored by your education in Classical Reform, which was anti-Zionist?
I was never a hot Zionist. I never joined a Zionist organization. I lived for a summer in the 20s in Mandate Palestine. I came back much impressed. I wrote two articles, one in *The American Scholar* and one in *The Open Court*. (*The Open Court* was the University of Chicago's liberal paper, a paper for cultured people.) In both of those, I was extremely sympathetic. But I never joined a Zionist organization because I don't want anybody to tell me what to do. I belong to only one Jewish organization, and that is B'nai B'rith. They never tell me what to do except to write a check. And I write the check. They do good work and they're innocuous.

So you stay away from ideological groups?
Yes. Because I have my own ideology. I can't belong to a group if I don't agree with them.

And liberal Judaism permits the idea of being Jewish without subscribing to an ideology?
That is correct. I am willing in my Judaism to reach out and to take ideas from everybody, as long as I can take them and use them as I see fit. I am closest to Reconstructionism in this sense: my theism is my own definition. I'm way over on the left. I am a humanistic theist, but I am a theist. But humanistic, with a more or less transcendental concept. I am a Diaspora nationalist, strongly. And therefore I have been profoundly influenced by the writings of Dubnow, particularly his philosophy of Jewish history. I am sympathetic to Orthodoxy in the sense that I observe some Orthodox customs. My kiddush, my mezuzuahs, my Passover haggadah— which is strictly Orthodox according to Minhag Maxwell.

Maxwell House?
Yes. And in many respects I go along with the Conservative Jews. I believe in the doctrine of "salutary neglect" when it comes to certain observances.

Is there any sine qua non of Judaism then?
Actually there are today in America close to 5,600,000 Judaisms.

All kosher? All permissable?
All permissable. So now you want to ask what makes a man a Jew? This is the definition I use in all my classes: any man is a Jew who *says* he is a Jew. No matter his color or creed. And as long as he identifies with the Jewish *people* and contributes to causes concerning which there is a consensus for that decade.

So like Mordecai Kaplan, you put peoplehood first?
Yes. But I didn't get it from him. I had these ideas in 1913 when he was just learning to be a modern American, long before his books.

Let's go back: What's your working definition of humanism?
I believe there is intelligence in the universe. Intelligence. Beyond that I can say nothing. I don't believe in immortality. Although I can conceive that a man does have a soul and that soul lives on eternally somewhere. You can believe that if the world is infinite.

Why humanistic?
Because I emphasize ethics. I am an ethical monotheist. People poo-

pooed it in my day, people used to make a joke about it. He's a Reform Jew, he's an ethical monotheist. Well, that's what I believe. There is benign intelligence in the universe. Otherwise I would have to conceive of the possibility of accepting satanism instead of theism.

Was your acceptance of change and evolution hard to come by?
There was a writer that I used to like as a kid, I think his name was Grinnell. He wrote boys' books, dealing with wild animals. And he referred to people who had all sorts of ideas about what animals did, rather fanciful ideas, and he referred to them as "nature fakers." I am not a nature faker. I don't really know what I believed as a child because I am not trained in abstract thinking, or philosophic thinking. I don't think I'm capable of it. I've had courses in philosophy and I minored in philosophy at the University of Berlin but I memorized the book of the professor who quizzed me and got through with flying colors. I was clever enough to get him to do all the talking.

The early essays you wrote were all about European Jewry. When did you become interested in America?
I began to write in 1916 and I wrote six items in that year. I was twenty years of age. And the first thing I wrote that was published was called "The Spiritual Center of Jewry."

Meaning America?
America. I wrote it for the Jewish Community Bulletin of Wheeling, West Virginia.

So in establishing American Jewish history as your main interest you were returning to an earlier pre-occupation?
I wouldn't say so. In those days I established that this was going to be the world center. But after that I wasn't working on any American material for a long time. Now, I'd like to know myself how I came to go into the American field. People ask me, and I answer rather superficially. But it might not be a superficial answer. I realized in the 40s that Europe was dead as a great center. And I didn't want to concern myself with a dead Jewry.

And you didn't feel that your task as an historian was memorializing the community?
That's correct. I wanted to work for the live community. Germany had been a live community when I determined to devote myself to it. The important event was in the summer of 1942. Then I gave the first required graduate course in an academic institution in American Jewish history. A required course. As far as I know I am the first scientist to work in the field, to make it a full time job in an academic institution of caliber. And almost immediately, either that year or the next year, the American Jewish Committee called a conference on American Jewish history. So from then on, the ball began to roll.

Was there any difficulty convincing the College that American Jewish history should be required?
Well, it was in the days of Morgenstern and he was very pro-America. And he was glad to have it, I'm sure. The boys were glad to have the course prior to '42, all my modern history courses had considerable American material. I was never divorced from it. But things moved fast. I induced the head of the Jewish Welfare Board to take the American Jewish Historical Society and adopt it. I did a number of things like that. I had already gone to Rothman, the HUC librarian, and I said, "I want to start a collection of Americana," and he cooperated. Then in '47, I went to Gleuck. I said we ought to start a national archives. I told him I want the building. He said "Take the building." He didn't know and didn't care. But whatever I asked for was all right.

Was that because you were friends?
Friends. And he knew that I knew what I was doing. Or he thought I knew what I was doing. And I thought I knew what I was doing. I didn't realize I had a tiger by the tail. Because then I got the building and I didn't have any money at first.

Not a penny. Not one cent. And then I went to a member of the board, who was a very difficult person, and yet, a very, very important person, and he thought it was a beautiful idea. He found out there was $10,000 in a book budget that wasn't being used. He had the $10,000 assigned to me. And I was in business. And then I got a famous female historian who's still living, Mrs. Eugene (Selma) Stern-Taeubler, very famous. A woman now about 80, to be my assistant. The College paid her salary. And then I started writing for documents. And people were going to throw all this stuff out, things nobody had any use for. And their records began to pour in.

What kinds of things?
The minutes of the congregations.

Is that where you started—with congregational minutes?
Minutes. B'nai B'rith minutes. Anything. "Send it to the College; what do we need it for?"

When did the private collections start coming in? You know, the Schiff papers, the Warburg stuff?
Very early. The minute they found out there was a place that would take it. I made some egregious errors. I didn't take certain papers I could have gotten. Egregious errors. But I learned.

Can I ask what?
The Otto Kahn papers. Then in a period of 10 years or 15 years, American history had so caught on we began to have local societies all over the country. Today, there are about 30 of them. I gave impetus to it, through the American Jewish Archives.

The timing was good, wasn't it? Because of the 300th anniversary of the first settlement.
That isn't the reason why it was '54. The reason was there was a Holocaust. The Holocaust was beginning to come out in '42. And came out in '43. Europe was dead. This was obviously the great center. And here is a point I want to make: after

15 years congregations refused to send me their minutes. No congregation today sends me minutes.

Why?
Because "These are valuable historic documents! We're not going to give them to you!" It was garbage before that. At the same time, or actually about a decade later, in about '55, I created the American Jewish Periodical Center and I literally rescued Jewish periodicals that were about to be masserated. Thrown into the garbage heap.

From public libraries?
No. From the owners who had closed the papers and had them lying around and wanted to get rid of them.

With an important collection, like, say the Schiff collection, what other options did the family have for donation? What does the Archives compete with?
They could have given them to the New York Historical Society, which would have taken them. They may even have tried to give them, but they made a condition that all economic papers, fiscal papers of the banking firm, be destroyed. The banking, which is the core of the collection. I destroyed them. That was the deal we made, so I destroyed the banana, the fruit, and kept the peel. But a peel is better than nothing. The Warburg papers I got complete. No, except this. They spent weeks going through and picking out anything of a personal nature. But I still have 200,000 pages.

Didn't it bother you to destroy documents you knew were important?
What choice did I have? If I can get a half a loaf of bread and I'm starving, it's better than refusing the half a loaf because they won't give me the whole loaf.

Somebody would have destroyed them, whoever took them ultimately?
Yes. It really was a revolution. I'm amazed—it grew like Topsy. Today we have five or six million pages.

What's the most significant paper you have in the building?
That's a document that was issued to me when I came out of the United States Army. You've seen the document, haven't you?

Your honorable discharge?
Oh, no, please! I've put my own picture in as a Lieutenant Acting Company Commander in the 145th United States infantry. And then there's a document underneath that. "This is to certify that Lieutenant Jacob Rader Marcus is entirely free of lice and veneral disease."

Actually, we have a letter signed by Daniel Boone to his employers who were the owners of the largest store in Richmond, Virginia—Korn & Isaacs. We have a signed letter of Weizmann given to Glueck in which he agrees to partition. We have a number of things like that. Nothing of *supreme* importance.

What is your principle for accepting or rejecting materials?
That it should throw light on the Jewish social experience. Actually, we don't turn down anything. I'm interested in criminals just as I am in rabbis.

In the writing of American Jewish history, what needs to be done now?
Nobody has yet written a scientific history of the American Jew. In all the one-volume histories, the elements are correct, but many of the facts are wrong. And they are not acceptable from the point of view of a trained historian.

I set out to do the volume, to do that book. About 12 years ago. I called it MOV—Marcus One Volume. I worked for a year or so, two years, and realized you cannot write one volume until you know the field. And I'm now working on the history of the American Jew.
I have four volumes and manuscripts. From 1776 to 1921. I have to stop at the first immigration act because I'll never live to finish it. I'm not sure I'll live to finish it as it is, and I work on it all the time.

That's exclusive of the colonial work you've already done?
Exclusive. That's been done. For a generation, nobody's going to touch it. I spent 15 years on the colonial period. I think that's when I started to do the MOV and 15 years later, all I had was the colonial period. And 1600 pages printed. Now, I'm working on the revolutionary post-revolutionary periods to 1921.

Who's been your model? What books have been your models as you write?
My model is Jacob Rader Marcus. There's no Irish history or German history to please me. I do not know of any ethnic history, though I've made no special study of ethnic histories, that is acceptable to me. I think that my approach will be unique, that the Jews are unique. You're dealing here with an extended middle class, the bulk of whom came as immigrants. They were either poor or impoverished, and have become the most affluent group in the United States today. Not the wealthiest, but the most affluent *group*. The difference is there are no Hunts with billion-dollar silver purchases.

How long will the book be?
At least four volumes. Running about 400 pages a volume. If I finish. I've got to have the *Kadosh Baruch Hu* with me. You see, we always have a partner. If you're a businessman you have a partner. A man with a long beard called Uncle Sam. He takes his share of everything. You're a literary man, your partner is always *Hakadosh Baruch Hu*. He decides whether you're going to finish it or not.

How did you have the spirit to keep on going in your career, after your book on German Jewry proved wrong?
All that was proved wrong was one paragraph. Three lines. All the rest was correct. I was only extrapolating and I extrapolated wrong. But the facts were all right.

You didn't in any way try to recall the book, or—
Why should I recall it? I simply said I can't imagine he'll kill the Jews. *He did.*

What are your feelings about the Holocaust?
I don't like the way it's been commercialized. I will not look at pictures of these dead Jews. I will not listen to the television because Hitler killed my father. Though my father did not die in the Holocaust. But the Jews in every picture I have seen of Jews about to be executed looked like my father. I refuse to go to Germany. I was invited to go to Germany, by a semi-official agency under the patronage of the State Department to talk to the German people, and I told the people who contacted me I wouldn't touch them with a ten-foot pole. When Miriam slandered Moses, they locked her up in a concentration camp for seven days, just for slander. And he killed six million; we could ignore them for a generation or two.

To go back to your work. You've just finished a book on the American Jewish woman.
It will be out this spring. About 1,100 pages altogether, I guess.

What brought you to deal with women's history?
This is a very important question. My secretary said, "You ought to do it." And my associate in the Archives, Abe Peck, said, "You ought to do it." And I knew where the female bodies were buried. So, the book. That's how a book is written; you don't sit down and assume the East European intellectual pose looking off into space. Books are not written that way. Maybe Shelly had an itch somewhere and he wrote "To a Skylark."

How many years on the women's book?
Less than two. In an hour, I could assemble half the documents. Then I started to work as a scientist. There were two or three first class essays with good bibliographies. I dug out every one of those articles. And the result is, I have a documentary that I think will last for at least 40 years. My *Jew in the Medieval World* was published about 1940 and is still selling, still a textbook. If people are still interested in women, academically, they'll use that textbook. And the introduction is important. Two hundred pages. That's the history. Straight history.

The introduction is separate?
A separate volume, no relation. It's the first time that anybody has scientifically taken the majority of American Jewry—who are females—and has attempted to study them. I had to begin with periodization.

Was it different from the periodization of general American history?
Sure. These are women making history. They make it differently.

But aren't the waves of immigration—that sort of thing—the same?
I don't deal with Germans and East Europeans. They are all in there. But that isn't my principle of organization. My organization is chronologically, continuously, sociohistorical. What were women doing? Who were their leaders? Did they have any "culture"?

What were the key dates when things changed?
In the history, I began with 1654 when the first Jewish woman landed. And then I go to 1819. In 1819, for the first time we have a woman's organization, and I maintained it's unconscious consciousness-raising. I go from 1819 to 1892, and show how women are beginning to reach out. In 1892, we have a national organization and these women know definitely what they want to do. And then there was a break. I go to 1962, 1963, with Betty Freidan's *Feminine Mystique*. From then on you have real feminism. With a lot of Jews among them. And then I take from '62 to the present day in which you're heavily involved with feminism. But it is not a history of feminism. It's a history of the woman.

And the experience of the woman?
Yes. And it's excellent, if I say it myself. I'm very proud of it. Some documents I *had* to put in because they're historically important. Others I loved! They were unknown.

Jacob Rader Marcus

They were buried in magazines. "How Women First Became Human Beings," is one I discovered. Magnificent. This is the first woman in the world to get a Ph.D. in a German university. An American girl.

What year was that essay?
1892 or 1896, I think. "No skirts shall ever enter my laboratory," said the German professor. But she managed. She persisted.

What's your reaction to the more contemporary manifestations of women's feelings, like the women's movement?
Well, I've had correspondence with women writers who started telling me what I should do. Nobody can tell me what to do. I point out in the history that feminists are trying to change a history that goes back at least 10 thousand years, the patriarchial system. And I have a very gloomy view of that in our time.

Do you mean of the effort to change that, or of patriarchial system?
Whether they'll have any success. I must say that I became very sympathetic towards the women. I've always liked women, but for different reasons. I tried desperately to be fair.

We've talked before about the problems with the use of the word "Jewess" in writing the book.
It's used by every Jewess in my anthology.

But it's not a contemporary word. And it's fallen into disfavor because of the suffix.
In the Third International Dictionary it is not a term of reproach. It's only a term of reproach in the Random House, bootleg dictionary.

So you still feel comfortable it?
Oh, yes. Because it bothers me that we read any noun ending with "ess" referring to a female as unacceptable. We don't say "Negress" either. That bothers me. Because if I'm ever lucky enough to have a mistress, I'll have to say that I'm sleeping with my mister.

I think it's perceived that the ending of "ess" is diminutive. For example, when a male writes, he's a poet, but a woman who writes is a poetess, which suggests diminishing her achievement.
Not in my opinion. My generation was never bothered by it. I looked it up in the OED. Incidentally, because there's been such a stink about it, I have written two and a half paragraphs, which I have here in my galleys, in the preface. In the 19th century, the word "Jew" was a term of contempt. But the Jewish man has turned it into a patent of nobility. Nobody's ashamed of the word "Jew" today.

So you value the word "Jewess" because the world "Jew" is in it?
I'm bringing to light the majority of Jews who have always been ignored. So I'm not hiding them under a male term. We're rising through a term so that people know we're talking about females, who have been non-persons to the present day.

Let's move on to this question: I am wondering about your own plans to write a memoir.
The answer is very, very simple. I have been asked that frequently. I don't think I ever will write a memoir, and I'm being very serious. I've had a very uneventful life. I've never met any of the great, number one. Number two, any of the so-called great whom I have ever met, some have been very decent people, but they've all been human beings and some have had clay feet that reached all the way to their groin, if you know what I mean.

So you don't want to expose anybody, is that it?
That's it. And since I have been the recipient of many confidences, if I really wrote what I know, and I made a very interesting book, it would be a *chronique scandaleuse*. And that I refuse to write.

If anybody ever wanted to write a history of the American rabbinate, the story you have to tell, minus the confidences, would be significant.
I could only write a history of the Reform rabbinate. When I joined the Central Conference of American Rabbis there were less than 100 rabbis in the Conference, as far as I know. I'm not sure there's a complete list—the records were very inadequate in 1920 when I joined up as a rabbi. Today, there are about 1200 or maybe even 1400. I think I could write a history but to do a scientific job, I would want to consult a lot of bulletins. Then I would be immersed in scholarly research, quantitative research. I wouldn't want to fool with that.

But if you called it a memoir, that would release you . . .?
But it would be very difficult for me to write it because I wouldn't be able to make any moral judgments except in a paragraph to dismiss all the pecadillos of the rabbis who've been messing around. But basically, I could sum it up in a sentence or two: Reform rabbis were the most important clergymen, most cultured clergymen, in their communities in the old days. And may still be. And they were frequently the leading clergy, not really the most cultured, but the leading clergymen in their cities. The Krauskopfs, the Emil G. Hirsches, the J. Leonard Levys, the Ed Magnins. Nobody comparable to those people in the Christian clergy. So I've said it all and you don't need any memoir.

Come on. You're getting off the hook too easily.
There's another psychological reason. If you have enough strength to write a memoir, then you have enough strength to finish your scientific work. That has to be done first.

Isn't it possible to do a memoir as we're doing now, talking on a tape?
No, because I have still another book over there all ready to go and for two months I haven't touched it. That's a primer, a primer for the American Jewish historian. "If I'm interested in American Jewish history, whether I'm a Jew or a Gentile, how do I work myself into the field?" I haven't got the time! I have to take a month out just to finish the

primer. In the meantime, I'd have to stop the big book. I'm disturbed about it. Because at night I get tired. I'm in my 85th year. And what the French call "Kayach"—strength—I don't have after 6 or 7 o'clock.

Of all the people I know, you are the one who best combines respectability and earthiness. How do you maintain that attitude of spirit?
Well, my father had a sense of humor and was an earthy person. And I was in the Army for two years, in the first World War. And I didn't live in the city and I'm not an intellectual. I'm primarily a fact man, with a capacity to interpret the facts properly. I don't want to cut myself down. I don't ruminate. I'm not interested in philosophic abstractions. I believe, and of course this is sour grapes, a great deal of philosophic thinking is sheer verbiage. Playing with words. And as I say, I've lived in small towns all the time. And living in the Army I was associating with people where I was the only college man in the whole company of 250 people. You have to live on their level. And I've lived on their level. But, I also am an academician. When I get excited I speak like an academician and not like a common ordinary human being. Though I never, never resort to academese. Never use gobbledygook. That annoys me. Clarity is important. If a sentence isn't absolutely clear I can't write it. I try to be absolutely exact and use no equivocation.

You're Honorary President of the CCAR now?
As long as I live.

What is the meaning of that and what is the feeling of it?
May I say to you that I wanted that more than anything else I ever wanted in this world as far as honors are concerned. I had to have the Ph.D as a passport. The world that means most to me is the rabbinical world. I have no family. Out of the 12 or 13 hundred Reform rabbis, there are a hundred that I'm very fond of. There are five or six or seven who are my intimate friends. That's my world. When I lost my family, my daughter, the only child I had, people said to me in the funeral sermons, you now have 500 sons. *That's my world.*

You actually pursued it?
Yes. It's the one thing I wanted and I asked three people, rabbis, and said "That's the honor I want." And I got it. And I've been very pleased. That meant something to me. You ask me to analyse why it means something to me. Now this is a very confidential thing, but (most of the rabbis pay no attention to it) in my opinion, it's the highest honor your colleagues can give you. Electing you for life to be their spiritual *beau ideal*. That meant something to me. It flattered me. In the long run, Bentham was right, all idealism or ethics are selfish, are self-concerned. I wanted that recognition. It sustains me to the present day. I still have my doubts about myself. And I say it in all seriousness. Because I know the defects in my education and the defects in my capacity for erudite thinking. Real thinking. The important thing is to do what you can with what you've got and to know your limitations. To look in that mirror and really see yourself. I can do that now.

What's your secret of longevity?
My mother. My mother's genes. She lived to be over 100. My grandparents on her side lived to be in the 90s. You've got to pick the right mother if you want to live a long time. You want to be a rich man, you have to pick the right father. ✡

Jacob Rader Marcus

MOMENT INTERVIEW

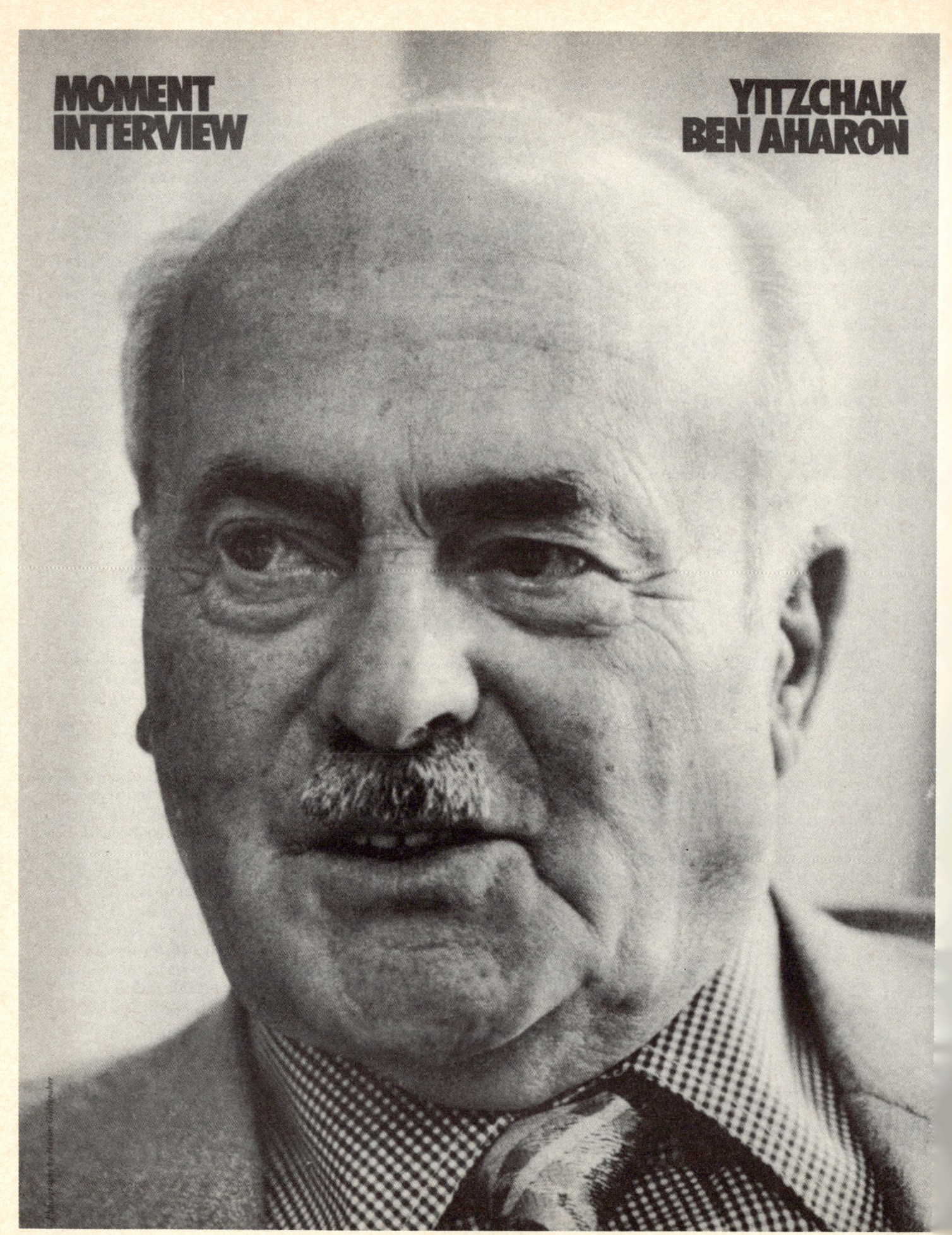

YITZCHAK BEN AHARON

Yitzchak Ben Aharon is the former Secretary General of the Histadrut, Israel's giant trade union.

MOMENT: **The Histadrut used to be widely perceived as one of Israel's most vigorous and creative institutions. Today, it is widely perceived as part of an entrenched establishment, a trade union which fights for higher wages and benefits for its members but is not interested in such problems as worker productivity or inflation. Is this change in perception fair? Has the Histadrut remained true to its own vision?**

Ben Aharon: The Histadrut will be sixty years old next year. Its name is sixty years old, and much of its terminology is sixty years old. But the circumstances in which it operates are new. The Histadrut of 1980 is not the Histadrut of 1920 any more than Israeli society today is the same as it was then.

Sixty years ago, there were 4,800 people who elected the delegates to the first Histadrut assembly—137 delegates. That was the working class in Israel—4,800 people. And of those 4,800, 60 percent were unemployed and a good number were unemployable. The delegates to the conference came to Haifa for four days, and ate herring and bread, and did what they did. There were altogether 60,000 Jews in Palestine at the time. And the delegates had a dream. They had a dream, but they had no reality.

In general, you will find, the smaller the reality, the bigger the dream. There was nothing to limit the dream—no state, no organization, no Jewish people, no Zionism, no money, no class. All there was was a crazy dream.

And so they spoke about a new society, a collective society. They spoke about building all of the workers of Israel into one commune. It wasn't a Marxist approach; it was an anarchist-syndicalist approach.

They were driven by two tremendous revolutionary events. The first of these was the Russian revolution. Remember that the Russian revolution back in 1920 did not mean Stalin, it did not mean concentration camps, it did not mean Siberia, nor hierarchy, nor oppression. It was the dream of a new world, a new society, and not only in Russia, but internationally. The dream was articulated by great visionaries and by great idealists, and they were credible.

The other great event was the Balfour Declaration, which was only three years old at the time. What a dream that expressed! The dream of a national Jewish home.

So there were those in Palestine who thought to join the two dreams, and to create a Jewish socialist state. And that is what they had, all they had—a dream, a vision. One trembles if one tries to imagine it. I wasn't there then; I didn't come until seven years later. But when you read the minutes and the literature, you get the jitters, you tremble. How could those people have dreamed that kind of a dream on an empty stomach, barefoot? They knew quite well that the Jewish people wasn't with them and didn't give two hoots about them. They were ridden with malaria. What there was of a Jewish economy in the country, mainly a handful of farmers, wouldn't consider employing them; they were viewed as charlatans. They were terrific at declarations, at debates, at platforms—but they couldn't do a day's work with a hoe, and nobody would give them a job.

And here they were, speaking of kibbutzim and moshavim, speaking of a state with millions of Jews, of hundreds of thousands of Jewish workers.

Now you ask what's happened during the sixty years. Is it less than they dreamed, or is it more?

One thing is clear: you can't measure the achievement by the criteria of 1920. In many ways, much more has been achieved than they dreamed. The Histadrut is, after all, a very considerable reality, a reality with 1,200,000 members. The Histadrut enterprises have balance sheets in the billions, and represent about 25 percent of the total economy of the country. We have 250 kibbutzim and 300 moshavim. We are a tremendous power reservoir — people, money, equipment, services. The Histadrut is, in fact, what its critics say it is — a state within a state.

But it is a state that has no legislative power; it can't coerce, it can't force a thing. But still, it can be very important. Today you can see that easily. One of the election pledges of the present-day government was to break the power of the Histadrut, to reduce its spending, to block its expansion. And this really means a confrontation between the government and the society, because the reality is that these are not 1,200,000 abstract members the Histadrut has. They are the bones and the muscle of the society. Whatever the policy-makers decide, people are getting up in the morning to do a day's work. By the time the bureaucrats wake up, somebody has already baked the bread, has cleaned the streets, has opened the offices and the factories, has taken out the tractors, opened the hospitals and the schools, the research institutions and the army. And this, after all, is what the Histadrut is, who the Histadrut is.

Usually we think of the Histadrut as an institution, a hierarchy, a bureaucracy. They are there, of course. Hierarchical and bureaucratic institutions are the blot of our modern society. We don't know what to do without them, we don't know what to do with them. But the buildings and the officials and the heads of the trade unions—these are not the Histadrut, not really. The people of Israel are the Histadrut. So when the government confronts the Histadrut, it confronts the people, and the Histadrut is a very important barrier to an all-powerful government; it is a way of insuring that the society remains more important than the government, which is as it should be.

But if I were to tell you that all those wonderful members of the Histadrut go off to work in the morning with a living vision of a different tomorrow in their hearts, that they think in ideological terms, or in messianic terms — that would be a lie. That does not describe the real man or woman you meet in the street or on the shop floor.

At the same time, to tell you that those people could have gone through sixty years without tremendous faith—a faith which many of them would be reluctant to define, maybe unable to define— that, too, would be a lie.

There is a great reluctance to talk in ideological terms. It's all too flowery; it's what the sabras call "*Ivrit shel Shabbat*"—the special Hebrew that is spoken on Shabbat. Talk ideology, talk theory or engage in intellectual analysis, and people will say you are talking "*Ivrit shel Shabbat*," something beyond day-to-day realities. This new generation doesn't like such talk. They are engineers.

I sometimes think that's why they shun the political field, and the public service field as well. They see something tainted in living at the expense of the public. They want to put their mind, their body and soul into creative action. They want to feel the impact their day's work makes on the world in a very direct way; the political world is too abstract for them.

And that brings me back to your question. Today's Histadrut is more a reality than a vision. Yes, it is sometimes a fossilized reality. But I would say that it is objectively realizing and materializing the original vision more than the founders who described that vision so eloquently.

That doesn't mean that the founders weren't important. In a way, we are still parasites, living off of their vision. If you look for the roots, for the sources of the very existence of our material circumstances today, you must see that they are to be found in the vision of the few. Societies are not shaped by majorities. Majorities make laws, they prohibit things and allow things and allocate budgets and so forth. But majorities don't create countries and cultures and civilizations. This is the task of minorities.

And the crucial question you must ask of a country or of a civilization is whether it contains such a minority, a minority that works not only for bread, for its own enhancement, but for an idea, a belief, a faith, a mythos.

If you travel about Israel today,

you will still find such a minority, those meshugaim (madmen) who are the salt of the earth and the shapers of our destiny. People of my generation don't often admit that. People in their 70's go around bewildered; they can't find a common language with the new generation. Everyone speaks Hebrew, but it's not the same language. Everyone uses the same words, but they don't have the same meanings. But if you move around, you find that everywhere you go— the university, the hospital, the kibbutz, the army, the factory— everywhere, you find among the masses who are dedicated only to earning their daily bread a kernel of creative people who are determined to make their activity a vehicle to some higher aim, in their profession and beyond it. And that is what keeps us going.

In the political field also?

Less than in other fields. The creative idealistic minority is less involved in politics, in part, I think, because people tend to avoid public service before they're fifty or so. First they want to make it on their own, to make a name for themselves, to achieve something; then, perhaps, they'll think about public service. But the problem is that we want them in their 30's, because we need young blood. And I am sorry to say it, because it's a harsh word, but the fact is that what we get in political life and in public service is mainly the dropouts, those who haven't made the grade in academic life, in the army, in economics, in the arts or in literature, those who have stopped short on the ladder of achievement and can't go any farther—they are the ones who turn to public service.

And the result is that the quality of public service in Israel is to a very large degree inferior to the quality of the basic services that make and build the country and keep it going. There just isn't very much of a correlation between what's going on in politics and the underlying creative forces of the country. And sometimes, people come to a mistaken conclusion about us because of that. They look at the public services, which are so highly visible, and they conclude that there is no dynamism in the country, no vision. But they are wrong.

I don't mean that everything outside of politics is wonderful. Our country isn't one country yet, our society isn't one society, there isn't one Israel, one nation. We are still engaged in nation-building. We are still many tribes. Everything about us is determined by the waves of immigration we've experienced. Even our class structure is more than a sociological category, it's tied up with our immigrant experience.

Take, for example, the revelation we've had with the new influx of Russian Jews. The Russian Jews who came fifty years ago were very different men and women from those who have come fifty years after the Russian revolution. The ones who arrive today have no social conscience. It's really quite fantastic: here come people from a Communist state, where everything is run by the state and its institutions, and they have no social conscience, they are complete egoists. What they want is to have money in their pocket and to spend it. They want to be free and to be unethical, not to care two hoots about who came before them and who is still underprivileged. So long as they get their housing, and their cars, and whatever they need—and they do, far beyond the standard of all the people who have been in the country for twenty or thirty years—they're happy. They have no conscience, they don't care at all about their neighbors who live in different conditions. If things aren't exactly right for them, they complain. In time, of course, they will change. But for now, that is how it is.

And that's only one example of how much we still have to do by way of nation-building. Now you can't really discuss worker productivity without taking such things into account. Productivity is a very serious problem, even though there are some branches of the economy where we are actually world leaders. Who would ever have expected that

Yitzchak Ben Aharon

we would lead the world in cotton, in terms of productivity, efficiency, price and quality? Or in dairy farming, or in citrus? Fifty years ago we probably couldn't tell the difference between a cow and a bull, and now we are ahead of Holland and the United States in dairy farming. The same holds for our electronics industry. Our rubber and plastics industries don't need any subsidies; they can compete effectively anywhere in the world.

Still, there are areas that are very much in the development stage, and the economists keep telling us that maybe they shouldn't be developed at all. Ever since the time of our grandfathers, the economists have been saying that there's nothing worth growing in this country, that everything costs too much to develop here. The only thing they think we should grow is more economists—provided, of course, that you can supply them with dollars.

We really need to concentrate on the power industry, and on some other sectors, and we have to do this under very difficult conditions—specifically, the dearth of capital we face. We have no capital, we have no capitalists, and the cost of capital these days—30 percent, 40 percent interest rates—makes it very, very difficult for us. We don't have an accumulation of capital that we can use. Black market practices, and tax evasion, and even some aspects of government policy have contributed to this. We've had to move fast, to deal with the enormous pressures of defense and security and immigration and employment. And the way we dealt with them was to act, and not to ask long-range questions, not to ask ourselves what the costs were. Anybody who could get the job done got the price he asked, and you didn't waste time investigating.

The result was that we enriched a certain sector of society, and contributed to great inequality in the country. And I'm talking about the Labor government now. And that doesn't help the matter of productivity either.

Was there a decision taken, somewhere along the line, to satisfy the demand for a Western standard of living even though the economic infrastructure that would support such a standard was not yet in place, had not yet been developed?

Most definitely. I'm not sure we thought of it as a "Western" standard particularly. We thought of it as a fair standard, and we thought that from the outset. It wasn't because of our socialism; it was because of our realism. You see, we wanted to turn the Jew into a working person. And we didn't want just one generation of Jewish workers; we wanted a genuine transformation, a social revolution. In order to perpetuate that revolution, in order to turn the individual from a middleman or a businessman into a worker or a farmer, we had to offer a fair standard of living. Otherwise, the higher standard of the middle class would act as a magnet, would draw the person back.

We haven't won that battle yet. People are still drawn atavistically to the old occupations. Most of the working class in Israel is a first generation of workers, and they don't want their children to be construction workers and metal workers and so forth; they want their children to go to the university. That is a very powerful thing with us. So we have a permanent struggle with revolutionizing the Jew in this country, in creating a new man, a new woman.

And we have to begin with a fair standard of living. Otherwise, we will never succeed.

In addition, there is an economic incentive for all this. We have to emphasize scientific work and high technology. Ours is a country with no natural resources. We have had to create an artificial economy—just like Japan or Switzerland. So your only real resource is people. If you place your emphasis on people, and on high technology, there is a chance to make a decent living. So our emphasis on good wages, on a fair standard, was not so much a way of giving in to people's greed as it was a very realistic and cool-headed assessment of the way to develop the country.

We're still climbing the hill. The struggle to normalize the Jewish people remains a vision, an aim which must be worked at day and night. And I believe that this is one of the great services of the Histadrut to Jewish history. Of course, like any trade union, we care about wages and the standard of living and social benefits. But beyond all that there is a confrontation with Jewish history, with our past and our future, with the question of creating and maintaining a people that does its own labor.

Now we face a new danger in this regard. The dream of our managers and our bourgeosie is that we can expand the economy by employing Egyptian labor, just as we now employ 60 or 80 thousand Arabs from the occupied territories. But the notion of open borders will raise a very grave danger for us. We cannot let ourselves become Rhodesia or South Africa. But unless there is a tremendous pioneering movement, an idealistic movement in this country, we will lose the battle. We will slide backwards, and return to the idea of a Jew as a person who lives by his wits, by his intellect, rather than by his hands. This is one of our biggest hangovers, and it is still very lively in the hearts and minds of the people.

Can it be different in an economy that depends on high technology?

High technology is not only a matter of formulas in the classroom. High technology is implemented on the shop floor. High technology means good machines, good tools. Somebody has got to produce them. Who will produce the machine? Who will run the machine?

I would say that this problem, the problem of maintaining the reality of Jewish workers, should disturb our sleep, because it is the most dangerous problem we face.

But does the Histadrut really contribute to a solution to this problem? Are workers in Histadrut enterprises more satisfied than workers in private enterprise? Is the Histadrut really more than a politically active trade union, one whose members see it as their Establishment fighting the enemy Establishment?

You know, it's an interesting thing that in the last general elections, Histadrut employees voted just about the way the country as a whole voted. That means, of course, that they voted for the Likud, against Labor. But when it came to elections in the Histadrut itself, they swung right back, and they voted for the Labor candidates for Histadrut leadership.

I don't mean to suggest that there is a complete identification between the worker and his place of work just because his place of work is owned by the Histadrut itself. He still may feel alienation, he still may feel oppressed by management, by the hierarchy. But we've now turned about 50 percent of all Histadrut enterprises into self-managed institutions, in which the workers themslves elect their directors and share in the profits. The powerful trend is to self-management and profit-sharing, and that has begun to change the atmosphere on the shop floor. It has begun to create a new atmosphere of dedication and higher productivity. And we are speaking here of sizable numbers, of perhaps 50,000 people out of 100,000 workers in Histradrut enterprises.

You suggested earlier that there is a kind of retardation in the political sector, a lack of enterprise and innovation. The conventional explanation is the party system. Do you agree with that?

Yes. I wish there were some other way of organizing a democracy. I wish we could handle democracy without parties.

You've remained an anarchist after all.

Yes, I am an anarchist at heart. Remember that I'm a kibbutznik, and that, too, makes me an anarchist. I believe that the kibbutz

Yitzchak Ben Aharon

is the ideal community, the right community. It is small, it is self-managed, there are no hierarchies, no bureaucracies, no rules, no governments, no orders, no privileges.

But for a nation-wide democracy, you must, of course, have the right of free expression and the right of free organization, and this means parties. Especially in a new country, a raw country, such as ours, where politics is not always a matter of ideology or even of classic material interests. Israel is the best proof that material explanations are not enough, that man does not live by bread alone. We see here the impact of religious notions, of different approaches to security problems, of mythologies of all kinds, prejudices of all kinds, this whole load of experience we've accumulated over the centuries. Much of what happens in Israeli politics and party life is a consequence of things that happened to us long ago, of reactions and responses we developed in different settings. We learned not to trust people, to disbelieve agreements, to think of the world as a pack of wolves waiting to swallow us up. We learned that the law is oppressive, and that we should not live by it, we learned not to be honest with the wolves, not to keep our agreements with them.

Our parties reflect these things even now. They are hardly the acme of morality; they suffer from personality cults, they suffer from the lust of individuals for power, they are manipulative institutions.

Still, parties are the only vehicle for mobilizing people around ideas, for mobilizing debate into rational channels. By and large, there is no alternative, and the question is what kind of parties you are going to have, not whether you are going to have them. And that depends, in turn, on the political culture of the nation. It depends on how long you've been living under a democratic regime. Is it 15 years, or two years, or 200 years?

Very few citizens in Israel have a tradition of democratic regimes. The general notion which seems to be axiomatically accepted in America and England, the notion that one of the preconditions for human happiness is the freedom of the individual to organize himself into parties and to express his views—that axiom is a fantasy for many people in the world, for the masses, the majority of the people in the world. It is hardly their highest priority, their greatest need. Still, for Israelis, personal freedom does rank very high. We have the priority, the need—but not yet the tradition. Our people are not yet used to a true democratic life.

A true democratic life doesn't rest on a parliament or a government. It rests on the involvement of the individual, on his belief that his involvement has value, that it carries weight. And in Israel, people still depend far too much on professional leadership, on others who take care of things, who tell what to do and what not to do. The citizen is satisfied with that, even though he may grumble and criticize.

In one important respect, we are getting better. The party system is being refined. We started with more than twenty parties, but now we're down to only three blocks that matter—right wing conservative, religious, and labor. All the attempts to create splinter groups with very fine ideals, with finely chiseled ideas, whether hawkish or dovish or whatever, groups with less compromise, less of a mixture—they have all faded. They were not accepted by the public. And this is a great achievement and a great hope for the development of Israeli political democracy.

But political democracy is not the highest goal of a democratic commonwealth. Parliament may have the power of life and death, but political democracy alone does not guarantee economic democracy, industrial democracy, communal democracy. These must be underpinned by new development within the welfare state. The questions we must ask are how to devolve responsibilities on the people, how the population can organize itself into autonomous communes. We have something called the kibbutz, and there is nothing in the world to match it. Even the moshav and some of our villages in the development areas do very well in this respect. But how can we do it with large populations? How can they be made into manageable self-governing groups?

Is this notion of communalism the answer a socialist gives when he's asked how he can remain a socialist in the face of what we have now learned about bureaucracy?

Yes. I believe that one of the great failures of social democratic regimes in Europe has been the attempt to lead the economy and society by huge hierarchies of bureaucratic establishments. Social democracies are paying the price for that. The problem is not restricted to the social democracies, but it is worse there, because we developed a welfare state and social services which brought about the growth of a tremendous overhead, which is expensive, which is inefficient, which is alien to the feeling of the people. The social democracies don't have much time; they should hurry to interpret their intentions properly.

What we must learn is that political democracy is not specific to socialism. Political democracy is an idea which was created by liberalism. And when the social democracies take over the liberal conception, and make the welfare state their ideal, that leaves people cold as far as their own lives are concerned.

To my mind, the problem of alienation is the outstanding problem—even crisis—of modern society, and one of the objectives of modern socialism must be to build up entities for self-management in every sphere, so that people are more than a number, more than ants.

It is happening, for objective reasons. You can't have a regime that provides free education and have a working force that will be satisfed with the assembly line. The nature of production within the plant has got to be changed from mass employment to communal groups. This is already being tried, and sometimes with tremendous success. In the huge, automated places of work, productivity has come to a standstill. Our economy and our way of thinking must be adapted to a society of educated people. You have to provide jobs for people with higher education. Can you expect them to work in Chaplinesque fashion? No, you cannot. We must find a way to the commune—that is what will give meaning to democratic socialism in our time.

Is that the message of the kibbutz movement?

The kibbutz is a living example of it. Our problem is how to interpret the kibbutz experience in ways that apply to masses, to perceive the kibbutz as an example rather than as a ghetto which is appropriate only for certain conditions. I believe that elements of the kibbutz ways can be translated and planted in every walk of life. That is the great challenge for the kibbutzim today, and it is our great challenge, too. ✡

JANE FONDA

The megastar—and mentsh—tells of her visit to the USSR to meet with Ida Nudel, Guardian Angel of the Prisoners of Conscience.

A MOMENT INTERVIEW

Photographs by Bonnie Burt

In September 1984, MOMENT's editors spoke with Jane Fonda about her April visit with refusenik and former Prisoner of Conscience Ida Nudel. Herewith, Fonda's report on that encounter.

Whence your interest in Soviet Jewry? Where did it all start?
I became aware of the issue first-hand when I was in Leningrad making a movie called *Bluebird*, which was the first—and I *think* the last—Soviet-American co-production, in which Ava Gardner, Elizabeth Taylor and a lot of stars participated. Everyone visiting the Soviet Union is assigned a guide from the government tourist agency, Intourist. We were there for a couple of months, and the last day—she waited until the last day—when we were outside, on the street, where nothing could be taped, our guide said, "I'm Jewish." She then spoke about what it meant to be Jewish—

On October 22, 1984, in Washington, D.C., Jane Fonda received the Solidarity Award of the National Conference on Soviet Jewry.

the limitations, the strictures, the sense of isolation. It was the first time that any Soviet Jew had ever spoken to me that way. This was in 1977. It was also then that my husband Tom [Hayden] met with some dissidents in Moscow.

But it really wasn't until four and a half years ago, when I was in Israel, that it all came together. The last day of my visit to Israel, I went to the Yad Vashem Museum, and as I came out of the museum, the way one invariably comes out, which is like a walking wound, there was this group of women, including Ilana Friedman, who is Ida Nudel's sister. The group was called I-WIN—Israeli Women for Ida Nudel. I had never heard of Ida Nudel. The group sat me down, and for about an hour and a half, they talked to me about Ida Nudel's case, and they gave me a lot of stuff to read. I took it with me, and I read it.

What really impressed me about Ida was her actions that led to her being described as the Guardian Angel of the Prisoner Movement. She had created this network between the prisoners and the families of the prisoners, so that if someone would be exiled to Siberia, when they would arrive at their barracks, they'd find a package of warm clothes, of socks, of food, of letters—from Ida! No one quite knew how she managed to do this, how she would find out where people were going to be, but she did. She seemed to be the kind of glue that held it all together for a period of time. She really kind of launched what she later described and what I came to understand as the second wave of the movement of prisoners of conscience and refuseniks.

So anyway, she sounded like the kind of woman that I am interested in and like to know more about and like to identify with. So I took on her case.

And, with the help and encouragement of Havi [Scheindlin], who at that time was working for the Committee on Soviet Jewry within the Jewish Federation in Los Angeles, I did what everyone does when he or she adopts a prisoner. I wrote my letters to American officials, and to our congressmen and senators, as well as to the Soviet officials. In the beginning, calls that I would place to Dobrynin would be returned by his underlings, and then pretty soon, I couldn't even get callbacks. No one would even talk to me on the phone. And I spoke on Ida's behalf at several different rallies in New York and in Los Angeles, participated in the Annual 10K Run for Soviet Jewry, the last time carrying a big poster of her, which I would hold up every time a TV camera was around. I communicated—wrote lots of letters to her. She was obviously aware of my involvement.

Her sister came to the United States three or four years ago, and met with me in California, with an interpreter. At that time she said to me, "Ida has come to feel that you are her only hope, that you are critical in her case."

Well . . . what a responsibility!

And then Ilana said, "We think that you should go to Moscow."

At the time, it seemed completely out of the question. We're sort of conditioned to think that if you do something, you expect *this* result, and that if you don't think you're going to get that result, then you don't understand why you should do it. To some extent, that was operative even as I was leaving for Moscow in May. And if it weren't for Havi, as well as for this growing sense of responsibility to this woman that I didn't know, I'm not sure that I would have done it, because I didn't think we'd get her out.

But I had said to my Soviet contact, Anatoly Mishkoff, the consul-general of San Francisco, "If you won't let her out, then I'm going to go there," hoping that that would prompt them to let her out. And of course it didn't, so I had to go. And then I didn't think they'd give me a visa, and they did. So I had to go! And I was still not sure—"Well, if I don't get her out, and I don't think I will, in fact, I'm not even sure I'm going to see her, what will the purpose of the trip be?" I didn't understand it.

Of course, now I realize what I didn't realize then: that there are many, many, many ramifications of such a trip, other than getting her out, that are terribly important, both for her, and for me, and for the movement.

There is no question about the fact that Ida's life has changed as a result of the trip. She is safer. She's not harassed. The quality of her life has improved. She is getting more letters. She has visitors. She has more mobility. It picked up her spirits. It gave her hope. It was a tremendous boost to the movement. All of those things.

And it made me feel good. It gave more meaning to my life, it gave me another role model—once again proof of the value of commitment and courage.

Whether or not it will ultimately lead to her getting out, I don't know. But it certainly can't hurt.

Let's back up just a second, to position all this. When did she first apply for her visa?
In 1971. Ida was an economist who worked as an accountant in the Department of Hygiene within the Ministry of Microbiotics. She and her sister and her sister's husband and son applied for visas. Ilana and her family got the visas; Ida's was denied on the grounds of access to state secrets. She has subsequently been told by Soviet officials that they know she didn't have direct access to state secrets, but that she might have overheard them. But it has to be pointed out that it was 13 years ago that she had this job. Since that time she has not had access to anything. So that if she *had* overheard secrets, she could have passed them on to anyone that she had contact with between that time and the time that she was exiled. So it doesn't hold up that they continue to use access to state secrets as a reason for denying her an exit visa.

Tell us about the encounter with Ida.
The very first moment of seeing Ida was really quite charming. We had sent a telegram telling her when we were arriving in Kishinev and where we were going to be. She wasn't there, so we assumed she didn't get the telegram—which she didn't. We didn't know how much she knew about where we were staying or when we were arriving. We were not able, even after hours and hours of trying, to get a call through to Bendery. And we were almost at a point where we were thinking, "We've come all this way, and . . . nothing. We may not see her."

We were exhausted. I went to bed—and I'd no sooner gotten undressed and gotten into bed when there was a knock at the door.

I just somehow sort of knew, but I didn't dare believe. . . .

I said, "Wait a minute! Wait a minute!" and I quickly threw my clothes on.

Knock again, and, "Wait, wait, wait, wait!"

I ran to the door, and I opened it, and there was Steve Rivers (one of our group), who's not very tall—he's shorter than I am—standing there, and I looked, and there was no one next to him.

And then I looked down.

There she was, all four foot seven of her, looking very different from the pictures I had been studying of her. Although she turned 53 the next day, she had blue jeans on, her hair was in a ponytail, and she had a huge smile. She looked like a little girl. She was *so* happy.

And then she said, "Jane! Finally! Jane!" Her voice, in presence as much as over the phone all those thousands of miles from Bendery to Santa Barbara, had a strength and a power. It's a unique voice. All of her courage and what she is, her gestalt, is in that voice. It was just like a bundle of contradictions. Small, vulnerable, and yet potent and powerful. And a laughter like a little girl. Just a bell-like laughter.

We spent the day in Kishinev talking and walking around and speaking in the parks so that we wouldn't be overheard, at which time she really described to me what it had been like growing up in the Soviet Union as a Jew. I'll just give you one of the examples, the one that struck me the most:

It was right around the time when Stalin began to really whip up anti-Semitism, the time of the Doctor's Plot, which you know about more than I do. She was a part of a group of friends from school that was very, very tight. They were best friends. There were about six of them, boys and girls together, and two of the girls were Jewish. They would hike together, and they would camp out together — Ida was a very outdoorsy person — and they would play games together, and they would go to parties. In a conversation one day, they got on the subject of Jews. One of the friends said, "I think Hitler was right. Jews should be killed."

Ida told me that it was like her heart died. She died inside. She could not see them anymore. She completely withdrew, and went through tremendous emotional upheaval. Now the other Jew in the group reacted very differently. She pretended she didn't hear it, and continued to socialize with these people. But for Ida, it was the end. She had no more friends. And it was the beginning of having to re-identify what her identity was. And life was never the same for her.

The turning point, the final break, was later, when she and her family began to study Hebrew, they began to read and learn everything they could about Israel. She said that one day her sister's son Yaakov came home from school and said that he had been taunted. People had shouted "Jew" at him. And Ida said, "That's it. That's it. We're going to Israel. We're not going to take this any more." And they applied for exit visas.

Now this is a fundamental point about Ida: She said to me that when you become a refusenik, your weak link is the children in your family. The children are used to try to break your spirit. She said, "I could not have done what I have done if I had had children. They suffer too much."

It's like she was destined to be the kind of leader she is. You know, there are many leaders in the world who have no children. The movement is their children. Her movement is her children. And the prisoners are her children. She nurtures them. She's like their mother. It's true, it's her destiny.

She waited until Ilana and her son and her husband got their visas and left, before she became an activist. The moment they left, she started. Her first act was to send a telegram, with more than 150 signatures, to a Jewish refusenik who was in prison. Her analysis was that the prisoners were the issue that had to be focussed on. As she described it: "The first wave had already been imprisoned and exiled, the brave ones that led the way, and the movement had really come to a halt. A movement is like a chain. You have to keep it going. I decided that this issue was the weak link for the Soviets, both because of the suffering of the prisoners themselves but also because this is the issue that could galvanize world opinion and give a link to the outside." And so that's what she chose to focus on, and she began to build this network, finding more and more creative and inventive ways to get words of encouragement into the prisons. Letters . . . I don't understand precisely how she did it, but I think what she said is that she would write a letter to a particular prisoner, in Russian of course, and she would hide Hebrew words in it in different places, and if you spoke Hebrew, and you could link the words together, it was a message, like "Keep your spirit," or this and that, and this and other methods would be little ways of doing it. You know, you see how the littlest thing, the littlest sign, symbol, of Jewish heritage, of your religion, of your homeland, would do it. *That* was what you would try to pass around like a flame. And that's what she's been doing.

Ida Nudel

On June 1, 1978, refusenik Ida Nudel hung a banner reading, "KGB, give me a visa," from her Moscow flat window. She was arrested on the charge of "malicious hooliganism," and at a closed trial on June 21, was sentenced to four years' exile. She told the court: "I am standing trial for all the past seven years, the most glorious years of my life. During these seven years I have learned to walk proudly with my head high as a human being and as a Jewish woman."

Jane Fonda with Ida Nudel, Kishinev

Born on April 27, 1931, the Moscow economist first applied for an exit visa in 1971. She was refused then, and numerous times since, due to "state interests." After her sister's family emigrated in 1972, she embarked on a one-woman campaign on behalf of Soviet Jewish prisoners of conscience. Ida, who soon became known as the "Guardian Angel of the Prisoners of Conscience," wrote to the prisoners regularly, provided them with emotional and material support and made protests and declarations on their behalf.

Ida finished her term in Siberia in March 1982, at which time she returned to Moscow, hoping to leave for Israel at last. There, she was refused not only an exit visa but even the right to live in Moscow. Eventually, she was able to get a residency permit in Bendery, a small town in Moldavia, where she has been living since the beginning of 1983.

The following are excerpts of Jane Fonda's conversation with Ida on Ida's 53rd birthday. Fonda was the first Westerner to visit Ida in six years.

Jane Fonda: When you applied in 1970-71 for a visa, did you have any idea of what lay in store for you? Did you think that you might still be here, a refusenik, 12 years later?
Ida Nudel: No. Never.

I never thought about it. It was impossible to imagine, because before '71, there were no patterns set.

Fonda: When you made the decision to become active on behalf of the prisoners, did you think that you might also become a prisoner?
Nudel: Of course, I thought of it the first time, when I went to the post office to deliver a telegram for prisoners with more than 150 signatures. It was for some Jewish holiday, and I decided to send them the telegram, to make their spirits go up. And when I took the telegram, in my thoughts, I was shaking. I thought, many, many KGB men will come and arrest me. But nothing happened.

Later, a fellow who had been in that prison told me how the telegram worked. He said that the whole prison camp was shaking, not only Jews, but non-Jews, because so many people knew about their situation and were sympathetic and gave them their attention. It didn't matter to the prisoners that the telegram wasn't for them personally. One of their fellow prisoners got it, and they were shaking. It was a shock for the prison camp. When I decided to make public protests, of course I did not imagine that I would be punished and would go to prison. It was beyond my imagination.

Fonda: Ida, What happened to you after you were arrested?
Nudel: I was sentenced. I was put in prison in Moscow. I was kept there about 20 days. After that it was terrible. I was put on a train and we went through prison camps and every town that had a prison. I went through five prisons. The train went through town in a special convoy, a special class. They would take people out of the trains and put them in cars with dogs and go far from town to the prison, and the prisoners were kept two or three days in the prison. After that they would send you out in another train and bring you to another town and so on, going east, east, east. . . .

I was by myself, with the prisoners. I had with me a little sack, where I kept my clothes, and a little food. I went with it through all the prisons. When a prisoner is brought into a prison, they give him a blanket and coat, clothes and a pillow, and a little spoon with no handle. And you need to carry all this yourself. For me it was very, very difficult to bring all the things together. I took the blanket and the pillow and when I went, I dropped one of them and I did not have the strength to go up the stairs. And then I took my pillow and blanket and brought them down and then I went back and took my sack, and it was full, and I was exhausted. And I went back and forth, and the policewoman shouted, "It is terrible! You are moving too slow!" I told her, "Beat me. I cannot do anything. Beat me." And she was terrified. Nobody had spoken with her like that before. I said, "You see, I cannot go make it. Beat me." She took my sack and carried it, and left me to carry the other things.

All the officials in prison were very surprised. "A Jewish woman as hooligan? We never saw a Jewish woman as hooligan. You don't look like a hooligan. Who are you?" I told them, "I am not hooligan. I am political prisoner." "Political? In our country nobody's political. But you don't look like hooligan. What is going on?" I told them, "I want to emigrate." "Emigrate! Israel! This fascist country!"

What to speak about. . . . It is easy to tell, but it is not so easy to go through.

I was beaten by children criminals. First of all, they disliked me because I am a Jew. The second reason was that I had some food in my sack. . . .

I was also poisoned with rat poison, where I lived in barracks in Krivosheino, Siberia. . . .

I worked in an organization for draining swamps, and the workers were only men. I lived in this barrack for the workers, with 20 to 30 men, and many times I was the only woman in the barrack. Five days a week they kept them in the swamps and they worked. And two days, they were in the barrack. When they were in the barrack, they were drunk and they wanted to rape. They were as drunk as possible. And so they behaved. . . . most of them were former criminals who had been released after the ends of their terms but their families refused to take them. They were homeless.

Their psychology was: "Woman, alone. If she doesn't belong to someone, it means she belongs to me." And so I had to go through this difficult new situation, to make them understand that I didn't belong to them. That a person belongs to him or herself. They have no right to go in my little room. They have no right to take my hand, and to do with me.

Fonda: Could you make them understand?
Nudel: Yes. I succeeded. After some experience, I succeeded. Because I told them, "You are human beings. I speak with you as human beings. Try to understand." And explain to them my own position. In spite of . . . they are human beings; they have some mind, some understanding. But they don't do this kind of love. "If she is a woman alone, she belongs to me." But I showed them that it is not so with me. And after some experience, very difficult and very depressing for me, they understood. They understood that I am a person, not to be touched. And they accepted me. And once my door in my little room was broken, and I asked them, "Help me, I cannot open my. . . ." and they ran and they did everything they could and everyone of them tried to be first.

Fonda: What is the thing in your life now that gives you the most sustenance? From where do you draw strength?
Nudel: I think from the idea that Jews now have a place; they have a homeland. They have their own house. This house needs to be built up and built up only with our own faith. And so Jews need to be reunited with their homeland. Here in the Soviet Union I think that we have maybe three or four or six million Jews. And many of them, I don't know how many, want to go to Israel. Especially the young ones. And I believe that this idea will succeed. So I understand my meaning in the movement. I understand my position. I understand now that I am a symbol of emigration movement from Soviet Union. It gives me strength.

Fonda: I can understand that. The most important thing in life is to know that your life has meaning. Then anything is possible.
Nudel: Thank you, Jane. Not everybody understands my position. It's not for fame that I fight. I fight for home.

Fonda: Today we're celebrating your 53rd birthday. It is really a blessing that we are here with you. Every year in Los Angeles, the women, the men, too, celebrate your birthday.
Nudel: I thank you.

Fonda: Is there some message that you'd like to tell them that can ring from Los Angeles to Jerusalem and to New York and back to Los Angeles again? What would you like us to tell them?
Nudel: I would like to tell them that I believe in our victory as Jews. I believe that this time we will be equal with all nationalities in our own homeland. I understand that to achieve this equality is not so easy and they need to go, they must go through many troubles and turbulences. But I believe in my people, I believe that we will succeed. With help of every one of us, with help of every woman, with help of every man, with help of every boy, with help of every girl, we'll have a strong house with dignity, with human faith, and we will bring our share in our civilization, the heritage of all people living in this world, our world, when we leave it now.

Also, I would like to use this opportunity to tell them I am very thankful to everybody, I am very thankful not only to Jews who are involved in helping their brothers, also I am very thankful to every person who is a non-Jew, who feels herself or himself responsible for all people, for people all over this world. I think that the good spirit of civilization will succeed this time.

So she came to the hotel, and you saw each other. How long was that visit?
That first day, we were together from noon until about 7:30 p.m. She had been followed by the KGB the day before she came to Kishinev. The day we arrived in Kishinev, she and another refusenik from Bendery went to the airport to meet us. Now this other refusenik was, I believe, a schoolteacher. He had asked for leave for a day, to come with her. The next day, he was told that he might not have his job anymore. I asked him what will happen, and he said, "They told me that I will be a street cleaner because of this."

Anyway, they travelled to Kishinev from Bendery, which Ida had never been allowed to do before. They knew the plane, they knew the flight number. They went to the airport to meet the plane, but the authorities kept her from getting up to the plane. Even while Marshall and Steven and I were getting off the plane, and Ida knew we were getting off the plane, the Soviets wouldn't let her get to the plane. So she then had to take the bus all the way back to Kishinev, and then make her way into the hotel. And it took so long, that we had already been in the hotel for hours by the time she finally got to our room.

We spent the day in Kishinev, until she had to get the bus back to Bendery, talking about the history, the background of the movement, of anti-Semitism, of the Russian policy vis-a-vis emigration, which I found quite interesting. In the beginning, she said, it was an unheard of thing that a Soviet citizen would apply for an exit visa. There was no policy to govern this. They were taken by surprise. And the KGB wondered—I can just hear her voice telling me this—"What to do? What to do?" The KGB couldn't figure it out. So they would meet with the refuseniks, asking, "Why do you want to leave?" Then they decided that the thing to do was to bring the refuseniks before a tribunal of their peers in the workplace, in the offices, in the factories, and that they should tell the people what they were doing, and that they wanted to leave. Ida said that of course, there were different reactions from different people. Some were very frightened, and would sort of disguise their reasons for wanting to go, talking about health, family health, mother-in-law getting older, family there, whatever. But there were some, like Ida, who stood up and said, "I am a Jew, and I have lived with discrimination and isolation and all this for too long, and I consider Israel my homeland. I want to be able to practice my religion, I want to live among my people. That's why I want to go." She made a very brave and eloquent statement, in fact, she was applauded in her place of work when she made her statement. They applauded her! And there were other Jews, as well, who got this kind of response.

The Soviets stopped having these "tribunals" after a certain number of years. One of the primary internal problems for the Soviets is that there are many nationalities. How to stamp it out? How to stamp out national identities? These presentations were giving too many ideas to too many people, not all of whom were Jews, but others who would want their own national identities.

So the next phase was: Get rid of the troublemakers, just let them leave. And there was a very large exodus that took place. Some went to Israel, and a lot of people came to the United States or went elsewhere. They wrote letters back, of course, telling what life was like outside of the Soviet Union, and more people wanted to go. Ida said that from the Soviet point of view, the Soviets weren't getting anything in return. It was not good press, no one was saying nice things about the fact that they were let out. The Soviets are very sensitive to the fact that people who leave then travel around and criticize the Soviet Union. Ida knows that, we'd been told that, Havi's probably heard that on *numerous* occasions. I've been told it directly: Why should we let her out, when she'll just come here and make one of these tours around the United States the way others have? They're very angry about that.

And so, little by little, the Soviets began to shut the doors. I guess for a while there were some negotiations, so that they could try to get something for allowing emigration, and still, I guess to some extent that goes on, but it's pretty much stopped altogether now.

Ida, of course, didn't know what the emigration figures were. When we told her on the last day . . . it was like she'd been afraid to ask. She finally asked: "How many got out last month?" The month before we'd been there, it was about 50 or 60. Both Marshall and I were struck by her reaction. She turned white. Her head dropped and her eyes closed. And she said, in almost a whisper, "It's over."

You just got this visceral sense of despair.

And the next day you went to Bendery. . . .
The next day, they gave us a government car, as if it was the most normal thing in the world—"We'd like a car to go to Bendery, we want to see a friend."

Did you know when you asked for it that this was unusual?
Oh yes, absolutely.

So, the car was there, and off we went to Ida's house, with a government driver in a government car. On the way, we wrote a telegram that we wanted to send to Chernenko, saying that we wanted to meet with him about the case of Ida Nudel on our way back through Moscow. We assumed that we wouldn't get the meeting, but it was just a little more escalation in the pressure we were trying to put on.

So we got to her house and we asked her to translate this telegram into Russian. And then we all got back into the car, and this time, with Ida in the Intourist car, we drove to the Bendery telegraph office. There, we finally got to someone who sends telegrams.

There's no way to explain how difficult everything is in the Soviet Union. No matter what it is that you want to do, there's at least an hour's worth of "nyet." It's like what you're asking—say you want to send a telegram—is absolutely impossible. No one understands what it is you're saying. It's never been done. We don't do that here. There's no room that is unlocked. . . . You think, "I'm talking to a brick wall!" There's a Russian with you, who speaks Russian, but still. . . . The people there are the most wonderful people . . . but the moment you get close to a bureaucrat: Nyet!

Finally we got to the room that we were supposed to send the telegram from, and a large, peasant-looking woman with a babushka looked at this telegram. Now what's wonderful about the Russians is that you see *nothing* happen on their faces. It was as if sending this telegram was the most normal thing in the world. There was just a flicker of an eye looking up, and then the woman casually left the room, and then, casually, about three more people strolled by about 15 minutes later, and just kind of looked.

So the telegram was sent. We didn't realize the impact it would have. Bendery is not a little country town, it's a small city. But word travelled very rapidly that Jane Fonda is in Bendery with Ida Nudel and they are demanding a meeting with Chernenko.

Ida became very popular. Lots of people came to see her, were very interested in what was going on. What's nice is that they were able to see her, whereas before, people were harassed into not seeing her. You see, in the year or so before, she had been celebrating the Jewish holidays with the young children of some of the refusenik families—Purim, Chanukah—she made them costumes, she made little star of David candleholders and other things. She taught them songs and rituals. And the families were so harassed afterwards that they got frightened, and with the singular exception of this one man and his family, they stopped coming to her house. She was isolated.

Now that's changed, which is one of the good things that came from the trip.

In general, visiting refuseniks, you've said, has mutual benefits. Could you tell us what it means for them, and, in this particular case, what it's meant for you?
I don't think there's any way that anybody in the United States, rich or poor or in between, can understand what it takes to apply for a visa for Israel when you're a Soviet citizen. From the moment that you do that, your life is changed. It is a major sacrifice of yourself, of your family, of your children. You lose your job, you work below your ability. Doors are slamming all around you.

What you do have is a dream. What you have is a small circle of friends in the Soviet Union, co-refuseniks—and you may even be isolated from them—who share the dream. And, from time to time, if you're lucky, you have visitors—Jews and non-Jews, but mainly Jews—from the United States and elsewhere, who come and who are your link to your dream. And that's what brings courage and hope. It sustains you. I guess it would be analagous to someone who is in prison, who is locked away from everything that he or she ever knew or wanted, having a visitor. There's no question in my mind now—and Ida certainly reinforced this impression, and does everytime I hear from her via her sister or speak to her on the phone—that it's crucial for the movement for people to keep the issue to alive, and to go there.

Now what you get in return, I think, is equally important. People don't think about that, but you do get something in return.

You get a deepening of your life. You get a renewed sense of what courage is. We don't often get an opportunity, as Americans, to exhibit courage or to rub shoulders with courage. I know, from many, many experiences in my fortunate life, that there's nothing more important. You *may* be put in a situation where you can prove to yourself that you have courage. But if that doesn't happen, the next best thing is to meet someone who is truly courageous and to try to understand what human courage is and what it means.

I'm not a Jew, but I would think that the experience of visiting refuseniks would deepen for a Jew the sense of what Jewishness and Judaism mean, and the preciousness of them. For a non-Jew, it opens the window. It opens a vista onto the meaning of what I think is one of the richest parts of our patchwork in this country, and onto part of the richest patchwork of the world comforter, which is Israel.

So that's what you get out of it. You get the sense of doing good, which we all need, and you get a deepening of your life. It's an opportunity, and it doesn't happen too often that one has the opportunity to confront such courage.

I recently spoke to a large number of members of the Philadelphia Jewish community about my visit with Ida. Quite a few people came up to me and said, "We were frightened to go, but now we think we're going to go. But we're scared." And I want to say to people who may be hesitating because they're frightened: the worst that could happen is that you'll have your books taken, or you'll be questioned. As American citizens, no harm will come to you. *No harm will come to you*. It's all *their*—the Soviet Jews'—risk. You have nothing to truly fear, but if you are frightened, then you have the benefit of having stood up to that fear. To go out of this context to a Katherine Hepburn lesson, which I wrote about in my workout book: "Overcoming fear," Katherine Hepburn said, "is the most important thing. If you don't do that in your life, you become soggy." The experience of doing something that you're frightened about makes you a different person. So even if you're frightened, then there's all the more reason to do it—to visit refuseniks in the Soviet Union.

I encourage as many people as possible to go. And for those who can't go, writing letters—writing letters to refuseniks, writing letters to Soviet officials, writing letters to senators and congresspeople, writing letters to the President—can't be emphasized enough. Ida told me that when she got out of exile, and she went to the town on her way back, she was given 11,800 letters that had been written to her, that had collected while she was in prison. She didn't need to tell me, "This meant so much to me." All I had to do was look at the expression on her face, which said something like: those years of suffering meant something. The photograph that Marshall Grossman, who travelled with me, took of Ida showing me the letters is just wonderful. She pulled out the letters, and the fact that they were from Catholics and Christians as well as Jews, and from Manila, and Japan, and Argentina, and all over the world, meant so much to her.

Ida has a book that clearly has been read a lot. I read a little bit of it, and was very struck by it. It's written by a Jewish psychologist, and it's about the meaning of suffering. What is the value and role of suffering? I realized that Ida's life is about suffering. Her life is about deprivation, about giving up. She has to find a meaning and a reason for what has been done to her, and the letters help that.

It's very hard for us, because we write letters and we get no feedback. I'm sure that almost none of the 11,800 people who wrote her have any idea whether she got the letters or not. I view that as part of my role now: I have to let them know, in every forum that I can, that she did get them, and that it mattered.

But chances are that most people will never know, they won't get any feedback. There are no pats on the back or anything. I'm a newcomer to this movement. Some of you have been in it many, many years, and I know people get tired. Ida talked a lot about chains, links one to the other. I'm like a link in the chain. My role is to say to people who were in it long ago and who made it possible for me to get involved—because without a Soviet Jewry movement, I never would have gotten involved—my role is to say: Don't get tired. It's very easy, because we get very little reinforcement. But when you start to get tired, just think of Ida, after 13 years, still sitting there, writing her letters.

And Ida won't stop, either.

How does she retain hope?
Real concretely.

I asked her, "How do you keep going?" And—this is what I love about her—she's so human!—she said, "My garden. Growing things. You can't know how important it is for me to be able to grow things. My dog. . . ."

Let me tell you the story about her dog, which is one of my favorite Ida stories.

After she'd been in Siberia for a while, she told me, she "needed friendly eyes." So she asked her friends if they could somehow get her a dog. *Lassie* was playing in the Soviet Union at the time, it was a big, very popular movie. So they sent her a collie puppy. And this dog became her "friendly eyes."

She would go for walks in the town with her dog, after school hours. You have to understand that there are no TVs, no movies there; the children in this Siberian town have very little distraction. So a dog to play with is wonderful. And she would let the children play with her dog after school.

Now, understand, the people in this town had been programmed to hate her. They were told literally that this woman was the devil. That she was an enemy of the state. That she was evil. And they would yell at her and taunt her, scream at her.

But the children would play with her dog, and they would go home, and they would tell their parents about this nice woman who would let them play with her dog. And it became something that they would look forward to every afternoon. And little by little, she said, first the children would smile at her, so it was not just the dog's friendly eyes, but also the children's friendly eyes. And then she said that as the months would go by, she could begin to see in the eyes of the parents little signs of friendship. She told me, in her wonderful accent, "And I became more popular. Through my dog." And their eyes became friendly.

Again, it's these tiny little things that you do that are links to hope. Growing a vegetable, getting a dog, the dog is then a link, the meaning of friendly eyes, the criminals that she. . . . You know, if you were in a situation like that, exiled in a town together with hardened criminals, you'd react one way. Her choice, to treat them like human beings and insist that they treat her that way—which says so much about her—paid off. They began to respect her. And as a result, *they* became better people. It's this dialectic. I don't know how it is that some people know that. But that's the kind of person she is.

The truth is in the details. . . .
It always is!

And you can't learn that sitting in America talking about it theoretically. You've got to go. You've got to meet them. You've got to read what they say. The people who go, get to the details! They can ask the most silly, little, personal, human questions—cause that's where you really begin to identify.

They're just human beings like us. So that means we could be like them, if push came to shove, right?

Jane, our time's up. You've got to go to your meeting with the governor.
Well, you'll print the interview, and eventually this will all go back to Ida. The links in the chain continue. . .✱

For more information about Soviet Jewry activism, contact:

The National Conference on Soviet Jewry, 10 E. 40th Street, New York, NY 10016, (212) 679-6122;

The Union of Councils for Soviet Jews, 1819 H Street NW, Suite 410, Washington, DC 20006, (202) 775-9770;

or your local Federation or Soviet Jewry council.

Readers are encouraged to write to Ida Nudel directly, at ul. Sovietskaya 69/2, Bendery 278100, Moldavskaya SSR, USSR.

Jane Fonda

ALL THE MIDDLE EAST NEWS THAT'S FIT TO PRINT?

After five years and one Pulitzer Prize reporting from Beirut, Thomas L. Friedman is—at 31—Israel bureau chief for the New York *Times*

A MOMENT INTERVIEW

Six weeks before the Israeli invasion of Lebanon, in April 1982, the New York Times *sent Thomas Friedman to Beirut as its foreign correspondent there. Friedman stayed in Lebanon until June 1984, when he transferred to the Jerusalem bureau.*

After receiving his BA in Mediterranean Studies from Brandeis University, Friedman went on a Marshall scholarship to St. Anthony's College, Oxford, where he earned a Master's of Philosophy in Middle Eastern Studies and Arabic. He was hired by UPI in London and served as the news service's Lebanon correspondent from June 1979 to May 1981, when he was hired by the Times. *He returned to New York, where he spent close to a year working in the business section of the paper before going back to the Middle East.*

This interview took place in Jerusalem on April 17, 1985.

MOMENT: The actual mileage from Beirut to Jerusalem is not that great. Isn't there something almost surrealistic about driving a few hours and moving from the terrible violence of Beirut to the westernness of Jerusalem?
Friedman: It's less than a tankful of gas from the one city to the other—five hours by car on a good day. When I left Beirut, when I was all done, I got in a car one morning, I kissed my driver good-bye—he was my closest friend—and I drove to Jerusalem. And that was it, that's how it ended.

One thing that always strikes you when you come to Israel from Lebanon, which I did frequently when I was there, is the contrast. Lebanon is sort of all agricultural fields. There aren't any street lights and everything's kind of a mess, and then you cross the border and there are traffic lights and straight roads and agricultural fields perfectly aligned. You know immediately that you're in an ordered society, and out of the chaos of Beirut. I was driving down the coastal highway one day, near Caesarea, and there on the highway was a road sign that read, "Beware of strong winds"—and it just blew my mind. I said, "Holy mackerel, I just came from a society where they kill people like flies every day and here they warn you about strong winds." To me, that really summed up the difference between the two places.

Still, I find Israel much more Middle Eastern than people would think. I tend to see the area in general as part of one long continuum. I do not make the distinction that Israel is this isolated pocket of westernness in the middle of a whole sea of I-don't-know-what. It's very much a part of the area. Things that are happening in the Arab world are happening here. Israel's involved obviously in Arab politics; Arab politics are involved in the politics here. They print the Jordanian TV listings in the *Jerusalem Post,* and the larger phenomena—the return to religion, for instance—that you find in the Arab world, you find here as well. Israel's very Middle Eastern. They spit sunflower seeds in the theaters in Beirut just like they do in Jerusalem. And the phones don't work in Beirut just like they don't in Israel some days. And Tel Aviv looks like Alexandria, it looks like Beirut. It's a Mediterranean city. People here shout from balcony to balcony just like in Beirut, and the same attitude towards public space that you find in the Arab world in many cases you find here: Inside the apartment everything is perfectly clean, but they'll throw their ice cream cups on the lawn right outside the door, put their garbage on the stairways or whatnot.

Before we talk about Israel, can we talk about Lebanon for a minute? We shouldn't miss the chance to talk just a bit about that most miserable place, that most Hobbesian country, that war of all against all.
It's way beyond Hobbesian because in Hobbes's world the law of the jungle applied. In Lebanon, you can't even count on the law of the jungle. It's beyond that. To me the metaphor for Lebanon was something I saw one day on the beachfront in West Beirut near where I lived. A Red Cross office, where they stored supplies, had gotten some new trucks. Somebody fired into the cabin of one of the trucks and smashed it. The whole cabin was smashed and mangled. And behind it, perfectly intact, was the storage area of the truck with the big red cross on

294/Moment

it. And I said, "That's Lebanon. In Lebanon even the Red Cross gets fired upon." That's how depraved the place was. At least in the jungle the Red Cross was spared. But not there.

In the articles you were writing two years ago, especially the ones about the psychologist, you depicted people saying that it's not possible anymore, one can't adjust. It's two years later, and things have gotten worse. It's a country that keeps on hitting rock bottom, and you say, "Okay, at least it can't get any worse," and then it sinks lower. And it plays tricks on people because it gives them a little bit of hope for a couple of weeks. So why isn't there a greater exodus, a higher suicide rate, and so forth?
The real suicides will come when the war is over. Right now people are mobilized. All their energies are directed at simply surviving. But if and when a day comes when the war is over and people hold up the mirror and realize they've lost 10 years of their lives to this, that's when the real depression and the real suicide and the real psychological trauma will come. You know, they found that during the summer of 1982 the crazy people in the Beirut insane asylum got better during the bombings. All your energies are mobilized and focused during a life-threatening event, but when the bombing stops and you have to deal with the aftermath, that's when the crisis comes.

I think as far as Lebanon is concerned, the party is over. The fat lady done sung her song. Lebanon is no longer a crisis waiting for a solution—it has become a way of life. This is how the story ends. And just as nobody speaks anymore about the Northern Ireland crisis, so no one will speak anymore about the Lebanon crisis. They'll just say Lebanon, and everyone will know what they mean, and eventually the word will enter the dictionary. We'll say things like, "Such and such a country went Lebanon." It'll become a metaphor for a country perpetually at war with itself.

I say that with enormous sadness, because I have friends there and I really like the place, but I think that's what its future is: Its future is nil.

Thomas Friedman

You are the first Jewish correspondent the *Times* has had here in Israel. Was your appointment an issue for the *Times*?
Basically, there had been a policy at the *Times* in the late 1950s and early 1960s that you don't send a Jewish correspondent to Israel. The *Times* is very sensitive about its image, and there might be any number of accusations from any number of sides, and the person himself might be exposed to certain pressures that another person wouldn't. When Abe Rosenthal took over as executive editor he decided this was a silly policy. If you had confidence in someone as a journalist you sent him no matter what his religion was. So he decided he was going to change the policy, and he sent David Shipler to Israel. And he said, boy, am I glad I got rid of that stupid policy. Then someone came to him and said, sorry Abe, but David Shipler's a Presbyterian or whatever David is—I forget, but he is certainly a Christian. Rosenthal was shocked. I mean, he really thought he had sent a Jew. So this time they didn't take any chances.

But I have no illusions. There were 16 people standing in line for this job and they could have chosen any one of them. They no more sent me because I was Jewish than they didn't send me because I was Jewish. It was a neat dovetailing. They felt it would be beneficial for our readers to have someone who had my perspective of the Arab world to go to Israel and have it be a unique experiment, and the fact that I was Jewish fit into another agenda but it was not the prime motivation at all.

Back when Barry Goldwater was running for President of the United States Harry Golden said, "I always knew that the first Jew to be President of the United States would be an Episcopalian." And one might have expected, if one were sitting down to write a scenario 10, 15 or 20 years ago, that the first Jewish correspondent for the *Times* in Israel would look very WASPy, and be a very assimilated Jew. That doesn't seem to describe you.
I'm a very Jewish Jew. First of all, I lived on kibbutz for all three summers of high school. I spent a semester abroad, during my sophomore year at Brandeis, at the Hebrew University on a Young Judaea program. I also did a semester abroad at the American University in Cairo.

But in Beirut everyone knew who I was, what I was. I made no effort to hide it. I was not among any reporters who went around bad-mouthing Israel in order to ingratiate myself with my local hosts. I've always been very up-front with who I am and what I am. I identify very strongly with the State of Israel, and at the same time I identify very strongly with the rights of the Palestinians to national self-determination. So I am who I am. And nobody tries to lean on me, because they know I didn't come here as an unknown from the Detroit bureau of some obscure newspaper, I came here after reporting for close to five years on the most sensitive press story Israel has been involved in since its creation as a state.

And you came with a Pulitzer Prize for your coverage of that story.
So they have confidence in me. I came here with a reputation for fairness towards Israel on a very hot story. People liked and were interested in what I said from Beirut. So what I find in coming here, instead of hostility because of my time in Lebanon, or people trying to turn me one way or another, is just the opposite. People really seek me out to talk about the Lebanon situation. They are very interested in my perceptions. I'm interviewed constantly in the Israeli press. I don't say this to brag, but to describe the way I've been received here. People have been very interested and curious.

This is very typical. You can always talk to Israelis in a way you can't talk to American Jews because Israelis are tempered by reality. They live with it every day. It's never Israelis who wonder how people receive you or whether they are hostile. It's always American Jews, because it's what they assume would be the reaction. Let me give you an example: A very senior official called me last night and said, "I've got some ideas about Lebanon, come on down to Tel Aviv, I'd like to bat them around with you." This is always in the context of reporting, but I get something out of it and I'm always happy to engage in the analysis of where events are going on the basis of my own experience.

I want to add one thing. It's an observation my editor made and one of which I'm very proud. Certain people come out to the Middle East and say, "Well, both sides condemn me," or, "Both sides like me"–"so I must be doing something right." And one of the points Abe Rosenthal made is that my reporting is hot. It's not neutral at all. I really get into things and get under people's skin. And what I'm most proud of is that I do that and I'm still perceived as fair. A lot of people who get under people's skin aren't perceived as fair. In fact they engender just the opposite response.

Let's stay on that for a minute. You're a person not merely of considerable reportorial skill but also of very strong convictions. So let's talk about journalism and ethics and responsibility and objectivity. How do you juggle them?
First, my personal view of objectivity. Most reporters confuse what objectivity is, I think. They imagine that objectivity and ignorance go together. We want to have an objective reporter in the Middle East, so we're going to take some guy from the Montana bureau and put him here. He couldn't have any feelings either way. That'll be our most objective reporter. They compare objectivity, if you want to put it in legal terms, to a jury. The most objective reporter is like a juror; he sits there as a *tabula rasa* to be inscribed upon. I say the objective reporter is like a judge. He provides a careful balance of disinterest; he doesn't have anything personally at stake in the outcome one way or another and he has understanding–sympathetic understanding or understanding that borders on sympathy. And it really has to be a balance all the time between his disinterest and his sympathetic understanding. Disinterest without understanding lapses into banality and we know just that kind of reporting. Understanding, bordering on sympathy, without disinterest lapses into commitment–and we sure know that kind of reporting. I think the best kind of reporting, and what I strive for, is a tension, where you're always walking that tightrope between the two. That is what objectivity is to me.

My philosophy of journalism, in general, is that the best sources are in people's minds and moods. That's where history stops and starts as far as I'm concerned. When I was in Beirut and I wanted to know what the limits of politics were, when I wanted to know where things were going, I interviewed my maid, I interviewed my barber, I interviewed my driver, I interviewed the shopkeeper down the street. I'm very much a grass roots reporter. If you look at my reporting for the last four years in the Arab world you'll find I interviewed maybe one head of state, maybe two. I couldn't care less. The last person I'm interested in talking to in a society is the head of state because usually–and this is not in reference to Mr. Peres in any way–I find that the head of state is the most removed and out of touch person in any society. And so I start from the bottom up and once I've done that then I know the limits of politics. I know where things are going. No one has to tell me what the public is thinking.

I came here and I felt that the mood about Lebanon had really changed, that Lebanon in the mind of Israel had undergone a transformation. I did a magazine article about it that happened to come out the week that the Lebanon withdrawal decision was announced. So the decision to withdraw didn't surprise me in the least. In fact, I worked on the article two months earlier; it just happened to come out then. But I felt I did my readers a service. I told them what the background of the decision was: It wasn't the government leading the people, it was just the opposite. It was the government detecting the sharp change in the public mood and taking it from there.

So I personally believe it's as importantly journalistically to be the first to say there's been a change in the mood as it ever is to say something like, "Sources report that there's going to be a summit between these two guys," or, "American aid is going to go up," or things like that. I'm not interested in those kinds of stories. When they write the history of Lebanon 1979-1984, a very important turning point in the Middle East, if they want to get the facts they can go to the *Washington Post,* the *Los Angeles Times,* the *Chicago Tribune,* Reuters, you name it. When they want to know the mood they're going to have to read me because that's what I focused on and that to me is the stuff of history. And that's really my view of journalism. I tend to feel that most stories are more interesting for their psychology than their politics. My best sources in Beirut were psychologists and those were the people I talked to.

When nothing "big" is happening and you're filing softer stuff, what proportion of what you file sees the light of day?
I would say 99 percent. I can think of only one story in the last four years that I filed that was not run and it was not run because it ran into the Chad crisis. It was a news analysis and it just got overwhelmed by events. It's very rare that you'll write a piece that they'll throw out–and that goes for every reporter, not just for me.

You have some sense of how much material they can absorb.
Exactly. And so I'm very conscious of that and I pick my slants very carefully. I largely believe that in this business your only asset is your byline and you can abuse it. It can become debased currency–just like Israeli shekels, to use a handy metaphor. And so I'm very careful when it comes to what I choose to write about. There are certain stories I would never write about. Dick Murphy arrives and meets the Prime Minister? That's something we might record in the *Times* because we're a newspaper of record. But to me it's a wire service story. Then there are certain stories I always write about. Say, for example, cabinet crises. And in between I have a huge area of choice. And it's there that a reporter really leaves his mark–where you go in that world of choice.

Do you read the Israeli press?
I get it in translation because my He-

brew's not good enough to read it directly. So I see a very wide range of things in translation. And I seek it out.

But don't you miss the nuances, the illuminating vignettes?
I've always got my ear up for such things. I clip little things and over time when the file becomes thick enough I will be pregnant with that story and put it up. But I'm always talking to as many people as I can. I have an assistant whose only job is to listen to the radio and read newspapers and tell me about those things and I hired her precisely for her sensitivity to the odd, the quirky, the anecdotal. So I have someone doing just that. She's very, very good at it.

Let's go back–within the limits of decorum–to the issue of your colleagues. And before we even get to the larger question of bias let's talk about competence. One has the feeling that there are a lot of people from the Montana bureaus of the world out here. Is that your sense?
It's certainly not my sense in Israel. I would say that this is perceived as a very important bureau for any newspaper in the world, especially a major American newspaper that has a foreign staff. Jerusalem is certainly up there with Moscow and London in terms of importance. And I know at the *Times* they only have sent senior people. I'm not trying to elevate myself but they take this bureau very seriously–and that's true of the *Washington Post* and the *Los Angeles Times* and the *Boston Globe* and the wire services as well.

I find that my colleagues here–and this is not just for public consumption–are top journalists. They're people who have all done well and have proven track records. Take Dan Fisher. He was the Moscow bureau chief. Dave Shipler was the Moscow bureau chief as well, and believe me it was not a step down for either of them to come here.

Now the real problem comes in with the firemen, I think–people who just sort of parachute in. The place looks easy, the people speak English, it's a hot story, bang, I can do it. But it's a lot more subtle than it looks, if you mean to do it well. Any "shmo" can pretend to do it. But that goes for Vietnam or any place. Doing it well is a different matter.

As far as the people working on it day to day, and this went for Beirut as well, I would say in most cases–not in all cases, because in Beirut you had a much younger press corps and it was much more of a cowboy-like environment–you have really top people here.

I think the core press was very solid in Beirut, too, but you had people who came in and thought it was a Mafia story and they covered it like a Mafia story. And I think they missed a lot and probably did a disservice to all of us who were there.

Now to get into the issue of press bias. There has been considerable anger in very many parts of the Jewish community in America towards the press coverage in the Middle East. What's your view of that ongoing controversy?
There are several issues here. Were mistakes made during the Lebanon war? Undoubtedly. Was the press responsible for Israel's negative image during that summer? I would say never. Israel was responsible for its own image and it was not the result of some writer inserting in the first draft or the tenth draft of his or her story one day an erroneous casualty figure. It was the result of a policy and a war that did not have a consensus domestically, that we now see was launched for fraudulent reasons, reasons that are now widely recognized here in Israel as having involved public deception as to the objectives and real intentions of the war. Maybe that was a lot more apparent to the reporters in Beirut at the time, and maybe there was a dissonance between Israel's claims at the time and its actions on the ground.

I resent a lot of the criticisms of the press, for a number of reasons. First of all, because they come from people who have never covered a two-alarm fire–and I happen to take my craft very seriously. I think a lot about it. It took me a long time to get where I am, and I resent some ding-dong who sits in a think tank somewhere, who knows nothing about the way a reporter works or the process of gathering information under deadline, selectively going through my reporting or someone else's. I resent it when he or she renders judgment. Second, I found the critiques of the press to be far more tendentious and biased than anything I read in the press itself. Some guy wrote a critique of me, in fact, in which I was criticized for a profile I did of Yasir Arafat, the basic thrust of which was why he was so popular with his own people. I was accused of being starry-eyed or whatnot. But when David Shipler wrote a similar piece about Begin, which was mentioned in the same critique, he was praised for getting into Begin and his psychology.

This brings up another point and that is that the critics of the press, to me, were as obsessed with the Palestinians as were the worst Likudniks who launched this war. This war was launched on the basis of an obsession with the Palestinians and it was that obsession with the Palestinians that forced Israelis to lose sight of the dynamics of Lebanese politics, that it was a mosaic of different communities in which the Palestinians were only one dimension and not even the most important dimension in terms of Lebanon's instability. And they then went around saying that because we weren't equally obsessed with the Palestinians, we must be biased.

I can give you a perfect example: the PLO's so-called reign of terror in southern Lebanon. After the war–and this was all covered, my colleague David Shipler wrote a very good article about it–everyone said to me, "Why didn't you cover that? You didn't cover the PLO's reign of terror in southern Lebanon. That proves that you were biased, you wanted to cover it up." But the fact is that I was sitting in Beirut and when I looked around from Beirut all I saw were reigns of terror. I had two militias fighting for control of my neighborhood. We had people shot on my doorstep. I was there during the Phalange reign of terror, when Christian Phalangist militiamen on July 7, 1980, wiped out Camille Chamoun's militia while they were swimming in the pool. It took them a week to get all the blood off the pool. I was there when the Phalange intimidated the

Armenians on the green line. If you were sitting in Beirut all you saw were reigns of terror and the PLO's was just one more, no worse in my opinion, no more evil and no less evil than any of the others. It was one part of the Lebanese mosaic. That's how it looked from Beirut.

But of course some Israelis, for ideological reasons, had to build it up out of all proportion, in order to justify an invasion that had nothing to do with peace for Galilee and everything to do with peace for the West Bank. That's what this war was about. It was, as several Israeli Likudniks have said quite openly, to remove the Palestinian cloud that was hanging over their head. They wanted to hit the home-run ball. And because we refused to see the conflict in those terms we were then criticized. So any piece about Arafat that humanized him in any way for whatever legitimate journalistic reasons—say, for example, to understand the dynamics that make this man a political figure—was by definition illegitimate.

That's not serious criticism as far as I'm concerned. I have never responded to any of the critiques because I find them juvenile and ideologically motivated and simplistic and proffered by truly ignorant people. And that goes for all the critics, bar none. I have given one lecture on this subject—at Tel Aviv University a month ago—in which I said everything I have to say on this subject. Anyone who wants to read it can read it.

What about the technical question of the intimidation of foreign correspondents in Lebanon by the PLO?
As I've always said, and I said it in that lecture, the intimidation was there, it was real, and anyone who denies that fact (and I've written this in the *Times*) is simply fooling himself. He's either a fool or a liar. I think neither the press critics nor the press itself has been honest about this issue. The press critics have taken the view that all of us were intimidated, hence none of us wrote the truth, hence the truth didn't get out, hence Israel's image in the world was skewed. The press took the view, "Intimidated? Me? Intimidated, macho me? Why, bullets bounce off my chest." But that's equally disingenuous.

In fact, the truth is somewhere in between. The press was intimidated, you did at times pull your punches, but at the same time you found unconventional ways to get the stories out. It wasn't perfect, it wasn't "truth even unto its innermost parts," to use the Brandeis motto, but it was not a cover-up. You show me one major story of any import during this period that did not get out in some way, shape or form. Was it perfect? Again, no, never. But under the circumstances we did everything to get the story out—with no byline or under a different dateline or whatever. Many times I wrote stories I just hoped wouldn't get played back because I knew the PLO never got the New York *Times* until months later and by then maybe they'd have forgotten about it. Or the Syrians or somebody else.

I wrote a story near the end of the Beirut siege when I was the only Jew in West Beirut. It was an analysis run on the front page of the *Times* in which I said that had the Israelis not bombed the PLO into the Stone Age they never would have left West Beirut. The Israeli embassy reprinted that story; I got royalties from it. And I wrote that when I was the only Jew in West Beirut. I'm as proud of that story as I am of my profile on Arafat. So nobody is going to tell me that I was biased or intimidated because the fact was I found ways to get my stories out. I went to Hamma as soon as the city was re-opened and I wrote, under a Hamma dateline, a story about the Syrian massacre there. The piece appeared on the front page of the New York *Times*—and the Syrians probably wanted to hang me for it. And when I was in Beirut I wrote some devastating pieces about the Syrians.

Did I write everything I knew all the time? Absolutely not. Was there intimidation? Absolutely. You were in a lawless environment. For $1.98 and 10 green stamps anyone could have you killed. And you knew it. But anyone who knows anything about reporting and reporters knows that the way reporters react to that kind of situation is not to go home and cower in a corner or curl up at the Commodore Bar. Their reaction is to find ways to get the stories out. And any honest reporter in Beirut did that. Were there dishonest reporters there? Were there some thoroughly biased anti-Semites there? Yes. Did they do us all a great disservice? Yes. So I see it all as more complicated. There is definitely truth to that claim. It had a very serious effect on the news—but no one wants to look at the other side.

Do you have any interesting hypotheses, given everything that you've said, as to why American Jewry is so agitated about press bias?
I think that the American Jews took out on the press their enormous anxiety and discomfort about what Israel was doing in Beirut. Since they were either too afraid or unwilling to express that anxiety directly to the Israeli government at the time, they took it out on the press. I'm not saying this was the greatest example of American journalism. There were things that I read in press critiques after the war that horrified me. There was a TV reporter for one of the major American networks who one day said, "Six square miles of West Beirut are dust and rubble"—and that was a complete and utter fabrication. That guy should be fired as far as I'm concerned. He does us all a disservice. So there are legitimate claims here. But the press critics aren't interested in a legitimate analysis of the press, its strengths and weaknesses. They're interested in making an ideological argument to justify Israel's invasion and what was ultimately a failed policy, and that's what bothers me. I'm ready to listen to any legitimate critique but not one that says it's legitimate to write an internal profile of Menachem Begin and not legitimate to write one of Yasir Arafat.

There was a conference in Jerusalem where a guy stood up and said John Le Carré was an anti-Semite. David Shipler went up to him and asked, "How can you say that about Le Carré? Have you actually read *The Little Drummer Girl*?" And the guy said, "No, I haven't read it." Now if I were to get up and say a similar thing I would be run out of town. But these guys do it. They're far more biased and tendentious than anyone in the press.

If you do go through the criticisms, you'll see that the New York *Times* is barely mentioned. We're only the most important newspaper in the U.S., the one followed most closely and read most closely by more people. So we didn't count, we were okay. They focused instead on the Poughkeepsie I-don't-know-what, or the South London I-don't-know-what. But all I know is I have a clean conscience.

I'll give you another example. A senior Jewish official after the war came to Des Moines, Iowa, to give a speech. It happens that my mother-in-law comes from Des Moines. This guy went in front of the Jewish community there and said all the reporters who stayed at the Commodore Hotel had their bills paid for them by the Saudis. This guy must have felt he was safe—after all, it was Des Moines, who would know? But who happened to be in the audience? The mother-in-law of the New York *Times* Beirut Bureau Chief. She stood up and she said that's just not true, that's a lie. And this guy patted her on the head, went to another seminar that day, and repeated the same thing. So don't talk to me about bias. I see the same kind of thing of McCarthy-like tactics, unfairness, underhanded use of information on the side of the critics. So I'm really not interested in the whole debate.

There's one related issue of some interest and since we've spent so much time on it let's at least deal with it for a moment. One of the elements of the critique is, "Look how much attention gets focused on Israel whenever Israel does anything out of the ordinary." The classic example is the Hamma massacre where the Syrians killed 10 or 20 thousand people. The Israelis are implicated for indirect responsibility in the killings of some hundreds of people at Sabra and Shatila and the story plays on the front pages for many, many days. But the Syrian massacre is an inch on an inside page. What is that about?

First of all, Israel demands to be judged by different moral standards. It makes a moral claim to the U.S. We don't give the Syrians three billion dollars a year. We don't give the Syrians $600 for every man, woman and child. They make no moral claim on us. We give Israel money because we feel it's the 51st state in the very best sense of the word, that it is like us, that it's a society that's worth supporting, that it is truly a friend in need and it's a value worth preserving. And Israel makes that claim to us. So when we in the press judge Israel by a different yardstick than we judge the Syrians I find nothing particularly surprising about that.

To the contrary, I say God save us from the day when I cover Syria like I cover Israel. It's a double-edged sword. Last week, for instance, I had two articles in the Sunday paper. I had 3,000 words in the Sunday paper about Israel. There wasn't any country in the world that got 3,000 words in that whole week, let alone that one day. One was a tough weekend review piece about Lebanon and the mistakes Israel made there, and I'm sure that made some supporters of Israel cringe. The other was about a guy in Jerualem who's got an archaeological dig under his house and how this guy is digging for his roots in the Holy Land.

Why do we like Israel? Because Israel is familiar. And that is the basis for our link with Israel. We know Israel with all its warts, with all its problems, but we know Israel is like us. And we know that because one day Tom Friedman is writing about its warts and the next day he's writing about this crazy guy who's digging in his basement for his roots. Or writing about kibbutzim raising crocodiles. I never wrote any kibbutz crocodile stories out of Syria. I used to go there very often but I never wrote any such stories, not out of intent, but because the Syrians make it so hard to get stories out that humanize the Syrians in any way, shape or form. So it's a double-edged sword to be sure. For every Sabra and Shatila story, in my opinion, there are 12 travel articles about Jerusalem, Israel's high-tech industry, stories that humanize Israel and underline the point to every American reader that this place is like us. These people are like us and they're worth supporting.

So I say, really, God save Israel from the day that it's covered like the Arab world is covered . . . with the same ignorance, and the same narrow-mindedness and the same stereotypes. Israel is covered differently because it's viewed differently. It's held to a different standard because it aspires to a different standard. It gets more space because, out of the sense of closeness with it, people are more interested in it. ✡

Thomas Friedman

A MOMENT INTERVIEW WITH FATHER THEODORE HESBURGH

An uncommon man talks about "the ultimate obscenity"

Odds are that you'll miss it the first time you walk into his office on the Notre Dame campus. But if you do, he'll call the m'zzuzah *on his doorpost to your attention as you leave. And you might be inclined to conclude therefrom that Father Theodore Hesburgh is a Judeophile. Which may be so, but which misses the central point about this most uncommon man, this thorough* mentsh: *Father Ted is an anthropophile, a lover of humankind. Nor is that love an abstraction. It has led him to undertake mission after mission in the service of people, from work on civil rights to work on technology transfer, from work on immigration to work on education, and now, energetically, skillfully, prayerfully, to work on peace.*

Readers of this magazine know that we do not normally bother to introduce our interviews. I do so in this instance not because a Catholic priest is an unfamiliar guest in these pages, but because this Catholic priest is so special a person. One mark of that specialness is that he was Lyndon Johnson's candidate to head the space program and Richard Nixon's to head the poverty program—two jobs he didn't accept—as well as Chairman of the Civil Rights Commission (to which he'd first been appointed by Eisenhower) as well as the Rockefeller Foundation as well as and so forth and so on—a servant of the public weal. A more telling mark, perhaps, is the number of people, across the land, who find hope and inspiration in his example of disciplined devotion to a better, a more decent world.

I am among those people. I had travelled to South Bend to speak with Father Hesburgh about the nuclear freeze, knowing how actively the Catholic Church has engaged with that issue, and knowing as well that there's not much of that kind of thing that happens in the Church to which Father Ted's not connected. Our conversation, however, began with some talk of the Jerusalem peace academy that Father Hesburgh's working on.
—L.F.

Hesburgh: I have an academy in Jerusalem—actually, it's a couple of hundred yards short of Rachel's tomb, but it's within the city limits of Jerusalem—that I set up 15 years ago at Pope Paul VI's request. He felt that the greatest benefit he'd derived from Vatican II was that he got to know so many other Christian theologians he wouldn't have met otherwise. With the Council over, he said, the only way these Christian theologians are going to get together is if we have some place where they can live together and pray together and study together. And so he said to me that I ought to try to make that possible in Jerusalem, where it all began.

So we have a program in existence, and at our last meeting of the advisory board, in Jerusalem last April, we decided that it's a nice thing to help get Christians together, but we have a much deeper problem facing us, and maybe this is the place where we can address that problem. Maybe we could get a broad ecumenical group from all the religions of the world to meet there to talk about peace and things relating to peace, and bring in scientists and social scientists—the kind of thing people have talked about establishing here in this country, a peace academy, but that hasn't gotten off the ground here. Sure, it would be tough at first to get Jews and Moslems together in Jerusalem, so maybe we'd have to hedge by starting in Cairo. And there are some people around, some friends of mine, with experience at getting Jews and Moslems together, and it can be an amazing thing.

I remember so clearly what happened about five years ago, at Bellagio, where we got Christians and Jews and Moslems together, about 30 fairly high-level academic people. We sort of threw them all together, and it was interesting that the Jews and the Moslems got together much more quickly than either the Jews and the Christians or the Moslems and the Christians. We would take turns at the prayers that closed the sessions, and I used to close my eyes, and often I wasn't able to figure out whether it was a Jew or a Moslem praying. I'd think I was hearing a Jew quoting Isaiah, and it would turn out to be a Moslem quoting the Koran.

Well, at the end of the last session, when we were all ready to leave, Bishop Paul Moore was to give the closing prayer. We had been together for four days, morning, noon and night, and we'd been talking mostly about justice in our traditions, and how our search for justice in the whole world, and particularly in the Middle East, should bring us together as brothers. And I'd noticed that over at the end of the table, where Shlomo Avineri was sitting next to a Moslem scholar from Egypt, each time the Moslem would speak, Avineri would swing his chair around and just look at him, and each time Avineri was speaking, the Moslem would do the same. They were watching each other; this was before the Sadat visit, incidentally. And then, just before Moore got up at that last session, Avineri got up and said that he had to say something. And what he said was that he'd come to the conference with great suspicion, but that sitting next to his brother—that's how he put it—he found that he had agreed with everything the Egyptian had said. And then the Egyptian got up and said the same thing, that there was no disagreement between them and that they were, indeed, brothers. And they turned and embraced each other. And at that point, Bishop Moore—like the rest of us—was too choked up to say anything, and he finally managed to say, "I guess that embrace was our closing prayer."

If you go back in history, you discover that there was a time before this bitter enmity when Jews and Moslems worked very well together, when they were very close and there was great mutual respect. I was curious about the contacts between the two, and since I know a great deal about both Christianity and Judaism but very little about Islam, I booked myself on a French tanker last summer and spent 28 days, completely isolated, reading the best books I could find on Islam. I just read them one right after the other, going all the way from the year 622 right up to today. And I was amazed at how many points of contact there are in the development of all religions. You've had fanatics in every one, and the adventurers, and the swashbuckling types, the imperialists, the academic types—the universities of the Middle Ages were really fantastic places—and you've had reform movements in every one, and the proponents of popular religion when things got too legalistic, the way they did with us in the Middle Ages. I think I could plot the course of these three religions and find absolute points of contact among all three.

And the thought struck me that if we're going to get peace in the world—I don't just mean in the Middle East, but in the larger world as well, which finds in the Middle East a kind of surrogate war, with the Russians blocking whatever we try to do just because we're trying to do it, without ever asking whether what they're doing is good for the peace of the world, and the result is just devastating for everybody, for them and for us, it's bad news for everybody—thinking of all this, I decided to do something about it. And I decided to start by getting some of the top scientists in the world together to declare themselves on the nuclear threat to humanity. Our theology here isn't adequate, there's nothing we have that can cope with it. Pacifism and war and peace aren't enough to serve as props for dealing with the issue. Pacifism is a very thin stream in the Christian tradition, and just war doctrine was developed to deal with bows and arrows and spears, not with thermonuclear ICBMs. So I got them together and we had six or seven meetings in Vienna, and I got the Pontifical Academy involved, and we had our last session at the Vatican in September. They came up with what I thought was a fine scientific statement in which, *inter alia*, they said that there's no scientific answer to the problem, that ultimately it's a matter of morals and ethics.

And then I got a group of religious leaders together in Vienna, and they came up with a statement, and it's interesting to see how completely the two statements dovetail. And next I'm going to meet with the Buddhists, in Kyoto, and then with the Hindus in Bangalore, and I'm working up to getting the Moslems and Jews together on this, and Christians as well. What I dream of is being able to invite them all to this academy in Jerusalem, which Teddy Kollek says is the best building built in Jerusalem by any outside group since World War I. And then we can really concentrate on the nuclear threat.

MOMENT: Let's talk about that threat. One of the things that must strike any Jew who reads the bishops' letter is what you've already mentioned, the points of identity in the two traditions. I'm struck, for example, by the bishops' use of the idea that "we must build a barrier against the concept of nuclear war as a viable strategy for defense." That is essentially the same as our notion of *gedder*, of a fence that must set certain things apart, a concept that Saul Berman has used in discussing these same things.
Occasionally I have some Jewish people come to mass, at a wedding or a funeral, and I always try to use the occasion to tell them to pay attention to the words. When we offer the bread, or the wine, it's with words you know: "Blessed are You, Lord of all creation, through Your goodness we

have this wine to offer, fruit of the vine. . . ." There's very much of that, and I think you have to build on it. I'm under no illusion that Jews are going to become Christians, or vice versa, but the fact is that we have a very rich tradition that we've shared. We've grown up together.

In a way, I've used this same argument with the Russians. One of the people at our scientific meetings was a very senior Russian named Velikhov. He's the Vice Chairman of the Academy of Sciences in Moscow. And I said to him one day that there are certain things that are very hard to do, even though doing them is totally to everyone's advantage, and the best example is to achieve a measure of peace in the world. That's not a Russian problem or an American problem. Now, for the first time in human history, we have the capacity to reverse Creation. We have the capacity to take this beautiful world that God created, the beautiful people that He created, plus everything that we've created—culture, art, music, science, human institutions—and wipe it all out, turn this beautiful planet into a cinder. If you want to know what we could be, look at Venus, look at Mars, look at the Moon. We alone have that fragile balance of qualities that makes life and growth possible. The terrible thing is that God gave us a beautiful world, and we have not only encumbered it with ugliness, but now we are about to destroy it.

I'm not talking in the abstract. The means for that destruction are already manufactured, they are poised on delivery systems. They are hair-triggered to computers, which are notably faulty. When I fantasize about the problem, I sometimes think that the only way we might get mankind and womankind and allkind together would be to arrange for an invasion from outer space; maybe that would lead us to rally and save our planet.

But it's very hard to arrange for an invasion from outer space. Still, maybe from this great evil that we have created there can come a great good, as the old scholastics might have thought. Maybe we can use this great evil to realize that our salvation is together, that we have to do it together. We may come at it with dozens of different ideologies and dozens of different religions, but we have so much in common. We want to save this earth as a habitable place, and we want to save all the beauty that has been created.

These were the things I said to Velikhov, and he responded by asking me why he should be as worked up about it as I. And I said to him, "Because you have a grandson. Do you want to see him vaporized? That's the reason you ought to be concerned. Our lives are mostly lived, but these people are coming along, and people after them. Do you want to wipe out the whole process?"

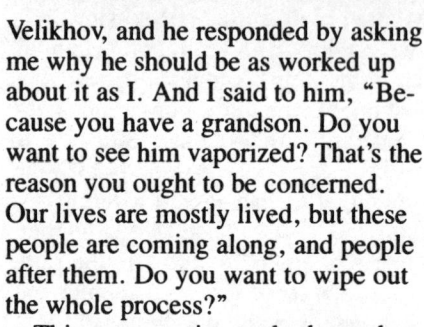

This conversation took place when we were walking around outside the hotel in Vienna. At our final meeting, he said to me, "You know, I've been thinking about what you said yesterday. And I am convinced that the problem is not out there somewhere, but in here, inside ourselves. Until we can purge the evil within, we won't get rid of the evil without." And, a few months later, when he came to the meeting at the Vatican, he reached into his pocket and pulled out a picture of a beautiful little boy sitting in a field of yellow flowers. "My grandson," he said, "the one you talked to me about."

It's interesting that you would use the image of "the reversal of Creation." That's also the image that Arthur Waskow, who has taken a leadership role in the Jewish community on these matters, uses.

Now let's shift, if we may, to the bishops' letter.
If I can put it in its broadest context, it's meant first as a theological and scriptural challenge, it's meant to comment on the greatest moral issue that's ever faced humanity. In theological language, this is, again, the first time we've been able to reverse Creation, to turn it off and destroy it, to fling it back at the Creator, if you will. Nuclear war is the ultimate blasphemy—as, rationally, it's the ultimate insanity.

Now the bishops have a tradition of commenting on everything from A to Z—abortion, pornography, all sorts of aspects of modern life. But all those things fade away when you compare them to the moral issue we're facing here. It's a moral issue that makes questions of sex look minuscule; we're talking here about survival. And I think the bishops felt that if they didn't comment on this, they'd lose the right to comment on anything.

But they had very little to go on. There is no elaborate theology of peace in the Church. You do have an elaborate theology on the problem of just wars coming out of Augustine, but there really isn't an elaborate theology of peace except in the sense that peace is at the foundation of most religious thought and most religious orientation.

So they drained as much out of the existing theology as they could. They looked at the theology of pacifism, which has been a fairly thin stream in most religions, and they looked at just war theology, which doesn't tell you much that's helpful about proportionality in an age of ICBMs where even if you choose to target only military-industrial targets, you're going to kill 80 million people in the first ten seconds. The idea of discrimination, or of surgical strikes and that kind of thing, becomes somewhat ridiculous in the modern context, even before you get into downwind radiation and other effects.

So they felt they had to say something about this, as every religious person does. For the last year and a half, I've wanted to get out of everything else and just think and talk and speak and act about this one issue, and to do something to bring people together on it, especially scientists and religious people. You see, when religious people speak on nuclear issues, people say they're naive, they don't know what they're talking about. And when the scientists speak, people say they speak with poor grace, since they're the ones who created the problem. But put them together, and the scientists will keep the theologians honest on their facts, and the theologians will give moral credibility to what the scientists have to say. It becomes a very productive symbiotic relationship. It has its limits, and it's got to be tied into what the physicians are doing, and what the lawyers are doing, and what everybody's doing.

There aren't any easy answers here, but there are a few basic principles. There is no reason on earth that can justify killing millions of innocent people deliberately, or even indirectly. We're now at a place where defending yourself means committing suicide. So we ask a further question about that. Deterrence is an accepted doctrine, because it's worked for the last 40 years, but if by virtue of the doctrine of deterrence you keep building the stockpiles higher and higher with more and more sophistication, and you end up with many times more force than any rational nation would require in order to defend itself— why, then, perhaps deterrence only makes sense on a temporary basis, and the ultimate framework has to be to get rid of these monsters entirely, lest we destroy ourselves by accident, if no other way.

So what the bishops have tried to do is to take a very, very difficult subject where there is very, very little precedent to work with—no big moral tomes to work with, just a few novels—and to place the issue in the context of faith. How do our policies stack up against what we believe? And, in addition to the context of faith, the context of reason—what is a reasonable approach to this horrible problem?

And they say, quite modestly, that the principles are easy. We don't expect a big argument from Catholics or from anyone else about the fact that there is no moral justification for killing hundreds of millions of innocent people. We are all aghast at the Holocaust where six million people were killed without any moral justification, simply because they were Jews. We can't now turn around and offer reasons for killing hundreds of millions; there is no reason that would support it, and it is ghastly even to consider.

And then they said, We want you all to talk about this. We want everybody, down to the parish level, to start discussing this. And while we all agree on principle, there are going to be people who disagree on the application of the principle, especially as it may seem to run counter to the policy of the highest officials of the nation. And that ought to be discussed openly and frankly.

Even more, we've got to start discussing with our adversary how we can develop peace. Peace is the work of justice, and there is very much injustice in the world today, and until we get rid of it we are not going to achieve real peace. In a sense, I think the best quote here is from Einstein, after the bomb: "Once this thing happened, everything changed—except our ability to think about ourselves and our world." Well, unless we can learn to think differently about ourselves and our world, we are facing an unimaginable catastrophe. I think the bishops are simply trying to follow Einstein's lead, to get people to think differently.

In approaching the matter, some Jews have suggested that we have a special witness to bring, since for us the Holocaust is not merely a possibility, but a memory as well.
Yes, I understand that. Actually, I was on the Holocaust Commission, and it was while working on it that I was struck that you could take all the problems I've worked on—higher education, or the Third World, or human rights, or refugees, or immigration, a whole series of very tough human problems, all with a moral dimen-

sion—and solve them in a moment. You could eliminate all the human problems by eliminating all the human beings. And that's what we're facing here; if we don't solve this problem, all the others are moot, because it's all over.

That's why I sometimes think this may be God's way of bringing us together as human beings. We have a great evil facing us, the greatest we've ever faced; we have a great moral problem facing us, the greatest we've ever faced. And we have great differences between us. But now we can see that we have to make common cause as human beings on a single Earth. Our total interdependence is so highlighted by this threat that is so great and so unprecedented; maybe it can be the greatest civilizing thing we've ever come across.

As a sidelight, I might say that I've been working with some scientists about the possibility of finding extraterrestrial intelligence, and in our conversations we've talked about what we would ask if we encountered a superior race out there—as any race that could communicate with us would obviously be. And the common question that everybody wants to ask, that everybody came to privately, without any discussion, is, How have you become so advanced without destroying yourselves through nuclear war? That's a pretty important question, and it reflects the feeling of the scientists that at the rate we're going, we might not be able to pull it off.

Obviously, religion has often separated peoples, and ideologies have certainly separated peoples, and race has separated peoples, and geography, and material possessions—and the people we remember as truly great are those who have brought others together in a common endeavor.

Blessed are the peacemakers?
Yes, blessed are the peacemakers. You can't beat that. Blessed are those who can relieve, in a real way, the fears of our children. I was talking not long ago with the daughter of a friend of mine, and I asked her whether she thinks about this, and she said, "All the time. I grew up like most girls my age, thinking of a romantic wedding, a nice house with a picket fence, children in the yard—the American dream. And now I'm faced with the stark reality of wondering whether it would be moral for me to bring children into a world where they might be vaporized."

After the Holocaust, when the survivors began to have children, that was the sign that they were healing. Otherwise, they wouldn't have, they wouldn't have wanted to expose another human being to this lousy world.

When the Pope was asked about our work with the scientists and the religious leaders, he thought it was a great idea, but he counselled us to go beyond the gloom and doom, to include in the statement a word of hope. In his mind, the greatest threat is that in the face of the problem, people are giving up. And maybe, as I've said, what all of us are doing can help revitalize our theology as well. In our theology, the notion of reconciliation is fundamental. Everybody is forgivable. And now we need to learn how to sit down and talk with the Russians, to try to draw their humanity out of them, to somehow get to the core of the thing and have them see that we are all up against a common evil. Reconciliation—the ability of one human being to talk to another even after being burned, to be able to say, "OK, it is terrible and I wish it hadn't happened but I forgive you"—maybe we can learn that now. We have it in the Lord's Prayer: "Forgive us our trespasses as we forgive those who trespass against us." That puts the monkey on our back, because it asks that we be shown mercy to the extent that we show it to others. That's the heart of the thing. If we wait for the problem to be settled in geopolitical terms, it won't be settled.

That's why the bishops call on us to discuss it, on all of us. The only thing they come down hard on is that there is no way you can justify killing a hundred million people; as to the rest, let's have what they call a "public moral dialogue." ✡

A MOMENT INTERVIEW WITH 'BOOKIE'

THE NEO-CONSERVATIVES MAY HAVE WON THE BATTLE, BUT HYMAN BOOKBINDER, WASHINGTON REPRESENTATIVE OF THE AMERICAN JEWISH COMMITTEE, CONTINUES TO FIGHT THE WAR.

Here it is, April, and the new Administration is off and running. What's the mood among the defenders of the old-time liberal religion, which, I presume, includes you?
Yes, I still proudly wear the label "liberal," even though it becomes less and less clear just what the label stands for. I think what we're finding, especially over the course of the last few weeks, is that the liberals really lost the election. In some ways, it's rather stark: budget cut proposals, confusion over human rights and things like that. But it's still too early; no absolute assessment is possible or is being offered at this point. And that's in part because the liberal leaders, in Congress and elsewhere, have not yet provided anything that resembles a coherent alternative. The battle is being waged on specific things, but no one is saying "This approach is better than what we now see coming from the Administration."

Doesn't that suggest that liberals have been without a comprehensive program for some time? This disarray is not merely political; it's ideological, too. The election merely revealed a condition that existed before the election, didn't it?
I wouldn't put it that way. With all the confusion and ambiguity that surrounds the so-called liberal program, I believe that even during these difficult, uncertain years, there was a basic liberal credo that has held up. I know that's unfashionable to say these days, but the idea that our complicated economic and social system requires a significant amount of federal intervention and involvement still holds true, despite the disappointments we've had over certain aspects of that intervention. The liberal believes that the major social goals—a greater measure of justice and equity, and so on—require a fairly active federal involvement. The other side—call it conservative, call it what you want—believes that the last 15 or 20 years prove that such intervention is not helpful. I personally, in my traditional view, hold to a position somewhere between these two: there is need for major intervention to secure social justice, but we've become lazy and unimaginative and uncreative in examining and evaluating and modifying specific programs as we go along. And that's given the whole idea of intervention a bad name.

But doesn't that suggest that it's time to go back to the drawing boards and rejustify the liberal program, a kind of ideological sunset act? For if what you're saying is correct, the last years of liberal power were fueled by inertia rather than by coherent approaches.
I think that's true, but another thing that's true and that modifies what you've said is that there really haven't been substantial failures in the programs the liberals have put forward these past years. I do not know of any major failure. What are the areas where there have been major failures, or major misconceptions? The generalized indictment comes because we look at America in 1980, in 1981, and we see that there's still a lot of unemployment, there's a growing underclass, there's a breakup of families—we look at these horrible, disturbing facts and then we come to a generalized assertion that everything we've done over the last 15 or 20 years has not prevented these conditions, and therefore the things we've done haven't been good. Is Social Security not a good thing? Is feeding the poor not a good thing? Is Headstart not a good thing? Is Medicare not a good thing? Is minimum wage not a good thing?
I really don't know what it is that's considered not a good thing. It could be that what the critics are in effect doing, without realizing it, is saying that the trouble with all these programs is not that they were not good, but that they were not good enough. We are close to having eliminated the kind of poverty we used to find 16 years ago or so when I was involved in the Poverty Program. Of course, poverty is a relative thing. But we had a definition back then, in 1964, and if you take today the financial income and services in kind that the poor receive, I think we've done a good

Moment/305

thing, and not a bad thing. We've reduced the number of people who are really, in fact, poor—homeless and hungry—to very, very few. I think America ought to be proud of that record.

Let's turn for a minute to Hyman Bookbinder. How long have you been in Washington?
Thirty-one years. I came at the beginning of the Korean War for what I thought would be a one year stint. I was a labor advisor to the Korean War Program. I was a legislative representative for the CIO and then the AFL-CIO—that was after I left government service in 1952, and then I went into the Kennedy administration in early 1961, where I served as a Special Assistant to the Secretary of Commerce. Then, in 1962, when Eleanor Roosevelt died, at the White House request, I took a leave of absence from government and spent the year organizing the Eleanor Roosevelt Memorial Foundation. At the end of about a year of that, the War on Poverty started, and I was asked to come back to government service in Washington where for three years I served as assistant director to OEO. At the same time, for two of those years, I was a Special Assistant to Vice President Hubert Humphrey.

Then, in '67, interestingly enough, a few months after the Six Day War, I was finally persuaded to leave government and to come join the American Jewish Committee. I might tell you—I'm sensitive to this now because I'll be celebrating my 65th birthday in a few weeks, and I've been doing some reflecting on these last years, and it might be suggestive of what happened in this town of Washington to remind you and remind myself—that the year before I came here, in 1950, I remember trying to have lunch with a black friend of mind, George Weaver, a man who ten years later became Assistant Secretary of Labor. When I tried to make a lunch date with him through a phone call from New York, and I suggested we go to the Statler, he said "no," and then I suggested the Occidental restaurant, and he said "no," and I finally realized what was going on and I was very embarrassed, and I said, "OK George, tell me where we can have lunch," and we ended up in a small Chinese restaurant. That was only thirty years ago.

I rather suspect that most people have only a very imperfect idea, if any at all, what it is that a Washington representative does.
In a way, since we like to think we're unique, we do it differently, but what we do is what a number of other people in this town do, people who represent Jewish and other public-spirited organizations. I serve as a two-way medium. I try to react to government and to other institutions in Washington, and be an advocate and an informant for views that we hold. And in the other direction, I try to keep our people informed about the thinking and the policies and the actions of government and of other major institutions. The word that describes that in common parlance is "lobbyist." I'm not a registered lobbyist, but that is in effect what I am. I'm an advocate, an explainer of policies, and, to the extent that we can participate in the shaping of policy on behalf of the AJC, that's what I do.

Crisis periods aside, what proportion of your effort is invested in Israel-oriented lobbying or advocacy?
It does fluctuate, as your question implies. I would say, with satisfaction on the one hand and with much dismay on the other, that activity on Israel's behalf clearly takes up the bulk of my time. I'm pleased because it's gratifying to play a role in shaping American policy towards Israel and in trying to improve the America-Israel relationship. I want to be involved in that; it is obviously our top priority, by far. On the other hand, it's disturbing that in the thirteen years I've been in this work, while there have been ups and downs in that relationship and in Israel's situation, Israel continues to be a crisis issue. Some days are quieter than others, but maintaining the proper attitude towards Israel and strengthening the bonds between our two countries is far and away the most important and the most time-consuming task we have.

There are, as you intimated a while back, a number of representatives of Jewish organizations who work in Washington. We hear a great deal about duplication and overlap. What kind of a relationship do you have with your colleagues who represent other Jewish agencies and organizations?
Mostly we work independently. We're together in that we try to meet often enough to exchange perceptions and information, and there I feel proud of the role I played in prompting the regular meeting of all the Washington reps back when I first started with AJC. It had not happened before. So we do have coordination of sorts, and we all work with AIPAC (America-Israel Public Affairs Committee), which is a unique organization, not a membership organization. It's a lobbying group, officially. And we all work with AIPAC, cooperate with AIPAC in thinking through the best possible legislative and political strategy on behalf of American–Israel cooperation. And we do work together in other ways, but we also have reflected on the Washington scene what is true of the Jewish community as a whole. I don't mean this in an accusatory way, but there is a good deal of institutional rivalry and competition. There are times it's disturbing—as when actions are taken or things are said as much to gain institutional credit as to advance our goals.

Reflecting on all these years, can you point to something you regard as your most satisfying success?
That presumes that I have a lot of successes to point to. I want to make an impersonal point here, and I hope it doesn't sound too self-serving if I say it in a personal way. I suppose the greatest satisfaction I have is that through these years and through these many, many great crises, whether it be the Yom Kippur War or the aftermath of Andy

Young, or the UN vote, I have always insisted to myself, to all of my colleagues here in Washington or in New York and in the Jewish community generally that, predominant as the Israel issue is, we dare not ever abandon totally or significantly our other commitments—to social justice, to economic equality, to making America a better place for all people, including Jews. First, that's because we're called upon to do that out of our own tradition and beliefs, and because it's right to do that. And also because our own efforts on behalf of Israel would be adversely affected if we were perceived as being solely a pro-Israel advocacy group. Therefore, busy as we might be, distressed as we might be over this emergency or that emergency affecting Israel, or even Jewish interests generally, we've got to be seen participating in the work of the Leadership Conference on Civil Rights, in the groups fighting poverty, in the groups fighting for civil liberties. If we expect people to be interested in our Jewish agenda, we've got to show an interest in other people's agendas—consistent, of course, with those agendas being compatible with what we generally believe.

That brings us to the vexing question of coalition. In the old days, the partners were clear—the trade union movement, the blacks, the Democratic party. That coalition, obviously, is in considerable disarray these days, and many Jews believe that it cannot be resurrected. It's not just the specific issues that have divided us, such as affirmative action; it's more a sense of fatigue, and a growing belief that the interests of the erstwhile partners—at least when narrowly defined—may not be truly compatible.
This may sound like a cliché, but we must never forget that Jews are not only Jews; we're also people. Jews are therefore not immune from general shifts regarding major issues in this country. And there has been a general fatigue and resentment and backlash regarding a wide range of black aspirations and civil rights issues. Jews are not immune from all that, from the resentment over the loud rejection of white participation in the civil rights movement. And Jews are not only people; they're white people, so Jews act like whites, and even when they don't, they are perceived to act like whites. But I believe that all the surveys, studies and analyses show that Jews still remain more pro-civil rights, pro-integration, pro-civil liberties, than other white Americans. I'm pleased about that, even as I am displeased by the degree of backlash that I note in the Jewish community.

You indicated that affirmative action is a major issue in the deterioration of the black-Jewish relationship, but on our Washington political scene I see much less of this disarray in the relationship between blacks and Jews than is reported elsewhere. The old political coalition of the civil rights movement is in fairly good shape here in Washington. The Leadership Conference on Civil Rights continues to function; we put aside controversial issues such as affirmative action, but we work together on things like fair housing, voting rights, implementation of the civil rights laws. Things aren't quite as bad here as they are in our communities.

And I only wish that the people back home, and the readers of MOMENT, would note and note well that with all the difficulties we've had with the Andy Young situation and Congressman Fauntroy in Washington and so on, the record over these years, including this last year, of the votes cast by black members of Congress on issues related to Soviet Jewry and Israel is almost perfect. They have a much better aggregate voting record on these so-called Jewish issues than do white members of Congress.

That's very interesting—and not well-known at all.
Moreover, there was a study done recently that deserves a fair amount of attention, a study that compares the voting records of various groups in Congress not just on Jewish issues, but across the board, in an effort to see which groups were closest and which were farthest apart. The correlation in voting records between the black members and the Jewish members is higher than between any other two racial or religious groupings in the Congress.

So what you're saying is that there's really no pressing need to seek out new coalition partners; the old coalition still has some life in it.
Absolutely. One of the dimensions of this problem is that there is disarray in the black leadership. There used to be a time, when A. Philip Randolph would speak out, or Roy Wilkins, and they were speaking for *the* black community, and usually they spoke out in ways that didn't raise any special problems for the Jews—I'm speaking now of those "golden" days of fifteen, twenty years ago. But now, more often than not, the media are interested in having a charismatic figure like Jesse Jackson presumably speak for the black community, and Jesse Jackson does indeed say distressing and sometimes hateful things. Many Jews are put off by that, and start to think of the black community as being Jesse Jackson. But I do not think he speaks for them.

Is there a generational thing at work here, too? Is the new generation as ready for coalition?
That's part of it. The fact that they're young means that they were not physically present and never saw the rabbis and the Jewish seminary students and the others who went down to Selma and participated in the early struggles. They know about that chapter only through assertions made by middle-aged people like myself, and that's not good enough.

But more important, there's a new assertiveness among the younger black leaders. Still I don't despair, as some others do, about the prospect that even the younger blacks will eventually see the appropriateness and the wisdom of cooperation and trust.

Does the prominence of Jews in the neo-conservative movement bother

the non-Jews you work with? Is that an issue?
Yes, especially on some recent issues like affirmative action or human rights—that curious new definition of human rights that distinguishes between "authoritarian" regimes and "totalitarian" regimes and all that jazz—I think we do see some of what you're suggesting. And there'll be more of it, because Jews are indeed prominent in neo-conservative circles. But it's important to remember that they also remain prominent in liberal and even the way-out liberal circles.

But that's dog bites man; it's not as remarkable. One statement by a leading Jew on the advisability of working with the Moral Majority is likely to draw ten times more attention than a statement from an equally prominent Jew attacking the Moral Majority for its anti-pluralist bias.
Yes, you're probably right. But people should know that the whites involved in the Leadership Conference on Civil Rights are virtually all Jews. That still exists. And the Jews who are involved with these causes are also deeply involved in the Jewish community, so it shouldn't really be a secret. And I'm very pleased and very proud when I see that.

Would you want to say something about the Moral Majority?
In just a second. But it occurs to me that so far in this discussion I may have given the impression that I'm entirely naive, that I've seen no changes and that I see no problems, that there are no conflicts. I don't want to give that impression. There are indeed problem areas. And I don't even mean things like affirmative action, which are reflections of the problem and not the problem itself. The most basic problem is that over these last ten years the economy hasn't grown, and therefore it became so much more difficult for the minorities to make real progress, and there's been a competition for the opportunities there have been. And as the blacks became more confident and more assured in their racial identity, we also became more assertive of our Jewish identity. I'm not unaware of these basic trends and developments—but I do reject the notion that our agendas are that far apart, that our interests are so far apart, that our antagonisms are so great that we have to operate on the premise that black-Jewish cooperation is not possible any more. I reject that premise.

That's a helpful reminder. And now, the Moral Majority?
It's very difficult for the Jewish community to decide to what extent we have to modify our visceral reactions. I would hope that we can find a way to feel and to say that if the Moral Majority or other groups like that do in fact, for whatever reason that motivates them, have a position on Israel that's compatible with ours, that we say "glory be"—we're not going to reject their help. We'll welcome it, and commend them for having that view. But we ought also to note that they've come to that view not in order to do us a favor. It's their belief, and as long as it's compatible with us, fine. And in areas where we disagree, we would hope that they would not, as some people suggest, be tempted to change their own convictions on Israel because we disagree with them on prayers in the school or abortion rights or any other issues. And I would hope that individual Jews would continue to be able to express both of these attitudes.

I have no problem with those Jews or others who agree with the positions of the Moral Majority. I'm much less interested in discussing whether the Moral Majority has the right to do what it is doing than in discussing whether it is right in what it is advocating—and there, let's have honest and frank discussion about the issues. And on most of the issues, I think most Jews have some genuine disagreements. But over and above that, the principal problem that I find with the whole movement of militant evangelical advocacy is that, whether they mean it or not, and despite all their vehement protestations about not being anti-Semitic, they really are seeking a Christianization of America. And in that sense, they're anti-Jewish—not anti-Semitic in the traditional use of that word. When they say that Christian ideals are ipso facto American ideals, I think we've got to resist that, and I resent it. For them to say that there is a Christian test on the Panama Canal Treaty or SALT, there's an arrogance there that we've got an obligation to speak out against.

Generally, how would you summarize your reaction to the domestic policies of the new administration?
During these days and weeks of looking at the federal budget, I too make the usual comment first that I want to see an end to inflation, and I too think that government has gotten out of hand, and so forth, and I really do believe those things, but I must say that I am distressed at what I see, as the wholesale gutting of programs that will affect the opening up of opportunities for our disadvantaged, whether they be black or white or Jewish—and there are many more disadvantaged Jews than many of us realize. But I have as well a very personal reaction to these things. I have never, not for a single day, permitted myself to foget my beginnings. When I was going to City College in New York, after my first year, if I had not then gotten a fifteen dollar a month federal stipend for work in the library, I would have had to drop out of college. That provided me the carfare and the lunch money that I needed, because my family could not have given me even the carfare. That made the difference between an education and no education.

And I am arrogant enough and proud enough of my life to think that maybe I've paid the society back for its investment in me. So anytime I see programs that reduce the effort we finally started making in this country to open up opportunities for people, to help them through their difficulties, I have not only a general philosophical resistance to it, but also a very personal reaction. ✡

A MOMENT INTERVIEW WITH HELEN SUZMAN

In May 1977, an honorary Doctor of Laws degree was conferred upon Helen Suzman by William J. McGill, president of Columbia University. The degree citation expresses most eloquently the essence of this great human rights advocate who was in the U.S. in November on a speaking tour.

"Illustrious stateswoman and educator, born in South Africa, educated at Witwatersrand University where you later taught economics, you have been an exemplar in the endless struggle for human rights and social justice.

"As a member of South Africa's parliament and founder of the Progressive Party, you have seized every opportunity since 1953 to speak in support of your country's disfranchised non-white majority. It has been said that as a minority of one in the Parliament, you represent more South Africans than all the other members combined. You courageously opposed the sabotage act in 1962, condemned the government of Rhodesia when it unilaterally declared its independence from Great Britain and spoke out against restrictions on foreign newsmen in South Africa. You have supported your cause with the logic of your careful research at the Institute of Race Relations, where you showed that apartheid flew in the face of economic sense. You have never deviated from your goal of a multi-racial society.

"For your moral courage, your scholarship and your wisdom, Columbia University is honored to confer upon you the degree of Doctor of Laws, honoris causa."

As part of her lecture tour in this country, Mrs. Suzman spoke at the 92nd Street Y, participating in their series on Dissent. She also graciously visited MOMENT's offices where the exclusive interview which follows took place. We are proud to share it with our readers.

When we last spoke, back in 1973, you indicated that you were thinking of retiring. And here it is, 1980, and you're still very much at it.

I sing the same refrain before every election—and then, inevitably, something happens and I stay on. What happened in 1974 was that my party expanded from just one member of Parliament—myself—to seven, and then we picked up two more seats in the by-elections. And then the United Party split up, and we picked up much of their support, so that by the 1977 elections we became the official Opposition.

It's true that I've had enough. I've been in Parliament for 28 years now, and that is a very long time. But what I'm waiting for is someone who will show the same interest in the fields that I cover—and those are not very popular fields—such as prisons, police action, detainees. That sort of thing requires a great deal of attention and care, and you've got to be prepared to confront ministers. So when I find someone who can do this job really briskly, it will be easier for me to go.

How did you get started in politics?

It's really not a very interesting story. I've always had a thing about the injustices of the system. Let me assure you that I have no sentimentality about blacks. I'm not a bleeding heart liberal who goes around moaning about the noble savage and all that rubbish. I have black friends and we argue and fight just as fiercely as I do with my white friends.

But the injustices are so patently obvious to anybody who has the eyes to see, and it has always worried me. Actually, I was not at all interested in politics until quite late. While I was growing up, World War II was the issue. And, as a Jew, I was particularly worried about what was going to happen if Hitler were to win the war. My husband was in the army, and I had my two children during the war, and that was what concerned me at the time. The Smutz government was in power, and one hoped that after the war there would be liberating ideas in South Africa so far as color was concerned. All the indications were there.

And just before the war ended, I took up a lectureship at Witwatersrand, dealing with the economic history of South Africa. That was my field, and I was asked to prepare evidence for a government commission appointed by Smutz to investigate the laws applying to urban Africans. I did six months of intensive research on the subject, and by the time I was done I was so apalled by what I had learned—the handicaps on mobility, the restrictions on the right to live with one's family, all the aspects that affected the right of Africans to enter the modern industrial economy. And I thought to myself that I must get into politics and do something about this.

So I started by joining a branch of the United Party, and I went to Party congresses and moved resolutions, and while the Party was not a liberal party and Smutz was not a liberal man, there was still a certain sense of what was just and what was unjust, and Smutz knew that the post-war world would not put up with racialism and that some changes would have to be made in South Africa.

Well, Smutz accepted the recommendations of the report—but he was put out of power, just as Churchill was, and the new government came in and has been in power ever since.

By 1952, when we were preparing for the next elections, I was quite well known in the United Party. I had done a good deal of speaking for the Party. And I was asked to stand for election. At first I refused, because I had a job that I enjoyed at the University, and I had a husband and two children, who were then age 13 and 19, and a home in Johannesburg, and serving in Parliament in South Africa—Parliament meets in Capetown—means spending five or six months a thousand miles away from home.

But my husband insisted that I was crazy, that I had to stand. I've always had dark suspicions about his reasons, but what he said was that this is what I had stood for and worked for over a period of five years. And so I agreed to stand for Houghton, which is the seat I still represent. To my utter amazement—at the time, rather to my dismay as well—I won the nomination against the sitting member, who had held the seat for 14 years. I presume the constituents were aware that he didn't represent the liberal views they held. And I won the seat.

By the time of the next elections, I was unopposed both for the nomination and in the election. In the meantime, there was a great deal of turmoil in the United Party, and we broke from the Party in 1959 to form the Progressive Party because we wanted a party that would be unequivocally opposed to race discrimination of any kind on the statute books.

And then we had an unexpected election in 1961 because South Africa had become a Republic and had left the Commonwealth, and that's when my colleagues—there were twelve of us who left the United Party to form the Progressives—were defeated, and only one of us was returned to Parliament as an M.P., and that was me. And that situation continued until 1974. In my first campaign as a Progressive, I won by only 564 votes, but I've won by increasing majorities with every subsequent election, and in the last election, in 1977, I was unopposed. But it's quite a change now, after all those years of being the solitary member, to be one of the 16 members of the official Opposition. Sixteen out of 165; we're very small, but we are very vocal and very active.

Actually, when I used to sit alone, I had the government representatives opposite me and across from me and next to me and behind me, and then the United Party over on my right, and I was literally surrounded by these people. It's very unnerving to look around and see all these beady eyes fixed on you, looking at you with unmistakable hostility. But you get used to it.

And you've not been exactly shy about reciprocating the hostility.

Not at all. You must be referring to the time last year when, just after the information scandal, we were involved in a very late-night session, and I had already made my speech and I was sort of nodding off happily on my bench when I suddenly heard P.W. Boetha's rasping voice referring to me. "It is well known," he said, "that the honorable Member from Houghton does not like me." And I sat up with a start and said, "Like you? I can't stand you!" Just like that. It was a completely natural reaction.

He went on to give me the blazes because I was about to come over here and receive an award from the United Nations on Human Rights Day. I was off, he said, to receive an award from South Africa's worst enemies. And on the way home I realized that I should have said, right then, that Boetha had left us with no friends so we have to accept awards from our enemies.

No, the Prime Minister and I are not renowned for our friendly attitudes towards each other. It's quite mutual; he can't stand me, either. I believe he's a very limited and a very irritable and unpredictable man, and he's anything but liberal by conviction. He's been making these atypical noises about how we must "adapt or die," and has proposed that the Immorality Act should be amended, and the Mixed Marriages Act, but all that's not because these are his natural convictions. Instead, he's been persuaded that unless he makes some changes that indicate that reform is coming and that will give Africans a better life, we are going to have increasing confrontation. I think his army chiefs have persuaded him that it's very difficult to contain troubles on our borders, which stretch from the Atlantic to the Indian Ocean. There really is quite widespread unrest across the bottom part of Africa.

So he has in fact encouraged the changes which have come about, such as granting the urban blacks the right to a 99 year leasehold on their homes, which gives them a sense of permanency they did not have before. Until that change, the blacks were officially viewed as temporary sojourners, even though it was perfectly obvious to anyone who took the trouble to look that many of them were third-generation in the places they lived, that they were there to stay. And the government has also voted very much more money this year for black education and technical training, this because of the shortage of skilled workers which creates a real bottleneck in the economy. You can't run a modern industrial economy with four million whites and 23 or 24 million unskilled blacks. So they've started to admit blacks to registered trade unions, which allows them to take part in the machinery of collective bargaining and become skilled workers. And I believe that this will provide the blacks with the economic muscle they need to be able to make further demands for the extension of their political rights.

That, in fact, is why I am not in favor of divestment, of pressing American and other foreign companies to withdraw their investments from South Africa. I'm in favor of economic development, because it will force the country to draw the blacks into the skilled labor force. And that is actually what's happening now. Because of the increase in the price of gold, we've had a terrific rejuvenation. After the 1976 riots in Soweto, we had a recession, but now the economy is booming. We are awash with money, because of the price of gold and other minerals. And the blacks are becoming skilled workers.

This is a point we've been pressing for years, and now the government is catching on. If we wait long enough, they may even discover the law of supply and demand. It really is quite unbelievable to me that I now hear in Parliament from right wing nationalists the same speeches I made twenty years ago—you know, you've got to expand the economy and if a black man is able to rise up the economic ladder, that does not mean that a white man will have to lose his job. So now the right has picked this up as a way to assuage the fears of its own constituents about the reforms the government is introducing. Remarkable.

Isn't that the best path to reform, the best way to get more justice?

I'm all for it. I know that it's late, but it may not be too late. Everybody is always saying that it's only five minutes before midnight in South Africa. But the fact is that the hands never strike twelve. That's because power is held by a very determined minority, which has armed itself very efficiently, with all the military and the police. People here in the States talk glibly about a black revolution and things like that, but that reflects abysmal ignorance. South Africa is not Guinea. We are a heavily fortified and competent industrial state. And we are not Zimbabwe, with only a quarter of a million whites, and with no resources. And we are not Iran, where the army finally wouldn't shoot on its own people. Our army is white.

But if you're talking about gradual relaxation, primarily as a result of the absorption of blacks into the labor force, can you avoid the revolution of rising expectations and demands which is bound to result? Can you reform a little bit at a time without people coming to insist on a rapid acceleration in the pace of reform? If the Nationalists want to man the gates, and say that some gates can be entered, but others cannot be, are they realistic?

No, but they can hang on for a very long time. The point is that the whites are in power, and while the blacks can say—they do say—"We want more," the whites can say "Only so far, and no further," and they can make it stick. Oh, there will be an increase in urban violence, a bomb here, a derailed train there, that sort of thing. But that's not the bloodbath everybody is predicting.

Is there a likelihood of massive passive resistance, of strikes and so forth?

Well, you've got to organize things like that, and the leaders get picked up right away and put under banning orders, or they get detained without trial. Unless you've lived in a country without habeus corpus, without a bill of rights, it's very hard for you to understand what power the government has. Here you have to understand our peculiar condition: We have habeus corpus. If I were to steal a bicycle, I'd have to be produced in court and charged within 48 hours. But if the government suspects that I am inciting, or that I am a subversive, or just doesn't happen to like my political views for any reason at all, they could pick me up and detain me without trial, hold me in solitary confinement for an indefinite period with nobody at all having access to me—not the courts, not the judges, not anybody.

Well, the government obviously doesn't like your political views. Why don't they pick you up?

I have certain tacit protection. It's not written into the law, but I am a Member of Parliament, and I was elected by a white electorate, and that gives me certain status, certain protection. I've never been afraid they'd move against me. I've been saying these things for so many years that everybody must be used to them by now. And maybe they regard me as a kind of safety valve. Or maybe they see me as an exhibit for democracy. Or maybe they just don't take me seriously. Or maybe they don't want to make a martyr out of me—not that anybody thinks a flotilla of ships would come to my rescue, but there would be a bit of a fuss.

So you just work away, saying the things you say. It must be terribly frustrating.

No, it's less frustrating than it is plain hard. During all the years I was our only M.P., I had only one researcher and one secretary, and there were over a hundred bills that were put before us in every session, and I had to learn to be selective, I couldn't deal with every issue. So I stuck pretty much to matters dealing with race relations, with all the abrogations of the rule of law which were so numerous right through the 1960s, all the laws that were introduced that granted the government the right to ban people, to detain people without trial, to restrict people in all sorts of ways.

I can't say that I've got any fundamental amendments attached to these laws, but I think it was enormously important to keep the issues alive and not to allow them to go by default. On many of the issues, I was the only person who voted against. And I think I did something for the morale of the people outside Parliament who opposed the government. Please don't think that I was the only such person. I had the forum of Parliament to use, and I used it to the best of my ability, but there are many, many thousands of people in South Africa who hate the system of apartheid. And I'm not talking only about blacks, who hate it almost to a man. (When I say almost, I mean that there are always a few Uncle Toms around.) There are hundreds of thousands of whites who hate it, and they value a voice talking up and voting the way I did. So my work has had that effect. And the press was extremely good to me, because the English language press—except for the one English newspaper the government itself set up—is all anti-government, and I was saying things most of the editors felt should be said.

And I also believe that black people appreciated having a spokesman, even though they'd clearly have preferred to say these things for themselves in Parliament, which they are perfectly capable of doing—but which is forbidden to them.

And maybe, when it's all over, *après le deluge,* the fact that people were speaking up during these times, were resisting as far as they were able in non-violent ways, will make the transition easier.

And, quite frankly, there's another aspect of my work that is less visible, but that provides me with a certain satisfaction. I am, after all, a senior Member of Parliament, after 28 years, and that gives me tremendous access to the Ministers. So I can intercede—and I do, almost daily—on behalf of people who are disenfranchised or who, though they have the vote, cannot get to the Ministers. So people who are detained, or banned, people who cannot get passports, people who want to change their ethnic classification—all these are "my" cases. Last year, for example, a new piece of legislation was introduced laying down heavy penalties on employers who employ blacks "illegally" in urban areas. So the blacks were in danger of being dismissed. I managed to persuade the Minister in charge of these things to declare a three month moratorium during which the "illegals" could be registered as employees with their current employers, and 84,000 people were registered during the moratorium. It may be frustrating to be seen as the spokesman on black affairs when that agenda is so very long, but it also gives me the chance to make a difference for quite a number of people. Not enough of a difference, not enough people, not enough of a chance—but it does add up.

There has been a very dramatic relaxation in petty apartheid, hasn't there? I mean in that whole network of gratuitously discriminating laws that have no relationship to the grand scheme of separate development to which the Nationalists are committed.

Yes, to quite an astonishing degree. But the basic cornerstones of the policy remain intact, and I don't see any change in prospect. The race classification rules that designate your "group," the group areas laws which say where you can live and own property, the pass laws, and the sharing of power—there is no change in these. Within the framework of these fixed points, there has been and will be change. There is more money for education, and for housing and technical training and that sort of thing. Some of the change is more comprehensive, some of it is disappointing, but none of the change envisages the dismantling of the cornerstones.

Now, South Africa—white South

Africa—will have to come around to the idea of sharing power with blacks or there is going to be a steady increase in violence and ultimately a real confrontation. I don't think such a confrontation is around the corner, but we cannot refuse forever to share power. And the notion of genuinely separate development simply makes no sense. The country is economically intertwined, dependent on the mineral resources of one province and the agricultural produce of another. The reality of South Africa is that 80 percent of the population is black, and unless you're prepared to accept that reality and to deal with it and adapt to it, you're going to have increased violence.

Here in the States, you have about 20 million blacks and 200 million whites, so the situation is completely different. And yet you had quite a struggle here to get your civil rights laws passed, so you can imagine what it is like for us, where the whites are such a small minority.

Especially given the degree to which South African whites benefit from the huge black underclass.

Yes, the fact of cheap black labor is important. Yet I must tell you that these days, it's the employers—the industrial employers—who are anxious to push the blacks up the economic ladder. They feel that way out of enlightened self-interest, first because there is such a shortage of skilled labor that it's difficult for them to function, and then because they know that the whole consumer market depends on blacks being able to purchase consumer goods, and also because they don't like the monopoly the white trade unions have. That kind of monopoly is not good for productivity. So the old view that apartheid and cheap labor was in the interests of capitalists just doesn't hold any more. Our economy isn't based on mining and agriculture, where cheap labor was useful, in nearly the degree it was. It is now coming to depend on a stable and skilled labor force, and that must mean a stable and skilled black labor force.

It's all so paradoxical. The same country is part police state and part modern democracy. We do, after all, have a press which is strongly critical of the government, so we are not a police state in the usual sense, and we do have an Opposition and we do have free elections. In our country, the white electorate could put the government out of power. It won't, obviously, but in theory, it could, if enough whites felt that way. And we are part a modern industrial economy and part a third world country, because if you go and visit the Homelands or the Bantustans, as they used to be called, you would see a primitive agriculture and polygamy and customs which definitely don't go with a modern industrial country—and these are overpopulated areas, to boot, since we've set aside just 13 percent of the land for the blacks.

Aside from the industrialists you've referred to, is there any sign that more people are coming to your view?

Surely the increase in the strength of our party provides some indication of that. Although the new boundaries that have been drawn around parliamentary seats in the recent redistricting will hurt us quite badly. Still, we've not advocated the replacement of an all white government with an all black government. We hope for multi-racial government and we propose certain protections for minorities—a bill of rights, a minority veto in parliament and so forth. But all that would depend on a real consensus, and that means one must get together quickly with those blacks who have remained moderate. Otherwise, the confrontation is inevitable.

How do the Jews vote?

I can't say, but I would suppose that most of the Jews, a majority, vote for the Progressives. Altogether, we won about 16 percent of the total vote in the last election. But the Jewish aspect is a bit complex. Jews are much more sympathetic to the government nowadays because of the Israel-South Africa connection. The Jews of South Africa are keen Zionists, and the South African government has been generous in its dealings with Israel in regard to funds being allowed to go out despite exchange control, and in regard to the exchange of know-how and exports and so forth, and all that influences Jewish opinion. I rather doubt that all that has made it easier to lobby for Israel either in Washington or at the United Nations, but it certainly has made my job easier. I can't tell you how popular I was in Parliament after the Six Day War. Nationalists who had never greeted me before slapped me on the back and said, "Well done!" It was wonderful, getting all the credit for Israel's victory in the Six Day War, especially from people who used to interject in the middle of my speeches and shout, "Go back to Israel!" There used to be quite a bit of that. But now, of course, Israel is thought to be much too good for me, so they say, "Go back to Moscow!"

It's really very funny, since what it says is that anybody who believes in equal opportunities for black people must be a Communist. And the result is that they are building up grand propaganda for Communism in South Africa by identifying everything that's anti-apartheid with Communism. So naturally blacks are inclined to reckon that Communism is probably a good thing, and many of the younger blacks consider themselves Marxists. That's been helped along by what's happened on our borders, in Angola and Mozambique and Zimbabwe where the liberating forces from white minority rule have had Russian help.

The network of dissidents around the world is painfully small, isn't it?

I'm not in the same league with people like Sakharov and Timmerman. I don't say that with false modesty: I've never been under the kind of threat they've lived with, and I've not been imprisoned or restricted in any way. I have a passport, I travel, I talk, I say the same things here that I say at home. And the government knows it. I've no doubt that wherever I speak, somebody informs the government on what I've said: they have a whole network of informers. I mean, they even open my mail, which must be very boring for them. There's nothing in my mail they don't know about me already, at least as far as politics are concerned, and the rest is none of their damned business.

Does the Reagan victory mean much in South Africa?

I have no doubt the champagne corks were popping in Preatoria on the fourth of November, because the government considered the Carter administration very hostile. Too much emphasis on human rights, you know. And it's not just the government; there are many ordinary South Africans who are not necessarily supporters of the government who take the attitude that South Africa's domestic affairs are her own affairs, and they were pleased when Reagan came in.

But I think they're wrong. I wonder very much whether any government in America today, Reagan or any other, can afford to give the impression that it is pro-apartheid. I think there are considerations that must operate whether it's the Democrats or the Republicans who are in power. Your relationship with black Africa is one consideration. The black vote in the States is a second. There may well be a slackening of the opposition to South Africa, but there can't be much more than that. After all, we are the one country in the world where race discrimination is entrenched by statute. There is discrimination all over the world, and there's no doubt that America has applied a double standard in its pursuit of human rights, closing its eyes to human rights violations in China while attacking small countries you can afford to offend. But we are unique, and it's not merely expedient to oppose us; it's also just.

Thank you very much. ✦

A MOMENT INTERVIEW WITH IMMANUEL JAKOBOVITS, CHIEF RABBI OF ENGLAND

For openers, just what is a "chief rabbi"?

In Britain, this office goes back originally to 1696, with the rabbinate of the Great Synagogue in London, and assumed its present form with the appointment of Nathan Adler as Chief Rabbi in 1844. So it's a fairly old and well-established office. Out of it have grown virtually all the major institutions in the country, including the United Synagogue, Jews' College, the Board of Guardians (now called the Jewish Welfare Board) and many others.

It's a tradition so remote, so distant from anything we know in the States.

It's the States rather than Europe and other countries that represent the exception, because Chief Rabbinates today exist in France, in Holland, in Belgium, in virtually all European communities, as well as South Africa, and of course Israel. So that it is only in this hemisphere that Chief Rabbinates have not been established, other than in some South American countries.

In Britain, the office has a special character in that it wields greater authority over all other rabbinates. That is unique. For instance, no marriage can be performed at any of the 200-odd synagogues under my jurisdiction without an authorization being issued by my office. That is a legal requirement. No synagogue rabbi can perform a marriage without receiving such an authorization, just as he must have a civil license before he can register such a marriage.

The Chief Rabbi is also, by law, the Chairman of a Rabbinical Commission that endorses shochtim, and no one can practice ritual slaughter in the country without such authorization. All appointments of religious officials in congregations under the Chief Rabbi's jurisdiction require the Chief Rabbi's approval; he is nominally, therefore, the spiritual head of all these congregations. I have no synagogue of my own which would be my regular pulpit, though I have a seat in all synagogues and preach there on pastoral visits or other special occasions.

Now that is as far as constitutional, or official assignments, are concerned. But in effect, by virtue of the seniority of his office, the Chief Rabbi is the religious spokesman of the entire community and that would include even elements of the community that do not come under his jurisdiction, as far as representation or spokesmanship is concerned.

However, in my own case, none of these functions has the priority that education does. All my other work would be of little significance if I didn't insure that there was another generation of Jews to take over, and this can only be achieved by strengthening Jewish education. Therefore, over half my domestic time, I would say, is devoted to education. I founded the Jewish Educational Development Trust, which now for the first time attends to Jewish educational requirements, especially at school level, on a community-wide basis. We are now raising millions of pounds, for both new school construction, and extension of existing schools, and above all, for intensification of Jewish studies at these schools, by way of better teaching, teacher-training facilities, and so on.

Does that mean that all schools supported by the Trust must be Orthodox?

It so happens that in Britain, which is a predominantly traditional community, all day schools are Orthodox. Some are more intensive than others, but they are all Orthodox; they would all accept the religious orientation to which I subscribe, and therefore no problem at that level exists. We have now something like 25 percent of all our children of school age attending Jewish day schools, as compared with 16 percent when I took office 13 years ago. The schools range all the way from what we call Zionist day schools, but which are also religiously oriented, to Chassidic schools, like Lubavitch schools and other "right-wing" schools.

Moment/315

Does that increase in day-school population reflect growing dissatisfaction with the grammar schools, as it often does in the States?

Not to the same extent. It does reflect, I think, a growing fear by parents that if they lose their children as Jews, they're likely to lose them as human beings as well, because of vice, of the drug culture and of other forms of escape from the values that they cherish. But I think that the negative factor of the low level of education at the general schools is not the major motivation for parents to send their children to Jewish schools—although it is, of course, a factor. There is equally a desire by many parents today to give their children what they themselves missed out on, and while formerly parents thought of this only in material terms, wanting children to get the benefits that were denied to them when they were children, they now feel that not having had the advantage of a good Jewish education themselves, at least their children should.

If I can go back to the issue of the Chief Rabbinate for a moment, how does one come to be elected, appointed, named as Chief Rabbi, and how does one, if at all, come to be removed from the office?

There is a kind of College of Electors, made up of representatives of all the congregations in the United Kingdom as well as in Australia and New Zealand which recognize the jurisdiction of this office. As I said before, there are something like 200 in number, and their representatives then elect an executive that makes the choice, and eventually issues a call to the favored candidate. In my case, that call was unanimous. There was no contested election, although other candidates had been considered.

And is it an election for life, or is it periodically re-ratified?

It's virtually a life sentence. Until my predecessor, the late sainted Sir Israel Brody took office, it was a life appointment. Since his time, there is a retirement age of seventy, and he in fact retired at seventy, and I was the first Chief Rabbi ever to assume office in the lifetime of his predecessor.

Prior to this position, you were in the States for a while. Can you walk us through your own personal history?

Yes, sure. I have been around a little. I was born in Germany. I studied in England and held my first three positions in London until 1949, when I was called to assume the Chief Rabbinate of Ireland, in succession to Chief Rabbi Herzog, who had left thirteen years earlier to become Chief Rabbi of the Holy Land. I stayed in Ireland for ten years until 1958, then became the first rabbi of New York's Fifth Avenue Synagogue, was there for a further eight years, and then returned to London on my appointment as Chief Rabbi, assuming office exactly thirteen years ago.

Therefore, there are few people who could observe as precisely the differences between English Jewry and American Jewry. I'm wondering, in particular, to what degree the non-separation of Church and State in England affects the character and culture of the community?

Remarkably enough, although the bulk of Anglo-Jewry is made up of the same wave of immigrants from Eastern Europe as eventually reached the shores of America, the development of the two communities, across the Atlantic, and indeed the mentality that characterizes them, is entirely different. In the United States, when this wave arrived, they did not already find a community structure into which to integrate. As a result, the fragmentation was far too great to allow for any offices such as, for instance, a Chief Rabbinate or a United Synagogue, which is a very closely-knit synagogue organization, to be set up—or indeed even for a Board of Deputies, such as we have it. Whereas in England, that wave, although much larger than the number of native Anglo-Jews at the time, nevertheless completely integrated into the existing order, and eventually became part of it; by and large, all our institutions today are of 19th century origin. Now this has a bearing on the question that you put to me.

The British Jews—as indeed do European Jews generally—at all times accepted not only that they were a minority, but that all they were seeking was equality as individuals, and not equality as a group, or as a community. There's no British Jew in his senses who would take umbrage at the fact that the Queen is the Head of the Church of England, and that England is a Christian country. Hence, the British Jew feels that his struggle for emancipation, which was quite acute in the 19th century, when he sought the right to be elected to Parliament and other civil rights, is now behind him; as a result he feels completely at ease in his environment, and accepted by it, and able to make his due contribution to its advancement.

In America, I find the situation is different, because of this state-and-church issue. The American Jew wants to achieve something that is in a way unattainable—that he will be granted equal rights not only as an individual, but that as a group the Jews must also enjoy equality. He wants, whenever reference is made to priests and ministers, rabbis to be mentioned in the same breath, or churches and synagogues. But constituting less than three percent of the total society, it is not likely that he will ever achieve actual equal status with the remaining ninety-seven percent. And therefore there is a greater degree of self-consciousness about being Jewish in the United States than I find to exist in Britain. For instance, in any American election, if the candidate is Jewish, this will not only be known, but presumably be an election issue, whereas here in Britain, you would hardly know if a Jewish person stands for Parliament. Often neither his constituents, nor the rest of the Jewish community, would be aware of the fact, and it certainly wouldn't be an election issue. So that there is a greater degree of integration and acceptance because of the virtual absence of self-consciousness about being Jewish.

That's curious. One would suppose that a greater degree of integration and acceptance would lead to more assimilation. Yet you cite a statistic on day schools which is astonishing from the American perspective.

Well, I think it is *because* attention is no longer given to the struggle of emancipation, that Jews here were able to attend to the more important struggle for self-preservation. And of course England itself is a very traditional country, and this has both advantages and disadvantages in terms of Jewish vitality. It does make for a far greater sense of stability in Jewish life in Britain. For instance, we have over 60 percent of the total community affiliated with synagogues, and of that number, over 80 percent belong to Orthodox synagogues, which is quite exceptional, and probably has no parallel anywhere else. So it is a profoundly and staunchly traditional community, and I could give any number of criteria to bear this out—the number of households that would be strictly kosher, and so on. Hence, the traditional element is still fairly strong, though mainly by virtue of the momentum of the past. In that respect, tradition, the addiction to tradition, works in our favor. On the other hand, because it is a community with a long and venerable history, it tends to be backward-looking rather than forward-looking, so it is far less enterprising than American Jewry.

Also, we don't have the competitiveness of each congregation being a law to itself, having to assert itself, and so there isn't the same sense of rivalry that sparks the energies or the dynamics of progress. British Jews don't like innovation and experimentation. They prefer to take the tried paths of past experience rather than the uncertainties of unknown ways. And that, of course, makes for a certain resistance to the adjustments that are necessary in order to maintain the commitment of the rising generation. And that is one of my problems, because whenever I make a new suggestion, the first reaction is, we've managed for three hundred years, why rock the boat?

That sounds very much like the classic debate in industry between centralizers and decentralizers.

It probably has its parallels.

Is the British diffidence that is so striking to Americans manifested at all in the philanthropic endeavor of the community?

We probably cover a rather wider network of contributors than would be the case in America. But in our allocation of resources, Israel takes a far higher priority than it does for you. The main instrument of fund-raising, which is our JIA, unlike its counterpart in America, the UJA, does not include domestic causes at all, and therefore the main energies today, both in terms of manpower and in terms of motivation, are generated by Israel, which is by far the principal dynamic of Anglo-Jewish life. And Israel-oriented causes have also been able to mobilize by far the most dynamic human resources. Israel commands not just a special type of contributor, but a worker and a fund-raiser of a level and of an intensity probably far superior to what we're able to command in the spheres of, say, welfare, or synagogue administration. The quality of leadership there is superb.

That sounds familiar. Roughly, what does JIA raise annually?

The JIA raises something in the region of 15 million pounds sterling, which would correspond to some 35 million dollars. To this, you must add the numerous Israeli institutions that have their Friends working very actively in Britain—all the universities, most of the yeshivot, hospitals, and so on. So that the total amount raised for Israel is many times as high as what we raise for domestic requirements, even including education.

How many Jews are we talking about in total?

The present estimate is just over 400 thousand. These are informed guesses, because we have no absolute gauge for counting the number of Jews in Britain, but it is fairly reliable. The number is somewhat on the decline, for reasons, of course, that apply to virtually all other Jewish communities today, notably our unconscionably low Jewish birth rate.

I recall, to stay with the philanthropic endeavor for a moment, that you once observed that there are stylistic differences between American Jewish philanthropists and their English counterparts.

Well, that, again, is one of the characteristic contrasts between the Anglo-Jewish and the American Jewish mentality, and I think it reflects the attitudes of society at large. The American Jew is outgoing, he is an extrovert. He loves not only exposure, but often overexposure. In any public issue, he would like to see Jewish opinion presented on the front page of the New York *Times*, and rabbis and an assortment of other leaders would try and make sure that they so appear, whether the issue concerns Vietnam or civil rights, or Watergate, or anything that is on the public agenda.

In England, the attitude is the opposite, in that, if anything, they like underexposure, or the "typical British understatement." They're reticent and discreet, and they prefer *not* to obtrude onto the front pages of the newspapers or on the television screens. And this attitude also is reflected in philanthropy.

If a man in the States has 100 thousand, he would like to appear as if he had 200 thousand, and therefore buys a car which looks accordingly, and gives donations which make it appear as if he had 200 thousand. In Britain, he likes to understate his wealth, and therefore if he has the 100 thousand, he would like to appear as if he had 50 thousand. He runs a car which looks like a 50 thousand earnings car, and gives charity accordingly, too.

One of the two things that we look at with a measure of awe, and certainly with envy, is the existence in England of a national Jewish newspaper of some quality, which is something that our community does not have. How important is the *Chronicle*?

Well, that again of course is a reflection of the difference between the high degree of centralization in England and the fragmentation that obtains in America. *The Jewish Chronicle* is now the oldest Jewish newspaper in the world. It was founded in the year of the appointment of the first of the present series of Chief Rabbis, in 1844. And it exercises a very considerable influence, not so much I think by the opinions that it happens to represent editorially—as by the fact that you get a very balanced presentation of both domestic and world Jewish news, with special emphasis, of course, on events in Israel. And therefore, the average English Jew is far better informed about Jewish affairs than I find the average American Jew to be. And he can therefore form more solid opinions, make more mature judgments, and not jump to conclusions on the basis of facts and opinions conveyed to him in sheets that hardly merit the title "newspaper."

Do you find, speaking of that, that the quality of debate on Jewish matters in the United Kingdom is significantly different?

It is more mature. One must not of course forget that the system of government in Britain does not allow for the influence of lobbying in the same way as it does here, and therefore the function of the Jewish community in expressing its views on, say, notably Israel, or even Soviet Jewry, or other burning issues of the day, is quite different from what it is in the States. That influences the level of the debate as well. But, in terms of *issues* that are under discussion, both at the leadership level and at the ordinary lay level, the degree of seriousness, and of balanced judgment, and even of a willingness to listen to opinions that one doesn't share, is greater in Britain than it is in the States, where discussions are often far more superficial and slogan-ridden, and also more subject to whimsical changes. In other words, American opinion is more volatile. It can change from one extreme to another overnight by just one announcement or so, and it hasn't the same depth and validity as in England.

I have in mind in particular, of course, your own political statements. They have provoked considerable controversy in Israel, in England, and in the States. In your most recent statement you suggested that the silent majority of English Jewry shares your relatively dovish views on Israel. Do you have anything more than intuition to go on in making that claim?

Well, in England itself, of course, I get around. I mean, I meet literally thousands of people every week, because of my multifarious activities that take me up and down the country, and enable me to meet virtually every grouping within the Jewish community at least once a year, in one form or another. So I have plenty of opportunity for feedback, and also partly through the organization that I head, notably my colleagues, ministers with whom I meet, and who supply me with a certain amount of assessment of public opinion. The reactions to debates of any kind, as I said, vary greatly from country to country, and in this particular controversy I had this very dramatically illustrated to me. Our discussion in Britain, first of all, was fed by far more reliable information. I mean, in the States people discuss things that have never been said, and that don't even in the remotest represent my actual views, whereas in Britain, the reports were fairly accurate, and therefore at least the discussion is on what actually was said. Hence in Britain, by and large, deep as this controversy strikes into highly committed people on both sides, nevertheless it was conducted in a relatively low key, and opinions on either side found the fullest expressions; there was no attempt at *any* kind of intimidation, no effort to suppress the expression of opinions. Of course, some people question the wisdom of expressing any controversial opinions on these matters. I greatly respect their view, though again I cannot share it. But in the States, the entire debate takes place in a vacuum; when those who have expressed themselves publicly are challenged it turns out that they've not even read what I've actually stated, although my statements are available, and have been expressed and presented to the public in very, very full and comprehensive forms. But people don't bother to check their facts, or their allegations, and that is something that you wouldn't find on quite the same scale in Britain.

You said a few minutes ago that the fact of an MP's Jewishness is really coincidental, is not widely registered. When the community does seek to make its views not only known, but also felt, in the councils of government, is it not Jewish MP's, typically, who are asked to carry the ball?

Sometimes. We have something in the region of 40 Jewish MP's, and quite a number of them are very committed Zionists, and certainly belong to the Friends of Israel Parliamentary Committee, to which, of course, non-Jewish MP's also belong. But it would not be automatic that because an MP happens to be Jewish he would be expected to, or indeed would respond to an expectation that he support the cause of Israel. And therefore, while we do rely largely on Parliamentary friends to make their opinions felt, and give expression to them both inside and outside Parliament, we would not limit this to what you might term the "Jewish lobby." This would often include a very eloquent non-Jewish spokesman as well, who would speak on exactly the same level as his Jewish counterparts. But again, it is not by way of representations in the form that they are made in the States, because of the difference of the system of government, which in Britain is simply less amenable to lobbying pressure of this kind.

Presumably because the party is so very much stronger in England than in the States.

Exactly. Once you elect a party, they don't need every three weeks to take a straw vote on public opinion. They can carry on for the five years, more or less without constant reference to the changing fads of public opinion.

If I can shift now, for a moment, to the question of Orthodoxy and its future, let me ask you a purposely provocative question. In the 1960s, the common prediction was that Orthodoxy, faced with the temptations of secular culture, would continue to erode. There's a certain degree of surprise, certainly among the non-Orthodox, and I suspect among the Orthodox themselves, that here in 1980 Orthodoxy has not only held its own, but appears to be gaining strength and confidence and adherents. Nor does it seem, as one might think, that Orthodoxy had adapted to its secular environment; the fundamentalist religious sense appears intact. And that sense often correlates with a political fundamentalism. In that regard, specifically—take, for example, Gush Emunim in Israel, or the Jewish Defense League—is there, in your view, a necessary correlation between religious fundamentalism and fundamentalist—or reactionary—politics?

I don't think it is inherent at all. The resurgence of Orthodoxy is one of the most astounding phenomena of the post-war Jewish world. That is something that has been my major theme in various addresses and writings over at least the past 20 years or so. I think the significance of this phenomenon has been largely overlooked, or insufficiently recognized. To my mind, this resurgence will determine the entire shape and composition of the Jewish people in just one or two generations. We are now faced with an extraordinary form of polarization whereby vast numbers of Jews get lost and the overall demographic trends of our people indicate a minus-zero growth rate, by virtue of both a phenomenally low birth-rate and a startlingly high defection rate by assimilation and intermarriage. In other words, there is here a self-liquidating process, whereby the less committed are not just opting out, but are heading for disappearance, physically as well as otherwise.

But in the staunchly and intensely committed section of the community, the opposite factors operate—that is, an extraordinarily high birth-rate, and, virtually for the first time in our modern history, the almost non-existence of any drop-out rates, rates which were very significant until, say, 10 or 20 years ago. Orthodox parents then would usually have children who were less committed. Today, the children, by and large, are far more committed than their parents, and the grandchildren even more so. And this is quite an extraordinary phenomenon. It is partly, I think, a reaction to the Holocaust, which leads to disillusionment with the values of the secular society. Also, it reflects a surrender of the faith in the inevitable progress of man which was once so widely shared, notably in countries like Germany. That faith was shattered with the Holocaust. So Jews became more inward-looking, less concerned with the outside world, certainly less confident that if they only joined hands with the outside world, they'd become part of this inevitable progress towards the Utopia of human brotherhood that they were aiming for. And, in Jewish religious terms, this has been expressed by a return, by a search for roots and identification of the most committed sort.

Here there may be a point of contact with the fundamentalism to which you made reference, which of course also is an expression of a disdain for the outside world, an indifference to it. That disdain springs from similar factors, from an experience of a cruel world that, as it were, has betrayed not only its trust, but its debt to the Jewish people over the years. So there are extraneous factors here that have had something to do with this remarkable phenomenon of both religious resurgence, or Orthodox resurgence, and of a certain tendency within this resurgence towards what you might term "fundamentalism." But one should not forget that these represent fringe elements on the Orthodox horizon. The great bulk of the element that has now enjoyed such a remarkable comeback is made up of two major sections. One is what we loosely term the "Yeshiva" community, with its enormous and burgeoning, flourishing institutions in Israel and in America and in England and throughout the world. This is more or less a purely intellectual movement of *very* intensive studies, conducted often for periods of 10 years or so, full-time, on a scale certainly never seen before in the Western world. And there is the Chassidic community, which also has undergone a remarkable upswing. The phenomenon is all the more remarkable since both these worlds, the Yeshiva world and the Chassidic world, had been virtually destroyed in the Holocaust. While the rest of our people lost one-third of their number, *they* may have lost as much as 90 percent of their fortifications, of their institutions, of their sages, their leaders, and their heartland. This makes the upsurge of these elements all the more extraordinary. Now in these two elements the "fundamentalist" expression—certainly as far as its political form is concerned—is very, very minimal. Therefore the mainstream of the staunchly Orthodox element today I would still regard as being within, call it broadly, the moderate rather than the extremist camp.

My own sense is that the social

or ideological pendulum swings in rather wide arcs. It's never very easy to calibrate, and throughout the Jewish world today, most notably in Orthodox circles, but visibly in other quarters of the community as well, perhaps in a reaction to the earlier and somewhat naive secular messianism, there is a somewhat distorted emphasis on the "*im ein ani li mi li*" element of Jewish life—"if I am not for myself, who will be for me"—to the detriment of the commitment to the "*u'ch'sheani l'atzmi mah ani*" element—if I am only for myself, what am I?". It is as if, in correcting for the past mistake of over-universalism, we've over-corrected, moved to over-particularism. Is that a view that you share?

Yes, to some extent. And one of the themes that has run through my various presentations over the past three years has been not just my regret, but my criticism over the gradual loss of the universalist dimension, or the Prophetic dimension, in the contemporary presentation of Jewish values. I recognize that this is so while at the same time acknowledging that there are valid reasons for this being so; above all, as I said earlier, the disillusionment with a world that has betrayed us. The values in which we believed have been shown to be not only nonexistent, but in fact they have been replaced by a form of decadence and brutality that we hadn't suspected to exist in such a vicious form. So there are good reasons for opting out from our wider Prophetic assignment as a light unto the nations, for abandoning our sensitivity and responsibility to moral standards in the world at large, and eventually the brotherhood of man, in all its ramifications. I suspect that this can only be a passing phase, because it is clearly a distortion of the Jewish message. Eventually, we will have to recover our balance, come to terms with what clearly is an imperfect world, and perhaps feel all the more challenged to contribute towards its perfection, as we did in the past. But that this distortion is, at the moment, a fact of Jewish life, and one which I regret and seek to redress, I cannot deny.

It is almost as if we have created a generation of specialists. There are those who specialize in the defense of the Jews, devil-take-the hindmost, and others whose concern is with the wider society, the universalist values, and who ignore the importance of Jewish continuity. It's as if we assign different missions to different groups within the community, and that's not the way it was supposed to be.

This doesn't reflect a process of deliberate choice. Unhappily, those who look upon themselves as, in your words, specialists in the area of attending to the wider world-view, have very few Jewish insights and perceptions to offer to the betterment of the human order. In other words, the content of their assignment as Jews is not derived from their Jewish heritage, which is virtually unknown to them, but from the conglomerate of general values that they absorb in the course of their presumably rather shallow education. Therefore, by no stretch of the imagination do they in fact translate the accumulation of Jewish teachings and Jewish insights into the wider arena of the world experience today. When I read letters, say, of Jewish participation in debates on moral problems such as abortion or euthanasia, which happen to be areas of special interest to me, I find that those who participate on the universalist basis, on the general basis, have no Jewish insights or commitments to offer whatsoever. In fact, they are usually ignorant of the Jewish stand in these areas.

If I can shift for a moment to a somewhat related question having to do with Jewish pluralism, and specifically with religious pluralism, one of the problems that some of us have with the institutionalization of the Orthodox perspective in Israel is that it appears to give young Israelis an either/or choice. Either you do it our way, or you don't do it. I wonder, for example, whether the fact that such a large proportion of younger Israelis prefer to think of themselves as Israelis rather than as Jews, may not be because Orthodoxy asserts a monopoly on the meaning of the word Jew. Is that a proper concern, or is that a concern you share? How do you feel in general about the political role of the Orthodox movement in Israel?

It is my impression that any non-Orthodox form of religious commitment in Israel will never be indigenous there, because these are, after all, specifically "galut" manifestations of response to pressures that were unique to the Diaspora experience.

I mean, for instance, the Reform movement originally grew up in Germany, and later on in the United States, because of the need felt to adjust to external pressure for praying in the same language as did the others, of doing away with reference to our national restoration in Zion. These were all factors that could only be experienced in a Diaspora condition. And to some extent the same goes for the Conservative movement which to this day has remained more or less limited to the American scene. It doesn't exist in Britain, for instance, or in most other European, and other overseas, communities. So I cannot quite see that there is a vacuum to be filled in Israel by people in search of religious values and not finding them in Orthodoxy.

I do recognize that there is a vacuum, that Orthodoxy in Israel, for a variety of reasons, partly institutional, and partly intellectual and ideological, cannot meet the groping for spirituality and for religious bearings of an increasing number of young people who are disillusioned with the purely secularist sense of values in which they've been brought up. But I would imagine that if an answer is to be found for such people, it would eventually have to be an indigenous Israeli answer, probably finding expression by some broadening of the Orthodox message. Institutions such as Bar Ilan University which, after all, represented initially an element that was far off the mainstream of Orthodox life in Israel, and denounced as such, have a special role here. Look at the very significant growth of the so-called Baal T'shuvah movements, now commanding quite a variety of institutions specifically geared to people who are groping, who've had no Jewish background and seek a new form of commitment, based of course on Orthodox traditional values. These may, perhaps, eventually produce new nuances of orientation, such as we've seen in 19th century Germany with the rise of the so-called Neo-Orthodox movement of Samson Raphael Hirsch. So I do think that the present situation in Israel is far from fossilized; there is a certain mobility and dynamic in the present situation. But I cannot see that a purely alien import, not only alien in the sense that it happens to come from abroad, but that it is conditioned by circumstances abroad, is going to be the answer to this problem.

I'm struck by the fact that if you're correct, one would assume that the best political solution to the current controversy would be for the Orthodox to permit the Conservative and Reform movements their day, on the theory that they would then quickly simply crumble of their own lack of weight. Instead, Orthodoxy appears to be operating out of a sense of insecurity.

Well, de facto, this is already the case. There's nobody to prevent anyone from establishing a Conservative or Reform congregation in Israel. In fact, there are quite a number of them, but they're mostly for American Jews.

Let's assume that your predictions about the growing centrality of Orthodoxy, given the birthrate, given the very high morale of the Orthodox movement, are correct, and that within a generation or so, there is in effect a return to that time when there was no such thing as Orthodox Judaism, because the two words were synonymous.

It was the only expression of Judaism.

Exactly. Is Orthodoxy ready for that kind of power? Having lived for so many years now, in such critical years in our people's history, as one of a *group* of contending movements, is it ready for the grace that needs to attend power?

Well, only potentially so. I'm sure that it would require very major changes to condition the Orthodox community to assume reins of leadership that will govern the overall destiny of our people, inside and outside Israel. Partly this will require a great deal of work in the purely technical aspects of the Halachah. If we have to run a modern state, then obviously pioneering and research work will have to be done to see how the timeless principles of Jewish law can be applied to the timely conditions involved in the administration of a modern state. Much is being done on this, and considerable progress has been made, but the process would have to be greatly accelerated. And the same goes for every other area of the Orthodox experience—its relation to the thinking, the science and technology, indeed the culture of our age. But, of course, the fact is that until the last century that was the situation, and it was the authentic tradition, now called Orthodoxy, that in fact did insure Jewish continuity, and determined the destiny of our people. I once said that so long as rabbis were in control of the Jewish destiny, the one problem that Jews never faced, never even raised on their national agenda, was the problem of Jewish survival. And now that rabbis have surrendered the ultimate control of Jewish affairs to an assortment of politicians, communal "machers" and public relations experts, we, for the first time in our millenial history, are haunted by the threat to Jewish survival. This is an indication of what happens when the mystique of Judaism, and of the Jewish people, gives way to norms which are entirely alien to us.

I gather that your belief, based both on the empirical data and on your own ideological conviction, is that Jewish survival is not really in jeopardy.

Oh, I am absolutely convinced that we are the people of eternity, and will prevail over any future tribulations, as we've done in the past. To me, this is no problem. The question is not whether we will survive, but who and how many will survive. And this will depend on the degree to which we can try and recapture the masses of our young people to the thrills of Jewish learning and Jewish living. Hence my concern to devote the bulk of my interests and time to the promotion of intensive Jewish education. ✡

MOMENT INTERVIEW WITH ARIE ELIAV

REFLECTIONS OF ISRAEL'S LEADING DOVE

ON THE BEGIN GOVERNMENT AND THE AMERICAN JEWISH COMMUNITY

Moment: You are widely regarded as Israel's number one dove these days. Is that a lonely place to be?
Eliav: I'm used to it. I've been doing it for ten years, and I long ago decided that what I'm doing is good for Israel, and good for Zionism, and good for the Jewish people. Of course, there's a price to be paid. I could have sat back and said nothing, and stayed in a position of power under Golda Meir. I would have been the obvious pretender, since I came before Rabin and Peres in the Labor Party hierarchy. But power is not the most important thing in a man's life. I believe in something. And over the last ten years, the things I believe in have become increasingly important to us, and I am worried that more people didn't listen when I and others started saying them. Maybe our whole situation would be different today.

M: What was the process that led you to break with the establishment? How did it all start?
E: I was born in Russia, and I came to Israel, which was then Palestine, at the age of two. I was a very ardent Zionist, and so I convinced my parents to come with me. I grew up in Tel Aviv, and I joined the Haganah when I was very young. My generation was involved in a number of bloody skirmishes at an early age. I was fifteen when I joined the Haganah, back in 1937. Then I joined the British army, where I served from 1940 to 1945, fighting with the Jewish Brigade in Montgomery's army and ending up in Germany. After the war, I remained in Europe where I was one of the organizers of the illegal immigration efforts. I was the captain of some of the vessels that brought survivors of the Holocaust to Palestine. I was imprisoned on Cyprus a number of times, and on one of the boats I met my wife, who was a survivor of the Holocaust.

Then came the War of Independence, and I served in the Israeli army, and after the war I went into resettlement, into the planning and building of development towns and villages for Jewish immigrants from wherever they came. This was during the '50's. I was one of the original planners of the Lachish area, I was in charge of building Kiryat Gat, and then a very beautiful desert town called Arad. That was my baby. I had many babies. And then, in 1956, there was another war, and I volunteered to head a rescue mission to save the Jews in Port Said, behind enemy lines.

Later, in 1958, I was sent to Moscow, where I served for three years as First Secretary of the Israeli Embassy, and my mission then was to meet the Jews of the Soviet Union and to spread the word. It was quite an assignment, and when I came back, I wrote a book about the Soviet Jews.

A while later, I went into politics, and became the Secretary General of Mapai, which was, of course, the party in power. I was Golda's right-hand man when she was Prime Minister, and I served twice as a Deputy Minister in her government. In short, I really was a part of what you call "the establishment." But after the 1967 war, about 1969 or 1970, I began to develop my "dovish" policies, and I began a parting of the way with Golda Meir. It was simply a question of different ideologies. And I started a debate within the Labor Party, which became a struggle, until I couldn't stand it anymore, and finally broke from the party, after the Yom Kippur War.

You asked about loneliness? For the last three years, I've been in a kind of political wilderness. Until Sadat, the doves in Israel were very much in the closet. But not me. I was never in the closet. I ran for the Knesset three times on the Labor ticket. The fourth time I ran, I headed the ticket of the Israeli peace movement, Sheli, and we got two seats. Thirty thousand people voted us in. But obviously, I'm no longer close to where the decisions are made.

M: Who are the 30,000? What kinds of people?
E: Unfortunately, they are Israel's elite. They are intellectuals, the university professors, many of our young people. But they are not enough. The fact is that I'd much rather have 300,000 not so elite.

M: Any Arabs?
E: Yes, there are some, but we really got started too late to have a real movement among Israeli Arabs. Sheli was constituted as a peace movement only two months before the elections. Most Israeli Arabs voted either Communist—not because they are Communists but because they are nationalists, and that was the outlet for them—or according to their older patterns, for one of the traditional parties. Only a few voted for Sheli. Sheli was a new phenomenon, and now, if we want to get more of the Arab vote, we'll have to work for it, to explain our position. Actually, out of our 30,000 votes, about 4,000 were from Israeli Arabs—which is roughly in the same proportion as their numbers in the general population.

M: What's the core of the Sheli position?
E: I think you have to start at the beginning. The Palestinian problem is the central problem of the entire conflict between us and the Arabs. And the recognition of its centrality was very late in coming. After the Six Day War, it was fashionable to say, "Let's not talk about it," as if by not talking about it the problem would go away. And I, and people like me—not too many—kept saying, "This is the central problem, and we cannot escape from it." The Palestinians are like our shadow, like our Siamese twin. And this was the first issue where I had great differences with Golda. She and the others kept insisting that the problem simply did not exist.

My colleagues and I, on the other hand, set about to diagnose the malaise which is the source of the Middle East problem in terms of two national liberation movements. One is the Jewish, the Zionist movement, which claims the whole of Eretz Yisrael. We say that from a historical point of view, from a moral point of view, the whole of the Land of the Bible—Israel, the West Bank, the Gaza Strip, even parts that are today Jordan—all of it is ours. But there is another national movement, the movement of the Palestinian Arabs, and they claim the same land. We say that we have historical rights, and they say that they have historical rights. We say that it is the land of our fathers, and they say that it is the land of their fathers.

So where my colleagues and I stand is that we say, "Yes, we have a right to it, but so do they." And the minute we said "so do they," we became doves.

Now you must understand that the Israeli peace movement and the dovish phenomenon there has nothing in common with the doves in America ten years ago. The war in Vietnam was not a life-or-death issue in America, 10,000 miles away. There is not a single dove in Israel who does not believe that war is vital. All the people who head the list of doves in Israel have impeccable military careers, and none of us is ashamed of that. I don't say this by way of boasting! I am just trying to explain that we are not far away from the issues of war and peace. In fact, if anything, the doves want a stronger Israel.

But the doves also want to find a compromise. And if you start from the position that we have rights and they have rights, then the solution comes by itself. You must halve the loaf. We won't get it all, neither will they. And in supporting that kind of solution, we believe that we follow in the footsteps of Jewish thinking, of Zionist thinking, of Jewish moralist teaching. You can halve a *tallit*, a piece of cloth, you can go to a judge and he can tell you to halve a room or a house. Land is not a baby; a baby you cannot cut in half. But land? Territory? Why not?

So our theoretical solution is that Israel should have made a declara-

Photographs by Michael Fein

tion of principle ten years ago, after 1967, saying we know that this is a major problem, and the way to solve it is to halve the loaf, meaning that we are prepared to recognize the Palestinian right to self-determination in the West Bank and Gaza, and to permit the Palestinians to determine for themselves whether they are going to link up with Jordan, and what the nature of the link will be. That part of it is their business. But in return, we require true peace. And there are some pre-conditions. First, we need some moderate Palestinians with whom to negotiate. Second, they must understand that their concern for sovereignty is matched by our concern for security. So they can have, they should have, border police, maybe even light infantry, but they cannot have, in this new entity, any heavy armaments. It should be demilitarized.

Now this has been our concept for ten years. Today, I don't think there's a person in his senses who says that the Palestinian problem does not exist. Many more people today realize that is it *the* issue, and that we'll not solve our problems here until this issue is settled. It's not only a political problem, an international problem, a military problem. It's more than that. It's also a social and moral problem, because if we don't solve it, our whole society will change.

Imagine what it would mean if we were to continue indefinitely, or for a very long time, the occupation, this rule over more than a million people whom we have now ruled for ten years. Our society is already changing because of it. Three million people ruling over another million? It deforms our whole body politic. It's not that the Palestinians are slaves; there's no need to exaggerate the matter. But they are non-citizens. From their economic standpoint, the situation is not bad. But from our standpoint, it is very dangerous. This is not what Zionism is about. This whole thing is an anti-Zionist phenomenon, and eventually it will erode our very core. And that's another reason we have to find a solution.

We won't find it tomorrow, we'll not find partners on their side tomorrow, but one way or another, we must find a solution.

M: What about the Begin self-rule proposal?
E: It may be a step forward for Begin, but in political reality it's a non-starter. A national movement, and the Palestinians are a national movement, as we are, has as its goal a nation, a state. They want a government, they want a parliament, they want freedom of assembly, they want flags and coins and medals, they want everything the Zionists want. And when people ask me what's so important about a flag and a passport, I tell them this is why my parents brought me here, to have a flag and a passport. And these things they, too, should get. Otherwise, they will not acquiesce. And our only pre-condition should be our own security.

M: But that's where the argument starts, isn't it? Many people acknowledge the social issue, the moral issue—but on security grounds, refuse to accept the prospect of Palestinian self-determination.
E: We think we have an answer for that. Security will come about as a result of demilitarization, with inspection, and with international guarantees, and with American guarantees, and with a very strong Israeli army. With all of these in place, I'm ready to take the chance. Because otherwise, there is no solution at all.

M: What about the settlements issue? Just now, this seems to be the major stumbling block. Why do you think the Begin government has taken the position it has?
E: Well, this, too, is a complicated issue. Let's talk first about the general problem of the settlements in the occupied territories. I and my friends said, after the Six Day War, "Okay, now we have acquired these territories, on all fronts, after a great victory. Let's keep all these territories as a surety for peace. Let's sit there, with the army, with

tanks, with guns, and wait for moderate Arabs with whom we can talk about how to return them, eventually, for a full-fledged peace—and not for anything less. Let's not 'create new facts' in the meantime."

But, as in so many other things, the majority wouldn't listen, and Golda Meir's government began to create a whole new set of facts, with settlements on the Golan and on the West Bank.

Not too many settlements. Seventeen. But it became a symbolic issue. Now, to my mind, and for others who believe as I do, the security value of these settlements is zero, and sometimes subzero. They are a liability rather than an asset.

Take the Golan, for example. We must keep the Golan until there is a true peace. But we have to keep it militarily, with guns and with tanks. You can't keep it with civilian settlements, with kindergarten children. The Golan should be an open place so that the military can maneuver.

The same holds for the other places. Sinai should be secured with tanks. Civilian settlements don't enhance security one iota. Not a drop. The security value of the settlements is nil.

Some people say that these are sacred places, especially the West Bank—Judea and Samaria. But peace is even more sacred, and we shouldn't be making a mishmash there which will be impossible to untangle when we come to negotiate. And I'm afraid that's what's happening now.

Before Sadat came, and the negotiations began, the argument was "We don't have anyone to talk to on the other side, so why play chess with ourselves? Let's stay where we are." After we started negotiations with Sadat, I think it was simply uncivilized and indecent to create more settlements. I'm not talking about the existing settlements. Somehow or other, they must be negotiated. One day, if we have others to talk to, the settlements that exist in Sinai could be negotiated. Some could be dismantled. Some could be incorporated into Israel under the heading of minor mutual adjustments, and some might stay on under Egyptian sovereignty. These are relatively minor issues. But to build new ones once the negotiations have started? I said, in the Knesset, to Sharon—and he is the one in charge of them—that it is not only indecent, it's wrecking the whole peace process.

So why did the Begin government do it? First of all, I think that Begin was not the master of his own house. I'm not sure that he agreed to all the settlements—which still doesn't justify them. But we have a situation where the Prime Minister cannot put his foot down.

Second, there is the Begin of 40 years of an ideology which says that we have to annex everything. It's only now, after Sadat, that he has some new concepts. Before that, he wouldn't even talk about it.

And third, I think the main reason was that a group of right-wingers, from outside and inside the government, headed by Gush Emunim—Sharon being the spearhead inside the government—are doing these things which should not be done. I think they should stop—immediately—the creation of any new settlements while the negotiations are taking place. The word *sensitive* is inbred in the process of negotiation. So we have to declare, loud and clear, that while negotiations are taking place, no more settlements.

M: How would you assess the role of the Labor party on this issue? Is there an opposition in the Knesset?
E: Labor is simply not playing a big role now. They have yet to recover from their defeat. They are bad losers; they begrudge. I applauded Begin when I thought he was going in the right direction. Labor is divided in its own midst between hawks and doves. There is no longer a common denominator. When they led the government, the common denominator was power, but there is no longer a common ideology, and they don't have recognized leadership. All in all, after

Arie Eliav

a year of being out of power, they haven't learned very much. They haven't yet taken on the proper role of the opposition.

M: What about Begin himself? As you pointed out, at the beginning, following the Sadat initiative, he seemed to be headed toward some movement in his personal philosophy.
E: He definitely was. Especially at the time of the Sadat visit, and then for a short while afterward, he surprised even people like me with his flexibility, and we gave him credit. And we, who had always been diametrically opposed to him, came to the Knesset and we said, "Go ahead. Do it. And we'll help you." And, in a round-about way, we did help him. Maybe too much so. There were some cartoons and jokes in the press that said he was really a Sheli man, but that years ago we planted him in Likud so that when he became Prime Minister, he'd come out of hiding.

But he's definitely made changes, and I think it's good, because it shows that the man is not all that rigid. Yet that only lasted for a very short period. After a while, the whole thing got sour. And one of the reasons it got sour was over the settlements. I don't have enough strong words to denounce it. It is really a minor thing, in itself, but it is a great irritant. We shouldn't have done it. And the other problem was that President Sadat became impatient. Maybe because of the great thing he did, he wanted quick results. But he shouldn't have expected quick results, either from Begin or from me. Even with Sinai, which is a very large peninsula and the largest military base in the Middle East, there has to be a process of negotiation. To demilitarize, to hand it back to the Egyptians, just like that? People are not all for it. It takes time, and patience. General has to sit with general. And a dovish Prime Minister would do the same thing.

So, Sadat became impatient, and the whole thing began to go sour. We had our share in it, and they had their share. Begin now has to change more. His positions before Sadat were non-starters. After Sadat's visit, he took two positions that could start the process. He said we would give back Sinai, for true peace, and that on the self-rule issue, we would be more forthcoming. I think he understands it. Whether he'll do it or not, I don't know. What he did after Sadat gives me hope that if he is persuaded by the administration here, by legislators and by American Jews who should be more forthcoming and outspoken, he can be more flexible. I think he has quite a lot of leeway within Israeli public opinion. He has a clear majority to pursue the road to peace. And American Jews should now play a much greater role in telling Begin what they think. I've now been here three weeks, and I think I know what the leadership of the American Jewish community thinks. So they should tell it to him.

M: What is it that you're hearing from the leadership of the Jewish community here?
E: I have a good sample. Not all of it, but there is no doubt that continued support of Israel is very strong. American Jews want the community of Israel to flourish, to be strong socially and economically and militarily. All this we know, and it's good. But most of the leaders I've spoken with in the American Jewish community cannot understand the current Israel policy in general, do not know where Israel is headed, and in particular, they cannot understand the position on the whole settlement issue. They don't understand it, they cannot justify it, and they cannot defend it. And I think that what they told me, they should tell Begin in so many words. This is what they told me, one after another, *in camera*. It's time for them to come out, and speak up. Because to my mind, they're doing harm to their own cause and to Israel if they don't say, "This cannot be done. It's not sensible. It's not defensible to the general public in America or in Congress or anywhere." And I think this will make

Begin more realistic. You have to know the facts of life.

M: So you're saying that many of the leaders you've talked to are agreeing with your position, even if only in private. But what about their constituencies? Did you get similar expressions from the community in general?
E: Well, I think that a great leader molds the constituency, not the other way around. I only had a small sample this time. A synagogue here, a temple there. And I saw a small number that showed me that the constituency is also confused. Maybe there are some die-hards among the right-wing here, or in some very Orthodox groups, or other very conservative ones. But on the whole the constituents are as bewildered as the leaders. They don't swallow the settlement position at all. And I think the test of leadership will be if they are willing to tell their constituencies. It's a two-way process, of course.

M: What do you think it will take for the leadership to speak out?
E: Courage. Some courage. Begin won't eat them for breakfast. I'm not telling them to dictate to him—God forbid. Just to tell him their views. I didn't come here to convince people. They told me, and you can quote it. Many of them said, "Are you meshugah? Is Israel getting meshugah?" And if they said that to me, they should say it to the Prime Minister.

M: The basic fear, I think, is that any kind of public questioning will erode support for Israel.
E: It's the other way around, to my mind. Support is being eroded anyway. Non-Jewish legislators understand the policies even less than Jews. So the erosion is there. And you can only stop it, to my mind, by telling Israel's leaders that we'll continue to support you; on the issue of selling arms, we are with you; on the issue of maintaining the balance of power, we are with you; about keeping Israel strong, we'll be with you. But, there are certain things that make your position, and our position as American Jews, unbearable. And the more so because the settlement issue, I am convinced, is a minor issue. It is an issue where there are some crazy elements, and the American Jewish community is supposed to be, on the whole, liberal and open-minded and tolerant. Why should they stand to attention and defend the policies of some nit-wit generals?

M: But American Jews continue to go to Israel to visit, and they talk to people, and they come back and say, "The people of Israel are behind Begin 100 percent." These are bright people, who visit often, well-connected in the Jewish community here. Who are they talking to?
E: First of all, it's not 100 percent. Yes, the majority of people are behind Begin. But they are behind a Begin who will be flexible. I supported Begin in the Knesset as a dove. But the ones who are opposing Begin now are the zealots who are doing the settlements, and Begin is a prisoner in his own house, to his own, old ideologies, and to extremists to his right. So people here should help him to unshackle himself. People should be behind a Begin who will bring Israel to peace, not behind a Begin who will bring a collapse of the talks.

M: Do you see this kind of public stance coming from American Jewish leadership in the near future?
E: You know, in these things you have to have the first one or two or three courageous leaders who are willing to speak out, come what may. They have to be willing to say, "What I want is for the good of Israel." People whose records are impeccable must stand up and say, "This is what I have to say about *this* issue. Not about all the issues in Israel, but about certain issues." I wouldn't suggest they speak this way if I hadn't heard from so many of them that this is how they feel. Why should we in Israel be expected to be the only courageous Jews? Let the American Jews also be courageous. We need that. ✦

The last aristocrat, Dr. Nahum Goldmann, is President of the World Jewish Congress, and was chief architect of the German reparations agreements. He was the founder, and for eight years the first president, of the Conference of Presidents of Major Jewish Organizations. At the age of 82, he is one of the preeminent Jewish leaders of the century. The following is extracted from an exclusive MOMENT interview with Dr. Goldmann. Photographed by Bill Aron.

You say that American Jewish life is governed by the very wealthy, that intellectuals are not adequately involved. Isn't that the way the Israelis have wanted it? Doesn't that make it easier for them?

You touch on a very delicate problem, but since I am now out of the competition—anyway, I never paid much attention to public opinion or to reactions to what I said—I can speak frankly. I've written a book which hasn't appeared yet in English. In French, it's called *Où Va Israël?* Where is Israel going? And in that book I say that two things went wrong. It's not Ben-Gurion's fault, with all the mistakes he made, nor is it Golda's or the others'. Two things happened that we simply never foresaw.

The one was the Holocaust. We thought we'd have millions of Jews as a reservoir, and then we'd never have had the problem of aliyah, which has brought us to a day when, in the United States, it seems there are more *shlichim* than there are *olim*.

And then the war with the Arabs. Who would ever have dreamt that Israel would begin with a war? I tried to prevent it; I suggested that the proclamation of independence be postponed. I was one of the great fighters for partition. Ben-Gurion, even though in his heart he was also for partition, couldn't say much—he was Chairman of the Agency, and he had to be careful. We foresaw that without partition, there would be one war, two wars, three wars, and the whole thing would be different. And that's what happened. Israel has to invest its main efforts in war, in the army, because first of all you have to survive. Otherwise you cannot create anything.

So things also went wrong with the Diaspora. Nietzsche said it: great victories are more dangerous to a people than great defeats. I think the victory in the Six-Day War was a catastrophe for Israel. When I said that after the war, I was almost crucified, but many people today agree. But even the first victory, in the War of Liberation, created a problem. For most people, it was a miracle.

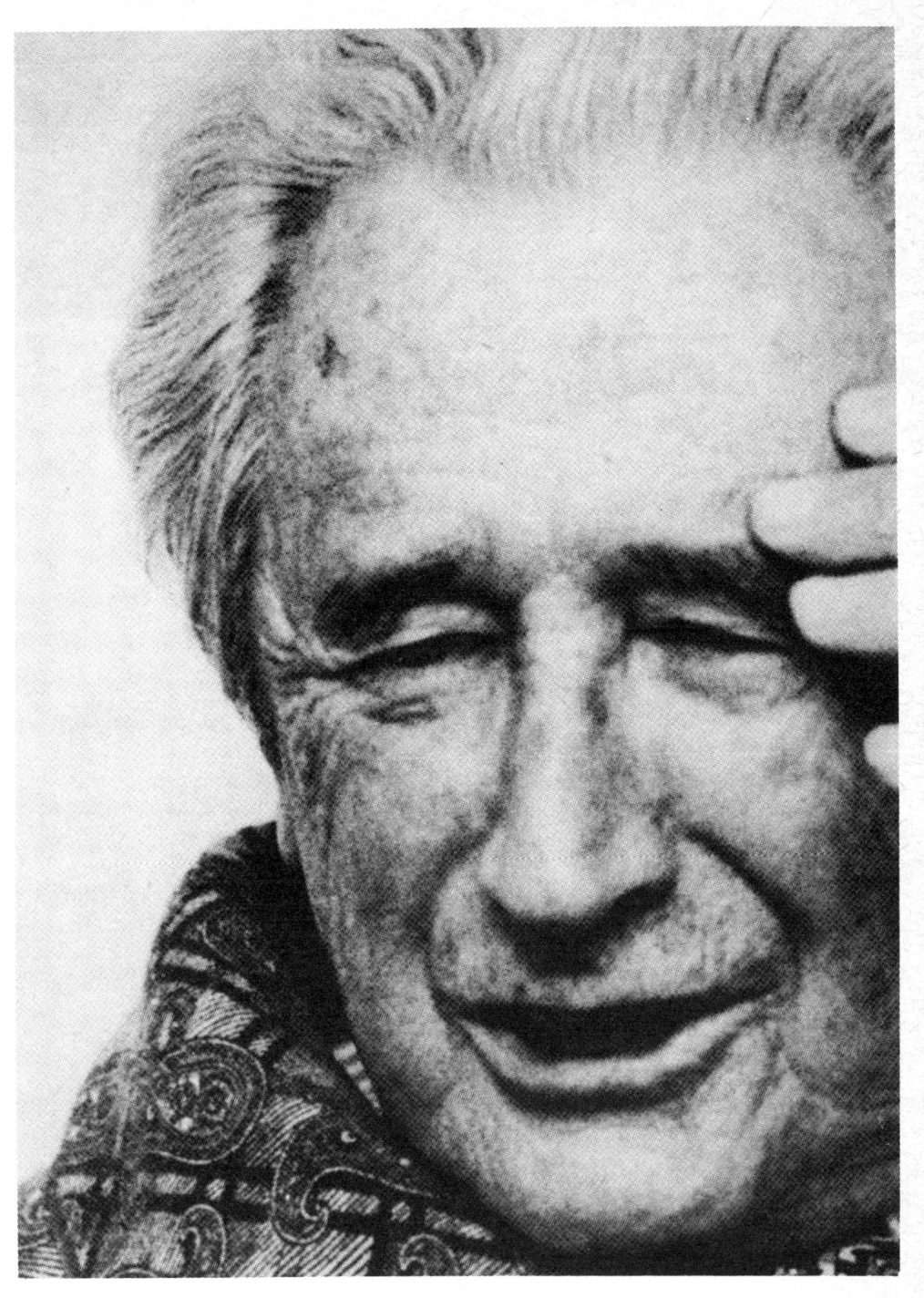

I believed in a state even before that war, and Ben-Gurion believed in it, but very few people believed in it. I remember my great friend, my greatest friend in America, [Rabbi] Stephen Wise. Just after the Second World War, I said to him, "I believe we shall have a Jewish state." And he began to cry, and he said, "Do you say that to comfort the people, or because you really believe in it?" And I said, "I believe in it, Stephen," and he wept. For him, it was a miracle. And miracles go to people's heads. So the Israelis, after the miracle, felt they didn't need the Diaspora. "Let them give us some money, and we will do everything."

That was Ben-Gurion's approach, too, until the last years of his life. In addition, he was a very strong personality. He didn't let the *Israelis* mix into policy; why should he allow the Diaspora to mix in? I used to say it often in his presence. He was the one great personality Israel created, with all his weaknesses—after all, a great man also has great weaknesses. And in his time, democracy in Israel was a joke—and he knew it. He used to say to me, "Nahum, your greatest sin is that you don't come to Israel and create a real opposition to me. Begin is a joke. If you come, I'll fight you to the death, and I expect to win, but win or not, we'll have democracy. Today there is no democracy. I do what I want." He knew it very well. And he was right, but I didn't go—because I knew I would lose. I am a man who hates parties. It is a weakness of mine. *Le Monde* once called me "*l'aristocrate du judaïsme mondial*," because they felt that by nature, I am not really a democrat. I am a democrat by conviction, not by nature.

So they felt they didn't need the Diaspora and wanted a certain kind of domination over it. This was never official, of course. But you know how it works—a *shammes* is always worse than a *gabbai*. The ambassadors are worse than the ministers, the consuls are worse than the ambassadors; the smaller the official, the greater his vanity, and when you told Ben-Gurion that the consul in Philadelphia or Atlanta was mixing in too much, there wasn't much he could do. He wasn't for such things, but he didn't really care that much about *galut* life.

And the Jews were so enthusiastic about this miracle that everything the state did was sacred, as it is even up to today. With all the mistakes and the corruption and the failures, whatever the state does is good; one is not supposed to criticize. And that is a disaster for the state. Intelligent Jews will not accept such blind obedience.

As long as Israel said, "The main thing is money—we don't need your advice, we don't need your intellectual cooperation, we can do everything, we know everything better—all we need is money," it was natural for the fund raising organization to become primary. When I tried to create an enlarged Jewish Agency, I wanted it to include the political organizations—the Committee, the Congress, and so on—and I failed. My friend [the late Jewish Agency Chairman Louis] Pincus did it the easy way: he went to the fundraisers and told them that they represented the Jewish people. But that won't go on for very long. I don't believe that all the welfare organizations and the religious denominations will accept that the chairman of the UJA is the chairman of the Agency, because they know that Israel is built not only by Jewish money.

So far, Israel has encouraged the emphasis on money, and of course that feeds the American tendency to have rich people play too much of a role. In Europe it is a little better. Not so much in France, because of the Rothschild tradition, which holds that every organization must be headed by a Rothschild. I told my old friend Guido Rothschild just a few weeks ago, "It's fortunate we have only three Rothschilds, because if we had eight, we'd have to create five more organizations to be headed by Rothschilds." But in England and in other countries, it's not just rich people who lead the community. There is a problem of leadership everywhere, but in America it's worse, because there is simply no other country where money plays such a role.

And Israel has encouraged it and will encourage it until there's peace. Generally, I'm afraid, as long as there's no peace in Israel, the main effort of Jewish life will be directed to helping Israel. I can understand that. I don't blame anyone. I myself have made hundreds of fund raising speeches. All the energies of the Jewish people, the great energies and the great resources, must today be concentrated on saving Israel and the Russian Jews. Perhaps it is wishful thinking, but I hope that if there should be peace, and we won't have to worry every day about Israel, other energies will be released for much more creative purposes. I understand why we concentrate on raising money and on political pressure; I don't say this critically. But these are unproductive directions.

Do you think, given the emphasis that's been placed on these things, that the American Jewish community could handle peace in the Middle East? Some people say that we couldn't function without the ever-present crisis that has become so familiar.

Well, I may say a word about this, too. It will probably not make me any more popular than I am with many of them. I really think that American Jews are wonderful for Israel; they have a generosity which no other community has. But politically, I think they have had a positive and a negative effect. On the whole, they are even more extreme than Israel's Jewry today. It's very easy for them. They don't go to war, they pay only with money.

I'll give you an example: I was lately at a meeting where we were considering a grant to WUJS, the Jewish student organization, and one of the people objected to the grant because, he said, "WUJS is ready to accept a Palestinian state." So I said, "My dear friend, what will you do when *Israel* will accept a Palestinian state. Will you stop giving money to Israel? We give 50 percent of our budget to Israeli institutions." He said, "Israel will accept such a thing?" And I said, "Sure. You will attack Israel, but they will accept it one day."

I can imagine that if America begins to pressure, or whatever you call it—it's all words—to bring about a settlement, with great concessions on the part of Israel, that many American Jews will fight the Israel government for agreeing. But I don't think it's of lasting importance—once Israel accepts, in three years American Jews will also be happy. But American Jewry politically, because its leadership is not in the hands of people who understand political science, or intellectuals, is generally very much inclined to demagoguery.

I know it, I was for 20 years one of the leaders of American Jewry; I was for eight years president of the Presidents' Conference; and Jews have no political experience. Political experience has to be learned. It took England a hundred, two hundred years to learn how to handle world politics. With Jews, it's still the first generation. The trouble with the Jewish people is—you know the old Lord Acton saying, "power corrupts"—it's worse still if a powerless people becomes powerful overnight. That's what happened to the Jews: Hitler, the climax of Jewish lack of power, and then, suddenly, a state, and power. You have to learn how to manage that.

When you come to this country, whom do you meet with?

When I come here I see my people of the World Jewish Congress, naturally. I see the leaders of the Conservative and Reform and Orthodox movements, I see regularly the Secretary of State. That was easy with Kissinger, who was an old friend. Before that I saw Dean Rusk, whom I hope to see again next week—he's still influential, close to Carter. So I see the Secretary of State, the Assistant Secretary of State, the head of the Middle East Desk, Atherton, Saunders. Then I always see Dobrynin, for hours. Then I like to see important journalists. I learn more from them than almost anyone—Kraft, Frankel, Brendan—first-class journalists. They know a lot; they have good judgment, too. That's really all. I don't see Arabs or others here—them I see in Europe, or I see the king of Morocco, I see Ceaucescu. It's really the Russians and the State Department, primarily.

When you meet with State Department people, how do they relate to you?

This is a personal relationship. My Israelis are sometimes angry. My way has always been to establish personal relationships. That's the trouble of Jewish diplomats to this day: they're interested only in their own problems. Let's say Adenauer. Erhardt once said to Adenauer when he was Vice-Chancellor, at a public reception, when Adenauer had just seen me and was saying very nice things about me, Erhardt said, "Mr. Chancellor, if I didn't know that you were such a religious and moral figure, I would be sure that Goldmann is your illegitimate son, you love him so much"—you know, you sometimes love illegitimate children more.

I have a knack to be very friendly. I am a great friend of Brandt, of Schmidt. I was a great friend of Sumner Wells. Not of Cordell Hull, who was an anti-Semite and a terrible guy. I was for years a friend of Dean Rusk, for twenty years. He was the head of the UN division when I represented the Agency; the whole discussion of partition was between the two of us. Kissinger is because of my son, who was his assistant.

So it's all personal relationships. And I never arrange the meetings through an organization; my son's office telephones, and they say that I will be here, can we arrange a meeting? I don't speak on official business, or as a representative of any organization. Or if I come to London, I see Wilson. Callaghan wants to meet me. I haven't seen him yet. I'm not keen on it. First of all I want a little bit to reduce my traveling, and second it begins to bore me, fifty years of diplomacy—but this was always the case with me.

That is what Jewish diplomats often lack. They concentrate everything on their own agenda. When I met Adenauer, I never talked agenda at the beginning; at the beginning I talked about music, religion, and then I began to talk about *tachlis*—a few hundred new millions and so on.

You say that's a problem of Jewish diplomats, but the fact is that outside the Israeli foreign service, you're the only Jewish diplomat there is.

Sure, and even in Israel, there are very few. It has to be learned, that's clear. The Jews are not by nature diplomats. Jews are a very stubborn people. First, they take themselves too seriously. I intend now to write a book on the philosophy of Jewish humor, with a hundred and fifty

Nahum Goldmann

Jewish stories as illustrations, where my theory is that Jews have been able to survive their seriousness—the chosen people, one God, everything else—only by their humor, by making fun of themselves. Otherwise they wouldn't have survived it psychologically. Jews take themselves too seriously, and are stubborn, and insist on every little point; and many I know, especially Americans, have a very poor impression of Israeli diplomats.

Rabin was a good ambassador. The best they had here was Yaacov Herzog. The State Department was enthusiastic about him. He was religious, he was very cultured, he was an extraordinary man. A pity that he died so young—if he hadn't been chief of Golda's cabinet he would have been alive today. He was an extraordinary fellow, one of my two or three closest friends. And Rabin wasn't bad. But in general they are too stiff, not sure of themselves, insist too much, fight for small things.

If you had accepted Ben-Gurion's offer way back, what would the opposition have been about?

First of all, real democracy. You know Ben-Gurion never made a constitution because it would have limited his power; he couldn't make a constitution based on dictatorship. Second, he had not only a theoretical pretext. He said a constitution would lead to a *kulturkampf* with the religious, and there was some truth in that. But the main thing was that he really didn't want it. So I would have fought for real democracy.

Second, I would have fought for a different and better relationship with the Arabs. I mean I don't want to boast, I cannot prove it, but I would have made peace ten or fifteen years ago. It's not that Ben-Gurion didn't want peace; he didn't want the conditions of peace. Naturally, everybody wants peace. The question is, what are you ready to pay for it?

I was the first to fight for partition. I was violently attacked, by [Abba Hillel] Silver, by [Emanuel] Neumann, even a part of Hadassah, whom I finally convinced. Ben-Gurion was for it, but he allowed me to do the fighting, because he was Chairman [of the Agency]. Sharett was for it, no question. I was convinced that the Russians would vote for a Jewish state. When Gromyko made his famous speech at the UN, Sharett was sitting next to me. He nearly fainted. I said, "Moshe, for years I've been telling you the Russians will be for a Jewish state, to get rid of the English."

The Russians in a certain way were fooled. I had discussions on the Jewish state with Litvinoff, Gromyko, ten or fifteen of them. They said, "Why should we be for a Jewish state? It's true we want to get rid of the British, but the Jews will be pro-Western; all the money will come from America." But I argued—this was before Auschwitz—"the manpower, which is not less important for a Jewish state, will come from the East, so Israel will have to be neutral, with people from the East and money from the West." And this convinced them. So when Israel became pro-Western, because the [Jews in the] East didn't exist any more, they felt they'd made a mistake.

Today they're not for the destruction of Israel. They honestly want Israel, because otherwise they're finished: all the Arabs would be pro-American.

When the Russians also voted for a Jewish state, the Arabs were in the same position that Israel is in today, except that today at least America is for Israel; at least she has one major supporter. And there was a hint—I got a message from the Egyptian embassy, not from the ambassador—that a secret meeting might be arranged between Sharett and me (we were the moderates) and Nokrashi Pasha, who was Farouk's foreign minister. Not to get them to agree to a Jewish state—this they wouldn't have done—but to prevent a war. And there were discussions, to meet in Malta, or Cyprus; and Truman was informed, and offered us his personal plane to fly. But the Executive of the Agency, under Silver—he had the majority, not me, and Rose Halpern, who was with me against Silver, was in this respect with Silver—voted it down.

So I sent Sharett to Israel. Sharett was a wonderful man, but not a strong man. I always said, "Moshe Sharett is the most first-rate second-rate man I ever met." He had no effect; he collapsed when people were mad. He was a man of wonderful character, decent; but he broke down when he came to Israel. When I came to Ben-Gurion four weeks later, I said, "*Gazlan!* Why didn't you postpone it for four weeks and give us a chance?" He said, "Look here, Nahum, you, sitting six thousand miles away in New York, could have a cool head. If you'd been here, with people fainting in the streets, dancing all night, crying, you'd have done the same."

I understand it. I have always said that psychology is much more important than ideology. If Marx had been a multi-millionaire he wouldn't have written

Das Kapital. And so we started with a war. I have been told by—I won't name them—people who were in Rhodes, at the time of the first armistice agreements, that with small concessions we could have had a real peace treaty. I can't judge that, because I wasn't there, but very serious people told me.

So a war, and another war, and another, and so on. I'll give you another example: after the Sinai Campaign, when Eisenhower agreed with Khrushchev regarding withdrawal, Ben-Gurion showed his greatness by changing his own policy in twenty-four hours. Nobody else, neither Rabin nor Golda, would have been able to do that, nor did they have the authority. So they withdrew, and Hammarskjöld wanted the border to be guaranteed by UN troops that could be called back only by the UN. So Nasser said, "All right, but then I want you to be on the Israeli side of the border as well as on my side, to be on their side for half a kilometer." But Ben-Gurion said, "That's out of the question. We are a sovereign state."

That was nonsense, the business of a sovereign state. Germany is also a sovereign state, and lives with occupation, and trembles that maybe, God forbid, the Americans will cease the occupation. Ben-Gurion simply wanted to have the right to march in when he wanted to. I knew the guy. He was the shrewdest politician there was—and a statesman, too.

So I came to Nasser—I was a mediator between Nasser and Ben-Gurion, who weren't on speaking terms—and he said, "All right, but if they're only on my side of the border, then I must have the right to recall them." And that's why the Six-Day War happened, because Bunche gave in to Nasser's demand which he shouldn't have done. Hammarskjöld would never have done it. Ben-Gurion always wanted to leave all his options open. And American Jewry supported him. So my main fight would have been on that. But I felt that I would lose the fight, because Ben-Gurion was much more a Jew. I always say I am a *goy*.

I was sitting once with my friend [Maurice] Couve de Murville, who is a very cultured man—not a great friend of Israel, pro-Arab, but very decent—so one day around the Six-Day War he said to me, "I know you don't like parties, and Israel is a small country while you are a citizen of the world, but you have to sacrifice, Nahum, you have to." So I said, "Look here, first of all Israel is a parliamentary democracy and I have no party. I once supported the Independent Liberals, but I never ran for the Knesset."

Begin once came to me and tried to make a coalition with me to bring down Mapai, where I would be number one and he would be number two. He's a very decent man, Begin,....

So I said, "Suppose they were to invite me as a foreign minister. I would resign in two months." So he said, "Why?" I said, "Because you may know that Israel is a Jewish state, and I am a *goy*." So he said, "*Qu'est-ce que c'est qu'un* goy?" So I said, "The fact that you don't know what *goy* means means that you are a super-*goy*." And I explained that what I meant was that I am not stubborn, I am not a fanatic, I am flexible, I understand the other fellow's point of view, I am tolerant, and that's not the Jewish character. So I would in two or three months get disgusted. They wouldn't give me full power. I would lose my position in the Diaspora and the possibility of working here. So what's the point? And I was right.

I'll tell you a nice story. It was during the Sinai Campaign, when Eisenhower and Dulles were threatening us with sanctions. Now, Ben-Gurion hated Hammarskjöld. He used to write open cables: "What does the Nazi want us to do now?" It was only later that they became friendly. Hammarskjöld was a close friend of mine; I was one of only eight people that he was *per du* with. He was a very complex man, not a homosexual as some people have said, but asexual, a very complex and interesting man.

One Sunday morning, at half past seven—I wasn't even dressed yet—my phone rings, and Hammarskjöld says, "Nahum, can you come over?" "Sunday morning?" I said. "Yes. I am alone in the office. I come every morning at seven and now I have time—the office is closed—and I want to talk fundamentally about the Arab-Israel problem."

So I got dressed, and I came over, and I tried to explain to him. "You must understand Jewish psychology. I am with you against Ben-Gurion on this issue, but you must understand: a persecuted people, that believes that every *goy* is an anti-Semite—and rightly so, after Auschwitz, after the way the democracies behaved—their experience is terrible, two thousand years of it. So give them some time. You say you are a better statesman than Ben-Gurion? What's the great achievement? It's clear—your father was prime minister, your grandfather was finance minister, you are the tenth generation of officials and ministers. Ben-Gurion's father? He was a little lawyer in a small town. Give them one or two generations and they will learn it, too."

I spoke, and he said, "Now I understand. But may I ask you a personal question? Sometimes when you leave me, after offering all kinds of compromise, I ask myself how come you are not at all Jewish? You are tolerant, understanding, are ready to make a compromise." I said, "There is only one explanation, Dag: probably one of my ancestors must have had an affair with a Hammarskjöld." So he blushed. He was very, very funny in these things.

And it's true. I wouldn't have won in Israel. And that's why I declined the invitation to be in the first cabinet. At that time it was an honor. Today it's not a great thing to be a Jewish minister in Israel, but the first after two thousand years? It took me two weeks, and then I felt I would be the opposition to Ben-Gurion, and I hate parties, I won't have the support of a party, he has Mapai, the strongest party at that time, and so I will waste my time.

I know my weakness; I am a very spoiled child. I never fought for any position. I never wanted to be president of the Zionist Organization—Ben-Gurion forced me into it, and I regret that I ever took it. The World Jewish Congress came by nature—forty years and I can't get rid of it. The Memorial Foundation? I established it and I am President until today. I am looking for a successor. My *yetzer hara* is very easily satisfied. It was satisfied in my youth already. I was a *wunderkind*. I made speeches at fifteen and sixteen. And from the *yetzer hatov* you don't go into politics.

When you say that you're a *goy*, is that true also at the cultural level?

Yes. I wouldn't say a world citizen, but I regularly, as far as I can, follow more or less the important productions of German, French, American literature. Hebrew a little less. I learned *Gemora* a little as a young man, but I couldn't learn today a *blat Gemora*. I know a bit of Jewish history, but I'm far from a scholar. I edited the *Encyclopaedia Judaica*, but I wasn't the scholarly editor. That was Klatzkin and Ellenbogen and so on, and now it's the people in Israel. So I am really a cosmopolitan.

And even if I could bring all the Jews to Israel, I would prevent it. Diaspora is more characteristic of the Jewish people than the state, but the normalization of Jewish life requires a state in the center and a big diaspora around the state. And our record in state building is not very great. The great eras of Jewish history were the prophets, and the Rambam, and Yochanan ben Zakai, not Bar Kochba, the Maccabees. All right, Masada is very nice, it's wonderful to write good books about, it's a very dramatic thing, but what maintained the Jewish people was not our performance in war or in state building.

To come back to the Arab question, it's part of the conventional wisdom these days that the early leaders of the Yishuv simply ignored the fact that there were Arabs to deal with. You remember the great statement, "A land without a people for a people without a land"—you were around in those days.... How do you remember them?

I didn't do enough. I try to be objective about myself—I don't belong to those who always think they're a hundred percent right. I once said to Golda, "The difference between us is that I never believe that I am a hundred percent right in anything, and you believe that you are, in everything."

When the Balfour Declaration was published, in 1917, I was twenty-two years old, and I wrote an article in a German-Jewish paper. As a matter of fact, I tried to find it recently, and it's not so easy—many archives were burned. I wrote then that the Balfour Declaration, given by the greatest empire in the world (England after the First World War was not England today; it was number one) was a great historical document. When the day comes that the Arabs give us a Balfour Declaration, it will be ten times more important.

So, I was attacked: a crazy, they said. Who are the Arabs? Just Bedouin. There was just one Arab state, Egypt, and Egypt did not want to be regarded as Arab. When I was at the League of Nations in Geneva, when I told them, "you are Arabs," they said, "No, we are not Arabs, we have a much older culture." And that's the truth; they have five thousand years of culture. So they said to me, "How can you compare the Bedouin to the world's greatest empire?" They were laughing at me.

So I always had this idea—it was my one consistent line—but I blame myself for not having fought for it enough. I didn't really have that much influence, either. It takes time to gain influence. I didn't do enough, even though I don't think I would have achieved it against Ben-Gurion. He was much stronger. We very often had talks until three in the morning. We were really close friends and close opponents. And he knew that I admired him, and he admired me for my courage in standing up to him.

Once he said, "I'll tell you, Nahum, why you cannot lead the state, despite all your great qualities. There were moments in the War of Liberation when I gave an order and I knew three hundred of our best young people would be killed that night, and you wouldn't have done it." So I said, "You are right, but I have a different advantage. I might have prevented the war more easily than you."

He had much more strength, specific gravity, than I. And you know he was in his heart...—it's worthwhile American Jews should know it—in his head he agreed with me. If I live long enough I may write a book, *Intelligence and Character in Statesmen*. Kissinger was ruined by his character despite the brilliance of his mind. I could prove it with many.

Same with Ben-Gurion. He knew better than I that without a settlement with the Arabs there cannot be a Jewish state. I was sitting once with him until three in the morning—it was a wonderful night—and Paula was sitting there, mixing in. He always said to me, "Paula is in love with you, not with me." Paula was my greatest *hasidah*. She once said, "Why didn't you ever try to flirt with me? I'm the only one who really loves you. I don't want anything from you, not to marry me, not to make love to me, not to take me on trips. I am your only real lover." So he said, "Tell her to go to bed—you tell her, she'll do it, me she doesn't listen to." So I told her, "Go, do me a favor, we have to have a very serious talk."

So it was about half past twelve, she went to bed, he made coffee and sandwiches, we were sitting in his kitchen, and we had a heart-to-heart talk. He said, "If you ask me why I want arms and strength, it's simple. Why should the Arabs make peace with us? Crazy? If I were an Arab, I would accept Israel? They have stolen our country. God promised us? What has that to do with the Arabs? What is it their business? Hitler? What's their responsibility? We came and stole their country. Why should they make peace." So I was shuddering, and I said, "How do you see the situation?" So he said, "I'll tell you."

I remember when it was, although usually I have no memory for dates, because he mentioned his seventieth birthday. He said, "I'll be, in two-three months, seventy. If you ask me if I will die and be buried in a Jewish state—I will live ten more years, maybe 15—I think yes. My son Amos will be fifty in October. If you ask me if he will die and be buried in a Jewish state, at best he has a fifty percent chance." I'll never forget it. So I said, "BG, how can you sleep at night being the Prime Minister with this prospect?" So he said, "Who told you I sleep at night?" You know he had a throat condition; every two hours he had to drink; he really never slept very long.

So why didn't he make peace? Because of his character. He wasn't a man who could make concessions, either to Jews or to Arabs. The best proof is—I said it once in the Actions Committee in a eulogy—that when he was no longer Prime Minister, he was for retreat, for giving back everything—except Jerusalem, which I wouldn't give, either. He wanted Eshkol to do what he couldn't bring himself to do. His character prevented him from doing what his intelligence told he him he had to do. Now I didn't have this character, so it was easier for me.

How much of Israel's abandonment by the world is realpolitik and how much of that is residual anti-Semitism?

I don't think it is because of anti-Semitism. I think it is Arab oil, it is for many the recognition that the Palestinians deserve a part of the country, and it is the anger at Jewish stubbornness, that whatever they grab they don't want to return. Anti-Semitism plays a minor role. Even with the Russians. The Russians are not anti-Semites. They may become anti-Semites if this goes on, this violent campaign against them. A man like Dobrynin, a man with whom I am friends, tells me often, "I call together my whole staff every two or three months and warn them against becoming anti-Semitic" because of the yelling, the picketing, the scandals and so on, Kahane and all that. And in Russia there is growing anti-Semitism. If God forbid détente fails in a cold war, I tremble for the future of the Russian Jews. I hope that détente will go on, but that's another story.

I'll end with a nice story, on Carter's fight for human rights. Brandt was here, and he is a good friend, and then he came to Paris and I had him and Mendès-France in my home in Paris, and he said, "Well, Carter's fight for human rights is wonderful and so on, but whenever I think about this I am reminded of a story which Goldmann told me.

"A tank commander in Israel was instructing his troops and said to them, 'Imagine you are in a war; you fall into a trap with the Egyptians; from all sides bullets. What do you do, Moishe?' Moishe said, 'I immediately lie down in the valley so the bullets shouldn't hit me.' So the commander said, 'Yes, but what will happen to the tank? That's not a very good answer. What will *you* do, Chaim?' 'I will tell you the truth,' answered Chaim, 'I am married and I have five children, so to hell with the tank. I jump down, crawl under the tank and save my life.' So the commander said, 'That's very irresponsible. Yosel, what about you?' And Yosel answered, 'I'll give full gas, blink to the right and go to the left.'" That's human rights—human rights is one thing, détente is another.

Part VI

The Editor's Pen: Leonard Fein

IN THE WAKE OF PEACE

LEONARD FEIN

It has come time to search for an idea that will help us to understand ourselves, to be ourselves. This essay is offered as an introduction to that search. It tries to explain why the search is necessary now, and to propose a framework for its pursuit.

I know that prayers are not meant to be taken literally. Still, after all these years of reciting "Grant us peace, Thy most precious gift," there was a part of me that expected a UPS delivery, a package wrapped and ribboned. A small package: peace is an exquisite gift, no larger than a gem. And though infinitely soft, as perfectly shaped.

Actually, I don't know much about peace. Not counting Vietnam, where peace was the name given to getting it over with at last, the times I remember are the surrenders: MacArthur on the *Missouri*, General Jodl at Reims. The peace treaties got signed much later, almost as afterthoughts. (It was only this week that China and Japan signed the peace treaty marking the end of their war, which stopped being fought thirty-plus years ago.)

And as to peace in the Middle East, peace for Israel at last, I know even less. There is no memory of non-war to fall back on, no time of plowshares and pruning hooks to remember. All my life, the Jews have been a beleaguered people, and all its life, Israel a threatened state. I gave my first formal speech on Israel's behalf in 1955, and adjusting for change in the details, I've been giving the same speech ever since: Israel is beseiged, the innocent victim of mindless hostility, of primitive enmity. Israel deserves better. Some day, things will get better. In the meantime, it needs our support, our love, our money, our understanding.

The truth is, now that I stop to think about it, that I never expected to have to change that speech. "Some day" meant always a time closer to the end of days than to this day. Even when I have been most critical of one or another aspect of Israel's own policy, I have known that the bottom line remains Arab perversity, an intractable which could accommodate interruptions to the fighting but not to the core hatred. You learn to live with it, as you learn to live with any malady that's chronic. And you take as your job seeing to it that "chronic" doesn't mean "fatal."

You learn to live with it because you can't really flesh out the picture of its alternative, or any way of getting from here to that alternative. And you even develop a certain style, a talent for living with it gracefully, the way some people with chronic lung disease manage to cough where the punctuation marks belong. You notice it only when the coughing stops.

And now, ladies and gentlemen, it's time for peace. Maybe they'll sign the thing at the foot of Mt. Sinai, although I expect (and hope) that the rumor they will is just a reporter's fantasy. Maybe they'll sign it in Washington, maybe in Oslo. Maybe they'll sign it this month, maybe not until next year, but they'll sign it, because now that we know it's a possibility, there's no going back. (Well, not quite. The language of peace is still less familiar than the language of war, and if the thing were to fall apart now, we'd revert to the old language with ease and even a measure of relief, having been spared the burden of learning a new language.)

So, peace. The entrepreneurs are already busy, planning Tel Aviv-Cairo excursions. The lunkheads of the Right are busy denouncing the agreement as a ruse, a sell-out, a prelude to disaster. The lunkheads of the Left are busy denouncing the agreement as an imperialist ploy that leaves the basic problem unresolved. And the rest of us are still holding our breath, trying to figure out what it may come to mean.

It is already clear that it will not mean, not for a while, a total reversal in every aspect of Israel's life. Terrorism will continue. Weighty foreign policy debates, focused especially on the West

Bank problem, will continue. Massive military expenditures will continue. There will be no sudden stomach cramps, for we shall emerge from the depths in stages. Nonetheless, it is time to craft a new speech, which means a new way of thinking, not only about Israel and its neighbors but also about the Jewish condition itself.

For as long as we can remember—since the year 70 anyway—we have lived with the knowledge that disaster was imminent. That has been a central element in the self-understanding of the Jew, that is a large part of what we have meant by the term "the Jewish condition." Each year, at Pesach time, we have read the *V'hi She'Amdah*—"It was not merely one enemy who rose up to destroy us; on the contrary, in every generation, 'they' rise up and seek to destroy us." "They," of course will not disappear with the signing of peace, for "they" include the Soviet brutes, the PLO, the anti-Semites everywhere. It is not yet time to rewrite the Hagaddah.

But it is time to think about a Jewish life whose central metaphor is something different from disaster. It is time to begin the task of shaping a Jewish life that is more than a response to threat. For more than thirty years, the best evidence of the Jewish peril has been the fury of the Arab hostility to Israel, a fury far beyond the logic of international conflict. "We will drive them into the sea," and all that. But now the most consequential exhibit on the table of evidence is in the process of being withdrawn. The peril continues, but it is considerably mitigated; more important still, there is now the seed of reason to believe that peril is not our permanent condition. It has lasted two millennia, to be sure, and it may continue for a time. But we can no longer assume that it is a fixed condition of Jewish existence. Accordingly, it can no longer be taken as the central metaphor of Jewish self-understanding.

With what, then, shall we replace it? And with what shall we replace all the network of activities and understandings which derive from it?

Consider: Ask a Jew to remember the high points of Jewish life over the course of the last decade or so, and he will first say "1967," meaning thereby just six days of that year. He will talk of the Yom Kippur War, of Munich and of Entebbe. Closer to home, he will recall Skokie, "Holocaust," Shcharansky, the Zionism-as-racism resolution, Jews in trouble, always in trouble. And the trouble becomes the source of our inspiration: "in spite of everything," "against despair," "survival." And watch the marginal Jews, those who don't belong, who don't work, who don't give. How is it that we know them as Jews? Because they, too, tremble in times of terror.

Have we not, all of us, ourselves debated whether Jews could survive without oppression? And left the question hanging, knowing that it was wholly hypothetical?

Yes, it is still hypothetical. Shcharansky languishes, trouble in Argentina, trouble in Uruguay, trouble in Ethiopia, trouble in a dozen different places that year, in a dozen new ones next. Trouble, still, in the West Bank. Trouble enough to spare, trouble to last the rest of our lives. Trouble, the Jewish connection.

But less acute. Aches and pains, not mortal threats. So let us begin to ask what the glue that will take us to the year 2000 will be, what new connection there can be.

Israel. Obviously, Israel should and almost surely will continue to matter greatly, deeply. Yet there will be dislocations if and as the sense of chronic crisis passes. In the past, the level of our Israel-directed philanthropy has mushroomed in time of active war, shrunk in time of relative quiet. Nor is it only our giving that has been affected by Israel's clear and present danger; it is also our understanding of the basis of our partnership with Israel. The recession of that danger will inevitably leave a void. If all's well, why care? Why give? Why go?

The immediate temptation will be to answer these questions by arguing that the crisis is not, in fact, over. If the guns fall silent, we will look for other elements of crisis; one does not give up a central metaphor so quickly. And if we look hard enough, we will find evidence; there is always enough to satisfy the pessimists and paranoiacs and those who would exploit pessimism and paranoia.

But the answer that may, in time, emerge, is that it is not Israel's peril that engages our attention and our energy; it is Israel's promise.

For what is this Promising Land about? Israel is the Jewish people's collective effort to demonstrate that, left to our own devices, we can create meaning and decency and law and justice where there was, as there is everywhere, futility and ugliness and chaos and evil. Israel's most dramatic challenges, its most exciting years, lie in its future, not in its past, however heroic that past has been.

Nor are these merely phrases to take heart from. There is a vision that has inspired our people since its inception. It has inspired some—very few—of our people all of the time, but it has inspired all of our people some of the time. It is a vision of how things are supposed to be, in a world made right, in a world that works. The State of Israel is the principal arena for the translation of that vision into a present reality.

That does not mean that all Israelis are soon to become holy men and women, any more than all have been heroes in Israel's wars. But as the Israelis have risen to the occasion when the occasion called for excellence at warmaking, so—perhaps—will they rise to the more constructive occasion that now begins.

It will not be easy. The temptations lie in other directions. From 1967 to 1973, years when national attentions might have been turned to the quality of public life, most of Israel's energies, public and private, were being invested in aping the least appealing aspects of American lifestyles. Barbecue pits and swimming pools are as enticing a substitute for meaning in Ashkelon as they are in Orlando. Nor

> Whether our response is born of commandment or of culture, it is the fact of our response that bridges all the gaps and all the ideologies, that gives meaning to the term "Jewish people."

is it seemly for those of us who eat, swim and are merry in all the Orlandos to sneer at those who yearn for pits and for pools in all the Ashkelons. We shall have to repress the urge to ask of the Israelis that they continue to compensate us for our own sense of deficiency, that they be our surrogates in peace as they have been in war. In war, they were our heroes while we prepared balance sheets, and we found ourselves walking with a touch of swagger. Shall we now demand that they be our paragons while we mix drinks, warmed by the delicious tingle of vicarious virtue?

No, what we must hope for and help with is not any more than we are prepared to ask of ourselves: a stumbling search for something better, for meaning beyond making it. And what we are entitled to expect is very sometime success, for the effort to craft a nation-state that brings out the best in people, that translates prophetic vision into workaday behavior is improbably ambitious. That effort will require—and deserve our material and moral support for decades to come. It will also require and deserve our continuing critical appraisal, and, if the partnership is working right, that appraisal will be welcome, so long as it is offered with sensitivity, with modesty, with full awareness that when those who eat from the flesh-pots preach ascetic virtues to those who still eat crusts, their advices are suspect.

Many American Jews, of course, will ask for less. They will want only that Israel's hotels should be comfortable, the waiters efficient, the beaches well-maintained.

But whatever our hopes and our entitlements, whatever the balance between virtue and venality, it is not likely that an Israel that gropes its way toward decency can excite our imagination as has the Israel whose very survival was at stake. Cannon and gore are more riveting than slum clearance projects, than medical insurance programs, than modest acts of kindness. It will take our best effort to resist a falling away, an erosion of the connection, as war is replaced by welfare. With wisdom and work, *we shall remain powerfully connected to Israel, but we shall no longer be able to look to Israel to provide our connection to one another.* Israel as the common denominator of Jewish identity, the one glue that binds all Jews, will fade as the guns fall silent.

That is bound to confuse those who know no other connection to Jews. But, on balance, it may not be a bad or unhealthy thing. Israel was meant to be a place, a cause, an opportunity—not a theology. In the inevitable post-Auschwitz confusion about Jewish theology, Israel neatly took up the ideological slack. But it would have been wrong, it is wrong, to see Zionism as Torah, to see devotion to Israel as a fully adequate expression of Judaic conviction and intention. Necessary, yes; but not sufficient.

God. What then of God, the traditional connector, the nominator and denominator of the Jews? Can we look to a renewal of religious sensibility and, more important, of religious conviction, to a restoration of God and Torah as the core elements in Jewish identity?

There are some signs that we can, even now. The astonishing staying power of Orthodox Judaism, and its apparent increased appeal to those who had been thought immune to such appear—both in Israel and in the United States—suggests the possibility. Moreover, we are approaching the year 2000, and it is almost certain that millennial fantasies will seize the imagination of vast numbers of people, Jews and non-Jews. As consciousness of the approach of so auspicious a time grows, so will religious strivings, especially among the hitherto untempled. At the very least, there will be a sharpening of the debate—quite likely, an increase in its nastiness—between those who contend that there is but One Way and those who cannot or will not walk that way. The problem for those who reject the One Way is that will no longer have Israel to fall back on as evidence of their Jewish connection and commitment. And the question then becomes, having lost Israel, will they find God, or will they lose Judaism?

Or stake out some new path for themselves. That, too, is a possibility. We have never been an especially theological people. Our concerns have centered not on the properties of God, but on the condition of His world. Obviously, very many Jews have responded to that concern, have devoted large parts of their lives to the repair of His world, our world. They have done so under noble banners: civil rights, science and medicine, socialism, civil liberties, liberal reform, the arts, law, a hundred others. It is impossible to conceive what America would be like today had not Jews devoted themselves with such enthusiasm to its betterment; clearly, the Jewish contribution has been a major shaping element, the Jews who have made that contribution an ongoing lobby for humaneness.

In the Wake of Peace

Yet few of the reformist banners are inscribed with the Magen David. Insofar as Jews have chosen to pursue justice, they have—in the main—marched in a polyglot parade. We may believe about them, they may even know about themselves, that they would not have marched at all had they not been Jews; the statistics of Jewish participation certainly so indicate. But having chosen to march, they have made common cause, and properly, with all those others who have, for other reasons, chosen the same path. There is no Jewish monopoly on decency. Therefore, even were there now to be a swelling of the ranks, a rebirth of civic commitment, a resurgence of liberalism, and even if the Jews were to emerge from their decade of hibernation and re-involve themselves in such matters, beneficial fall-out to the Jewish collectivity would not necessarily ensue. On the contrary: insofar as Jews choose to act out their parochial motives in universal arenas, they tend to wander away from their roots. You don't have to be Jewish to love justice. And, loving justice, pursuing it, Judaism becomes less a motive force than a residual category, a way of organizing the calendar and the lifecycle, but not the day, not the life.

Back, then, to God. But not really God, to Torah. To study, to commandments, to daily devotion to ritual behavior. If Zionism, narrowly defined (the creation of a Jewish State) is now less compelling, and if secularism, broadly defined (saran wrap, napalm, but also open heart surgery) is now more problematic, and if neither provides adequate glue, why resist the motive and the method that has informed most Jews since the first?

Primarily because God-as-Glue is a *consequence* of belief, not a *reason* to believe. God is not a name you give to Jewish identity. It stands history, logic and theology on its head to argue, "I want to be Jewish, therefore I will believe in God." That is not a belief, that is a make-belief. God is a premise, not a conclusion. If the premise comes to be widely shared, yes, it provides cohesion as well. But you don't, can't and shouldn't come at all those who suffer from breach of premise with the argument that God is necessary if we are to make it as a cohesive people. Not even if you accept the argument of those who insist that only the One Way will keep us alive. (Given the attitudes and behavior of the One Way exponents, we would soon enough become a cult rather than a people. That would resolve the problem of glue easily enough, but it would leave most of us unstuck.) In short, God—more broadly, religious conviction—may once again become the core of the Jewish self-understanding, but it cannot be forced into happening.

Stiff-neckedness. One of the primary reasons that the Jews have not folded their tents and gone away is because that is what they have been expected to do by those who have wished them ill. There is some cohesive power to stubbornness. Aerial bombing doesn't break the moral of the bombed, it raises their morale. But it is a tasteless source of cohesion, and one of limited utility as well. So long as we lived in a world where anti-Semitism was endemic, where there was no escaping it, perhaps the act of resisting it—that is, of staying Jewish—was a decisive and self-defining act. But we no longer live in such a world. There are escapes aplenty. Or do we really mean to argue to our youngsters that they should stay Jews because "it might happen here?" What kind of an answer is it to a child who asks "Why?" to respond "the Ku Klux Klan," or even "Shcharansky?" It is no answer at all. If it is an answer, if Judaism is a reaction to others' meanness, then those of us who care that the Jewish people lasts are bound to wish that meanness last as well. (Some of us come close to doing just that, sniffing everywhere for evidence of meanness, then, finding it, brandishing it with glee: "We told you so!" Some triumph.)

Ethnicity. How can we doubt the

Either we pursue justice, for ourselves and all others, *as* Jews, or we destroy our distinction. We are not Jews *and* human beings; we are Jews, and that is the way in which we choose to be human beings.

adhesive power of ethnicity when everyone is into roots, when the Lower East Side has become a piece of chic nostalgia, when every marginally Jewish college sophomore wants to take his Presbyterian girlfriend to meet his still-accented grandfather, knowing she will then invest him with a mystique that outdoes the most potent aphrodisiac? Jewishness is in, no?

Yes, but so what? A culture requires experience, not merely recollection. *A people requires ambition, not merely memories.*

Tikun Olam. Is there, then, no glue that can be prescribed?

To find the glue, we must move beyond dependence on events. We live in history, the secular unfolding of time. But we are informed by Revelation, which stands outside history. We study Revelation not as history nor as current events, but as the always Current Event. Hence we do not "study" Revelation, or even remember it; we experience it. The ancient midrash that holds that all Jews—the living, the dead, the still unborn, therefore we as well—were present at Sinai does not mean that we were there on that day, at that hour. It means that Sinai is here, on this day, at this hour, if we are open to it. And that is why what we have managed to accomplish, at our best, has been to link the sacred understanding to the secular unfolding.

It is that understanding which is required if the world is to be healed of its fractures. I do not know that the Jews are unique in their possession of the understanding. I hope we are not, even though I sometimes fancy that we have a special calling for it. But it is not necessary that we lay exclusive claim to that understanding in order for it to provide an entirely adequate foundation for Jewish identity, for Jewish consciousness, for Jewish connectedness. Tikun olam—the repair of the universe—is still the stuff that binds secularists, religionists, Zionists, all who would be thoughtful Jews. For in the end, it does not matter, not a whit, whether the Revelation happened; it matters only that it happens. Whether we respond to our calling because it was God who called us, or whether we respond because the work is so uplifting, or whether we respond because we know no other way, whether our response is born of commandment or of culture, it is the fact of our response that bridges all the gaps and all the ideologies, that gives meaning to the term "Jewish people," a people otherwise so diverse in its beliefs and its behaviors. And in all of secular time, there has been no more dependable vessel of concern for and commitment to the healing of this world than the Jewish people. There is no more certain way of transmitting that concern to our children than to make Jews of them.

Judaism is not a room where we meet to discuss Jewish interests. The world is not a place we enter only after having cleansed ourselves of our particularity. Either we pursue justice, for ourselves and for all others, *as* Jews, or we destroy our distinction—as well as our raison d'etre. We are not Jews *and* human beings; we are Jews, and that is the way in which we choose to be human beings.

We are Jews, and there are questions that cry for answers. It is the pursuit of the answers that warrants our survival. And it is the pursuit of the answers that creates the prospect for our survival.

What, for example, of the bioethical questions which now emerge? What of the right to life as opposed to the right to one's own body, what of euthanasia, what of DNA research, what of the distribution of medical care? And what, for example, of the family, of its sudden restructuring, what of loneliness and fear, what of disarray and of moral uncertainty? And what of old age and of inflation, and what of Jewish learning? What of racism and of quotas, what of worship and tradition, what of poverty and what of pollution? What of the Third World, what of Rhodesia, what of crime and what of prisons? What of taxes, what of gays, what of privacy and what of order?

What, in short, of a world we profess to care about, to whose repair we are called, we are pledged?

Are these questions less urgent than what the range of the next generation of missiles will be? Is the pursuit of their answers less exciting than reciting the Kaddish still again? Is the joy of our calling less cementing than the fear for our lives?

To these questions, different constellations of Jews will bring different kinds of answers, each drawing from its own experience and resources. In Israel, the answers will be offered by the agencies of the State as well as other groups. Here, the Orthodox will seek to apply answers from other times and other places, answers which may still illuminate. The secular liberals will bring answers from the hurly-burly of contending groups and the non-Orthodox religious will try to carve out a new Halachah, a code for themselves and for the rest of us. And periodically, we will all pause, together, and offer praise and thanksgiving, it mattering little whether we agree on the address, praise and thanksgiving that we see things as we do, that we are priviledged to care.

If those on the one side, who would cloister themselves in yeshivot and fight a rearguard action for Jewish survival, condemning all the rest of us for trafficking with heretics, or if those on the other side, who would throw themselves into the arena with no regard for whence they come, with no concern for the transmission of the tradition, for the structure and welfare of our community, if either of these were to "win," or if, as is more likely, they were both to "win," leaving us with an either-or choice—either Judaism or justice—our people will lose, be lost. There is no corner of the world where we can hide and stay a people. There is no need, on entering the world, to resign our peoplehood. We have been since our beginning, a people parochial in its structure, universal in its ideology and its concerns. Both the structure and the ideology merit attending.

By now, then, it will be clear that it does not matter very much whether the troubles will go away quite so quicky as we hope, or whether they will linger for generations more. The prospective treaty does not alter the character of the Covenant. *It never was the fear that brought us to this place; it was the pity.* We are *rachmanim b'nei rachmanim,* a people that cares, children of those who cared, and now, with wisdom, parents of those who are still needed, always will be, to care. It was not the terror that kept us together, but our messianic madness, our intoxication with justice, and with mercy. It was not the peril that made us cling to one another, but a shared vision, a vision seen too often through eyes abrim with tears. And if there will now be less reason to weep, then that vision may be seen—and reclaimed—more clearly, more resolutely, than ever.

VITAL SIGNS
LEONARD FEIN

Definition: A Jewish telegram is one which reads, "Start worrying. Letter follows."

I have told that story to Jewish audiences very many times. Each time, it works; people laugh in appreciative self-recognition. They understand the story: to be a Jew means to worry. We worry about Israel, we worry about intermarriage, we worry about our survival, we worry about anti-Semitism, we worry about Soviet Jews, we worry about Jewish identity. We worry about war, and we worry about peace. When the day is so glad that the poet announces, "All's right with the world," we know that something must be wrong; he has overlooked the cloud, the flaw, the imminent crisis. He has been lulled; the storm is brewing just out of sight, we can feel it in our ancient bones.

A sixth sense that can alert to danger is a very handy resource—unless it is so enlarged that it lacks all capacity to discriminate, unless it erodes the five fundamental senses. One who smells danger with every sniff does not have a super-sensitive nose; he is a nasal drip.

By any rational standard, the story of the Jewish people this past decade or so has been and continues to be a marvelous success story. We have endured diverse threats and assorted crises, and appear able—if not always willing—to deal sensibly with the problems we now face. Those problems—there are many of them—are interesting and challenging. But they are problems, not crises. They are the kinds of problems that all peoples have. They cannot be ignored, but they should not be exaggerated.

The Jewish success story. In the late 1950's and early 1960's, it was commonly supposed that the American Jewish community was doomed. Look Magazine had published its famous essay, "The Vanishing Jew," and new intermarriage statistics indicated that we were rapidly succumbing to the lure of assimilation. It was obvious that the native born generation which was soon to come of age was no match for the generation of immigrants that had shaped and directed the community since its inception; the new generation had neither the will nor the way to take over.

Elsewhere? Soviet Jewry languished. Even had there been a basis for confidence that the Jewish instinct remained intact among the Jews of the Soviet Union, it was perfectly clear that the Russians would not permit their Jews to leave. And Israel, of course, was surrounded by utterly implacable enemies; no comfort there. All in all, a bleak picture, amply reflected in the journals and symposia of the day.

And still reflected, in 1979, in our journals and symposia, despite dramatic change in our circumstances. Consider, for example, that between 1968 and the end of 1979, according to the best present estimates, some 225,000 Jews will have left the Soviet Union for freedom. That works out to about one of every twelve Soviet Jews. If the pessimist wants to insist that the glass of Soviet Jewish emigration is still more than ninety percent empty, he has the facts on his side. Nor can we be confident that this year's total of 50–60,000 emigrants will be permitted again next year. But is it not a signal success that we debate whether there will be "only" 25,000 or whether there will be 50,000 permitted out next year? Is it not a cause for jubilation that there are 225,000 out already? Ought we not be proud that our own persistent efforts, from noisy street demonstrations to sophisticated Washington lobbying to continued encouragement of the Soviet Jews themselves, those marvelously courageous people, have been so visibly rewarded?

Give us a silver lining, and we set off in search of the cloud: Too few of the Russian Jews are going to Israel, those that come here don't want to identify with the community, the costs of resettlement are astronomical. Worry, worry, worry. What can we, the tiny, oppressed, impotent Jewish people do?

Are we afraid that if we permit ourselves to admit that we have won a wonderful victory we will relax our

> As a people, we do not know how to deal with success: it is a stranger, and when it enters our home, we do not know its name.

effort and lose our will? That is part of it, no doubt. But the larger part is that we have had a sense of failure and foreboding bred into our bones. We do not know how to deal with success; it is a stranger, and when it enters our home, we do not know its name.

Consider: After thirty years of war and near-war and blind, stupid, murderous hostility, Israel's most potent Arab neighbor signs a peace treaty with Israel. Yes, the peace is fragile; yes, the problems that remain to be dealt with are far more complex than those that have been resolved; yes, the PLO persists; yes, the future is far from secure. But Egypt and Israel HAVE SIGNED A PEACE TREATY!

Our reaction is to schedule symposia on "The Crisis of Peace."

In Boston, a special committee was created after Camp David to prepare for a community-wide celebration of peace. Finally, after all the months of diplomatic bickering, the committee moved into high gear. A rally was planned for the day after the signing, a rally in downtown Boston, outside historic Faneuil Hall. Had the rally been called on the eve of war, with no time for planning or preparations, ten thousand Jews would surely have assembled. But to note the miracle of peace, after months of planning, we managed eight hundred—half of them bused in from our captive day schools.

Another day, another peace treaty? Not quite. It is not that we are jaded. And it is surely not that we are realistic; there is no realism in chronic, instinctive suspicion. It is, quite simply, that we have no ritual, no lively precedent for welcoming success. It does not suit our vale of tears. While we have no problem with success as individuals, as a community it is the bell of alarm rather than of jubilation that we have been taught to ring.

Consider: over the course of the past decade, leadership in every important arena of Jewish life and expression in this country has passed from the hands of the immigrant generation to the hands of the native born. The transfer has been accomplished with grace and with skill. It was a transfer that was thought unlikely: How could we expect the native born to care as deeply, to remember as lavishly, to sigh as profoundly as their parents? Yet it has happened, and there is no reason at all to believe that we are any the worse for it. On the contrary: In terms of professional competence, Judaic knowledge and commitment, or virtually any other relevant standard, the new leadership often represents an impressive advance.

Consider, too, the growing evidence that the dispersal of American Jews from the old cities of the Northeast to the sunbelt region, a dispersion which was once thought would lead inevitably to the disappearance of whole communities, has lead instead to the development of important new centers of Jewish life and activity. Think, for example, of Los Angeles. There was a time when it appeared that the Jews who flocked to Los Angeles were eager to find a city that matched their own rootlessness. Aside from Fairfax, home to the poor and the elderly, there was no such thing as a Jewish neighborhood in Los Angeles. And today? Today there are Orthodox, Conservative, and Reform seminaries in Los Angeles which, in selected areas, outshine their mother institutions back East; there are synagogues whose important innovations are attended nationwide; nowhere has the fight for Soviet Jewry been pursued as aggressively or as imaginatively; there is, in this community of nearly half a million Jews, an emerging Jewish life of quality and purpose.

Consider Jewish studies programs on dozens of campuses, consider the continuing philanthropy of the community, consider the increase in conversion to Judaism, consider the evidence that growing numbers of Jews have come to view Judaism not as a condition, but as an aspiration.

Yet note that none of this is mirrored in our self-image and self-understanding. Just the opposite: We continue to distort the information we are given, to squeeze it into the mold of failure we know so well. The most enduring illustration of that distortion is our response to the very interesting data we now have on intermarriage. Everyone "knows," of course, that intermarriage is a calamity, a calamity of epidemic proportions. It is, therefore, especially interesting—and instructive—to examine the statistical foundation for this perception.

We do not have precise data on the present rate of intermarriage. The best estimate we have derives from the National Jewish Population study, which found that in the period 1966–72, 32.7 percent of all new marriages involving at least one birthright Jew involved only one birthright Jew.

Now that seems a very cumbersome way to say that during those years, the intermarriage rate approached one-third. The reason for the cumbersome formulation, however, is that the intermarriage rate did *not,* in fact, approach one third. The statistic describes marriages rather than individuals, and a brief excursion into the difference will show how sloppy citation begets sloppy perception.

Imagine, for example, a hundred Jews who are about to be married. Fifty of them are men, and fifty of them are women. (Note, therefore, that the maximum number of Jewish-Jewish marriages these one hundred people could accomplish would be fifty.) Now imagine that ten of the men and ten of the women decide to marry people who were not born Jews. Twenty Jews, in all, marrying "out"; twenty Jews, twenty marriages. The remaining forty men and forty women do marry each other, and so produce forty Jewish-Jewish marriages. Thus we have forty endogamous marriages—born Jew to born Jew—and twenty "other" marriages. Forty to twenty; two-thirds to one-third.

That is the situation, roughly, which the National Jewish Population Study found. Accordingly, it is a mistake to say that one-third of the Jews prefer to marry non-Jews. That is simply not the case. Twenty out of one hundred is not one-third. The fact is that the "one-third rate of intermarriage" represents a condition in which four out of every five born Jews who get married choose a born Jew as their mate. And even if the statistic has grown from one-third to 40 percent since 1972, as some observers have suggested, we are still dealing with a condition in which three of every four Jews marry other Jews.

Moreover, the rate of conversion to Judaism has increased, and dramatically. That figure, in the context of intermarriage, now approaches one-third. Accordingly, if we go back to our hypothetical 100 people, and look at the twenty of them whose spouses were not born Jews, we find that about seven of those twenty marriages involve a conversion to Judaism. Those seven belong with the forty Jewish marriages, not with the twenty intermarriages—and that gives us a total of 47 Jewish marriages (out of an original maximum of 50) as against 13 mixed marriages. And, finally, we know that in a substantial number of those remaining 13, there will be some effort to raise the children as Jews even in the absence of conversion.

In short, the much-lamented "one-third rate of intermarriage" describes a situation which most likely involves no loss whatsoever of potential Jewish family units.

That is not to say that intermarriage is not a problem. Minimally, the Jewish commitment of the intermarried cannot be taken for granted. (For that matter, neither can the Jewish commitment of the non-intermarried.) There are many aspects of intermarriage which need to be studied, considered, dealt with. *But a problem is not a crisis*. We can deal with intermarriage far more intelligently if we understand it for what it is—a problem that flows from our full-fledged participation in an open society—and refuse to be panicked into perceiving it as symptomatic of wholesale rejection of and defection from the Jewish community.

The origins of failure. We have problems galore. Our birthrate is a problem, and our birthright is a problem. Israel's safety is a problem and Jews in diverse other countries live in varying degrees of danger. Now and again, some of our problems flare up into crises, which the dictionary defines as decisive turning points. But we do not careen from turning point to turning point, not except by our own choice and distorted sense to things. "Gevald!" is not a proper slogan for a people that has lived productively for 4,000 years.

The choice of words here makes a difference. The Jewish people has not simply "survived" for 4,000 years. We have done considerably better than that. We have not merely "endured" for all this time. We have made love, and written books, and dreamed dreams—some of which we have realized—and we have tried, and sometimes succeeded, to be decent. Survived? Endured? What sort of mealy-mouthed language is that to describe the noble past to which we are heir?

The much lamented "one-third rate of intermarriage" most likely involves no loss whatsoever of potential Jewish family units.

But then how is it that we see things in the shadowed way we do?

In our own generation, the most obvious answer is the Holocaust. There is no understanding, not now, not ever, of how such horror could be visited upon us. One can hardly be surprised if a people that has witnessed the butchery of one-third of its number loses its sense of balance, becomes nervous and apprehensive. Earlier generations of Jews had a lengthy chronicle of disaster to deal with; we have that whole chronicle, and the crushing added weight of its grotesque climax.

But if we use the Holocaust to prove that only the cynic is a realist, we pervert the message the slaughtered poets left for us, the message which has in fact informed our behavior since the Kingdom of Darkness. To understand the past, you have to know its future. The future of the Jewish people after the Holocaust has not been to cast itself down into mourning. We remember, oh yes we remember. We remember, and we build. We remember, and we plant. We remember, and we laugh, and have children, and worship God. That is what we *do,* what we insist on doing. Call it defiance, call it affirmation, call it stiff-neckedness; we will not, we have not, let ourselves become a victim people.

We do not behave as victims; then why do we think of ourselves as victims? Why, when we look in the mirror, do we not see ourselves as we are, vigorous and vital?

It is not just the Holocaust that haunts us and distorts our image of ourselves. It is also the way in which our history is read and taught. Salo Baron once referred to the "lachrymose interpretation of Jewish history." According to that interpretation, encountered everywhere, our history consists of an unending series of calamities and catastrophes, some actually experienced, the rest narrowly escaped. In every age, our enemies rise up to destroy us; too often, they succeed. Ours is a dismal religion: its weather is a steady drizzle, interrupted only by occasional thunderstorm or hurricane; its costume is the shroud; its companion is fear; its teary vision sees only the grim half-emptiness of the glass of life. Exile, pogrom, auto-da-fé, martyrdom, persecution, persecution, persecution. At the height of our joy, we break the glass, and we know that the broken glass is the real metaphor for our lives.

Is it not so? Is this not what we have been taught? Do we not know that joy is ephemeral, ours on loan, that suffering is our authentic destiny? "In this world," goes the song, "pain and sighs; in the next world, Shabbat and rest."

But it is in this world, of course, that the State of Israel has been attesting our competence and our skill for thirty-one years, and it is in this world that Russian Jews have insisted upon freedom, and it is in this world that America's Jews have achieved distinction in philanthropy and have recently rediscovered Jewish learning. In this world.

Unfortunately, it is also in this world that old traditions and old perceptions die hard, and that some leaders and some teachers think it a clever tactic to encourage the sense of foreboding we carry with us. There are leaders and teachers who do not trust their people, their students; they fear the consequence of freedom, of normalcy. And so they sow the seeds of panic, in the hope that a frightened community will draw together. They see us straining at the leash, and they think we want to run away. They seek to tether us with Judaism; untethered, they suppose, we will stray, we will escape. They cannot understand that it is a strangling leash they bind us with, that we will choke on their diet of garlic and tears. We want to know the whole of it, not just the parts of sorrow and of woe. We want a piece of the dream, not just the fear and foreboding.

We do not want to be managed and manipulated by hyperbole, nor do we need to be. When a swastika is daubed on a tombstone, we take notice: somewhere, there is a vandal, perhaps a maniac. But a random swastika is not a resurgence of anti-Semitism. The case for Jewish education does not need to be made in alarmist terms. Neither anti-Semitism generally, nor the Holocaust specifically, need to be invoked as arguments in favor of Jewish identity or Jewish philanthropy.

Of course we are a wounded people. Numberless tragedies are tattooed on our hearts. We have seen the abyss. But we have also seen Sinai. The waters once parted for us. In the midst of madness, we have found meaning. If we introduce the story of the Jewish people as conclusive evidence of cruelty, of the inevitability of disaster, we misread that story and mislead its audience. The history of the Jewish people is a proof text for hope, for redemption, for faithfulness to a compelling vision of a world made right. It is the hope we represent and not the fear we nurture that is the inducement, the incentive, the motive. It is the hope that binds us.

Last month, a columnist for the *Jerusalem Post* wrote that "It is extremely doubtful that within a few generations there will be many Americans who have remained Jewish in any meaningful sense of the word. Any thoughtful observer of American Jewry cannot but be struck by the ravages of assimilation."

The columnist's ignorance must be forgiven. It comes about, presumably, because he has read what we have written and heard what we have said about ourselves. He is also, most likely, the bearer of ideological bias: Classic Zionist theory cannot accommodate the possibility that there can be a Jewish life in the Diaspora that is safe and meaningful.

But that is *his* problem. *Our* problem is that when we read his words, we are most likely to nod our assent. And the danger of that assent is that it becomes a self-fulfilling prophecy. Yet what strikes the genuinely thoughtful, as distinguished from the merely instinctive, observer of American Jewry is how persistently we refute the grim predictions of our imminent demise. I think of the lawyers in Los Angeles who meet during their lunch hour to study Jewish law, of the housing for the elderly in Baltimore that has been built adjacent to several of the synagogues of that community, of the Russian Jew in Shreveport who insisted on making a significant contribution to the UJA campaign just six months after his arrival, of the rabbis who have walked with Cesar Chavez, and of those who have chained themselves to the White House gates on behalf of Soviet Jewry, of the wisdom and the beauty in the new prayer books of the Reform and Conservative movements, of the emergence of a cadre of Jewish communal workers whose training in Judaism has at last been recognized as no less essential to their jobs than the traditional social work skills, of a hundred stories that belie the doomsayers, of a hundred songs, some old, some new, that we are learning how to sing. It is time for us to hear the music we are making. ✦

ISRAEL, SUMMER 1979 A VISITOR'S JOURNAL

LEONARD FEIN

I had heard before I went, of course, that the reaction of Israelis to the peace treaty was remarkably subdued. But nothing I had heard prepared me for what I in fact encountered. I had expected that after all the back and forth of the negotiations, and on the eve of negotiations still more complex and consequential, the mood would be both weary and wary rather than exultant. I had anticipated that the economic morass in which the country is bogged down would have drained such energy as the diplomatic haggling had not.

But the Israel I encountered in the summer of 1979, on this, my seventeenth trip to that land, is in far deeper crisis than I had imagined. It is a crisis that goes well beyond Begin and his demagogic posturing ("There will be many more Eilon Morehs"), beyond the administrative incompetence of his government. It is a crisis that goes beyond an inflation rate that is heading to the hundred percent level. It is a crisis of the spirit, of the soul. It is a crisis one friend summarized quite neatly when suddenly he asked—he, a young man of the Right, a pragmatic sabra, not an old-fogey relic, not an ideologue left over from the 1920's—"Where did we go wrong? Where, where did we lose the thread?"

Ever since 1953, the year of my first visit, I have become used to a peculiar strain of angst which affects the Israeli spirit. It is not restricted to the generation of warrior-prophets who laid the foundation; sabras, at least of my generation, carry the germ as well, though it is often well-disguised.

When, therefore, so plaintive a question is put to me, it should not surprise. It may even be that residue of the golus-Jew, the ghetto mentality, that makes communication between us so easy. Children of parents reared in the same East European households, children, as well, of the Holocaust, we have unspoken questions in common, questions to which there are responses but never answers. For all that our experiences these last 31 years have been so radically different, the unspoken questions are a bridge between us.

But *this* question was spoken, and an answer was awaited. It was not a rhetorical complaint, not an existential sigh. It came on the final day of my visit, in the final hour of an extended conversation with a marvelously intelligent Israeli I had met just two days before, and who thought, I suspect, that my visitor's eye might have caught sight of a specific that had escaped his own considerable attention. An answer was awaited.

My visit had begun with questions of a different and more modest kind. I arrived in Israel during the week the Israeli Cabinet, by a vote of 8-5, approved the settlement outside Nablus (also known as Shchem) called Eilon Moreh, and stayed on during the week the controversy over Eilon Moreh raged forward. I came wanting to know more about Begin's autonomy plan, and wanting to know whether Eilon Moreh was merely, as I hoped, a sop Begin threw to his own right wing on the eve of his party's convention, and wanting, more generally, to know what the political sense of the place was two years into the Begin government. I wanted to know whether Labor was using its time out of office to get its act together, and whether Shalom Achshav (Peace Now) was still alive, and whether Gush Emunim (The Bloc of the Faithful), which has been relentless in its pressure for more West Bank settlements, and more, was making inroads or only headlines. And other things: Whether Bet Hatfutsot (The Museum of the Diaspora) was everything I'd heard, and whether the dispute between the Jewish Agency and the Ministry of Housing over Project Renewal was really resolved, and whether Israeliness and Jewishness were drawing closer or were still compartmentalized, the one the way of the secular, the other of the Orthodox.

Big questions, these, but not nearly so big as the kind I used to ask in Israel, of Israel. Years back, my questions were about nation-building, not about statecraft, and identity and meaning and such. But now, thirty-one years into independence, it seemed to me that once-tenuous assumptions should have ripened into undoubted axioms, that one could and should take Israel for granted at last. You don't need more of a reason to get up in the morning than the fact that it's morning, and a country doesn't have to rationalize its existence anew with every dawn, even if that country is Israel.

I was wrong. It took ten surprising days to find that out, to learn that Israelis still believe they have a rendezvous with destiny—but feel they have forgotten where it was they were to meet. Rush, rush to the rendezvous—but where was it to be, and is it not too late? After thirty-one years, the old questions, the largest ones, still press for answers, more insistently than ever. On the one hand,

348/Moment

the pushing and shoving in Israeli queues, the dangerous rudeness of Israel's automobile drivers, the venom of its political debate; on the other hand, the sense that this country has been assigned a higher purpose, that everything that happens here matters; in the tension between the two, my friend's haunted and haunting question is born. I heard his question, in one version or another, everywhere I went. And here and there, during the course of my visit, I heard or saw a piece of the answer—not just the analytic answer, that dissects the past and is satisfied with explanation, but the existential answer, the one that still insists upon tomorrow, the answer that is built on bits of hope.

I went to Eilon Moreh with the protesters. The Cabinet had approved the settlement on June 3 (Yadin, Dayan, and Weizman among those opposing), the first time private land had been expropriated (except for security reasons), the first civilian settlement so close to a major center of Arab population. The settlers arrived on June 7; twenty tents, a flag, and a generator, perched on the top of a barren hill less than two miles from Shchem. In the good old days, settlements were erected overnight—a fence and a watchtower—in order to elude the British authorities, and there are those who see in the Gush Emunim settlers this generation's authentic heir to the tradition of pioneering self-sacrifice. My own impressions, gained from earlier conversations at Kadum, the settlers' base camp, are less favorable. I see, with a few exceptions, a small group of fanatic fundamentalists who thrill to asserting their superiority over the surrounding Arab villagers—a superiority entirely dependent on the Israeli army rather than on their own devices—and whose pseudo-sophisticated geopolitical arguments are as fatuous as they are fervid. (Later in the week, Yehuda Hellman, Executive Director of the Conference of Presidents of Major American Jewish Organizations, will visit the settlers and report that their sincerity and conviction brings tears to his eyes.

Does he know that one of their leaders has described the settlers' purpose as the sabotage of Begin's "Satanic autonomy plan"? Does he know that the government has promised these would-be saboteurs fifty million pounds of investment in the next two months, and that new settlements in the Negev and the Galilee go begging?)

I am at the parking lot of Binyanei Ha'umah, from which the Jerusalem protesters are to leave, at the appointed hour. The smallish crowd is scruffy, and my first reaction is that they are as much a fringe element as the settlers whose actions they mean to oppose. That reaction is strengthened during the endless ride to the settlement site, for I share the back seat of the car to which I have been assigned with a young woman who insists that almonds alone provide an adequate diet, that all machinery is evil, and that all politicians are facists. The driver vehemently disagrees; even if coffee and tobacco destroy the system, he says, he is not prepared to give them up. Each time he disagrees, he turns to face my seatmate; each time he turns, the car careens to the side of the road. Other cars in the caravan, seeing our erratic path, pass us, curious heads turning as they do. I have visions that we will be passed by them all, that we will be alone in the West Bank, through which we are now driving, that we will be lost. The argument ebbs at last; now the driver's attention is on his pipe, which will not stay lit. I huddle in my corner, wishing Nablus to appear. But the army has blocked the main road, so we are diverted to a patrol path, and for the next hour we bounce rather than drive towards our destination. Up and down from the road, side to side from the pipelighting, through a barren moonscape over which nations may yet go to war.

We arrive, at last. It is not the middle of nowhere, not at all. It is five minutes or less from Nablus. A crude road has been bulldozed through a cornfield, and a centipede of people is winding its way up the hill the road traverses. I see that the Jerusalem contingent is small, that there are some thousands of people who have arrived before us, and I begin panting my way up, to the top. We pass sullen police, soldiers. It is a forty minute climb, and when it is done, we are a hundred yards from the crude fence which surrounds the settlement. Nothing can be seen of the settlers or their settlement. Here the soldiers block any further advance, and here, therefore, the organizers of the protest reveal their plans. No confrontation will take place. Instead, the protesters will go back down the hill, and set up camp. They will try to seal the road, to prevent any supplies from reaching the settlers. They are to avoid conflict with the authorities, to rely on passive resistance. The language is familiar, and even the faces, from days of civil rights and Vietnam. The protest has been organized by Shalom Achshav, overwhelmingly an Ashkenazi movement. The soldiers we pass are dark-skinned, Sephardim. They look more disgusted than menacing; it is Shabbat, and but for the protest, they would be on home leave for the day.

Down the hill, then. Along the way, with cheers, huge boulders are heaved onto barriers. Children—there are many—add stones. No one thinks these barriers will slow the bulldozers, but one wants to do *something* more than marching up a hill and then back down again. The police do not intervene. Hearing a New York accent, I turn and see Z., who once taught at Brandeis and has, for some years, been living and teaching in Haifa. This is his first active protest, he tells me. The confiscation of private lands, the location of this new settlement in the midst of a densely populated Arab region, the irrelevance of the settlement to any legitimate security need—these have combined to bring him here from Haifa. His children are busy dumping stones and rocks in the road. I am happy to see him, to see that there are Americans on this side of the issue. Many of the Gush Emunim people are Americans, and some of them are among the most extreme elements of the settlement movement. Just a couple of weeks back, some of Meir Kahane's goons broke into several Arab homes in Hebron, breaking up furniture, beating and shoving the occupants around. (Two weeks later, the Prime Minister will get around to issuing a public apology for this pogrom. It "brings shame on us all," he will say, and he will offer to pay compensation for the damages done.) Mainline Gush elements rarely engage in such outright hooliganism; nonetheless, they seek to impose their annexationist fantasies on the government, and are not much troubled by the niceties of the law or the accepted norms of democratic behavior.

Back at the bottom of the hill, the protesters mill about, police cars come and go, the organizers huddle. Some speeches, brief, as dusk falls, and then the crowd dissipates, leaving behind only a scattering of hardy souls who will sleep on the road to insure that it stays blocked. The rumors that a large contingent of Gush supporters are on their way from Tel Aviv prove groundless; there will be no confrontation this evening. In the meantime, I have found A., another old friend from America, and am to go back to Jerusalem in his car. The ride back is a breeze, and the conversation is familiar: we talk Zionism, for A. and R., his wife, are among the purely classic Zionists I know. Israel is the center, we the periphery. I argue that five and a half million Jews, bursting with Jewish vitality, cannot be classified as peripheral. It is amiable; we have been having such arguments with each other or with one another's friends, for decades. We do not discuss the protest at all. What is there to say? Tomorrow, the papers will duly report the event. That day, or the next, the road will be cleared, and the settlement will go forward. The courts may yet stop it, but a couple of thousand assorted Saturday afternoon pickets will not. I invent a rule: If a melange seeks to defeat a movement, it needs a numerical advantage of better than a hundred to one. Or it needs to become a movement.

(Later, I will learn that the Military Governor of Nablus ordered the area closed some hours after we left, and that the several score demonstrators who had stayed on through the night feared they would be bodily removed. A few hasty phone calls later, two Knesset members arrived—in the very early hours of the morning—and they, in turn, convinced Defense Minister Weizman to put in an appearance on Sunday. Upon his promise to raise the issue once again at the Cabinet level, the protesters broke camp. Later that day, Weizman failed; Begin did not allow the matter to be added to the Cabinet agenda.)

Back in Jerusalem. Was there ever a city at once so majestic and so intimate? This jewel glistens more brightly, more richly, each time I enter it. What a piece of good fortune we and all the generations to come have been granted in Teddy Kollek, its mayor, who has caused parks to happen suddenly and unexpectedly, who has removed the scar where the city was once cut in half, who has polished the streets. The Jerusalem I knew 26 years ago was a picturesque but squalid place; today's Jerusalem is a triumph.

I wander the city center, missing the blind beggar in front of Fefferberg's, the one whose daughter used to come to lead him home each afternoon; stopping to see my cousin at the municipality's tourist office; zig-zagging towards Rechavia and thinking, as I always do in this place, how gracefully Jerusalem carries the weight of its centuries. I pause at the balcony of the King David Hotel, waiting for Eva Marie Saint to appear, which does not happen; do Paul Newman and she know how many of us they continue to disappoint by their absence?

Much later, I walk through the alleys of a movie set called the Old City, through the Armenian Quarter to the Jewish Quarter, all too perfect. Living here, can there ever come a time when the sense of privilege is lost, when the edge of expectation dulls?

And, at the same time, not a museum. The traffic jams are real enough, and now the city stays open at night. Fink's and My Bar were once the only comfort of insomniac visitors; now there are bars and all-night eateries and even some very, very good restaurants.

My hosts take me to one they like especially, a Chinese restaurant not far from Yad Vashem. The restaurant is owned by Vietnamese, and the food is awful. They are pleased to be taking me to dinner; for me, a Chinese restaurant in a Jewish neighborhood is no novelty. Yet I am mildy amused at the curious juxtaposition; Jerusalem's juxtapositions have always pleased me. There is music playing, pop music. The record is changed; June in Jerusalem, our unknowing Vietnamese restauranteurs are now playing a medley of Christmas carols. To the strains of The First Noel, I dissolve.

This cannot be the same Jerusalem where terrorists plant bombs. But tonight, as we leave, I notice some books resting on top of my friend's car. I reach out to remove them, and he rudely shoves my hand away. He examines them from every side, and very, very gingerly touches them before he picks them up. Yes, they are books. We get into the car, and enter the stream of traffic.

I do not want Eilon Moreh to occupy my week. The foolishness of Begin-Sharon's settlement policy has been obvious to me for many, many months. An isolated outpost in the midst of a densely populated Arab area is not a contribution to Israeli security; it is a provocation. The Jerusalem Post editorial on Sunday summarizes my views on the matter: "Eilon Moreh, and the international furor it creates, only provides additional ammunition for the forces ranged against Israel . . . There is no genuine security argument for introducing scores of Gush Emunim zealots into the outskirts of Nablus . . . The unfortunate resort to the security argument where it does not apply runs the risk of undermining all credibility in Israel's legitimate security arguments in other areas."

No, I want to dig beneath a single damaging episode, to try to understand what part of the government's policy is based on domestic political considerations, what part on ideological conviction. More, to understand how people I know and respect view the prospect of peace, what they imagine the coming months will bring.

My hosts in Jerusalem have

arranged a reception for me, inviting not only some of our mutual friends but also some people they think I'd be interested in hearing. One of these, the son of a distinguished Jerusalem family, in whose childhood home Arab visitors were commonplace, is described to me as especially interesting. He is, they say, a militant annexationist, but an intelligent one. I am a courteous audience, although I suspect he mistakes my courtesy for agreement. When, after half an hour, he proposes that Israel's only serious recourse is to threaten atomic retaliation for any attack, I decide that there are more interesting ways to spend time. Later in the week I will have dinner with a former Chief of Staff who perversely favors Begin's policies. These, he argues, will surely cause Egypt to renege on the peace treaty, and that is what he wants. The treaty was a mistake. Any treaty is a mistake. Arabs cannot be trusted. My problem, he says, is that I do not understand *hamentaliut ha'aravit* — the Arab mentality.

"The Arab mentality" is the last defense of all the zealots, including that not insubstantial number who are part of the Labor Party. I do not doubt that there are important cultural differences among nations and peoples, but I am frightened by the casual racism of those who depend on such sloppy phrases as "the Arab mentality" to support their position.

I am frightened as well that Sunday, the day after the protest, by Mr. Begin's response. Don't the protesters realize, Mr. Begin asks, that if we have not the right to Shchem, we have not the right to Jaffa or Ramat Aviv?

This is, of course, Arafat's argument turned upside down. It suggests an all-or-nothing approach which seems to me reckless in the extreme. The debate over Eilon Moreh or the other settlements is not a debate over rights. Of course Israel has a right to Shchem, the U.S. State Department notwithstanding. But not every right a person has — or a nation — need be exercised. Those who live in Shchem also have a right to the place, and the question is not which right a court of law may find superior, but how the two rights may be accommodated. That has been the question between Israel and its neighbors for many years now; it is Arafat and Company who have insisted on arguing from right rather than from reason. And Begin, by adopting their frame of reference, has fallen into their trap. The world community will never accept the priority of Israel's right to the West Bank over the Arabs' right to govern themselves. Begin's case — Israel's case — must be built on a foundation of legitimate security requirements, not on a foundation of technical legal arguments. Mr. Begin is still arguing against the Partition Plan of 1947, and that is a very dangerous thing to be doing in 1979 — for if the principle of partition were to be rejected, it is not at all clear that the rejection would be in Israel's favor.

Enough, I hope, of politics; my primary concern, during this visit, lies in a very different direction. I want to know about Judaism in Israel, I want to know whether any new choices have developed, whether there is some stopping point between fullfledged Orthodoxy and absolute secularism. I have for years been hounding my Israeli friends with a question they now know I am incapable of not asking: What will our children have to say to each other, how will they feel and be connected? We, those of my generation, can still find a common language. But what of our children? And must not the answer lie somewhere in the unexplored territory of Judaic idiom and expression?

On my first Shabbat, my hosts — who have been my guests in Boston, who know, therefore, of my ritual for welcoming the Sabbath — do me the courtesy of asking that I chant the kiddush. I decline, knowing it is not their way, not wishing to perform. I appreciate their courtesy. They explain that it is not for courtesy's sake, but for their children's. Later, they will argue that the signs and symbols we depend on in America are gratuitous in Israel. We need the candles and the kiddush to remind us of the Shabbat; in Israel, on Friday afternoon, one knows, the very air reminds; the candles are gratuitous.

Of course one knows. Offices and shops close early, and there will be chicken on the table and guests after dinner. Children will come home on leave from the army. What more is there to know, to do?

But last summer, my oldest daughter spent six weeks working in a kubbutz; though she enjoyed the work, she missed the Jewish atmosphere of summer camp.

So I go to Bet Hatfutsot, the Museum of the Diaspora, about which I have heard nothing but praise and which may be a piece of the answer I am looking for. This new museum, on the campus of Tel Aviv University, is a celebration of 2,000 years of Jewish life. As Abba Kovner, whose idea it was, explains, "Yad Vashem describes the destruction; Bet Hatfutsot describes *what* was destroyed."

I am not disappointed. I know little of museums, but it is clear, first of all, that this one *works*. It is filled with surprises, with computer consoles that quiz you and with buttons to press and earphones to lift; it draws you in. And the exhibits are clever. There are no original works here; Bet Hatfutsot is not intended as a repository for things that have somehow survived. It is manifestly a teaching museum, and what it teaches is how vast our experience has been, and how faithful we have stayed. Detailed reproductions of synagogues — from Vilna, from Cochin, from Amsterdam, from Kai Feng, from Lutzk, and from Toledo (Spain, not Ohio) and from Elkins Park — films on the Jewish communities of Salonika, of Fez, of a "typical" shtetl, a brilliant recapturing of the richness of the Jewish past. It is a museum filled with surprises.

In one room, there are drawings of Jewish dining rooms from a dozen different places, a dozen different times. The table settings change with time and place, the architecture of the rooms changes. But in each room, on each table, there are candles. The time is always Friday evening, erev Shabbat. Wherever we have been, whenever, there have been these constants.

But in Jerusalem, last erev Shabbat, when I self-consciously chanted the kiddush, there were no candles.

Eilon Moreh will not leave me alone. Begin is angry: He is angry with the New York *Times,* which on Sunday has published a lead editorial called "Begin's Fears, Eban's Hopes" (the Eban reference is to his article in the May MOMENT), he is angry with his critics in the Knesset. He lashes out: "There will be more Eilon Morehs, we shall continue to establish new settlements in Judea, Samaria, the Gaza Strip, and the Golan." On Wednesday, there is a raucous Knesset session. Ariel Sharon's provocative defense of Eilon Moreh ("no fifth column will halt the march of Zionism") is interrupted by catcalls from Knesset members; even by the Knesset's own dismal standards, the debate is crude and rowdy. That night, Begin attacks the "hysterical screams" which have marked the session. Those who interrupted, he says, will soon be forgotten; no sign will remain that they ever lived. But for generations, every child in Israel will learn of the heroism and leadership of Ariel Sharon.

This is the kind of hyperbole at which Begin excels. For him, politics has always been theater, in the grand manner. On stage, which is where he prefers to be, he is destiny's child, the Maker of History whose critics are merely petty partisans devoid of vision. He is most comfortable with slogans: Those who oppose Eilon Moreh "follow the evil paths of the enemies of our people." (Weizman? Dayan?) Those who disagree with his policies engage in "incitement." Words like "never" and "always" roll off his tongue, and he leaves Dayan to pick up the pieces of his excess. Let others dabble in politics and government, let others fret over Israel's domestic problems; Begin presides over History. After all those years in hiding, and all those years in impotent opposition, after all those years of suffering Ben Gurion's refusal to pronounce his name ("that man," B.G. used to call him), his time has come. But the sulking resentments of all those years have taken their toll:

Later in the week, still angry, he will denounce Max Fisher's opposition to Eilon Moreh: "Were Jewish leaders accustomed to saying such things in the days of the Labor Government? Does he think that his subsidies and donations entitle him to influence our policies and actions? The State of Israel can survive even without these moneys . . ."

Other things are on most people's minds this week: Israel is doing well in the European basketball championships, and the annual Book Fair is opening, and "nirmul" goes forward. "Nirmul" is the Hebrew neologism for "normalization," the unfolding process of accommodation with Egypt. The Jewish people being what it is, Hebrew lacks a word for "normal." Hence "to normalize" becomes "l'narmel."

And, as always, family affairs. My friends in Israel are now of age to have children in the army. There is much talk of that. People postpone sabbaticals and extended trips abroad; they want to be around while their children are serving. Israel's is not just a citizen's army; it is a family army. The kids come home for the Shabbat, and they are still kids, combat boots and Uzi submachine guns notwithstanding. Their fathers are, of course, in the reserves—forty-five days of active duty a year—but it is the children who are learning to use the latest equipment. Even civil defense, provided by volunteers, is a family affair. R. and L., an over-age Israeli couple, do a midnight shift twice a week; given their busy professional schedules, it's the one time of the day they get to see each other. And when I leave the Jerusalem Theatre after a Habimah performance, I watch the guards who have stood duty during the performance walk away: a mother and her two teenage children, rifles dangling from their hands.

A friend shares his good news with me: "Our son has been accepted to a first-rate officers' training course. He's really lucky; his buddies who were rejected will be serving in regular units, and that means mostly with Moroccans, so they won't have anybody to talk to."

I recognize the importance of what he has said. In the 1950's and on into the 1960's, it was assumed that the mass of Near Eastern immigrants (for which "Moroccans" has come to be a kind of shorthand) could best be dealt with through a "Generation of the Desert" strategy. Wait for the parents to die, invest in the education and acculturation of the children. With proper schooling, with army service, the ethnic divide will be bridged, there will be one Israel.

But it hasn't happened that way, and it's not at all clear that it's happening. The President is a Sephardic Jew, and there are other Sephardim sprinkled throughout every element of Israel's elite, but that was never the problem. There was always a Sephardic aristocracy, and its scions were hardly thought of as "Moroccans." The problem was, and is, the Second Israel—the relatively poor, relatively uneducated, relatively left out. In some ways, the Israeli experience parallels our own these last twenty years: a surge of attention and investment, and then a withdrawal. The right laws are on the books, and the right policies are in place, an occasional statistic suggests progress, but the problem seems frozen, intractable. Suddenly, it is accepted as one of the continuing dismal conditions of modern life, like traffic jams and terrorists.

The difference—one of the differences—between Israel and the U.S. is that the Israeli "minority" problem is not a minority problem at all. The Second Israel is already larger than the First, and is growing more rapidly. And it contributes over 90 percent of the youthful offenders in Israel's jails. The issue goes well beyond such catch-phrases as racism, or bigotry, or discrimination. There are two cultures (more, really) and they simply are not merging. My friends' daughter, of thoroughbred Polish ancestry, wants to be a Moroccan. She will not be, of course, but she is only 12, and she does not know that yet. She will go on to college, and her friends, the ones who teach her the swear-words her mother does not like, will likely not. I hear all this, and think of the essays I have read—and some I have written—on the subject, all those fancy analyses which invariably conclude that there is much that is worth preserving in all cultures, that Israel should be searching for an amalgam, and other such pleasant liberal sentiments. But then whom do you talk to when you're in the army? Social theory has a devilish way of collapsing at the threshold of the family home. The existence of two Israels is no longer a problem to be solved; it is a fact to be endured. I have a dozen friends in Israel's universities who labor mightily to alter that fact; I have dozens more who are hoping their children will be accepted at officers' training schools, so they "can have somebody to talk to."

I wonder about these things, and worry about them. I am sitting in a new bistro in North Tel Aviv, a few blocks from hotel row, an area that was recently slum. Now it is filled with cutesy boutiques and coffee shops, and Tel Avivians on the make. The women are costumed, the men v-chested with necklaces. Somewhere in my head I carry that old photograph of Meir Diezengoff and his hardy band standing on top of a Jaffa sand dune with picks and shovels, beginning to build Tel Aviv. The images jar. No, Diezengoff did not imagine that it would come to this. But why must I be so judgemental? How long can you pick at a sand dune before a city happens, and then boutiques and bistros? Must everyone play chess and listen to Mozart?

I do not know Europe; perhaps this is all very European. To me it appears veneer American, imitative. In so many ways, Israel seems to insist on repeating every American mistake. I want to pick these people up and shout at them, "Hey! We've been there, and it doesn't work! Find a different way!" I don't; I can't. "Starsky and Hutch" and "Hawaii Five-O" are the most popular television programs here, and they wouldn't believe me.

My own television performance happens on Thursday, and therein lies a tale. I have been invited to appear on Alei Koteret (Behind the Headlines), Israeli TV's most popular talk show. I am to say some things about American Jewry, and I am happy for the chance to rebut the obituaries which are so regularly pronounced over us here in Israel. But this is a politically charged week. In an effort to win support for Eilon Moreh, Begin has invited a delegation from the Conference of Presidents of Major American Jewish Organizations to meet with him. The delegates are known to me; some are close friends. They arrive on Tuesday, and I have been asked by the Peace Now people to arrange for a meeting. I promise to try, and meet with Ted Mann, the Chairman of the Conference. He is three hours off the plane, and still groggy. While we talk, he is getting ready for his first press conference, a suit-and-tie appearance. I, who have been here five days already, have gone native—open-collar shirt and khakis—and feel entitled to brief him on the mood. He asks that I have the Peace Now people call him after he has met with Begin; as Begin's guest, it would be rude of him to speak with them first.

On Thursday morning, the press reports that the delegation has told the Prime Minister that they find it "difficult to explain the government's timing for the settlement in Eilon Moreh." But they will be spending the day, it turns out, touring the West Bank, and visiting Eilon Moreh itself in the company of Ariel Sharon.

Sharon is a blustering enigma. He has brought to his work as Minister of Agriculture and Chairman of the Ministerial Settlement Committee the same style which won him renown as a military leader. He is blunt, single-minded, always on the offensive. He and Rabbi Moses Levinger, leader of Gush Emunim, are the most potent—and most peculiar—team in Israeli politics today. The one a burly outdoorsman, the other a sallow scholar, the one entirely lacking in religious conviction or sentiment, the other a staunch fundamentalist, they share a single-minded ferocity of character and a passionate annexationist conviction. And they provide each other much-needed support: Levinger's zealots are Sharon's shock troops; Sharon's office is Levinger's protection.

I doubt that Sharon will sway the delegation, but they will meet with Begin again before leaving, and he will surely work very hard to win them over.

In the meantime, I am off to the television studio. I am terribly tense; I speak Hebrew, but I do not control it as I control my English. It is not the embarrassment of middling fluency that distresses me; it is the fear that I will be spending my energy on the words rather than on the ideas.

There is time, before the program begins, to chat with my host, Yaron London. I have been warned that he can be tough, a kind of Mike Wallace with subtlety. But over the inevitable grapefruit juice, he seems entirely harmless. I am to be one of four guests this evening: After our interview, there will be a performance by a mandolin band, then an interview with a pop artist, then back to the mandolins, and then on to an Israeli dentist who has recently returned from two years of treating natives in the Amazon jungle.

We rehearse, for voice levels and camera angles and such. I have never seen such sober mandolin players. They pluck away without facial expression, and Mendelssohn comes out. The dentist shows off his blowspear. What am I doing here?

What I am doing here, once the program begins, is talking about Eilon Moreh. Even had I no substantive objections to that place, I would by now oppose it on purely personal grounds: enough, already.

But London wants to know by what right American Jews think they can determine Israel's foreign policy. I explain that none of us, whether he opposes that policy or supports it, presumes that he can or ought to be able to "determine" it. Begin, however, appears interested in the views of American Jews, else he would not have invited the Presidents' Conference delegation. In light of that interest, I describe what I believe to be the American Jewish reality: profound support for Israel, profound concern for its security, substantial difference of opinion over its current settlement policies. I express agreement with the delegation's assertion that it will be difficult to "sell" Eilon Moreh to

American Jews. We go on, at last, to other topics.

I ask London "my" question: What will connect my child and his? He stares at me blankly. "And so what if nothing connects them?" he asks. "The end of the Jewish people," I say. "And so?" Whereupon I talk for a bit about the notion of mission, a lamp unto the nations, pursuing justice, and all that. He looks at me incredulously, and I see that he wants to change the subject.

At which point the producer walks on camera, and hands London a note. Shlomo Nakdimon, Mr. Begin's press advisor, has just called the studio with the text of the Presidents' Conference public statement at the conclusion of their visit. London reads the statement aloud; at first hearing, it sounds like a warm endorsement of Eilon Moreh. "I wish to emphasize," Nakdimon's statement says, "that the delegation expressed the full support of the majority of American Jewry for the government's policy." (Only later will I have the chance to read the delegation's statement itself, and understand that it is deftly worded to avoid reference to Eilon Moreh. It says, instead, that the delegation believes settlements on the West Bank are legal and also essential for Israel's security. That, of course, is not the issue at stake on Eilon Moreh.) London asks for my reaction. I am disappointed, since I believe that Begin will use this alleged endorsement by the American Jewish community in the battle with domestic opposition to his settlement policy. As I see it, the Israeli national consensus accepts the importance of an Israeli security presence on the West Bank; it has never embraced the notion of Jewish civilian settlements in densely populated Arab regions. Most Israelis, I suspect, oppose such settlements; at the least, very many oppose them. I see no reason for American Jews to be used as a weapon in the debate, or to feel bound to defend this very controversial departure. Nor do I believe that the delegation's endorsement of Eilon Moreh accurately represents American Jewish opinion.

(Later, after the Israeli press has joined in my misinterpretation of what the delegation has said, Ted Mann will issue a clarifying statement delicately balanced between endorsement of settlements in general and rejection of Eilon Moreh in particular. But that will not happen before next week. In the meantime, people will wonder what it was that caused the delegation to change its mind between Wednesday and Thursday. Was the change real, or was it a result of Begin's pressure, or his charm? Much conversation over the next three days will be devoted to this topic, imagining different scenarios to account for the change. Most of them, imagined by people who do not know Ted Mann, propose that Begin, through a combination of charm and pressure, has invited the delegation to an ego trip. But I cannot accept this; Ted is uncommonly immune to such temptations. When, finally, I have the chance to talk to three participants in the meeting, I learn that it was Begin's fury that placed the delegation on the defensive and caused them to frame their statement in a manner that could so easily be interpreted as an endorsement.)

The television interview meanders along. I am by now exhausted, impatient for the mandolins. No one should be required to speak Hebrew after ten o'clock. At last—it turns out that we have completed one of the longest interviews Alei Koteret has ever done—we are through, and I stagger into the control room. A fistful of telephone messages is handed me: the studio switchboard has been lit up since I began. All my friends, those who did not know I was in the country, many whom I have not seen in a dozen years, have been calling. What a grand way to let people know you're in town! But right now, I am talked out; I need some grapefruit juice.

It is Friday evening, erev Shabbat once again. This time I am with perhaps two hundred people, delegates to an international conference. We are in the dining room of the kibbutz guest house where the conference is taking place, and the American delegation, of which I am one, has decided that at our table, we will welcome the Shabbat with the kiddush. We do so, quietly, unobtrusively. At another table, a very prominent Israeli labor leader rises, raps on his glass for attention, and then says, "I don't have a yarmulke, but we can still welcome the Shabbat properly." Raising his glass of wine, he says, "L'chaim!"

Before those at my table, for whom the assertion of the tradition has become a point of stubborn honor, have had a chance to react, still another corner is heard from: again a prominent Israeli, but this one evidently more sensitive to the peculiar ways of the Diaspora, rises and asks for silence. Then he unabashedly, and with full dramatic emphasis, declaims the kiddush.

No, there are no candles. A motto for Israeli and American Jews alike: It is better to light two candles than to curse a lapsed Jewish consciousness.

I have spent the day Friday being recognized. In a country with one television station, I have become a bit of a celebrity. My cab driver takes me the long way around; he wants enough time to explain his position on Shchem and Eilon Moreh, on Sharon and Peres and such. The President of Israel, to whose home the cab finally takes me, tells me that he watched the program. I cannot bask, however; I am too conscious of the answers I might have given, but did not. "Trepverter"—the clever phrases that come to you only after a conversation, too late to use.

Friday morning papers feature the Presidents' Conference "endorsement" of Eilon Moreh. It is front page news. By late Friday afternoon, however, the radio is broadcasting the news of a critical letter that has been sent to Begin signed by fifty-nine American Jews, a letter condemning Eilon Moreh. The list of signers includes several prominent community leaders, although it is top-heavy with academic types. It is a solid rebuttal to the Presidents' Conference statement; the timing is near-perfect, and, if Begin's advisors are sensitive to the who's who of American Jewry, they will understand that there are important defections here, that Eilon Moreh does not easily commend itself to the American Jewish community. (Instead, as I will later learn, those advisors are insisting that the statement was instigated by the U.S. State Department. It is hard for me to accept that they cannot believe the opposition is fully genuine, harder still for me to accept that they are merely seeking to discredit it by their canard.)

At the very least, the Israeli public is now at last aware that American Jews are divided, as are the Israelis themselves. How could it be otherwise? Begin has already announced that there will be "many Eilon Morehs." Clearly, he intends a rapid expansion of Jewish presence precisely in heavily populated Arab areas; he has, in fact, said exactly that to the Presidents' Conference delegation. When Begin talks security, he means sovereignty, and his hope is to "establish facts" over the course of the next five years that will validate Israel's claim to sovereignty over the West Bank.

This is a radical departure from the existing Israeli consensus. It may enjoy majority support—even that is doubtful—but it will be bitterly opposed by very many Israelis, as well as, obviously, by the international community. Can the American Jewish community suspend its own judgment and permit itself to be used as an instrument of a policy it perceives as mistaken, and even dangerous?

My specific fear is that in the course of his efforts to mobilize Israeli opinion, Begin is planning to use the presumed solidarity of American Jewry as one of his supporting arguments. But there is no such solidarity, not on these new departures, not on the claim to Israeli sovereignty over the West Bank. That must be made clear to Begin; more important, it must be made clear to the Israeli public, which will otherwise contemptuously conclude that American Jews are robots, woodenly moving off in whatever bizarre direction they are pointed. So I am pleased about the letter, proud to be among the signers.

My fears are renewed on Sunday when the press reports that Begin is now fuming with the Jewish Telegraphic Agency. The JTA is the principal source of news for the Jewish press world-wide. It is supported by its clients, as well as by the organized Jewish community, which appreciates the importance of the service it renders. But Begin—so says his advisor for foreign information, Harry Hurwitz, who recently immigrated to Israel from South Africa—thinks that the editors are "too leftist." Accordingly Begin is considering the possibility of setting up a competing news service, or even a substitute.

What I suspect Mr. Hurwitz means is that the JTA accurately reports the very deep divisions that now exist within Israel. Mr. Begin would prefer—what politician would not?—that these divisions be ignored. It cannot please him that the audience which watches his performance on the world stage may be aware of the bad notices he gets back home. And those notices—Israel has a free and hypercritical press—have been very bad of late. Accordingly, a government news agency.

I envy no politician who must suffer the vituperations of the Israeli press. Israel's accepted journalistic traditions virtually guarantee that no Israeli prophet will be honored in his own country. But the proposal that the government replace the JTA with its own news agency is, of course, a cure far more sinister than the disease, another symptom of government by anger.

Late Friday night, I am collected from the kibbutz by a Jerusalem relative. He takes me to the home of his friend in Ein Karem, where several couples will gather to talk into the night. We sit in the domed living room of an exquisite house, and the talk is light, diverting. It is a relief to be away from Eilon Moreh and the world of politics. The assembled are quiet and confident and bright. They are Israelis who have made it, and they wear their success well. An engineer, a senior security official, an economist, two teachers, an agronomist, two housewives, they manage the country, they are beyond the bluster of the still-climbing.

And then, perhaps because I am there, the talk becomes reflective. "How can we complain?" V. asks wistfully. "There is nothing that we lack," her arm in a sweeping motion that embraces the house, its large and lovely yard where we will later sit, the ancient grape arbor it embraces. "We have two cars, and every appliance, and trips abroad, and education for our children."

It is so. She and these others live well not simply relative to other Israelis, but even when measured by American standards. Not wealthy, but quite comfortable. Yet the wistfulness suggests that there *is* a complaint; it is an invitation to comment.

And the others do. Yes, we live well, they say, but something is amiss, something beyond war and politics, beyond terrorism and tensions. We search for the something, I with questions, they with vague musings. I suggest the endless war, the anxiety that is bred when you live in a place that others revile. No, that is not it. I propose the crazy-quilt economy, the maddening inflation, the insecurities that result. Not that, either.

And then I remember. I remember the bitter-sweet taste of success, the confusing realization that this last new appliance has added nothing, has raised the spirits for just an hour, just a day, no more. I remember the gropings of those who are sated with things and now search for meanings.

Last night, on television, the interviewer asked how American Jews prefer to think of Israelis: Do we want them hardy and heroic, or needy and besieged? Now it occurs to me that I should have said we want them to have the courage of our convictions. Is not one of the great unstated assumptions of American Jewish life that so long as the Israelis, plow in one hand and gun in the other, live at the center of history, we can continue, checkbook in one hand and tickets to Las Vegas in the other, to half-live at its fringes? Our expectation is that Israel matters; it stands for something, and by extension—rather than by our own behavior—so, vicariously, do we.

But if *these* eight warm and winsome people stand for something, they do not know its name. We talk of the quality of life, of the dirty streets and traffic, the shouting and the high level of aggression. I wonder what they mean. In Israel, virtually every Jew is armed. Tens of thousands of people move freely and pacifically around the country carrying submachine guns. And there is almost no crime that involves those weapons. The streets? Not as clean as London's, but cleaner by far than Boston's. The infuriating bureaucracy? Let them stop in Chicago's City Hall; Israel does not suffer by comparison.

Slowly, our conversation moves from the question of quality, from the chronic complaints of modern life, to the question of content. It is not, after all, that something is amiss; something is missing. This nation was built on a dream, and the dream has dried up, has atrophied. There was a time, not very many years ago, when those who spoke of the dream, of any dream, were ridiculed—perhaps even by these same now-wistful people. The old dream—"We have come to the land to build it and to be rebuilt by it" and all that—no longer compels. But no new dream has been pronounced that would replace it, and now, come to successful mid-life, a dream is wanted.

So our talk turns to dreams, and what they might be, and where they might come to be discovered.

We talk of an Israel transformed into a lamp unto the nations, but that is too weighty a dream, and too distant. This morning, a large call-girl ring has been exposed in Tel Aviv; this morning, the income tax people have revealed that half the nation's shopkeepers under-report their business receipts; yesterday, a member of the Knesset resigned his seat after being sentenced to a three and a half year jail term for bribery; earlier in the week three men were indicted for their armed robbery—armed with grenades, an Uzi, revolvers—of a Ramat Aviv bank; last week, 17 people were killed in traffic accidents, and 105 more were injured; a new poll shows that half of Israel's Arab citizens reject Israel's right to exist, and that nearly two-thirds regard the Zionist movement as racist. A lamp unto the nations? Measured against the present reality, that is no dream; it is a fantasy.

I talk a bit about the American dream, and its souring. I know what it is to be without a dream, but I know it in a country so large and so well-established that one can turn inward without guilt; the system works, more or less, even when left unattended. And I try to make excuses for my friends: You expect too much, this place is still too raw, too pressured, too self-conscious. I tell the story of the English baron and his guest: The guest asks how so marvelous a lawn has been achieved, and the baron decribes the watering, and the cutting, and the raking, and adds, "When you've got all that in place, then what you must do is wait 400 years, and you, too, can have this green a lawn."

But my excuses do not fill the empty space where once there was a dream. And finally, we come to the stuff of the Israeli dream, the battered dream that was called Zionism, that same Zionism which their parents and teachers and leaders spoke about in Russian and Polish accents, that same Zionism they have long since assumed was done.

The Russian Jews do not come; two-thirds of them prefer America. And America's Jews refute Zionist theory and prediction: We have not been pogrommed to death, we have not assimilated ourselves to death. On the contrary: We persist, and find ways of being Jewish. Our persistence is a continuing rebuke to classic Zionist theory—and 300,000 Israelis have chosen to make their homes with us. Will Israel one day become merely a half-way house for Jews in trouble, waiting for a better place to go? Can the pressure of life in Israel be endured if the purpose of life in Israel is obscured? And if the central purpose—to be a home for us all—continues to be rejected, what purpose is left?

I reject the question. Why must everything be so weighty, so burdened? Here and there, a shard of meaning; is that not enough? Where in the world is there more than that, who else in the world insists that there be more?

But this is Israel, and these are Jews. The religious monopoly enjoyed by Israel's Orthodox establishment has left a yawning void; in Israel, you are either religious (read: Orthodox) or you are secular. But religious or secular, there is still the lingering sense of a people chosen, of expectations of self and of nation that will not go away. And that is why the word for what I hear is not despair; it is *disappointment*. Somewhere, something precious has been lost. It is trapped in the innards of the bureaucracy, in the divide between the two Israels, in the perception of the kibbutz by the 97 percent of Israel's population who don't live there and wouldn't as a nice place to visit, in the laws of parliamentary immunity which are regularly exploited by members of the Knesset to avoid paying parking tickets. Bequeathed a dream they once scorned, whose content they do not recall and whose contours they cannot define, these, Israel's successful, are disappointed.

It is late now, very late. My cousin drives me back to the kibbutz guest house where I am to spend the night. In the small lobby, I bump into an Israeli acquaintance who insists on talking. I am impatient, talked out, and eager for sleep. But he has a story to tell me, and he must be heard. It is the same story I have just come from hearing, told briefly and with passion. He is an education officer in the army, and he has just returned from a session with a group of young officers. His job is to provide them the ideological background that will justify their effort. He is good at his job; he has been doing it for fifteen years. But it no longer takes. There is, he says, "no motivation." The officers, he says, are adrift, men of marvelous technical capacity and nothing else. And then he takes from his pocket a leaflet he has brought with him from Los Angeles, where he has just spent a year of study. The leaflet announces the creation, in Northern California, of a moshav. "Join us, and explore the possibility of a rich Jewish life lived in a cooperative fashion." There is a phone number for "further information." He calls the number; it is an Israeli who answers. "What," he says to me, "will become of us?"

My cousin, during our drive, had also told that story. Here is his version: "In 1947, my father took me for a walk on Mt. Scopus. *Me'al pisgat Har Hatsofim* — from the top of Mt. Scopus — we looked down at all of Jerusalem, and he said to me that there would soon rise in this place the Third Jewish Commonwealth. 'The first two failed, and they did not fail because they were conquered, but because we never learned how to live with one another. This Third will also be an experiment,' my father said, 'and I am thrilled beyond words that it will happen. But I am not at all confident that we have learned how to make it work.' " I do not see the point of the story until my cousin continues: "That happened in 1947, and from then until 1978, the story was tucked away among all my childhood memories. Never once did I actively remember it, never once did I have occasion to share it with anyone. But this past year, I have remembered that story and told it half a dozen times."

Saturday has come now, and my agenda for this day is fixed. Tonight, there is to be a mass rally of protest against Eilon Moreh. It is sponsored by Shalom Achshav; it will take place in Tel Aviv. I have been asked, in the kindest possible way, to speak. By "kind" I mean that those who asked, after telling how much they felt my appearance might mean, were quick to add that they would understand perfectly well if I thought it best to decline. They know something of the nature of American Jewish communal life, and they had heard of the ugliness that followed on the sending of a cable of support for their effort by 37 American Jews last spring. They did not, they said, want me to expose myself to risk.

The risk, such as it is, was of little concern to me; I was far more concerned with the proprieties. By what right does an American Jew address a public meeting in Israel on matters which affect the life and death of his audience, but not his own?

Yet it is they who have invited me; if they do not feel a presumption here, why should I? More, word has now leaked out of the Begin meeting with the Presidents' Conference delegation: Begin has flatly stated that Eilon Moreh is the beginning of Israel's effort to assert sovereignty over the West Bank; it has nothing to do with security. So it may well be that land rather than life is the issue, and — because there are 750,000 Arabs who live in the West Bank, and another 350,000 in the Gaza Strip — Israel's future as a Jewish state.

Still, I do not accept the invitation to speak until after the press has had its heyday with the Presidents' Conference statement, has made of that statement a blanket endorsement of West Bank settlement, *including* Eilon Moreh. Given the raging debate going on within Israel on these matters, such an interpretation is itself an intervention. If these are life-and-death issues, the Presidents' Conference has already intervened — or been used. Is it right that the Israeli public be permitted to believe there is an American Jewish consensus on Eilon Moreh when there is not?

So I agree to speak, and know that I must choose my words with care. I am, withal, a guest in this house, and good manners point to restraint. I want to say just three things: First, that there are very many of us, back home, for whom Israel is a precious place, and whose natural tendency is to defer to Israeli judgment on issues affecting Israel's security: we take no pleasure in criticism. Second, that there is, in fact, a major rift among American Jews on the matter of Eilon Moreh, and that insistence on Eilon Moreh's importance to Israel's security may well damage Israel's credibility when, down the road a piece, *genuine* security decisions must be taken. Third, that the cause of the split is not lack of concern or flagging energy; the cause of the split, quite clearly, is a policy which goes beyond the established consensus, and one cannot expect a policy so divisive in Israel to be accepted with absolute calm back in the States. Loyal we are, but not mindless.

So I work at a text, and then at a translation. And as the Hebrew fills the pages, I relax: Have not the critics back home, those who believe it is forbidden to American Jews to dissent, most often added that if one has criticism to offer, it should be offered in Israel? And is this not Israel, and are these words not in the language of the place?

The rally is scheduled for seven, and I am to be there by half-past five. A ride has been arranged, and I am collected from the kibbutz at four thirty. A pleasant couple and their dog are my companions — everyone in Israel, it seems, keeps dogs these days, and a bright cultural anthropologist could surely do a dissertation on how the classic Jewish phobia for all things canine has so suddenly been transformed — and we chat amiably during the hour's ride.

At the plaza of the Tel Aviv Museum, where the rally is to be held, preparations are under way. Here signs are being readied, there tables for the sale of T-shirts and bumper stickers are set in place. In a far corner, the organizers are conferring. They are terribly serious. They greet me, pass me over to someone else's care, and resume their conversation.

The someone else is Julie Neriya, who is known to me but whom I have not met before. Julie is the wife of Yuval, one of the original organizers of Shalom Achshav and, a year ago, the subject of an article in MOMENT. I try to remember the details of the article as we walk across the plaza, while she introduces me to her friends. She is an uncommonly beautiful woman, a frail, ethereal beauty, and she is also a most gracious hostess. If I am her "assignment," she is doing very, very well. And the article begins to come back to me: Yuval is one of eight men in all of Israel's history to have been awarded the Ot Hagvurah, equivalent to the Congressional Medal of Honor or the Victoria Cross. His heroism during the Yom Kippur War, as a tank commander, is legendary. As one tank and then another was shot out from under him, he found new tanks to command, organizing and improvising new tank companies along the way, until, commanding his fifth tank and crew, he was severely wounded.

And I step away from Julie as it dawns on me that this young woman, this lovely person, herself a lieutenant in the army, has been to war. Real war. And I look about, at the crowd that has begun to assemble, and it dawns on me—how could I ever have forgotten, even for a second?—that this is no American-style peace rally. The issues at stake here are not going to be played out in distant places with strange-sounding names, and the actors will not be other people's children. The place is this place; the actors are here, before me. And they have already fought their wars, seen death, and may again. This peace movement is not on its way to Canada; no draft cards will burned here. Last month, next month, all these brave young men will don their fatigues, and be off to their duty in the reserves. And if there is another war, they will fight in that war, and some will live and some will die, and their women, these women, and their children, these children, will worry and weep.

It is an honor, wholly undeserved, to be standing with them, with these who had worried for me that I might by speaking be exposed to risk.

The organizers are concerned: It is almost seven, the crowd is sparse, Israel's basketball champions are playing against Czechoslovakia tonight in Italy, people may be staying home to hear the game. Then quite suddenly, the mass is there; between seven and a quarter past, the crowd swells from three thousand to thirty thousand, perhaps forty. A torch is lit, there is a reading from Brecht, and the speeches start. There will be six in all, four or five minutes each.

I am to be the second speaker. I listen carefully to the first. This young man, this veteran of the battle on the Golan Heights, this dreamer, cries out in passion. His words excite the crowd, which stretches back behind the signs that block our view. I watch the crowd, the parents and their children, the old folks, the people of the dream and of the disappointment. Not far from the dais, I see two of my relative's friends from the night before, and I think it right that this is where they have come in the course of their search for meaning.

And Adi Ophir, the speaker, voice cracking, cries out: "General Sharon: If we are not Zionists"—for that is what Sharon has said of those who disagree with him just two days ago, in the Knesset—"who is it, General Sharon, that you will send to the next war?"

There is a slogan, a motto here tonight: "Hakibbush Mashchit"—"Conquest Corrupts." At first, I think it just another phrase. But I notice where it is the crowd applauds the most, and each time it is when reference is made to the price that Israel pays for its occupation of the disputed lands. Begin has said it clearly: cede the lands, and each of us becomes a target for the terrorists. These people know that risk; they will be targets no less than any other. But they know as well the price Israel pays, and has paid for twelve years now, as the master of the lands and of those who dwell therein. The price is the dream.

Ben Gurion, the one time we spoke at length, insisted that the single most important chapter in Zionist history was the chapter known as "The Conquest of Labor"—the demand by the early pioneers that Jews do their own work, with their own hands, and not enter this land as colonizers. Now it is West Bank and Gaza Strip Arabs who do the nation's dirty work. Now, in the Lachish area, once Israel's showplace of human reconstruction, it is Arabs who are hired to do the farming, and Jews become effendis.

Conquest corrupts. It is not, in the first instance, justice for others that these protesters demand; it is their own right to self-respect. Jews know too much, remember too well, to respect themselves as rulers of another people. It is their right to self-respect that they want back, and security as well. But those assembled here believe that genuine security cannot be achieved so long as Israel rules the West Bank. Some have one plan, others a second, a third, a tenth they believe will preserve, even extend Israeli security after Israel withdraws. But all are agreed that without significant withdrawal, there can be neither peace nor security nor self-respect. There will be some zealots on some hills, and a dream gone awry.

With what words, on my return to America, will I be able to convey the pride and the heartbreak of Adi Ophir, or the hope of this assembled mass? Dreams grow like wildflowers in this land; they have since time began. Madmen and prophets have competed for attention, and nameless masses have prayed and plowed, have planted and reaped, for the sake of this dream or that. Freud, a sometime Jew, believed that our dreams are an extension of our reality; Herzl, Zionism's father, believed that our reality is an extension of our dream. But which dream shall it be? Is it the dream of Gush Emunim, to stand astride another people and offer prayers to God? Shall it be the dream of Ariel Sharon, a dream of fortress Israel? Is it to be Begin's dream, a dream that in the name of security destroys consensus, that makes no distinction between security and power, that sows hope among Israel's enemies and confusion among its friends?

Is it the dream that has been planted a mile from Shchem, in a place called Eilon Moreh, or is it the dream I see in this thronged plaza?

The words are these: Near the beginning of our time, the Bible tells us, a man named Shchem raped Dinah, daughter of Jacob, our father, and Leah, our mother. And Dinah's brothers were most angry. But Shchem offered to marry Dinah, because he was much taken with her, and Dinah's brothers, the sons of Jacob and Leah, agreed, requiring only that Shchem and his men be circumcised, and that Shchem's people and Jacob's people, our people, become one. And Shchem and his men consented, and every male among them was circumcised, and on the third day, when they were still in pain, Simon and Levi, Dinah's brothers, "took each man his sword, and came upon the city unresisted, and slew all the males therein." Then they plundered the city; all its wealth they took, and its little ones and its women.

And then it was that Jacob said to

them, "You have brought trouble upon me and made me odious."

It is Adi Ophir who alludes to this story, reminding us that this is not the first time in our history that the name of Shchem has been linked to our darker instincts, that the deeds we do there bring trouble and odium upon us.

And I, who have wondered where Judaism can be found in this, the Land of Israel, and where the dream, now know.

No, I answer my friend the next day, my last, when he asks his haunting question, the thread has not been lost. It is tangled and twisted, but it is not lost. All the vulgar and trivial temptations of modernity, all the incessant pressures of hostility, all the complexities of a developing economy have snagged it, but it is not lost. For it never was an isolated thread; it did not begin in 1882, and it did not end in 1948. It was, and is, a part of the tapestry we know as Jewish life.

Go to Yad Vashem, and turn from the museum and the monument to look out at the hills of Jerusalem and its environs; see what this bereaved people has built and planted.

Go to Rishon L'Tzion, and stop at the Malben center for the elderly; see what this restless and rushing people still remembers to do for its parents.

Go to Afula, and look for the boat people; see what this preoccupied nation has done to make the Vietnamese feel themselves at home.

Go to Bet Hatfutsot and see the imagination, go to a dozen different hospitals and see the kindness, to a hundred different kibbutzim and see the industry, to a thousand and a hundred times that many homes and see, and feel, the love this beleaguered and confused and frenetic people still make manifest.

Or come to Boston, to Shreveport, to Kansas City, to Los Angeles, and attend the devotion, regardless of conviction, that is turned toward this place.

Or stay, stay here in Jerusalem, the heart of the tapestry, city of threads and of weavers, city of dreams, and listen to your question; so long as the question is asked, the thread is not lost. ✡

THE ANDREW YOUNG AFFAIR... TO BE CONTINUED

LEONARD FEIN

How very real are our fears, and how very little can we expect others to understand them.

What can it possibly mean to anyone who is not a Jew when we say that we have felt the lash and smelled the acrid flesh and stood in the abyss, that we bind ourselves in fear? Who can comprehend it? We, the Jews of Englewood Cliffs and of Beverly Hills, of Shaker Heights and of all the other high places, the Jews with the Cadillacs and the Mercedes, the Jews with the M.D.'s and the J.D.'s and the Ph.D.'s, the Jews with connections, with lobbies, whose lives are splashed with the smell of success; we, afraid?

No, we do not all live in the high places. Some of us are postal clerks, and some of us are nurses, and some of us are schoolteachers, and some of us are penny-ante hustlers. We don't own the banks, and we don't control the press. And even when we know success, all but a very few of us, after the cologne has worn off, hear the things all mankind hears, the things that go bump in the night.

And we hear other things as well, things our neighbors do not, things that may be there and may not be there, and please God let us never find out whether it is only our haunted memories and our crazed imaginations that echo with the sound of the jackboots or whether they have reached our block. Across the crowded restaurant, he whispers the word "Jew," and at our table all conversation stops: What is he saying? Is he with Us, or with Them? What is he saying, what are They saying in their board rooms, in their locker rooms?

In the board rooms, the authorities; in the locker rooms, the vandals. Here is Nat Hentoff, a decade back: "Rationally, we 'know' that there can be no pogroms here; but if the lead headline in tomorrow's paper were to say, ALL JEWS ARE TO REPORT AT THE NEAREST ARMORY BY SUNSET FOR TRANSPORTATION, would those of us Jews over thirty-five . . . be *totally* surprised?" And here, Mordecai Richler's Jacob Hersh, who waits, as do we all, for "the coming of the vandals. Above all, the injustice collectors. The concentration camp survivors. The emaciated millions of India. The starvelings of Africa . . . the demented Red Guards of China . . . followed by the black fanatics . . . the thalidomide babies, the paraplegics. The insulted, the injured. Don't bother barring the door, they'll spill in through the windows." One way or the other, Hentoff's authorities or Richlers' vandals, and most likely both together, we'll get it. Our destiny. We live between the rock of the powerful and the hard place of the powerless, and survive by learning how to slither.

That's why those blacks who, in the aftermath of the Andrew Young Affair, alleged that we had been for civil rights only when it was in our interest so to be, were entirely accurate. We care about justice and other such good things, but the thing we care about most is civil rest, social peace. We are for civil rights, and we are for justice, because without civil rights and without justice the peace of society is a deceptive calm, because when the storm comes, as it surely will without justice, we are in trouble, the boots come closer. They have come from the right, from the left, from the top, from the bottom. Hitler was a National Socialist, whatever that was supposed to mean, and Stalin was a Communist, whatever that was supposed to mean, and don't forget Torquemada and the Czars. Most of the time, we've known that our best odds were with the evolutionary left, with those who have sought reform and amelioration, equity and decency. And some of the time we've sold out to self-deception or to fatigue, or just hedged our bets, and thrown in with the powerful, endorsed the status quo—and held our breath. Self-interest? Absolutely. For if the pot be left to boil over, the others will merely be scalded; we will die.

But how can we expect anyone to understand all that? Show "Holocaust" on compulsory television for an entire year, and they will not; build a thousand memorials to all

> **Looking across the chasm that separates us, can they tell that we are not anemic whites, that we are wounded Jews?**

our tragedies, require daily attendance, still they will not. And how, if the comfortable others cannot be expected to understand, how can we ever expect the blacks to understand?

For do they not have their own special fears? It is not so hard to suppose what they hear in the dark of the night: rats, real ones, and crosses burning, real or imagined, and the hiss of the descending whip, remembered. Looking across the chasm that separates us, can they tell that we are not anemic whites, that we are wounded Jews? Can they see the fear, the fear we speak of only when we are sure there is no one to overhear, the fear we hide so well?

Even without the chasm of their own preoccupation, how shall they know that we are Jews? So much of the time we are simply what we seem to be: white. So much of the time, *we* do not know, do not even want to know, that we are Jews. Do not know, save for the gnawing fear.

Ah, but Selma. Don't they remember Selma? Doesn't Selma prove that we are Jews? All those resolutions we passed, and Heschel, and Lelyveld, and Schwerner and Goodman, those who marched and sometimes died.

Sorry. Vicarious virtue won't do. Where were the rest of us then? Where have we been since? Where are we now? No great and noble coalition came undone in August of 1979; it's been a while, a long while, since there was anything left to come undone. Here and there, a joint project, a working relationship, but none of the old sense of common agendas, shared destinies. We've been busy with other things—with cults and with the PLO and with Skokie and with State Department reassessments and with recovering from the exhaustion of the sixties. And we've been troubled and confused, because we keep turning affirmative action inside out and upside down and all we can see are quotas, and we don't think, we really don't think that quotas are good for anybody, except maybe in the very short run, and sure, it's about our own kids and medical school, but it's about other and bigger things than that, too. And we've been disenchanted with the housing projects that haven't worked and the welfare programs that haven't worked and all the other programs that haven't worked. When it comes to voting, we're still the closest friends and the stanchest allies of the blacks, but we're confused, and yes, we dropped out, we took time off as just about everybody has for Vietnam and Watergate and for some overdue house-mending of our own.

Last time we found ourselves shouting at each other—it was back during the New York City school strike of '68—the soothsayers tried to calm us. They told us it wasn't blacks and Jews, it was blacks and whites. "Negroes are anti-Semitic because they're anti-white," James Baldwin said. And some of us tried to listen, tried to believe that it was just an accident that Jewish storekeepers got caught in the burning cities, just a coincidence that the teachers' union was mostly Jewish.

This time, it's different. What was it that Kenneth Clark said when the black leadership met near the end of August to pronounce on the Young affair and related matters? "This is our independence day." No ambiguity there; it was independence from the Jews that Clark was talking about. That's what Julian Bond talked about, and that's what Richard Hatcher talked about, and that's what Franklin Williams talked about when he said, "Blacks are deeply affronted by the inherent arrogance of some Jewish groups," in responding to the Young affair.

No, there's no hiding place this time. This is about blacks and Jews, head on head.

How can that be? However derelict we've been, we're still not the enemy. Bull Connor—whatever happened to Bull Connor?—is the enemy, and inflation's the enemy, and the galoots that burn down houses on Long Island and in Yonkers, they're the enemy.

Is it just that we're handy targets? Low risk targets, that's what we are. Call us names, and we rush to our phones and our mimeograph

The Andrew Young Affair...To be Continued

machines and our conferences and our congressmen. Wanna get a rise? Pick on a Jew. See the one over there, the one who looks well-fed and oh so smug? Wanna have some fun? Call him a racist. Tell him Arafat's a freedom fighter and Dayan's a Nazi. He'll choke on his food, and it's safe, 'cause he won't hit back.

But no. It's not the vandals, the unwashed, the slum-dwelling hordes. Not this time. It's the middle class blacks, the best and the brightest of Black America, the ones who are supposed to know better. What in the world can account for that?

Not Andy Young. That one just doesn't add up. One loud-mouthed Jewish leader (and the blacks know as well as we that the loud-mouthed can't be restrained) called for Young's dismissal. The whole affair, from the time of the revelation to the time of the "resignation," took less than forty-eight hours. Young is out because he stood there with his truth shaved, and there may be more to the story, but that's why he's out, and nothing else. And they know it.

So it's something else, something deeper, more festering, a wound waiting for an excuse to erupt. It was James Baldwin, I think, who back then said that the real tragedy of being black in this country is that when you fail, you don't know why—you don't know whether it's because you're flawed or because you're black. This time, it's the flipside of that tragedy: it's the ones who've succeeded, and don't know why, don't know whether it's because they've earned it or because they're black.

Sure, if you've got to pick a tragedy, better to pick the story of success rather than the story of failure. It's a mark of some progress, after all, that there are so many blacks around who have made it, whatever the reasons, whatever the routes, whatever the mix of personal merit and of social mandate that has brought them there. But it's not an easy thing to live with; it, too, emasculates. Kenneth Clark has resented the Jewish intellectuals for all these years, and so have a bunch of others, the ones who are breaking into the employment areas where we predominate, and are working their way up, and are filled with anxiety and resentment and all the rest, and here we are, the Jews, the white Jews, the ones with Israel, potent Israel to identify with, and nobody's firebombing our houses, just a few swastikas here and there, mostly in cemeteries, and always sticking together and being so damned tolerant, so smooth, so clever, so satisfied, and talking about how we understand, how persecuted we are and how well we know what it's like and all that stuff on our way to the airports and to the safe suburbs and to the air conditioned malls.

Messrs. Young, Clark, Hooks, Jackson, et al.:

If what you're saying is that the rats are still biting your kids, and you can't afford for us to drop out, ok. That's fair. But that's not what we're hearing. Instead, we're hearing a lot of dumb garbage about the PLO and the Middle East and how arrogant we are and how patronizing and how selfish and about how independent you can be and how moral and oh how righteous.

You want to lecture to us about the virtues of non-violence, about the merits of the PLO? Tell you what: Let's talk about the PLO on the outskirts of Safed, where the kids who were massacred at Ma'alot are buried. Or will you call it cheap sentimentality that we react that way to the murder of our women and children, yes, *our* women and children? Ah, you will say, the innocents of Lebanon are no less innocent, somewhere the cycle must be broken, the endless violence that begets violence.

Cycle? Terror and counter-terror? Not for a second. Not for a second can you contend that there would be Israeli air strikes over Lebanon if the murderers of the PLO were not bent on the shedding of Israeli blood. I do not like the air strikes. (Neither does Moshe Dayan, incidentally.) I think they are a mistake. I think Israel should stop them. But how in the name of simple reason one can equate the provocation with the response I shall never understand. Cycle of violence indeed! There is no cycle here, none at all. There is a chain that can be broken at any time, and there is only one way for it to be broken, and that is for the PLO to renounce its policy and practice of murder. Do you contend that were Israel to cease its efforts to interdict the terror, the PLO would likewise be tamed? Recent history refutes you. Do you imagine that were the PLO to cease its villainy, Israel would nonetheless continue its raids? Not a shred of evidence supports that view.

Is it that these miserable terrorists appear to you as freedom fighters, heroic battlers against mighty odds? These well-funded murderers heroic? Let us talk of their heroism in Kiryat Shmonah, in the apartment building where they left nineteen dead Jews, nine of them children, as tokens of their heroism. No, we will have none of it. Yassir Arafat is a mass murderer. In a plausible world, he would be tried before a world court for crimes against humanity. This is not a plausible world. He will not be tried, nor will Mr. Terzi, another active member of this conspiracy to commit homicide and politicide. The one will hold joint press conferences with Kreisky and Brandt, the other will walk the streets of New York and the halls of the U.N. in peace.

That worries me. Forgive me, but I worry about a world in which people are so very ready to assume that the more horrible the atrocity, the more compelling the cause that must have brought it on. I worry about a world which chooses to sanitize the PLO, which teaches Jesse Jackson's children—and mine—that there are ample rewards to terrorism. I worry about a world whose international organization confers formal observer status upon a movement so loathsome in its intention and in its behavior.

Not to worry, you say? Just talk: what harm can come of that?

Let us be clear: I accept that responsible people, people who care about peace and such, should talk

> When you sit for photos with the murderers of innocents, you imply that they are welcome in civilized company.

with anyone at all with whom a bargain may be struck. If you want to bring peace to the Middle East, there's not much point in talking with the IRA. Willie Sutton robbed banks, he said, because that's where the money is. Moshe Dayan has now begun to meet with members of the PLO, presumably because that's who the enemy is. But, you see, I can depend on Dayan to know that he's dealing with the enemy. The problem with Kreisky and Brandt and Young and all the others who know what's best for Israel is that they don't deal with the PLO as an enemy. And that's a problem with very dangerous moral and political consequences.

When you sit for photos with those who boast of the murderers of innocents, you imply that they are welcome in civilized company. Perhaps you feel sullied by the encounter, but think it's worth the discomfort. What of those who see the pictures later? Will they know of your mixed feelings, or will they conclude that the PLO is acceptable in decent circles?

And what will the Palestinians themselves conclude? Whatever slim chance there may be that other and more civilized men and women will step forward to state the Palestinian case vanishes the moment you have public truck with the crazies.

As of this time, the cause of the PLO remains the destruction of the State of Israel. That is their formal commitment, and it is regularly repeated and translated into foul behavior. In time, that commitment may change, and the PLO may come to terms with a more modest goal, or may be displaced by other Palestinians who are prepared to live amicably with Israel. But each time well-meaning bystanders seek dialogue with the PLO, they postpone that time. For under such circumstances, why should any alternative Palestinian voice be raised? Not for fear of retribution, but for lack of incentive. So long as the PLO is encouraged by the whores of Europe and the hypocrites of the Arab world and by misguided souls in this country, why should any Palestinian set forth a moderate position? Why negotiate minimal demands? The world has become more impatient with Israel than with the PLO; why interfere with the process?

But Israel itself is not without responsibility for the silence of the moderates, you say. It has done far too little to encourage them, it has drawn so hard a line that the moderate position has been entirely subverted. I agree. But do you not see, can you not tell, that the encouragement of the PLO merely increases Israeli anxieties over the fate of the West Bank? If Israel is disposed to regard the risks the world encourages it to take as life-threatening, is the source of its anxiety not plain?

Yes, there is blame enough to go around, blame for everyone. But the fact that none is perfect does not mean that all are equally culpable. There is, withal, a difference. There is a difference between the mistakes that America and Israel have made and the cowardice which Europe and the Arab world have displayed on these matters. And there is a difference between these and the inhumanity of the PLO. That is what Mr. Young seems to have forgotten. That is what Mr. Lowery of the SCLC apparently never learned. And that is what Jesse Jackson proposes to deny.

Yes, Israel is cast in the role of the mighty, the Palestinians in the role of the dispossessed. Surely, you argue, it is time for us to take the fact of Israel and of its power and of its capacity to survive for granted, and move on to other and more pressing needs. Curious, is it not, that there seem to be only two places left where Israel's existence is *not* yet taken for granted: among the PLO, which does not want to, and within Israel, which cannot afford to.

So please, no sanctimonious sermons to us. If you need to declare your independence, find a different issue. This one strikes far too close to the bone, and all those storied guilt feelings you expect to elicit from us you can just forget about. Maybe we do feel guilty about our success, and maybe we do feel guilty

The Andrew Young Affair...To be Continued

about your situation, and maybe we feel guilty about Cambodia and the Kurds and the parents we don't write to and the kids we don't spend enough time with, and maybe we even feel guilty about the raw deal the decent Palestinians are getting, but there's one thing we don't feel a gram of guilt about, and not all your preaching, not all your preaching and the preaching of the World Council of Churches and Vanessa Redgrave will change that, will cause us to crawl. For the State of Israel, for a free and fallible home for the Jews, no guilt. No apologies.

Declare your independence if you must, if you will. Tell us that you've changed, that you can no longer abide our good wishes and our advices, show us how far you've come. But note: We've changed, too. We've watched for ten years as the world has fallen for the Big Lie, has rejected the notion that Jews can take care of themselves, has abandoned Israel and dignified the brute, and, meaning no rudeness, we're no readier than you to apologize for living, to excuse ourselves for acquiring, here and there, a bit of power.

It would have been nice, how nice it would have been, back when we were all singing "We Shall Overcome" together, if we had managed to sing just a bit louder, loud enough to make the walls of injustice tumble down. We didn't, they wouldn't have. So now, a decade later, when instead of singing we've begun to shout, you want to see who can shout the louder? Does that help? Maybe it does. Maybe the Libyans will send you more cash, or maybe it just raises your morale to hear us yelp. But it's dumb. It's dumb not because our enmity, if that is where this episode comes to rest, is such a danger to you, any more than our friendship has been all that helpful of late. It's dumb because it's a diversion, a wildly wrong turn for both of us. The end of it will be to make it legitimate for our racists and for your anti-Semites to say out loud the words they were taught it was wrong to say, the words that decent people frowned upon. Now no guilt need attach to their utterance. Is that what you want? But you must know better: let loose the always straining dogs of bigotry, and there is no calling them back.

The Klan must be chortling. We're not the Klan, and you expect more from us? Good. We're used to being held to a higher standard; for some thousands of years, we've bound ourselves to a higher standard than anyone else has yet managed to impose upon us, a higher standard than we've yet been able to meet. But if it's equal treatment you want, then listen: We expect more from you, as well. We have the misfortune that we take our own rhetoric seriously, and we really believe all that stuff about the brotherhood of the ex-slaves—we in Egypt and in the camps, you in the South and in the Arab countries. We expect more from you. Not more favors, not more sermons; more recognition. Because some—not all, but some—of those special noises that you hear we also hear, and because some of those terrible places you have been we have also been, because fear haunts us both.

Fear and, at our best, a common dream. In this mishaped world, dreams ought not be casually dismissed. In Cambodia, two million people may die of starvation in the next few months. Four million Kurds in Iran may die at Khomeini's hands. In Thailand last week, a man sold his rib, extracted without anesthesia, for forty dollars, so that he could buy food; the rib will be used by plastic surgeons for women who want their noses to look more European. Your kids are still being bitten by rats, and our people languish in prisons in Argentina and in Russia, and our children in Israel's schools and marketplaces are still at risk, the sandboxes in the playgrounds must still be searched carefully for explosives each morning. Half the world is starving, and the other half is in Las Vegas. Too poor to dream, too rich to care. There aren't very many dreamers left, maybe not enough to make it work. So think twice before you finger us as the enemy.

No, we won't always agree. Our interests are not identical. Sometimes it will be easy for us to work together, and sometimes it will be hard, and sometimes it will be impossible. If there are issues where we part company, let's try to see to it that they aren't the vital issues, the ones that are rock-bottom for one or the other of us. (You'd do well to remember that even on affirmative action, our record is not what you've made it out to be: On the DeFunis case, the Union of American Hebrew Congregations and the National Council of Jewish Women, among others, stood with you; on Bakke, all three major Jewish defense organizations opposed your views, but on Webber only one did. The issues may distress us, but we've tried to behave with reasonable sensitivity.) So let's see to it that we confine our partings, if partings there must be, to real issues, and that we not make such differences as there are between us into occasions for generalized denunciations. Oh, it's a delicate and hazardous business, this business of insisting on the dream, and of sharing it. The crazies and the bigots in both our communities will try to throw us off, and the demagogues will try to wreck it for us all.

But the least that you should know about us by now is that we are seized of the dream. You frighten us just now, with your loose accusations and your superficial analyses. You frighten us and you offend us. But we won't let go the dream. You think we want your gratitude for favors past; you are mistaken. We want your respect for our authenticity, no less than you want the same from us, your respect for the complex authenticity of our confusion and our commitment. But even if, for passing reasons of your own, you withhold that respect, we will not let go the dream; we do not know how.

We are not your patrons. We are not even your brothers. We are not more than co-conspirators with you in the fight for decency. And if you choose to side with the brute, or in other ways reject our hand, that will be a shame and a waste.

How will we react? As best we can, we will fight on alone. ✡

AUTUMNAL REFLECTIONS

LEONARD FEIN

This fall has been filled with temptation. Large things have happened, are happening, and there are powerful reasons to try to misunderstand those things and what they portend.

I. The Temptation to Withdraw
On election night, at Republican headquarters, one of the principal organizers of the Jewish vote rushed into the room with the latest estimate of how the Jews were voting: "The California exit polls show that we're getting 70 percent of the Jewish vote," he announced. "Seventy percent! We don't even lie that high!"

No they don't, although they do tend to inflate. Mr. Reagan did respectably well among the Jews, but not nearly so well as some of his more enthusiastic supporters would have us believe. The CBS/New York *Times* exit polls estimate that some 39 percent of the Jewish vote was cast for the Reagan-Bush ticket; other neutral estimates add a couple of points more. Let's assume that the actual figure was 40 percent. That's higher than the Jewish vote for the Republican nominee in any recent election; until now, 35 percent was the record, set on two occasions—the Nixon vote in the 1972 election, and the Ford vote in the 1976 election. The apparent 14 percent growth in the Jewish Republican vote suggests that the Jews are, as many observers have recently been suggesting, moving to the right.

Moving to the right? There are at least three good reasons to hesitate before accepting that conclusion:

First, a careful analysis of the

Jewish vote suggests a record level of abstention. Apparently, even the Anderson option did not satisfy many regular voters who rejected both Carter and Reagan. Some stayed home, others left the Presidential ballot blank. It does not take very many abstentions to confuse the statistics. Suppose, for example, that 10 percent of those Jews who normally vote for President held back this time. Instead of 100 Jewish voters, there were only 90. And suppose, further, we use the 40 percent pro-Reagan estimate. That's 40 percent of 90, or 36 votes. On that basis, it appears that Mr. Reagan did no better than Nixon and Ford—a respectable showing, to be sure, but not one which warrants sweeping conclusions about major shifts in Jewish voting behavior.

Second, one needs to look at the specific precincts where Mr. Reagan did especially well. The data here will take many months to analyze, but it seems clear that Jewish support for the Republican nominee was heaviest among two very different kinds of groups; first, among those "legitimately" Republican Jews whose economic status has for some time led them to support conservative candidates—about three out of every five of Reagan's Jewish votes fall into this category—and, second, among very Orthodox Jews in places such as Boro Park. Indeed, it is quite likely that if there was a net increase in the number of Jews who voted for the Republican nominee, much of it can be accounted for by the Orthodox shift. That shift does not represent a move towards economic conservatism. Instead, it is a reflection of the political fundamentalism which was so prominent an aspect of this election. For many years, the specific ties between the Jewish community and the Democratic Party were so tight that even right wing Orthodox Jews, whose cultural orientation was manifestly illiberal, were swept along by it. But those ties have weakened considerably of late. Further, the Republicans this time around did not try to disguise their conservatism behind liberal rhetoric. These circumstances, together with the more specific issues of the Middle East—issues on which some elements within the Orthodox community find Mr. Begin too dovish for their taste—led the precincts of Boro Park, for example, to go two and three to one for Reagan. (*The Jewish Press,* a kind of newspaper with a mass circulation in Orthodox Brooklyn, endorsed Reagan and D'Amato—and claims now that its endorsement of both made the crucial difference.) Yes, that is a Jewish swing to the right, but it is rather a different kind of swing from the one that is supposed to have happened. It is not a swing among middle and upper middle class Jews who have finally learned the folly of their liberal ways. It is a swing among Orthodox Jews who have finally recognized the contradiction involved in supporting aid to parochial schools, opposing abortion, and generally endorsing conservative perspectives, while continuing to vote for Democrats.

Finally: Imagine that this last election had not been between Mr. Reagan and Mr. Carter, but had, instead, been between Mr. Reagan and Hubert Humphrey, or even Walter Mondale. Can it be doubted that the Jewish vote would have split 80-20 or so in favor of the Democratic nominee? The fact is that almost all the Jews who voted for Carter in 1976 and did not vote for him in 1980 either abstained or voted for John Anderson. Very, very few ended up pulling the Reagan lever—and for at least some of those who did, it was not fondness for Reagan but antipathy to Carter that moved them. A credible liberal candidate would have restored the traditional Jewish voting pattern.

There is, in short, no reason to conclude, on the basis of this election, that the Jews of America have deserted their liberal disposition. For years now, there has been no coherent spokesman for that disposition. In 1960, when John Kennedy defeated Adlai Stevenson for the Democratic nomination, it was generally believed that Kennedy was not a liberal. Jews perceived him as his father's son, and the overwhelming margin of support they gave him was as much an anti-Nixon vote as this year's returns were an expression of opposition to Carter. Lyndon Johnson, in 1964, may have been widely perceived as a liberal—but had the good fortune, whatever the perception, to run against Barry Goldwater. The Jews stayed true. The Hubert Humphrey of 1968 was a Humphrey neutered, temporarily, by President Johnson, and, in the specific context of that election, Humphrey could not be regarded as a liberal's delight. Yet, even so, the Jews voted overwhelmingly in his favor. Nineteen seventy-two? McGovern was surely liberal, but as surely lacked coherence. He fared badly with the Jews, even though they supported him more than almost any other population group—as, incidentally, was also the case with Mr. Carter. And as to 1976, whatever good things may be said about Jimmy Carter, he did not present himself then as a plausible carrier of the liberal banner.

That tattered banner has not been nobly lifted for many years, and the reason may have less to do with the quality of the people who are enticed into politics than with the fact that the banner itself is badly frayed. Liberalism may remain our disposition, but there is a difference between a disposition and a program, and the content of the liberal program is very hard to define these days. Not since the heady days of the Great Society has there been a sense of genuine possibility, of excitement regarding the liberal prospect. Since then, we have stuttered and sputtered, and it is evident that the old slogans no longer will do. There is none among us who can any longer deny that government by regulation is stultifying, no matter how benign the instincts that give rise to the regulation. No one can sensibly stay blind to the malignance of the Soviet Union and the need to protect against its spread. Nor ought anyone dismiss as Neanderthal the belief of many Americans that moral issues cannot any longer safely be ignored by the society. Liberals cannot avoid asking how their tradition of reliance on government can be reconciled with the manifest clumsiness of government, how their instincts for pacific détente can be reconciled with the warring malice of the USSR, how their insistence on moral freedom can be stayed from inviting moral license.

At the same time, the old questions remain. They will not go away. How shall this great and generous nation finally come to grips with the gross inequities that persist within it, inequities that have never much troubled conservatives? How shall we deal more effectively with crime, and with poverty, and with sleaziness, and with health? Opposition to the death penalty is good liberal doctrine, and so is endorsement of national health insurance, but a series of random convictions, or even of coherent sentiments, does not add up to a persuasive program. We can choose to sulk out the next four years, or to revel in opposition, but neither will repair the banner—much less produce the needed program.

I suspect that many of us will be tempted simply to distance ourselves from the world of politics, which has been so disappointing a world these past years. Such distancing, if it leads to a serious investment of energies in good works, cannot be condemned. (Later in these pages, Harold Schulweis makes a powerful case for that kind of investment.) On the assumption that a conservative President and a conservative Senate and a more conservative House of Representatives will cut back the dollars available for social programs, the need for voluntarism will grow dramatically. The sick will not stop being sick, and the old will not vanish. Our contributions of money and time to help care for them will have to grow, and if those to whom such matters have always been of concern are moved, in a period of government retrenchment, to fill the gap, that will be a productive fringe benefit of the recent elections.

But only a fringe benefit. The problems are too vast and too complex to be solved by goodness alone. Government remains the intended expression of our collective goodness, not as a substitute for personal involvement but as an institutional expression—utterly essential—of our commitment to decency. The American people have not turned their backs on that commitment; they have merely become bored and disillusioned with the stumbling ways in which government has sought to give it life. They can scarcely be blamed for that; cynicism is fostered with almost every news broadcast. But it will be a terrible error to suppose that because yesterday's social strategies are no longer persuasive, the beliefs which gave rise to them have been discarded. The political imagination of a mature democracy is shaped by its sense of political possibility. If the liberal possibility can be persuasively represented, it will once again fire our political imagination.

II. The Temptation to Consort

How can one speak of liberal possibilities in the age of Jerry Falwell and Bailey Smith? Fundamentalism is everywhere ascendent, and the United States is not immune. The so-called Moral Majority is no longer dismissable as a fringe group of trogolodytes; it feels itself triumphant—tomorrow the world—and its success in establishing itself as a political force creates very serious problems for those of us whom it would consign to the immoral minority.

For Jews especially. The heart of our problem is obvious; in the view of the so-called Moral Majority, this is a Christian country. (The specific remark of Reverend Bailey Smith, president of the Southern Baptist Convention, which evoked so much furor back in August was, "It is interesting at great political rallies how you have a Protestant to pray and a Catholic to pray, and then you have a Jew to pray. With all due respect to these dear people, my friends, God Almighty does not hear the prayer of a Jew." The Jewish response was predictably indignant, though it is questionable whether very many Jews think that God hears our prayers—or anyone's—and it is indignant because we understand precisely what is at stake. It is not our place in heaven that is in dispute; it is our place in the United States.)

But while the heart of the matter is the legitimacy of a plural society, which is an entirely straightforward question, there are specific aspects of the matter which make it painfully complex.

Jews have not fared well, recently, at the hands of liberal Christians. The general sense within the Jewish community, encouraged in a major way by the call of the National Council of Churches for the recognition of the PLO, is that our erstwhile allies on the moderate left have abandoned us, that they are insensitive not only to Israel's plight but also to the dangers of anti-Semitism. Among the Evangels, however, there is much support for Israel and its safety, support which holds that the Second Coming depends on the ingathering of the Jews in the Holy Land—followed, to be sure, by their conversion to Christianity.

Some of the Evangels are in the business because it is lucrative, others because they believe it. The Christian Right is hardly monolithic; it consists of a very loose and often competitive group of private entrepreneurs, and the temptation is to try to take advantage of their disarray and of their disposition to support Israel by embracing those who indicate a readiness to work with us on matters of common interest.

It is an understandable temptation. A people that feels itself friendless wants to find allies. A people that thinks itself sophisticated assumes that it can control the alliance, protect against its obvious dangers. And so, in mid-November, under the aegis of the Jabotinsky Foundation, and in the presence of Menachem Begin, and with the tacit endorsement of Jewish leaders from dozens of Jewish organizations, Jerry Falwell, the so-called Moral Majority's leader, was awarded a medal for his "distinguished service to the State of Israel and to the Jewish people."

I am unaware of any service whatsoever that Falwell has performed for the State of Israel, save for not attacking it—but my files are incomplete, and it is possible that he has done something praiseworthy. But I am quite certain that Mr. Falwell has performed no service whatsoever for the Jewish people, and it is demeaning to suggest that he has. Frank Church, whose service to both the State of Israel and to the Jewish people are a matter of long and exceptional record, was also slated to receive a Jabotinsky medal, but he had the spine to refuse the "honor": "While I greatly appreciate the award you have conferred upon me," he cabled the evening's sponsors, "I regret that I cannot accept this honor at the same time that you are citing Jerry Falwell. Mr. Falwell has attempted to distort the American political process by imposing his views of morality as a political litmus test of a man's moral fitness to hold office.... Our political and religious freedoms are cornerstones of our system and should not be undermined. Israel's security and America's freedom are inextricably bound together. I shall continue to fight for both."

Church was saying what almost all of us know: An America governed by Jerry Falwell's perceptions would be no friend to Israel, let alone to the Jews. But there are those among us who imagine that by seeking to ingratiate ourselves with Falwell et al., we will blunt the mischief of which they are capable. They will reason that some on the Christian Right—Pat Robertson of the Christian Broadcasting Network, for example—are genuinely friendly, and, more important, do not seek to mold our body politic to conform to their theological perceptions. Some leaders of the Christian Right are among Israel's warmest friends in this country today. Good. Good to have friends everywhere. That is not the issue. The issue is the wisdom of making common cause with those whose most basic understandings are so radically at odds with ours. Not all Evangels, by any means, accept the currently fashionable theopolitics of Jerry Falwell; it is that theopolitics, and not Christian fundamentalism as such, that threatens us, and that we should have both the good sense and the self-respect to oppose.

For if we do not oppose it—if, worse, we lend it respectability in the name of temporary advantage—we shall lose our claim to the friendship of those whose friendship matters more, and with whom we more naturally belong. There is no more important issue on the Jewish political agenda these days than the development of new coalitions. The old combination of Jews, Blacks, and the trade union movement has come unglued, and it is not at all likely that it can be put back together. Neither we nor the Israelis can look to the traditional coalitions with the kind of confidence we once felt. But the notion that the militants of the theopolitical Right are our new partners is absurd; it is absurd for us; it is absurd for the Israelis. It reflects a failure of imagination rather than a new sophistication. As much as we have been disillusioned by the Left, and as complicated as it is to figure out with whom we ought now to be working, those who urge us to turn so sharply rightward must suffer from amnesia. There is no comfort there for us. Such a turn would merely insure an end to our credibility with the center and Left, and would alienate still further a host of our own people, all those who correctly viewed the award to Falwell as an embarrassment rather than as a clever device.

There is anti-Semitism on the Left, and there is anti-Semitism in the center, and these disgusting aberrations are most unnerving. But the anti-Semitism of the Right is no aberration; it springs from a venerable tradition, and its practitioners are not fools. We may imagine ourselves clever enough to use them; odds are it is we who will be used.

III. The Temptation to Evade

Anti-Semitism. A few weeks back, a friend of mine, a ranking official of one of our national defense agencies, was expostulating on the present danger. The Pope has attacked us on Jerusalem; in Paris, the bombings; in England, a sudden flurry of "episodes"; in dozens of American cities, scores of incidents—spray-painted swastikas on our schools, vandalization of our synagogues and cemeteries. It is not hard to weave a fabric out of all that has been happening, and to feed the conspiratorial fantasy. On August 16 last, the Lake Grove Jewish Center on Long Island was burned to the ground. On October 28, swastikas, obscenities and five-foot high KKK inscriptions were painted on the walls of the Great Neck North Senior High School. Erev Yom Kippur, the walls of the Ramaz School in New York City were defaced. Just a couple of weeks back, the Solomon Schechter school my daughter Jessica attends was the hooligan's target, and a swastika was painted on its window.

Something is clearly happening. We know very little about why it is happening, but the events themselves cannot be denied. Yet there seems no reason at all, other than our own constant apprehension, to suppose that what is happening is in any sense at all the product of conspiracy. In the offices of the Anti-Defamation League, I imagine, careful files are kept. Each new incident is meticulously logged, indexed, cross-referenced, stored. Perhaps by now a computer is required to keep track. But all the episodes do not add up to a pattern. Here a disgruntled employee, there a troubled youngster, now an ideological anti-Semite, then a drunken gang. This is not Argentina, where 2500 Jews have been caused to "disappear" by agents of the State over the course of the last three years; this is not France, where the anti-Semitic Right has become fashionable, and where PLO assassins ply their trade; this is manifestly not the USSR, where anti-Semitism has been adopted as a policy of the State. No, this is America, and America, of course, is different.

Those of us who were children before the Second World War had hoped and expected that it would be more different than it has turned out to be. We had been called the distorted names back then, and more, and we thought it would be different for our children. Away from the urban cauldrons, in the insulated safety of our single family homes and condominiums, in the sympathetic aftermath of the Holocaust, we expected that our children would know anti-Semitism only secondhand. It is a terrible disappointment to find that we were mistaken.

A disappointment, but far from a tragedy. Anti-Semitism in America is hardly an epic phenomenon, even though it is encouraged by the attacks on Jews elsewhere. Anti-Semitism here is an attitude rather than a doctrine, much less a movement. It is a measle, not a tumor.

I do not mean that we should be content merely to scrub the walls clean and repair the broken windows, comfort our children with stories about the inevitability of it all, and go on about our business. Attitudes, too, have consequences, and measles are infectious. Some part of our energy must always be devoted to preventing the development of anti-Semitism, or, if we cannot, to containing it. And this we do, assigning vast sums and some of our best personnel to the Anti-Defamation League, to the American Jewish Committee and the American Jewish Congress and the National Community Relations Advisory Council, to dozens of local community councils.

Perhaps, in light of what appears to be happening these days, the budgets of these organizations should be increased, their methods improved, their operations more precisely targeted. Perhaps more attention should be paid to what was once quaintly called "inter-group relations," or to ecumenical outreach. Perhaps more studies of the extent and the roots of anti-Semitism should be commissioned, so that we understand more exactly just what is happening, and why.

But one thing is clear, or should be, amidst all the "perhapses": If we permit the new outbreak of hooliganism to divert us from the other issues on the Jewish agenda of our time, we will have needlessly abetted the insult it offers, helped to convert that insult into an injury we can ill afford.

The temptation is powerful. If the anti-Semites still roam about in the night, our fight against them can free us of the need to ask the hard questions that urgently await our attention, questions that cannot be answered by looking through a window daubed with a swastika, questions that can be answered only by looking in the mirror.

For the Jewish people to survive, we must be able not only to repel the anti-Semites, we must be able to develop satisfying responses to the enemy within, to the confusions and uncertainties that plague our understanding of what Judaism and Jewishness are and ought to be about. The cements that once bound us to one another have dried out. Save for the sense of common threat, there is little that defines our common destiny. Neither the Jewish God nor the Jewish calendar nor the Jewish language(s) nor the Jewish culture draws us together as once each did; the Jewish consensus has come to depend almost wholly on external stimuli. We lean into one another in our anxieties; these replace the erstwhile connections.

Anxiety is a powerful magnet, but it is as dangerous as it is compelling. We are witness today to a resurgence of the Jewish appetite such as none had foreseen, none predicted. For a wide variety of reasons, more Jews than anyone had thought likely want to be Jews, want to connect with their past, with their future, with each other. The appetite is there—but not the nourishment. So the temptation is to use the threat of anti-Semitism. What connects one Jew to another? Our common destiny. What defines that destiny? Our common enemy.

Danger is so comfortably familiar to a generation that has been schooled in fear and lamentation. It is Munich, not Entebbe, that confirms our vision of Jewish destiny; it is not the pride of June 1967, but the terror of May 1967 that draws us together. Fear is our Stradivarius, and we are virtuoso fiddlers.

But a condition is not a vocation. It is not Rome that burns as we fiddle our fears; it is our dreams. Anti-Semitism is a blight which, unattended, can lay us waste. But over-attended, it will ravage us more certainly still. For anti-Semitism can also become a crutch, an especially appealing crutch to a generation that is just learning how to walk. If we permit it to divert us from our urgent business, then, when the hooligans are gone at last, we shall not have learned how to walk, we shall not know of what to speak. Better to stumble our way to dignity and meaning than to rely on the crutch our enemies so conveniently offer us.

How easy it would be to draw together in outrage and in apprehension rather than to figure out how to make Jewish education work, and how to make Jewish culture happen, and how to make Jewish thought come alive. The pain that is caused by anti-Semitism, real though it is, is a fraction of the pain that is caused by loneliness; why should the one be treated as urgent and the other ignored? Even in the short run, surely in the long, a community that offers its members respite and succor in a careening world will hold its members more certainly than a community that knows only to huddle together against the enemy's stones. I do not accept that we need the threat, that we depend on it, not even as a substitute while we learn to wrestle with God again. Yes, we are a threatened community, and yes, therefore, we need a radar system that will warn us when the missiles fly. But yes, as well, yes, in the first place, we need a gyroscope that will allow us to stay on course, that will permit us to determine for ourselves the ways we choose to travel. It is not for the hooligans to tell us how to spend our time or money, much less to tell us what we have in common. We have more important things in common than their enmity. Unless we believe that, we might as well pack it in. And unless we start figuring out what those things are—say, for example, an obsession with making this world work better—then we have no good reason to insist upon our own survival as a people. ✶

ISRAEL AT 33

On a kibbutz in Israel's heartland, a kibbutz that is home to 160 families, there is a factory whose high-technology products are (via a third country) exported to the Union of Soviet Socialist Republics. The factory is just eight years old; its machines and its materials are all imported; it is staffed by some 40 members of the kibbutz, which hires no outside labor in any of its branches, and never has. The manager of the factory is one of my oldest friends.

Sitting in his apartment near the end of a two hour visit—to the factory and the fields, the children's houses and the flower gardens, the library and the cultural center—we talk of hopes and fulfillments, of satisfactions and disappointments. We have known each other since our mid-teens, almost 30 years ago, and we have kept in touch ever since, through the birth of his three sons and my three daughters, their growth, and each other's, the assorted flowerings and contractions of our adolescent ambitions. In 1953, we picked olives together, and spoke of an Israel that might yet be, and that night, in this same kibbutz, we collapsed exhausted on the cots in the huts that were our temporary home. He stayed for a second year, and then for good, while I came back to school in the States, and today he is the force behind a factory that earns 60 percent of the revenues of his kibbutz and sells its produce to a dozen foreign countries, and he is very, very proud.

An F-15 fighter plane costs $42 million dollars, more or less. The United States has offered to let Israel buy ten more F-15s. But Israel's foreign debt now stands at some $185 billion; Israel cannot afford to buy all the planes, tanks and sundry other weapons systems America is now prepared to sell. In the short term, the solution may be to negotiate more favorable credit terms from the United States, or perhaps to defer once again much-needed investment in Israel's domestic economy. That would solve the problem of the ten more F-15s. But what of the next ten, or fifty? What of the next generation of fighter aircraft?

Beyond the short-term, there is only one way for Israel to maintain its military superiority over a hostile Arab world that is now able to afford whatever it wants. (One argument that is advanced by proponents of the F-15 enhancement package the Saudis now seek is that if America denies the Saudis, they will buy the French Mirage 2000/4000 or the European Toronado, which are both more lethal than the F-15.) That way is for Israel to depend on a direct American shield for its protection.

According to Hirsh Goodman, the respected military correspondent for the *Jerusalem Post,* the new generation of sophisticated military equipment is "idiot-proof"; it does not require sophisticated personnel for its operation or its maintenance. Accordingly, Israel's qualitative advantage will, as these new systems come on line, mean much less than it has until now. The quality will matter less, and the quantity will no longer be affordable. So, an American shield, perhaps even a treaty of alliance.

There were two arguments for an independent Jewish state. The first was the need for a refuge, a haven, a safe harbor for the Jews. There needed to be one country, at least, that would unconditionally open its door to Jews in trouble. Israel is that country. But the Jews, even those in trouble, have not flocked to it. (In February of 1981, a total of 857 newcomers arrived in Israel.) Instead, it has become a refuge of last resort; it is honored in prayer but not in practice. The wrenching disappointment of the last 33 years is that so few Jews have associated themselves with Israel in the way that matters most, through aliyah, immigration to the land. They have instead preferred to view Israel as if it were an insurance policy, dutifully paying their premiums—and hoping they'd never have to make a claim.

There are those who complain that Israel is too problematic a place to attract Jews. Beset by enemies without, confused by disarray within, why should Jews—yes, even those in trouble—want to make Israel their home? But this is no argument at all. First, there is no evidence whatever that immigration to Israel has suffered because it has seemed inadequately attractive. Second, and more important, Zionist theory never contemplated that Israel would be a charming resort to which distant Jews would happily repair out of desire for milk, honey and sunshine. Israel was not Miami Beach; it was not supposed to be. It was, and is, supposed to be a place of challenge, affording an energetic people the opportunity to be pioneers in the rebirth of Jewish independence.

That was, in fact, the second argument for Zionism. Refuge aside, the idea was that Jews should be able to control their own agenda, set their own priorities, make their own mistakes. Some Jews would come out of need, and others, in the hundreds of thousands, would be attracted by the nobility of the endeavor. But even if there were no flood of immigration, even if most Jews inertially stayed put, the enterprise would go forward. Jewish independence would be asserted, Jewish autonomy, at last, enjoyed.

What is at stake in the Middle East today is not merely war or peace, as if these issues were not large enough. More than Israel's security is threatened by developments, actual and impending, in weapons systems. Jewish independence and autonomy are at stake as well. For an Israel that is moved inexorably towards dependence on the United States for its protection is an Israel that moves as certainly away from control over its own destiny. What independence is there for a nation that must beg its instruments of survival from a distant power?

Obviously, there are ways in which this unhappy movement has already begun. America's capacity to exert fierce pressure on Israel, and to impose its judgment on a reluctant Jewish state, has already been exercised any number of times. But Israel has managed to retain a reasonable freedom nonetheless. In part, this freedom is the gift of Israel's supporters in the United States. American governments have been reluctant to force Israel to accept every aspect of American doctrine for fear of political backlash that would inevitably ensue. (Count Israel's capacity to mobilize its friends in this country—by no means only Jews—as one of its more important strategic assets.)

In more important part, Israel's freedom of political maneuver has been supported by Israel's military capabilities, as evidenced by its unbroken string of impressive military success.

But the past may not be prologue to the future. It is hard to imagine how, by the 1990s, Israel's military capabilities will be as significant as they are today. Accordingly, it is hard to feel confident that Israel's freedom, its independence, will be maintained.

Modern weapons are Israel's life-support system, and without life, there is no independence. But is there independence when someone else can pull the plug?

Time, therefore, is not on Israel's side. The country grows stronger with each passing year, yet its strength does not bring it more freedom, more certain independence, more autonomy. Its agenda is still heavily burdened by the impositions of its neighbors, and its policies are increasingly fixed by what is acceptable to the United States. It is comforting to know that current American strategic doctrine places so high a value on Israel's power, but the comfort is bittersweet. For we had hoped, still hope, that Israel's independence would not be the product of Pentagon assessments, that Israel would be more than a piece in someone else's puzzle. The Zionist vision of the Return has been subverted by the Jews; the more compelling aspect of the Zionist dream, the goal of genuine autonomy, is in the process of being done in by the exigencies of the arms race and the East-West conflict. It was not a client state the Zionists envisioned.

A pawn with a flag is still a pawn.

Israel's 33rd is an occasion for celebration. The vast accomplishments of this troubled land are an inspiration to those who seek evidence of mankind's capacity for steadfastness and creativity. But it is no secret that those accomplishments are threatened by a series of distressing developments within Israeli society. The Israeli economy is in acute crisis; the political system is marked by clumsy and costly compromise; the society is increasingly fractious. Mid-course corrections are urgently required in almost every sphere, yet the ability of the nation to contemplate such corrections is powerfully restricted by the crushing weight of the arms race. Soon, Israel will no longer enjoy even the right to make its own mistakes. Hence there is something wistful about this year's celebration of Israel's independence.

Those who care for Israel will continue to insist that it be assured the capacity to defend itself against its enemies. Yet they will know there is a curse embedded in the blessing. There is no military solution to the continuing conflict; there is only, if at all, a political solution. Israel's independence, not for a day but for eternity, cannot rest on an American view of the world that time and circumstance may change; its achievement and its guarantee will be the product not of military prowess but of political genius.

I try to visit my friend on his kibbutz each time I come to Israel. There is a reality here that is harder to grab hold of in ethereal Jerusalem or in sweaty Tel Aviv. Outside the room where we sit, the sprinklers swirl, watering flowering vines and flowering bushes and flowering plants, and just plain flowers, in a profusion of shape and color and perfume such as I have never seen, and high-pile lawns that say more about pride and even independence than the words of my friend, than any words can.

How far this is from the daily headlines and the tortured analyses of international affairs that frame the context of most discussion of Israel today. The "real" Israel is, to be sure, the Israel that is excoriated in the UN and defined as a strategic asset in the White House, the Israel of triple-digit inflation and of political confusion, of a rising crime rate and a declining rate of immigration. But it is also the Israel of my friend's factory, these lawns, this pride. Some of the children on my friend's kibbutz can visit with their great-grandparents, for the kibbutz is among Israel's oldest, and some of the children who were born here have died of natural causes and others have been killed, in automobile accidents or in the wars of 1948, 1956, 1967 or 1973, or in the times of non-peace between wars. There is a room in the library where the pictures of the war-dead are displayed, and their memorabilia, and one of the pictures is of J., the closest friend of my friend, with whom we lounged and laughed together on the lawn one evening back in the summer of 1973, before the dark days.

It is not the clouds of death and loss that have brought on the darkness, for they are fleeting clouds, the kind that cause at worst a transient chill. Neither memories nor fear of war intrude, as such, on the days's trivial calamities and trivial celebrations, any more than do the muggings and the ripoffs here at home. Time is framed by the boys growing up and the harvest and the arrival of the automated lathe, by the paunch and the graying, by the sweetness of these grapes. Somewhere, a bomb went off today, or did not; somewhere, my friend's first-born is being made into a warrior. But the bomb was far away, and no one was hurt; my friend's first-born will be home for the Shabbat, and will play with his brothers in the awkward way of men with boots and guns come back to their mother's warm embrace and their father's rough kiss. This is the Valley of Jezreel, once a swampland, now a riot of flowers and a precision of high-tech exports.

Dusk falls. Nearby, a lamb bleats. Far off, a jet roars past. I walk with my friend to the factory; it is time for the second shift. Soon it will be dawn.

THINKING ABOUT LEBANON

LEONARD FEIN

I write on July 4, four weeks to the day since Israel moved into Lebanon. A few hours from now, just a few blocks from here, the Boston Pops will play its annual Independence Day concert that culminates with the "1812 Overture" and the synchronized explosion of cannon and fireworks over the Charles River. In Beirut today, July 4, a far more ancient ritual drags on; there, the sounds that served Tchaikovsky as his raw material are still untamed. Tomorrow, next week perhaps, soon in any case, the ritual will end. Eyes that have followed the cannon in their steady northward movement, that for ten days now have been fixed on West Beirut, will move outward again, to all of Lebanon, back to the Galilee and to the West Bank, back to the Palestinians, to the Arab-Israel conflict, back to war and peace, back to the tragic imperfections of humankind.

For war is a tragedy, all war; there is no escape from that. Killing people, whether the people are those we call "innocent bystanders" or those we call "the enemy" (who are in fact usually children) is a terrible thing, a tragic thing. We do not rejoice, we are forbidden to rejoice, at the death of our enemies. And if on the death of our enemies we are forbidden to rejoice, then surely we are bound to mourn the death of the bystanders.

But tragedy is not the same as evil, not at all. It is one thing to lament the killing, another to condemn it. The pictures of the mothers and children fleeing in terror, of the old men sitting in confusion and despair amidst the rubble, haunt us, and they become, inevitably, a part of the equation. But they are not the whole of it. Because we are tragically imperfect, there is war, and war is senseless, and war is cruel, but some wars, at least, are about things worth fighting for, and some wars therefore we call "just." Israel's war in Lebanon is entitled to be judged, as all wars are, analytically. In any such analysis, the tragedy must be figured in, a heavy cost of war. But no matter how deeply we feel, no matter how wrenching the pictures and the agony they bespeak, we are required to *think*, not just to feel. Minds made soggy by flowing emotion are as useless as hearts drained by austere analysis.

Some of my friends, people I care for and from whose decency I draw strength, do not seem to understand that. The pictures hypnotize them; they cannot move beyond. All of us abhor violence, but some of us seem to me to be heirs to a dismal diaspora tradition that comes very close to making a virtue of Jewish impotence. I, too, am proud that we are not a hunting people, yet I vastly prefer—the world being what it is—that we are today non-hunters who have guns rather than disarmed non-hunters. It takes no special virtue, after all, to refrain from hunting if you've not been given weapons for the hunt. This way, this ugly way, we have the weapons, and that helps solve a problem to which we Jews have historically been particularly susceptible, the problem of being murdered. It also helps create a problem, for now our virtue is directly on the line in ways it was not, could not have been, back in the days of our castration. On balance, I'd rather confront the new problem than the old; I do not regard the centuries of Jewish impotence as the "good old days," and I do not join in the celebration of Jewish powerlessness. Our grandfathers may have been as sweet and gentle as we like to think, and I am happy we praise them for such qualities; they also tended to die from unnatural causes. Jews without guns are not—as some seem to think—more authentically Jewish. Impotence was merely our circumstance, not our destiny.

It is shameful, criminal even, that in this world there must be victims and victors. But if such there must be, as the old saying goes, we've been both, and victor's better. The unadorned fact that the Jews of Israel have been engaged in killing does not make them guilty of anything more than living in this world, does not even provide grounds for indictment.

Yes, it is ironic, even cruelly so, that in the Jewish State, where we'd hoped to develop our finest talents, so much of our energy has perforce been turned to warmaking. As my visitor from Israel put it just last month, here in America Jewish parents compare notes on the colleges to which their children have been admitted; back home, on his kibbutz, the talk is not of colleges, but of officer training

Is there a proportionality between the havoc and the good that's meant to come of it?

courses. His own son had just been graduated from the most demanding of these, the Harvard of warmaking, summa cum laude; in Lebanon, he's put his new knowledge to practical use. He is, as his father wistfully says, "an expert in ruining." With his father, I curse that we have had to learn such things, worse yet teach them to our children; with his father, I rejoice that we have learned them so well.

It cuts both ways: Others of my friends have lost their sense of irony. They see nothing awry, no distortion, in the triumph of muscles over morals. It is time, they argue, to shuck our super-sensitivities; the world is a mean and brutish place, where nice guys are finished first. No more sheep to the slaughter for us, no more dreamy martyrdom. Never again. If your enemy rises up to kill you, go out to kill him first, and don't feel that on your return you've got to write gentle poems to prove your decency. No need to strut, but no need either to turn up your nose at the smell of the tanks, the roar of the jets. Those are Jewish tanks and Jewish jets, the smells and sounds of civilization. Nations cannot live on poems or on dreams, and we're a nation now.

And I wonder: If you stop writing poems and dreaming dreams, if you stop knowing irony, if you stop retching at death, won't you start hunting for sport?

This is the first war that Israel has fought where its survival was not immediately at stake, the first war where battles raged in heavily populated places. Our instinct has always been to rally 'round Israel's flag in times of trouble, but that flag has been carried to the suburbs of Beirut, and that's a bit far to go on instinct alone. Twenty-five miles, maybe—but not this far.

So for once, just this once, let's set aside our anger at a calloused world that has no regard for Jewish safety, our anger at the media distortions, at the double-standarding to which Israel is so subjected. Of course it is true that the others have expressed far greater outrage at Israel's actions in Lebanon than they did, say, a few months back when Syria was destroying Hamma. But *thinking* about Lebanon is not advanced by our resentments. Unless we fear the harder questions, and the harsher answers, why seek to have the case dismissed on the grounds that the witnesses against us are impeachable, biased, incompetent? Winning on such technical grounds is not much of a victory. If it's the best we can do, so be it—but it does Israel little service and less credit to imply that we have no stronger argument, that we are reluctant to take the stand in our own defense. Ought we not do Israel the courtesy of imagining that its actions might be valid in their own terms? Or do we mean to argue merely that a world that failed to condemn Syria has not the right to condemn Israel? But the world's wrongness does not establish Israel's rightness. Is it really by the expectations that people have of Syria that we insist Israel now be judged? Can Israel and its supporters not risk more rigorous judgment?

So. This war was meant, from its start, as a war against the PLO. Minimally, its aim was to clear the area south of the Litani River of a terrorist presence. If Israel had been able to go no farther, *dayenu*—that would have been sufficient in the eyes of Israel's planners. But the plan, from its inception more than a year ago (so Chief of Staff Eitan informed us last week) called for a far more comprehensive victory, called for an Israeli move all the way to Beirut and the destruction of the PLO as an effective organization. There was never any question that, left to its own devices, Israel could do what it planned to do. The question was whether Israel would be left to its own devices, how, that is, others—especially the United States—would react. In the event, the United States blessed Israel with faint rebuke, and the Israelis pressed forward, well beyond the Litani.

How can one oppose a war against so scurrilous a gang as the PLO? Surely there has never been a more contemptible collection of nationalist leaders, people who send 12-year-olds off to do battle, who hold their own kinsfolk hostage in order to save their own lives, who kill those of their own people who deviate from their rejectionist line, people, above all, who have no sense of opportunity, of reality.

For if they had, they would have entered the autonomy negotiations from the start. Had they done so, they would have opened irreversibly the door to self-determination. Thoughtful people in Israel, from both left and right, knew exactly that; that is why the left supported the autonomy, and the right opposed it. Even later in the day, after Prime Minister Begin eviscerated the original proposal for "full autonomy," Palestinian participation in the talks would have initiated a process bound to culminate in self-determination. But no, the PLO could not see that, or did not want to.

PLO apologists claimed, with some plausibility, that it was Syria that vetoed Palestinian participation in the talks, as it was Syria that forced the PLO to reverse its initial endorsement of the Fahd plan. But these last two weeks or so, the PLO has not had to submit to Syrian demands. Suppose that on the morrow of Israel's encirclement of Beirut, Mr. Arafat had declared that the military option was now closed, that he therefore accepted President Mubarak's invitation to move to Cairo and establish there a Palestinian government-in-exile? Would not his prospects and those of the people he leads have risen quite dramatically? Would not the dilemma facing Mr. Begin with regard to Palestinian self-determination have been substantially compounded?

But Mr. Arafat, it turns out, is simply not a serious person. As a terrorist, he may be a giant; as a nationalist leader, he is a pygmy, a betrayer of the people he leads. He is fueled by fantasy, not by vision; he is adept at managing factions, inept at exploiting facts. Little wonder that no Arab country wants to receive him and his comrades.

It is shocking that some Western observers suggest a moral symmetry between Arafat's exclusivism and Begin's exclusivism. What symmetry, either moral or intellectual, is there between a "revolutionary" who would rather kill than win, who sends small children to the front and abandons them there, and a leader who, myopic though he be, pursues his faulty vision with some sense of responsibility and even—by comparison—restraint?

A terrorist to others, a traitor to his own: Can there be any question that this war was justified?

Yes, there can be—there is—such a question. We do not make war against people simply because we do not like them, or because they are not likable, we do not make war against people even when those people are our enemies. War is not about likes and dislikes, even when these are entirely justifiable. It is about threats that cannot be removed in any other way, it is about goals that are large enough to warrant the heavy costs of war and that cannot be achieved by more pacific means. A surgeon with a knife in the operating room deftly slices open a patient, and we approve. The same surgeon, with the same knife and the same deftness, slices open a person on the street. This time, it is assault with a deadly weapon he has committed, not surgery performed.

There has to be a reason for the killing, a reason beyond hate.

And more than that. The larger the scope of the killing, the maiming, the dislocation—that is, of the ravages of war—the more compelling the reason must be.

That is a brutal way to put it, but I know no other. In a different world, each of the dead has a name, and neither death nor suffering can be aggregated; the second cadaver cannot be added to the first. In our world, there is no way around summing up the costs, and then the benefits, and thus arriving at judgment.

That sounds more callous than it is, for we are free to assess the costs as we choose. It seems to me, for example, that in whatever crude equation we develop, the death of the innocent bystander must be doubly weighted. Governments have the right to expose their own citizens to risk, and their enemies. But only the most compelling reasons will justify the incidental killing of people who are neither citizens nor enemies, merely hapless witnesses.

The status of those exposed to death matters, and their numbers do as well. That we know from our own tradition, which very early on teaches us that it is wrong, as Abraham put it, "to make the innocent perish with the guilty," and that Sodom was ultimately destroyed by God because the number of its innocents was not large enough. The larger that number, then, the more compelling must be the reason for the destruction.

We cannot know what would have happened had there in fact been ten innocent people in Sodom. According to His promise, God would have spared the city for the sake of those ten, but perhaps the evil that was in Sodom would then have infected the entire country. We cannot know, because that is not the story or the lesson we were meant to learn. Instead, the redactors of the Bible meant for us to learn—at the least—restraint.

As with so much of what has come down to us, we have adapted the ancient lesson. We do not accept it as an absolute teaching that brooks no compromise. We will slay the innocent along with the guilty for the sake of the greater good, as we see that good, if there is no other way. But the story of Sodom reminds us to pause before so doing, to consider well what we are about to do, perhaps to draw back from the doing of it. It reminds us that we must—where innocents are involved—meet a higher burden of proof before we let loose the dogs of war.

If it were possible to remove the threat of terrorism with no attendant loss of life, who would oppose its removal? No cost, much benefit. But even if we count the lives of PLO fighters (12-year-olds?) for nothing, there are all those other lives—Israeli soldiers, Palestinian and Lebanese civilians. They count, and it is our way—our law—to count them. If we are forced to play God, to decide who shall live and who shall die, we are bound as well to play Abraham, from whom, it sometimes seems to me, we have truly descended. And Abraham, trembling, interceded.

I can hear the murmuring. "Sloppy sentimentalism," "bleeding heartism." But, no, I will not accept it. I will instead insist that the case be made, that this war be defended not by epithets or instincts, but by cold analysis. I will not accept a hardened heart as a substitute for a tough mind. I want us to examine the costs, and to examine the benefits, and I will not allow us to omit the bodies of the bystanders from the calculation of the costs.

It *does* matter how many were killed and maimed in Lebanon. Things that can be justified when the cost in lives is low cannot be justified when the cost soars. Some would have it that because each life is sacred, because each single life contains the entire universe, each life taken is an unacceptable excess. At the other extreme, some would shrug their shoulders, as did one writer in a local Jewish newspaper last week, and say, "*C'est la guerre.*" Both evade the wrenching problem that haunts the rest of us: Where is the limit? Where do we draw the line and say, "With the very next death, you have crossed the boundary from justice to injustice"? Nor is that problem solved if, like Abraham, we count by tens.

Still, we are not quite so unpleasantly confronted, reduced. This is not an arithmetic exercise, a moralistic body count. It is not precision we seek but proportion. Long before we reach the question of how much is too much, we reach the rough sense of it. Is there, we simply need to know, a proportionality between the havoc and the good that's meant to come of it? Little comfort to the dead and the bereaved, but for us, the central question.

Not all the costs of Lebanon are known. The number of the dead is not yet known, not even of the Israeli dead. As of this day, 271 Israeli soldiers are dead, and some 30 are missing, and some of the wounded will not recover, and some will be scarred. There are as well the homeless, and it is not enough to say that the world has grossly exaggerated their number. There are the traumatized, and there is, on all sides, the coarsening that comes with killing.

And there are other kinds of costs. Justly or not, the likelihood is that the next time an AWACS-type vote comes before the Senate of the United States, we will lose by more than two votes. The Hatfield proposal that aid to Israel be stopped forthwith will not prevail, but the erosion of support for Israel will accelerate. For those who wince at the inclusion of another people's dead as a cost to our people, here is a practical item that must be included.

More generally, Israel's good name must be seen not merely as a knee-jerk obsession of Jewish sentimentalists, but as a critical resource in its struggle for survival. This generation of American legislators increasingly remembers Vietnam rather than World War II, and the pictures of the fleeing families evoke unpleasant recent memories. We may believe that Israel has done the West a favor, and yet another favor to American military planners. But who can be so confident that such favors will be recognized, let alone remembered, as to be indifferent to the support Israel derives not from its strategic contributions to the West, but from the values for which it stands—and according to which it behaves?

We know to our regret that Israel has an "image problem." Some of my friends argue that since, no matter what Israel does, it will be condemned, Israel should simply plunge forward, doing what it feels it has to do in order to survive. Yet the "image problem" cuts the other way as well, suggesting that Israel must be doubly certain, before it acts in ways its enemies will exploit, that its action is unavoidable.

No, we are not done with the costs, not yet, not even if we note in passing the nearly three billion dollars this war has so far cost Israel, and the higher taxes its citizens must now pay. And there are future costs, as well, though these are still speculative. I have yet to encounter even one Middle East scholar who thinks there is any chance that the Lebanese, left to their own devices, free at last of foreign intervention, can pull off stability on their own. What, for example, will it mean if that "strong central government" everyone has suddenly decided the Lebanese deserve can be maintained only through periodic Israeli intervention—or, more likely, through the appointment of a de facto Israeli proconsul for Lebanon?

And what of the sharpened divisions the move beyond the Litani has meant within Israel? Some number of Israel's soldiers have now fought a war that was, to put the matter plainly, optional, have killed, that is, not because Israel was immediately and severely threatened, but because Israel's government decided it was time. For some of these soldiers, that is a heavy burden to bear, and so must be counted a cost.

And so forth.

But a tally of the costs, no matter how extensive, does not settle the question. One must look to the benefits as well.

It is no small thing that the children of the North will now be able to sleep in their own beds, in security. And it is no small thing to have captured such massive amounts of arms and ammunition, many times more, we are told, than the PLO could possibly have put to use. If Lebanon is freed of Syrian troops and of the PLO, that, too, is a major benefit. This war was not, in short, for nothing.

But about wars, man's last resort, we must ask not only whether they were about something, but whether they were about enough, and about the right thing.

This war was, for example, neither about peace nor about the Galilee, though peace for the Galilee is one of its important fringe benefits. It was not about peace for the Galilee because there had been relative peace in that region for the 11 months before the war, because even the children in the shelters, had they been asked to name a fair price for the right to sleep in their own beds, would have thought the lives of 300 Israeli soldiers too high a price to pay, and some of them might even have added the lives of the bystanders to the price. It was not about peace for the Galilee because such a peace could have been secured after the first three days of fighting, when only 25 Israelis and commensurately fewer others had fallen.

And it was not about independence for Lebanon, desirable a goal as that might be, for Israel has not been charged with the responsibility to impose independent governments in its region.

No, this war was about the PLO and its destruction.

It would be comforting to think that what Mr. Begin and his colleagues had in mind was the replacement of the PLO with a more moderate Palestinian leadership, with which Israel might now negotiate an honorable and enduring resolution of the Palestinian question. After all, the reason that Mr. Begin has given us in the past for his rejection of Palestinian self-determination—the only basis for an honorable and enduring resolution—is that a Palestinian state on the West Bank would surely be a PLO state, a base for continuing terrorist activity against Israel. Now that the PLO has for all practical purposes been destroyed, what will Mr. Begin say?

It would be comforting to think that Mr. Begin and his colleagues genuinely believed that the circuitous road to peace passed through Beirut, and now that the first part of that road has been traversed, the second half of the journey may begin. For Mr. Begin and his colleagues cannot be unaware that there will be no honorable peace in Zion until there is a negotiated solution to the Palestinian question, a solution based on a return to the principle of partition. For those many thoughtful people, lovers of Zion in and outside Israel, who so believe, partition is no miracle cure, no guaranteed antidote to all the problems that afflict the region. It is merely the only plan that might yet bring an end to violence, for while partition is no guarantee of peace, exclusivism is a guarantee of war. Palestinian nationalism will not go away; it does not depend on the PLO.

It would be comforting to think that Mr. Begin and his colleagues know these things, and, knowing them, will act accordingly. Yet it is far more likely that the purpose of this war was less to bring peace to the Galilee than to bring silence to the West Bank. More Israelis were killed during the last year in the West Bank than in the Galilee, more, far more danger to the safety of the State was there encountered. Danger to the safety of the State, and danger to Mr. Begin's vision of a West Bank tamed, its national aspirations deflected, its territory incorporated into Israel.

It is plainly the case that Israel's leadership entered this war before it had exhausted all other alternatives, before, that is, it had adequately explored the possibility of a political resolution to the conflict. Perhaps no such solution was possible; surely, the PLO did not contribute to its development. But neither did Mr. Begin, and only by his future actions can he relieve the dark suspicion that the reason for that is that he wants no political solution. This is not Egypt, and the Sinai; this is the West Bank, and the compromise here called for if a serious political solution is sought would necessarily mean, for Mr. Begin, a compromise of his most fundamental beliefs, an end to his self-willed imprisonment by futile slogans.

Yet if Mr. Begin is not now prepared to compromise those beliefs, to adjust to the new facts his own policies and actions have created, then this war in Lebanon was fought for folly, the dead have died in vain. There is no way around that. It is grisly to observe that out of havoc, new opportunities arise—but to ignore such opportunities is worse than grisly. It is obscene. It must not be that this war was fought for timid and trivial reasons, for reasons that were not part of the compelling needs of the Jewish State, in the name of a vain idea that threatens the Jewish body not less than its soul. If the repression of Palestinian nationalism and the incorporation of the West Bank into Israel were the goals of this war, then vanity is its proper name and bitter fruit its evil harvest. Its costs will haunt us for years to come.

No, there is only one adequate offsetting benefit which might yet make sense of the tragedy, and that is peace between the Palestinians and Israel. And it is time to say plainly that such a peace requires that there be a Palestine. The strongest argument against Palestine—terrorism, the PLO—has been dealt a mighty blow; there is a new and urgent argument in its favor, the need to make retrospective sense of the war in Lebanon. It is either that, or a war that was far darker than tragedy, and a future that is no better. ✦

WHAT, THEN, SHALL WE DO

The mood on the eve of Israel's 35th birthday is grim. Here, MOMENT's editor reports on his recent visit, and reflects on independence, on Ariel Sharon, on West Bank settlements, on peace and on Israel's future.

LEONARD FEIN

Remember how it used to be? Wonder upon wonder, a modern *dayenu* as overflowing with gifts as the old: Not just a State, which would itself have sufficed, but swamps drained, deserts reclaimed, language reborn, lives redeemed. "The beginning," so said the prayer, "of the flowering of our redemption"—Jewish workers and Jewish farmers, Jewish skyscrapers and Jewish symphony orchestras, a Jewish army and a Jewish diplomatic corps, the remarkable achievements of a remarkable people finally free to turn its genius to nation-building. It was magic, or miracle, and it took the breath away.

So: On the eve of Israel's 36th year of independence, Amos Oz asks, "What else must happen before we all understand that our people is liable to shatter to pieces from within?"

And my friend, a senior official in Israel's security establishment, writes to me: "How have we fallen? For years, we've been asking in despair what happened to the dream. But now it's no longer just the dream that's in jeopardy—it's the reality, it's what we've actually achieved."

And a youngster of my acquaintance here in America, product of, as we say, "a good Jewish home," has come to view Israel as "a place where bad things happen."

What went wrong?

I.
One version: Nothing went wrong. The only thing that's wrong is that there are some Jews who are still trapped, whose minds have never left the ghetto. They ask their soulful questions without realizing how silly those questions are, how craven. Their tortured questions are symptoms of self-doubt and even self-hate. The reality we face is hardly perfect, but it is surely normal, and "normal" is what Israel was established to allow us to be.

There are two problems with this version. The first is that if asking "What went wrong?" is a symptom of abnormalcy, there are very, very many abnormal Jews in Israel and around the world these days. The disappointment with the way things are turning out is almost palpable, especially in Israel. If that's a sign that we're still ghettoized, even in Israel itself, then whoever said "you can take the Jew out of the ghetto, but you can't take the ghetto out of the Jew" had a point.

The second problem with this version is that Emil Grunzweig is dead.

Grunzweig was murdered by a hand grenade while participating in a Peace Now demonstration in front of the Prime Minister's office. Inside, Israel's Cabinet had convened to consider its response to the Report of the Commission of Inquiry. Most of the editorial writers and columnists who addressed themselves to the episode in the ensuing days expressed horror at what they described as "the first political murder in Israel's history." Initially, it seemed rather premature to use so loaded a word as "first," intimating thereby that now that this threshold had been crossed, there would be more to come. But then reports began arriving from all parts of the country that wherever Peace Now demonstrators, honoring their fallen comrade, had gathered in silent vigil, passersby would shout—or mutter— "The next grenade's for you." "First" began to feel right.

Avrum Burg was near Emil when the grenade exploded, and he was among the nine who were wounded. I'd have guessed he'd be there, for late one Jerusalem afternoon, this last December, Avrum and I had spoken at length of these things—of the dream (one cannot escape the metaphor) gone astray, of a future as ominous as the winter sky, of Avrum's move, during the course of the summer, to political activism. We had even talked of the growing violence between the opposing camps, the pushing and the shoving he'd experienced as one of the founders of "Soldiers Against Silence."

"They hate us," he had told me. "They cannot stand it that we ask questions, and they hate us." He'd been to a demonstration in front of the P.M.'s offices once before, back during the endless summer, a demonstration of wives and mothers against the war, and he'd seen the pushing and the fists, felt them, heard the curses. "I know from our sources that *sinat chinam*—baseless hate—was one of

> The point about doing the right thing is that most of the time, it's also the smart thing to do.

the reasons for the destruction of the Second Temple. And I feel, deep in my heart, in my bones, that this *sinat chinam* exists here and now, as well, that you just have to scratch a little to uncover it."

Is that the voice of the ghetto? Avrum Burg, who is the son of Dr. Joseph Burg, Israel's Minister of Interior; who walks with a cane because of the spinal injury he suffered in a parachute jump some years back; who nonetheless volunteered to rejoin his combat unit when the war in Lebanon began. The voice of the ghetto?

If so, then whose is the voice of Israel?

No, it makes no sense. Ariel Sharon, born without umbilical cord, with no inhibiting connection to any civilized tradition, be it Jewish or secular democratic—Ariel Sharon yes and Avrum Burg no?

Here's Burg: "It's not that having all that power pushes you to use it; it *makes* you use it. In *Pirkei Avot* (*The Ethics of the Fathers*) we read, '*Eizeh hu gibor? Hakovesh et yitzro*'—'Who is a hero? The one who can control his instinct, his might.' That's not just a phrase. That's not just aimed at the private instincts, at the passions, it's not just about sex. It's a challenge for all of us here, for the whole society: Can we control our force, our power?

"They say the world is unfair to the Jews, that it demands that we behave better than everyone else. But that's not the point. *We* demand that of ourselves. One of the arguments against the Jews has always been, 'Your Torah is very theoretical. It's nice, but no one can live up to those standards.' It's like the story Yehuda Halevi tells in his *Hakhuzari*. When the King of Khuzar asks the Jewish philosopher what's special about Judaism, the philosopher answers that the Jews don't kill, they don't even kill their enemies. And the King says, 'When you find the strength, you, too, will kill.'

"The real challenge for us is to make the Torah come alive, to show that now that we have the strength, we can still try to live according to our highest values, and, more than that, to show that those values are practical, that they can be the basis for daily life."

And here's Sharon, asked by one of his commanders how to respond to Arab disturbances: "Cut off their testicles."

II.

A second version: "Practical values? Away with such drivel! When the Arabs are ready to make peace, then come with your values, and I won't even mind if they're impractical. For now, values are a luxury. You Jews in the Diaspora sit in moral judgment over us, as if this were some theological debating club instead of a battlefield. In the trenches, there's no time for scruples. What went wrong, you want to know? What went wrong is that they hate us and they want to kill us, that's what went wrong. You expect us to build Utopia while the bombs are falling? Go dream your aimless dreams—but bear in mind, please, that if we start dreaming along with you, there'll be nobody left to guard the house."

How to respond to such profoundly realized frustration? You can't simply trot out Ahad Ha'Am—or Avrum Burg—and expect their pretty words to provide a sufficient response. In fact, Ahad Ha'Am's reasoning might be enlisted to explain the frustration rather than to relieve it. It was in 1898 that he wrote his essay, "The Transvaluation of Values." There, he observed that "on the one hand, there still lives within us, though it be only in the form of an instinctive feeling, a belief in that moral fitness from which we were chosen from all the nations, and in that national mission which consists in living the highest type of moral life, in being the moral Supernation. But, on the other hand, since the day when we left the Ghetto, we cannot help seeing that our superiority is merely potential. Actually we are not superior to other nations even in the sphere of morality. We have been unable to fulfill our mission in exile, because we could not make our lives a true expression of our own character, independent of the will or opinion of others."

Ahad Ha'Am believed that with the rebirth of Jewish independence, we'd at last have the chance to "make our lives a true expression of our own character." But here it is, just 15 years from the centennial of his essay, 35 years into the independence he sought, and we've still not managed it. Endless enemies later, countless dead later, they still don't leave us alone, leave us be. Is it a wonder that we are frustrated? The Jewish State came to provide the framework for our genuine independence, but the agenda of that State is imposed upon it; it is not yet freely chosen. The Jewish citizens of the Jewish State are therefore no more free to set their own course than are the scattered Jews of the Diaspora.

That's pretty compelling stuff, but it invites a somewhat skeptical response. It's too easy, too self-serving. Yes, the enemies are there, and they provide an explanation. But not an excuse, for that would be both a sacrilege and a distortion. Judaism has insisted, from its beginnings, that morality is *not* an indulgence, but a way of life. We do not, we are not permitted to, set aside our values "for the time being," while we see to the building of our house. Morality is a resource, not a luxury; it is a prescription, a perspective, a path to proportion. And practical, too: If the early Zionists had not so believed, the house would never have been built, it would never have been sufficiently compelling to attract the needed resources. Remember that, lest by abandoning that belief today, the house is caused to come tumbling down.

Besides, despite all the confusion and constraint, it just won't do to say that circumstances do not permit us to make our lives a true expression of our character. Duress may be the forge of our character, but we hold the anvil in our own hands. Even outside the Land, the Jews have wielded that anvil with imagination and with energy. And though the State of Israel is less independent than we might have wished, it is by no means without choice, and the chance to choose is what independence is finally about. Hail Israel's achievements; they are not merely the mechanical response to external stimulus. Neither, then, are its failures.

No, our history and texts do not permit, nor does our present condition require, that we choose between morals and muscles. (My sign in the next demonstration: AN END TO FALSE DICHOTOMIES!) It's especially infuriating to hear American Jews, often the same American Jews who object to anyone on this side of the ocean "telling" Israel what to do, condemning Israel's doves, urging upon Israel a blind hardness they would denounce as insane in their own country. As if morality were a form of etiquette, required only when you're in a stranger's house; at home, you can belch away to heart's content.

No, no, morals are not manners. Without manners, we are boors; without morals, we are meaningless. I mean that specifically: The Jews mean nothing without morals. That is what the commandments teach, that is what the history shows. (I know: The brute doesn't inquire before he rapes and slaughters. But though morality doesn't guarantee individual life, its absence does guarantee communal death.)

A small test: Which did more to promote and insure Israel's survival, and that of the Jews—the Lebanese adventure, or the rally of the 400,000? The siege of Beirut, or the Report of the Commission of Inquiry? Perhaps it's not, as I think it is, a clear choice—but it's at least close enough to show that security is not simply a function of muscle. The point about doing the right thing is that most of the time, it's also the smart thing to do. That's one of the really neat things about the way the world works.

III.

Perhaps it's only that the wolves still eat the lambs, that the swords are not yet plowshares, that the dreams are beginning to feel like fantasies, that this isn't the Heavenly Jerusalem after all. The whole thing started with expectations so extravagant they were bound to be disappointed, even in the best of worlds—which this, assuredly, is not.

Another version: The reason things haven't turned out the way they were meant to is that the wrong people came. As one senior civil servant put it to me recently, "Our great disappointment is that the American Jews stayed put. That changed the character of the country, and brought on the terrible manpower crisis we now face. The manpower crisis, and the deeper crisis, the crisis in the streets."

The crisis in the streets: On December 23, 1982, a police bullet killed Shimon Yehoshua, son of a Yemenite Jew who came to the Land on the wings of a silver eagle 35 years ago. The facts of the tragedy don't matter much; what matters is that in reaction to the violence, Sephardi Jews went on a bit of a rampage, painting swastikas and such on identifiably Ashkenazi homes and institutions. (The painted slogans included "Ashkenazim to Auschwitz," "Ashke-Nazi," and so forth.)

Nor does the hatred move in only one direction across the ethnic divide. I don't know that any Ashkenazim have ever shouted, "Why don't you go back to Morocco?" to a group of Sephardi demonstrators, but if they haven't, it's not for lack of bigotry, it's for reasons of style. Ashkenazi bigotry gets expressed in subtler ways, as befits the group in power (and the group with higher education). Over and over again, one hears from Israeli Ashkenazim these days a sigh of resignation, followed by language about "we" and "they" and about "their mindlessness" or "intolerance" or "primitivism." One hears—in polite company—references to *frankim*, a word disturbingly akin to "nigger." Or, more veiled, one hears about the desperate need for immigration from the West. Those Israelis who had imagined Israel as an outpost of Western civilization in the Middle East, a fulfillment of Herzl's vision in *Altneuland*, who did not and for the most part do not understand *Jewish* culture, or, understanding it, eschew it in favor of *fin de siècle* Viennese, lament what they euphemistically refer to as "the manpower crisis."

And the reference is not always euphemistic. Here's part of a recent letter from an Israeli friend, an attorney, the kind of liberal person who, had he lived in America, would be for all the right things. "The 'other Israel' no longer lives in immigrant camps, its economic situation is generally good, but it's still the 'other Israel.' They don't think the way we do, they don't act the way we do, they don't care

> Within Israel, there are five times as many Jews as Arabs. Add in the West Bank and Gaza, and the ratio changes dramatically.

whether the war in Lebanon was justified, Sabra and Shatilla mean nothing to them, corruption in the government does not interest them. Begin, who knocks the Ashkenazim, the kibbutzim, the intellectuals, who shows the Arabs and the world how powerful we are, he is the King of Israel. Their vocabulary does not include 'Diaspora Jewry.' They get their kicks out of disturbing meetings of the Opposition. When Begin says in the Knesset, 'We will go to the people, let the people decide,' he's not referring to me and my neighbors, and not to the kibbutznikim and not to the intelligentsia, he's referring to this embittered group, because he knows that the more he lies and misleads them, the more he splits the Jewish people, the more support they'll give him."

It's a fact that there is a political correlate to all this, that 70 percent of the Sephardi voters cast their votes for the Likud in the last elections, while 75 percent of the Ashkenazi voters cast theirs for Labor. But it's a dreadful and dangerous mistake to assume that Sephardim are hawks and Ashkenazim are doves. Much of the split owes to the politics of resentment rather than to ideological predisposition. Some of it owes to the fact that so long as the Arabs are around, the Sephardim are not, as they fear they otherwise would be, Israel's niggers. And much of it owes to the infuriatingly patronizing perspective even liberal Ashkenazim adopt when trying to think about the problem.

Here, for example, is the thinking of one of Israel's most distinguished champions of human rights, a man widely known and respected in the West for his commitment to liberal values, for his urbanity and civility. Our conversation in December was devoted mostly to "the situation," but it touched for a bit on the ethnic problem as well. "It's too late now," he averred. "We simply have to make the best with what we have. When the State of Israel was established, we assumed, as a matter of course, that it would enjoy large-scale immigration by Jews from all over the world, including the West. Not only catastrophic immigration from people who had to come because they were persecuted, but idealistic immigration from people who wanted to come because they wanted to join the effort. If we'd had such large-scale immigration, as we thought we would, then there would be today no majority for Mr. Begin. The image of the State would be entirely different. Instead, we are saddled with immigration from the Oriental countries only, and we are eating the bitter fruit of that. I have nothing against these people; I very well understand their complexes. But, if in addition to them we had another three or four million people from the West, we would look very different."

No Sephardic Jew in Israel, so far as I'm aware, has yet written a letter from a region of his mind, or described what it means to be a man-child in the truly Promised Land; that is, no one has written the kind of book that would suddenly alter the consciousness of the Ashkenazi community, as, for a time at least, some books altered our consciousness here in the United States 20 years or so ago. So the Sephardim—some of them— shout their vulgar imprecations and daub their swastikas, and the Ashkenazim, some of them, grumble about life's unfairness, and do not understand, do not begin to understand, the depths of Sephardic bitterness, any more than they understand the deeply Jewish elements in the non-secular, non-liberal, non-Western culture of the Sephardim. And Jews hate Jews. In both directions.

What went wrong? Reality intruded. The "wrong" Jews came and the "right" Jews stayed put, according to one reading; the "Establishment" was insensitive and the Ashkenazim are bigots, according to another; the inevitable historical process, the consequence of the revolution of rising expectations, has finally overtaken the early romantic assumptions, according to a third; the dynamite's been there, and Begin has seen fit to light its fuse, according to a fourth. And, ingathered, Jews hate Jews.

IV.

What went wrong? Another version:

In 1937, the Peel Commission, appointed by His Majesty's Government to propose a solution to the continuing conflict in Palestine, recommended the partition of the land between the Mediterranean and the Jordan. The Arabs rejected the notion out of hand; after bitter debate, the Jews, meaning in this case the World Zionist Organization, accepted it. From 1937 to 1977, partition remained the formal doctrine of the Jewish people and of the Jewish State. In 1977, after 40 years of continuing Arab rejection, the Jewish State changed its mind. It elected a new leadership, committed to the retention of all the Land.

Well, what of it? The Zionist movement has a proud record of seizing historic opportunities, and not just of seizing them, but of creating them. Long before Moshe Dayan coined the phrase, the doctrine of "establishing facts" was at the core of the Zionist enterprise. That doctrine holds that by your actions on the ground, you can alter the political environment. Let the diplomats and politicians waste their time in intricate negotiation; in the meantime, we will move, move, move, we will bring people to the land, we will build new settlements, we will create new facts the negotiators will have to deal with. We did not seek to extend our boundaries in 1967, and, having extended them, we were prepared to reduce them again, but the Arabs persisted in their obduracy. Why spurn the opportunity?

Because you can't make a fact out of a fantasy, and it is a fantasy to suppose that there can be both extended boundaries *and* peace. There may not be much chance for peace with partition, but there's no chance at all without it.

But why shouldn't Jews be permitted to live in *all* parts of their historic homeland? And why should Israel permit an enemy "entity" to be established at its doorstep? And what about Camp David, which insures that the final disposition of the "territories" will be the subject of negotiations that have yet to take place?

And so forth. If scoring points is the purpose of the exercise, those who defend Israel's claims are in good shape. But if the purpose is peace, with security, points won't take us there. We may argue first causes and original sins from now until midnight, but save as we move beyond such sterile argument, the dawn will never break. Suppose, for example, that we establish that Israel's claim to the West Bank is superior to all other claims. Suppose, further, that we manage to convince the world of that superiority. Does that necessarily mean that Israel is wise to press its claim? No, it does not, not unless it can be shown that the exercise of that claim is to Israel's advantage—which means that it is consistent with Israel's desire for peace. For what profit can there be in winning the right to do yourself in?

That's what it's come to be about, be our eye on the future or on the present. Those who press Israel's claim must take account of the costs of its exercise.

Let us speak of future costs: For years we've known of what's come to be called "the demographic problem," by which is meant the simple fact that there are today somewhere between 710,000 and 800,000 Palestinian Arabs who live on the West Bank, and another 450,000 in the Gaza Strip. Within Israel proper, Arabs come to some 16 percent of the population. Add to these the Arabs of the West Bank and Gaza, and you move from 16 percent to 35 percent, from a ratio of more than five Jews to one Arab to a ratio of two Jews to one Arab. Incorporation of the West Bank and Gaza into Israel, whether by formal annexation or de facto arrangement, radically alters the composition of the population of the Jewish State.

That's not a "new" problem; it's been discussed and debated at great length in Israel ever since 1967, and still more vigorously since 1977, when the Likud government came to power with its promise of permanent retention of the West Bank and Gaza. Several years ago, Prime Minister Begin was asked how he proposed to deal with the problem, was asked, more bluntly still, whether he intended to preserve the Jewishness of the Jewish State by denying its Arab residents the vote. No, replied Begin, not at all; instead, he said, he was confident that in conditions of peace, there would be massive immigration to Israel of Jews from the West, enough of them to "redress" the de-

If the West Bank is retained, is there any way to avoid Israel becoming a "secular democratic state"?

The newspaper complained that on the bus from Ariel, Arabs sat while Jews were standing.

mographic imbalance.

These days, other Israelis of annexationist bent make a rather different point, a point that is both more plausible and more ominous. They note that for all that the Arabs of the West Bank have a birth rate roughly twice that of Israel's Jews, their number does not increase. It does not increase because there is a continuing and substantial emigration of Palestinian Arabs from the West Bank. It would not take much by way of policy to "encourage" the departure of Palestinians, to cause a dramatic acceleration in the rate of emigration. Accordingly, one is not necessarily talking about an eventual Arab majority in the expanded Jewish State.

But we do not need to contemplate an Arab majority to foresee a bitter and essentially insoluble problem. A one-third minority is not easily digestible, even if the appetite is large. (Black Americans, who live in a country that is not located in Africa, and who are not heirs to a doctrine of conquest, come to about 12 percent of this nation's people. For over a hundred years, the United States has announced its intention of integration. Yet there is still a considerable distance to go before that intention is adequately realized.) And in the event that sufficient energy and effort is devoted to making it work, to making it possible for so large a minority to be fully integrated into the life of the country, are we not then talking, essentially, about a bi-national state, or, to use the contemporary phrase, about a secular democratic state? About, then, an end to Jewish independence? Under those circumstances, is it not likely that there would be voices raised within Israel demanding that democracy be "attenuated" in order to preserve Jewishness?

That is why there are some Israelis who have said, bluntly, that even if the Arabs were tomorrow morning to change their mind, and to announce their readiness to live with an Israel that reaches from the Mediterranean to the Jordan, and even if the entire family of nations were to give its blessing to Israeli rule over the West Bank and Gaza, still they would object. The matter, as they see it, is not law, or justice, or right, but self-interest. In their view, the question ought not to be how Israel can persuade the Arabs or the world of its entitlement, but how Israel can insure its safety once the West Bank is relinquished. That's not an easy question, but, as they observe, given that hardly anyone accepts that Israel is, in fact, entitled to hang on to the territories, there's no more insurance of safety in retention of the territories than in their devolution. Perhaps less, for to retain them is to prescribe permanent war.

Listen, if you will, to Avrum Burg once more:

"I love Eretz Yisrael, all of it. And I know what it means. My mother was born in Hebron. Half of her family was massacred by the Arabs there in 1929. (But I have to remember that she and her father and two of her sisters were saved by Arabs. So if I think of Hebron, I think not only of the lives that were lost but of the lives that were saved, and by whom.) And I've walked through all the valleys and the hills of Judea and Samaria. I love the land, all of it.

"But I'm ready to trade it for something more valuable. I don't mean just peace. Peace is only a start, it would give us the chance to begin to rebuild, to rebegin, our society. That's the work that's waiting. If we hang on to the land, I'm worried. I'm not concerned mostly with the political challenge of having so many Arabs. I'm concerned with the spiritual challenge. We can't absorb them at this stage, we can't digest them; they will destroy us, because we haven't yet established our foundations.

"The government says they're against partition, they believe in *shlemut ha'aretz*, the 'integrity of the Land.' But what they want will mean partition, because it will mean taking in partners in running the country— either that, or an end to democracy. And when I ask myself which I prefer, the partition of the Land or the partition of the soul of the people, the answer is simple. I'd rather have a tiny, little state of Jews than a big state that is shared.

"Sure, I'd like it if Eretz Yisrael were empty and all the Palestinians were on the other side of the Jordan and we could be Eretz Yisrael as the

Prophets described it, within the borders that were promised to Moses in *Bamidbar* 34. But I take seriously what our Chief of Staff has said, that we are in a situation where for the next hundred years there will be a war every ten years. We are becoming heirs to the blessing that Jacob gave Esau: *'Al charbechah tichyeh.'* ('By your sword you shall live.') That's Esau's blessing, and I don't want it. That's no blessing, that's a curse."

Some might say—some do say—"Let the future take care of itself, it's all speculation anyway, in the meantime the present is more than enough to contend with, and there's nobody to talk to, to make peace with, so we really have no choice but to do what we're doing."

Let us speak of the present. Let us talk not of distant and necessarily speculative scenarios, but of a present that is oh so tempting to ignore. Let us ask what the continuing occupation of the territories, which means the continuing rule over a hostile population, is doing; what, specifically, it is doing to the occupiers.

I don't relish this next, but I have much in mind these days a lesson taught us by the Kahan Commission (the Commission of Inquiry): "We do not say that the decision to have the Phalangists enter the camps should under no circumstances have been made and was totally unwarranted. Serious considerations existed in favor of such a decision . . . and had the decision-makers and executors been aware of the danger of harm to the civilian population on the part of the Phalangists but had nevertheless, *having considered all the circumstances*, decided to enter the camps while taking all possible steps to prevent harm coming to the civilian population, it is possible that there would be no place to be critical of them, even if it had emerged that the decision had caused undesirable results and had caused damage." [Emphasis added.]

"*Having considered all the circumstances . . .* " We ignore those circumstances at our peril, moral and physical.

So: Ariel is a new city in the West Bank. In mid-January, we are informed by Hirsh Goodman (military correspondent of the *Jerusalem Post*), the newspaper published by the settlers in Ariel carried an item complaining that local Arabs were using the Dan bus service rather than the bus service provided for Arabs. Worse yet, Arabs were seen to be sitting on the Dan buses while Jews stood.

How shall we relate to such a report? Obviously, it is disgusting. Perhaps, however, we may dismiss the episode it describes as atypical, simply the cranky expression of bigotry that might be—and is—found anywhere and everywhere. Why bother, then, to bring it to the attention of readers of the *Jerusalem Post*? Why to the readers of MOMENT?

Because, dear readers, that is how it starts, and there is not a Jew alive who does not know that, who has not made that very point to others. About others. But if there is any learning that ought have come to us these past years, it is that being Jewish does not of itself provide absolute immunity against the nastiness that afflicts mankind.

Nor, as it turns out, does the newspaper of Ariel describe an isolated episode.

On February 17, 1983, a military court in Israel convicted four of seven soldiers arrested for aggravated assault on Arabs in the Hebron area last spring. I shall spare you the grizzly details of the behavior which led to their indictment. It is sufficient to say that the heart of the matter was that the soldiers had engaged not merely in gratuitous violence, but also in utterly despicable acts of humiliation against Arabs.

In defending themselves, the soldiers pleaded that they were merely following standard orders regarding the proper response to disturbances. Those orders, detailed during the course of the trial by the testimony of officers all the way up to the Chief of Staff, call for the harassment of local Arabs.

In Israel, however, there are limits to how far one can press the defense of "higher orders." Ever since the tragedy of Kfar Kassem in 1956, the precedent has been established that a soldier is forbidden to execute a patently illegal order. (That precedent was most dramatically confirmed during the Eichmann trial, in 1961.) In the case at hand, Col. Ya'akov Hartabi, former military commander of the West Bank, had ordered his men to drive people out of their homes and beat them, to shoot into the reflectors of rooftop solar heaters and to break the residents' watches. (These were not, however, the acts with which the men on trial were charged. The acts in question were considerably more base.)

Lest it be thought that Col. Hartabi was merely a trifle overly enthusiastic in his manner, it must be added that his orders were based on directives issued by Israel's Chief of Staff, Rafael Eitan, who last spring recommended that unrest be dealt with by such things as the punishing of parents of disorderly students, depriving the inhabitants of areas where rioting has occurred of the right to purchase cement or fuel, the arrest and detention of instigators of disturbances (where formal charges cannot be brought against them for lack of evidence) for a few days, followed by their release and then their re-arrest. Collective punishment, arbitrary imprisonment, economic sanctions—all orders that became a matter of public record only during the course of the trial.

Is it, then, that we are dealing here with the familiar case of orders from on high being a bit too literally interpreted at each lower echelon? Is Eitan the villain, are the convicted soldiers merely victims?

I think not. Like the soldiers, Eitan is both villain and victim. Their shared villainy is that they ignore the civilizing perception that power must be clothed in restraint, else it is naked power, and naked power is indecent. But they are also all victims. As the *Jerusalem Post*, no fan of Eitan, said in an editorial on his directives on January 23, 1983, Eitan is a "victim . . . like the society as a whole, to the corrosive effects of military occupation." Indeed, even Ariel Sharon, this time around, is not the villain.

(A brief digression: It is altogether too easy to blame Sharon, but that's not the way things work in a democracy. Sharon holds onto office at the pleasure of his colleagues. It may be, as we are told, that his presence gives them little pleasure, but that's their problem, not his. It's also their problem that while the Cabinet prepares to annex the West Bank, Sharon has already annexed the Cabinet. Outsiders might have expected that a man so roundly chastised by the Commission of Inquiry would have seen fit to offer up some visible, if modest, act of contrition, if only to make it easier for his colleagues to play musical ministries, shifting him as they did to a different post within the Cabinet in order to provide the appearance of compliance with the Commission's recommendations. But Sharon knows his colleagues well; easier or harder, they'll come to heel. The rest of the country, hawks and doves alike, scrambles at the edge of a nervous breakdown, dozes fitfully through a national nightmare; Ariel Sharon bulls merrily, and ferociously, along, perhaps the only adult in Israel who sleeps well.)

The tragedy of the occupation—I use the word "tragedy" pointedly—is that what is happening in the West Bank, from the bigotry of a settler in Ariel to the vulgarity of the incumbent Minister Without Portfolio, from the unlawful behavior of soldiers of the I.D.F. to the unlawful behavior of vigilante settlers, is roughly what is bound to happen under circumstances such as these, independent of the actors and their motives. Oh, it is likely the case that the "get tough" policy pursued by Sharon and Eitan of late reflects their distinctive styles and intention, and it may even be the case that their policy was intended to encourage Arab emigration from the West Bank. Now, there are signs of change: In the first weeks of his tenure as Minister of Defense, Moshe Arens, the hawk who replaced the vulture, has moved rapidly to curb the excesses of the vigilantes, has sought to demonstrate that the policy of settlement need not be accompanied by cruelty and lawlessness. But he will not, because he cannot, curb the bigotry, the corruption of the soul that comes of being an occupying power. Worse, it is probably safe to assume that ugly episodes will continue. The fact is that they did not begin with Sharon, or, for that matter, with the Likud; they began before, when others were in charge, back in the days of the Labor government. Circumstance overwhelms intention.

Is all this too harsh? After all, we are not talking about a Boy Scout jamboree, but about a tense and volatile area. What, after all, is one to do with troublemakers? As the military tribunal said in its verdict, "The Israeli Defense Forces cannot be expected to handle rioters with silk gloves."

What one is to do with troublemakers I do not know. I do know, however, some things one is *not* to do. One is not, for example, to roust them from their beds in the middle of the night and then, using a ballpoint pen, inscribe numbers on their forearms. And that, too, was done by Israeli soldiers in the West Bank two months ago.

I hesitated for quite some time before writing this last paragraph. It is a detail, ugly though it be, less sinister, in the end, than the continuing killings in the West Bank, than the continuing vigilante terrorism there, and one would like to believe that it is an entirely exceptional detail. I decided, finally, to tell about the numbers on the forearms not because I think the incident "typical," but in order to shock us out of our willful lethargy. It is easier by far to turn a blind eye to these things, to fancy that the occupation is just another chapter in the difficult history of Israel's continuing war of independence. But it is a chapter that has gone on for nearly 16 years now, and it has done things to us, to all of us. Among those things, it has desensitized us. Some there are who will have read all the rest and who will still be wondering why others of us are so upset. I hope, and believe, that there is no Jew, anywhere, who can read this last, this thing about the numbers, and not feel sick to his/her stomach. Nobody ordered it. But it happened, and it, or things like it, will happen again. That is what the continuing occupation of the West Bank means, right now.

What went wrong? We sought to rule over a people that did not and does not and will not welcome us. Some day, that will mean yet another war. In the meantime, it means a different kind of horror.

V.
An interlude for a commercial message: Here on my desk is a sales brochure for apartments and houses in a place called Emanuel, a new town in the West Bank. "Emanuel, City of Faith" is what it's called, 10,000 homes and apartments for religious folk. As the brochure says, "Yeshivot, Girl's Seminars, Mikvaot" in a city that has "received the blessings of the most prominent rabbinic leaders of our time, who see in the building of this 'City of Faith' a hope and a solution for the thousands of religious families blessed with children." What that means, I'm told, is that B'nei Brak, just outside Tel Aviv, is full-up, and here, just a 25 minute drive away, the adult children of B'nei Brak can have low-cost housing and still live near their parents. And that's not all: Emanuel features "an urban transport system based on a modern technological approach as the definitive solution to noise, air pollution and road safety." It is "surrounded by springs and natural reserves, with a magnificent panorama of the seashore and the Shomron Hills" and it "is replete with clean air." Best of all, it "lies in the heartland of Israel."

And the price is right, less than half what comparable apartments, were they available, would cost in older areas within Israel proper. (Five bedrooms in Emanuel will set you back just $66,000.)

Those Americans who've not visited the West Bank recently may be somewhat taken aback by this. Say "settlements" and we conjure up visions of a few austere buildings atop a dusty hill, some dozens of hardy settlers who command respect for their audacity if not for their balance. But here we're talking about a suburb rather than a settlement. No dust, no ideology; just clean air and low-cost housing, cheaper by far than what's available within the Green Line (the pre-1967 boundaries). These days, it takes ideology to stay out of the West Bank, not to move into it.

A clever ploy to force the Jordanians to the negotiating table? Tell that to the 10,000 families—that's 50,000 people—of Emanuel, and to the families of Ma'Aleh Adumim and of Ariel and of Nofim and of Tsavta and

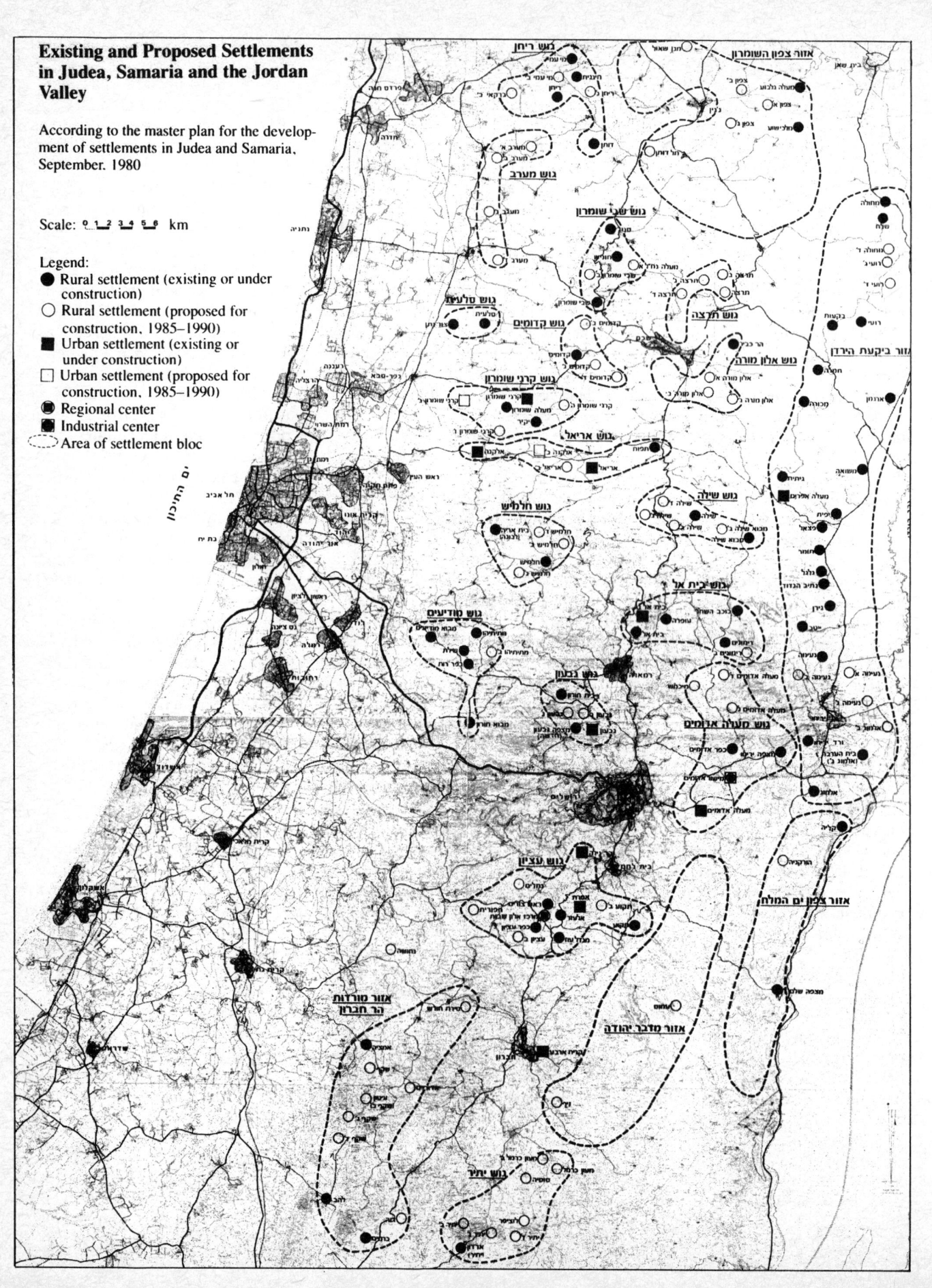

Existing and Proposed Settlements in Judea, Samaria and the Jordan Valley

According to the master plan for the development of settlements in Judea and Samaria, September, 1980

Scale: 0 1 2 3 4 5 6 km

Legend:
- ● Rural settlement (existing or under construction)
- ○ Rural settlement (proposed for construction, 1985–1990)
- ■ Urban settlement (existing or under construction)
- □ Urban settlement (proposed for construction, 1985–1990)
- ▣ Regional center
- ▪ Industrial center
- ⌐ ⌐ Area of settlement bloc

> Renunciation of the Sinai was intended to facilitate retention of the West Bank.

of Alfei Menashe. They, those already there and those to come, don't see it that way. Nor, for sure, do the relevant officials in the Ministries of Interior and Defense. A couple of months ago, they held a planning session, seeking to determine Israel's needs in the year 2010. The people from Interior projected 250,000 Jews in the West Bank by then; the Defense people predicted 500,000.

Ah, but the 500,000 aren't there yet, nor even the 50,000; if Jordan were to join the talks *now*, it might preempt all that. And, indeed, it might. (Although from Hussein's perspective, the prospect of endless months of negotiation during which new settlements continue to be created and old ones expanded cannot be very appetizing.) But given the repeatedly stated position of Israel's government, it seems plain that it is history's hand rather than Hussein's that Israel seeks now to force. Yitzhak Shamir, Israel's Foreign Minister, who voted against Camp David: "Judea, Samaria and Gaza are part of Eretz Yisrael, and what is part of your country you do not annex." Menachem Begin, Prime Minister of Israel, speaking in Ariel in 1981: "I, Menachem, the son of Zev and Hasia Begin, do solemnly swear that as long as I serve the nation as Prime Minister we will not leave any part of Judea, Samaria, the Gaza Strip and the Golan Heights."

Still, that's the same Menachem Begin who traded the Sinai for peace. Except, of course, that retention of the Sinai was never part of Begin's fundamental commitment, and retention of Judea and Samaria is. Indeed, the link between the Sinai and the West Bank is not that the renunciation of the one provides a precedent for the renunciation of the other, but that the renunciation of the one was intended to *facilitate* the retention of the other. That's been a popular assumption among students of these matters ever since the Camp David negotiations; now we have confirmation from Eliahu Ben Elissar, Chairman of the Knesset Foreign Affairs and Defense Committee, and a member of Israel's delegation to Camp David. Writing in the Herut magazine *Yoman Hashavua* last December, Elissar informs us that,

"Israel sacrificed for the sake of this peace [with Egypt]. It was absolutely clear to Egypt why we were doing this. We did it for the sake of peace, but not only for the sake of peace: also in order to preserve our control of Judea, Samaria and the Gaza Strip. We did not hide that from the Egyptians, and when we signed the Camp David accords, in September '78, and later, in March '79, the peace treaty—the Egyptians knew, in the clearest possible way, what Israel is prepared to sacrifice and what it is not prepared to sacrifice . . . In the negotiations for peace, we knew exactly what we wanted: Israeli rule over Western Eretz Yisrael."

And what they wanted seems to be what they're getting. One of Israel's leading experts on the West Bank is Meron Benvenisti, former Deputy Mayor of Jerusalem, now Director of something called "The West Bank and Gaza Data Base Project." His interim report on his research has created a major stir in Washington as well as in the Arab world, and we talked at length during my December visit:

"At most, there are three or four years left. At most. After that, we'll have to view Israel as a permanently polarized society, one where there can be no surgery, where you cannot achieve partition."

"For partition to work, the map must be drawn along demographic lines—Jews here, Arabs there. The more the two populations become intermingled, the harder it will be. So if you continue putting major Jewish settlements in Arab areas, you finish the possibility of partition. It becomes impossible—unless, of course, you're willing to create yet another refugee problem.

"When Labor started building settlements, there wasn't much to it. They established a bunch of dots, involving very few people. They were expensive political demonstrations, an effort to repeat the experience of the 30s and 40s, controlling the land by creating settlements.

"The Likud has very cleverly changed the whole strategy. They're still putting the rural settlements there, but they don't really care whether they're viable. They're talking about

140 rural settlements, which is probably an exaggeration. So let's assume a hundred. What does that amount to? Multiply that by 600 or so per settlement, and you're talking about 60,000, maybe even 80,000 people. And that will take quite some time, and it will require ideologically motivated people, and they don't exist, not in those kinds of numbers. And even if they did, that would still leave you with a ten-to-one ratio of Arabs to Jews in the West Bank. No, the only reason for the rural settlements is so that people will look at the map and say, 'Look how many dots there are!' And in the meantime, they're busy opening up areas for urban sprawl.

"When they do that, they immediately have an unlimited number of people. And they also have access to private investment. Take Ariel, for example. The first piece of land there was bought by a private person. He bought some thousand dunams from an Arab. Then the government came along and invoked a clause from Ottoman law—it's from Article 103 of the Turkish Land Code—that reads, 'Vacant land, such as mountains, rocky places, stony fields . . . and grazing ground which is not in possession of anyone by title deed, nor assigned *ab antiquo* to the use of inhabitants of a town or village, and lies at such a distance from towns and villages from which a human voice cannot be heard at the nearest inhabited place is called *mawat* (dead) land . . . anyone who is in need of such land can, with the leave of the official . . . cultivate it on the condition that the ultimate ownership shall belong to the Sultan.' You see, you don't need to make a security claim any longer. About two-thirds of the land of the West Bank is 'vacant,' unlisted in the Land Registry. And if an Arab wants to dispute Israel's claim that the land is *mawat*, the burden of proof is on him, a burden he must meet before an Appeals Board headed by the legal advisor of the Israel Land Authority—not exactly a neutral observer.

"In any case, using the Ottoman code, the Israeli government claimed about 30,000 dunams [one dunam = one quarter acre] on which they plan to build Ariel, a city of 150,000 people. The land will remain government land, and people will lease it from the government on 49 year renewable leases. Now, the value of the land to start with is about 20 percent of the value of the same kind of land 15 miles down the road in Israel proper. Then the government gives it to the contractor for about five percent of its value, which means, for all practical purposes, that the contractor is getting it for nothing. He's paying about four percent of what he'd have to pay in Israel. The government, for the most part, takes care of the infrastructure—roads, water, public spaces and such. And, to top it all off, the mortgage rates are very low, and there are loans and grants available that make it almost irresistable. People who now live in a two bedroom apartment in Rishon L'Tzion can get, for the same price, a three-level detached villa in Ariel, with a quality of life you can't find any more in Israel proper, not unless you're ready to move quite a distance from the urban centers. Ariel, after all, is just a 40 minute drive from downtown Tel Aviv.

"People abroad think that because the West Bank is so famous, it must be at least the size of France. But the whole of the West Bank is the size of the state of Delaware. It's not a vast area that can be neatly divided. So you cannot say that what will remain in Arab possession will be viable. Even under the Labor plan, what was left to the Arabs was not viable. To cut even more deeply into it? Nothing will remain.

"People say that Jordan is Palestine, that a majority of the Jordanian population is Palestinian. But that's true because there are so many refugees in Jordan. To use that as an argument is to raise the question, *haratzachtah v' gam yarashtah?*—you've killed, and now you propose to inherit? You can use any argument you want, but not that one. It's too self-serving.

"And beyond that, you must understand that the Palestinians will not shift their focus from Jerusalem to Amman. The fact is, like it or not, that they developed the same kind of emotion to Jerusalem, towards the rest of the places here, as we did. They don't have the literature we do, but one of the reasons for that is that when you live with your beloved, you don't bother to write her letters. It's when you're far away, as we were, that you do that. It would be—it is—a profound mistake for us to conclude that just because their being here is inconvenient for us, it's not important to them."

Benvenisti says three years, maybe four. There are those who think him an optimist. Here, for example, is what Dani Rubenstein, West Bank reporter for the daily *Davar*, wrote a year ago: "There is no chance that Israel will be able to give up as much as one meter in the West Bank and Gaza even if it wishes to do so . . . The extensive settlement operations in the territories, the confiscation and acquisition of land, the Israeli Defense Forces deployment there, the bases, the emergency stockpiles, the training fields, the economic integration of the territories, all have been perpetrated by Israel's latest government in a way that even a partial renunciation thereof will lead the entire country to collapse."

VI.

What went wrong? Another version:

We forgot what we were supposed to know so well it didn't even need remembering. We forgot that Judaism doesn't teach us to distinguish between God and Caesar. The Jews are commanded to be a holy people *all* the time, not just when it's convenient. As important, we're taught that the only way the world will ever work the way it's meant to, which is to say the only way there'll ever be security, is if we take God's work as our own.

We're taught that when the world's working right, what's good is good for the Jews. And when it's not working right, which is all of the time, we're supposed to know that we can't use its malfunction as a license to pursue evil. The malfunction, instead, is to cause us to redouble our efforts *l'taken olam*, to repair, to fix, to make whole.

What went wrong is that we were seduced by all the glitzy technology, and came to believe that hardware could serve as a shortcut to security. But no nation, not even the megapowers, can make it on hardware alone. And Israel, independent/dependent Israel, for sure cannot. There are so very many other elements that go into security's equation—the morale of the people, the health of the economy, the strength of the alliances, even the moral stature of the country. Is it not relevant to Israel's security, for example, that during each of the last two years, more Israelis left the country for good than were replaced by new immigrants?

Jews stand at a peculiar but ingenious intersection, the intersection of two questions that do not seem to fit together, but which we ask in one breath: If I am not for myself, who will be for me? And if I am only for myself, what am I?

I need to stop here briefly, lest the clichés obscure the content. We do not say, first let us look to our own health and then, with what's left over, to the health of everybody else. We say that each depends on the other, that in this world there is no health for self save as there is health for the other, that in this world, the particular and the universal must both be nurtured if either is to be sustained.

We don't say all that because our hearts are bleeding, or because we're mushy. We say it as diamond-edged wisdom, the accreted wisdom of a people that can speak to the relationship of the particular to the universal, of the self to the other, with greater experience and authenticity than any other.

"But why blame the victim?" they will ask. "Blame instead the fears and prejudices that inform Saudi behavior, the venality and thuggery of the PLO, the timid wisdom of King Hussein, the awesome feuds of the Lebanese, the machinations of the Soviet Union, the vacillations of the United States."

Blame enough to go around, if it's a verdict we seek. But suppose the jury files back, and announces its verdict: "These are the guilty, those the innocent." So what? Is it vindication we seek, or a way out of the morass?

I think, sometimes, that we are still not used to power, to the meaning of our having re-entered history, that we still imagine the whole thing is about words. That's how it was, of course, for most of the two thousand years of our wanderings, when debate was all there was for us to win, when words were all we owned. We had memories, and we had dreams; we had a past, we had a future.

But we knew that others owned the present.

Zionism came to give the Jews a present tense. A here. A now. The earthly Jerusalem is necessarily more complicated than the heavenly Jerusalem; the one is messy, the other messianic. That's what coming back to history means. In real time, in the here and now, in the cave of shadows where the best you can hope for is a crude approximation of your dreams, winning debates doesn't count. All that counts is owning your choices.

"Can you say nothing good about Israel?" they will ask. I can say, in fact, very much that is good about Israel, and the very best thing I can say is that Israel *does* have choices, that for all its travails, and with all the constraints, it is an independent State. Zionism was a success.

So the question now is how to insure that success, how to act in ways that will protect it, how to choose, and choose wisely. What is it that we want to see in the Middle East, all of us? Let the mind roam a bit, away from the bombs and away from the quarrels. What all of us want is an Israel free to discover what the Jewish people can accomplish, what it can make of its new nation. And for this, there must, of course, be peace. Real peace. Not—even the roaming mind cannot roam so far from reality—a love feast, but the kind of peace that is marked by decent neighborly relations.

The dread that haunts us these days owes to the belief that such a peace, such a freedom, grows less likely day by day. Events converge, and become trends; trends converge, and become history. And one day, unmarked, unnoticed, the last trend falls into place, the one that makes the tale complete, the one that closes the chapter, the one before which there is still time, there is still choice.

Not, as is often claimed, a choice between naive idealism and hard-headed realism. No dove I know proposes that Israel can make it on sweetness alone, that if only Israel were more forthcoming, the Arabs would suddenly welcome the Jews in their midst. Doves are as self-centered as hawks; in their hard-headed assessment, retention of the land endangers the safety of the state.

Writing of these things in his *The Bar Kokhba Syndrome*, Yehoshafat Harkabi, former Chief of Military Intelligence in Israel and no romanticizer of history's complexity, has this to say: "A realistic orientation includes an awareness of one's ability accompanied by a recognition of one's limits . . . Such realism is not belittling oneself, or folding up one's tents and retreating, but is taking a balanced view of the world. On the other hand, unrealism, on which policies of vainglory are founded, is an exaggeration of one's capabilities; its end is failure."

What went wrong? Yossi Klein said it in these pages two months ago: It was preposterous to suppose that the Jewish people could move from the traumas of its recent past to the time of the wolf and the lamb, the time of the plowshares and the pruning hooks, without stumbling somewhere along the way. It was wrong to think that the nightmare would not overtake the dream, somewhere. It was wrong to suppose that we, so deeply wounded, could set aside our fears and pretend the world's a playing field.

But on the occasion of the anniversary of Israel's independence, yesterday's mistakes are less interesting than tomorrow's opportunities. Those who choose now to reject the Israel of the nightmare also abandon the Israel of the dream. Those who decide for themselves that the dream is dead decide that for others as well, they change the odds for all of us, and thereby insure its death. What went wrong is that we stumbled. But stumbling is permitted, is to be expected. The question is what we do next. Having stumbled, we can collapse, lie there waiting for someone to stretch out a hand—or a dagger—or we can pick ourselves up and move on, this time in a more promising direction. That's what being truly independent means.

★

THE 91ST MOMENT
An editor's notes

LEONARD FEIN

One night last June, more apprehensive than there was any good reason to be, my three daughters and I climbed Masada. We wanted to reach the top by sunrise, which we'd figured for six-thirty or so; six, to be safe. Friends had told us that the climb, via the Snake Path, usually takes an hour, but, as out-of-shape Americans, we should allow for two, just to be sure. That meant we had to start the climb by four; estimating an hour's drive from Jerusalem, we had to be on the road by three—but, taking no chances, we planned to leave by two. And when we discovered that we were all up and eager by half-past one, we decided we might as well be on our way.

Which put us at Masada at two-thirty, and, after dawdling at its base until three, on top at 3:58(!). By the time the darkness began to break apart nearly two hours later, we were too weary, by far, to appreciate the remarkable restoration of the Zealot fortress. Besides, the truth is that we were too filled with our own achievement to have much room for the Zealots', or for Professor Yadin's. We'd come alone, and climbed alone, the moon lighting our way. It was my first Snake Path climb in 30 years, and I had not become more lithe over the decades; for the girls, it was their first ever, and used to climbing mountains, even small ones, in the foreign dark they're not. For the four of us, it was warming confirmation of our capacity for mutual support and, thereby, collective achievement. Neat-o.

So when, on the eve of our return to America, a cousin asked the girls—Rachel, Nomi and Jessica—what of all they'd seen and done in Israel impressed them most, I expected them to say our climb.

Or, perhaps, Yad Vashem. There, as I'd tried to set a fairly rapid pace, the girls had lingered, insisting on seeing each photograph, reading each legend. There we had sat near "the corner of the children," with its infinitely sad statue of Janusz Korczak and the children of his orphanage, and talked of those times and of these. (Though later in our trip we were to visit the more compelling Ghetto Fighters' House, we'd run out of time and down in energy by then, and the visit to Yad Vashem was clearly the more memorable.)

I was, therefore, somewhat surprised when each of my daughters responded that it was our visit with Miriam Mendilow and her Lifeline for the Old—at the very beginning of our trip—that had most moved her.

Briefly: Mrs. Mendilow, a tiny woman in her 70s, decided some years back that it is wrong for us to discard the elderly. Single-handed, she set out to establish workshops where they might be employed, permitting them to continue to live independently and usefully. Several hundred elderly, including not only the healthy but also the physically and mentally disabled, now work in Lifeline's shops. My own favorite of the more than half-dozen workshops is the book bindery, where damaged elementary school texts are rebound and a book plate then inserted: "A gift to the children of Jerusalem from its old folks."

There are, I suppose, other such workshops, but there can scarcely be another such whirlwind of energy, compassion and intelligence as come together in Miriam Mendilow, who has packaged these in one of the most attractively conniving personalities I've anywhere encountered. I've met first-time tourists to Israel, come to the country with schedules fit for presidential candidates, who've made the mistake of stopping at Lifeline early in their trip—only to discard their programs and to spend the balance of their time helping out at Lifeline. She gets to you, this woman Mendilow, with her breathless single-mindedness; her world is so full and so intense it's hard to remember there's another.

But days later, Masada and Yad Vashem and two dozen other places later, I was nonetheless surprised when of all we'd seen, the girls chose Lifeline as the high point of our visit.

We've talked about it since. As nearly as I can understand it, it comes to this: Rachel and Nomi and Jessica cannot volunteer to commit suicide on Masada, nor can they volunteer to enter the gas chambers depicted at Yad Vashem. But they can, and plan to, volunteer, next summer or later, to lend a hand to Miriam Mendilow. The heroism and martyrdom of the Jewish past are interesting, moving, inspiring, but the stuff of the Jewish present, of Jewish life, is, among many other things, helping sweep the floors of rooms where old folks renew books for children.

With this issue, we inaugurate MOMENT's tenth anniversary year. Back in 1974, when the magazine was gestating, there were those who asked to see its manifesto. But there was no manifesto then, and there is none now. The stories and the poems, the essays and reports of a monthly magazine—these are a more useful guide to the intentions of its editors than their pronouncements.

Yet I am not indifferent to our arrival at Year Ten. Though manifestos are not our style and summaries would be premature, surely a Big Thought or two may be in order? Or, at least, some clues to the things that preoccupy us here.

I write on the very eve of the 1984 elections. There's been much talk in the months of this campaign about selfishness and selflessness. Many of us—I include myself—have found the presidential campaign especially depressing because of the reported intention of the young to vote for Reagan-Bush—and, more to the point, because of the reasons they tend to give for that choice. I can, sort of, understand the not-young. Those (very few) of my friends, middle-aged and older, who plan to vote for Reagan-Bush have a kind of logic on their side: They really do have interests to protect. We disagree on the definition of those interests, and on how they may best be defended, but I understand their decision.

But the young? They are supposed to be moved by other things. Whatever happened to the classic pattern of youthful radicalism, reconfirmed so massively during the 1960s? (Maybe the 1960s is what happened to it.) The young cannot have grown tired of the demands of the liberal commitment, as have so many of their elders; they haven't been around long enough to be worn out. Nor have they, upon disinterested reflection, concluded that conservatism is the better way.

My hunch is that we now witness the specifically political translation of a decade of "looking out for number one" and similar claptrap, the narcissistic psychojunk that came to fill the post-60s vacuum. After the assassinations, after the burning cities, after Vietnam, after Watergate, it was a bit much to expect the tradition of civic commitment to retain its vigor. The young, with no tradition of civic success to fall back on, became profoundly skeptical of society's ability to deliver on its diverse reformist promises, let alone its utopian rhetoric—conservative or liberal.

And so it is that very many of them—not all—seek to avoid commitment, and, with it, risk. Better never to care about the public weal than to experience disappointment, caring's inseparable companion. They hear Mario Cuomo's "tale of two cities," and they are not inspired by it; instead, it merely reinforces their insistent ambition to insure that *their* city is the one on *top* of the hill, fat city.

We've taken to calling this crippling cynicism "selfishness," and contrasting it with the "selflessness" that seems so much more appropriate and charming an attribute of youth.

But that is, I think, a mistaken way to state the issue. Classically, we do not interpret "Love thy neighbor as thyself" as a plea for selflessness. The focus of the words is on the link between love of self and love of other; if you are to love your neighbor "as yourself," you'd better love yourself well. Otherwise, you do your neighbor no favor by loving him.

That's not merely hoary ethical insight; it's also potent psychological theory. Which means that the purpose of an ethical education is not to teach "selflessness," not at all. It is to educate towards a self that derives pride and pleasure and satisfaction from reaching out to others, a self sufficiently secure to delight in sharing and caring and touching.

Among other things, MOMENT tries to be about ethical education. In the contemporary context, that evidently means to buck the tide.

Jewish history may easily be—and often is—taken as an invitation to radical cynicism, to a kind of collective narcissism. To resist that invitation, to insist instead upon an ethic of altruism, to assert not merely the burdens of such an ethic but its joys, not merely its nobility but its pragmatism, is to defy the present trend, to appeal to a truth that goes beyond history, that goes, if you will, to religion in its broadest sense.

This morning, I received in the mail an announcement of a day of outreach that has been planned by a Jewish institution in another city, an institution with a proud history of involvement in the "larger" world. The program is meant to attract people in their 20s and 30s, and it includes four one-and-one-half hour time slots, during each of which those who attend may choose from any of 14 or 15 concurrent seminars—57 seminars in all.

Fifteen of the seminars deal with issues of personal growth—"How to Survive the Break-Up," "How Do You Rate as an Achiever?" and "Survival Cooking" illustrate this group. Another eight focus on career: "Getting Your Face and Name in the News" and "Getting to the Top" reflect their orientation. There are six that deal with personal finances, and another six on miscellaneous subjects, such as "Wine and Cheese—the Perfect Partners."

The remainder, 20 in all, are more or less about matters of explicit Jewish interest. Here we have one each on marriage, intermarriage and conversion; one on the *Bet Din* (religious court), one on the *mikveh* (ritual bath), one on the woman in traditional Judaism; one is about the *havurah* (Jewish fellowship) and another on Jewish spirituality and another on Reconstructionism; there's one on genealogy, and one on Jewish travel, and one on Israeli artists; three are Bible-based, and four deal, more or less, with "current" issues—Jewish PACs, "American Jewish Women—Then and Now," "How to Instill Judaism in Kids" and "Giving Honor and Dignity to the Jewish Dead."

There's a long-standing debate in the Jewish community about the propriety and wisdom of Jewish

The 91st Moment

sponsorship of essentially secular projects. Why should Jews, as Jews, meet to discuss retirement planning? To which the answer is that Jews are, or try to be, a community, and not merely a group that meets for limited purposes. On the whole, I accept this answer, believe that we may share all our interests without feeling that the sharing must have explicit Jewish content, be Jewishly "justifiable."

So if I have problems with the 57 seminars that have been so carefully planned, so enthusiastically designed to offer something for everybody, those problems are not about what they include, but about what they exclude. Every presentation by a Jewish agency or institution is, in its way, a statement about what matters to Jews. With 57 presentations, we may also draw some conclusions about what does not matter.

Among those the program is meant to reach, are there none who would be turned on by a seminar on economic justice, or on the relationship between ritual and ethics, or on national health insurance, or on relations between the Jewish community and the black, or the Hispanic, or, for that matter, the Italian, Greek, Polish or Irish community? None concerned with Central America, none with famine in Ethiopia, none with nuclear proliferation, none with terrorism? None with apartheid in South Africa, or divestment? None with Simpson-Mazzoli, none with the bag ladies and street people?

How can it be that we accept that Jews—as Jews—are entitled to talk together, and care together, about wine and cheese ("An open discussion on pairing the perfect wine and cheese as well as when and where to serve the combination") but not about welfare and abortion and church-state relations?

Well, maybe it's just a ruse to attract the young, to seduce them into the building; once seduced, we'll start feeding them the other stuff, the stuff from the real agenda. There is one clue that points in that direction: Except for a seminar on Israeli artists, there's not a single seminar on Israel. There's nothing on Israel's economy, or its politics, or its conflict with its neighbors. Yet it simply cannot be the case that the sponsors are indifferent to Israel. It must, therefore, be that the sponsors assume that those they mean to attract are indifferent—to Israel, as also to the whole of the civic culture.

Some of them surely are. But we cannot have failed so miserably in our educational effort that all of them are. By implying such widespread indifference, we alienate those non-indifferent young who don't give a tinker's damn about "Applying Business Techniques to Managing Your Life"—and we encourage the indifferent young to think they're whole, that the top is where the good life is and that getting there is all that counts.

If the civic culture is to be repaired, if a new generation is to be inducted into the ethic of civic responsibility and given the opportunity to experience its intensity, we shall have to overcome the ethic of futility and indifference that now subverts it.

That, as it happens, is a Jewish agenda. Jewish survival is incompatible with an ethic of futility, cannot be protected where there is no sense of public purpose, of a civic culture.

Among other things, MOMENT tries to be about Jewish survival. The surest way to subvert that survival is to trivialize the Jewish agenda; the surest way to protect it is to concentrate on the redemptive understandings that have characterized Jewish thought through the ages, and on the ways in which those understandings can inform our lives. Ways like sweeping floors in workshops for the elderly. Yes, and ways like "Promoting a Healthy Sexuality" and "Giving Honor and Dignity to the Jewish Dead" and giving food to the African hungry and promoting justice for the South African blacks and worrying about how to resolve the conflict between Arab and Jew in the Middle East.

Which is a different way of saying that a people that is preoccupied with survival for survival's sake is not likely to survive. It is the ambitions of a people that sustain it—if those ambitions are sufficiently uplifting and inspiring to excite the imagination and loyalty of its members. And if they are insistently and persuasively communicated.

The language we speak is, therefore, a matter of considerable importance in our ongoing effort. The figures of speech we invent and employ tell a good deal about us— as, even more simply, does our basic vocabulary.

Some years ago, the "hot" text for teaching Hebrew was something called *Elef Milim*—a one thousand word vocabulary list that was supposed to prepare the student for simple communication in Hebrew. As best I can recall, successful completion of the text enabled the visitor to Israel to find a bathroom or order a salami sandwich.

There *is* a basic Jewish vocabulary, a list of words that has the capacity to unite Jews wherever they are. But it is not about food and comfort stations. It is about hunger and justice, about melancholy and ecstasy and, above all, about hope. It includes such words as *almanah* and *yatom*—the widow and the orphan—as *tzedakah* and *tz'niyut*—righteousness and modesty—and so forth, a thousand words and more.

What have Jews, as Jews, to do with such a vocabulary?

When all the dreams are fractured, you can desist from dreaming—or you can try to heal the fractures. Were we to stop using the vocabulary we invented, a vocabulary that has moved humankind to pity for more than two millenia, we would begin to forget why we are and want to be who we are.

When, for fear Club Med is as close as they can come to community, we withhold the words from our young, we insult, then injure them; we leave them ignorant of the rich inheritance that is theirs by right. Nor are the words alone enough: Save as we seek to live our language, we become castaways from past and future; we are, all of us, diminished.

Among other things, MOMENT tries to sustain the classic Jewish vocabulary, that there may flourish a Jewish civic culture, that through the ongoing enrichment of that culture Jewish dreams be sustained and life be preserved. And that thereby, the repair of the world go forward. ✡

Part VII

Just a Moment . . .

HOW TO READ A YIDDISH POEM

SETH WOLITZ

The Poem	The transliteration
דער קוש	Der Kush

יעדער האָט זיך זײַנע טנועס און האַוואַיעס.
אוּן רעב ניסל שאַיעס,
דער גבֿיר דער שיינער,
ער געהאַט אַ טבֿע: תּמיד נאָכן עסן
זיך בײַם טיש געזעסן
און געצמאָקעט ביינער.
צמאָקעט ער אַ ביין אַזוי און נאָגט,
און דער ביין דערפֿרייט זיך און ער זאָגט:
— טעלער, שיסל, גרויס און קליין!
זעט נאָר, ווער סע קושט מיך! דער באַלבאָס אַליין!
גלעזלעך דינע,
רוקט אײַך אָפּ, מעכילע!
איר פֿאַר קינע
קענט דאָך פּוקען נאָך, כאָלילע!
ווי ער צמאָקעט, לעקט מיך מיט די ליפּעלעך די רויטע!
— אײַ, דו שויטע,
(ענטפֿערט אים אַ שיסל)
וואַרט אַביסל,
ביז רעב ניסל
וועט דעם מאַרעך דיר אויסנאָגן —
וואָס וועט איר, רעב בײניש, דעמאָלט זאָגן?

Elyezer Shteynbarg (1880–1932)

Yeder hot zikh zayne tnues un havayes.
Un reb Nisl Yeshayes,
der gvir der sheyner,
er gehat a teve: tomid nokhn esn
zikh baym tish gesesn   5
un getsmoket beyner.
Tsmoket er a beyn azoy un nogt,
un der beyn derfreyt zikh un er zogt:
—teler, shisl, groys un kleyn!
Zet nor, ver se kusht mikh! Der balbos aleyn! 10
Glezlekh dine,
rukt aykh op, mekhile!
Ir far kine
kent dokh puken nokh, kholile!
Vi er tsmoket, lekt mikh mit di lipelekh di royte! 15
—Ay, du shoyte,
(entfert im a shisl)
vart abisl,
biz reb Nisl
vet dem marekh dir oysnogn— 20
Vos vet ir, reb Beynish, demolt zogn?

Mesholim, I (Czernowitz: Komitet af aroystsugebn Elyezer Sheynbargs shriftn, 1932), p.18 Rpt. (Buenos Aires: Besaraber landslayt-fareyn in Argentine, 1949), p. 36.

The literal line by line translation	A poetic attempt at translation
## The Kiss	## The Kiss

1. Each one has his gestures and grimaces	Each one has his quirk and grimace,
2. And [so does] Reb Nisl Yeshayes,	And so does dear Reb Nisl Shayes,
3. The upstanding rich man,	Rich, esteemed, who, after every meal
4. [Who] He had a habit: always after the meal	Had a habit, I'll reveal,
5. [remained] seated by his place setting	Of sucking bones piled on his plate.
6. and sucked on bones.	Once he sucked and licked a bone
7. He sucked and gnawed a bone so [much]	Which wanted known
8. [that] the bone took such pleasure and said	Its happy state:
9. "Dish, bowl, big and small!	"Hey plate and platter,
10. Just look who's kissing me, the boss himself.	Big and small
11. Thin glass [cups]	Just look who's kissing me:
12. Move over, if you please,	Our master!
13. From envy you	Move over glass! What *is* the matter?
14. Might even crack, God forbid!	You could crack and splatter (God forbid!)
15. How he sucks [and] licks me with his red lips!"	From envy. Pardon me!
16. "Oh you fool,"	How our master loves to nibble me with lips so red!"
17. (a bowl replies)	"Oh, you fool,"
18. Wait a little	Said the bowl:
19. Until Reb Nisl	"Just wait a little
20. will gnaw the marrow out of you,	'Til Reb Nisl
21. What will you say then, Mr. Bone?"	Will gnaw your marrow away.
	Then, Mr. Bone,
	What will you say?"

A fable helps to face a bitter truth indirectly. By making animals and animated objects act human, the aesthetic distance permits the readers to observe and laugh at the human condition as superior beings while recognizing the inescapability of human nature. Eleazar Shteynbarg needed the aesthetic distance of a fable to present his vision of life: a world not built on justice but on power. In this world only the master counts. The servant exists for his pleasure. There is neither mercy nor room for fools. Survival demands the recognition of power and the ability to bend. The fable becomes an aesthetic interlude and social protest: a mediation in time to resharpen the perception of social reality, a locus of renewal for psychic energies preparing to reenter the fray, a forum to denounce and laugh scornfully at the absurdity of life and an act of assertion to demand human dignity. A Shteynbarg fable rips off the mask of social amiability, good form, protocol and civilization to reveal the bitter lot of the oppressed squabbling among themselves and eventually crushed from above. Relentless in its denunciation of social injustice, a Shteynbarg fable functions

Seth L. Wolitz is the Gale Professor of Jewish Studies, Professor in the French-Italian Department and Professor of Slavic Languages at the University of Texas in Austin.

like a forlorn hope to change the human condition, if not human nature.

Shteynbarg is the finest craftsman of fables in Yiddish. Like La Fontaine and Krylov, he treats the fable as drama, conflict and ironic resolution. The last line, a *pointe*, reduces the opponent to humiliating silence. Usually Shteynbarg pits two or three against one another and eventually a master emerges. In the third person singular, the poetic narrator sets the stage, orders the props, places the protagonists in their battle positions and retires quickly, ending the exposition. Direct discourse develops immediately. The animated objects do not converse; they command, they order and argue. Irony floats on every syllable—particularly on the Yiddish interjections. Shteynbarg uses free verse with calculated skill to speed or retard the delivery, building rich rhymes to further the sarcasm of the antagonists. Each personage is typed by his language and rhythms. The vocabulary Shteynbarg employs retrieves old Yiddish terms, quaint Hebrew, Aramaic and Slavic words, folk expressions and idioms.

In our fable, *The Kiss*, the title beguiles with innocence and affirmation. The narrative voice ushers in the fable with a trite generalization (v.1) more normally saved for the conclusion. The second verse provides an *exemplum* of the generalization in the person of Reb Nisl Yeshayes, the master of the house and *agent provocateur* of the ensuing drama. Names in Shteynbarg fables are never innocent. Nisl may be a diminuative of *Nissim* but *nisl* is also a nut and *Yeshayes* is *Yeshaye* or Isaiah with the possessive: *Isaiah's nut*. But Isaiah means salvation. (Can a nut look upon its consumer as its salvation?) The name Reb Nisl Yeshayes contains, as it were, the meat of the fable. After dinner ("from soup to nuts"), it was traditional in Europe to "crack nuts" and eat the contents. Reb Nisl obviously has his *gestures* and *grimaces* as well as *habit*, namely—a folk tradition—of gnawing bones after dinner. The intention and act, however, are the same. (But what happens to the shells?) Around this seemingly innocent habit, the drama begins. A rich complacent man comfortably seated at his dining table provokes "a tempest in a teapot" by repeatedly "sucking on bones" (v. 6–7). Verse eight transposes the reader from the world of men to the lilliput world of animated objects. (Shteynbarg is unique among the world fabulists in preferring to animate objects rather than to anthropomorphize animals.) The narrator retires as he animates the bone and table setting.

Verses 9–15 boom with the arrogance and false pride of the bone boasting of his service to *the boss* (v. 10) and "lording it" over the other "servants." The kiss of the title is now only too ironic: the kiss of death. The foolish bone, ignorant of the fatal attentions, usurps power and rights based on false premises. Space (v. 12) becomes hierarchical for the bone. Veiled threats to the fragility of the glass and its possible envy reflect, in fact, the mirror image of the bone's physical and psychological make-up. The central image of "cracking" (v. 14) prepares the *denouement*. The heavy repetitive trochaic accent in Yiddish (long-short) of verses 11–14 with the rich monotonous alternating rhymes in short lines: *dine, mekhile, kine, kholile,* reveal Shteynbarg's virtuoso use of language and prosody to delineate the vaunting personality of the Bone. Meanwhile Reb Nisl continues (v. 15) to "suck and lick with his red lips."

Verses 16–21 contain the rebuttal and savagely ironic resolution. The bowl speaks for all the place setting with the lesson that puts the bone back into its proper place—the fool. Why is the bowl the chief spokesman? As the marrow is scooped out of the bone, leaving it empty and useless as a nutshell, so the bowl, useful by having its cavity filled, sharpens the shared image but draws the opposite functional distinction. The prosody also helps underline the rebuking sarcasm. The short verses 17–19 mimic the heavy trochaic meter and rhyme of lines 11–14 in order to mock the bone's haughty style and to maintain the continuous gnawing rhythm of Reb Nisl's kisses.

The normally diminuative final /l/ in the rhyme adds a further "come-uppance" to the belittling mono-rhyme: shisl, bisl, Nisl. The scorn increases in the language play of address. In line 20 the bone is addressed as *dir* ("you"), the second person singular (indirect pronoun), which is used for intimacy but expresses here inferior status: the bowl now asserts authority. With the loss of marrow, the bone's *raison d'etre* ceases as much for itself as for Reb Nisl. The rhyme, *oysnogn*, to gnaw away, juxtaposed to the rhyme *nogt*, to gnaw, of verse 7 subverts cruelly the high point of the bone's delusion of grandeur. In fact, the two rhymes, v. 20–21, recall the rhymes of v. 7–8, conjugated verbs of *nogn* and *zogn*, in order to dramatize the rapid descent. The underling pays with his life for the attentions of the master.

Line 21 is the only interrogative sentence after the series of imperatives. Its impact rests with the withering silence that trails the question mark. By having the bowl address the bone in the formal *ir*, you, the second person plural, as well as adding the title of respect, *Reb*, mister, to the bone, Shteynbarg suddenly raises the language register, recalls the bone's own use of the form (lines 10, 12, 13 *zet, rukt, ir*) and exaggerates the bowl's ironic use of "high tone" in order to reveal, through language play, the foolishness and megalomania of the bone at the moment of its final degradation and humiliation. The name *Reb Beynish* is actually a pun on *Beyn Nish(t)*, *Bone-not* or *Mr. Bone-no-longer*! At the end of the fable the thin glass remains intact but the marrowless bone is cracked open and vacant: the fate of boasting fools. Meanwhile Reb Nisl, unaware, is still blissfully consuming. The rich and powerful continue to rule, such is the human condition. The typical Shteynbarg fable mediates through humor and fantasy, the horror of a seemingly daily civilized dining scene transmogrified before our eyes into an abattoir and finally an ossuary.★